Conte

Introduction

However many cookery books you have on your shelf, everyone has one favourite – the one that contains all their everyday recipes as well as special-occasion dishes. With 1000 delicious and stylish recipes in this book, it is guaranteed to become a favourite. It contains everything from simple soups to exotic main courses, from family puddings and snacks to desserts for the most lavish of dinner parties, all simply arranged so that you can find everything you need quickly and easily, and convenient for browsing when you are looking for something new. Dip into this tremendous range of recipes and you'll be sure to find everything you need.

Notes on the recipes

- Do not mix metric, imperial and American measures. Follow one set only.

- All spoon measurements are level: 1 tsp = 15 ml; 1 tbsp = 15 ml.

- Eggs are medium unless otherwise stated. If you use a different size, adjust the amount of liquid added to obtain the right consistency.

- Always wash, dry and peel, if necessary, fresh foods before use.

- Seasoning and the use of strongly flavoured ingredients, such as onions and garlic, are very much a matter of personal taste. Taste the food as you cook and adjust seasoning to suit your own taste.

- Herbs are fresh unless dried are specifically called for. If you wish, you can substitute dried for fresh, using only half the quantity or less as they are very pungent, but chopped frozen varieties give better results than dried. There is no substitute for fresh parsley and coriander (cilantro).

- A fresh bouquet garni is traditionally made up of sprigs of thyme, parsley and a bay leaf tied together with string or wrapped in muslin (cheesecloth) and is used in slow-cooked dishes. Sachets of bouquet garni are readily available in supermarkets.

- Use a good-quality oil of your choice for cooking. Corn or groundnut (peanut) oil is best for deep-frying as they can be heated to high temperatures.

- Use butter or a margarine of your choice in the recipes. Since some margarines or spreads are best for particular uses, check the packet before using for the first time.

- Use your own discretion in substituting ingredients and personalising the recipes. Make notes of particular successes as you go along.

- Use whichever kitchen gadgets you like to speed up preparation and cooking times: mixers for whisking; food processors for grating, slicing, mixing or kneading; blenders for liquidising.

- All ovens vary, so cooking times have to be approximate. Adjust cooking times to suit your own appliance, especially if you have a fan oven.

- Some recipes, such as Mayonnaise, include raw eggs. You should follow the current health advice on using raw eggs.

Starters and snacks

Starters can vary from a simply prepared prawn (shrimp) salad to a lavish and expensive dish. What all have in common is that they whet the appetite for the main course and the flavours complement the food to follow. It is therefore a good idea when planning a meal to choose the main course first, then go back and find a suitable starter to introduce the style and tastes to come. When serving a starter, remember that you do not usually need large quantities of food – that may well result in your family or guests struggling to eat their main meal. Presentation is very important. Whether stylish and sophisticated or robust and homely, the starter will set the tone and atmosphere for your meal. Of course, as our lives become ever busier and our meal patterns change, we often want just a light meal or perhaps to serve a selection of recipes to a group of friends so that they can dip into what they fancy. This chapter offers many recipes that are ideal for just that, or you can serve individual dishes with a crisp green salad and some crusty bread to make them a meal in themselves.

Smoked haddock mousse

SERVES 4

450 g/1 lb smoked haddock fillet, cut
    into pieces
1 small onion, sliced
250 ml/8 fl oz/1 cup milk
1 bay leaf
25 g/1 oz/2 tbsp unsalted (sweet) butter
15 g/½ oz/2 tbsp plain (all-purpose) flour
2.5 ml/½ tsp cayenne
Salt and freshly ground black pepper
15 ml/1 tbsp powdered gelatine
30 ml/2 tbsp water
Grated rind and juice of 1 lemon
150 ml/¼ pt/⅔ cup double (heavy) cream
½ cucumber, sliced
Thin slices of buttered wholemeal or
    granary bread, to serve

Put the haddock, onion, milk and bay
leaf in a saucepan, bring to the boil,
cover and simmer for 10 minutes.
Strain the fish and reserve the cooking
liquor. Remove the skin and bones
and flake the fish finely. Melt the
butter over a low heat, then stir in the
flour and cook for 2 minutes until the
mixture is very light golden. Whisk in
the milk and cook, stirring, for
3 minutes. Season to taste with
cayenne, salt and pepper, then
remove from the heat, cover and
leave to cool.

Mix the gelatine and water in a
small heatproof bowl, then place the
bowl in a pan of hot water until the
gelatine is transparent. Whisk the
cream until stiff. Fold the flaked fish
and gelatine, lemon rind and juice and
cream into the sauce. Pour into a
soufflé dish and leave until set.
Garnish with the cucumber slices and
serve with thin slices of wholemeal or
granary bread.

Salmon mousse

SERVES 4

15 ml/1 tbsp powdered gelatine
150 ml/¼ pt/⅔ cup water
200 g/7 oz/1 small can of red salmon,
    drained
Juice of ½ lemon
150 ml/¼ pt/⅔ cup soured (dairy sour)
    cream
Salt and freshly ground black pepper
150 ml/¼ pt/⅔ cup double (heavy) cream
1 cucumber, peeled and diced
Thinly sliced wholemeal bread and
    butter, to serve

Mix the gelatine with 45 ml/3 tbsp of
the water in a small heatproof bowl,
then place the bowl in a pan of hot
water until the gelatine has dissolved
and become transparent. Place the
dissolved gelatine in a food processor
or blender with the remaining water,
the salmon, lemon juice and soured
cream and purée until well blended.
Season to taste with salt and pepper.
Turn into a bowl and leave until just
beginning to set. Whisk the cream
until just stiff, then fold into the
mousse with the diced cucumber.
Turn into a very lightly oiled 900 ml/
1½ pt/3¾ cup mould and chill until
set. Turn out and serve with thinly
sliced wholemeal bread and butter.

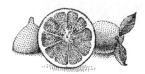

Chinese almonds

SERVES 4

15 ml/1 tbsp oil
225 g/8 oz/2 cups unskinned almonds
30 ml/2 tbsp soy sauce
5 ml/1 tsp chilli oil

Heat the oil in a frying pan (skillet).
Add the almonds and stir until coated
in oil. Add the soy sauce and chilli oil
and stir-fry over a high heat for
3–4 minutes. Remove from the pan
and leave to cool before serving.

Garlic olives

SERVES 4

225 g/8 oz black olives
60 ml/4 tbsp olive oil
3 garlic cloves, crushed
½ lemon, thinly sliced
15 ml/1 tbsp chopped thyme
Salt and freshly ground black pepper

Mix together all the ingredients in a
screw-topped jar and shake to mix
them well. Chill for at least 24 hours,
shaking occasionally, before serving.

Avocado and tuna mousse

SERVES 4

1 avocado, peeled, stoned (pitted) and
   halved
5 ml/1 tsp lemon juice
200 g/7 oz/1 small can of tuna, drained
30 ml/2 tbsp plain yoghurt
5 ml/1 tsp Tabasco sauce
Freshly ground black pepper
Crisp or melba toast, to serve

Purée the avocado flesh and lemon
juice in a food processor or blender,
then add the remaining ingredients
and process until smooth. Taste and
add more pepper and Tabasco, if
liked. Pile into a serving dish and chill
before serving with crisp or melba
toast.

Taramasalata

SERVES 4

12 slices of white bread, crusts removed
300 ml/½ pt/1¼ cups milk
200 g/7 oz/1 small can of smoked
   cods' roe
1 shallot, chopped
Juice of 2 lemons
250 ml/8 fl oz/1 cup olive oil
Warm pitta bread, to serve

Soak the bread in the milk until soft,
then squeeze out the excess moisture.
Purée the bread in a food processor
or blender with the cod's roe, shallot
and lemon juice. With the motor
running, gradually pour in the oil
through the feed tube until the
mixture becomes smooth and creamy.
You may not need to use all the oil.
Turn into a serving bowl, cover and
chill thoroughly. Serve with warm pitta
bread.

9

Hummus

SERVES 4

400 g/14 oz/1 large can of chick peas (garbanzos), drained
1 onion, very finely chopped
1 garlic clove, chopped
150 ml/¼ pt/⅔ cup plain yoghurt
10 ml/2 tsp lemon juice
15 ml/1 tbsp olive oil
2.5 ml/½ tsp ground cumin
Salt and freshly ground black pepper
Pitta or crusty bread, or Crudités (page 10), to serve

Place the chick peas, onion and garlic in a food processor or blender and process until smooth. Add the remaining ingredients, seasoning to taste with salt and pepper, and process again until well mixed. Turn into a serving bowl, cover and chill overnight before serving with pitta or crusty bread or crudités.

Tzatziki

SERVES 4

½ cucumber, peeled and diced
Salt and freshly ground black pepper
150 ml/¼ pt/⅔ cup plain firm-set yoghurt
1 garlic clove, crushed
15 ml/1 tbsp chopped mint
Warmed pitta bread or Crudités (page 10), to serve

Place the cucumber in a colander, sprinkle with salt and leave to stand for 30 minutes. Rinse, drain well and pat dry on kitchen paper (paper towels). Place in a serving bowl and mix with the remaining ingredients. Cover and chill in the fridge before serving with warmed pitta bread or crudités.

Crudités with minted yoghurt dip

SERVES 4

150 ml/¼ pt/⅔ cup plain yoghurt
150 ml/¼ pt/⅔ cup soured (dairy sour) cream
30 ml/2 tbsp Mint Sauce (page 256)
5 ml/1 tsp lime juice
30 ml/2 tbsp ground almonds
2.5 cm/1 in piece of cucumber, peeled and chopped
Salt and freshly ground black pepper
A pinch of paprika
1 red-skinned eating (dessert) apple, cored and sliced
5 ml/1 tsp lemon juice
12 baby sweetcorn (corn) cobs
1 red (bell) pepper, sliced
2 celery sticks, cut into matchsticks
2 carrots, cut into matchsticks

Mix together the yoghurt, soured cream, mint sauce, lime juice, ground almonds and cucumber and season to taste with salt and pepper. Spoon into a serving bowl and sprinkle with the paprika. Toss the apple slices in the lemon juice to prevent discolouring. Arrange the apple, baby sweetcorn, pepper, celery and carrots on a serving plate and serve with the dip.

Spicy salami dip

SERVES 4

100 g/4 oz salami, chopped
175 g/6 oz/¾ cup full-fat soft cheese
30 ml/2 tbsp Mayonnaise (page 277)
15 ml/1 tbsp tomato ketchup (catsup)
30 ml/2 tbsp olive oil
15 ml/1 tbsp Worcestershire sauce
5 ml/1 tsp mustard powder
Salt and freshly ground black pepper
Savoury biscuits (crackers), to serve

Purée all the ingredients in a food processor or blender, checking and adjusting the seasoning to taste. Turn into a serving bowl and chill thoroughly. Serve with savoury biscuits.

Black olive pâté

SERVES 4

250 g/9 oz stoned (pitted) black olives, coarsely chopped
1 garlic clove, crushed
Finely grated rind and juice of 1 lemon
25 g/1 oz/½ cup fresh breadcrumbs
50 g/2 oz/¼ cup full-fat soft cheese
Salt and freshly ground black pepper
1 lemon, cut into wedges, to garnish
Ciabatta bread or crisp toast, to serve

Blend or mix together the olives, garlic, lemon rind and juice, breadcrumbs and cheese. You can do this by hand or in a blender or processor, but if you use a machine be careful not to make the mixture too smooth. Season to taste with salt and pepper. Chill for several hours before serving with ciabatta bread or crisp toast.

Chicken and mushroom pâté

SERVES 4

65 g/2½ oz/5 tbsp butter or margarine
1 onion, chopped
225 g/8 oz chicken livers
15 ml/1 tbsp dry sherry
30 ml/2 tbsp double (heavy) cream
100 g/4 oz/1 cup cooked chicken, finely chopped
100 g/4 oz mushrooms, thinly sliced
Crusty bread or savoury biscuits (crackers) and a few salad leaves, to serve

Melt 25 g/1 oz/2 tbsp of the butter or margarine in a frying pan (skillet) and fry (sauté) the onion until soft but not brown. Add the chicken livers and fry for 8–10 minutes until just cooked. Stir in the sherry, then add the cream and a further 25 g/1 oz/ 2 tbsp of the butter or margarine. Mix well, then transfer to a food processor or blender, add the chicken and purée until smooth. Spread the remaining butter on the base of a 450 g/1 lb loaf tin (pan). Arrange half the mushrooms on the base, then spread with half the pâté. Top with the remaining mushrooms, followed by the remaining pâté. Cover with foil and place the tin in a baking dish and pour boiling water into the dish to come half-way up the sides of the loaf tin. Bake in a preheated oven at 180°C/350°F/gas mark 4 for 30 minutes. Remove from the dish of water and leave to cool in the tin. Place weights or food cans on top and chill overnight. Turn out, cut into slices and serve well chilled with crusty bread or savoury biscuits and garnished with the salad leaves.

Country pâté

SERVES 4

1 onion, finely chopped
1 garlic clove, crushed
100 g/4 oz streaky bacon, rinded and
    finely chopped
225 g/8 oz lambs' liver, chopped
225 g/8 oz lean pork, finely chopped
25 g/1 oz/2 tbsp butter or margarine
2.5 ml/½ tsp ground mace
30 ml/2 tbsp single (light) cream
Salt and freshly ground black pepper
Granary bread or toast, to serve

Mix together all the ingredients,
seasoning to taste with salt and
pepper. You can vary how finely you
chop the ingredients depending on
whether you like a smooth or coarse
pâté. For a really smooth pâté, use a
food processor or blender for mixing.
Spoon the mixture into a 1.2 litre/
2 pt/5 cup ovenproof pâté dish or
terrine, cover with foil and stand the
dish in a baking tin (pan). Pour in
boiling water to come half-way up the
sides of the dish. Bake in a preheated
oven at 180°C/350°F/gas mark 4 for
1½ hours. Remove from the baking tin
and leave to cool. Place weights or
food cans on top and chill overnight.
Slice and serve cold with granary
bread or toast.

Mackerel pâté

SERVES 4

225 g/8 oz smoked mackerel fillet,
    skinned
Juice of ½ lemon
50 g/2 oz/¼ cup butter or margarine,
    melted
45 ml/3 tbsp soured (dairy sour) cream
Freshly ground black pepper
Crudités (page 10) or savoury biscuits
    (crackers), to serve

Flake the mackerel into small pieces
and purée in a food processor or
blender with the lemon juice, melted
butter or margarine and soured
cream. Season to taste with pepper,
then turn into a serving dish and chill
before serving with crudités or
savoury biscuits.

Bruschetta

SERVES 4

8 slices of ciabatta or crusty bread
2 garlic cloves, halved
4 ripe plum tomatoes, sliced
A few basil leaves, torn into pieces
60 ml/4 tbsp olive oil
Salt and freshly ground black pepper

Toast the bread slices until crisp. Rub
the surfaces of the bread with the
garlic cloves, then rub the tomato
slices over the bread, squashing them
with a fork. Sprinkle with the basil,
drizzle with the olive oil and season to
taste with salt and pepper. Leave to
stand for a few minutes before
serving.

Stuffed eggs

SERVES 4

6 hard-boiled (hard-cooked) eggs,
   halved
3 parsley sprigs, thick stalks removed
200 g/7 oz/1 small can of tuna, drained
100 g/4 oz/½ cup full-fat soft cheese
50 g/2 oz/¼ cup butter or margarine,
   melted
Freshly ground black pepper
1 bunch of watercress
2 tomatoes, thinly sliced
1 lemon, thinly sliced

Ease the egg yolks from the whites
and place the whites in a bowl of
water to keep them soft. Purée
together the egg yolks, parsley, tuna,
cheese and butter or margarine in a
food processor or blender. Season to
taste with pepper. Drain the egg
whites and pat dry on kitchen paper
(paper towels). Spoon or pipe the
mixture into the egg whites. Arrange
the watercress on a serving plate, lay
the eggs on top and garnish with the
tomato and lemon slices.

Nut and soured cream eggs

SERVES 4

½ lettuce, shredded
4 hard-boiled (hard-cooked) eggs, sliced
300 ml/½ pt/1¼ cups soured (dairy sour)
   cream
25 g/1 oz/¼ cup chopped mixed nuts
15 ml/1 tbsp chopped parsley
Salt and freshly ground black pepper
Wholemeal or granary bread, to serve

Arrange the shredded lettuce on
individual plates and arrange the egg
slices on top. Mix the cream with the
nuts and parsley and season to taste
with salt and pepper. Spoon the sauce
over the eggs and serve with slices of
wholemeal or granary bread.

Melon with sweet ginger mushrooms

SERVES 4

225 g/8 oz button mushrooms
300 ml/½ pt/1¼ cups ginger wine
20 ml/1½ tbsp soft brown sugar
1 small honeydew melon
A few mint leaves, to garnish

Put the mushrooms, ginger wine and
sugar in a saucepan, bring slowly to
the boil, then cover and simmer
gently for 10 minutes until the wine
has reduced and become syrupy. Pour
into a warm jar, put the lid on loosely
and leave to cool. When cold, screw
down the lid tightly and keep in a cool
place until required. The mushrooms
will keep for several days.

   Cut the melon flesh into small
cubes, or use a melon baller to make
tiny spheres. Just before serving, toss
the melon with the mushrooms and
syrup and serve garnished with mint.

13

Smoked duck with broccoli and almonds

SERVES 4

250 g/8 oz broccoli florets, cut into small
   sprigs
25 g/1 oz/¼ cup flaked (slivered)
   almonds
45 ml/3 tbsp sherry vinegar
60 ml/4 tbsp hazelnut (filbert) oil
60 ml/4 tbsp olive oil
45 ml/3 tbsp sunflower oil
Salt and freshly ground black pepper
350 g/12 oz smoked duck breast, thinly
   sliced

Blanch the broccoli in boiling salted
water for 1 minute, then drain and
rinse under cold running water. Drain
and pat dry on kitchen paper (paper
towels). Toss the almonds in a dry
frying pan (skillet) for about 1 minute
until golden, then leave to cool. To
make the dressing, whisk together the
sherry vinegar and oils, seasoning to
taste with salt and pepper. Add the
cool broccoli and leave to stand for
30 minutes. Stir in the almonds.
Arrange the duck slices on individual
plates and spoon the broccoli mixture
over. Grind plenty of black pepper
over and serve.

Tomatoes with herbs and crème fraîche

SERVES 4

4 beefsteak tomatoes
Salt and freshly ground black pepper
150 g/5 oz/⅔ cup full-fat soft cheese
30 ml/2 tbsp crème fraîche
1 garlic clove, crushed
30 ml/2 tbsp snipped chives
30 ml/2 tbsp chopped parsley
30 ml/2 tbsp chopped cress
Juice of ½ lemon
A few drops of Worcestershire sauce
1 head of radicchio, shredded
1 head of chicory, sliced
A few drops of raspberry vinegar
5 ml/1 tsp olive oil

Cut the tops off the tomatoes, scoop
out the seeds and place upside-down
on a rack to drain. Sprinkle the insides
with salt and pepper. Mix together the
cream cheese, crème fraîche, garlic,
herbs, cress, lemon juice and
Worcestershire sauce. Season to taste
with salt and pepper. Fill the tomatoes
with this mixture. Arrange the
radicchio and chicory on a serving
plate and sprinkle with the raspberry
vinegar and oil. Stand the tomatoes
on top and serve at once.

Peperonata

SERVES 4

15 ml/1 tbsp olive oil
1 onion, sliced
1 red (bell) pepper, sliced
1 green pepper, sliced
1 yellow pepper, sliced
1 garlic clove, crushed
200 g/7 oz/1 small can of tomatoes,
    chopped
Salt and freshly ground black pepper
Ciabatta bread, to serve

Heat the oil and fry (sauté) the onion
until softened but not browned. Add
the peppers and garlic and fry gently
for about 15 minutes until the
peppers are tender. Stir in the
tomatoes and season to taste with
salt and pepper. Turn into a serving
dish and leave to cool. Serve with
crusty ciabatta bread.

Tomatoes with pesto

SERVES 4

350 g/12 oz cherry tomatoes
200 g/7 oz/scant 1 cup Mozzarella
    cheese, drained and chopped
1 avocado, peeled, stoned (pitted) and
    chopped
30 ml/2 tbsp Pesto Sauce (page 254)
Salt and freshly ground black pepper
A few small parsley sprigs

Halve the tomatoes and scoop out the
centres. Place upside-down on a rack
to drain. Meanwhile, mix together the
Mozzarella, avocado and pesto sauce
and season with salt and pepper.
Arrange the tomato halves in a circle
on a large serving plate and spoon
the filling into the centres. Garnish
with parsley sprigs.

Italian-style bean, egg and spring onion salad

SERVES 4

225 g/8 oz French (green) beans
2 hard-boiled (hard-cooked) eggs,
    chopped
3 spring onions (scallions), finely
    chopped
15 ml/3 tbsp balsamic vinegar
120 ml/4 fl oz/½ cup olive oil
Salt and freshly ground black pepper

Bring a large pan of salted water to
the boil, add the beans and boil for
about 5 minutes until just tender but
still crisp. Drain, rinse in cold water,
then leave to cool. Transfer to a
serving bowl and sprinkle with the
eggs and spring onions. Whisk
together the vinegar and olive oil until
well blended and season with salt and
pepper. Pour over the salad and toss
well before serving.

Italian antipasti

SERVES 4

4 ripe plum tomatoes, thinly sliced
15 ml/2 tbsp extra virgin olive oil
A few basil leaves, torn into pieces
Freshly ground black pepper
4 slices of Parma ham
4 slices of mortadella
4 slices of bresaola (cured beef)
4 ripe figs, quartered
1 ogen melon, seeded and cut into
  wedges
50 g/2 oz stoned (pitted) black olives
Extra olive oil and pepper (optional)

Place the tomatoes in the centre of a
serving plate, drizzle with the oil to
taste, sprinkle with basil leaves and
season with pepper. Arrange the
meats and fruit around the tomatoes
and sprinkle with the olives. Serve
with a little extra olive oil and pepper
for guests to drizzle over their own
portions, if liked.

Tropical fruit cocktail

SERVES 4

1 avocado, peeled, stoned (pitted) and
  sliced
15 ml/1 tbsp lemon juice
1 papaya (pawpaw), sliced
2 kiwi fruit, sliced
1 bunch of spring onions (scallions),
  sliced
225 g/8 oz/2 cups Gouda (Dutch)
  cheese, diced
100 g/4 oz cherries, stoned (pitted)
For the dressing:
45 ml/3 tbsp cider vinegar
5 ml/1 tsp clear honey
30 ml/2 tbsp walnut oil
Salt and freshly ground black pepper
15 ml/1 tbsp sparkling white wine
A little angostura bitters

Toss the avocado in the lemon juice,
then carefully mix together all the
remaining cocktail ingredients.
To make the dressing, mix together
the cider vinegar, honey and oil and
season to taste with salt and pepper.
Pour over the salad, toss carefully and
leave to chill for 30 minutes. Arrange
the salad in cocktail glasses, add a
dash of sparkling wine and sprinkle a
little angostura bitters over before
serving.

Prawn and dill avocados

SERVES 4

60 ml/4 tbsp full-fat soft cheese
60 ml/4 tbsp crème fraîche
30 ml/2 tbsp horseradish sauce
15 ml/1 tbsp chopped dill (dill weed)
Salt and freshly ground black pepper
100 g/4 oz cooked, peeled prawns
  (shrimp)
30 ml/2 tbsp lemon juice
2 avocados
4 dill sprigs, to garnish

Mix together the cheese, crème
fraîche, horseradish and chopped dill
and season to taste with salt and
pepper. Fold in the prawns and half
the lemon juice. Halve the avocados,
remove the stones (pits) and brush
with the remaining lemon juice. Pile
the prawn mixture into the avocados
and serve garnished with dill sprigs.

Cream cheese nectarines

SERVES 4

½ iceberg lettuce, shredded
4 nectarines, halved and stoned (pitted)
225 g/8 oz/1 cup full-fat soft cheese
30 ml/2 tbsp single (light) cream
100 g/4 oz/1 cup chopped mixed nuts
Salt and freshly ground black pepper
50 g/2 oz/1 small jar of lumpfish roe

Arrange the lettuce on individual plates and place the nectarine halves on top. Beat the cheese with the cream and nuts and season to taste with salt and pepper. Spoon the mixture on the top of the nectarines and garnish with the lumpfish roe.

Strawberry and melon salad

SERVES 4

½ iceberg lettuce, shredded
1 melon, skinned, seeded and cubed
100 g/4 oz strawberries, sliced
¼ cucumber, sliced
60 ml/4 tbsp French Dressing
   (page 276)
30 ml/2 tbsp chopped mint
Salt and freshly ground black pepper
50 g/2 oz/½ cup flaked (slivered)
   almonds

Place the lettuce on a serving plate and arrange the melon, strawberries and cucumber attractively on top. Mix the French Dressing with the mint and season to taste with salt and pepper. Just before serving, pour the dressing over the salad, then sprinkle with the almonds.

Gingered melon and parma ham

SERVES 4

1 honeydew melon
100 g/4 oz Parma ham, thinly sliced and
   cut into strips
25 g/1 oz stem ginger, chopped
30 ml/2 tbsp ginger syrup
5 ml/1 tsp lemon juice
45 ml/3 tbsp olive oil
Freshly ground black pepper

Quarter the melon lengthways, remove the seeds and skin and cut the flesh into long slices. Wind the ham round the melon slices. Arrange on a serving plate. Whisk together the remaining ingredients until thoroughly mixed, then pour over the melon. Cover and chill for 1 hour before serving.

Greek tomato platter

SERVES 4

6 ripe plum tomatoes, sliced
100 g/4 oz/½ cup Feta cheese, crumbled
8 black olives, stoned (pitted) and sliced
15 ml/1 tbsp dried oregano
15 ml/1 tbsp white wine vinegar
15 ml/1 tbsp olive oil
Freshly ground black pepper

Arrange the tomato slices on individual plates and scatter the cheese, olives and oregano over. Whisk together the wine vinegar and olive oil, then drizzle it over the tomatoes. Season generously with pepper before serving.

Courgette and parmesan bake

SERVES 4

3 courgettes (zucchini), sliced
2 eggs, beaten
75 ml/5 tbsp single (light) cream
15 ml/1 tbsp chopped mint
Salt and freshly ground black pepper
50 g/2 oz/½ cup Parmesan cheese, freshly grated
30 ml/2 tbsp French Dressing (page 276)
2 tomatoes, sliced
½ box of cress

Bring a large pan of salted water to the boil, drop in the courgettes and cook for 5 minutes, then drain well. Purée in a food processor or blender. Stir in the eggs, cream and mint and season with salt and pepper. Pour into greased individual ovenproof dishes, sprinkle with the Parmesan and bake in a preheated oven at 180°C/350°F/ gas mark 4 for 30 minutes until set. Leave to cool, then chill. Turn out on to individual plates and spoon the French Dressing over. Serve with the tomato slices and cress.

Cheese courgettes with Parma ham

SERVES 4

2 large courgettes (zucchini), halved lengthways
50 g/2 oz/½ cup Cheddar cheese, grated
1 hard-boiled (hard-cooked) egg, chopped
50 g/2 oz/½ cup Parma ham, chopped
5 ml/1 tsp chopped parsley
Salt and freshly ground black pepper
15 ml/1 tbsp freshly grated Parmesan cheese

Using a teaspoon, scoop out the centres of the courgettes to create boat shapes and arrange the shells, skin-side down, in a shallow ovenproof dish. Chop the flesh roughly, then mix with half the Cheddar, the egg, ham and parsley and season to taste with salt and pepper. Spoon into the courgette shells and sprinkle with the remaining Cheddar and the Parmesan. Bake in a preheated oven at 190°C/375°F/gas mark 5 for 30 minutes until golden brown.

Goats' cheese with lemon

SERVES 4

100 g/4 oz goats' cheese
5 ml/1 tsp grated lemon rind
Salt and freshly ground black pepper
30 ml/2 tbsp olive oil
1 garlic clove, crushed
A few basil leaves, torn into pieces
Crusty bread or Crudités (page 10), to serve

Place the cheese in a shallow bowl and sprinkle with the lemon rind, salt and pepper. Mix together the oil and garlic and pour over the cheese. Sprinkle with the basil leaves. Leave to stand at room temperature for at least 1 hour before serving with crusty bread or crudités.

Grilled goats' cheese salad

SERVES 4

100 g/4 oz mixed salad leaves
8 baby plum tomatoes, halved
25 g/1 oz/¼ cup walnuts, chopped
45 ml/3 tbsp olive oil
45 ml/3 tbsp hazelnut (filbert) oil
30 ml/2 tbsp balsamic vinegar
Salt and freshly ground black pepper
225 g/8 oz firm goats' cheese
8 thick slices of French bread

Mix together the salad leaves and tomatoes and arrange on individual plates. Sprinkle with the walnuts. Whisk together the oils and vinegar and season with salt and pepper. Drizzle over the salad and toss together gently. Cut the cheese into eight slices and place on top of the bread. Grill (broil) for about 4 minutes until bubbling and golden. Place on top of the salad and serve.

Blue cheese bites

MAKES 30

50 g/2 oz/½ cup wholemeal plain (all-purpose) flour
25 g/1 oz/¼ cup plain flour
75 g/3 oz/⅓ cup unsalted (sweet) butter, softened
Freshly ground black pepper
75 g/3 oz/¾ cup Stilton or other blue cheese, crumbled
30 ml/2 tbsp beaten egg
45 ml/3 tbsp plain yoghurt
30 ml/2 tbsp celery or sesame seeds

Mix together the flours, then rub in the butter until the mixture resembles breadcrumbs. Season with pepper. Mix in the cheese, then blend to a soft dough with the egg. Wrap the dough in clingfilm (plastic wrap) and chill for 1 hour. Roll out the dough to 3 mm/⅛ in thick, cut into 5 cm/2 in rounds with a biscuit (cookie) cutter and place on ungreased baking (cookie) sheets. Brush with the yoghurt and sprinkle with the celery or sesame seeds. Bake in a preheated oven at 180°C/350°F/gas mark 4 for 12 minutes until crisp and brown. Cool on a wire rack, then store in an airtight container until required.

Vine-leaf fruit parcels

SERVES 4

225 g/8 oz/1 medium can or packet of vine leaves, drained
175 g/6 oz/1½ cups cooked long-grain rice
1 onion, finely chopped
100 g/4 oz/⅔ cup no-need-to-soak dried apricots, finely chopped
50 g/2 oz/⅓ cup sultanas (golden raisins)
A pinch of ground cinnamon
A pinch of allspice
15 ml/1 tbsp chopped mint
15 ml/1 tbsp lemon juice
300 ml/½ pt/1¼ cups orange juice
150 ml/¼ pt/⅔ cup water

Rinse the vine leaves and pat dry on kitchen paper (paper towels). Arrange a few leaves on the base of a deep casserole dish (Dutch oven). Mix together the rice, onion, apricots, sultanas, spices, mint and lemon juice. Place spoonfuls of the mixture on individual vine leaves and fold up, then roll into tight parcels. Arrange half the parcels in a single layer in the casserole dish, then cover with a few more vine leaves. Repeat the layers with the remaining parcels and vine leaves. Pour in the orange juice and water and bake in a preheated oven at 160°C/325°F/gas mark 3 for 1½ hours, then either serve immediately or cool and chill before serving.

Aubergine and pesto rolls with goats' cheese

SERVES 4

2 aubergines (eggplants), diagonally
   sliced
Salt and freshly ground black pepper
60 ml/4 tbsp Pesto Sauce (page 254)
225 g/8 oz/2 cups mild goats' cheese,
   cut into chunks
75 ml/5 tbsp extra virgin olive oil
30 ml/2 tsp lemon juice

Place the aubergines in a colander,
sprinkle with salt and leave to stand
for 30 minutes. Rinse in cold water,
then pat dry on kitchen paper (paper
towels). Spread the aubergine slices
with the pesto sauce, then season
with salt and pepper. Roll the slices
round the chunks of goats' cheese
and secure with cocktail sticks
(toothpicks). Arrange in a shallow
ovenproof dish. Whisk together the oil
and lemon juice, then sprinkle over
the aubergine rolls. Bake in a
preheated oven at 180°C/350°F/gas
mark 4 for about 30 minutes until
tender and lightly browned. Serve hot.

Prawn fritters

SERVES 4

225 g/8 oz/2 cups plain (all-purpose)
   flour
A pinch of salt
100 g/4 oz/½ cup butter or margarine
2 egg yolks
45 ml/3 tbsp single (light) cream
225 g/8 oz cooked, peeled prawns
   (shrimp)
30 ml/2 tbsp lemon juice
Oil, for deep-frying
1 lemon, cut into wedges

Mix together the flour and salt, then
rub in the butter or margarine until
the mixture resembles fine
breadcrumbs. Stir in the egg yolks
and cream and work to a smooth
dough. Wrap in clingfilm (plastic
wrap) and chill for 30 minutes.
   Sprinkle the prawns with the lemon
juice and leave to stand. Roll the
dough into a long cylinder shape and
slice off 2 cm/1 in pieces. Press a
prawn into each slice, then work the
dough round the prawn to make little
balls. Heat the oil to 190°C/375°F,
when a cube of day-old bread sinks to
the bottom, then rises to the top and
browns in 1 minute. Add the dough
balls and fry (sauté) for a few minutes
until golden brown. Drain well on
kitchen paper (paper towels) and
serve hot with the lemon wedges.

Spanish prawns in garlic

SERVES 4

45 ml/3 tbsp olive oil
250 g/9 oz large raw prawns, peeled but
   with tails intact
2 garlic cloves, sliced
A pinch of chilli powder (optional)
Salt and freshly ground black pepper

Heat the oil in a large frying pan
(skillet), add the prawns, garlic and
chilli, if using, and fry (sauté) for a
few minutes, tossing and shaking the
pan frequently, just until the prawns
turn pink. Season with a little salt and
plenty of pepper and serve at once.

Scallops with red pepper sauce

SERVES 4

Juice of 2 limes
175 ml/6 fl oz/¾ cup olive oil
8 large scallops, sliced into thick discs
Salt and freshly ground black pepper
175 g/6 oz/1 jar of red (bell) peppers,
    drained
1 garlic clove, crushed
A few coriander (cilantro) sprigs

Reserve 15 ml/1 tbsp of the lime juice and whisk the remainder with 90 ml/ 6 tbsp of the oil. Pour over the scallops, season generously with salt and pepper and leave to marinate for 30 minutes. Purée the peppers and garlic with the reserved lime juice and 75 ml/5 tbsp of the remaining oil in a food processor or blender, then season to taste with salt and pepper. Drain the scallops and pat dry on kitchen paper (paper towels). Heat the remaining oil and fry (sauté) the scallops quickly over a high heat for about 2 minutes on each side until just golden. Transfer to individual plates, arrange a spoonful of the puréed sauce on the side and serve garnished with the coriander sprigs.

Scallops with dill

SERVES 4

12 scallops
300 ml/½ pt/1¼ cups milk
Salt and freshly ground black pepper
25 g/1 oz/¼ cup plain (all-purpose) flour
25 g/1 oz/2 tbsp butter or margarine
6 dill (dill weed) sprigs

Remove the scallops from the shells, cut away and discard the black parts and wash them thoroughly. Place in a greased ovenproof dish, pour over the milk and season to taste with salt and pepper. Bake in a preheated oven at 190°C/375°F/gas mark 5 for 45 minutes. Meanwhile, mix the flour and butter or margarine to a paste in a small saucepan, adding a little extra milk if the mixture is too stiff. Transfer the scallops to a warm serving dish and keep warm. Add the liquor from the cooking dish to the saucepan, a little at a time, until the mixture is smooth, then bring to the boil and simmer for 4 minutes, stirring continuously, until the sauce is smooth and thickened. Reserve one sprig of dill, then chop the remainder and stir into the sauce. Season to taste with salt and pepper, pour over the scallops and garnish with the remaining dill.

Shrimp toasts

SERVES 4

5 slices of bread
100 g/4 oz cooked, peeled prawns
    (shrimp)
50 g/2 oz/¼ cup butter or margarine
2.5 ml/½ tsp curry paste
A pinch of ground coriander (cilantro)
4 parsley sprigs

Reserve one slice of bread and flatten
the others with a rolling pin. Cut into
rounds with a pastry (cookie) cutter
and toast lightly. Reserve a few
shrimps for garnish and chop the
remainder. Break the remaining slice
of bread into crumbs. Blend the
chopped shrimp with the butter or
margarine, then stir in the curry
paste, breadcrumbs and coriander.
Spread the mixture over the toast
rounds and grill (broil) under a hot
grill (broiler) for 5 minutes until
golden. Garnish with the reserved
shrimps and a sprig of parsley.

Mozzarella and Parma ham dreams

SERVES 4

8 slices of day-old bread, crusts removed
25 g/1 oz/2 tsp butter or margarine
200 g/7 oz Mozzarella cheese, cut into
    four slices
4 slices of Parma ham
3 eggs, lightly beaten
45 ml/3 tbsp milk
Salt and freshly ground black pepper
Olive or sunflower oil, for deep-frying
Tomato Sauce (page 253), to serve

Lightly butter the bread and sandwich
together with the Mozzarella and

Parma ham, pressing the edges
together firmly. Halve diagonally, if
preferred, then wrap in clingfilm
(plastic wrap) and chill for 30 minutes
if possible.

Lightly beat the eggs with the milk
and season with salt and pepper. Dip
the sandwiches in the egg mixture
until well coated. Heat the oil until a
cube of day-old bread browns in
30 seconds. Add the sandwiches, one
or two at a time, and deep-fry for a
few minutes until golden brown on
both sides. Fry (sauté) the remaining
sandwiches and serve hot with tomato
sauce.

Hot tomato and Mozzarella salad

SERVES 4

100 g/4 oz Mozzarella cheese, sliced
2 beefsteak tomatoes, sliced
Salt and freshly ground black pepper
50 g/2 oz stoned (pitted) black olives,
    finely chopped
30 ml/2 tbsp olive oil
25 g/1 oz/¼ cup Parmesan cheese,
    freshly grated
A few basil leaves, to garnish

Layer slices of Mozzarella between
and on top of three tomato slices,
seasoning with salt and pepper and
sprinkling with olives as you go.
Arrange the stacks in a flameproof
serving dish, drizzle with the oil and
sprinkle with the Parmesan. Season
again lightly with pepper. Place under
a hot grill (broiler) for a few minutes
until the Mozzarella begins to melt.
Garnish with the basil and serve at
once.

Asparagus with herb butter

SERVES 4

750 g/1¾ lb asparagus
50 g/2 oz/¼ cup unsalted (sweet) butter
15 ml/1 tbsp chopped parsley
5 ml/1 tsp chopped thyme
15 ml/1 tbsp snipped chives
5 ml/1 tsp lemon juice
Freshly ground black pepper

Wash and trim the asparagus and tie in a bundle. Stand the bundle in a pan of lightly salted water, cover with foil or a lid and bring to the boil. Simmer gently for about 10 minutes, then remove from the heat and leave to stand for 5 minutes. Meanwhile, melt the butter with the herbs, lemon juice and plenty of pepper. Drain the asparagus and arrange on warm serving plates, pour over the herb butter and serve at once.

Garlic bread

SERVES 4

1 baguette
100 g/4 oz/½ cup Garlic Butter
   (page 260)

Cut the baguette diagonally into thick slices without cutting right through the base. Spread all the cut sides with the garlic butter and wrap the loaf in foil. Bake in a preheated oven at 180°C/350°F/gas mark 4 for 20 minutes. Serve alone, with dips or with a main course.

Stilton tarts

SERVES 4

50 g/2 oz/¼ cup butter or margarine
25 g/1 oz/2 tbsp lard (shortening) or
   vegetable fat
175 g/6 oz/1½ cups plain (all-purpose)
   flour
75 g/3 oz/¾ cup Stilton or other blue
   cheese, crumbled
45 ml/3 tbsp water
1 bunch of spring onions (scallions),
   chopped
300 ml/½ pt/1¼ cups single (light) cream
2 eggs, beaten
Salt and freshly ground black pepper

Rub the butter or margarine and lard or vegetable fat into the flour until the mixture resembles breadcrumbs. Mix in a third of the cheese and add enough of the water to bind the mixture to a firm pastry (paste). Roll out on a floured surface and use to line four greased 10 cm/4 in flan tins (pie pans). Sprinkle the onions into the flan cases. Beat together the cream and eggs, then season with salt and pepper. Stir in the remaining cheese and pour the mixture into the pastry cases (pie shells). Bake in a preheated oven at 200°C/400°F/gas mark 6 for about 20 minutes until golden brown. Serve hot or warm.

23

Filo parcels with chestnut mushrooms

SERVES 4

75 g/3 oz/⅓ cup butter or margarine
1 garlic clove, crushed
250 g/9 oz leeks, trimmed and thinly sliced
200 g/7 oz/1 medium can of chestnut pieces
60 ml/4 tbsp crème fraîche
25 g/1 oz/¼ cup Parmesan cheese, freshly grated
15 ml/1 tbsp chopped parsley
Salt and freshly ground black pepper
12 sheets of filo pastry (paste)
Mixed salad, to serve

Melt 25 g/1 oz/2 tbsp of the butter or margarine and fry (sauté) the garlic and leeks for about 4 minutes until softened but not browned. Turn into a bowl and stir in the chestnuts, crème fraîche, Parmesan and parsley. Season to taste with salt and pepper. Melt the remaining butter and lightly brush a little over a sheet of filo pastry. Place a spoonful of the filling on one corner, then fold over into a triangle. Brush the top with butter, then continue folding and brushing until you have wrapped the filling into a triangular parcel. Repeat to make the remaining parcels. Arrange on a greased baking (cookie) sheet and bake in a preheated oven at 180°F/350°F/gas mark 4 for about 20 minutes until crisp and golden. Serve hot with a mixed salad.

Ham gougère

SERVES 4

15 ml/1 tbsp oil
1 onion, chopped
100 g/4 oz mushrooms, chopped
175 g/6 oz/1½ cups honey roast ham, chopped
Salt and freshly ground black pepper
75 g/3 oz/⅓ cup butter or margarine
200 ml/7 fl oz/scant 1 cup water
100 g/4 oz/1 cup plain (all-purpose) flour
3 eggs, beaten
50 g/2 oz/1 cup fresh breadcrumbs
100 g/4 oz/1 cup Cheddar cheese, grated

Heat the oil and fry (sauté) the onion and mushrooms until softened but not browned. Add the ham and season to taste with salt and pepper. Put to one side. Heat the butter or margarine and water in a saucepan, bring to the boil, then tip in the flour all at once and beat until the mixture comes away cleanly from the sides of the pan. Leave to cool slightly, then gradually beat in the eggs, a little at a time, to make a choux pastry (paste). Spread half the pastry on the base of a greased 20 cm/8 in pie dish and pile the rest round the edge. Spoon the ham mixture into the centre and sprinkle with the breadcrumbs and cheese. Bake in a preheated oven at 200°C/400°F/gas mark 6 for 30 minutes until well risen and golden brown.

Red pepper soufflés

SERVES 4

225 g/8 oz Shortcrust Pastry (page 164)
30 ml/2 tbsp olive oil
1 red (bell) pepper, seeded and sliced
15 ml/1 tbsp chopped mixed nuts
15 ml/1 tbsp caster (superfine) sugar
A few drops of balsamic vinegar
Salt and freshly ground black pepper
For the soufflés:
175 ml/6 fl oz/¾ cup milk
100 g/4 oz/½ cup goats' cheese
10 ml/2 tsp cornflour (cornstarch)
2.5 ml/½ tsp cayenne
3 eggs, separated
15 ml/1 tbsp snipped chives

Roll out the pastry (paste) on a lightly floured surface to about 5 mm/¼ in thick and use to line four greased 7.5 cm/3 in flan tins (pans). Cover with greaseproof (waxed) paper, fill with baking beans and bake blind in a preheated oven at 200°C/400°F/gas mark 6 for 10 minutes. Remove the paper and beans and keep the pastry cases (pie shells) warm.

Meanwhile heat the oil in a frying pan (skillet) and fry (sauté) the peppers until golden. Stir in the nuts, sugar and vinegar and season with salt and pepper.

To make the soufflés, heat the milk and cheese gently together just until the cheese melts. Mix the cornflour to a paste with a little water, then stir it into the milk with the cayenne and season with salt and pepper. Bring to the boil, stirring continuously, and stir until the sauce thickens. Remove from the heat and leave until cool. Beat the egg yolks into the sauce. Whisk the egg whites until stiff, then fold into the sauce. Pour into four greased 7.5 cm/3 in ramekins (custard cups) and bake in the preheated oven at 180°C/350°F/gas mark 4 for about 7 minutes until well risen and golden brown. Spoon the pepper mixture into the pastry cases and top each one with a soufflé. Serve garnished with the chives.

Pancakes with wild mushrooms

SERVES 4

25 g/1 oz/2 tbsp unsalted (sweet) butter
30 ml/2 tbsp extra virgin olive oil
450 g/1 lb mixed wild mushrooms, thinly sliced
1 garlic clove, crushed
2 shallots, chopped
120 ml/4 fl oz/½ cup double (heavy) cream
Salt and freshly ground black pepper
4 Pancakes (page 187)
15 ml/1 tbsp chopped parsley

Heat the butter and oil in a saucepan and fry (sauté) the mushrooms over a high heat, stirring continuously, until the liquid has evaporated. Stir in the garlic and shallots and cook for a few minutes, stirring, until the shallots are golden. Stir in the cream, season to taste and simmer gently for a few minutes until the sauce thickens. If you have just made the pancakes, keep them warm, otherwise warm them in the oven or in a frying pan (skillet). Divide the mushroom mixture between the pancakes, roll up and serve at once sprinkled with the parsley.

Mushrooms in batter with herb sauce

SERVES 4

15 g/½ oz/1 tbsp butter or margarine
1 onion, chopped
100 g/4 oz/1 cup plain (all-purpose) flour
5 ml/1 tsp tomato purée (paste)
200 g/7 oz/1 small can of tomatoes, chopped
150 ml/¼ pt/⅔ cup Chicken Stock (page 28)
5 ml/1 tsp white wine vinegar
A pinch of paprika
Salt and freshly ground black pepper
30 ml/2 tbsp chopped parsley
30 ml/2 tbsp chopped chervil
30 ml/2 tbsp chopped watercress
300 ml/½ pt/1¼ cups milk
1 egg, separated
5 ml/1 tsp olive oil
Oil, for deep-frying
225 g/8 oz button mushrooms

Melt the butter or margarine in a saucepan and fry (sauté) the onion until softened but not browned. Stir in 15 ml/1 tbsp of the flour and the tomato purée, then add the tomatoes, stock, vinegar and paprika. Season to taste with a little salt and plenty of pepper. Add the herbs and watercress, bring to the boil and simmer for 10 minutes. Purée the sauce in a food processor or blender, then place in a small serving dish.

Meanwhile, beat together the milk, egg yolk, olive oil and remaining flour until smooth. Whisk the egg white until stiff, then fold into the batter. Heat the oil to 190°C/375°F, when a cube of day-old bread sinks to the bottom, then rises and browns in 1 minute. Dip the mushrooms in the batter, then shake off any excess.

Fry immediately in the hot oil for 5 minutes until golden brown. Remove and drain well on kitchen paper (paper towels) before serving with the sauce.

Thai fish cakes

SERVES 4

For the fish cakes:
750 g/1¾ lb cod or haddock fillet, skinned and flaked
1 egg
30 ml/2 tbsp Thai fish sauce
175 g/6 oz cooked, peeled prawns (shrimp)
45 ml/3 tbsp chopped fresh coriander (cilantro)
20 ml/4 tsp Thai red curry paste
Salt and freshly ground black pepper
30 ml/2 tbsp plain (all-purpose) flour
Oil, for shallow-frying
For the dipping sauce:
30 ml/2 tbsp Thai fish sauce
15 ml/1 tbsp dark soy sauce
10 ml/2 tsp sesame oil
15 ml/1 tbsp lime or lemon juice
5 ml/1 tsp soft brown sugar
A pinch of chilli powder
Mixed green salad, to serve

To make the fish cakes, put the fish, egg and fish sauce in a food processor or blender and process until well mixed but still fairly coarse. Transfer to a bowl. Process the prawns until chopped and add to the bowl with the coriander and curry paste. Season with salt and pepper. Shape into walnut-sized balls and roll in the flour. Shallow-fry for a few minutes until golden on all sides.

To make the dipping sauce, mix together all the ingredients. Serve with the fish cakes and a mixed green salad.

Stocks and soups

Some people like to make their own stocks to ensure the very best quality and ingredients, and it is simple to do as well as very satisfying. However, if, like me, you lack the time – and often the inclination – you can buy excellent stocks, which taste just like home-made, from the chill cabinet of your local supermarket. I also keep some good-quality stock cubes or a bottle of concentrated stock in the storecupboard to use on an everyday basis. There's a vast range to suit all kinds of flavours, but chicken or vegetable will be fine for most uses. Remember that some stock cubes can be very salty, so seek out the best you can find.

If you do make your own stock, remember to skim it carefully by sliding a shallow spoon across the top to lift off any scum. To remove any fat from stock, leave it to cool so that any fat solidifies on the top, then lift it off with a shallow spoon. To remove fat from hot stock, run a clean cloth under the cold tap until it is very cold, then wring it out and use it to line a colander. Pour the hot stock through the colander and the fat will solidify when it touches the cold cloth, leaving the fat-free stock to strain through into a bowl. Always cool stock quickly, then chill it and use it within a day or so. To freeze home-made stock, boil it to concentrate the stock and reduce the quantity by about half, then cool it quickly and freeze it in ice-cube trays or other small quantities for convenience. Soups make great starters for a meal, or you can team them with Croûtons (page 33) or crusty bread and a side salad to make a complete meal. Keep some part-baked loaves or rolls in the freezer and you are always prepared. This selection offers a variety of thin and chunkier soups as well as some delicious iced soups for warmer days.

Stocks

Vegetable stock

MAKES 1 LITRE/1¾ PTS/4¼ CUPS

2 carrots, sliced
1 onion, sliced
2 celery sticks, sliced
1 turnip, chopped
1 litre/1¾ pts/4¼ cups water
6 black peppercorns
1 bay leaf

Place all the ingredients in a large saucepan, bring to the boil, cover and simmer gently for 1½ hours. Strain.

Chicken stock

MAKES 1 LITRE/1¾ PTS/4¼ CUPS

1 kg/2¼ lb cooked or raw poultry bones and trimmings
2 onions, sliced
5 ml/1 tsp salt
450 g /1 lb vegetables (carrot, celery, leek, onion, etc.), roughly chopped
1 bay leaf
8 black peppercorns

Place the bones and meat in a large saucepan and cover with cold water. Bring to the boil and add the remaining ingredients. Bring back to the boil and simmer very gently, uncovered, for about 2 hours, topping up with boiling water as necessary. Strain and skim off any fat before using.

Beef stock

MAKES 1 LITRE/1¾ PTS/4¼ CUPS

1 kg/2¼ lb cooked or raw beef bones and trimmings
2 onions, sliced but not peeled
5 ml/1 tsp salt
450 g /1 lb vegetables (carrot, celery, leek, onion, etc.), roughly chopped
1 bay leaf
8 black peppercorns

Place the bones and meat in a large roasting tin (pan) and roast in a preheated oven at 200°C/400°F/gas mark 6 for about 30 minutes until browned. Transfer to a large saucepan and cover with cold water. Bring to the boil and add the remaining ingredients. Bring back to the boil, cover and simmer very gently for about 3 hours, topping up with boiling water as necessary. Strain and skim off any fat before using.

Giblet stock

MAKES 1 LITRE/1¾ PTS/4¼ CUPS

Giblets of 1 chicken, turkey or goose
1 onion, sliced
1 carrot, sliced
1 bunch of mixed herbs
1 litre/1¾ pts/4¼ cups water

Place all the ingredients in a large saucepan with just enough water to cover. Bring to the boil, skim, then cover and simmer gently for 2–3 hours. Strain and skim off any fat before using.

Fish stock

MAKES 1 LITRE/1¾ PTS/4¼ CUPS

1 kg/2¼ lb bones, skins and heads from
    filleted fish or other white fish
    trimmings
1 litre/1¾ pts/4¼ cups water
5 ml/1 tsp salt
1 onion, chopped
1 celery stick, chopped
6 white peppercorns
1 bouquet garni sachet

Wash the fish and discard the eyes.
Place all the ingredients in a large
saucepan, bring to the boil, cover and
simmer gently for 40 minutes. Strain.

Soups

Scotch broth

SERVES 4–6

700 g/1½ lb scrag end neck mutton or
    lamb
1.75 litres/3 pts/7½ cups Chicken Stock
    (page 28)
100 g/4 oz/generous ½ cup pearl barley
50 g/2 oz peas
1 large carrot, diced
1 large onion, diced
1 turnip, diced
2 celery sticks, diced
Salt and freshly ground black pepper
5 ml/1 tsp chopped parsley

Put the meat, stock and barley in a
large saucepan, bring to the boil,
cover and simmer for 1 hour,
skimming as necessary. Add the
vegetables, season to taste, cover and
simmer for a further 1 hour, stirring
occasionally. Remove from the heat,
take out the bones and skim off the
fat. If you wish, leave the soup to cool
at this stage so that it is easier to
remove the fat, which will solidify on
the surface. Add the parsley, adjust
the seasoning if necessary, and reheat
to serve.

Curried apple soup

SERVES 4

25 g/1 oz/2 tbsp butter or margarine
1 onion, chopped
25 g/1 oz/¼ cup plain (all-purpose) flour
15 ml/1 tbsp curry powder
900 ml/1½ pts/3¾ cups Chicken Stock
    (page 28)
750 g/1¾ lb cooking (tart) apples,
    peeled, cored and sliced
15 ml/1 tbsp lemon juice
Salt and freshly ground black pepper
90 ml/6 tbsp plain yoghurt

Melt the butter or margarine in a large saucepan and fry (sauté) the onion until soft but not brown. Stir in the flour and curry powder and cook for 1 minute, stirring. Add the stock, apples and lemon juice and bring to the boil, stirring continuously. Season to taste with salt and pepper. Simmer for 10 minutes until the apples are soft, then purée in a food processor or blender. Return to the pan to reheat, then ladle into warm soup bowls, add a swirl of yoghurt to each one and serve.

Apple and wine soup

SERVES 4

75 g/3 oz/⅓ cup caster (superfine) sugar
A pinch of salt
600 ml/1 pt/2½ cups water
1.5 kg/3 lb cooking (tart) apples,
    peeled, cored and chopped
50 g/2 oz/1 cup fresh breadcrumbs
1 cinnamon stick
Thinly pared rind of 1 lemon
Juice of 2 lemons
450 ml/¾ pt/2 cups dry red wine
45 ml/3 tbsp redcurrant jelly (clear
    conserve)
60 ml/4 tbsp plain yoghurt

Put the sugar, salt and water in a large saucepan, bring to the boil and add the apples, breadcrumbs, cinnamon and lemon rind. Simmer for 10 minutes, stirring occasionally, until the apples are soft. Remove the cinnamon and lemon rind and purée the apple mixture in a food processor or blender. Return the mixture to the pan, add the lemon juice, wine and redcurrant jelly and simmer gently, stirring, until the jelly dissolves and the soup is warmed through. Ladle the soup into warm soup bowls, add a swirl of yoghurt to each one and serve.

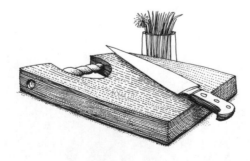

Dutch bacon and pea soup

SERVES 4

25 g/1 oz/2 tbsp butter or margarine
100 g/4 oz streaky bacon, finely
    chopped
1 garlic clove, chopped
225 g/8 oz/1 cup dried peas, soaked
    overnight in cold water
1 litre/1¾ pts/4¼ cups Vegetable Stock
    (page 28)
5 ml/1 tsp chopped mint
Freshly ground black pepper

Melt the butter or margarine in a large saucepan and fry (sauté) the bacon until crisp, then remove the bacon and keep it warm. Add the garlic to the pan and fry until just golden. Drain the peas and add to the pan with the stock and mint and season to taste with pepper. Bring to the boil, then simmer gently for 1 hour until tender. Purée in a food processor or blender, then return the soup to the pan and reheat gently. Serve sprinkled with the bacon pieces.

Beetroot soup

SERVES 4

25 g/1 oz/2 tbsp butter or margarine
1 onion, chopped
1 celery stick, chopped
4 raw beetroot (red beets)
225 g/8 oz tomatoes, skinned
600 ml/1 pt/2½ cups Vegetable Stock
    (page 28)
Salt and freshly ground black pepper
30 ml/2 tbsp soured (dairy sour) cream

Melt the butter or margarine in a large saucepan and fry (sauté) the onion and celery until soft but not brown. Add the beetroot, tomatoes and stock, bring to the boil, cover and simmer gently for about 1 hour until the beetroot are tender. Purée in a food processor or blender. Return the soup to the saucepan, season to taste with salt and pepper and reheat. Spoon into warm soup bowls, add a swirl of the soured cream to each one and serve.

Bouillabaisse

SERVES 4

450 g/1 lb fish bones and trimmings
900 ml/1½ pts/3¾ cups water
1 onion, finely chopped
30 ml/2 tbsp chopped parsley
1 bouquet garni sachet
600 ml/1 pt/2½ cups milk
Salt and freshly ground black pepper
1 egg yolk, beaten

Place the fish, water, onion, parsley and bouquet garni in a large saucepan, bring to the boil, cover and simmer gently for 45 minutes. Strain and return the liquor to the pan. Add the milk, season to taste with salt and pepper and stir in the egg yolk. Heat through before serving, but do not allow the soup to boil.

31

Smooth carrot and coriander soup

SERVES 4

15 ml/1 tbsp sunflower oil
1 onion, chopped
1 garlic clove, chopped
450 g/1 lb carrots, chopped
600 ml/1 pt/2½ cups Chicken Stock
    (page 28)
A pinch of sugar
Salt and freshly ground black pepper
150 ml/¼ pt/⅔ cup single (light) cream
15 ml/1 tbsp chopped coriander
    (cilantro)
Croûtons (page 33), to serve

Heat the oil in a large saucepan and
fry (sauté) the onion and garlic until
soft but not brown. Stir in the carrots,
then add the stock and sugar and
season to taste. Bring to the boil,
then simmer for 15 minutes until the
carrots are soft. Purée in a food
processor or blender, then return the
soup to the pan and stir in the cream
and coriander. Heat through gently
and serve hot with croûtons.

Celery and shallot soup

SERVES 4–6

25 g/1 oz/2 tbsp butter or margarine
1 head of celery, chopped
6 shallots, chopped
2 large potatoes, chopped
600 ml/1 pt/2½ cups Chicken Stock
    (page 28)
300 ml/½ pt/1¼ cups milk
150 ml/¼ pt/⅔ cup single (light) cream
Salt and freshly ground black pepper
30 ml/2 tbsp chopped mint or parsley

Melt the butter or margarine in a
large saucepan and fry (sauté) the
celery, shallots and potatoes until soft

but not brown. Add the stock, bring
to the boil, cover and simmer gently
for about 20 minutes until the
vegetables are tender. Purée in a food
processor or blender, then return the
soup to the pan and add the milk and
cream. Season to taste and reheat.
Serve sprinkled with the mint or
parsley.

Simple chicken noodle soup

SERVES 4

15 ml/1 tbsp olive oil
1 onion, finely chopped
1 garlic clove, crushed
1.5 litres/2½ pints/6 cups Chicken Stock
    (page 28)
15 ml/1 tbsp tomato purée (paste)
Salt and freshly ground black pepper
225 g/8 oz/2 cups cooked chicken, cut
    into slivers
75 g/3 oz thin egg noodles

Heat the oil in a large saucepan and
fry (sauté) the onion and garlic until
soft but not brown. Add the stock and
bring to the boil. Stir in the tomato
purée and season to taste with salt
and pepper. Add the chicken and
simmer for about 5 minutes until
heated through. Add the noodles,
return to the boil and simmer for
about 8 minutes until just tender.

*Smoked duck with broccoli
and almonds (page 14)*

Leek and pasta soup

SERVES 4

25 g/1 oz/2 tbsp butter or margarine
6 leeks, thinly sliced
1.2 litres/2 pts/5 cups Chicken or
    Vegetable Stock (page 28)
50 g/2 oz vermicelli
Salt and freshly ground black pepper
150 ml/¼ pt/⅔ cup single (light) cream

Melt the butter or margarine in a large saucepan and fry (sauté) the leeks until soft but not brown. Add the stock, bring to the boil, cover and simmer for 30 minutes, stirring frequently. Add the vermicelli and cook for a further 15 minutes until just tender. Season to taste, stir in the cream and reheat gently before serving.

Cream of chicken soup

SERVES 4

50 g/2 oz/¼ cup butter or margarine
1 onion, finely chopped
1 carrot, finely chopped
1 celery stick, chopped
1 garlic clove, crushed
1.5 litres/2½ pints/5 cups Chicken Stock
    (page 28)
225 g/8 oz/2 cups cooked chicken,
    chopped
30 ml/2 tbsp chopped parsley
Salt and freshly ground black pepper
250 ml/8 fl oz/1 cup single (light) cream

Melt the butter or margarine in a large saucepan and fry (sauté) the onion, carrot, celery and garlic until soft but not brown. Add the stock and chicken and bring to the boil. Simmer for about 10 minutes until the

*Seafood stir-fry with mangoes
(page 47)*

vegetables are very tender. Add half the parsley and season to taste with salt and pepper. Purée the vegetables in a food processor or blender, adding enough of the stock to make a thick soup. Return to the pan, add the cream and adjust the seasoning to taste. Reheat gently and serve sprinkled with the remaining parsley.

Curried chicken and lentil soup with croûtons

SERVES 4

For the soup:
15 ml/1 tbsp sunflower oil
1 onion, chopped
10 ml/2 tsp curry powder
15 ml/1 tbsp dry sherry
1.2 litres/2 pts/5 cups Chicken Stock
    (page 28)
4 carrots, cut into sticks
225 g/8 oz/2 cups cooked chicken,
    chopped
100 g/4 oz/⅔ cup lentils
Salt and freshly ground black pepper
For the croûtons:
120 ml/4 fl oz/½ cup sunflower oil
4 slices of wholemeal bread, cut into
    1 cm/½ in cubes

To make the soup, heat the oil in a large saucepan and fry (sauté) the onion until soft but not brown. Stir in the curry powder and fry gently for 1 minute. Stir in the sherry, then add the stock, carrots, chicken and lentils. Bring to the boil, then simmer for 15 minutes until the carrots and lentils are tender. Season to taste.

To make the croûtons, heat the oil and fry the bread until crisp, then drain on kitchen paper (paper towels) and serve with the soup.

Ham and sweetcorn chowder

SERVES 4

25 g/1 oz/2 tbsp butter or margarine
1 onion, finely chopped
45 ml/3 tbsp plain (all-purpose) flour
75 g/3 oz/⅓ cup full-fat soft cheese
300 ml/½ pt/1¼ cups Chicken Stock
  (page 28)
150 ml/¼ pt/⅔ cup milk
400 g/14 oz/1 large can of sweetcorn
  (corn), drained
Salt and freshly ground black pepper
150 ml/¼ pt/⅔ cup double (heavy) cream
100 g/4 oz/1 cup cooked ham, finely
  chopped
Hot crusty bread, to serve

Melt the butter or margarine in a large saucepan and fry (sauté) the onion until soft but not brown. Stir in the flour and cook for 1 minute. Stir in the cheese, then whisk in the stock and milk. Add the sweetcorn, season to taste and simmer for 10 minutes. Stir in the cream and heat through gently, stirring occasionally. Sprinkle with the ham and serve with hot crusty bread.

Creamy mushroom soup

SERVES 4

225 g/8 oz mushrooms, diced
1 celery stick
1.2 litres/2 pts/5 cups Vegetable Stock
  (page 28)
600 ml/1 pt/2½ cups milk
30 ml/2 tbsp dry white wine
Salt and freshly ground black pepper
15 ml/1 tbsp plain (all-purpose) flour
60 ml/4 tbsp double (heavy) cream

Place the mushrooms, celery and stock in a large saucepan, bring to the boil and simmer for 15 minutes until the vegetables are tender. Remove the celery. Reserve 15 ml/1 tbsp of the milk, then stir the rest into the soup with the wine and season to taste with salt and pepper. Bring back to the boil. Mix the flour and the reserved milk to a paste, stir into the soup and simmer for 3 minutes until thickened. Stir in the cream and heat through gently before serving.

Lentil soup with lemon

SERVES 4

25 g/1 oz/2 tbsp butter or margarine
1 onion, chopped
1 carrot, chopped
2 celery sticks, chopped
225 g/8 oz/1⅓ cups lentils, soaked
  overnight in cold water, then drained
2 litres/3½ pints/8½ cups water
300 ml/½ pt/1¼ cups milk
30 ml/2 tbsp lemon juice
Salt and freshly ground black pepper
15 ml/1 tbsp plain (all-purpose) flour
  (optional)
Extra 15 ml/1 tbsp butter or margarine
  (optional)

Melt the butter or margarine in a large saucepan and fry (sauté) the onion, carrot and celery until soft but not brown. Add the lentils and water, bring to the boil and simmer for about 45 minutes until the lentils are soft. Purée in a food processor or blender, then return to the pan. Add the milk and lemon juice, season to taste and bring back to the boil. If the soup is not thick enough, mix the flour and additional butter or margarine to a paste, stir into the soup and simmer for a few minutes until thickened.

Minestrone

SERVES 4

45 ml/3 tbsp olive oil
1 onion, chopped
1 leek, thinly sliced
2 celery sticks, thinly sliced
2 carrots, chopped
1 courgette (zucchini), thinly sliced
2 tomatoes, skinned and roughly
  chopped
2 potatoes, peeled and diced
2.5 litres/2 pts/10 cups Vegetable Stock
  (page 28)
75 g/3 oz macaroni
200 g/7 oz/1 small can of cannellini
  beans, drained
15–30 ml/1–2 tbsp Pesto Sauce (page
  254) or use bought
Salt and freshly ground black pepper
25 g/1 oz/¼ cup Parmesan cheese,
  freshly grated

Heat the oil in a large saucepan and fry (sauté) the onion, leek, celery and carrots until soft but not brown. Add the courgette, tomatoes, potatoes and stock, bring to the boil, then simmer for 10 minutes. Add the macaroni and simmer for 5 minutes. Add the cannellini beans and continue to simmer for about 10 minutes until all the vegetables are tender. Stir in the pesto sauce to taste and season with salt and pepper. Serve sprinkled with the Parmesan.

Mulligatawny soup

SERVES 4

25 g/1 oz/2 tbsp butter or margarine
3 streaky bacon rashers (slices), rinded
2 onions, chopped
2 eating (dessert) apples, peeled, cored
  and chopped
1 carrot, chopped
1 turnip, chopped
1 bunch of parsley, chopped
15 ml/1 tbsp curry powder
50 g/2 oz/½ cup plain (all-purpose) flour
10 ml/2 tsp curry paste
1.2 litres/2 pts/5 cups Vegetable Stock
  (page 28)
30 ml/2 tbsp tomato purée (paste)
A pinch of cayenne
Salt
1½ lemons
225 g/8 oz/1 cup long-grain rice

Melt the butter or margarine in a large saucepan and fry (sauté) the bacon until soft. Remove from the pan, then fry the onions, apples, carrot, turnip and parsley until soft. Blend together the curry powder, flour and curry paste, then stir into the vegetables. Add the stock and tomato purée, season to taste with the cayenne and salt and bring to the boil. Quarter the whole lemon and squeeze the juice from the half lemon. Add the lemon juice to the soup. Meanwhile, cook the rice in boiling salted water for about 15 minutes until tender. Drain and serve with the soup and lemon quarters.

French onion soup

SERVES 4

50 g/2 oz/¼ cup butter or margarine
3 large onions, sliced
4 lean bacon rashers (slices), rinded and
    chopped
2 potatoes, chopped
1.2 litres/2 pts/5 cups Beef Stock
    (page 28)
Salt and freshly ground black pepper
50 g/2 oz/½ cup Cheddar cheese, grated
2.5 ml/½ tsp Dijon mustard
2.5 ml/½ tsp dried mixed herbs
½ small baguette, thickly sliced

Melt the butter or margarine in a
large saucepan and fry (sauté) the
onions gently for about 20 minutes
until golden brown. Add the bacon
and potatoes and fry until just
browned. Stir in the stock, bring to
the boil, cover and simmer for about
15 minutes until the potatoes are
soft. Season to taste.

Meanwhile, mix the cheese,
mustard and herbs and season to
taste. Spread on the bread slices and
toast under the grill (broiler) until the
cheese is melted and golden brown.
Float the bread on the soup to serve.

Oxtail soup

SERVES 4

50 g/2 oz/¼ cup vegetable fat
1 oxtail, jointed
1 onion, chopped
1 carrot, chopped
1.2 litres/2 pts/5 cups Beef Stock
    (page 28)
6 black peppercorns
Salt and freshly ground black pepper
5 ml/1 tsp lemon juice
15 ml/1 tbsp plain (all-purpose) flour
    (optional)

Melt the lard or vegetable fat in a
frying pan (skillet) and fry (sauté) the
oxtail until browned. Transfer the joints
to a large saucepan. Fry the onion and
carrot in the frying pan until browned.
Add to the saucepan with the stock
and peppercorns, bring to the boil,
cover and simmer gently for 5 hours
until the meat is thoroughly tender.
Strain the soup and skim off all the fat.
Return to the pan, season to taste
with salt, pepper and the lemon juice
and reheat. If necessary, mix the flour
with a little water, then stir it into the
soup and heat gently, stirring, until the
soup thickens.

Creamy fresh pea soup

SERVES 4

25 g/1 oz/2 tbsp butter or margarine
4 spring onions (scallions), chopped
4 streaky bacon rashers (slices), rinded
    and chopped
450 g/1 lb fresh shelled or frozen peas
1.2 litres/2 pts/5 cups Vegetable Stock
    (page 28)
30 ml/2 tbsp chopped parsley
6 mint leaves, chopped
Salt and freshly ground black pepper
Mint leaves, to garnish

Melt the butter or margarine in a
large saucepan and fry (sauté) the
onions and bacon until soft but not
brown. Add the peas, stock, parsley
and chopped mint, bring to the boil,
cover and simmer gently for
10–15 minutes until the peas are
tender. Purée in a food processor or
blender, then return the soup to the
pan, season to taste with salt and
pepper and reheat. Serve garnished
with mint leaves.

Split pea soup

SERVES 4

700 g/1½ lb/4 cups split peas, soaked
   overnight in cold water, then drained
2 onions, chopped
1 carrot, chopped
½ turnip, chopped
1 celery stick, chopped
2 parsley sprigs, chopped
1.5 litres/2½ pts/6 cups Vegetable Stock
   (page 28)
Salt and freshly ground black pepper
150 ml/¼ pt/⅔ cup single (light) cream

Place the split peas in a large
saucepan with the onions, carrot,
turnip, celery, parsley and stock. Bring
to the boil, cover and simmer for
about 30 minutes until soft. Purée in a
food processor or blender, then return
to the pan. Season, stir in the cream
and reheat gently before serving.

Pumpkin soup

SERVES 4

700 g/1½ lb pumpkin, diced
600 ml/1 pt/2½ cups water
600 ml/1 pt/2½ cups milk
25 g/1 oz/2 tbsp butter or margarine
Salt and freshly ground black pepper
15 g/1 tbsp caster (superfine) sugar
15 ml/1 tbsp chopped parsley
Croûtons (page 33), to serve

Place the pumpkin and water in a
saucepan, bring to the boil, cover and
simmer for about 20 minutes until
tender. Strain off the water, purée the
pumpkin in a food processor or
blender, then return it to the pan with
the milk and butter or margarine and
season to taste. Reheat, stirring
occasionally. Stir in the sugar and
sprinkle with the parsley before
serving with croûtons.

Seafood and lemon soup

SERVES 4

15 ml/1 tbsp oil
15 ml/1 tbsp butter or margarine
225 g/8 oz onions, diced
1 garlic clove, crushed
225 g/8 oz potatoes, peeled and diced
300 ml/½ pt/1¼ cups milk
350 g/12 oz firm white fish fillets,
   trimmed and cubed
15 ml/1 tbsp lemon juice
Salt and freshly ground black pepper
60 ml/4 tbsp double (heavy) cream
50 g/2 oz peeled prawns (shrimp)
15 ml/1 tbsp snipped chives

Heat the oil and butter or margarine
in a large saucepan and fry (sauté)
the onions, garlic and potatoes until
the onions are soft but not brown.
Add the milk, bring to the boil, then
simmer for about 5 minutes until soft.
Add half the fish and the lemon juice
and season with salt and pepper.
Simmer for 5 minutes until the fish is
cooked. Purée in a food processor or
blender, then return to the pan. Stir in
the remaining fish and the cream and
simmer for 5 minutes until the fish is
almost cooked. Stir in the prawns and
heat through. Serve sprinkled with the
chives.

Creamy rice and celery soup

SERVES 4

50 g/2 oz/¼ cup butter or margarine
2 Spanish onions, thinly sliced
3 celery sticks, chopped
30 ml/2 tbsp long-grain rice
600 ml/1 pt/2½ cups water
900 ml/1½ pts/3¾ cups boiling milk
30 ml/2 tbsp chopped parsley
Salt and freshly ground black pepper

Melt half the butter or margarine in a large saucepan and fry (sauté) the onions and celery until soft but not brown. Stir in the rice and water, bring to the boil, cover and simmer for 1 hour, stirring frequently. When the rice is quite tender, add the boiling milk and parsley and season to taste. Bring back to the boil and simmer for a further 5 minutes, then stir in the remaining butter or margarine and serve.

Cream of tomato soup

SERVES 4

25 g/1 oz/2 tbsp butter or margarine
2 onions, chopped
1 garlic clove, crushed
1 celery stick, chopped
1 kg/2¼ lb tomatoes, skinned and chopped
2 carrots, chopped
1.75 litres/3 pts/7½ cups Vegetable Stock (page 28)
Salt and freshly ground black pepper
150 ml/¼ pt/⅔ cup double (heavy) cream
Croûtons (page 33), to serve

Melt the butter or margarine in a large saucepan and fry (sauté) the onions, garlic and celery until soft but not brown. Add the remaining vegetables and the stock, bring to the boil, cover and simmer for 30 minutes until all the vegetables are tender. Purée in a food processor or blender, then return the soup to the pan. Season to taste, stir in the cream and reheat gently before serving with Croûtons.

Tomato and orange soup

SERVES 4

450 g/1 lb tomatoes, halved
1 potato, chopped
1 carrot, chopped
1 sprig of basil
900 ml/1½ pts/3¾ cups Chicken Stock (page 28)
Salt and freshly ground black pepper
Juice of ½ orange
150 ml/¼ pt/⅔ cup single (light) cream

Put the tomatoes, potato, carrot, basil and stock in a saucepan and season to taste. Bring to the boil, then simmer for 20 minutes. Purée in a food processor or blender, then return the soup to the pan, stir in the orange juice and reheat. Taste and adjust the seasoning, if necessary. Serve with a swirl of the cream in each bowl.

Thick cream of vegetable soup

SERVES 4

25 g/1 oz/2 tbsp butter or margarine
1 onion, sliced
3 carrots, sliced
3 celery sticks, sliced
1 turnip, chopped
1.2 litres/2 pts/5 cups Chicken Stock
    (page 28)
Salt and freshly ground black pepper
15 ml/1 tbsp caster (superfine) sugar
15 ml/1 tbsp single (light) cream

Melt the butter or margarine in a large saucepan and fry (sauté) the vegetables until golden brown. Add the stock, bring to the boil, cover and simmer for 1 hour. Purée in a food processor or blender, then return the soup to the pan. Season to taste with salt, pepper and the sugar, stir in the cream and reheat gently before serving.

Winter vegetable soup

SERVES 4

15 ml/1 tbsp oil
1 onion, chopped
1 garlic clove, chopped
1 potato, chopped
1 carrot, chopped
1 leek, chopped
1 celery stick, chopped
45 ml/3 tbsp dry sherry
900 ml/1½ pts/3¾ cups Chicken Stock
    (page 28)
5 ml/1 tsp dried mixed herbs
Salt and freshly ground black pepper
Grated cheese or Croûtons (page 33), to
    serve

Heat the oil in a large saucepan and fry (sauté) the onion and garlic until soft but not brown. Stir in the potato,

carrot, leek and celery. Stir in the sherry and stock, add the herbs and season to taste. Bring to the boil and simmer gently for 20 minutes. Serve hot with grated cheese or croûtons.

Watercress soup

SERVES 4

450 g/1 lb potatoes
1.2 litres/2 pts/5 cups water
5 ml/1 tsp salt
25 g/1 oz/2 tbsp butter or margarine
25 g/1 oz/¼ cup plain (all-purpose) flour
2 bunches of watercress, stems
    discarded and leaves finely chopped
Salt and freshly ground black pepper
Croûtons (page 33), to serve

Place the potatoes, water and salt in a large saucepan, bring to the boil and simmer for about 15 minutes until tender. Drain, reserving the liquid, then purée the potatoes. Melt the butter or margarine and stir in the flour until smooth. Add the potato purée and reserved cooking water, bring to the boil, cover and simmer for about 30 minutes. Add the watercress, season to taste and simmer for a further 5 minutes. Serve hot with croûtons.

Gazpacho

SERVES 6

1.25 kg/2½ lb ripe tomatoes, skinned,
  seeded and chopped
2 green (bell) peppers, seeded and
  chopped
1 cucumber, peeled and chopped
1 onion, chopped
30 ml/2 tbsp white wine vinegar
250 ml/8 fl oz/1 cup olive oil
225 g/8 oz/4 cups fresh breadcrumbs
Salt and freshly ground black pepper
Cold water and ice cubes, to serve

Reserve some of the chopped tomato,
green pepper and cucumber for the
garnish and place the remainder in a
food processor or blender with the
onion. Process until fine. Add the
wine vinegar, oil and breadcrumbs and
season to taste. Process again until
well blended. Transfer to a dish, cover
and chill. When ready to serve, thin
the soup with cold water to the
consistency you like, then float a few
ice cubes in the soup and serve with
the reserved garnish.

Chilled cucumber soup

SERVES 4

15 g/½ oz/1 tbsp butter or margarine
1 onion, chopped
1 cucumber, peeled and sliced
450 ml/¾ pt/2 cups Chicken Stock
  (page 28)
1 egg yolk, beaten
45 ml/3 tbsp plain yoghurt
10 ml/2 tsp cornflour (cornstarch)
A few mint leaves, chopped

Melt the butter or margarine in a
large saucepan and fry (sauté) the
onion until soft but not brown. Add
the cucumber and stock, bring to the
boil and simmer for 20 minutes. Beat
together the egg yolk, 15 ml/1 tbsp
of the yoghurt and the cornflour until
smooth. Add the hot soup, then
transfer to a food processor or
blender and purée until smooth and
creamy. Allow to cool. Pour into
individual dishes and garnish with the
remaining yoghurt and the chopped
mint. Chill before serving.

Jajik

SERVES 4

1 cucumber, peeled and halved
Salt and freshly ground black pepper
1 garlic clove, crushed
15 ml/1 tbsp chopped mint
2.5 ml/½ tsp chopped fennel
5 ml/1 tsp white wine vinegar
5 ml/1 tsp olive oil
450 ml/¾ pt/2 cups plain yoghurt
300 ml/½ pt/1¼ cups water
Ice cubes, to garnish

Using a teaspoon, scoop the seeds out of the cucumber and discard. Chop the cucumber flesh and sprinkle with salt. Leave to stand for 1 hour, then rinse and drain well. Mix together the garlic, 5 ml/1 tsp of the mint, the fennel, wine vinegar, oil and yoghurt. Add just enough of the water to make a thin cream, then fold in the cucumber. Season to taste. Chill for 2 hours before serving in chilled soup bowls, sprinkled with the remaining mint and with a few ice cubes in each bowl.

Chilled almond soup

SERVES 4

75 g/3 oz/¾ cup almonds
1 garlic clove, crushed
Salt and freshly ground black pepper
900 ml/1½ pts/3¾ cups water
100 g/4 oz/2 cups fresh breadcrumbs
90 ml/6 tbsp olive oil
25 ml/1½ tbsp red wine vinegar
Ice cubes
100 g/4 oz white seedless grapes

Pound the almonds, garlic and a pinch of salt to a paste with about 120 ml/ 4 fl oz/½ cup of the water. Gradually beat in the breadcrumbs, then beat in the oil a little at a time. Stir in the wine vinegar. Stir in enough of the remaining water to create the consistency you like and season to taste with salt and pepper. Serve in chilled soup bowls, each garnished with ice cubes and a few grapes.

Seafood

Quick and easy to cook, available in a variety of delicious flavours and textures, great tasting and good for you – what more could you want? This chapter includes a wide range of seafood recipes, from simple grilled (broiled) dishes to fish and shellfish baked in tasty sauces. All the recipes suggest a particular type of fish that is ideal for that recipe, but you can experiment with other basic ingredients as long as you choose an alternative type of fish with similar qualities. If you do not have haddock, for example, other white fish such as cod can be substituted.

Steaming is a great method for cooking fish as the fish stays whole and retains its delicious flavour. If you do not have a fish steamer, place the fish on a heatproof plate with about 30 ml/2 tbsp milk and a knob of butter or margarine and cover with another plate. Carefully rest the plates on top of a saucepan of boiling water and steam for about 15 minutes, depending on the size of the fish. The fish is cooked when it flakes easily with a fork. You can add the liquor around the fish to your accompanying sauce.

Fish cooks perfectly in the microwave. Add about 15 ml/1 tbsp of milk and a knob of butter or margarine to the dish, cover and microwave on High for about 4 minutes for 225 g/8 oz of white fish fillet, depending on the shape of the fish. Test the fish, then continue to cook until the fish flakes easily when tested with a fork, making sure you don't overcook.

Boiling is a bit drastic for the delicate flavour and texture of fish. If you do want to use this method, rub the fish with a little lemon juice before cooking and add a pinch of salt and a few drops of vinegar to the water. Use a slotted spoon to remove any scum that rises to the surface and only simmer very gently otherwise the outside of the fish will break up before the inside is cooked. Do not overcook or the fish will lose its flavour.

Shallow-frying is better for oily fish, such as mackerel, rather than white fish. Make sure the oil or oil and butter or margarine is hot before you add the fish, then cook over a medium heat. If you are cooking whole fish, the skin will protect the flesh and become beautifully crisp and golden. If you are cooking a skinless fillet, a light coating of batter or egg and flour will maintain the shape and flavour.

Use good-quality corn or groundnut (peanut) oil to deep-fry fish. It is best if the fish has a coating of batter or breadcrumbs to protect the delicate flesh – as in good old British fish and chips! The oil should be at 180°C/350°F, when a cube of day-old bread will sink, then rise to the top and brown in about a minute. If it is not hot enough, the batter will go soggy; if it is too hot, the oil will begin to burn and ruin the flavour, the outside will cook too fast and the inside will be raw. Do not add too much fish at a time to deep-frying oil otherwise the temperature of the oil will drop and, again, the fish will not be crisp.

Don't ignore baking as a trouble-free way of cooking fish, especially whole fish. Arrange the fish on an ovenproof dish, season to taste with salt and pepper, dot with butter or margarine and baste frequently while baking at about 180°C/350°F/gas mark 4 until the skin is crisp and the flesh flakes easily when tested with a fork.

Prawn and beansprout stir-fry

SERVES 4

30 ml/2 tbsp oil
1 leek, sliced
50 g/2 oz mushrooms, sliced
½ red (bell) pepper, sliced
100 g/4 oz cooked, peeled prawns
    (shrimp)
225 g/8 oz/4 cups beansprouts
30 ml/2 tbsp dry sherry
A few drops of soy sauce

Heat the oil in a wok or large frying pan (skillet) and stir-fry the leek until soft, then add the mushrooms and stir-fry until soft. Add the pepper and fry (sauté) for 2 minutes, then add the prawns and cook briefly until just golden. Add the beansprouts and stir well for 2 minutes until heated through but still crisp. Mix together the sherry and soy sauce and pour into the pan. Toss the ingredients thoroughly together for 1 minute, then serve immediately.

Prawns in beer batter

SERVES 4

150 ml/¼ pt/⅔ cup lager
1 egg, beaten
15 ml/1 tbsp oil
75 g/3 oz/¾ cup plain (all-purpose) flour
A little milk (optional)
A pinch of salt
A pinch of cayenne
Corn oil, for deep-frying
450 g/1 lb cooked, peeled prawns
    (shrimp)
1 lemon, cut into wedges
Chips (fries) and a green salad, to serve

Whisk together the beer, egg, oil and flour to make a smooth batter. Add a few drops of milk or a little more flour if the batter is too thick or too thin. Season with salt and cayenne. Leave to stand for 5 minutes, then whisk again. Heat the oil to 180°C/350°F, when a cube of day-old bread will sink to the bottom, rise and brown in 1 minute. Dip the prawns in the batter, shaking off any excess, then deep-fry a few at a time for about 5 minutes until crisp and golden brown. Drain on kitchen paper (paper towels) and keep the first batch warm while you fry (sauté) the remainder. Garnish with lemon wedges and serve with chips and a green salad.

Prawn, egg and tomato bake

SERVES 4

225 g/8 oz cooked, peeled prawns (shrimp)
2 hard-boiled (hard-cooked) eggs, sliced
4 tomatoes, skinned and sliced
50 g/2 oz/¼ cup butter or margarine
40 g/1½ oz/generous ⅓ cup plain (all-purpose) flour
300 ml/½ pt/1¼ cups milk, warmed
50 g/2 oz/½ cup Cheddar or other strong cheese, grated
Salt and freshly ground black pepper
15 ml/1 tbsp single (light) cream
Crusty bread and a green salad, to serve

Arrange layers of prawns and egg and tomato slices in a greased ovenproof dish. Melt the butter or margarine in a saucepan, stir in the flour and cook for 1 minute. Whisk in the milk and cook, stirring, until the sauce thickens. Remove from the heat and stir in half the cheese. Season to taste and stir in the cream. Pour the sauce over the dish and sprinkle with the remaining cheese. Bake in a preheated oven at 180°C/350°F/gas mark 4 for 15 minutes until heated through and golden brown on top. Serve with crusty bread and a green salad.

Creole prawns

SERVES 4

45 ml/3 tbsp oil
1 onion, chopped
1 green (bell) pepper, chopped
2 celery sticks, chopped
1 garlic clove, chopped
25 g/1 oz/¼ cup plain (all-purpose) flour
45 ml/3 tbsp tomato purée (paste)
5 ml/1 tsp lemon juice
2.5 ml/½ tsp Worcestershire sauce
A few drops of Tabasco sauce
1 bay leaf
300 ml/½ pt/1¼ cups water
Salt and freshly ground black pepper
450 g/1 lb cooked, peeled prawns (shrimp)
Rice or pasta, to serve

Heat the oil and fry (sauté) the onion, green pepper, celery and garlic until soft but not brown. Stir in the flour and cook for 2 minutes. Add the tomato purée, lemon juice, Worcestershire sauce, Tabasco sauce, bay leaf and water. Season to taste, bring to the boil, then simmer for 3 minutes. Add the prawns and stir well. Simmer for about 5 minutes until heated through and well blended. Discard the bay leaf. Serve with rice or pasta.

Prawn and cashew stir-fry

SERVES 4

15 ml/1 tbsp sunflower oil
1 garlic clove, crushed
5 ml/1 tsp crushed fresh root ginger
225 g/8 oz sugar snap peas or
  mangetout (snow peas)
225 g/8 oz cooked, peeled prawns
  (shrimp)
75 g/3 oz /¾ cup unsalted cashew nuts
30 ml/2 tbsp soy sauce
30 ml/2 tbsp orange juice
5 ml/1 tsp lime juice
5 ml/1 tsp clear honey
Salt and freshly ground black pepper

Heat the oil in a wok or large frying
pan (skillet), add the garlic and ginger
and toss for a few seconds. Add the
peas or mangetout and stir-fry for
2 minutes until coated in the
flavoured oil. Add the prawns and
nuts and stir-fry for 1 minute. Add
the soy sauce, orange juice, lime juice
and honey and stir-fry for 2 minutes
until all the ingredients are well
blended, hot and coated in the sauce.
Season to taste and serve at once.

Prawn and scallop kebabs

SERVES 4

225 g/8 oz large uncooked prawns
  (jumbo shrimp)
225 g/8 oz scallops
250 ml/8 fl oz/1 cup dry white wine
30 ml/2 tbsp olive oil
15 ml/1 tbsp chopped tarragon
15 ml/1 tbsp chopped parsley
50 g/2 oz/¼ cup butter or margarine,
  melted
A pinch of cayenne
Freshly ground black pepper
1 lemon, cut into wedges
Crusty bread and a salad, to serve

Peel the prawns and discard the
heads, tails and black intestinal
threads. Place in a bowl with the
scallops, pour over the wine and oil,
add the tarragon and parsley and toss
together until well covered. Cover with
clingfilm (plastic wrap) and chill for
about 3 hours.

Lift the prawns and scallops from
the marinade and thread on to soaked
wooden skewers. Brush with the
melted butter or margarine and
sprinkle with the cayenne and pepper.
Grill (broil) under a medium grill
(broiler) for about 10 minutes until
just cooked, turning and basting
frequently. Garnish with lemon wedges
and serve with crusty bread and
salad.

Seafood stir-fry with mangoes

SERVES 4

5 ml/1 tsp sugar
15 ml/1 tbsp cornflour (cornstarch)
225 g/8 oz squid rings
225 g/8 oz cooked, peeled prawns (shrimp)
225 g/8 oz scallops
30 ml/2 tbsp oil
5 shallots, sliced
10 ml/2 tsp grated fresh root ginger
1 garlic clove, crushed
200 ml/7 fl oz/scant 1 cup Chicken Stock (page 28)
30 ml/2 tbsp dry white wine
15 ml/1 tbsp soy sauce
5 ml/1 tsp sesame oil
30 ml/2 tbsp white wine vinegar
400 g/14 oz/1 large can of mango slices, cut into strips

Mix a pinch of the sugar with 5 ml/ 1 tsp of the cornflour and toss with the seafood until lightly coated. Heat the oil in a wok or large frying pan (skillet) and stir-fry the seafood for a few minutes until tender. Remove from the pan and keep warm. Add the ginger and garlic to the pan and stir-fry for 1 minute. Blend the remaining cornflour with the stock, wine, soy sauce, sesame oil, vinegar and remaining sugar, then stir into the pan, bring to the boil and simmer gently for 2 minutes. Stir the seafood back into the pan with the mango slices and stir-fry just until heated through. Serve at once.

Italian-style seafood roast

SERVES 4

450 g/1 lb small new potatoes
2 red onions, cut into wedges
2 courgettes (zucchini), cut into chunks
4 garlic cloves, halved
2 lemons, cut into wedges
3 small rosemary sprigs
60 ml/4 tbsp olive oil
350 g/12 oz uncooked prawns (shrimp)
225 g/8 oz squid rings
4 tomatoes, quartered

Place the potatoes, onions, courgettes, garlic, lemon wedges and rosemary in a large roasting tin (pan). Pour over the oil and toss until the vegetables are well coated. Cook in a preheated oven at 200°C/400°F/gas mark 6 for 30 minutes until the potatoes are tender, stirring occasionally. Stir in the prawns, squid and tomatoes and roast for 10 minutes until the prawns are pink and all the ingredients are tender and lightly browned.

Shrimp jambalaya

SERVES 4

4 bacon rashers (slices), rinded and chopped
1 onion, sliced
½ green (bell) pepper, diced
1 garlic clove, crushed
75 g/3 oz/⅓ cup long-grain rice
300 ml/½ pt/1¼ cups Chicken Stock (page 28)
200 g/7 oz/1 small can of chopped tomatoes
2.5 ml/½ tsp chilli powder
1 bay leaf
Salt and freshly ground black pepper
225 g/8 oz cooked, peeled prawns (shrimp)
8 green olives, stoned (pitted) and sliced
15 ml/1 tbsp chopped basil
Boiled rice, to serve

Fry (sauté) the bacon until crisp, then drain and set aside. Add the onion, pepper and garlic to the pan and fry gently until soft. Return the bacon to the pan with the measured rice and stir until the rice is coated in fat. Stir in the stock, tomatoes, chilli powder and bay leaf and season to taste. Bring to the boil, cover and simmer for 20 minutes until the rice is just tender. Stir in the prawns and olives and reheat, then discard the bay leaf. Sprinkle with the basil and serve with rice.

Dressed crab

SERVES 4

1 cooked crab
10 ml/2 tsp white wine vinegar
50 g/2 oz/1 cup fresh breadcrumbs
A pinch of grated nutmeg
25 g/1 oz/2 tbsp butter or margarine, diced
Salt and freshly ground white pepper

Remove the meat from the shell, discarding the soft gills from the side of the central body section. Clean the shell well and mix the meat with the other ingredients, seasoning to taste. Return the mixture to the shell and bake in a preheated oven at 190°C/375°F/gas mark 5 for about 15 minutes. Alternatively, for a cold dish omit the breadcrumbs and add 15 ml/1 tbsp oil and a little white pepper to the mixture.

Moules marinière

SERVES 4

1.75 kg/4 lb fresh mussels, scrubbed and bearded
1 sprig of parsley
1 sprig of thyme
2 shallots, chopped
Freshly ground black pepper
150 ml/¼ pt/⅔ cup dry white wine
15 ml/1 tbsp chopped parsley
100 g/4 oz/½ cup butter or margarine
1 garlic clove, crushed
Chips (fries), to serve

Wash the mussels in several changes of water and discard any that are open and do not close when sharply tapped. Put them in a large saucepan with the parsley, thyme and shallots and pepper to taste. Add the wine, bring to the boil, stir well, cover and heat over a high heat for a few minutes just until the mussels open. Discard any that remain closed. Transfer the mussels to a warmed serving dish and keep them warm. Boil the liquor until reduced by half, then stir in the parsley, butter or margarine and garlic. When the butter has melted, pour over the mussels and serve hot with chips.

Coriander mussels

SERVES 4

2 kg/4½ lb mussels, scrubbed and
    bearded
150 ml/¼ pt/⅔ cup Thai sweet chilli sauce
5 ml/1 tsp Thai fish sauce
50 g/2 oz coriander (cilantro), finely
    chopped
Crusty bread, to serve

Wash the mussels in several changes
of water and discard any that are open
and do not close when sharply tapped.
Put them in a large saucepan with the
chilli and fish sauces, cover and steam
over a high heat for about 4 minutes,
shaking the pan occasionally, until the
mussels have opened. Discard any
that remain closed. Add the coriander,
remove from the heat, cover and
shake the pan to toss all the
ingredients together thoroughly.
Transfer to a warm serving dish and
serve with crusty bread.

Mussels with red pesto

SERVES 4

1 shallot, finely chopped
250 ml/8 fl oz/1 cup dry red wine
1 sprig of thyme
1 bay leaf
Salt and freshly ground black pepper
900 g/2 lb fresh mussels, scrubbed and
    bearded
60 ml/4 tbsp red pesto
1 lime, cut into wedges
Crusty bread, to serve

Place the shallot, wine, thyme and
bay leaf in a large saucepan and
season with salt and pepper. Bring to
the boil, then add the mussels, cover
and simmer for about 4 minutes until
they have opened. Discard any that

remain closed. Drain the mussels,
remove the top shells and loosen the
mussels from the bottom shells.
Arrange the mussels in their bottom
shells in a shallow flameproof dish.
Spoon over the pesto sauce, squeeze
the juice from one or two lime wedges
over and season to taste with pepper.
Flash under a hot grill (broiler) for
2 minutes until the pesto bubbles,
then serve at once garnished with the
remaining lime wedges. Serve with
crusty bread.

Angels on horseback

SERVES 4

24 shell-on oysters
24 bacon rashers (slices)
15 ml/1 tbsp plain (all-purpose) flour
Salt and freshly ground black pepper
1 egg, separated
15 ml/1 tbsp melted butter or margarine
Oil, for deep-frying
4 parsley sprigs
2 lemons, cut into wedges

Open the oysters and free them from
the shells, then roll each one in a
rasher of bacon. Season the flour with
salt and pepper, add the egg yolk and
butter or margarine, beat well and
leave to stand for 30 minutes. Just
before it is needed, beat the egg
white until stiff, then fold it into the
batter. Heat the oil to 180°C/350°F,
when a cube of day-old bread will sink
to the bottom, rise and brown in
1 minute. Pick up each oyster on a
skewer, dip into the batter, then deep-
fry in the hot oil for a few minutes
until golden brown. Drain well on
kitchen paper (paper towels) and
serve garnished with the parsley and
the lemon wedges.

Squid with garlic and tomatoes

SERVES 4–6

60 ml/4 tbsp olive oil
1 garlic clove, chopped
600 ml/1 pt/2½ cups passata (sieved tomatoes)
Salt and freshly ground black pepper
900 g/2 lb squid rings
15 ml/1 tbsp pine nuts
30 ml/2 tbsp raisins
6 black olives, stoned (pitted) and halved
30 ml/2 tbsp chopped parsley
Ciabatta bread, to serve

Heat the oil and fry (sauté) the garlic for a few seconds, then stir in the passata and season with salt and pepper. Add the squid, pine nuts, raisins and olives. Bring to the boil, cover and simmer gently for about 40 minutes, stirring occasionally, until the squid is tender. Sprinkle with the parsley and serve with ciabatta bread, using the bread to soak up the juices.

Coquilles St Jacques

SERVES 4

50 g/2 oz/1 cup fresh breadcrumbs
50 g/2 oz/¼ cup butter or margarine
12 scallops
2 shallots, chopped
15 ml/1 tbsp plain (all-purpose) flour
150 ml/¼ pt/⅔ cup dry white wine
150 ml/¼ pt/⅔ cup double (heavy) cream
5 ml/1 tsp cayenne
Salt and freshly ground black pepper

Spread half the breadcrumbs on the base of a greased ovenproof dish. Melt half the butter or margarine and fry (sauté) the scallops gently for a few minutes until just coloured, then lay them in the dish. Fry the shallots until soft, then transfer them to the dish. Stir the flour into the pan and cook, stirring, for 1 minute. Stir in the wine and cream, bring to the boil and season to taste with the cayenne and salt and pepper. Cook for a few minutes, stirring, until the sauce thickens, then pour it over the scallops and top with the remaining breadcrumbs. Dot with the remaining butter or margarine and bake in a preheated oven at 190°C/375°F/gas mark 5 for 20 minutes until golden on top.

Scallops with mascarpone

SERVES 4

200 g/7 oz mascarpone cheese
25 g/1 oz/¼ cup Parmesan cheese, freshly grated
Salt and freshly ground black pepper
30 ml/2 tbsp olive oil
20 scallops
Pasta shapes, boiled and drained, to serve
30 ml/2 tbsp snipped chives

Gently melt the mascarpone over a low heat, stir in the Parmesan and season with salt and pepper. Heat the oil in a heavy-based frying-pan (skillet), then add the scallops and stir-fry for a few minutes over a high heat until they are opaque and just lightly browned on the edges. Season with salt and pepper. Arrange the pasta on warmed serving plates, spoon the scallops and oil over, then top with the mascarpone. Sprinkle with the chives and serve at once.

Sea bass parcels with wild rice

SERVES 4

50 g/2 oz/¼ cup brown rice, soaked in
   cold water overnight, then drained
50 g/2 oz/¼ cup wild rice
25 g/1 oz/¼ cup pine nuts
30 ml/2 tbsp sultanas (golden raisins)
15 ml/1 tbsp chopped dill (dill weed)
Salt and freshly ground black pepper
1 large sea bass, scaled and cut into
   four pieces
15 ml/1 tbsp lemon juice
1 onion, thinly sliced
2 bay leaves, halved
30 ml/2 tbsp dry white wine

Rinse the rices well, then place them
in a saucepan and add enough water
to come 2 cm/¾ in above the rice.
Bring to the boil, cover and simmer
for about 30 minutes until cooked.
Drain, rinse under cold water until
cool, then drain well. Mix with the
pine nuts, sultanas and dill and
season with salt and pepper. Sprinkle
the fish inside and out with lemon
juice, salt and pepper. Transfer to
large pieces of foil and stuff with the
rice mixture. Arrange the onion slices
on top of the fish, add a pieces of bay
leaf to each and sprinkle with the
wine. Twist the tops of the foil
together to make loose parcels,
allowing plenty of space for the fish.
Place in a baking tin (pan) and bake
in a preheated oven at 180°C/350°F/
gas mark 4 for 40 minutes until the
fish is cooked through and tender.

Baked bream with tomatoes and lemon

SERVES 4

1 × 900 g/2 lb bream
Salt and freshly ground black pepper
1 lemon, halved
30 ml/2 tbsp olive oil
1 onion, thinly sliced
1 garlic clove, thinly sliced
120 ml/4 fl oz/½ cup dry white wine
400 g/14 oz/1 large can of tomatoes
15 ml/1 tbsp ground coriander (cilantro)
15 ml/1 tbsp chopped parsley

Make three broad slashes across each
side of the fish and season on both
sides with salt, pepper and the juice
of one lemon half. Heat the oil and fry
(sauté) the onion and garlic until soft
but not brown. Stir in the wine and
boil for 1 minute. Stir in the
tomatoes, coriander and parsley and
simmer for 5 minutes, stirring
frequently, until well blended. Season
to taste with salt and pepper. Pour the
sauce over the fish. Slice the
remaining lemon half and arrange the
slices over the top. Cover and bake in
a preheated oven at 190°C/375°F/
gas mark 5 for 45 minutes until the
bream is cooked through and the
sauce is thick.

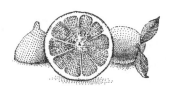

Bream with garlic butter

SERVES 4

75 g/3 oz/⅓ cup unsalted (sweet) butter
120 ml/4 fl oz/½ cup olive oil
4 garlic cloves, halved
1 small green chilli, seeded
25 g/1 oz/¼ cup plain (all-purpose) flour
Salt and freshly ground black pepper
4 sea bream, scaled
25 g/1 oz fennel fronds, chopped

Melt the butter with the oil in a large frying pan (skillet), add the garlic and chilli and simmer gently for 10 minutes to flavour the oils. Discard the garlic and chilli. Season the flour generously with salt and pepper. Dust the fish with the flour and shake off any excess. Raise the heat under the pan and fry (sauté) the fish over a high heat until browned on both sides, then reduce the heat and fry for about 5 minutes until cooked through. Transfer the fish to a warm serving plate. Raise the heat under the pan again, add the sauce and stir for 1–2 minutes until reduced slightly, then spoon over the fish and serve garnished with the fennel fronds.

Fish cakes

SERVES 4

225 g/8 oz cooked white fish, flaked
225 g/8 oz cooked mashed potato
15 ml/1 tbsp finely chopped parsley
A few drops of lemon juice
A few drops of anchovy essence (extract)
Salt and freshly ground black pepper
1 egg, beaten
100 g/4 oz/2 cups fresh breadcrumbs
Oil, for shallow-frying

Mix the fish with the potato and parsley and season to taste with the lemon juice, anchovy essence, salt and pepper. Bind with a little of the egg. Turn out on to a lightly floured surface and form into flat patties. Coat with the egg, then the breadcrumbs. Heat the oil in a frying pan (skillet) and fry (sauté) the fish cakes for about 10 minutes until golden brown on both sides.

Family fish pie

SERVES 4

750 g/1¾ lb potatoes, cubed
300 ml/½ pt/1¼ cups milk
50 g/2 oz/¼ cup butter or margarine
2.5 ml/½ tsp grated nutmeg
350 g/12 oz cod or other white fish
    fillets
25 g/1 oz/¼ cup plain (all-purpose) flour
15 ml/1 tbsp chopped parsley
Salt and freshly ground black pepper
50 g/2 oz cooked, peeled prawns
    (shrimp)
1 hard-boiled (hard-cooked) egg,
    chopped
25 g/1 oz/¼ cup strong, hard cheese,
    grated

Cook the potatoes in boiling salted
water for about 10 minutes until
tender, then drain and mash with
30 ml/2 tbsp of the milk, half the
butter or margarine and the nutmeg.
Poach the fish in 150 ml/¼ pt/⅔ cup
of the milk for 8 minutes, then lift the
fish from the pan, reserving the milk,
remove and discard the skin and flake
the flesh. Melt the remaining butter or
margarine in a saucepan, stir in the
flour and cook for 1 minute. Strain
the milk in which the fish was cooked
into the pan with the remaining milk
and cook, stirring, until the sauce
thickens. Add the parsley and season
to taste. Spread half the potato on
the base of an ovenproof dish and
cover with the prawns and chopped
egg. Spoon over the fish, pour on the
sauce, sprinkle with cheese and pipe
or spoon the remaining potato around
the edge of the dish. Bake in a
preheated oven at 200°C/400°F/gas
mark 6 for 25 minutes until hot and
lightly browned.

Creole fishcakes

SERVES 4

450 g/1 lb cooked haddock, flaked
15 ml/1 tbsp melted butter or margarine
225 g/8 oz/4 cups fresh breadcrumbs
1 large onion, chopped
1 garlic clove, crushed
15 ml/1 tbsp chopped parsley
5 ml/1 tsp chopped thyme
A pinch of cayenne
A little milk (optional)
1 egg, beaten
45 ml/3 tbsp oil
4 watercress sprigs

Mix together the haddock, butter or
margarine, 150 g/5 oz/2½ cups of the
breadcrumbs, the onion, garlic,
parsley, thyme and cayenne. Add a
little milk if the mixture does not bind
together. Shape into small, round, flat
cakes and coat with the egg, then the
remaining breadcrumbs. Heat the oil
in a frying pan (skillet) and fry (sauté)
the cakes for about 5 minutes on
each side until cooked through and
crisp. Serve garnished with
watercress.

Seafood soufflé

SERVES 4

225 g/8 oz haddock or other white fish
   fillet
150 ml/¼ pt/⅔ cup milk
15 g/½ oz/1 tbsp butter or margarine
15 g/½ oz/2 tbsp plain (all-purpose) flour
Salt and freshly ground black pepper
3 eggs, separated
100 g/4 oz cooked, peeled prawns
   (shrimp)
15 g/½ oz/¼ cup fresh breadcrumbs
25 g/1 oz/¼ cup Cheddar cheese, grated

Place the haddock and milk in a pan,
bring to a simmer, then poach for
about 8 minutes until the fish flakes
when tested with a fork. Lift out the
fish, reserving the milk, take off the
skin and flake the flesh. Melt the
butter or margarine in a saucepan,
stir in the flour and cook for
1 minute. Whisk in the milk in which
the fish was cooked, season to taste
and cook, stirring, until the sauce
thickens. Remove from the heat and
beat in the egg yolks, then add the
haddock and prawns. Whisk the egg
whites until stiff and fold them into
the sauce and pour into a greased
18 cm/7 in soufflé dish. Sprinkle with
the breadcrumbs and cheese and
bake in a preheated oven at 200°C/
400°F/gas mark 6 for 30 minutes
until well risen and golden brown.
Serve immediately.

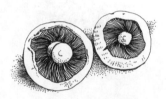

Tomato fish bake

SERVES 4

450 g/1 lb haddock fillet, skinned
50 g/2 oz/1 cup fresh breadcrumbs
50 g/2 oz/½ cup Cheddar cheese, grated
1 onion, chopped
2.5 ml/½ tsp dried mixed herbs
Salt and freshly ground black pepper
375 ml/13 fl oz/1½ cups milk
25 g/1 oz/2 tbsp butter or margarine
50 g/2 oz mushrooms, sliced
25 g/1 oz/¼ cup plain (all-purpose) flour
30 ml/2 tbsp tomato purée (paste)
5 ml/1 tsp lemon juice
A pinch of sugar
450 g/1 lb potatoes, chopped
15 ml/1 tbsp chopped parsley

Flake half the fish over the base of a
greased shallow ovenproof dish. Mix
together the breadcrumbs, cheese,
onion and herbs and season to taste.
Bind with 45 ml/3 tbsp of the milk
and spread over the fish, then cover
with the remaining fish. Melt the
butter or margarine and fry (sauté)
the mushrooms until soft. Add the
flour, the remaining milk, the tomato
purée, lemon juice and sugar and
season to taste. Bring to the boil,
stirring, and simmer until the sauce
thickens. Pour over the fish and bake
in a preheated oven at 190°C/375°F/
gas mark 5 for 20 minutes.
Meanwhile, cook the potatoes in
boiling, salted water until tender.
Drain and mash. Pipe a border of
mashed potato around the dish and
return it to the oven or place under
the grill (broil) to brown. Serve
garnished with the parsley.

St Peter's pie

SERVES 4

450 ml/¾ pt/2 cups milk
1 bay leaf
2 pinches of grated nutmeg
2.5 ml/½ tsp ground mace
225 g/8 oz cod fillet
225 g/8 oz smoked haddock fillet
50 g/2 oz/¼ cup butter or margarine
15 ml/1 tbsp plain (all-purpose) flour
Salt and freshly ground black pepper
15 ml/1 tbsp olive oil
30 ml/2 tbsp double (heavy) cream
1 garlic clove, crushed
2 hard-boiled (hard-cooked) eggs, sliced
25 g/1 oz/¼ cup Parmesan cheese,
    freshly grated
25 g/1 oz/¼ cup Gruyère (Swiss) cheese,
    grated

Bring the milk to the boil with the bay leaf, a pinch of the nutmeg and the mace. Place the fish in a casserole dish (Dutch oven) and pour over the milk. Cover and cook in a preheated oven at 180°C/350°F/gas mark 4 for 30 minutes. Strain and reserve the cooking liquor. Remove the bones and skin from the fish and flake the flesh.

Melt half the butter or margarine, stir in the flour and cook for 1 minute. Whisk in 300 ml/½ pt/1¼ cups of the milk and cook, stirring, until the sauce thickens. Add the remaining nutmeg and season to taste. Keep the sauce warm, stirring occasionally.

Stir the remaining butter or margarine and the oil into the fish, followed by the cream, garlic and 45 ml/3 tbsp of the remaining milk and season with salt and pepper. Transfer the mixture to a pie dish and cover with the egg slices. Fold the cheeses into the sauce, pour it over the fish and bake in a preheated oven at 220°C/425°F/gas mark 7 for about 5 minutes until the top is golden brown.

Halibut steaks in orange sauce

SERVES 4

4 halibut steaks
600 ml/1 pt/2½ cups Fish Stock
    (page 28)
15 g/½ oz/1 tbsp butter or margarine
15 ml/1 tbsp oil
1 onion, chopped
150 ml/¼ pt/⅔ cup frozen concentrated
    orange juice
5 ml/1 tsp chopped tarragon
15 ml/1 tbsp chopped parsley
Salt and freshly ground black pepper
10 ml/2 tsp cornflour (cornstarch)
15 ml/1 tbsp water
150 ml/¼ pt/⅔ cup soured (dairy sour)
    cream
1 orange, peeled and sliced

Place the halibut in a greased flameproof dish, pour the stock over, bring to the boil and poach for 10 minutes. Transfer the fish to a warm serving dish, remove the skin and bones and keep it warm. Reserve 150 ml/¼ pt/⅔ cup of the cooking liquor. Heat the butter or margarine and oil and fry (sauté) the onion until soft, then stir in the orange juice, reserved fish liquor and herbs and season to taste. Bring to the boil, then simmer for 4 minutes. Blend the cornflour to a paste with the water, then stir into the sauce and cook, stirring, until the sauce thickens. Remove from the heat and stir in the soured cream, then pour the sauce over the halibut and serve garnished with the orange slices

Soused herrings

SERVES 4

6 herrings
Salt and freshly ground black pepper
1 bay leaf, chopped
2 cloves
10 peppercorns
150 ml/¼ pt/⅔ cup water
150 ml/¼ pt/⅔ cup white wine vinegar

Bone the herrings and cut into
12 fillets. Sprinkle with salt and
pepper and roll up, skin-side
outwards. Place the herrings in an
ovenproof dish just large enough to
hold them. Sprinkle the bay leaf,
cloves and peppercorns over. Mix
together the water and vinegar and
pour over enough to cover the fish.
Cover and bake in a preheated oven
at 160°C/325°F/gas mark 3 for
30 minutes.

Soused mackerel

SERVES 4

Prepare as for Soused Herrings, but
substitute 6 small mackerel for the
herrings.

Mackerel with gooseberry sauce

SERVES 4

50 g/2 oz/1 cup fresh breadcrumbs
15 ml/1 tbsp chopped parsley
Grated rind of 1 lemon
1 egg, beaten
A pinch of grated nutmeg
Salt and freshly ground black pepper
4 mackerel fillets
50 g/2 oz/¼ cup butter or margarine,
    melted
225 g/8 oz gooseberries
45 ml/3 tbsp water
50 g/2 oz/¼ cup caster (superfine) sugar

Mix together the breadcrumbs,
parsley, lemon rind, egg and nutmeg
and season to taste. Place the stuffing
down the centre of the mackerel
fillets, then roll them up and secure
with cocktail sticks (toothpicks). Place
the fish in a greased ovenproof dish,
brush with half the butter or
margarine, cover and bake in a
preheated oven at 190°C/375°F/gas
mark 5 for 30 minutes.

Meanwhile, cook the gooseberries
in the water with the sugar and
remaining butter or margarine over a
medium heat for a few minutes until
they pop open. Purée the fruit in a
food processor or blender, or rub
them through a sieve (strainer), then
return to the pan to heat through.
Transfer the fish to a warm serving
dish and pour the sauce over.

Baked mackerel in mustard

SERVES 4

4 mackerel or large herrings
15 ml/1 tbsp plain (all-purpose) flour
25 g/1 oz/2 tbsp butter or margarine
10 ml/2 tsp Dijon mustard
30 ml/2 tbsp white wine vinegar
30 ml/2 tbsp water
Salt and freshly ground black pepper

Clean the fish and lay them side by side in a greased ovenproof dish. Mix together the flour, half the butter or margarine, the mustard, wine vinegar and water and pour over the fish. Season to taste and dot with the remaining butter. Cover and bake in a preheated oven at 190°C/375°F/gas mark 5 for about 30 minutes, basting occasionally.

Mackerel with lime and garlic

SERVES 4

4 mackerel
2 limes, sliced
2 garlic cloves, cut into slivers
30 ml/2 tbsp dry white wine
Salt and freshly ground black pepper
50 g/2 oz/¼ cup unsalted (sweet) butter

Make three large slashes on either side of each of the fish. Press the lime slices and garlic slivers into the slashes, then place the fish in a greased ovenproof dish. Pour over the wine, season lightly and dot with the butter. Bake in a preheated oven at 200°C/400°F/gas mark 6 for about 20 minutes until the fish is cooked through and the skin is crisp and golden brown.

Mullet with chives and fennel

SERVES 4

4 red mullet, scaled and filleted
1 fennel bulb, sliced and fronds reserved
150 ml/¼ pt/⅔ cup dry white wine
300 ml/1½ pt/1¼ cups Fish Stock (page 29)
1 bunch of chives, chopped
Salt and freshly ground black pepper

Place the mullet in a large saucepan skin-side up, sprinkle with the fennel and add the wine. Bring to the boil, then simmer gently for about 3 minutes until the fish is just cooked. Meanwhile, boil the stock rapidly until reduced by half. Reserve 15 ml/1 tbsp of the chives, add the remainder to the stock and season to taste. Transfer the fish to a warm serving plate, pour the sauce over and serve garnished with the reserved chives and the fennel fronds.

Thai monkfish with ginger

SERVES 4

700 g/1½ lb monkfish fillet
Juice of 1 lemon
15 ml/1 tbsp olive oil
A pinch of dried thyme
Salt and freshly ground black pepper
Rind of 2 lemons, cut into julienne strips
225 g/8 oz/1 cup butter or margarine, diced
3 spring onions (scallions), chopped
450 ml/¾ pt/2 cups Fish Stock (page 29)
120 ml/4 fl oz/½ cup dry white wine
60 ml/4 tbsp double (heavy) cream
Juice of 2 limes
15 ml/1 tbsp grated fresh root ginger
30 ml/2 tbsp chopped parsley
Tagliatelle or noodles, to serve

Place the fish in a glass or ceramic bowl. Mix together the lemon juice, oil, thyme and salt and pepper and pour over the fish. Cover with clingfilm (plastic wrap) and chill for 1½ hours.

Bring a small pan of water to the boil, add the lemon rind strips, return to the boil and blanch for 3 minutes. Drain well, rinse in cold water and pat dry on kitchen paper (paper towels). Melt 15 ml/1 tbsp of the butter or margarine and fry (sauté) the onions until soft. Lift the fish pieces from the marinade and fry for a few minutes until covered in the flavoured butter. Add the stock and wine, bring to the boil, then simmer gently for about 3 minutes until the fish becomes opaque.

Remove the fish from the pan and keep warm. Bring the sauce back to the boil and boil until reduced to about 30 ml/2 tbsp. Add the cream and boil to reduce again by half. Dice the remaining butter or margarine and whisk into the pan a piece at a time to create a smooth sauce. Add the lime juice, ginger and parsley and stir well, then season to taste. Return the fish to the pan to coat in the sauce, then serve with tagliatelle or noodles.

Plaice with cucumber sauce

SERVES 4

50 g/2 oz/¼ cup butter or margarine
30 ml/2 tbsp anchovy paste
750 g/1¾ lb plaice fillets
1 small cucumber, diced
5 ml/1 tsp chopped dill (dill weed)
275 g/10 oz/1 medium can of condensed mushroom soup
60 ml/4 tbsp plain yoghurt
1 tomato, skinned, seeded and chopped
Salt and freshly ground black pepper

Melt the butter or margarine in a pan and stir in the anchovy paste. Add the plaice and fry (sauté) for about 8 minutes until the fish is golden brown on both sides. Combine the remaining ingredients, seasoning to taste, and spoon over the fish. Cover and cook gently for 5 minutes. Transfer the plaice to a warm serving dish and pour the sauce over.

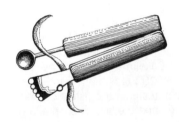

Goujons of plaice with tartare sauce

SERVES 4

100 g/4 oz/1 cup plain (all-purpose)
   flour
1 egg, separated
15 ml/1 tbsp oil
Salt and freshly ground black pepper
300 ml/½ pt/1¼ cups milk
450 g/1 lb plaice, skinned and cut into
   strips
Corn oil, for deep-frying
150 ml/¼ pt/⅔ cup Tartare Sauce (page
   256)

Reserve 15 ml/1 tbsp of the flour and
whisk the remainder to a batter with
the egg yolk, oil, a pinch of salt and
the milk. Whisk the egg white until
frothy, then fold into the batter.
Season the reserved flour with salt
and pepper and roll the strips of
plaice in it, shaking off any excess.
Heat the corn oil to 180°C/350°F,
when a cube of day-old bread will sink
to the bottom, rise and brown in
1 minute. Dip the fish in the batter
and fry (sauté) in the hot oil for about
5 minutes until crisp. Drain well on
kitchen paper (paper towels) and
serve with the tartare sauce.

Salmon cheesecake

SERVES 4–6

150 g/5 oz digestive biscuits (graham
   crackers), crushed
25 g/1 oz/¼ cup rolled oats, toasted
75 g/3 oz/⅓ cup butter or margarine,
   melted
100 g/4 oz/½ cup low-fat curd cheese
100 g/4 oz/½ cup firm tofu
60 ml/4 tbsp oil
15 ml/1 tbsp lemon juice
150 ml/¼ pt/⅔ cup plain yoghurt
3 eggs, separated
200 g/7 oz/1 small can of pink salmon,
   drained
15 ml/1 tbsp powdered gelatine
15 ml/1 tbsp water
Salt and freshly ground black pepper
½ lemon, sliced
¼ cucumber, sliced

Mix together the biscuit crumbs and
oats, then stir in the butter or
margarine. Press into a 23 cm/9 in
loose-bottomed flan tin (pan). Beat
together the cheese, tofu, oil, lemon
juice, yoghurt, egg yolks and salmon.
Sprinkle the gelatine over the water in
a small bowl, then place the bowl in a
pan of hot water and leave until
dissolved. Stir the gelatine into the
salmon mixture. Whisk the egg whites
until stiff, then fold into the mixture.
Season to taste, pour into the flan tin
and chill until firm. When set, remove
from the flan tin and decorate with
the cucumber and lemon slices.

Salmon mould with white butter sauce

SERVES 4

225 g/8 oz cooked salmon, flaked
2 eggs, beaten
25 g/1 oz/2 tbsp butter or margarine, melted
15 g/½ oz/¼ cup fresh breadcrumbs
1 shallot, finely chopped
30 ml/2 tbsp white wine vinegar
100 g/4 oz/½ cup butter or margarine, diced

Mix the fish with the eggs, butter or margarine and breadcrumbs and turn into a greased fish mould or shallow pudding basin. Cover with greased greaseproof (waxed) paper and tie with string. Transfer to a large saucepan and pour in boiling water to come half-way up the sides of the container. Cover and steam gently for about 1 hour until the mixture is quite firm.

Meanwhile, mix the shallot and vinegar and simmer gently until most of the liquid has evaporated. Add the butter or margarine, a piece at a time, stirring continuously, until the sauce thickens. Carefully turn out the salmon mould on to a warm serving plate, pour the sauce over and serve immediately.

Salmon croquettes

SERVES 4

400 g/14 oz/1 large can of salmon, drained and finely flaked
300 ml/½ pt/1¼ cups All-in-one White Sauce (page 250)
5 ml/1 tsp Worcestershire sauce
Salt and freshly ground black pepper
1 egg, beaten
100 g/4 oz/2 cups fresh breadcrumbs
Oil, for deep-frying
1 lemon, cut into wedges

Mix the salmon with just enough of the white sauce to make a thick mixture and season to taste with the Worcestershire sauce and salt and pepper. Shape into croquettes. Heat the oil to 180°C/350°F, when a cube of day-old bread will sink to the bottom, rise and brown in 1 minute. Dip the croquettes in the egg, then the breadcrumbs, then in the egg and breadcrumbs again. Fry (sauté) in the hot oil for about 4 minutes until crisp and golden brown. Drain on kitchen paper (paper towels) and serve with the lemon wedges.

Red snapper with wine and garlic

SERVES 4

75 ml/5 tbsp olive oil
45 ml/3 tbsp dry white wine
60 ml/4 tbsp water
2 garlic cloves, crushed
30 ml/2 tbsp chopped parsley
Salt and freshly ground black pepper
4 red snapper fillets

Put the oil, wine and water into a large heavy-based frying pan (skillet), add the garlic and parsley and season generously. Bring to the boil. Add the fish, cover and steam for about 8 minutes just until tender. Transfer the fish to a warm serving plate, spoon over the cooking liquid and serve.

Sole with white grapes

SERVES 4

4 sole fillets
Salt and freshly ground black pepper
16 seedless white grapes
25 g/1 oz/2 tbsp butter or margarine
15 ml/1 tbsp plain (all-purpose) flour
150 ml/¼ pt/⅔ cup milk
150 ml/¼ pt/⅔ cup single (light) cream
50 g/2 oz/½ cup strong cheese, grated

Season the sole with salt and pepper, lay the grapes along the top, roll up as tightly as possible and secure with cocktail sticks (toothpicks). Place the sole in a greased ovenproof dish. Melt the butter or margarine in a saucepan, stir in the flour and cook for 1 minute. Whisk in the milk and cream and cook, stirring, until the sauce thickens, then remove from the heat and stir in the cheese. Pour the sauce over the sole and bake in a preheated oven at 180°C/350°F/gas mark 4 for 30 minutes until cooked through.

Sole Provençale

SERVES 4

4 sole fillets
Salt and freshly ground black pepper
A pinch of grated nutmeg
30 ml/2 tbsp chopped parsley
50 g/2 oz/¼ cup butter or margarine
150 ml/¼ pt/⅔ cup dry white wine
15 ml/1 tbsp oil
4 onions, sliced
5 ml/1 tsp lemon juice

Season the sole with salt and pepper, the nutmeg and half the parsley. Place in an ovenproof dish, dot with half the butter or margarine and pour the wine over. Cover and bake in a preheated oven at 180°C/350°F/gas mark 4 for 30 minutes. Meanwhile, heat the remaining butter or margarine and the oil and fry (sauté) the onions until golden brown. Drain well on kitchen paper (paper towels). Arrange the onions round the fish and serve sprinkled with the remaining parsley and the lemon juice.

Skate with egg and lemon sauce

SERVES 4

2 carrots, chopped
1 onion, chopped
2 celery sticks, chopped
2 shallots, chopped
1 bay leaf
3 parsley sprigs
2 thyme sprigs
30 ml/2 tbsp lemon juice
300 ml/½ pt/1¼ cups dry white wine
750 ml/1¼ pts/3 cups water
Salt and freshly ground black pepper
450 g/1 lb skate wings
2 egg yolks
Juice of 1 lemon

To make the court bouillon, place the first ten ingredients in a large saucepan, seasoning to taste with salt and pepper. Bring to the boil, cover and simmer for 15 minutes, then leave to cool slightly and strain. Place the skate wings in a clean pan and pour over enough of the court bouillon to almost cover the fish. Bring back to the boil and simmer gently for 10 minutes until the fish is cooked.

Meanwhile, reheat 300 ml/½ pt/ 1¼ cups of the remaining strained court bouillon. Beat together the egg yolks and lemon juice and pour on a little of the court bouillon, beating all the time. Stir the egg mixture back into the court bouillon and heat, stirring, until the sauce thickens. Do not allow the mixture to boil. Arrange the fish on a warm serving dish and pour the sauce over.

Skate in wine and parsley

SERVES 4

450 g/1 lb skate wings
2 shallots, chopped
1 onion, sliced
Salt and freshly ground black pepper
50 g/2 oz mushrooms, sliced
30 ml/2 tbsp chopped parsley
150 ml/¼ pt/⅔ cup dry white wine
15 g/½ oz/1 tbsp butter or margarine
15 ml/1 tbsp plain (all-purpose) flour
50 g/2 oz/1 cup fresh breadcrumbs

Arrange the skate wings in a greased shallow, flameproof dish, sprinkle with the shallots and onion and season to taste. Mix the mushrooms and half the parsley with the wine and add it to the dish. Cover and bake in a preheated oven at 180°C/350°F/gas mark 4 for 45 minutes. Transfer the fish to a warm serving dish and keep warm. Mix together the butter or margarine and flour and stir it into the sauce, heating gently, until the sauce thickens. Pour the sauce over the fish and sprinkle with the breadcrumbs. Brown under a hot grill (broiler) and serve sprinkled with the remaining parsley.

Swordfish steaks with lime and coriander

SERVES 4

4 swordfish steaks
Juice of 3 limes
120 ml/4 fl oz/½ cup olive oil
1 bunch of coriander (cilantro)
50 g/2 oz/¼ cup unsalted (sweet) butter
1 lime, cut into wedges

Place the swordfish steaks in a shallow glass or ceramic bowl and sprinkle with the lime juice, oil and half the coriander. Cover with clingfilm (plastic wrap) and chill for at least 2 hours, turning the fish occasionally in the marinade. Remove the fish from the bowl, reserving the marinade. Brush the fish with butter and grill (broil) under a medium grill (broiler) for about 10 minutes until cooked through and golden, turning occasionally and brushing with butter as it cooks. Dot with any remaining butter, sprinkle with the remaining coriander and serve with lime wedges.

Trout with almonds

SERVES 4

4 trout
50 g/2 oz/¼ cup butter or margarine
50 g/2 oz/½ cup flaked (slivered) almonds
60 ml/4 tbsp lemon juice
Freshly ground black pepper
4 watercress sprigs

Make three slashes in the skin of the trout on each side, dot with the butter or margarine and grill (broil) for about 10 minutes, turning once, until the fish is cooked through and the skin is crisp. Transfer the fish to a warm serving dish and keep warm. Pour the butter from the grill (broiler) into a frying pan (skillet). Add the almonds and a little extra butter if needed. Fry (sauté) gently until the almonds begin to brown. Add the lemon juice and pepper and pour over the fish. Serve garnished with the watercress.

Tuna parcels

SERVES 4

225 g/8 oz/2 cups plain (all-purpose) flour
A pinch of salt
50 g/2 oz/¼ cup butter or margarine
50 g/2 oz/¼ cup lard (shortening) or vegetable fat
45 ml/3 tbsp water
100 g/4 oz/1 small can of tuna fish, drained
15 ml/1 tbsp tomato purée (paste)
15 ml/1 tbsp Worcestershire sauce
Salt and freshly ground black pepper

Mix together the flour and salt, then rub in the fats until the mixture resembles fine breadcrumbs. Stir in just enough of the water to make a smooth pastry (paste). Wrap in clingfilm (plastic wrap) and chill for 30 minutes. Thoroughly mix together the remaining ingredients and season to taste with salt and pepper. Roll out the pastry on a lightly floured surface and cut into small squares. Place spoonfuls of the filling mixture on each square, dampen the edges and seal into triangles. Place the triangles on a greased baking (cookie) sheet and bake in a preheated oven at 200°C/400°F/gas mark 6 for 20 minutes until golden brown.

Sweet and sour fish kebabs

SERVES 4

60 ml/4 tbsp clear honey
30 ml/2 tbsp lemon juice
15 ml/1 tbsp soy sauce
A pinch of chilli powder
750 g/1¾ lb whiting or red mullet fillets
2 onions, sliced
4 courgettes (zucchini), sliced
1 lemon, sliced

Warm the honey, lemon juice, soy sauce and chilli powder in a saucepan. Cut the fish into 4 cm/1½ in slices, then thread the fish, onions, courgettes and lemon alternately on to four skewers. Lay them in a shallow dish and pour the marinade over. Leave for at least 30 minutes, turning occasionally. Remove the skewers from the marinade and grill (broil) under a medium grill (broiler) for 15 minutes until cooked through and golden, basting with the marinade and turning frequently.

Creamy whiting

SERVES 4

4 small whiting
15 ml/1 tbsp plain (all-purpose) flour
50 g/2 oz/¼ cup butter or margarine
2 spring onions (scallions), chopped
15 ml/1 tbsp chopped parsley
150 ml/¼ pt/⅔ cup milk
30 ml/2 tbsp double (heavy) cream
Salt and freshly ground black pepper
1 lemon, cut into wedges

Dust the fish with flour. Melt the butter or margarine and fry (sauté) the fish for 10 minutes, turning once. Mix together the onions, parsley, milk and cream and season to taste. Pour over the fish, bring to the boil and cook for 5 minutes, stirring gently to avoid breaking up the fish. Transfer the fish to a warmed serving dish and pour the sauce over. Serve garnished with the lemon wedges.

Tuna fish curry

SERVES 4

4 tuna steaks
Salt and freshly ground black pepper
15 ml/1 tbsp olive oil
50 g/2 oz/1 small can of anchovy fillets, drained
50 g/2 oz/¼ cup butter or margarine
2 bananas, sliced
15 ml/1 tbsp plain (all-purpose) flour
15 ml/1 tbsp curry powder
300 ml/½ pt/1¼ cups Fish Stock (page 29)
15 ml/1 tbsp chopped parsley

Lay the tuna in a greased shallow, flameproof dish, season with salt and pepper and pour the oil over. Arrange the anchovies on top, cover and bake in a preheated oven at 190°C/375°F/ gas mark 5 for 25 minutes.

Meanwhile, melt the butter or margarine and fry (sauté) the bananas over a fairly high heat until soft and just browning on the edges. Arrange the cooked fish on a warm serving plate, place the bananas round the edge and keep warm. Stir the flour and curry powder into the pan and cook, stirring, for 2 minutes, then stir in the stock, bring to the boil and cook, stirring, until the sauce thickens. Pour the sauce over the fish and serve sprinkled with the parsley.

Veal saltimbocca (page 85)

Beef and veal

Many cuts of beef are expensive, and as most of us are trying to cut down on red meats, it makes sense to make the best of beef when you do eat it by preparing and cooking it carefully. Choose a good-quality beef, such as steak, for any quick-cook recipes; the cheaper cuts are best for recipes with long, slow cooking times that allow the meat time to tenderise. Trim the meat well before cooking to avoid excess fat. When choosing minced (ground) beef, select those with a lower fat content, or buy from a quality butcher where you can see the meat that is put into the mince.

Many classic beef dishes are cooked on the bone. However, due to the health risks associated with beef during the late 1990s, you may not be able or may not want to cook beef on the bone. Simply replace the joint of beef with a boneless joint, but do remember to protect the meat well during cooking and you may need to add a little more oil or water.

Veal is an extremely easy meat to prepare and as it is lean there is little waste. It has a subtle flavour that lends itself well to all kinds of recipes, from the classic Wiener Schnitzel to Vealburgers. Veal is readily available in supermarkets, usually as escalopes, mince, or cubed meat. As with mature beef, some veal recipes, such as Osso Buco, use veal on the bone which may not be available, although you can substitute a boned joint.

Lamb with redcurrant sauce (page 98)

Beef

Stilton steaks

SERVES 4

100 g/4 oz/1 cup Stilton cheese, crumbled
25 g/1 oz/2 tbsp butter or margarine, softened
50 g/2 oz/½ cup walnuts, finely chopped
Salt and freshly ground black pepper
4 sirloin steaks

Mix together the cheese, butter or margarine and walnuts and season to taste. Season the steaks with pepper, then grill (broil) them under a hot grill (broiler) for 4 minutes each side or until cooked to your liking. Remove from the grill and press the cheese mixture over the steaks, then return to the grill for a further 1 minute until browned.

Steaks with wholegrain mustard

SERVES 4

30 ml/2 tbsp wholegrain mustard
15 ml/1 tbsp plain (all-purpose) flour
4 sirloin steaks
30 ml/2 tbsp chopped parsley
30 ml/2 tbsp chopped thyme
Salt and freshly ground black pepper

Mix together the mustard and flour and spread on top of the steaks. Sprinkle with the herbs and season to taste. Grill (broil) them under a hot grill (broiler) for 5 minutes each side or until cooked to your liking.

Beef with charred shallots

SERVES 4

75 ml/5 tbsp olive oil
8–10 shallots, halved
2 garlic cloves, chopped
25 g/1 oz chopped thyme
Salt and freshly ground black pepper
4 rump steaks
Dijon mustard, to serve

Heat the oil in a flameproof and ovenproof dish and fry (sauté) the shallots, cut-side down, until browned. Turn them over and brown the other sides. Sprinkle with the garlic, thyme, salt and pepper, then toss the ingredients together. Transfer to a preheated oven and cook at 200°C/400°F/gas mark 6 for about 40 minutes until tender and brown. About 10 minutes before they are ready, preheat the grill (broiler), then grill (broil) the steaks for about 3 minutes each side until cooked to your liking. Serve the steaks and shallots immediately, garnished with mustard.

Brandy peppered steaks

SERVES 4

60 ml/4 tbsp green peppercorns,
    crushed
900 g/2 lb fillet steak, cut into four slices
25 g/1 oz/2 tbsp butter or margarine
15 ml/1 tbsp oil
25 g/1 oz/¼ cup plain (all-purpose) flour
250 ml/8 fl oz/1 cup Beef Stock
    (page 28)
30 ml/2 tbsp brandy
30 ml/2 tbsp single (light) cream
Salt and freshly ground black pepper

Press the peppercorns into both sides
of the steaks. Melt the butter or
margarine and oil and fry (sauté) the
steaks for about 4 minutes until
browned on both sides and cooked to
your liking. Transfer the steaks to a
warm serving plate and keep warm.
Stir the flour into the pan and cook
for 1 minute, then stir in the stock,
bring to the boil and simmer for
5 minutes, stirring, until the sauce
thickens. Stir in the brandy and
cream, season to taste and cook until
heated through. Pour the sauce over
the steaks and serve.

Peppercorn steaks with lemon cream

SERVES 4

30 ml/2 tbsp green peppercorns,
    crushed
4 sirloin steaks
50 g/2 oz/¼ cup butter or margarine
Grated rind and juice of 1 lemon
15 ml/1 tbsp snipped chives
30 ml/2 tbsp double (heavy) cream

Press the peppercorns into both sides
of the steaks. Melt the butter or

margarine and fry (sauté) the steaks
for 4 minutes on each side for
medium steaks, slightly less or more if
you prefer them rare or well done.
Transfer the steaks to a warm serving
plate and keep warm. Add the lemon
rind to the pan with 15 ml/1 tbsp of
the lemon juice and the chives and
cook for a few minutes until reduced
slightly. Remove from the heat and
stir in the cream. Pour over the steaks
and serve at once.

Baked mushroom-stuffed steak

SERVES 4

25 g/1 oz/2 tbsp butter or margarine
1 onion, chopped
100 g/4 oz mushrooms, finely chopped
50 g/2 oz lean bacon, rinded and
    chopped
25 g/1 oz/½ cup fresh breadcrumbs
10 ml/2 tsp chopped parsley
5 ml/1 tsp chopped thyme
Salt and freshly ground black pepper
900 g/2 lb piece of lean rump steak,
    trimmed

Melt the butter or margarine and fry
(sauté) the onion until soft but not
brown. Stir in the mushrooms and
bacon and cook for 3 minutes, then
remove from the heat and stir in the
breadcrumbs, parsley and thyme and
season to taste. Leave to cool. Slit the
steak in half lengthways and fill with
the stuffing, then tie round with
string. Roast in a preheated oven at
200°C/400°F/gas mark 6 for about
30 minutes until cooked to your
liking.

Beef olives with bacon stuffing

SERVES 4

450 g/1 lb rump steak, cut into four thin slices
50 g/2 oz lean bacon, rinded and finely chopped
50 g/2 oz/½ cup shredded (chopped) suet
100 g/4 oz/2 cups fresh breadcrumbs
30 ml/2 tbsp chopped parsley
2.5 ml/½ tsp dried mixed herbs
A pinch of grated lemon rind
Salt and freshly ground black pepper
1 egg, beaten
25 g/1 oz/¼ cup plain (all-purpose) flour
25 g/1 oz lard (shortening) or vegetable fat
1 onion, sliced
600 ml/1 pt/2½ cups Beef Stock (page 28)
15 ml/1 tbsp tomato ketchup (catsup)
1 carrot, sliced

Beat the steak slices flat and leave to stand for 30 minutes. Mix together the bacon, suet, breadcrumbs, parsley, herbs and lemon rind and season to taste. Bind together to a stuffing with the egg. Divide the stuffing equally between the steak slices, roll up the slices round the stuffing and tie with string or secure with cocktail sticks (toothpicks). Season the flour with salt and pepper and dust the rolls with the flour, shaking off any excess. Heat the lard or vegetable fat in a frying pan (skillet) and fry (sauté) the beef olives until browned on all sides. Transfer to a casserole dish (Dutch oven) and keep warm.

Add the onion to the pan and fry until browned, then add to the beef. Stir the remaining flour into the pan and brown for 1 minute, stirring well to scrape up the meat juices. Mix in the stock and ketchup, stirring thoroughly, then pour over the beef in the casserole, add the carrot and season to taste. Cover and cook in a preheated oven at 160°C/325°F/gas mark 3 for 2 hours until tender.

Pâté steaks

SERVES 4

4 slices of bread
50 g/2 oz/¼ cup unsalted (sweet) butter
15 ml/1 tbsp oil
4 tournedos steaks
60 ml/4 tbsp medium-dry sherry
100 ml/4 fl oz/½ cup Beef Stock (page 28)
30 ml/2 tbsp tomato purée (paste)
A dash of Worcestershire sauce
Salt and freshly ground black pepper
100 g/4 oz firm liver pâté, cut into four slices

Using a biscuit (cookie) cutter, cut the bread into rounds a little larger than the steaks. Heat 15 g/½ oz/1 tbsp of the butter with the oil and fry (sauté) the bread until crisp, then transfer to a warm serving plate and keep warm. Trim the steaks into neat rounds and seal them quickly on both sides, then put them on top of the fried (sautéed) bread. Stir the sherry, stock, tomato purée and Worcestershire sauce into the pan and season to taste. Bring to the boil and simmer for 4 minutes until slightly thickened, then pour into a sauce boat. Meanwhile, heat the remaining butter in a pan and fry the pâté slices until browned but not melted. Place them on top of the steaks and serve with the sauce.

Beef in red wine

SERVES 4

50 g/2 oz/¼ cup butter or margarine
2 onions, finely chopped
150 ml/¼ pt/⅔ cup red wine
60 ml/4 tbsp water
5 ml/1 tsp dried thyme
2 bay leaves
4 sirloin steaks
60 ml/4 tbsp brandy
Salt and freshly ground black pepper
150 ml/¼ pt/⅔ cup single (light) cream
30 ml/2 tbsp chopped parsley

Melt half the butter or margarine and fry (sauté) the onions until soft. Stir in the wine, water, thyme and bay leaves and simmer until the liquid has reduced by half. Melt the remaining butter or margarine in a separate pan and fry the steaks for a few minutes until browned on both sides. Add the brandy and cook for 4 minutes or until the steak is cooked to your liking. Transfer the steaks to a warm serving plate and season to taste. Pour the wine sauce into the pan in which you cooked the meat, stirring well to mix in the meat juices. Stir in the cream and heat through, then pour over the steaks and serve sprinkled with the parsley.

Stir-fry beef with ginger

SERVES 4

15 ml/1 tbsp oil
450 g/1 lb lean steak, cut into strips
25 g/1 oz fresh root ginger, peeled and grated
1 garlic clove, crushed
100 g/4 oz baby sweetcorn (corn) cobs
50 g/2 oz mangetout (snow peas)
1 red (bell) pepper, cut into strips
200 g/7 oz/1 small can of water chestnuts, drained
50 g/2 oz/½ cup cashew nuts
30 ml/2 tbsp soy sauce
5 ml/1 tbsp Chinese five spice powder
5 ml/1 tbsp sesame seeds
Egg Fried Rice (page 204), to serve

Heat the oil in a work or large frying pan (skillet) and fry (sauté) the beef, ginger and garlic until browned. Stir in the corn, mangetout, red pepper, water chestnuts and nuts and stir-fry for 3 minutes. Add the remaining ingredients and cook for 1 minute, then serve immediately with Egg Fried Rice.

Quick and tasty beef

SERVES 4

15 ml/1 tbsp olive oil
25 g/1 oz/2 tbsp butter or margarine
4 lean beef slices
½ red (bell) pepper, chopped
½ green pepper, chopped
½ yellow pepper, chopped
250 ml/8 fl oz/1 cup soured (dairy sour)
    cream
5 ml/1 tsp wholegrain mustard
10 green peppercorns
Salt and freshly ground black pepper
Rice or pasta, to serve

Heat the oil, then add the butter
or margarine. When the butter or
margarine has melted, add the beef
and fry (sauté) until browned on both
sides, then cook for 4 minutes. Stir in
the peppers and soured cream and
cook for 5 minutes. Then stir in the
remaining ingredients and season to
taste with salt. Heat through gently
and serve with rice or pasta.

Beef stroganoff

SERVES 4

50 g/2 oz/¼ cup butter or margarine
2 onions, chopped
100 g/4 oz mushrooms, sliced
15 ml/1 tbsp plain (all-purpose) flour
Salt and freshly ground black pepper
750 g/1¾ lb fillet steak, cut into strips
300 ml/½ pt/1¼ cups Beef Stock
    (page 28)
5 ml/1 tsp dried mixed herbs
15 ml/1 tbsp tomato purée (paste)
10 ml/2 tsp French mustard
150 ml/¼ pt/⅔ cup soured (dairy sour)
    cream
15 ml/1 tbsp chopped parsley

Melt half the butter or margarine and
fry (sauté) the onions until just
browned. Add the mushrooms and fry
for 2 minutes, then transfer the
onions and mushrooms to a dish and
keep warm. Season the flour with salt
and pepper and toss the steak in the
flour, shaking off any excess. Melt the
remaining butter or margarine and fry
the steak quickly until browned, then
transfer to the dish with the
mushrooms and onions. Stir the stock,
herbs, tomato purée and mustard into
the pan and bring to the boil, stirring
well to scrape up any pan juices.
Return the meat and vegetables to
the pan, stir in the soured cream and
heat through but do not allow to boil.
Serve sprinkled with the parsley.

Beef and vegetable stir-fry

SERVES 4

45 ml/3 tbsp olive oil
350 g/12 oz steak, cut into strips
6 spring onions (scallions), sliced
1 garlic clove, chopped
½ red (bell) pepper, cut into strips
½ yellow pepper, cut into strips
175 g/6 oz carrots, cut into strips
275 g/10 oz/1 medium can of baby
    sweetcorn (corn) cobs, drained
5 ml/1 tsp cornflour (cornstarch)
75 ml/5 tbsp dry cider
30 ml/2 tbsp soy sauce
150 ml/¼ pt/⅔ cup Beef Stock (page 28)
100 g/4 oz/2 cups beansprouts
Salt and freshly ground black pepper
Boiled rice, to serve

Heat the oil in a wok or large frying pan (skillet) and fry (sauté) the steak until browned on both sides. Remove from the pan and keep warm. Add the spring onions, garlic, peppers, carrots and sweetcorn and stir-fry for 3 minutes. Mix the cornflour with the cider and soy sauce, add to the pan and bring to the boil, stirring, until the sauce thickens. Stir in the stock, beansprouts and beef, season to taste and heat through. Serve with boiled rice.

Beef with pepper strips

SERVES 4

450 g/1 lb rump steak, cut into strips
10 ml/2 tsp cornflour (cornstarch)
60 ml/4 tbsp soy sauce
45 ml/3 tbsp oil
2 red (bell) peppers, cut into thin strips
10 ml/2 tsp chilli powder
1 onion, sliced
1 garlic clove, crushed
25 g/1 oz fresh root ginger, peeled and
    grated
5 ml/1 tsp caster (superfine) sugar
30 ml/2 tbsp dry sherry
Boiled rice, to serve

Sprinkle the steak with the cornflour and some of the soy sauce and leave to stand for 15 minutes. Heat 15 ml/1 tbsp of the oil and fry (sauté) the peppers, chilli powder, onion, garlic and ginger for 3 minutes. Remove from the pan and set aside. Heat the remaining oil and fry the meat for a few minutes until browned. Return the pepper mixture to the pan with the remaining soy sauce, the sugar and sherry and stir-fry for a few minutes to heat through. Serve with boiled rice.

Beef puchero

SERVES 4

200 g/7 oz/1 small can of haricot (navy)
  beans, drained
1 carrot, diced
½ turnip, diced
2 onions, diced
2 tomatoes, skinned and diced
225 g/8 oz lean bacon, diced
900 ml/1½ pts/3¾ cups Beef Stock
  (page 28)
1 bouquet garni sachet
15 ml/1 tbsp oil
900 g/2 lb stewing beef, cut into 4 cm/
  1½ in pieces
Salt and freshly ground black pepper
15 ml/1 tbsp plain (all-purpose) flour
  (optional)
15 g/½ oz/1 tbsp butter or margarine
  (optional)
Mashed potatoes, to serve

Place the beans, carrot, turnip,
onions, tomatoes, bacon, stock and
bouquet garni in a large saucepan.
Bring to the boil, cover and simmer
gently for about 2 hours to create a
rich stock. Heat the oil in a separate
pan and fry (sauté) the meat until
browned. Add the meat to the
saucepan, season to taste, cover and
simmer for a further 1 hour until the
meat is tender. Remove the bouquet
garni and adjust the seasoning if
necessary. If the gravy is too thin,
either remove the lid and boil until the
sauce thickens a little, or mix the flour
and butter or margarine to a paste,
stir into the puchero and simmer,
stirring, until thickened. Serve with
mashed potatoes.

Beef pot roast

SERVES 4

1.75 kg/4 lb brisket of beef, boned and
  rolled
Salt and freshly ground black pepper
25 g/1 oz/2 tbsp lard (shortening) or
  vegetable fat
1 onion
4 cloves
300 ml/½ pt/1¼ cups water
4 carrots, halved lengthways
4 small onions, halved
150 ml/¼ pt/⅔ cup Beef Stock (page 28)

Tie the meat securely, pat dry with
kitchen paper (paper towels) and
season with salt and pepper. Heat the
lard or vegetable fat in a flameproof
casserole dish (Dutch oven) and fry
(sauté) the meat until browned on all
sides. Stud the onion with the cloves
and add to the dish with the water.
Bring to the boil, cover and place in a
preheated oven at 150°C/300°F/gas
mark 2 for 2 hours, basting
occasionally. Remove from the oven,
lift out the meat and add the carrots
and small onions. Place the meat on
top, cover and return to the oven for
a further 1 hour. Remove the meat
and vegetables from the casserole,
discard the clove-studded onion, and
keep warm. Skim off any excess fat,
mix in the stock, stirring to scrape up
all the meat juices, bring to the boil
and strain the gravy into a gravy
boat. Serve with the beef and
vegetables.

Beef with green noodles

SERVES 4

175 g/6 oz green tagliatelle
15 ml/1 tbsp oil
1 onion, chopped
1 garlic clove, crushed
750 g/1¾ lb minced (ground) beef
100 g/4 oz mushrooms, sliced
25 g/1 oz/¼ cup plain (all-purpose) flour
150 ml/¼ pt/⅔ cup Beef Stock (page 28)
400 g/14 oz/1 large can of tomatoes, chopped
15 ml/1 tbsp Worcestershire sauce
15 ml/1 tbsp soy sauce
15 ml/1 tbsp tomato purée (paste)
5 ml/1 tsp dried oregano
Salt and freshly ground black pepper
25 g/1 oz/2 tbsp butter or margarine
300 ml/½ pt/1¼ cups milk
75 g/3 oz/⅔ cup Cheddar cheese, grated
50 g/2 oz/1 cup fresh breadcrumbs

Cook the tagliatelle in boiling salted water for 4 minutes until partly cooked. Drain and rinse with hot water, then place half the pasta in a casserole dish (Dutch oven). Heat the oil and fry (sauté) the onion and garlic until soft, then add the beef and fry until browned. Add the mushrooms, stir in half the flour and cook for 1 minute. Stir in the stock, tomatoes, Worcestershire sauce, soy sauce, tomato purée and oregano and season to taste. Bring to the boil, then pour over the pasta in the dish and cover with the remaining pasta. Melt the butter or margarine, stir in the remaining flour and cook for 1 minute. Stir in the milk, bring to the boil, stirring, and simmer for 2 minutes, then pour over the pasta. Mix together the cheese and breadcrumbs and sprinkle over the top. Cook in a preheated oven at 200°C/400°F/gas mark 6 for 30 minutes until browned and crisp on top.

Beef hot pot

SERVES 4

450 g/1 lb shin of beef, boned and cubed
30 ml/2 tbsp sherry vinegar
15 ml/1 tbsp plain (all-purpose) flour
Salt and freshly ground black pepper
225 g/8 oz pork sausages, cut into chunks
450 g/1 lb potatoes, sliced
1 eating (dessert) apple, peeled, cored and sliced
225 g/8 oz tomatoes, skinned and sliced
1 onion, sliced
300 ml/½ pt/1¼ cups Beef Stock (page 28)

Put the beef and sherry vinegar in a bowl, cover with clingfilm (plastic wrap) and leave to stand for 1 hour, stirring occasionally. Drain and pat dry on kitchen paper (paper towels). Season the flour with salt and pepper, then toss the meat and sausages in the flour, shaking off any excess. Place a layer of potato, apple, tomato and onion slices in the bottom of a casserole dish (Dutch oven), then add a layer of meat and continue layering until all the ingredients have been used up, finishing with a layer of potatoes. Add enough stock to come one-third of the way up the casserole. Cover and cook in a preheated oven at 160°C/325°F/gas mark 3 for 2½ hours or until the meat is tender. Remove the lid and turn the heat up to 200°C/400°F/gas mark 6 for 10 minutes to crisp the top.

Rich beef and mushroom cobbler

SERVES 4

30 ml/2 tbsp oil
1 onion, chopped
1 garlic clove, chopped
450 g/1 lb chuck steak, chopped
100 g/4 oz mushrooms, sliced
15 ml/1 tbsp plain (all-purpose) flour
450 ml/¾ pt/2 cups Beef Stock
  (page 28)
15 ml/1 tbsp tomato purée (paste)
5 ml/1 tbsp Worcestershire sauce
4 juniper berries, crushed
Salt and freshly ground black pepper
225 g/8 oz/2 cups self-raising (self-rising) flour
5 ml/1 tsp baking powder
50 g/2 oz/¼ cup margarine, softened
10 ml/2 tsp dried mixed herbs
150 ml/¼ pt/⅔ cup milk

Heat the oil in a large saucepan and fry (sauté) the onion and garlic until soft. Add the steak and fry until browned. Add the mushrooms and fry for 1 minute. Stir in the flour and cook for 1 minute, then stir in the stock, tomato purée, Worcestershire sauce and juniper berries and season to taste. Bring to the boil and simmer, stirring occasionally, for 15 minutes. Pour into a casserole dish (Dutch oven). Mix together the flour and baking powder, then rub in the margarine until the mixture resembles fine breadcrumbs. Stir in the herbs, then gradually add enough of the milk to form a soft dough. Roll into about eight small balls and arrange around the edge of the casserole. Bake in a preheated oven at 220°C/425°F/gas mark 7 for 20 minutes.

Oxtail ragout

SERVES 4–6

1.5 kg/3 lb oxtail, chopped
25 g/1 oz/¼ cup plain (all-purpose) flour
5 ml/1 tsp dried thyme
5 ml/1 tsp ground ginger
Salt and freshly ground black pepper
15 ml/1 tbsp pork fat, lard (shortening) or vegetable fat
100 g/4 oz belly of pork, rinded and diced
2 onions
10 cloves
1 leek, chopped
1 turnip, chopped
1 carrot, chopped
300 ml/½ pt/1¼ cups Beef Stock
  (page 28)
1 bouquet garni sachet
1 garlic clove, crushed

Soak the oxtail in water for 4 hours, then cover with fresh water, bring to the boil and simmer for 15 minutes. Drain and pat dry on kitchen paper (paper towels). Season the flour with the thyme, ginger and salt and pepper and toss the oxtail in the flour. Melt the fat, lard or vegetable fat in a flameproof casserole dish (Dutch oven) and fry (sauté) the belly pork until crisp. Add the oxtail and brown all over. Stud one onion with the cloves and chop the other. Add these to the pan with the leek, turnip and carrot. Stir in the stock, bouquet garni, and garlic and season to taste. Cover and bring back to the boil, then transfer the casserole to a preheated oven and bake at 140°C/275°F/gas mark 1 for 4 hours. Remove the bouquet garni and the clove-studded onion before serving.

Casserole Provençale

SERVES 4

900 g/2 lb stewing beef, cubed
100 g/4 oz belly of pork, rinded and
    cubed
1 onion, chopped
5 ml/1 tsp dried mixed herbs
Salt and freshly ground black pepper
250 ml/8 fl oz/1 cup red wine
25 g/1 oz/¼ cup plain (all-purpose) flour
30 ml/2 tbsp olive oil
2 garlic cloves, chopped
½ green (bell) pepper, chopped
60 ml/4 tbsp water
200 g/7 oz/1 small can of tomatoes,
    chopped
5 ml/1 tsp paprika
1 bouquet garni sachet
6 black olives, stoned (pitted)

Put the beef, pork, onion and herbs
in a dish, season to taste and cover
with the wine. Leave to marinate
overnight.

Remove the meat, pat it dry on
kitchen paper (paper towels) and toss
it in the flour. Heat the oil in a
flameproof casserole dish (Dutch
oven) and fry (sauté) the meat until
browned, then add the garlic and
green pepper and fry for 2 minutes.
Stir in all the remaining ingredients
except the olives and bring to the
boil. Transfer the casserole to a
preheated oven and cook at
140°C/275°F/gas mark 1 for 4 hours.
Remove the bouquet garni, leave to
cool and skim off any fat. When ready
to serve, bring the casserole back to
simmering point and add the olives.

Danish beef casserole

SERVES 4

10 shallots
30 ml/2 tbsp oil
750 g/1¾ lb braising steak
15 ml/1 tbsp plain (all-purpose) flour
300 ml/½ pt/1¼ cups Beef Stock
    (page 28)
60 ml/4 tbsp tomato purée (paste)
30 ml/2 tbsp port
A pinch of ground cumin
5 ml/1 tsp ground cinnamon
100 g/4 oz/1 cup Danish Blue cheese,
    crumbled

Cook the shallots in boiling water for
3 minutes, then drain and transfer to
a casserole dish (Dutch oven). Heat
the oil and fry (sauté) the steak until
browned, then transfer it to the
casserole. Add the flour to the pan
and cook for 1 minute, stirring well to
scrape up the meat juices. Stir in the
stock, tomato purée, port, cumin and
cinnamon, bring to the boil and pour
into the casserole. Cook in a
preheated oven at 180°C/350°F/gas
mark 4 for 1½ hours. Top the
casserole with the cheese and leave to
stand for 5 minutes before serving.

Hungarian goulash

SERVES 4

25 g/1 oz/¼ cup plain (all-purpose) flour
Salt and freshly ground black pepper
900 g/2 lb braising steak
30 ml/2 tbsp oil
3 onions, chopped
1 garlic clove, crushed
1 green (bell) pepper, sliced
30 ml/2 tbsp paprika
300 ml/½ pt/1¼ cups Beef Stock
  (page 28)
200 g/7 oz/1 small can of tomatoes,
  chopped
15 ml/1 tbsp tomato purée (paste)
1 bouquet garni sachet
150 ml/¼ pt/⅔ cup soured (dairy sour)
  cream

Season the flour with salt and pepper and toss the beef in the flour. Heat the oil and fry (sauté) the steak until browned, then transfer it to a casserole (Dutch oven). Fry the onions until soft, then add the garlic and green pepper and fry for 1 minute. Stir in the paprika and fry for 1 minute, then stir in the stock, tomatoes, tomato purée and bouquet garni, bring to the boil and season to taste. Pour into the casserole and cook in a preheated oven at 170°C/325°F/gas mark 3 for 2 hours until the meat is tender. Remove the bouquet garni and swirl in the soured cream before serving.

Pepperpot beef

SERVES 4–6

25 g/1 oz/¼ cup plain (all-purpose) flour
5 ml/1 tsp ground ginger
Salt and freshly ground black pepper
900 g/2 lb stewing steak, cubed
30 ml/2 tbsp oil
400 g/14 oz/1 large can of tomatoes,
  chopped
100 g/4 oz button mushrooms, sliced
5 ml/1 tsp chilli sauce
15 ml/1 tbsp Worcestershire sauce
25 g/1 oz light brown sugar
30 ml/2 tbsp red wine vinegar
2 garlic cloves, crushed
1 bay leaf
30 ml/1 tbsp chopped parsley

Mix together the flour and ginger and season with salt and pepper. Toss the steak in the flour. Heat the oil and fry (sauté) the steak until browned, then transfer to a casserole (Dutch oven). Stir in the remaining ingredients and cook in a preheated oven at 160°C/325°F/gas mark 3 for 3 hours. Remove the bay leaf and serve sprinkled with the parsley.

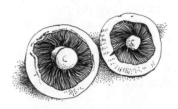

Spiced beef with kidney beans

SERVES 4

50 g/2 oz/½ cup plain (all-purpose) flour
5 ml/1 tsp ground ginger
Salt and freshly ground black pepper
750 g/1¾ lb braising steak, cubed
30 ml/2 tbsp oil
2 onions, chopped
1 garlic clove, crushed
15 g/½ oz fresh root ginger, grated
300 ml/½ pt/1¼ cups Beef Stock
  (page 28)
400 g/14 oz/1 large can of tomatoes,
  chopped
30 ml/2 tbsp red wine vinegar
15 ml/1 tbsp clear honey
15 ml/1 tbsp Worcestershire sauce
300 g/11 oz/1 medium can of red kidney
  beans, rinsed and drained

Mix together half the flour and ground ginger and season with salt and pepper. Toss the steak in the flour. Heat the oil and fry (sauté) the steak until browned, then transfer it to a casserole dish (Dutch oven). Fry the onions, garlic and grated ginger until just browned, then stir in the remaining flour and cook for 1 minute. Stir in the stock, tomatoes, wine vinegar, honey and Worcestershire sauce and season to taste. Bring to the boil, then pour into the casserole. Cook in a preheated oven at 160°C/325°F/gas mark 3 for 1½ hours, then add the kidney beans and return to the oven for a further 40 minutes until cooked through and tender.

Beef in beer

SERVES 4

30 ml/2 tbsp oil
750 g/1¾ lb chuck steak, cubed
100 g/4 oz gammon steak, rinded and
  cubed
2 onions, sliced
1 garlic clove, crushed
300 ml/½ pt/1¼ cups light ale
150 ml/¼ pt/⅔ cup brown ale
5 ml/1 tsp dark brown sugar
5 ml/1 tsp grated nutmeg
1 bouquet garni sachet
Salt and freshly ground black pepper
5 ml/1 tsp red wine vinegar
15 ml/1 tbsp chopped parsley

Heat the oil and fry (sauté) the steak and gammon until browned, then transfer the meats to a casserole dish (Dutch oven). Fry the onions and garlic until just browned, then add them to the casserole. Add the beers, sugar and nutmeg to the pan and bring to the boil, stirring well to mix in the meat juices, then pour it into the casserole. Add the bouquet garni and season to taste. Cover and cook in a preheated oven at 140°C/275°F/ gas mark 1 for 3 hours. Stir in the wine vinegar, remove the bouquet garni and serve sprinkled with the parsley.

Boeuf en croûte

SERVES 6

225 g/8 oz/2 cups plain (all-purpose) flour
A pinch of salt
150 g/5 oz/⅔ cup butter or margarine
30 ml/2 tbsp water
1.5 kg/3 lb fillet of beef
50 g/2 oz smooth liver pâté
5 ml/1 tsp thyme
1 egg
15 ml/1 tbsp oil

Mix together the flour and salt, then rub in 50 g/2 oz/¼ cup of the butter or margarine until the mixture resembles fine breadcrumbs. Add just enough of the water to mix to a soft pastry (paste), then chill. Grate 50 g/2 oz/¼ cup of the remaining butter. Roll out the pastry to a large rectangle and sprinkle with the grated butter. Fold the pastry into thirds, enclosing the butter, then roll out and fold again. Wrap the pastry in clingfilm (plastic wrap) and chill for 15 minutes, then repeat the rolling and folding three more times. Chill. Spread the remaining butter over the top of the beef and seal in a preheated oven at 220°C/425°F/gas mark 7 for 20 minutes, then leave to cool. The meat will be rare. If you prefer your beef well done, cook the joint for a little longer before wrapping it in the pastry.

Roll out the pastry to a rectangle large enough to enclose the meat. Spread the pâté on top of the meat and place it, pâté-side down, in the centre of the pastry. Sprinkle with the thyme. Fold the pastry round the meat, sealing the edges well. Turn the parcel over and decorate with pastry trimmings. Chill. Beat together the egg and oil and brush over the pastry. Stand the pastry on a damp baking (cookie) sheet and bake in a preheated oven at 220°C/425°F/gas mark 7 for 35 minutes until golden brown.

Hungarian beef

SERVES 8

1.5 kg/3 lb joint of beef
6 smoked bacon rashers (slices), rinded and halved
100 g/4 oz smoked sausage, sliced
1 onion, chopped
Salt and freshly ground black pepper
30 ml/2 tbsp oil

Cut some holes in the beef joint. Roll the bacon and sausage pieces and press them into the holes. Sprinkle the meat with the onion, season well and leave to stand for 1½ hours, then shake off the onion. Heat the oil and fry (sauté) the meat on all sides to seal the joint. Put the meat in a roasting tin (pan), cover and roast in a preheated oven at 180°C/350°F/gas mark 4 for 1½ hours, basting occasionally.

Boeuf à l'orange

SERVES 4

30 ml/2 tbsp oil
750 g/1¾ lb braising steak, cubed
225 g/8 oz shallots, sliced
1 garlic clove, crushed
100 g/4 oz button mushrooms, halved
15 ml/1 tbsp plain (all-purpose) flour
300 ml/½ pt/1¼ cups Beef Stock
   (page 28)
2 oranges
15 ml/1 tbsp tomato purée (paste)
45 ml/3 tbsp brandy
15 ml/1 tbsp black treacle (molasses)
Salt and freshly ground black pepper
15 ml/1 tbsp chopped parsley

Heat the oil in a frying pan (skillet) and fry (sauté) the steak until browned, then transfer to a casserole dish (Dutch oven). Fry the shallots and garlic until browned, then transfer to the casserole with the uncooked mushrooms. Stir the flour into the frying pan and cook for 1 minute, then stir in the stock and bring to the boil. Peel the rind from one orange, cut into thin strips and add it to the pan. Squeeze the juice from both oranges and add to the pan with the tomato purée, brandy and treacle. Season to taste and pour into the casserole. Cover and cook in a preheated oven at 160°C/325°F/gas mark 3 for 2½ hours. Serve sprinkled with the parsley.

Perfect roast beef

SERVES 8

1.75 kg/4 lb roasting joint of beef such
   as fillet, ribs, sirloin or topside
50 g/2 oz/¼ cup lard (shortening) or
   vegetable fat
Yorkshire Pudding (page 186), Roast
   Potatoes (page 226) and fresh
   vegetables, to serve

Clean the joint, dry it on kitchen paper (paper towels) and place it on a trivet in a roasting tin (pan) just large enough to take it comfortably with the fattiest side uppermost and largest cut surface exposed. Brush the meat with the fat and put two knobs of fat on top. Roast in a preheated oven at 220°C/425°F/gas mark 7 for 10 minutes to seal the meat, then turn down the oven to 180°C/350°F/gas mark 4 for 20 minutes per 450 g/1 lb plus 20 minutes extra for rare meat and 40 minutes extra for well done. Baste the joint frequently. Test the meat when you think it is ready by inserting a skewer into the thickest part or by using a meat thermometer (cooking times will vary depending on the shape of the joint, whether it is boned, rolled or stuffed, and your own taste). Allow the meat to rest for 30 minutes before carving. Serve with Yorkshire Pudding, Roast Potatoes and fresh vegetables.

Beefburgers

SERVES 4

450 g/1 lb minced (ground) beef
100 g/4 oz/2 cups fresh breadcrumbs
1 onion, finely chopped
10 ml/2 tsp dried mixed herbs
Salt and freshly ground black pepper
1 egg, beaten
30 ml/2 tbsp oil
4 baps or other large soft rolls
4 lettuce leaves
60 ml/4 tbsp cucumber relish
4 gherkins (cornichons), sliced
Chips (fries), to serve

Mix together the beef, breadcrumbs, onion and herbs and season to taste. Bind with the egg and shape into burgers. Heat the oil and fry (sauté) the burgers until cooked through and browned on both sides. Split the rolls and put the lettuce leaves on the bottom halves. Place the burgers on top and cover with the cucumber relish and gherkins, or other pickles of your choice. Top with the other half of the roll and serve with chips.

Nutty beef roll

SERVES 4

200 g/7 oz/1¾ cups self-raising (self-rising) flour
10 ml/2 tsp baking powder
A pinch of salt
100 g/4 oz/1 cup shredded (chopped) suet
A pinch of caraway seeds
30 ml/2 tbsp cold water
15 ml/1 tbsp oil
450 g/1 lb minced (ground) beef
1 onion, chopped
45 ml/3 tbsp mango chutney
50 g/2 oz/½ cup walnuts, chopped
25 g/1 oz/½ cup fresh breadcrumbs
Gravy, to serve

Mix together the flour, baking powder, salt, suet and caraway seeds. Add enough of the water to mix to a soft dough. Roll out on a lightly floured surface to about 28 × 33 cm (11 × 13 in). Heat the oil and fry (sauté) the mince and onion for 5 minutes. Stir in the remaining ingredients and spread over the pastry (paste) to within 1 cm/½ in of the edges. Dampen the edges and roll up the pastry from one short side, finishing with the seam underneath. Pinch the ends to seal, cover in greased kitchen foil, place on a baking (cookie) sheet and bake in a preheated oven at 160°C/325°F/gas mark 3 for 1 hour. Remove the foil and turn up to 190°C/375°F/gas mark 5 for a further 10 minutes to brown the pastry. Serve sliced with gravy.

Mexican meatballs with chilli tomato sauce

SERVES 4–6

750 g/1¾ lb minced (ground) beef
25 g/1 oz/½ cup fresh breadcrumbs
2 onions, finely chopped
10 ml/2 tsp dried oregano
1 egg, beaten
Salt and freshly ground black pepper
30 ml/2 tbsp plain (all-purpose) flour
40 ml/2½ tbsp oil
1 garlic clove, crushed
2 chilli peppers, chopped
2.5 ml/½ tsp caster (superfine) sugar
400 g/14 oz/1 large can of tomatoes
30 ml/2 tbsp tomato ketchup (catsup)
300 ml/½ pt/1¼ cups Beef Stock
   (page 28)
3 spring onions (scallions), chopped
Brown rice and tortilla chips, to serve

Mix together the mince, breadcrumbs, 1 onion, oregano and egg and season to taste. Divide the mixture into 16 pieces and shape into balls using floured hands. Heat 30 ml/2 tbsp of the oil and fry (sauté) the meatballs until browned and cooked through. Drain on kitchen paper (paper towels) and place in a warm ovenproof dish.

To make the sauce, heat the remaining oil and fry the remaining onion with the garlic and chilli peppers until soft. Add the sugar, tomatoes, ketchup and stock and season to taste. Simmer, uncovered, for 15 minutes until the sauce has reduced and thickened slightly. Mix in the spring onions, pour the sauce over the meatballs and bake in a preheated oven at 180°C/350°F/gas mark 4 for 15 minutes. Serve with brown rice and tortilla chips.

Crispy-topped minced beef pie

SERVES 4

100 g/4 oz/½ cup butter or margarine
1 onion, chopped
1 garlic clove, chopped
450 g/1 lb minced (ground) beef
100 g/4 oz/1 cup plain (all-purpose)
   flour
300 ml/½ pt/1¼ cups Beef Stock
   (page 28)
2.5 ml/½ tsp thyme
2.5 ml/½ tsp rosemary
2.5 ml/½ tsp grated nutmeg
Salt and freshly ground black pepper
100 g/4 oz/1 cup Cheddar cheese,
   grated

Melt 25 g/1 oz/2 tbsp of the butter or margarine and fry (sauté) the onion and garlic until soft, then add the meat and fry until browned. Stir in 15 ml/1 tbsp of the flour and cook for 1 minute, then stir in the stock, thyme, rosemary and nutmeg and season to taste. Simmer for 5 minutes, then transfer to an ovenproof dish. Rub 50 g/2 oz/¼ cup of the remaining butter or margarine into the remaining flour, then stir in the cheese. Spread the mixture on top of the mince and dot with the remaining butter. Bake in a preheated oven at 180°C/350°F/gas mark 4 for 45 minutes until golden brown and crispy.

Beef and ham roll

SERVES 4

450 g/1 lb minced (ground) beef
225 g/8 oz minced ham
175 g/6 oz/3 cups fresh breadcrumbs
15 ml/1 tbsp Worcestershire sauce
Salt and freshly ground black pepper
400 g/14 oz/1 large can of tomatoes,
    chopped
Boiled potatoes and a green vegetable,
    to serve

Mix together all the ingredients
except the tomatoes and season to
taste with salt and pepper. Form into
a roll and place in a greased loaf tin
(pan). Bake at 180°C/350°F/gas mark
4 for 40 minutes, then pour the
tomatoes over and bake for a further
15 minutes. Serve with potatoes and
a green vegetable.

Swedish meatballs

SERVES 4

50 g/2 oz/1 cup fresh breadcrumbs
10 ml/2 tsp cornflour (cornstarch)
1 onion, chopped
250 ml/8 fl oz/1 cup single (light) cream
250 ml/8 fl oz/1 cup milk
Salt and freshly ground black pepper
450 g/1 lb minced (ground) beef
30 ml/2 tbsp oil

Mix together the breadcrumbs,
cornflour, onion, cream and milk and
season to taste. Transfer to a pan
and cook gently over a low heat for
10 minutes, stirring well, then add
the meat and stir until browned.
Remove from the heat and roll the
meat into small balls. Heat the oil
and fry (sauté) the meatballs for
about 8 minutes until browned.

Meatballs in tomato sauce

SERVES 4

4 juniper berries, crushed
100 g/4 oz/2 cups wholemeal
    breadcrumbs
30 ml/2 tbsp chopped parsley
4 prunes, soaked, drained and chopped
450 g/1 lb minced (ground) beef
2.5 ml/½ tsp grated nutmeg
1 egg, beaten
Salt and freshly ground black pepper
30 ml/2 tbsp oil
400 g/14 oz/1 large can of tomatoes,
    chopped
3 basil sprigs, chopped
5 ml/1 tsp Worcestershire sauce
15 ml/1 tbsp dry sherry
15 ml/1 tbsp plain (all-purpose) flour
50 g/2 oz/½ cup Parmesan cheese,
    freshly grated
Pasta, to serve

Mix together the berries, breadcrumbs, parsley, prunes, beef and
nutmeg, bind together with the egg
and season to taste. Make the
mixture into 16 balls and place them
in an ovenproof dish. Mix together
the oil, tomatoes, basil, Worcestershire sauce, sherry and flour by hand
or in a blender until smooth. Pour the
mixture over the meatballs and bake
in a preheated oven at 200°C/400°F/
gas mark 6 for 30 minutes. Sprinkle
with the Parmesan and serve with
pasta.

Chilli con carne

SERVES 4

30 ml/2 tbsp oil
2 onions, chopped
1 garlic clove, crushed
550 g/1¼ lb minced (ground) beef
5 ml/1 tsp cayenne
5 ml/1 tsp chilli powder
10 ml/2 tsp dried oregano
300 ml/½ pt/1¼ cups Beef Stock
   (page 28)
400 g/14 oz/1 large can of tomatoes,
   chopped
225 g/8 oz/1 small can of kidney beans,
   drained and rinsed
30 ml/2 tbsp tomato purée (paste)
A few drops of Worcestershire sauce
Salt and freshly ground black pepper
Boiled rice, to serve

Heat the oil and fry (sauté) the onions and garlic until soft, then stir in the meat and fry until browned. Stir in the cayenne, chilli powder and oregano and cook for 1 minute. Stir in the stock, tomatoes, kidney beans, tomato purée and Worcestershire sauce, bring to the boil and simmer for 10 minutes. Season to taste. Part-cover the pan and simmer for 1 hour, stirring occasionally and adding extra stock if necessary. Serve with rice.

Mexican-style chilli

SERVES 4

30 ml/2 tbsp olive oil
1 onion, chopped
1 garlic clove, crushed
350 g/12 oz minced (ground) beef
2.5 ml/½ tsp ground cumin
5 ml/1 tsp chilli powder (or to taste)
100 g/4 oz button mushrooms, sliced
250 ml/8 fl oz/1 cup passata (sieved
   tomatoes)
Salt and freshly ground black pepper

Heat the oil and fry (sauté) the onion and garlic until just soft. Add the mince and fry until browned. Stir in the cumin and chilli power to taste, then add the mushrooms and passata. Bring to a simmer and simmer gently for about 20 minutes until the sauce has thickened. Taste and season with salt and pepper, if necessary.

Beef sausages with onion gravy

SERVES 4

15 ml/1 tbsp oil
450 g/1 lb beef sausages
4 onions, sliced
10 ml/2 tsp cornflour (cornstarch)
450 ml/¾ pt/2 cups Beef or Vegetable
   Stock (page 28)
Salt and freshly ground black pepper
Mashed potatoes and peas, to serve

Heat the oil in a large frying pan (skillet) and fry (sauté) the sausages for about 5 minutes until just beginning to brown. Add the onions and fry together over a low heat for about 10 minutes until soft. Raise the heat slightly and cook until the sausages are cooked through and browned and the onions are lightly golden. Stir in the cornflour and cook for 1 minute, stirring continuously. Gradually stir in the stock, bring to the boil and simmer until thickened. Season to taste and serve with mashed potatoes and peas.

83

Veal

Mozzarella veal with anchovies

SERVES 4

4 veal escalopes, flattened
Salt and freshly ground black pepper
25 g/1 oz/¼ cup plain (all-purpose) flour
15 g/½ oz/1 tbsp butter or margarine
15 ml/1 tbsp oil
25 g/1 oz/½ small can of anchovies, mashed
3 tomatoes, skinned and sliced
10 ml/2 tsp dried oregano
100 g/4 oz Mozzarella cheese, sliced
4 black olives, stoned (pitted)
15 ml/1 tbsp chopped basil

Season the veal with salt and pepper and toss in the flour. Melt the butter or margarine with the oil and fry (sauté) the veal until golden brown on both sides. Spread the veal thinly with the anchovies, cover with tomato slices, sprinkle with the oregano and top with the cheese. Place an olive on top of each and heat under a hot grill (broiler) until the cheese softens. Sprinkle with the basil and serve immediately.

Veal in Madeira

SERVES 4

4 veal escalopes, flattened
Salt and freshly ground black pepper
60 ml/4 tbsp Madeira
100 g/4 oz/½ cup unsalted (sweet) butter
1 shallot, finely chopped
100 g/4 oz mushrooms, finely chopped
4 tomatoes, skinned, seeded and chopped
300 ml/½ pt/1¼ cups double (heavy) cream
5 ml/1 tsp paprika

Season the veal lightly with salt and pepper. Lay it in a flat dish and spoon the Madeira over. Leave to marinate for 2 hours. Remove the meat and pat dry on kitchen paper (paper towels). Melt the butter and fry (sauté) the veal for about 4 minutes, turning once. Transfer the veal to a warm serving dish and keep warm. Pour off a little butter from the pan and chill. Add the shallot to the remaining butter in the pan and fry until soft, then add the mushrooms and cook for 5 minutes. Add the tomatoes and cook them to a pulp. Pour in the marinade, bring to the boil and simmer until the sauce has reduced and thickened slightly. Stir in the cream and paprika and season to taste. When the sauce is creamy, remove it from the heat and stir in the chilled butter, shaking the pan till the sauce is glossy. Pour over the escalopes and serve immediately.

Veal with tomatoes

SERVES 4

30 ml/2 tbsp oil
2 garlic cloves, chopped
4 veal escalopes, flattened
250 ml/8 fl oz/1 cup dry white wine
400 g/14 oz/1 large can of tomatoes,
    chopped
30 ml/2 tbsp tomato purée (paste)
2.5 ml/½ tsp Worcestershire sauce
5 ml/1 tsp dried oregano
5 ml/1 tsp marjoram
Salt and freshly ground black pepper

Heat the oil and fry (sauté) the garlic
for 1 minute. Add the veal and fry
until browned on both sides. Pour off
any remaining oil and stir in the wine
and tomatoes, bring to the boil and
simmer for 8 minutes. Stir in the
tomato purée, Worcestershire sauce,
oregano and marjoram and season to
taste. Simmer for 10 minutes, then
serve.

Veal Camembert

SERVES 4

40 g/1½ oz/3 tbsp butter or margarine
15 ml/1 tbsp oil
4 veal escalopes, flattened
1 onion, chopped
15 ml/1 tbsp plain (all-purpose) flour
300 ml/½ pt/1¼ cups Chicken Stock
    (page 28)
30 ml/2 tbsp red wine
5 ml/1 tsp dried mixed herbs
1 bay leaf
Salt and freshly ground black pepper
1 garlic clove, crushed
225 g/8 oz tomatoes, skinned, seeded
    and chopped
225 g/8 oz Camembert cheese, sliced

Melt 25 g/1 oz/2 tbsp of the butter
or margarine with the oil and fry
(sauté) the veal until browned on both

sides. Remove the veal from the pan
and keep warm. Fry the onion until
soft, then add the flour and cook for
1 minute. Stir in the stock, wine,
herbs and bay leaf and bring to the
boil, stirring to scrape up the meat
juices. Season to taste and simmer for
8 minutes until the veal is tender.
Melt the remaining butter or
margarine in a clean saucepan, add
the garlic and tomatoes and simmer
for 5 minutes. Transfer the veal to a
warm flameproof serving dish, remove
the bay leaf and pour over the tomato
sauce. Top with the cheese and place
under a hot grill (broiler) for
5 minutes until the cheese bubbles.
Serve the sauce with the escalopes.

Veal saltimbocca

SERVES 4

4 veal escalopes, flattened
100 g/4 oz Mozzarella cheese, sliced
4 sage leaves
4 slices of Parma ham
30 ml/2 tbsp olive oil
150 ml/¼ pt/⅔ cup dry white wine
Salt and freshly ground black pepper

Place a slice of Mozzarella on each
escalope, then a sage leaf and a slice
of Parma ham. Secure with cocktail
sticks (toothpicks). Heat the oil in a
large frying pan (skillet) and fry
(sauté) the escalopes for about
10 minutes until cooked through.
Remove from the pan and keep warm.
Add the wine to the pan and stir to
scrape up all the cooking juices.
Season to taste, pour over the veal
and serve.

Wiener schnitzel

SERVES 4

4 veal escalopes, flattened
1 egg, beaten
30 ml/2 tbsp oil
100 g/4 oz/2 cups fresh breadcrumbs
Salt and freshly ground black pepper
75 g/3 oz/⅓ cup butter or margarine
8 anchovy fillets, drained
4 lemon slices
15 ml/1 tbsp chopped parsley
150 ml/¼ pt/⅔ cup Chicken Stock
   (page 28)

Pat the veal dry on kitchen paper (paper towels). Beat the egg with a few drops of oil and dip the veal into the egg. Season the breadcrumbs with salt and pepper and dip the veal into the breadcrumbs, pressing them down firmly. Melt 50 g/2 oz/¼ cup of the butter or margarine with the remaining oil and fry (sauté) the veal for about 6 minutes each side, turning once. When cooked, transfer to a warm serving plate and arrange two crossed anchovy fillets on top of each escalope, then top with a slice of lemon. Stir the parsley, stock and remaining butter or margarine into the pan and bring to the boil, stirring to scrape up the meat juices. Serve as a sauce with the escalopes.

Danish veal

SERVES 4

50 g/2 oz/¼ cup butter or margarine
4 veal escalopes, flattened
100 g/4 oz button mushrooms
4 pineapple rings
300 ml/½ pt/1¼ cups double (heavy)
   cream

Melt the butter or margarine and fry (sauté) the veal until golden brown on both sides. Add the mushrooms and cook for a further 5 minutes. Remove the meat from the pan and arrange on a warm serving dish. Remove the mushrooms from the pan and keep them warm. Heat the pineapple rings in the pan for 2 minutes, then put one on each fillet and top with the mushrooms. Pour the cream into the pan and bring to the boil, stirring to scrape up all the meat juices. Pour over the meat and serve at once.

Veal stroganoff

SERVES 4

50 g/2 oz/¼ cup butter or margarine
1 onion, sliced
100 g/4 oz button mushrooms, sliced
30 ml/2 tbsp tomato purée (paste)
15 ml/1 tbsp plain (all-purpose) flour
4 veal escalopes, flattened and cut into
   strips
150 ml/¼ pt/⅔ cup soured (dairy sour)
   cream
30 ml/2 tbsp lemon juice
Salt and freshly ground black pepper

Melt half the butter or margarine and fry (sauté) the onion and mushrooms until soft but not brown. Stir in the tomato purée and flour and cook, stirring, for 1 minute. Remove from the heat. Melt the remaining butter in a clean pan and fry the veal until golden brown on both sides. Return the sauce to the heat, add the veal and stir in the cream and lemon juice. Season to taste, heat through and serve immediately.

New Zealand veal

SERVES 4

4 veal escalopes
350 g/12 oz/3 cups Cheddar cheese,
    grated
1 onion, finely chopped
15 ml/1 tbsp chopped parsley
4 streaky bacon rashers (slices), rinded
50 g/2 oz/¼ cup butter or margarine
25 g/1 oz/¼ cup plain (all-purpose) flour
300 ml/½ pt/1¼ cups milk
Salt and freshly ground black pepper

Flatten the escalopes with a meat
mallet or rolling pin. Mix together
three-quarters of the cheese with the
onion and parsley. Press the mixture
into the centre of the escalopes, then
roll up the escalopes and wrap a
bacon rasher around each one,
securing with cocktail sticks
(toothpicks). Melt half the butter or
margarine and fry (sauté) the meat
over a medium heat until golden
brown on all sides. Transfer it to a
shallow casserole dish (Dutch oven).
Melt the remaining butter or
margarine, stir in the flour and cook
for 1 minute, stirring continuously.
Whisk in the milk and continue to
cook and stir until the sauce boils and
thickens. Remove from the heat, stir
in the remaining cheese and season to
taste. Pour over the veal, cover and
bake in a preheated oven at 180°C/
350°F/gas mark 4 for 40 minutes,
then remove the lid and cook for a
further 10 minutes to brown the top.

Continental veal rolls

SERVES 4

4 slices of ham
4 veal escalopes, flattened
15 ml/1 tbsp olive oil
1 garlic clove, chopped
25 g/1 oz/¼ cup pine nuts
25 g/1 oz/3 tbsp raisins
25 g/1 oz/¼ cup Parmesan cheese,
    freshly grated
30 ml/2 tbsp chopped parsley
Salt and freshly ground black pepper
100 g/4 oz Emmental (Swiss) cheese,
    sliced
300 ml/½ pt/1¼ cups dry white wine
2 tomatoes, skinned, seeded and
    chopped
Boiled rice, to serve

Lay a slice of ham on each escalope
and brush with the olive oil. Mix
together the garlic, pine nuts, raisins,
cheese and half the parsley and
sprinkle over the meat. Season to
taste. Top with the slices of Emmental,
roll up and secure the meat with
cocktail sticks (toothpicks). Heat the
remaining oil and fry (sauté) the veal
until browned on all sides. Add the
wine, bring to the boil, cover and
simmer for 30 minutes until tender.
Transfer the veal to a warm serving
dish and keep warm. Boil the liquid
until reduced by half, then stir in the
tomatoes and the remaining parsley,
season to taste and spoon over the
veal. Serve with rice.

Veal in cream and mushroom sauce

SERVES 4

350 g/12 oz button mushrooms
Juice of ½ lemon
25 g/1 oz/2 tbsp butter or margarine
450 g/1 lb veal, cubed
1 onion, chopped
15 ml/1 tbsp plain (all-purpose) flour
150 ml/¼ pt/⅔ cup Chicken Stock
  (page 28)
150 ml/¼ pt/⅔ cup dry white wine
300 ml/½ pt/1¼ cups single (light) cream
5 ml/1 tsp paprika
Salt and freshly ground black pepper
Noodles and a green salad, to serve

Cook the mushrooms in the lemon juice for 2 minutes. Remove the mushrooms from the pan, reserving the cooking liquid, and keep warm. Melt the butter or margarine and fry (sauté) the veal and onion until lightly browned, then remove from the pan and keep warm. Stir in the flour and cook for 1 minute, then stir in the stock, wine and reserved mushroom juice and cook for 3 minutes. Stir in the cream, mushrooms and veal and heat through gently. Add the paprika and season to taste. Serve with noodles and a green salad.

Tarragon veal

SERVES 4

4 veal escalopes
Salt and freshly ground black pepper
100 g/4 oz/½ cup butter or margarine
30 ml/2 tbsp chopped tarragon
225 g/8 oz mushrooms, sliced
300 ml/½ pt/1¼ cups single (light) cream
2 tarragon sprigs

Flatten the escalopes with a meat mallet or rolling pin, then season with salt and pepper. Melt the butter or margarine and fry (sauté) the veal until browned on both sides. Transfer the veal to a warm serving dish and keep warm. Add the tarragon and mushrooms to the pan and fry for about 5 minutes, stirring occasionally, until the mushrooms are soft. Transfer to the serving plate. Stir the cream into the pan and bring just to the boil, stirring to scrape up the meat and vegetable juices. Pour the sauce over the veal and mushrooms and serve garnished with the tarragon sprigs.

Veal and leek casserole

SERVES 4

50 g/2 oz/¼ cup butter or margarine
45 ml/3 tbsp oil
750 g/1¾ lb lean veal, cubed
450 g/1 lb leeks, sliced
15 ml/1 tbsp plain (all-purpose) flour
90 ml/6 tbsp dry white wine
150 ml/¼ pt/⅔ cup milk
1 bouquet garni sachet
Salt and freshly ground black pepper
50 g/2 oz/⅓ cup sultanas (golden raisins)
15 ml/1 tbsp lemon juice

Melt the butter or margarine with the oil and fry (sauté) the veal until browned on all sides. Add the leeks and fry gently until soft. Stir in the flour and cook for 1 minute, stirring, then add the wine and milk and continue to cook, stirring continuously, until the sauce thickens. Add the bouquet garni and season to taste. Cover and simmer gently for 30 minutes, then remove the bouquet garni and stir in the sultanas and lemon juice before serving.

Vealburgers

SERVES 4

1 garlic clove
150 ml/¼ pt/⅔ cup canned ratatouille
Salt and freshly ground black pepper
2.5 ml/½ tsp chopped basil or thyme
50 g/2 oz/½ cup cooked white rice
450 g/1 lb minced (ground) veal
50 g/2 oz/½ cup cooked ham, finely
   chopped
30 ml/2 tbsp chopped parsley
1 egg, beaten
Plain (all-purpose) flour
25 g/1 oz/2 tbsp butter or margarine
15 ml/1 tbsp oil

Squeeze the garlic over the ratatouille in a saucepan, season with salt and pepper and add the basil or thyme. Bring to the boil and simmer for 5 minutes or until any free liquid with the ratatouille has almost evaporated. Mix together the rice and both meats and stir into the ratatouille with the parsley. Season to taste with salt and pepper. Mix in enough egg to bind the ingredients. With floured hands, shape into eight burgers and chill until needed. Just before cooking, sprinkle the burgers with flour and brush with the butter or margarine and oil. Grill (broil) under a medium grill (broiler) for 20 minutes until cooked through, turning once and basting occasionally with butter and oil.

Fruity veal olives

SERVES 4

4 veal escalopes, flattened
Juice of 1 lemon
Freshly ground black pepper
25 g/1 oz/½ cup fresh breadcrumbs
1 dessert (eating) apple, peeled, cored
   and chopped
350 g/12 oz onions, chopped
5 ml/1 tsp sage
1 egg, beaten
1 orange, peeled and sliced
25 g/1 oz/2 tbsp curd (smooth cottage)
   cheese
30 ml/2 tbsp oil
100 g/4 oz canned tomatoes, chopped
150 ml/¼ pt/⅔ cup Beef Stock (page 28)
15 ml/1 tbsp chopped parsley

Coat the escalopes in the lemon juice and sprinkle with pepper. Mix together the breadcrumbs, apple, onion, sage and egg. Chop all but two of the orange slices and mix into the stuffing. Spread the veal slices with the cheese, then cover with the stuffing mixture, roll up and secure with cocktail sticks (toothpicks). Gently fry (sauté) the olives on all sides in the oil until browned, then transfer to a covered ovenproof dish, cover with the chopped tomatoes and stock and bake in a preheated oven at 180°C/ 350°F/gas mark 4 for 30 minutes. Serve garnished with orange twists and the parsley.

Veal chops with Swiss cheese

SERVES 4

75 g/3 oz/⅓ cup butter or margarine
4 veal chops or steaks
100 g/4 oz mushrooms, chopped
50 g/2 oz/½ cup Gruyère (Swiss) cheese,
    grated
Salt and freshly ground black pepper
150 ml/¼ pt/⅔ cup port
225 g/8 oz pasta shells
50 g/2 oz ham, cut into strips

Melt 25 g/1 oz/2 tbsp of the butter or margarine and fry (sauté) the chops on one side, then remove them from the frying pan (skillet). Add the mushrooms and cook for 2 minutes, then stir in the cheese until it melts and season to taste. Spread this mixture on the cooked side of the chops. Melt 25 g/1 oz/2 tbsp of the remaining butter or margarine and cook the other side of the chops for 5 minutes. Place the chops in an ovenproof dish and bake in a preheated oven at 200°C/400°F/gas mark 6 for 10 minutes to glaze. Add the port to the pan, stirring to scrape up all the meat juices, then pour over the chops.

Meanwhile, cook the pasta in boiling salted water until just tender, then drain and rinse in hot water. Return to the saucepan with the remaining butter or margarine and the ham and season with pepper. Heat until the butter has melted and the mixture is thoroughly warmed through. Serve the chops surrounded by pasta shells.

Veal in sorrel sauce

SERVES 4

50 g/2 oz/¼ cup butter or margarine
750 g/1¾ lb veal, cubed
1 onion, chopped
1 garlic clove, crushed
1 carrot, sliced
450 ml/¾ pt/2 cups Chicken Stock
    (page 28)
10 ml/2 tsp thyme
10 ml/2 tsp marjoram
1 bay leaf
Salt and freshly ground black pepper
50 g/2 oz/½ cup chopped sorrel
15 ml/1 tbsp plain (all-purpose) flour
150 ml/¼ pt/⅔ cup single (light) cream
15 ml/1 tbsp lemon juice
Boiled potatoes and carrots, to serve

Melt half the butter or margarine and fry (sauté) the veal, onion, garlic and carrot, stirring continuously, until just browned. Stir in 300 ml/½ pt/1¼ cups of the stock and the herbs and season to taste. Bring to the boil, cover and simmer for 1½ hours until tender.

Simmer the sorrel in the remaining stock for 5 minutes. Leave to cool slightly, then purée in a food processor or blender. Melt the remaining butter or margarine, stir in the flour and cook, stirring, for 1 minute. Stir in the sorrel purée. When the veal is cooked, stir the purée into the casserole. Stir in the cream and lemon juice and season to taste. Remove the bay leaf and serve with boiled potatoes and carrots.

Veal in herbs

SERVES 4

50 g/2 oz/¼ cup butter or margarine
1 onion, chopped
2 carrots, chopped
1.25 kg/2½ lb veal joint, boned and
  rolled
150 ml/¼ pt/⅔ cup dry white wine
150 ml/¼ pt/⅔ cup Chicken Stock
  (page 28)
3 parsley sprigs
3 dill (dill weed) sprigs
Salt and freshly ground black pepper
150 ml/¼ pt/⅔ cup Mayonnaise
  (page 277)
5 ml/1 tsp Dijon mustard
60 ml/4 tbsp plain yoghurt
15 ml/1 tbsp chopped dill
15 ml/1 tbsp chopped parsley
15 ml/1 tbsp snipped chives

Melt half the butter or margarine and
fry (sauté) the onion and carrots until
soft but not brown, then transfer to a
casserole dish (Dutch oven) just large
enough to hold the meat. Melt the
remaining butter or margarine and fry
the veal joint until browned and
sealed on all sides, then transfer to
the casserole dish. Stir the wine and
stock into the pan, bring to the boil,
add the parsley and dill sprigs and
season to taste. Simmer for
2 minutes, then pour over the veal.
Cover and cook in a preheated oven
at 180°C/350°F/gas mark 4 for
1½ hours until tender. Lift out the
meat and leave it to cool. Strain and
reserve the cooking liquor.
  Place the mayonnaise in bowl and
beat in the mustard, yoghurt and
chopped herbs with 45 ml/3 tbsp of
the reserved cooking liquor. Serve the
veal sliced with the sauce poured over.

Veal in orange sauce

SERVES 4

900 g/2 lb veal joint
1 onion, sliced
1 garlic clove, crushed
Juice of 1 lemon
Juice of 2 oranges
15 ml/1 tbsp chopped basil
1 bouquet garni sachet
15 ml/1 tbsp oil
Salt and freshly ground black pepper
25 g/1 oz/2 tbsp caster (superfine) sugar
60 ml/4 tbsp white wine vinegar
1 orange, peeled and sliced

Place the veal in a bowl. Mix together
the onion, garlic, lemon and orange
juices, basil and bouquet garni, pour
over the veal and leave to marinate
for 12 hours. Lift the veal from the
marinade and pat dry on kitchen
paper (paper towels). Heat the oil and
fry (sauté) the veal until browned on
all sides, then transfer it to a
casserole dish (Dutch oven). Stir the
marinade into the pan, bring to the
boil and simmer for 4 minutes,
stirring to scrape up all the meat
juices. Season to taste, then pour over
the veal, cover and cook in a
preheated oven at 150°C/300°F/gas
mark 2 for 1 hour. Transfer the veal to
a warm serving plate and keep warm.
Dissolve the sugar in the wine vinegar
and whisk it into the stock. Remove
the bouquet garni, add the orange
slices and simmer for 3 minutes, then
spoon over the veal and serve.

Osso buco

SERVES 4

900 g/2 lb shin of veal, cut into 5 cm/
    2 in pieces
Salt and freshly ground black pepper
50 g/2 oz/¼ cup butter or margarine
1 onion, sliced
1 celery stick, sliced
1 carrot, sliced
1 leek, sliced
150 ml/¼ pt/⅔ cup dry white wine
400 g/14 oz/1 large can of tomatoes
150 ml/¼ pt/⅔ cup Chicken Stock
    (page 28)
15 ml/1 tbsp tomato purée (paste)
5 ml/1 tsp dried oregano
15 ml/1 tbsp chopped parsley
1 garlic clove, finely chopped
Grated rind of 1 lemon

Season the veal with salt and pepper.
Melt the butter or margarine and fry
(sauté) the veal until just browned,
then add the onion, celery, carrot and
leek and fry until just browned. Stir in
the wine, bring to the boil, then stir in
the tomatoes, stock, tomato purée
and oregano. Bring back to the boil,
cover and simmer for 1½ hours.
Transfer to a warm serving dish. Mix
together the parsley, garlic and lemon
rind and sprinkle over the dish.

Fricassee of veal

SERVES 4

450 g/1 lb fillet of veal, cubed
1 onion, sliced
1 sprig of parsley
6 peppercorns
1 strip of lemon rind
2.5 ml/½ tsp salt
300 ml/½ pt/1¼ cups boiling water
8 streaky bacon rashers (slices), rinded
25 g/1 oz/2 tbsp butter or margarine
15 g/1 oz/¼ cup plain (all-purpose) flour
150 ml/¼ pt/⅔ cup milk
1 lemon, cut into wedges

Put the veal and onion in a casserole
dish (Dutch oven). Tie the parsley,
peppercorns and lemon rind in a piece
of muslin (cheesecloth) and add it to
the casserole with the salt and boiling
water. Cover and cook in a preheated
oven at 160°C/325°F/gas mark 3 for
2 hours. Stretch the bacon rashers
with a knife, then roll them up and
spear on metal skewers and roast for
the last 15 minutes cooking time.
    Melt the butter or margarine, stir
in the flour and cook for 1 minute.
Stir in the milk and 150 ml/¼ pt/
⅔ cup of the liquor from the casserole
and bring to the boil, stirring, until
the sauce thickens. Transfer the meat
to a warm serving dish, pour the
sauce over and arrange the bacon
rolls and lemon wedges around the
edge.

Blanquette de veau

SERVES 4

450 g/1 lb fillet of veal
25 g/1 oz/¼ cup plain (all-purpose) flour
50 g/2 oz/¼ cup butter or margarine
150 ml/¼ pt/⅔ cup Chicken or Vegetable
    Stock (page 28)
2 cloves
1 bay leaf
Salt and freshly ground black pepper
8 small potatoes
15 ml/1 tbsp plain (all-purpose) flour
    (optional)
Extra 15 g/½ oz/1 tbsp butter or
    margarine (optional)

Coat the veal with the flour. Melt the
butter or margarine in a large
saucepan and fry (sauté) the veal until
well browned on both sides. Add the
stock, cloves and bay leaf and season
to taste. Bring to the boil, cover and
simmer for 1 hour. Add the potatoes
and simmer for a further 30 minutes.
    Remove the meat, slice it thinly
and arrange it on a serving dish with
the potatoes. Either add a little water
to the pan or thicken the remaining
gravy with the flour mixed to a paste
with the extra butter or margarine.
Stir well and strain over the meat.

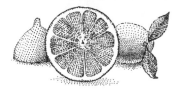

Lemon veal

SERVES 4

2 onions
6 cloves
50 g/2 oz/¼ cup butter or margarine
15 ml/1 tbsp oil
3 carrots, diced
1 garlic clove, crushed
750 g/1¾ lb cubed veal
25 g/1 oz/¼ cup plain (all-purpose) flour
150 ml/¼ pt/⅔ cup dry white wine
150 ml/¼ pt/⅔ cup Chicken Stock
    (page 28)
150 ml/¼ pt/⅔ cup water
Juice of 3 lemons
3 tomatoes, skinned, seeded and
    chopped
1 bouquet garni sachet
Salt and freshly ground black pepper
15 ml/1 tbsp chopped parsley

Chop one onion and stud the other
with the cloves. Melt the butter or
margarine with the oil and fry (sauté)
the onions, carrots and garlic until just
beginning to brown. Transfer to a
casserole dish (Dutch oven). Fry the
veal until browned on all sides, then
transfer to the casserole. Stir the flour
into the pan and cook for 1 minute.
Stir in the wine, stock and water and
bring to the boil, stirring to scrape up
the meat juices. Add the lemon juice,
tomatoes and bouquet garni and
season to taste. Bring back to the
boil, then pour over the veal, cover
and cook in a preheated oven at
180°C/350°F/gas mark 4 for 1 hour
until tender. Remove the bouquet
garni and clove-studded onion and
serve sprinkled with the parsley.

Lamb

Lamb is a versatile meat, delicious in slowly cooked stews and ideal for quick evening meals made with chops or cutlets. It can be a little fatty, but if well trimmed cooks quickly and simply in all sorts of dishes. It is suitable for roasting, grilling (broiling) and frying (sautéing).

Lamb in cider

SERVES 4

15 ml/1 tbsp oil
8 lamb chops
Salt and freshly ground black pepper
1 onion, sliced
1 garlic clove, chopped
1 red (bell) pepper, sliced
100 g/4 oz/1 cup plain (all-purpose)
    flour
300 ml/½ pt/1¼ cups dry cider
150 ml/¼ pt/⅔ cup Chicken Stock
    (page 28)
30 ml/2 tbsp chopped parsley
5 ml/1 tsp baking powder
50 g/2 oz/½ cup shredded (chopped)
    suet
30 ml/2 tbsp water
Crusty bread (optional), to serve

Heat the oil. Season the lamb with salt and pepper and fry (sauté) in the oil until browned on both sides, then transfer to a casserole dish (Dutch oven). Add the onion and garlic to the pan and fry until soft but not brown. Add the pepper and cook for 2 minutes, then stir in 15 ml/1 tbsp of the flour and cook for 1 minute. Stir in the cider and stock, bring to the boil, then stir in half the parsley, season to taste and pour over the lamb. Cover and cook in a preheated oven at 180°C/350°F/gas mark 4 for 1 hour.

Meanwhile, mix the remaining flour with the baking powder, suet and the remaining parsley. Stir in enough of the water to mix to a firm dough, then roll into eight dumplings. Skim any fat off the top of the casserole, add the dumplings, cover and cook for a further 30 minutes until the meat is tender and the dumplings are cooked through. Serve with crusty bread, if liked.

Lemon and mint lamb

SERVES 4

4 lamb chops
15 ml/1 tbsp plain (all-purpose) flour
30 ml/2 tbsp oil
1 onion, sliced
Grated rind and juice of 1 lemon
30 ml/2 tbsp chopped mint
15 ml/1 tbsp demerara sugar
300 ml/½ pt/1¼ cups Chicken Stock
    (page 28)
Salt and freshly ground black pepper
1 small sprig of mint, to garnish
Steamed couscous, to serve

Toss the chops in the flour, then heat the oil and fry (sauté) the chops until browned on both sides. Transfer to a casserole dish (Dutch oven). Add the onion to the pan and fry until soft but not brown. Stir in the lemon rind and juice, mint, sugar and stock and season to taste. Bring to the boil, then pour over the chops and bake in a preheated oven at 180°C/350°F/gas mark 4 for 1¼ hours until tender. Transfer to a warm serving plate, garnish with the sprig of mint and serve with couscous.

95

Noisettes of lamb with fennel

SERVES 4

Salt and freshly ground black pepper
4 noisettes of lamb or lamb chops
10 ml/2 tsp ground coriander (cilantro)
15 ml/1 tbsp oil
1 onion, sliced
2 fennel bulbs, chopped
300 ml/½ pt/1¼ cups Beef Stock
   (page 28)
15 ml/1 tbsp cornflour (cornstarch)
15 ml/1 tbsp water
50 g/2 oz/1 cup fresh breadcrumbs
50 g/2 oz/½ cup strong cheese, grated
2 fennel sprigs
Boiled new potatoes and French (green)
   beans, to serve

Season the lamb to taste with salt and pepper and sprinkle with the coriander. Heat the oil and fry (sauté) the lamb until browned on both sides, then transfer to a casserole dish (Dutch oven). Fry the onion until soft and lightly brown, then add the fennel and cook for a few minutes before spooning into the casserole. Stir the stock into the pan and bring to the boil, then pour over the meat, cover and cook in a preheated oven at 180°C/350°F/gas mark 4 for 1 hour until the meat is tender.

Transfer the meat and vegetables to a warm flameproof serving dish and keep warm. Transfer the pan juices to a saucepan. Mix the cornflour with the water and stir into the juices, bring to the boil and simmer, stirring well, until thickened, then pour over the meat. Sprinkle with the breadcrumbs and cheese and brown under a hot grill (broiler). Garnish with the fennel sprigs and serve with boiled new potatoes and French beans.

Piquant lamb chops

SERVES 4

225 g/8 oz/1 cup butter or margarine
15 ml/3 tsp capers, drained and
   chopped
10 ml/2 tsp light brown sugar
8 lamb chops
Salt and freshly ground black pepper
30 ml/2 tbsp clear honey
30 ml/2 tbsp white wine vinegar
Boiled rice and carrots, to serve

Soften half the butter or margarine and mix in the capers and sugar. Shape into a roll and chill. Season the chops with salt and pepper. Heat the remaining butter or margarine with the honey and vinegar until the fat melts. Brush both sides of the chops with the glaze, then grill (broil) them under a medium grill (broiler) for about 20 minutes, brushing frequently with the glaze. Transfer the chops to a warm serving plate and top with the chilled piquant butter. Serve with boiled rice and carrots.

Braised lamb with vegetables

SERVES 4

4 lamb chops
30 ml/2 tbsp oil
4 back bacon rashers (slices), rinded
15 g/½ oz/1 tbsp butter or margarine
100 g/4 oz carrots, sliced
2 onions, sliced
1 turnip, cut into wedges
2 celery sticks, sliced
1 bouquet garni sachet
Salt and freshly ground black pepper
300 ml/½ pt/1¼ cups Beef Stock
   (page 28)
15 ml/1 tbsp cornflour (cornstarch)
15 ml/1 tbsp water
Mashed potatoes, to serve

Trim the chops, heat the oil and fry (sauté) the chops until lightly browned on both sides. Remove from the pan and cover each one with a piece of bacon. Melt the butter or margarine and fry the vegetables until golden brown, stirring continuously. Add the bouquet garni and season to taste. Pour in enough of the stock almost to cover the vegetables, lay the chops on top, bring to the boil, cover and simmer for 40 minutes until the chops are tender. Transfer the chops to a baking tin (pan) and bake in a preheated oven at 220°C/425°F/gas mark 7 for 10 minutes until the bacon is crisp.

Meanwhile, transfer the vegetables to a warm serving dish and keep warm. Make up the cooking liquid to 300 ml/½ pt/1¼ cups with any reserved stock and discard the bouquet garni. Mix the cornflour to a smooth paste with the water, then stir it into the stock and bring to the boil, stirring, until the sauce thickens.

Arrange the baked chops on top of the vegetables and serve with mashed potatoes and the gravy.

Lamb cutlets with soubise sauce

SERVES 4

8 lamb cutlets
1 egg, beaten
100 g/4 oz/2 cups fresh breadcrumbs
45 ml/3 tbsp oil
2 onions, chopped
150 ml/¼ pt/⅔ cup water
25 g/1 oz/2 tbsp butter or margarine
25 g/1 oz/¼ cup plain (all-purpose) flour
450 ml/¾ pt/2 cups milk
15 ml/1 tbsp single (light) cream
Salt and freshly ground black pepper
2 parsley sprigs
Jacket potatoes and peas, to serve

Dip the lamb in the egg, then the breadcrumbs. Heat the oil and fry (sauté) the lamb until cooked through and golden brown, turning once. Transfer to a warm serving dish and keep warm. Put the onions and water in a saucepan, bring to the boil and simmer for 10 minutes, then purée in a food processor or blender. Melt the butter or margarine, stir in the flour and cook for 1 minute. Whisk in the milk and cook, stirring, until the mixture thickens. Remove from the heat and stir in the onion purée and cream and season to taste. Pour the sauce over the cutlets, garnish with the parsley sprigs and serve with jacket potatoes and peas.

Sweet and sour lamb

SERVES 4

25 g/1 oz/2 tbsp butter or margarine
8 lamb cutlets
1 onion, chopped
25 g/1 oz/¼ cup cornflour (cornstarch)
30 ml/2 tbsp white wine vinegar
5 ml/1 tsp soy sauce
400 g/14 oz/1 large can of pineapple rings
150 ml/¼ pt/⅔ cup Chicken Stock (page 28)
15 ml/1 tbsp chopped parsley
Salt and freshly ground black pepper
Boiled rice, to serve

Melt the butter or margarine and fry (sauté) the lamb for 10 minutes on each side until crisp and brown. Transfer to a warm serving dish and keep warm. Fry the onion until soft but not brown, then drain off any excess fat. Mix together the cornflour, wine vinegar and soy sauce and add it to the pan with the juice from the pineapple and the stock. Bring to the boil, stirring, and boil for a few minutes until the sauce thickens. Add the cutlets and parsley, season to taste and simmer for 15 minutes. Garnish with the pineapple rings and serve with boiled rice.

Lamb with redcurrant sauce

SERVES 4

150 ml/¼ pt/⅔ cup soured (dairy sour) cream
1 garlic clove, crushed
10 ml/2 tsp wholegrain mustard
Salt and freshly ground black pepper
450 g/1 lb lamb fillet
75 ml/5 tbsp red wine
45 ml/3 tbsp redcurrant jelly (clear conserve)
Sauté potatoes and mushrooms, to serve

Mix 60 ml/4 tbsp of the cream with the garlic and mustard and season to taste. Spread over the lamb and place it in a roasting tin (pan). Cook in a preheated oven at 180°C/350°F/gas mark 4 for 50 minutes until tender. Slice the lamb thickly and arrange on a warm serving dish. Add the wine and redcurrant jelly to the tin and bring to the boil, stirring to scrape up all the meat juices, then stir in the remaining soured cream and simmer until slightly thickened. Pour over the lamb and serve with sauté potatoes and mushrooms.

Lamb with chestnut mushrooms and herbs

SERVES 4

15 ml/1 tbsp oil
4 lamb leg steaks
1 onion, chopped
1 garlic clove, crushed
100 g/4 oz chestnut mushrooms, sliced
400 g/14 oz/1 large can of tomatoes, chopped
15 ml/1 tbsp chopped parsley
2.5 ml/½ tsp rosemary
2.5 ml/½ tsp chopped basil
2.5 ml/½ tsp sugar
60 ml/4 tbsp Chicken Stock (page 28)
Boiled new potatoes, to serve

Heat the oil and fry (sauté) the steaks until browned on both sides, then reduce the heat and fry gently until cooked through. Transfer to a warm serving dish and keep warm. Add the onion and garlic to the pan and fry until soft but not brown, then stir in all the remaining ingredients, bring to the boil and simmer, stirring occasionally, for 10 minutes until thick and well combined. Spoon over the steaks and serve with new potatoes.

Minted lamb steaks with sharp fruits

SERVES 4

1 dessert (eating) apple, cored and thinly sliced
15 ml/1 tbsp lemon juice
2 peaches, peeled and sliced
2 kiwi fruits, peeled and sliced
½ white cabbage, shredded
150 ml/¼ pt/⅔ cup Mayonnaise (page 277)
50 g/2 oz/¼ cup butter or margarine, melted
30 ml/2 tbsp chopped mint
4 lamb leg steaks
Salt and freshly ground black pepper
Boiled rice, to serve

Toss the apple slices in the lemon juice, then mix with the peach and kiwi fruit slices and the cabbage. Toss in the mayonnaise and chill.

Mix the butter or margarine with the mint and brush it over the steaks, then season to taste. Cook the steaks under a medium grill (broiler) for about 10 minutes each side until cooked through to your liking and browned on both sides. Top with the chilled minted butter or margarine and serve with boiled rice.

Sichuan-style lamb

SERVES 4

5 ml/1 tsp Sichuan peppercorns
250 ml/8 fl oz/1 cup golden (light corn) syrup
10 ml/2 tsp sesame oil
2.5 cm/1 in piece of root ginger, grated
3 star anise
5 ml/1 tsp Chinese five spice powder
2 racks of lamb
Steamed pak choy, to serve

Toss the peppercorns in a hot, dry pan for a few minutes until fragrant, then remove and grind coarsely. Warm the syrup in a pan, then stir in all the remaining ingredients except the lamb and leavel to cool. Rub this marinade into the lamb, then pour over the remaining marinade, cover and leave in a cool place overnight.

Lift the lamb out of the marinade and place on a rack in a roasting tin (pan) and baste with a little of the marinade. Roast in a preheated oven at 220°C/425°F/gas mark 7 for 15 minutes, then reduce the oven temperature to 190°C/375°F/gas mark 5 and continue to cook for a further 10 minutes or until cooked to your liking. Leave to stand for 10 minutes, then carve and serve with steamed pak choy.

Paprika lamb chops

SERVES 4

25 g/1 oz/2 tbsp unsalted (sweet) butter
8 lamb chops
2 onions, sliced
2 garlic cloves, crushed
30 ml/2 tbsp paprika
30 ml/2 tbsp tomato purée (paste)
Salt and freshly ground black pepper
300 ml/½ pt/1¼ cups Chicken Stock
  (page 28)
150 ml/¼ pt/⅔ cup dry white wine
1 bay leaf
15 ml/1 tbsp plain (all-purpose) flour
400 g/14 oz/1 large can of tomatoes,
  chopped
150 ml/¼ pt/⅔ cup plain yoghurt
30 ml/2 tbsp chopped parsley
Boiled potatoes and seasonal vegetables,
  to serve

Melt half the butter and fry (sauté)
the chops until browned, then add the
onions and cook until soft. Remove
from the heat and stir in the garlic,
paprika and tomato purée and season
to taste. Stir in the stock, wine and
bay leaf, bring to the boil, cover and
simmer for 50 minutes, stirring
occasionally, until the meat is tender.
Mix the flour to a paste with the
remaining butter and stir it into the
stew until the sauce thickens. Simmer
for a few minutes, then stir in the
tomatoes and heat through. Transfer
to a warm serving dish, remove the
bay leaf and stir in the yoghurt.
Sprinkle with the parsley and serve
with boiled potatoes and seasonal
vegetables.

Lamb in sweet sherry sauce

SERVES 4

50 g/2 oz/¼ cup butter or margarine
1 onion, chopped
1 celery stick, finely chopped
75 g/3 oz/1½ cups fresh breadcrumbs
75 g/3 oz/¾ cup chopped mixed nuts
Grated rind and juice of 1 lemon
Salt and freshly ground black pepper
1 egg, beaten
4 lamb fillets
25 g/1 oz/¼ cup plain (all-purpose) flour
300 ml/½ pt/1¼ cups Beef Stock
  (page 28)
75 ml/5 tbsp sweet sherry
Boiled new potatoes and French (green)
  beans, to serve

Melt half the butter or margarine and
fry (sauté) the onions and celery until
soft but not brown. Stir in the
breadcrumbs, half the nuts and the
lemon rind, season to taste and bind
with the egg. Remove from the pan.
Melt the remaining butter or
margarine and fry the lamb until
browned on both sides, then place
two of the fillets in a casserole dish
(Dutch oven) just large enough to
hold them. Spread the stuffing
mixture on top and top with the
remaining fillets. Stir the flour into the
pan and cook for 1 minute, then stir
in the stock and sherry, bring to the
boil and add the lemon juice. Season
to taste, then pour over the lamb.
Cover and cook in a preheated oven
at 180°C/350°F/gas mark 4 for
1½ hours until the meat is tender.
Slice the meat on to a warm serving
dish and sprinkle with the remaining
nuts. Strain the sauce into a sauce
boat and serve separately with boiled
new potatoes and French beans.

Lamb with cumin and sesame seeds

SERVES 4

30 ml/2 tbsp olive oil
Juice of 1 lemon
45 ml/3 tbsp sesame seeds, crushed
15 ml/1 tbsp cumin seeds, crushed
1 garlic clove, crushed
2.5 ml/½ tsp cayenne
Salt and freshly ground black pepper
4 lamb fillets
45 ml/3 tbsp chopped mint
150 ml/¼ pt/⅔ cup plain yoghurt
Pilau Rice (page 203), to serve

Mix together all the ingredients except the lamb, mint and yoghurt and spread the mixture over the fillets. Leave to marinate overnight. Bake in a preheated oven at 230°C/450°F/gas mark 8 for 15 minutes, then reduce the heat to 180°C/350°F/gas mark 4 for a further 15 minutes until cooked through. Cut the fillets into thin slices, season to taste and pour the meat juices over. Stir the mint into the yoghurt. Serve the lamb with the minted yoghurt and Pilau Rice.

Malaysian lamb curry

SERVES 4

50 g/2 oz/½ cup desiccated (shredded) coconut
2 dried red chilli peppers
15 ml/1 tbsp cumin seeds, toasted
15 ml/1 tbsp coriander (cilantro) seeds, toasted
6 green peppercorns
25 g/1 oz fresh root ginger, grated
2 garlic cloves, chopped
5 ml/1 tsp turmeric
30 ml/2 tbsp lemon juice
30 ml/2 tbsp oil
3 onions, chopped
450 g/1 lb lamb, cubed
200 g/7 oz/1 small can of tomatoes, chopped
Salt and freshly ground black pepper
Boiled rice, to serve

Purée the coconut, chilli peppers, cumin, coriander, peppercorns, ginger, garlic, turmeric and lemon juice in a food processor or blender. Heat the oil and fry (sauté) the onions until soft but not browned, then stir in the paste and fry for 4 minutes. Stir in the lamb and cook for 5 minutes, then add the tomatoes and season to taste. Bring to the boil, cover and simmer for 1 hour until tender. Serve with boiled rice.

Lamb ragout

SERVES 4

50 g/2 oz/¼ cup butter or margarine
900 g/2 lb leg of lamb, boned and
  cubed
3 onions, sliced
1 garlic clove, crushed
15 ml/1 tbsp paprika
15 ml/1 tbsp plain (all-purpose) flour
15 ml/1 tbsp tomato purée (paste)
150 ml/¼ pt/⅔ cup dry white wine
300 ml/½ pt/1¼ cups Chicken Stock
  (page 28)
1 bouquet garni sachet
Salt and freshly ground black pepper
Egg Fried Rice (page 204), to serve

Heat the butter or margarine in a saucepan and fry (sauté) the lamb until browned on all sides, then remove from the pan. Add the onions and garlic to the pan and fry until soft, then stir in the paprika and flour and cook for 1 minute. Stir in the tomato purée, wine and stock, add the bouquet garni and season to taste. Bring to the boil, cover and simmer for 1 hour until the meat is tender, stirring occasionally. Remove the bouquet garni and serve with Egg Fried Rice.

Sasaties

SERVES 6

1 garlic clove, halved
1.5 kg/3 lb leg of lamb, cubed
4 onions, quartered
30 ml/2 tbsp light brown sugar
300 ml/½ pt/1¼ cups milk
15 ml/1 tbsp oil, plus extra for brushing
15 ml/1 tbsp undiluted lime juice cordial
15 ml/1 tbsp curry powder
2.5 ml/½ tsp ground cloves
2.5 ml/½ tsp whole allspice
120 ml/4 fl oz/½ cup white wine vinegar
Salt and freshly ground black pepper
15 ml/1 tbsp plain (all-purpose) flour
15 g/½ oz/1 tbsp butter or margarine,
  chilled and diced
Boiled rice and a salad, to serve

Rub the inside of a large earthenware bowl with the cut sides of the garlic clove. Lay the meat in the bowl. Add two onions, the sugar and milk. Heat the oil in a frying pan (skillet) and fry (sauté) the remaining onions until lightly browned. Add the lime juice, curry powder, spices and wine vinegar and season to taste. Pour over the meat and leave overnight.

Remove the meat and onions with a slotted spoon and thread alternately on to six skewers. Pat dry with kitchen paper (paper towels) and brush with oil. Turn the marinade into a saucepan, sprinkle on the flour and stir in the butter or margarine. Bring to the boil and simmer, stirring constantly, until slightly thickened. Place the kebabs under a medium grill (broiler) and grill (broil) for about 20 minutes, turning frequently, until cooked through. Serve with rice and salad and serve the sauce in a jug.

Chelow kebab with rice nests

SERVES 4

750 g/1¾ lb leg or shoulder of lamb, boned
Salt and freshly ground black pepper
175 ml/6 fl oz/¾ cup plain yoghurt
4 tomatoes, halved
30 ml/2 tbsp oil
1 packet of tortilla chips
340 g/12 oz/1½ cups long-grain rice
4 egg yolks
50 g/2 oz/¼ cup butter or margarine

Cut the lamb into 18 × 5 cm/7 × 2 in strips and rub with salt and pepper. Beat them flat with a mallet. Place the yoghurt in a bowl, add the lamb and leave to marinate for 3 hours. Season the tomatoes with salt and pepper and brush with the oil. Weave the meat strips lengthways on to long skewers. Brush the kebabs lightly with oil, then grill (broil) under a medium grill (broiler) for about 20 minutes, turning frequently, until cooked to your liking. Add the tomatoes to the grill for the last 5 minutes cooking time. Warm the tortilla chips in the oven for 10 minutes.

Meanwhile, cook the rice in plenty of boiling salted water for 15 minutes until just tender, drain and serve in individual bowls with an egg yolk and a knob of butter or margarine in the centre of each bowl. The egg and butter are mashed into the hot rice and eaten with the meat, tortilla chips and tomatoes.

Lancashire hot-pot

SERVES 4

50 g/2 oz/¼ cup lard (shortening) or vegetable fat
900 g/2 lb potatoes, peeled and thickly sliced
750 g/1¾ lb middle neck of lamb, cut into pieces
2 kidneys, skinned, cored and sliced
2 onions, sliced
Salt and freshly ground black pepper
300 ml/½ pt/1¼ cups hot Chicken Stock (page 28)

Grease a casserole dish (Dutch oven) with half the lard or vegetable fat and put a thick layer of potato slices in the bottom of the dish. Add the meat, kidneys and onions and season to taste. Pour the hot stock over and cover with the remaining potatoes in an overlapping layer. Brush well with the remaining fat. Cover and cook in a preheated oven at 180°C/350°F/gas mark 4 for 2 hours until the meat and potatoes are tender. Remove the lid, raise the temperature to 220°C/ 425°F/ gas mark 7 and continuing cooking for a further 20 minutes until the top is lightly browned.

Lamb and red onion casserole with coriander

SERVES 4

700 g/1½ lb potatoes, thinly sliced
450 g/1 lb red onions, thinly sliced
900 g/2 lb neck or leg of lamb, boned
  and diced
50 g/2 oz/¼ cup long-grain rice
1 large bunch of parsley, chopped
1 large bunch of coriander (cilantro),
  chopped
2 kaffir lime leaves
5 ml/1 tsp chilli flakes
2 carrots, sliced
60 ml/4 tbsp olive oil
Salt and freshly ground black pepper
1.2 litres/2 pts/5 cups Chicken Stock
  (page 28)

Fill a large casserole dish (Dutch oven)
with layers of potatoes, onions, lamb,
rice, herbs, lime leaves, chilli and
carrots, sprinkling with oil and
seasoning with salt and pepper as you
go. Finish with a layer of potatoes and
sprinkle with the remaining olive oil.
Pour in enough of the stock to come
almost to the top layer of potatoes.
Cover and bake in a preheated oven
at 180°C/350°F/gas mark 4 for
2 hours. Remove the lid and return to
the oven for a further 30 minutes
until the top is crisp and browned.

Bordeaux-braised lamb

SERVES 6–8

1.5 kg/3 lb leg of lamb, boned
300 ml/½ pt/1¼ cups red wine
30 ml/2 tbsp oil
100 g/4 oz button mushrooms
1 onion, chopped
1 garlic clove, chopped
2 carrots, sliced
15 ml/1 tbsp plain (all-purpose) flour
150 ml/¼ pt/⅔ cup Chicken Stock
  (page 28)
1 bouquet garni sachet
Salt and freshly ground black pepper

Marinate the lamb in the wine
overnight.
  Remove the meat from the
marinade, reserving the marinade.
Drain the meat and pat dry with
kitchen paper (paper towels). Heat
the oil and fry (sauté) the meat until
browned, then transfer it to a
casserole dish (Dutch oven) and cover
with the uncooked mushrooms. Fry
the onion, garlic and carrots until just
browned, then add the flour and cook
for 1 minute. Stir in the stock and
150 ml/¼ pt/⅔ cup of the wine
marinade, bring to the boil, then pour
into the casserole, add the bouquet
garni and season to taste. Cover and
cook in a preheated oven at 150°C/
300°F/gas mark 2 for 2½ hours.
Remove the bouquet garni before
serving.

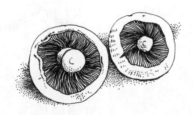

French-style roast lamb

SERVES 6

1.75 kg/4 lb leg of lamb
3 garlic cloves, sliced
A pinch of rosemary
A pinch of sage
A pinch of thyme
5 ml/1 tsp cayenne
15 ml/1 tbsp oil
300 ml/½ pt/1¼ cups Chicken Stock
(page 28)
120 ml/4 fl oz/½ cup red wine
2 tomatoes, skinned, seeded and
chopped
15 ml/1 tbsp Worcestershire sauce
15 ml/1 tbsp tomato purée (paste)
5 ml/1 tsp chopped mint

Pat the meat dry on kitchen paper (paper towels) and cut tiny slits in the surface of the meat. Push the garlic into the cuts and rub the meat with the herbs and cayenne. Roast in a preheated oven at 220°C/425°F/gas mark 7 for 15 minutes, then reduce the temperature to 180°C/350°F/gas mark 4 and roast for a further 30 minutes. Bring the stock and wine to the boil and pour it over the meat, then continue roasting for a further 30 minutes, basting frequently.

When the meat is cooked to your liking, transfer it to a warm serving plate and keep warm. Add the tomatoes, Worcestershire sauce, tomato purée and mint to the liquid in the tin (pan), bring to the boil and simmer, stirring well, until the liquid has reduced by a third. Strain the sauce, then return it to the pan to reheat. Carve the lamb and serve with the sauce spooned over the meat.

Butterflied lamb

SERVES 6–8

60 ml/4 tbsp lemon juice
150 ml/¼ pt/⅔ cup dry white wine
30 ml/2 tbsp Worcestershire sauce
30 ml/2 tbsp oil
2 garlic cloves, chopped
5 ml/1 tsp chopped basil
5 ml/1 tsp chopped marjoram
5 ml/1 tsp chopped rosemary leaves
Salt and freshly ground black pepper
1.25 kg/2½ lb leg of lamb, boned

Mix together all the ingredients except the lamb in a plastic bag. Open out the lamb into the shape of a butterfly, lay it in the marinade, close the bag securely and leave the meat to marinate for 24 hours, turning occasionally.

Bake the lamb in a preheated oven at 200°C/400°F/gas mark 6 for about 1 hour, basting occasionally with a little marinade, until cooked to your liking. Allow the meat to rest for 10 minutes before slicing.

Traditional roast lamb

SERVES 4

1.5 kg/3 lb leg of lamb
Salt and freshly ground black pepper
15 ml/1 tbsp oil

Season the lamb with salt and pepper. Grease a roasting tin (pan) with the oil and add the meat. Roast in a preheated oven at 220°C/425°F/gas mark 7 for 20 minutes, then reduce the temperature to 190°C/375°F/gas mark 5 and continue to roast for 1¼ hours until crisp on the outside and cooked to your liking. For different-sized joints, calculate the cooking time as 20 minutes per 450 g/1 lb plus 10 minutes.

Guard of honour

SERVES 6

900 g/2 lb best end of neck of lamb cut
    into two pieces, each having about
    6 chops
50 g/2 oz/1 cup fresh breadcrumbs
225 g/8 oz pork sausagemeat
50 g/2 oz mushrooms, finely chopped
10 ml/2 tsp lemon juice
2.5 ml/½ tsp made English mustard
Salt and freshly ground black pepper
4 tomatoes
15 ml/1 tbsp chopped rosemary leaves
50 g/2 oz/¼ cup butter or margarine
5 ml/1 tsp French mustard
1 garlic clove, crushed

Ask the butcher to cut the lamb into
two pieces, each having about six
chops, and to remove the chine bone
from the meat, then cut off the top
2.5 cm/1 in at the thin end, leaving
the bones exposed. Discard the fat.
Trim the meat between the bones and
scrape each bone to clean it. Chop
the meat finely, then mix it with the
breadcrumbs, sausagemeat,
mushrooms, half the lemon juice and
the English mustard and season to
taste. Halve the tomatoes and scoop
out the seeds. Stir these into the
stuffing. Use half the stuffing to fill the
tomato shells.

Stand the lamb so that the
exposed bones interlock. Form the
remaining stuffing into a thick sausage
and place in the middle of the two
pieces of lamb. Place in a shallow
ovenproof dish. Mix together the
rosemary, butter or margarine,
remaining lemon juice, French
mustard and garlic. Score lines on the
fatty side of the meat with a sharp
knife and spread the butter mixture
over the outside. Bake in a preheated
oven at 190°C/375°F/gas mark 5 for
30 minutes, covering the bones with
pieces of foil if they appear to be
burning.

Roast lamb with mint

SERVES 8

1.75 kg/4 lb leg of lamb, boned
Salt and freshly ground black pepper
3 garlic cloves, crushed
1 bunch of mint, chopped
45 ml/3 tbsp olive oil
Juice of 1 lemon
1 celery stick, finely chopped
1 carrot, finely chopped
1 onion, finely chopped
300 ml/½ pt/1¼ cups water

Open out the lamb, season to taste
with salt and pepper and sprinkle with
the garlic and half the mint. Roll up
and tie securely. Season the outside of
the joint and place it on a rack in a
roasting tin (pan), fat-side up. Pour
over the oil and lemon juice, surround
with the vegetables and roast in a
preheated oven at 230°C/450°F/gas
mark 8 for 20 minutes, then reduce
the heat to 180°C/350°F/gas mark 4.
Add the water to the tin and roast for
a further 1¼ hours until the meat is
tender and crisp on the outside.
Transfer the lamb to a warm serving
dish. Skim any excess fat off the pan
juices, stir in the remaining mint and
bring to the boil, then pour into a
sauce boat and serve with the lamb.

Apricot and chestnut lamb

SERVES 6

1 onion, finely chopped
150 g/6 oz/1½ cups fresh breadcrumbs
100 g/4 oz/⅔ cup no-need-to-soak dried
    apricots, chopped
100 g/4 oz frozen chestnuts, chopped
1 egg, beaten
Salt and freshly ground black pepper
1.5 kg/3 lb shoulder of lamb, boned

Mix together the onions, breadcrumbs
apricots, chestnuts and egg and
season to taste. Lay the lamb joint
flat and cover with the stuffing. Tie
round with string and cook in a
preheated oven at 190°C/375°F/
gas mark 5 for 2 hours, basting
occasionally, until tender.

Lamb meatloaf with taco topping

SERVES 4

2 onions, chopped
1 garlic clove, chopped
450 g/1 lb minced (ground) lamb
5 ml/1 tsp chilli powder
50 g/2 oz/1 cup fresh breadcrumbs
5 ml/1 tsp Tabasco sauce
Salt and freshly ground black pepper
100 g/4 oz/1 cup strong cheese, grated
150 ml/¼ pt/⅔ cup taco sauce
25 g/1 oz corn chips, broken into pieces

Mix together the onions, garlic, lamb,
chilli powder, breadcrumbs and
Tabasco sauce and season to taste.
Press half the mixture into a greased
900 g/2 lb loaf tin (pan), sprinkle in
half the cheese and top with the
remaining mixture. Cover and bake in
a preheated oven at 180°C/350°F/
gas mark 4 for 45 minutes, then

leave to stand for 10 minutes. Turn
the loaf out on to an ovenproof plate
and brush with the taco sauce.
Sprinkle with the remaining cheese
and the corn chips. Return to the
oven at 200°C/400°F/gas mark 6 for
10 minutes until the cheese has
melted. Serve sliced, hot or cold.

Grilled kofta

SERVES 4

3 slices of bread, crusts removed
45 ml/3 tbsp dry white wine
450 g/1 lb minced (ground) lamb
1 onion, chopped
1 egg, beaten
4 parsley sprigs, chopped
Salt and freshly ground black pepper
30 ml/2 tbsp olive oil
4 pitta breads, warmed
150 ml/¼ pt/⅔ cup Sharp Yoghurt
    Dressing (page 279)

Moisten the bread with the wine and
a little water if needed. Squeeze it
dry and put it with all the other
ingredients except the oil, pitta bread
and dressing in a food processor or
blender and process until smooth and
pasty. Using floured hands, shape into
rissoles the size of small eggs. Leave
to stand for 30 minutes, then thread
carefully on to shish kebab skewers
and brush with olive oil. Grill (broil)
under a hot grill (broiler) for 20
minutes, turning frequently, until well
browned on all sides. Serve with warm
pitta bread and Sharp Yoghurt
Dressing.

Crispy-topped lamb and watercress

SERVES 4

450 g/1 lb minced (ground) lamb
2 onions, chopped
2 bunches of watercress, chopped
5 ml/1 tsp dried oregano
40 g/1½ oz plain (all-purpose) flour
300 ml/½ pt/1¼ cups Chicken Stock
    (page 28)
60 ml/4 tbsp dry white wine
Salt and freshly ground black pepper
50 g/2 oz/¼ cup butter or margarine
600 ml/1 pt/2½ cups milk
225 g/8 oz/2 cups Cheshire cheese,
    crumbled
225 g/8 oz ready-to-use lasagne sheets

Fry (sauté) the lamb in a saucepan
until all the grains are brown and
separate, then add the onions and fry
until soft. Add the watercress,
oregano and 30 ml/2 tbsp of the flour
and cook for 1 minute, then stir in the
stock and wine and season to taste.
Bring to the boil, then simmer for
40 minutes, stirring occasionally.
Meanwhile, melt the butter or
margarine, stir in the remaining flour
and cook for 1 minute. Whisk in the
milk and cook, stirring, until the sauce
thickens. Remove from the heat and
stir in half the cheese. Layer the
mince, lasagne and half the cheese
sauce in a greased shallow ovenproof
dish, finishing with a layer of lasagne.
Pour over the remaining cheese
sauce, sprinkle with the remaining
cheese and bake in a preheated oven
at 190ºC/375ºF/gas mark 5 for
40 minutes until cooked through
and well browned.

Lamb samosas

SERVES 4

175 g/6 oz/1½ cups self-raising (self-
    rising) flour
75 g/3 oz/¾ cup shredded (chopped)
    suet
A pinch of salt
30 ml/2 tbsp water
1 onion, chopped
5 ml/1 tsp curry powder
15 ml/1 tbsp oil
175 g/6 oz/1½ cups cooked lamb, finely
    chopped
Salt and freshly ground black pepper
15 ml/1 tbsp sweet chutney, plus extra
    for serving
Corn oil, for deep-frying

Mix together the flour, suet and salt,
then bind to a firm dough with the
water. Roll out and cut into eight
rounds. Mix together the onion and
curry powder. Heat the oil and fry
(sauté) the onion until soft, then add
the lamb and cook for 5 minutes.
Season to taste and stir in the
chutney. Leave to cool. Put a spoonful
of the mixture in the centre of each
pastry (paste) round, bring up the
edges and pinch together to make a
pasty shape. Fry (sauté) in the hot oil
for about 5 minutes until golden
brown. Drain and serve with chutney.

Moussaka

SERVES 4

2 aubergines (eggplants), sliced
Salt and freshly ground black pepper
15 ml/1 tbsp oil
1 onion, chopped
1 garlic clove, chopped
350 g/12 oz/3 cups cooked lamb,
    minced (ground)
10 ml/2 tsp tomato purée (paste)
5 ml/1 tsp cornflour (cornstarch)
45 ml/3 tbsp dry white wine
150 ml/¼ pt/⅔ cup Chicken Stock
    (page 28)
5 ml/1 tsp dried oregano
25 g/1 oz/2 tbsp butter or margarine
25 g/1 oz/¼ cup plain (all-purpose) flour
450 ml/¾ pt/2 cups milk
75 g/3 oz/¾ cup Cheddar cheese, grated

Lay the aubergine slices in a dish,
sprinkle with salt and leave to stand.
Heat the oil and fry (sauté) the onion
and garlic until soft but not brown.
Stir in the lamb, tomato purée,
cornflour, stock and oregano and cook
until thickened. Turn the mixture into
an ovenproof dish. Rinse the
aubergines. Drain them, pat dry on
kitchen paper (paper towels) and layer
them on top of the meat. Melt the
butter or margarine in a clean
saucepan, stir in the flour and cook
for 1 minute. Whisk in the milk, bring
to the boil and simmer until
thickened, stirring continuously.
Remove from the heat and stir in half
the cheese, then pour the sauce over
the aubergines. Sprinkle with the
remaining cheese and bake in a
preheated oven at 200°C/400°F/gas
mark 6 for 30 minutes until golden
brown.

Lamb in rich spicy sauce

SERVES 4

15 ml/1 tbsp oil
1 garlic clove, chopped
1 onion, chopped
15 ml/1 tbsp curry powder
400 g/14 oz/1 large can of tomatoes
15 ml/1 tbsp tomato purée (paste)
15 ml/1 tbsp lemon juice
15 ml/1 tbsp mango chutney, plus extra
    for serving
10 ml/2 tsp garam masala
50 ml/2 fl oz/¼ cup plain yoghurt
450 g/1 lb/4 cups cooked lamb, diced
Boiled rice, to serve

Heat the oil and fry (sauté) the garlic
and half the onion until browned. Add
the curry powder and cook for
1 minute. Add the tomatoes, tomato
purée, lemon juice and chutney and
cook for 20 minutes. Blend in the
garam masala, then pour the mixture
into a food processor or blender and
process until smooth. Add the yoghurt
and process again until mixed. Return
the mixture to the pan, add the lamb
and remaining onion, bring to the boil
and simmer gently for 15 minutes.
Serve with rice and extra mango
chutney.

Lamb in pitta with cucumber sauce

SERVES 4

½ cucumber
250 ml/8 fl oz/1 cup plain yoghurt
1 spring onion (scallion), finely chopped
15 ml/1 tbsp lime juice
15 ml/1 tbsp chopped dill (dill weed)
15 ml/1 tbsp chopped mint
Salt and freshly ground black pepper
4 pitta breads
225 g/8 oz/2 cups cooked lamb, thinly
    sliced
2 tomatoes, thinly sliced

Peel the cucumber, halve it lengthways and scoop out the seeds with a teaspoon. Dice the cucumber flesh and mix it into the yoghurt with the onion, lime juice and herbs. Season to taste. Leave to stand. Warm the pitta breads either in a microwave for a few seconds or wrapped in foil in a warm oven for a minute or two. Split the breads and open them out to form a pocket. Divide the meat and tomatoes between the breads and spoon some of the yoghurt sauce into each one. Serve at once.

Pytt i panna

SERVES 4

50 g/2 oz/¼ cup unsalted (sweet) butter
15 ml/1 tbsp olive oil
450 g/1 lb boiled potatoes, chopped
450 g/1 lb/4 cups cooked lamb, diced
225 g/8 oz streaky bacon, diced
1 onion, chopped
Salt and freshly ground black pepper
15 ml/1 tbsp chopped parsley
5 ml/1 tsp Worcestershire sauce
4 eggs

Melt the butter with the oil and fry (sauté) the potatoes until golden brown. Remove the potatoes from the pan, drain well and keep warm. Fry the lamb, bacon and onion until the onion is soft but not brown, then stir the potatoes back into the pan and season to taste. Cook for 5 minutes, shaking the pan gently, then stir in the parsley and Worcestershire sauce. Meanwhile, fry the eggs lightly. Turn the lamb mixture into a warm serving dish and serve topped with the fried eggs.

Pork

Pork must always be thoroughly cooked, so take care to check that the meat is completely cooked through before serving. A slightly fatty meat, it should be well trimmed and works well when combined with sharper flavours, especially fruits or a little well-chosen alcohol. The leanest cuts of pork can be stir-fried or cooked quickly, but larger cuts should be allowed a longer, slower cooking time.

Pork in whisky

SERVES 4

25 g/1 oz/2 tbsp butter or margarine
15 ml/1 tbsp oil
4 pork chops
Salt and freshly ground black pepper
150 ml/¼ pt/⅔ cup whisky
150 ml/¼ pt/⅔ cup Beef Stock (page 28)
25 g/1 oz/2 tbsp light brown sugar
15 ml/1 tbsp Dijon mustard
5 ml/1 tsp cornflour (cornstarch)
15 ml/1 tbsp water

Melt the butter or margarine with the oil and fry (sauté) the chops until browned on both sides. Season to taste. Stir in the whisky and simmer until the aroma subsides, then stir in the stock, sugar and mustard, bring to the boil, cover and simmer for 15 minutes until the chops are cooked. Mix together the cornflour and water, stir into the sauce and cook until the sauce thickens.

Pork chops Avesnoise

SERVES 4

15 g/½ oz/1 tbsp butter or margarine
15 ml/1 tbsp olive oil
4 pork chops
Salt and freshly ground black pepper
100 g/4 oz/1 cup Gruyère (Swiss)
    cheese, grated
10 ml/2 tsp Dijon mustard
150 ml/¼ pt/⅔ cup single (light) cream
1 garlic clove, crushed
Crisp green salad, to serve

Melt the butter or margarine with the oil and fry (sauté) the chops until browned on both sides. Season to taste, transfer to a shallow casserole dish (Dutch oven) and bake in a preheated oven at 180°C/350°F/gas mark 4 for 45 minutes until tender.

Mix together the remaining ingredients and spread over the top of the chops. Return the chops to the oven for a further 10 minutes until the topping is golden. Serve with a crisp green salad.

Devilled pork chops

SERVES 4

15 ml/1 tbsp oil
4 pork chops
1 onion, chopped
½ green (bell) pepper, chopped
15 ml/1 tbsp plain (all-purpose) flour
400 g/14 oz/1 large can of tomatoes,
    chopped
10 ml/2 tsp Dijon mustard
15 ml/1 tbsp Worcestershire sauce
2.5 ml/½ tsp light brown sugar
Salt and freshly ground black pepper

Heat the oil in a large frying pan (skillet) and brown the chops on both sides. Transfer to an ovenproof dish. Fry (sauté) the onion and green pepper in the oil until soft but not brown, stir in the flour and cook for 1 minute. Add the remaining ingredients, seasoning to taste with salt and pepper. Bring to the boil, stirring constantly, until the sauce is thick and smooth. Pour over the chops, cover and bake in a preheated oven at 180°C/350°F/gas mark 4 for 30 minutes.

Pork foil parcels

SERVES 4

25 g/1 oz/2 tbsp butter or margarine
4 pork chops
1 onion, chopped
225 g/8 oz mushrooms, sliced
75 ml/5 tbsp dry cider
30 ml/2 tbsp lemon juice
150 ml/¼ pt/⅔ cup soured (dairy sour)
   cream
Salt and freshly ground black pepper

Melt the butter or margarine and fry (sauté) the chops until browned on both sides, then transfer them to four squares of kitchen foil. Add the onion and mushrooms to the pan and fry (sauté) until soft but not brown. Stir in the cider and lemon juice, bring to the boil and boil until reduced by half. Remove from the heat, stir in the cream and season to taste. Spoon over the chops, then fold up the foil and seal the edges into parcels. Place the parcels in an ovenproof dish and bake in a preheated oven at 180°C/350°F/gas mark 4 for 1 hour. Serve the pork in the foil and let everyone open their own parcel.

Pork in cider

SERVES 4

50 g/2 oz/¼ cup butter or margarine
4 pork chops
1 onion, sliced
350 g/12 oz cooking (tart) apples,
   peeled, cored and sliced
450 ml/¾ pt/2 cups dry cider
Salt and freshly ground black pepper
Boiled rice, to serve

Melt the butter or margarine and fry (sauté) the chops until browned, then transfer them to a casserole dish (Dutch oven). Fry the onion and apples until lightly browned, then spoon them into the casserole. Pour the cider into the pan and season to taste. Bring to the boil, then pour over the meat. Cover and bake in a preheated oven at 180°C/350°F/gas mark 4 for 50 minutes until the meat is tender. Serve with boiled rice.

Pork with apple rings

SERVES 4

4 pork chops
Salt and freshly ground black pepper
50 g/2 oz/¼ cup butter or margarine
1 onion, chopped
25 g/1 oz/¼ cup plain (all-purpose) flour
150 ml/¼ pt/⅔ cup Chicken Stock
   (page 28)
150 ml/¼ pt/⅔ cup milk
2 cooking (tart) apples, peeled and
   cored
15 ml/1 tbsp chopped parsley

Season the chops with salt and pepper and fry (sauté) in half the butter or margarine until lightly browned and cooked through. Transfer to a warm serving dish and keep warm. Gently fry the onion until soft but not brown. Add the flour and cook for 1 minute. Whisk in the stock and milk and bring to the boil, stirring continuously. Return the chops to the pan. Chop one apple and stir it into the pan. Simmer for 15 minutes. Meanwhile slice the second apple into rings and fry (sauté) lightly in the remaining butter or margarine. Serve the pork with the apple slices and garnish with the parsley.

Honeyed pork steaks

SERVES 4

150 ml/¼ pt/⅔ cup tomato ketchup
  (catsup)
30 ml/2 tbsp clear honey
30 ml/2 tbsp lemon juice
30 ml/2 tbsp oil
15 ml/1 tbsp Worcestershire sauce
4 pork steaks
4 tomatoes

Mix together the ketchup, honey,
lemon juice, oil and Worcestershire
sauce in a saucepan over a low heat
until warm through. Pour over the
steaks in a shallow dish and leave to
marinate for 30 minutes, turning
once. Cook under a medium grill
(broiler) for about 30 minutes,
basting frequently with the marinade
while cooking. Cut a cross in the
tomatoes and add them to the grill
for the final 5 minutes of cooking.

Sweet and sour pork steaks

SERVES 4

15 ml/1 tbsp oil
1 onion, chopped
100 g/4 oz mushrooms, sliced
30 ml/2 tbsp tomato purée (paste)
30 ml/2 tbsp demerara sugar
30 ml/2 tbsp lemon juice
30 ml/2 tbsp cider vinegar
30 ml/2 tbsp Worcestershire sauce
400 g/14 oz/1 large can of tomatoes,
  chopped
Salt
4 pork steaks
Green noodles, to serve

Heat half the oil in a frying pan
(skillet) and fry (sauté) the onion and
mushrooms until soft but not
browned. Stir in all the remaining

ingredients except the remaining oil
and the steaks, adding salt to taste.
Bring to the boil, cover and simmer
for 20 minutes. Brush the steaks with
the remaining oil and grill (broil)
under a medium heat for 7 minutes
on each side. Pour the sauce over the
steaks and serve with green noodles.

South sea spare ribs

SERVES 4

90 ml/6 tbsp soy sauce
60 ml/4 tbsp red wine
90 ml/6 tbsp tomato ketchup (catsup)
75 ml/5 tbsp pineapple juice
15 ml/1 tbsp chopped basil
5 ml/1 tsp chopped sage
250 ml/8 fl oz/1 cup oil
Freshly ground black pepper
1.5 kg/3 lb pork spare ribs

Mix together all the ingredients
except the pork, seasoning to taste
with pepper. Marinate the pork in the
mixture overnight, then drain and dry
well on kitchen paper (paper towels).
Put the pork in a greased baking tin
(pan) and bake in a preheated oven
at 180°C/350°F/gas mark 4 for
20 minutes, then turn the chops and
bake for a further 20 minutes, basting
frequently with the marinade. Drain
the pork and finish off under a
preheated grill (broiler) for 5 minutes
until glazed.

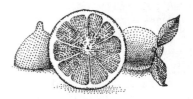

Pork with peppers

SERVES 4

15 ml/1 tbsp oil
15 g/1 oz/2 tbsp butter or margarine
1 onion, chopped
25 g/1 oz fresh root ginger, grated
1 garlic clove, crushed
4 pork steaks
1 red (bell) pepper, sliced
1 green pepper, seeded and sliced
1 yellow pepper, seeded and sliced
60 ml/4 tbsp dry sherry
30 ml/2 tbsp soy sauce
150 ml/¼ pt/⅔ cup pineapple juice
Salt and freshly ground black pepper
Boiled rice, to serve

Heat the oil and butter or margarine and fry (sauté) the onion, ginger and garlic until soft but not brown, then remove them from the pan. Add the steaks to the pan and fry until browned on both sides, then add the peppers, sherry, soy sauce and pineapple juice and return the onion mixture to the pan. Mix thoroughly and season to taste. Bring to the boil, cover and simmer for 15 minutes until the steaks are cooked through. Transfer the steaks to a warm serving dish and keep warm. Bring the sauce to the boil and boil to reduce and thicken the sauce, then pour it over the steaks and serve with rice.

Lemon pork

SERVES 6

15 ml/1 tbsp oil
900 g/2 lb pork fillet, cubed
300 ml/½ pt/1¼ cups dry white wine
30 ml/2 tbsp ground cumin
2 garlic cloves, crushed
Salt and freshly ground black pepper
1 lemon, sliced
10 ml/2 tsp ground coriander (cilantro)
Boiled rice, to serve

Heat the oil and fry (sauté) the pork until browned on all sides, stirring well. Stir in half the wine and the cumin and garlic. Season to taste with salt and pepper. Bring to the boil, cover and simmer for 30 minutes until tender. Remove the lid and add the remaining wine, the lemon slices and coriander and simmer until the sauce has reduced and thickened slightly. Transfer to a warm serving dish and serve with boiled rice.

Mississippi grill

SERVES 6

2 eating (dessert) apples, sliced
60 ml/4 tbsp oil
450 g/1 lb pork fillet, cubed
2 green (bell) peppers, cut into squares
100 g/4 oz button mushrooms
6 small tomatoes
Salt and freshly ground black pepper

Brush the apple slices with the oil as soon as you have cut them. Thread the pork, apple, peppers, mushrooms and tomatoes on six skewers. Brush generously with the remaining oil and season with salt and pepper. Grill (broil) under a medium grill (broiler) for 25 minutes until the pork is well cooked through.

115

Pork with orange and soy sauce

SERVES 4

15 ml/1 tbsp soy sauce
15 ml/1 tbsp clear honey
2 garlic cloves, crushed
15 ml/1 tbsp grated orange rind
2.5 ml/½ tsp paprika
2 pork fillets
15 ml/1 tbsp corn oil
Crisp rocket salad, to serve

Mix together all the ingredients except the fillets and oil. Cut the fillets through into thin slices, then add them to the marinade, coating the fillets well, and leave to stand for at least 30 minutes. Heat the oil in a frying pan (skillet). Remove the fillets from the marinade and fry (sauté) for about 20 minutes, turning occasionally, until cooked through on both sides. Serve with a crisp rocket salad.

Pork spare ribs in wine

SERVES 4

15 ml/1 tbsp chopped parsley
1 garlic clove, chopped
3 juniper berries, crushed
8 pork spare ribs
Salt and freshly ground black pepper
30 ml/2 tbsp oil
150 ml/¼ pt/⅔ cup dry white wine
300 ml/½ pt/1¼ cups Chicken Stock
    (page 28)
Juice of 2 oranges

Mix together the parsley, garlic and juniper berries and rub them into the spare ribs. Season to taste with salt and pepper. Heat the oil and fry (sauté) the spare ribs until browned on all sides, then stir in the wine and bring to the boil. Stir in the stock and orange juice, bring back to the boil

and simmer, uncovered, for 30 minutes until the meat is tender and the sauce has thickened.

Pork with pâté

SERVES 4

2 pork fillets, halved horizontally
125 g/4 oz smooth pâté
Salt and freshly ground black pepper
25 g/1 oz/2 tbsp butter or margarine
1 garlic clove, crushed
100 g/4 oz mushrooms, sliced
150 ml/¼ pt/⅔ cup dry sherry
150 ml/¼ pt/⅔ cup dry white wine
5 ml/1 tsp Dijon mustard
2.5 ml/½ tsp Worcestershire sauce
5 ml/1 tsp chopped parsley
45 ml/3 tbsp double (heavy) cream

Flatten out the pork and spread with the pâté, season with salt and pepper, then fold over and sew the edges, enclosing the pâté. Melt the butter or margarine and fry (sauté) the pork until browned on all sides, then remove it from the pan. Add the garlic to the pan and fry until lightly browned. Add the mushrooms and cook for 2 minutes, then stir in the sherry, wine, mustard, Worcestershire sauce and parsley and bring to the boil. Return the pork to the pan, cover and simmer for 40 minutes. Remove the pork from the pan and slice, discarding the thread. Arrange the slices on a warm serving plate and keep warm. Boil the sauce until thickened, then stir in the cream and heat through for 3 minutes before pouring the sauce over the meat to serve.

Stuffed pork fillet

SERVES 4

9 prunes, chopped
25 g/1 oz/½ cup fresh breadcrumbs
100 g/4 oz/½ cup butter or margarine, softened
5 ml/1 tsp dried mixed herbs
Salt and freshly ground black pepper
700 g/1½ lb piece of pork fillet
8 streaky bacon rashers (slices), rinded
Rice or pasta, to serve

Thoroughly mix together the prunes, breadcrumbs and 75 g/3 oz/⅓ cup of the butter or margarine, then stir in the mixed herbs and season to taste. Slice the fillet almost in half, fill the centre with the stuffing, then fold the meat over again. Stretch the bacon rashers with a knife on a board, then wrap them around the meat. Lay the rolls in an ovenproof dish and dot with the remaining butter or margarine. Bake in a preheated oven at 200°C/400°F/gas mark 6 for 30 minutes until cooked through and crispy. Serve with rice or pasta.

Pork fillet with orange sauce

SERVES 4

50 g/2 oz/¼ cup butter or margarine
450 g/1 lb pork fillet, thinly sliced
1 onion, chopped
15 ml/1 tbsp plain (all-purpose) flour
Grated rind and juice of 1 orange
30 ml/2 tbsp redcurrant jelly (clear conserve)
300 ml/½ pt/1¼ cups Chicken Stock (page 28)
Salt and freshly ground black pepper
Boiled new potatoes and carrots, to serve

Melt the butter or margarine and fry (sauté) the pork until browned on both sides, then remove from the pan. Add the onion to the pan and fry until soft but not brown, then stir in the flour and cook for 1 minute. Stir in the orange rind and juice, the redcurrant jelly and stock and season to taste. Bring to the boil, return the pork to the pan, cover and simmer gently for 15 minutes until the meat is cooked through. Serve with boiled new potatoes and carrots.

Caribbean pork

SERVES 4

30 ml/2 tbsp oil
30 ml/2 tbsp soft brown sugar
700 g/1½ lb pork fillet, cubed
5 ml/1 tsp allspice
5 ml/1 tsp thyme
1 onion, chopped
2 garlic cloves, chopped
15 ml/1 tbsp white wine vinegar
50 g/2 oz creamed coconut
300 ml/½ pt/1¼ cups water
100 g/4 oz mushrooms, sliced
1 green (bell) pepper, sliced
Juice of ½ lime

Heat the oil in a large frying pan (skillet), add the sugar and heat until caramelised. Add the pork and fry (sauté) until browned. Add the allspice and thyme, cover and simmer for 10 minutes. Stir in the onion, garlic, wine vinegar, coconut and water, cover and simmer for 20 minutes. Add the mushrooms and green pepper, cover and simmer for 10 minutes. Stir in the lime juice before serving.

Paprika pork

SERVES 4

50 g/2 oz/¼ cup butter or margarine
15 ml/1 tbsp oil
450 g/1 lb pork fillet, cubed
3 onions, sliced
15 ml/1 tbsp paprika
25 g/1 oz/¼ cup plain (all-purpose) flour
300 ml/½ pt/1¼ cups Chicken Stock
    (page 28)
15 ml/1 tbsp lemon juice
15 ml/1 tbsp tomato purée (paste)
400 g/14 oz/1 large can of tomatoes,
    chopped
50 g/2 oz/⅓ cup raisins
Salt and freshly ground black pepper
60 ml/4 tbsp soured (dairy sour) cream

Melt the butter or margarine with the oil and fry (sauté) the pork until browned on all sides, then transfer it to a casserole dish (Dutch oven). Add the onions to the pan and fry until lightly browned, then stir in the paprika and flour and cook for 1 minute. Stir in the stock, lemon juice, tomato purée, tomatoes and raisins, season to taste and bring to the boil. Pour the mixture into the casserole and bake in a preheated oven at 180°C/350°F/gas mark 4 for 1½ hours until the meat is tender. Swirl the soured cream into the casserole just before serving.

Pork curry with mango

SERVES 4

750 g/1¾ lb pork fillet, cubed
25 g/1 oz/¼ cup plain (all-purpose) flour
30 ml/2 tbsp oil
2 onions, sliced
1 red (bell) pepper, sliced
1 green pepper, sliced
5 ml/1 tsp turmeric
15 ml/1 tbsp curry powder
5 ml/1 tsp ground cumin
5 ml/1 tsp ground ginger
2.5 ml/½ tsp chilli powder
400 g/14 oz/1 large can of tomatoes,
    drained and chopped
15 ml/1 tbsp tomato purée (paste)
300 ml/½ pt/1¼ cups Chicken Stock
    (page 28)
450 g/1 lb small new potatoes, scrubbed
400 g/14 oz/1 large can of mango slices,
    drained
Boiled rice and mango chutney, to serve

Coat the pork in the flour. Heat the oil and fry (sauté) the pork until just browned. Add the onions and peppers and cook for 2 minutes. Add the spices and cook for 1 minute, stirring continuously. Stir in the tomatoes, tomato purée, stock and potatoes, bring to the boil, cover and cook for 20 minutes. Add the mango and cook for a further 5 minutes until the meat and vegetables are cooked through. Serve with rice and mango chutney.

Pork in calvados

SERVES 4

750 g/1¾ lb pork fillet, cubed
Salt and freshly ground black pepper
50 g/2 oz/¼ cup butter or margarine
225 g/8 oz mushrooms, sliced
60 ml/4 tbsp calvados
150 ml/¼ pt/⅔ cup Chicken Stock
   (page 28)
150 ml/¼ pt/⅔ cup single (light) cream
10 ml/2 tsp cornflour (cornstarch)
50 g/2 oz/½ cup chopped mixed nuts
15 ml/1 tbsp chopped parsley

Season the pork with salt and pepper.
Melt half the butter or margarine and
fry (sauté) the meat until lightly
browned, then transfer it to a
casserole dish (Dutch oven). Melt the
remaining butter or margarine and fry
the mushrooms for 2 minutes, then
stir in the calvados and stock, season
to taste, bring to the boil and simmer
for 3 minutes. Pour the sauce into the
casserole, cover and bake in a
preheated oven at 180°C/350°F/gas
mark 4 for 45 minutes until the meat
is tender. Mix together the cream and
cornflour and stir into the sauce, then
return the casserole to the oven for
10 minutes. Mix together the nuts
and parsley and sprinkle over the
casserole to serve.

Navarin of pork

SERVES 4

15 ml/1 tbsp plain (all-purpose) flour
A pinch of grated nutmeg
Salt and freshly ground black pepper
750 g/1¾ lb pork fillet, cubed
30 ml/2 tbsp oil
2 large parsnips, diced
½ turnip, diced
2 carrots, diced
1 onion, chopped
300 ml/½ pt/1¼ cups Chicken Stock
   (page 28)
5 ml/1 tsp Worcestershire sauce
1 bay leaf

Season the flour with the nutmeg and
salt and pepper and toss the meat in
the flour. Heat the oil and fry (sauté)
the meat until browned on all sides,
then transfer to a casserole dish
(Dutch oven). Add the vegetables to
the pan and fry until lightly browned,
then add to the casserole dish. Pour
the stock into the pan, add the
Worcestershire sauce and season to
taste. Bring to the boil, then pour it
into the casserole dish and add the
bay leaf. Cover and cook in a
preheated oven at 160°C/325°F/gas
mark 3 for 1¼ hours until tender.
Discard the bay leaf before serving.

Roast pork with apple and nut stuffing

SERVES 6

25 g/1 oz/2 tbsp butter or margarine
1 onion, chopped
50 g/2 oz/½ cup cashew nuts, chopped
2 slices of bread, cubed
1 cooking (tart) apple, peeled, cored
    and chopped
1 celery stick, chopped
15 ml/1 tbsp chopped parsley
2.5 ml/½ tsp savory
2.5 ml/½ tsp lemon juice
Salt and freshly ground black pepper
1.5 kg/3 lb shoulder of pork, boned
30 ml/2 tbsp oil
150 ml/¼ pt/⅔ cup dry cider

Melt the butter or margarine and fry (sauté) the onion and nuts until just browned, then stir in the bread, apple and celery and fry until soft. Stir in the parsley, savory and lemon juice and season to taste. Flatten the joint and spread the stuffing over the meat, then roll it up and tie securely with string. Place in a roasting tin (pan), brush well with the oil and sprinkle with salt. Bake in a preheated oven at 200°C/400°F/gas mark 6 for 20 minutes, then reduce the heat to 180°C/350°F/gas mark 4 and cook for a further 1½ hours until the meat is well cooked through. Transfer the meat to a warm serving dish and keep warm. Pour the cider into the tin and bring to the boil, stirring to scrape up all the meat juices. Simmer until reduced and thickened slightly, then pour it into a sauce boat and serve with the pork.

Fried pork with sweet and sour sauce

SERVES 4

450 g/1 lb minced (ground) pork
50 g/2 oz/1 cup fresh breadcrumbs
1 onion, finely chopped
2.5 ml/½ tsp sage
1 egg, beaten
Salt and freshly ground black pepper
45 ml/3 tbsp oil
400 g/14 oz/1 large can of apricots in
    syrup
15 ml/2 tbsp cornflour (cornstarch)
45 ml/3 tbsp soy sauce
45 ml/3 tbsp tomato purée (paste)
150 ml/¼ pt/⅔ cup Chicken Stock
    (page 28)
2 red (bell) peppers, chopped
15 g/½ oz fresh root ginger, grated
Crisp salad, to serve

Mix together the pork, breadcrumbs, onion, sage and egg and season to taste. Shape into small balls. Heat the oil and fry (sauté) the balls until golden brown all over and cooked through. Drain well and keep them warm. Meanwhile, drain the apricot syrup into a saucepan and mix in the cornflour, soy sauce, tomato purée and stock. Bring to the boil, stirring, then add the peppers and ginger and simmer for 5 minutes. Add the pork balls, stirring gently, and simmer for a further 5 minutes. Slice the apricots and add them to the sauce, heat through gently and serve with a crisp salad.

Boston baked beans

SERVES 4

350 g/12 oz/2 cups haricot (navy)
    beans, soaked overnight
450 g/1 lb belly pork, rinded and cubed
2 onions, sliced
10 ml/2 tsp salt
10 ml/2 tsp mustard powder
Freshly ground black pepper
30 ml/2 tbsp black treacle (molasses)
30 ml/2 tbsp white wine vinegar
6 cloves
15 ml/1 tbsp tomato purée (paste)
15 ml/1 tbsp chopped parsley

Drain the beans well, then mix with all
the other ingredients except the
parsley in a casserole dish (Dutch
oven). Add just enough water to
barely cover the ingredients, cover
tightly and bake in a preheated oven
at 150°C/300°F/gas mark 2 for
6 hours. Stir well, add a little boiling
water if the casserole is too dry, cover
again and bake for a further 1 hour.
Discard the cloves and serve sprinkled
with the parsley.

Spicy pork curry

SERVES 4

30 ml/2 tbsp oil
450 g/1 lb pork fillet, cubed
1 onion, sliced
2 garlic cloves, crushed
5 ml/1 tsp chilli powder
10 ml/2 tsp ground cumin
5 ml/1 tsp ground cinnamon
10 ml/2 tsp ground coriander (cilantro)
300 ml/½ pt/1¼ cups water
Salt and freshly ground black pepper
150 ml/¼ pt/⅔ cup plain yoghurt
Boiled rice, to serve

Heat the oil and fry (sauté) the meat
until browned on all sides, then

remove from the pan. Add the onion
and garlic and fry until lightly
browned, then stir in the spices and
cook for 1 minute. Stir in the water,
season to taste and bring to the boil,
then simmer for 1 hour until the pork
is cooked. Stir in the yoghurt and
reheat, then serve with rice.

Oriental pork

SERVES 4

30 ml/2 tbsp oil
450 g/1 lb belly pork, rinded and cubed
1 onion, chopped
15 ml/1 tbsp plain (all-purpose) flour
200 g/7 oz/1 small can of pineapple
    chunks
15 ml/1 tbsp white wine vinegar
1 green (bell) pepper, sliced
150 ml/¼ pt/⅔ cup Chicken Stock
    (page 28)
5 ml/1 tsp soy sauce
Salt and freshly ground black pepper
Boiled rice, to serve

Heat the oil and fry (sauté) the pork
and onion until browned on all sides.
Stir in the flour and cook for 1
minute, then stir in all the remaining
ingredients, seasoning to taste. Bring
to the boil, stirring, then cover and
simmer for 35 minutes until tender.
Serve with boiled rice.

Pork with beer sauce

SERVES 4

750 g/1¾ lb loin of pork
Salt and freshly ground black pepper
1 garlic clove, crushed
30 ml/2 tbsp oil
3 onions, sliced
450 ml/¾ pt/2 cups stout or brown ale
150 ml/¼ pt/⅔ cup single (light) cream
15 ml/1 tbsp cornflour (cornstarch)

Season the meat with salt and pepper and rub it with the garlic. Heat the oil in a flameproof casserole dish (Dutch oven) and fry (sauté) the meat until browned on all sides. Add the onions and fry until lightly browned. Stir in the stout or brown ale, cover and simmer gently for 1½ hours, basting occasionally. When the meat is thoroughly cooked, transfer it to a warm serving dish and slice it thickly, then keep it warm. Blend together the cream and cornflour and stir into the beer. Bring to the boil and simmer, stirring, until the sauce thickens. Season to taste and strain into a sauce boat.

Mustard pork roast

SERVES 6

1.5 kg/3 lb pork joint, boned and rolled
Oil, for brushing
Salt
30 ml/2 tbsp made English mustard
15 ml/1 tbsp clear honey
5 ml/1 tsp ground coriander (cilantro)

Brush the pork with oil and sprinkle with salt. Place in a preheated oven at 200°C/400°F/gas mark 6 for 10 minutes, then turn the heat down to 180°C/350°F/gas mark 4 and continue cooking for 35 minutes per 450g/1 lb. Mix together the remaining ingredients, pour them over the pork and return it to the oven for a final 30 minutes cooking.

Minced pork and potato pie

SERVES 4

450 g/1 lb minced (ground) pork
1 onion, chopped
400 g/14 oz/1 large can of baked beans
5 ml/1 tsp dried mixed herbs
450 g/1 lb boiled potatoes
50 g/2 oz/¼ cup butter or margarine
30 ml/2 tbsp milk
Salt and freshly ground black pepper

Heat the mince gently in a saucepan until the fat begins to run, then increase the heat and fry (sauté) until browned. Drain off any excess fat, add the onion and fry until soft. Stir in the beans and herbs, then transfer to a shallow ovenproof dish. Mash the potatoes with half the butter or margarine and the milk and season to taste. Top the pork mixture with the potato, fluff up with a fork and dot with the remaining butter or margarine. Bake in a preheated oven at 180°C/350°F/gas mark 4 for 45 minutes until golden brown and crispy on top.

Bacon, ham and sausages

A meal based on bacon or ham, with their distinctive flavours, makes a pleasant change from other meats. As it is a salty meat, take care to adjust seasoning as you cook, and team the meat with suitable vegetables to complement the strong flavours. You will find all sorts of fancy sausages and sausagemeats in the chill cabinet of your local supermarket, so give them a try – as well as enjoying that good old favourite, British pork sausages.

Bacon

Bacon roly poly

SERVES 4

350 g/12 oz/3 cups self-raising (self-rising) flour
125 g/5 oz/1¼ cups shredded (chopped) suet
A pinch of salt
75 ml/5 tbsp water
3 large onions, chopped
225 g/8 oz bacon rashers (slices), rinded and chopped
A pinch of dried sage

Mix together the flour, suet and salt. Gradually add enough of the water to make a light dough. Roll out the dough on a lightly floured surface to a rectangle about 1 cm/½ in thick and sprinkle with the onions, bacon and sage. Roll up like a Swiss (jelly) roll and curl into a greased pudding basin. Cover the basin and place in a large saucepan. Add boiling water to the saucepan to come half-way up the sides of the basin, cover and steam for 2½ hours, topping up with boiling water as necessary, until the pastry (paste) is cooked through.

Devils on horseback

SERVES 4

Prepare as for Angels on Horseback (page 49), but substitute stoned (pitted) prunes for the shelled oysters.

Bacon-stuffed cabbage leaves

SERVES 4

50 g/2 oz/¼ cup long-grain rice
8–10 large cabbage leaves
15 ml/1 tbsp oil
1 onion, chopped
25 g/1 oz mushrooms, sliced
225 g/8 oz lean bacon, rinded and chopped
200 g/7 oz/1 small can of pimientos, drained
50 g/2 oz/1 cup fresh breadcrumbs
50 g/2 oz/½ cup cashew nuts, chopped
Salt and freshly ground black pepper
400 g/14 oz/1 large can of tomatoes

Cook the rice in plenty of boiling salted water for about 10 minutes, then drain and rinse in cold water. Pour boiling water over the cabbage leaves and leave to stand for 5 minutes to soften. Heat the oil and fry (sauté) the onion until browned. Add the mushrooms and bacon and fry lightly, then remove from the heat. Chop half the pimientos and add them to the pan with the breadcrumbs and nuts and season to taste. Drain the cabbage leaves and lay them on a work surface. Divide the mixture between them, roll them up and lay, join-side down, in a shallow ovenproof dish. Purée the remaining pimientos with the tomatoes in a food processor or blender. Pour the mixture over the cabbage leaves, cover and bake in a preheated oven at 180°C/350°F/gas mark 4 for 45 minutes.

Bacon and kidney rolls

SERVES 4

12 streaky bacon rashers (slices), rinded
½ onion, finely chopped
15 g/1 oz/½ cup fresh breadcrumbs
100 g/4 oz lambs' kidneys, cored and
    chopped
2.5 ml/½ tsp dried mixed herbs
A few drops of Tabasco sauce
5 ml/1 tsp tomato purée (paste)
Boiled rice and a green salad, to serve

Stretch the bacon rashers with the
blunt side of a knife. Mix together all
the remaining ingredients. Place a
spoonful of the mixture on the end of
each piece of bacon and roll up. Grill
(broil) under a hot grill (broiler) for
about 10 minutes, turning once, until
crisp and brown. Serve hot with rice
and a green salad.

Bacon steaks with orange and peppercorn sauce

SERVES 4

4 gammon steaks
Grated rind and juice of 1 orange
150 ml/¼ pt/⅔ cup Chicken Stock
    (page 28)
15 ml/1 tbsp light brown sugar
5 ml/1 tsp green peppercorns
45 ml/3 tbsp orange marmalade
1 bunch of watercress

Grill (broil) the steaks until tender. Mix
together the orange rind and juice,
stock, sugar, peppercorns and
marmalade. Bring to the boil and
simmer for 8 minutes until thickened.
Transfer the cooked steaks on to a
warm serving dish, pour over some of
the sauce and garnish with watercress.
Serve the remaining sauce separately

Bacon and bean casserole

SERVES 4

30 ml/2 tbsp oil
450 g/1 lb bacon, chopped
3 onions, sliced
2 garlic cloves, chopped
1 red (bell) pepper, sliced
300 g/11 oz/1 medium can of kidney
    beans, drained
400 g/14 oz/1 large can of tomatoes,
    chopped
15 ml/1 tbsp dried oregano
450 ml/¾ pt/2 cups Chicken Stock
    (page 28)
Salt and freshly ground black pepper
30 ml/2 tbsp chopped parsley

Heat the oil and fry (sauté) the bacon
until cooked through, then transfer to
a casserole dish (Dutch oven). Fry the
onions, garlic and red pepper until
soft, then transfer to the casserole
with the kidney beans, tomatoes,
oregano and stock. Season to taste
and bake in a preheated oven at
200°C/400°F/gas mark 6 for
20 minutes, then reduce the heat to
150°C/300°F/gas mark 2 for a further
2 hours. Serve sprinkled with the
parsley.

125

Honey-glazed bacon

SERVES 6

1.5 kg/3 lb bacon joint, boned and
  rolled
1 bay leaf
1 blade of mace
4 black peppercorns
4 cloves
45 ml/3 tbsp clear honey
Juice of 1 orange
15 ml/1 tbsp cornflour (cornstarch)
Salt and freshly ground black pepper

Place the bacon in a large saucepan
with the bay leaf, mace, peppercorns
and cloves. Cover with water, bring to
the boil and simmer for 50 minutes.
Drain, reserving 300 ml/½ pt/1¼ cups
of the stock for the gravy. Place the
joint in a roasting tin (pan) and score
the rind into a diamond pattern. Mix
together the honey and orange juice
and slowly spoon over the bacon so
that the glaze soaks into the incisions
in the rind. Roast in a preheated oven
at 180°C/350°F/gas mark 4 for
1 hour until tender. Transfer the bacon
to a warm serving plate. Blend the
cornflour with a little of the reserved
stock, then pour with the remaining
stock into the pan, bring to the boil,
stirring, and cook until thickened.
Taste and season if necessary, but do
not over-season or the stock will be
salty.

Bacon chops in ale

SERVES 4

4 thick chunks of lean bacon
300 ml/½ pt/1¼ cups light ale or lager
Freshly ground black pepper
1 bay leaf
3 onions, sliced
15 ml/1 tbsp oil
60 ml/4 tbsp black treacle (molasses)
Juice of ½ lemon

Put the chops in a shallow dish with
the light ale or lager, pepper, bay leaf
and onions. Cover and chill overnight.
Using a sieve (strainer), strain off the
beer marinade into a saucepan,
reserving the onions and bay leaf.
Bring to the boil and simmer until
reduced by half. Meanwhile, start the
chops cooking under a medium grill
(broiler). When the marinade is ready,
brush the marinade over the chops
and grill (broil) for about 15 minutes.
Turn the chops, baste with the
remaining marinade and continue
cooking for about 10 minutes until
tender and glazed.

Meanwhile, remove the bay leaf
from the onions, heat the oil in a
frying pan (skillet) and fry (sauté) the
onions for a few minutes until soft.
Stir in the treacle and lemon juice
and continue to cook over a low heat
until soft and browned, stirring
occasionally. Cover the chops with the
onions and serve.

Ham

Pineapple grill

SERVES 4

4 gammon steaks
300 g/11 oz/1 medium can of pineapple
  chunks, drained
15 ml/1 tbsp clear honey
100 g/4 oz/2 cups fresh breadcrumbs
Salt and freshly ground black pepper

Grill (broil) the gammon steaks for
5 minutes, then turn them over. Chop
two-thirds of the pineapple finely and
mix with the honey and breadcrumbs.
Pile the mixture on top of the steaks
and season to taste. Grill for
10 minutes until crispy, then top
with the remaining pineapple and
serve hot.

Ham and cheese fingers

SERVES 4

100 g/4 oz/½ cup butter or margarine
225 g/8 oz/2 cups plain (all-purpose)
  flour
30 ml/2 tbsp cold water
100 g/4 oz/1 cup cooked ham, finely
  shredded
50 g/2 oz/1 cup fresh white breadcrumbs
5 ml/1 tsp tomato purée (paste)
A pinch of mustard powder
100 g/4 oz/1 cup Cheddar cheese,
  grated
1 egg, beaten

Rub the butter or margarine into the
flour until the mixture resembles fine
breadcrumbs. Add the water and mix
to a pastry (paste), knead lightly, then
roll out on a lightly floured surface to

a 30 cm/12 in square. Cut in half and
chill for 15 minutes.
  Place one rectangle on a damp
baking (cookie) sheet. Mix together
the ham, breadcrumbs, tomato purée
and mustard and spread the mixture
on the pastry, leaving a 1 cm/½ in gap
around the edges. Scatter the cheese
on top. Brush the edges of the pastry
with egg, lay the second pastry sheet
on top and press the edges together
to seal. Mark a criss-cross pattern on
the top with a knife and brush with
egg, then bake in a preheated oven
at 220°C/425°F/gas mark 7 for
25 minutes. Allow to cool, then cut
into fingers.

Spiced island steaks

SERVES 4

150 ml/¼ pt/⅔ cup pineapple juice
45 ml/3 tbsp soy sauce
2 garlic cloves, crushed
75 ml/5 tbsp clear honey
15 ml/1 tbsp dry sherry
2.5 ml/½ tsp paprika
1 small onion, chopped
4 cloves
1 bay leaf
5 ml/1 tsp lemon juice
A pinch of grated ginger
4 gammon steaks
1 kiwi fruit, sliced

Mix together all the ingredients
except the gammon and kiwi fruit,
bring to the boil and simmer for
15 minutes until slightly thickened.
Meanwhile, grill (broil) the steaks until
cooked through, then place them on a
warm serving dish and arrange the
kiwi fruit around them. Pour over a
little of the sauce and serve the
remaining sauce separately.

Ham cornets

SERVES 4

6 black peppercorns
1 bay leaf
1 onion, chopped
200 ml/7 fl oz/scant 1 cup milk
100 g/4 oz/½ cup butter or margarine
25 g/1 oz/¼ cup plain (all-purpose) flour
Salt and freshly ground black pepper
75 g/3 oz coarse pâté
2.5 ml/½ tsp Dijon mustard
60 ml/4 tbsp double (heavy) cream
8 thick slices of cooked ham

Place the peppercorns, bay leaf and onion in the milk in a saucepan, bring to the boil, remove from the heat and leave to infuse for 30 minutes. Melt 50 g/2 oz/¼ cup of the butter or margarine, stir in the flour and cook, stirring, for 1 minute. Strain the flavoured milk into the pan, season to taste and bring to the boil, stirring, until the sauce thickens. Pour into a food processor or blender. Dice the remaining butter or margarine and add to the sauce with the pâté and mustard. Blend until smooth. Allow to cool slightly, turn into a bowl and fold in the cream. Use the ham to line cornet moulds and support them upright, or roll the ham into cornet shapes. Pipe the mixture into the cornets and chill for 2 hours before serving.

Sweet and sour ham steaks

SERVES 4

4 gammon steaks
50 g/2 oz/¼ cup demerara sugar
10 ml/2 tsp mustard powder
10 ml/2 tsp water
1 lemon, cut into wedges
15 ml/1 tbsp chopped parsley
Creamed potatoes and mangetout (snow peas), to serve

Grill (broil) one side of the gammon under a hot grill (broiler) for 5 minutes. Mix the sugar, mustard and water to a smooth paste. Turn over the gammon and spread the mustard mixture on the gammon. Grill for 3 minutes until golden brown. Serve immediately with lemon wedges dipped in the parsley, and creamed potatoes and mangetout.

Roast pork with apple and nut stuffing (page 120)

Sausages

Sausage pickle

SERVES 4

15 ml/1 tbsp oil
450 g/1 lb pork sausages
4 onions, sliced
15 ml/1 tbsp tomato purée (paste)
45 ml/3 tbsp water
3 tomatoes, skinned and chopped
100 g/4 oz sweet pickle
Salt and freshly ground black pepper

Heat the oil and fry (sauté) the sausages gently for 10 minutes. Add the onions and fry for a further 10 minutes until the sausages are cooked. Remove the sausages and keep warm. Add the tomato purée and water, bring to the boil, then add the tomatoes and pickle and season to taste. Heat through, then serve with the hot sausages on the top.

Country sausage flan

SERVES 4

225 g/8 oz Shortcrust Pastry (page 164)
15 ml/1 tbsp oil
1 onion, chopped
2 leeks, chopped
3 bacon rashers (slices), chopped
100 g/4 oz mushrooms, sliced
450 g/1 lb pork sausagemeat
5 ml/1 tsp Dijon mustard
15 ml/1 tbsp chopped parsley
Salt and freshly ground black pepper
2 eggs, beaten

*Orange and tarragon
chicken (page 152)*

Roll out the pastry (paste) and use to line a greased 20 cm/8 in pie dish. Heat the oil and fry (sauté) the onion, leeks and bacon until the onion is soft. Add the mushrooms and sausagemeat and fry for 15 minutes, then stir in the mustard and parsley and season to taste. Turn the mixture into the pastry case (pie shell) and pour the eggs over the top. Bake in a preheated oven at 190°C/375°F/gas mark 5 for 45 minutes.

Cidered sausage skuets

SERVES 4

90 ml/6 tbsp medium dry cider
90 ml/6 tbsp clear honey
45 ml/3 tbsp tomato purée (paste)
Juice of 1 lemon
900 g/2 lb large pork sausages
12 streaky bacon rashers (slices), rinded
225 g/8 oz button mushrooms
15 ml/1 tbsp oil
Salt and freshly ground black pepper

Mix the cider, honey, tomato purée and lemon juice over a low heat until well blended. Pinch the sausages in the middle, twist them into two short links, then separate them. Wrap each in a bacon rasher and thread the stubby sausages on to kebab skewers alternately with the mushrooms. Brush with the oil and season lightly. Grill (broil) under a medium grill (broiler), turning frequently and brushing with the baste, for about 20 minutes until cooked through.

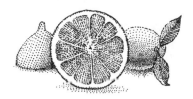

Sausagemeat moussaka

SERVES 4

50 g/2 oz/¼ cup butter or margarine
1 onion, sliced
450 g/1 lb sausagemeat
5 ml/1 tsp sage
1 garlic clove, crushed
400 g/14 oz/1 large can of tomatoes,
    chopped
Salt and freshly ground black pepper
450 g/1 lb potatoes, sliced
225 g/8 oz cooking (tart) apples,
    peeled, cored and sliced
25 g/1 oz/¼ cup plain (all-purpose) flour
300 ml/½ pt/1¼ cups milk
100 g/4 oz/1 cup strongly flavoured
    cheese, grated

Melt half the butter or margarine and
fry (sauté) the onion until soft. Stir in
the sausagemeat and fry gently for
10 minutes, stirring. Remove from the
heat, drain off any excess fat, stir in
the sage, garlic and tomatoes and
season to taste. Parboil the potatoes
for 10 minutes, then drain. Layer half
the potatoes on the base of a greased
casserole dish (Dutch oven) and
spread half the meat mixture on top.
Spread with the apple slices, then a
layer of meat and finally potatoes.

Melt the remaining butter or
margarine in a saucepan, stir in the
flour and cook for 1 minute. Whisk in
the milk and cook, stirring, until the
sauce thickens. Season to taste,
remove from the heat and stir in most
of the cheese. Pour the cheese sauce
over the casserole and sprinkle on the
remaining cheese. Bake in a
preheated oven at 190°C/375°F/gas
mark 5 for 30 minutes until browned
and crispy on top.

Smoked sausage hot-pot

SERVES 4

45 ml/3 tsp oil
1 onion, chopped
2 garlic cloves, crushed
1 red (bell) pepper, chopped
1 carrot, chopped
1 celery stick, chopped
225 g/8 oz/1 cup long-grain rice
400 g/14 oz/1 large can of tomatoes,
    chopped
15 ml/1 tbsp mild paprika
5 ml/1 tsp caster (superfine) sugar
450 ml/¾ pt/2 cups Vegetable Stock
    (page 28)
225 g/8 oz smoked sausage, cut into
    chunks
Salt and freshly ground black pepper

Heat the oil in a large saucepan and
fry (sauté) the onion, garlic, pepper,
carrot and celery for about 5 minutes
until soft but not brown. Add the rice
and stir until hot and shining. Stir in
the tomatoes, followed by the paprika
to taste, and the sugar. Stir in the
stock, bring to the boil, then simmer
for about 10 minutes until the rice is
tender and most of the liquid has
been absorbed. If there is still too
much liquid, boil for a minute or two
to evaporate. Stir in the sausage and
heat through, then season to taste
and serve.

Frankfurter and cheese roll

SERVES 4

For the pastry (paste):
275 g/10 oz/2½ cups plain (all-purpose) flour
20 ml/4 tsp baking powder
A pinch of salt
100 g/4 oz/½ cup butter or margarine
150 ml/¼ pt/⅔ cup milk
For the filling:
225 g/8 oz frankfurters, coarsley grated or chopped
225 g/8 oz/2 cups Cheddar cheese, grated
50 g/2 oz/¼ cup butter or margarine, softened
1 shallot, finely chopped
5 ml/1 tsp Worcestershire sauce
5 ml/1 tsp Dijon mustard
1 egg yolk
30 ml/2 tbsp milk
15 ml/1 tbsp chopped parsley

To make the pastry, mix together the flour, baking powder and salt, then rub in the butter or margarine until the mixture resembles breadcrumbs. Stir in enough of the milk to make a fairly stiff dough. Roll out on a lightly floured surface to a 35 × 25 mm/ 14 × 10 in rectangle.

To make the filling, mix together the frankfurters, cheese, butter or margarine, shallot, Worcestershire sauce and mustard. Spread evenly over the pastry, then roll up from one short end like a Swiss (jelly) roll. Place on a greased baking (cookie) sheet and cut into slices almost through to the base. Beat together the egg yolk and milk, then brush over the roll and sprinkle with the parsley. Bake in a preheated oven at 200°C/400°F/gas mark 6 for 20 minutes until well risen and golden brown.

Soudzoukakia

SERVES 4

50 g/2 oz/1 cup fresh breadcrumbs
75 ml/5 tbsp milk
450 g/1 lb pork sausagemeat
2 onions, chopped
1 garlic clove, chopped
Salt and freshly ground black pepper
25 g/1 oz/¼ cup plain (all-purpose) flour
30 ml/2 tbsp olive oil
400 g/14 oz/1 large can of tomatoes, chopped
5 ml/1 tsp caster (superfine) sugar
1 bay leaf
A pinch of ground cumin

Moisten the breadcrumbs with the milk and squeeze dry. Mix with the sausagemeat, one of the onions and the garlic and season to taste. Shape into little fat sausages and roll in the flour. Heat the oil and fry (sauté) the sausages until browned on all sides and cooked through, then drain well. Meanwhile, put all the remaining ingredients into a saucepan and simmer for 45 minutes. Remove the bay leaf and purée the sauce in a food processor or blender, then add the sausages and return to the pan to reheat.

Sausage-stuffed potatoes

SERVES 4

4 large baking potatoes
8 pork sausages
225 g/8 oz/2 cups Cheddar cheese, grated
30 ml/2 tbsp milk
50 g/2 oz/¼ cup butter or margarine
1 egg, beaten
15 ml/1 tbsp soured (dairy sour) cream
Salt and freshly ground black pepper

Prick the potatoes with a fork and bake in a preheated oven at 190°C/375°F/gas mark 5 for 1¼ hours until soft. Place the sausages in a roasting tin (pan) and bake with the potatoes for the last 45 minutes cooking time. Halve the potatoes lengthways and scoop out the insides. Mix with the cheese, milk, butter or margarine, egg and cream and season to taste. Pile half the mixture back into the potato skins, place a sausage on each, and pile on the remaining mixture. Return to the oven for 10 minutes until browned and crispy on top.

Toad in the hole

SERVES 4

450 g/1 lb pork sausages
300 ml/½ pt/1¼ cups milk
2 eggs
225 g/8 oz/2 cups plain (all-purpose) flour
A pinch of salt

Put the sausages in a greased baking tin (pan) and bake in a preheated oven at 200°C/400°F/gas mark 6 for 15 minutes. Thoroughly beat together the milk, eggs, flour and salt to a thick batter and pour into the pan.

Return to the oven and bake for 15–20 minutes until well risen and golden brown.

Barbecued bangers

SERVES 4

2 onions
200 g/7 oz/1 small can of tomatoes, chopped
75 ml/5 tbsp dry cider
45 ml/3 tbsp tomato ketchup (catsup)
15 ml/1 tbsp Worcestershire sauce
1 bay leaf
1 garlic clove, chopped
3 celery sticks, finely chopped
5 ml/1 tsp lemon juice
30 ml/2 tbsp Muscovado sugar
300 ml/½ pt/1¼ cups water
450 g/1 lb pork sausages

Chop one onion and cut the other into wedges. Mix together the chopped onion and all the remaining ingredients except the sausages and onion wedges, bring to the boil, cover and simmer for 30 minutes. Grill (broil) the sausages and onion wedges under a hot grill (broiler), turning frequently, until cooked through and golden brown. Discard the bay leaf and serve the hot sauce with the sausages.

Offal

Although many people do not often cook liver, kidneys or other types of offal, there is a great variety to choose from, and there are plenty of tasty recipes to bring out the best flavours. Most types of offal are also available frozen from supermarkets and, as these are ready prepared, they can save both time and wastage for the busy cook.

Old-fashioned liver and bacon

SERVES 4

15 ml/1 tbsp oil
4 onions, sliced
450 g/1 lb lambs' liver, sliced
15 ml/1 tbsp plain (all-purpose) flour
300 ml/½ pt/1¼ cups Beef Stock
    (page 28)
Salt and freshly ground black pepper
8 streaky bacon rashers (slices)
Potatoes and a green vegetable, to serve

Heat the oil and fry (sauté) the onions until just beginning to brown. Add the liver and fry gently for a few minutes until browned on both sides. Stir in the flour and cook for 1 minute, then stir in the stock and bring to the boil, stirring, until the sauce thickens. Cover and simmer for 10 minutes until the liver is tender. Meanwhile, grill (broil) the bacon rashers until crisp and browned. Transfer the liver and onions to a warm deep serving dish, surround with the bacon and serve immediately with potatoes and a green vegetable.

Liver and bacon with lemon sauce

SERVES 4

25 g/1 oz/2 tbsp butter or margarine
6 back bacon rashers (slices), rinded
    and halved
450 g/1 lb lambs' liver, sliced
15 ml/1 tbsp plain (all-purpose) flour
Salt and freshly ground black pepper
60 ml/4 tbsp red wine
450 ml/¾ pt/2 cups Chicken Stock
    (page 28)
10 ml/2 tsp lemon juice
15 ml/1 tbsp chopped parsley
1 lemon, cut into wedges

Melt the butter or margarine and fry (sauté) the bacon until crisp, then remove from the pan. Coat the liver in the flour and season to taste with salt and pepper. Add to the pan and fry for a few minutes until browned on both sides. Stir in the wine, stock, lemon juice and bacon, cover and simmer for 15 minutes until tender. Serve garnished with the parsley and lemon wedges.

Spicy liver with pasta

SERVES 4

50 g/2 oz/½ cup plain (all-purpose) flour
2.5 ml/½ tsp ground cinnamon
5 ml/1 tsp mixed (apple-pie) spice
Salt and freshly ground black pepper
350 g/12 oz lambs' liver, cut into strips
50 g/2 oz/¼ cup butter or margarine
2 onions, sliced
100 g/4 oz mushrooms
150 ml/¼ pt/⅔ cup Beef Stock (page 28)
150 ml/¼ pt/⅔ cup milk
15 ml/1 tbsp tomato ketchup (catsup)
15 ml/1 tbsp Worcestershire sauce
375 g/12 oz pasta spirals

Mix together half the flour, the cinnamon and spice and season with salt and pepper. Coat the liver in the seasoned flour. Melt the butter or margarine and fry (sauté) the onions until soft but not brown. Add the liver and mushrooms and fry for 10 minutes. Stir in the remaining flour and cook for 1 minute, then stir in the stock, milk, tomato ketchup and Worcestershire sauce. Bring to the boil, stirring, and cook until the sauce thickens.

Meanwhile, cook the pasta in boiling salted water for about 15 minutes until just tender. Drain and rinse in hot water, then serve with the liver.

Chicken liver and vegetable brochettes

SERVES 4

100 g/4 oz chicken livers, quartered
3 bacon rashers (slices), cut into squares
8 small mushrooms
4 small tomatoes, halved
Salt and freshly ground black pepper
45 ml/3 tbsp oil
1 bunch of watercress

Thread the chicken livers, bacon, mushrooms and tomatoes alternately on four skewers. Season to taste and brush with the oil. Bake in a preheated oven at 190°C/375°F/gas mark 5 for 15 minutes, turning several times, until cooked through. Serve garnished with watercress.

Liver with yoghurt and sherry

SERVES 4–6

25 g/1 oz/¼ cup plain (all-purpose) flour
Salt and freshly ground black pepper
750 g/1¾ lb calves' liver, diced
50 g/2 oz/¼ cup butter or margarine
300 ml/½ pt/1¼ cups plain yoghurt
30 ml/2 tbsp dry sherry

Season the flour with salt and pepper, then coat the liver in the flour. Melt the butter or margarine in a frying pan (skillet) and fry (sauté) the liver for 2 minutes on each side. Stir in the yoghurt and sherry and season to taste. Cook gently, without boiling, for about 10 minutes until the liver is tender, stirring continuously.

Calves' liver casserole

SERVES 4

25 g/1 oz/2 tbsp butter or margarine
750 g/1¾ lb calves' liver
2 carrots, sliced
2 onions, sliced
2 tomatoes, skinned and chopped
1 celery stick, sliced
30 ml/2 tbsp sherry
90 ml/6 tbsp dry white wine
150 ml/¼ pt/⅔ cup Beef Stock (page 28)
1 bouquet garni sachet
Salt and freshly ground black pepper
New potatoes, to serve

Melt the butter or margarine and fry (sauté) the liver and vegetables until the meat starts to colour. Add the sherry and wine and bring to the boil, then add the stock and bouquet garni and season to taste. Transfer to a casserole dish (Dutch oven), cover and bake in a preheated oven at 150°C/300°F/gas mark 2 for 2 hours. Just before serving, transfer the meat and vegetables to a warm serving dish and discard the bouquet garni. If the gravy is too thin, boil it down to reduce it a little before pouring it over the meat. Serve with new potatoes.

Stuffed baked liver

SERVES 4

450 g/1 lb calves' liver, sliced
75 g/3 oz/1½ cups fresh breadcrumbs
5 ml/1 tsp chopped parsley
2.5 ml/½ tsp dried mixed herbs
1 small onion, grated
Salt and freshly ground black pepper
30 ml/2 tbsp tomato ketchup (catsup)
6 back bacon rashers (slices), rinded
150 ml/¼ pt/⅔ cup Beef Stock (page 28)

Overlap the liver slices in a greased pie dish. Mix together the breadcrumbs, parsley, herbs and onion and season to taste. Stir in the tomato ketchup. Spread the stuffing over the liver and arrange the bacon in an overlapping layer on top. Pour the stock down the side of the dish, cover and bake in a preheated oven at 180°C/350°F/gas mark 4 for 45 minutes, then remove the lid and bake for a further 15 minutes to allow the top to crisp.

Liver with garden herbs

SERVES 4

50 g/2 oz/¼ cup butter or margarine
1 onion, finely chopped
450 g/1 lb calves' liver sliced
45 ml/3 tbsp chopped sage
30 ml/2 tbsp chopped parsley
Salt and freshly ground black pepper
30 ml/2 tbsp dry sherry
45 ml/3 tbsp oil
450 g/1 lb potatoes, diced

Melt the butter or margarine and fry (sauté) the onion until soft but not brown. Add the liver, sage and half the parsley, season to taste and fry until browned and tender. Transfer the liver to a warm serving plate and keep warm. Add the sherry to the pan, bring to the boil, stirring, and simmer for 1 minute, then pour over the liver. Meanwhile, heat the oil and fry (sauté) the potatoes until golden and tender. Drain well, arrange on the serving plate and serve sprinkled with the remaining parsley.

Hearts with butter and parsley

SERVES 4

4 large lambs' hearts
Salt and freshly ground black pepper
45 ml/3 tbsp chopped parsley
50 g/2 oz/¼ cup butter or margarine
150 ml/¼ pt/⅔ cup Beef Stock (page 28)
5 ml/1 tsp Worcestershire sauce
8 small new potatoes

Cut the excess fat off the hearts and snip out any tubes and membranes. Season with salt and pepper and half-fill each one with parsley and a knob of butter or margarine. Close the tops with cocktail sticks (toothpicks). Melt the remaining butter or margarine and fry (sauté) the hearts until browned on all sides. Add the stock and Worcestershire sauce, bring to the boil, then transfer to a shallow casserole dish (Dutch oven), add the potatoes, cover and bake in a preheated oven at 180°C/350°F/gas mark 4 for 1–1½ hours until tender.

Tripe and onions

SERVES 4

450 g/1 lb dressed tripe, cubed
2 onions, chopped
Salt
4 black peppercorns
8 parsley sprigs
450 ml/¾ pt/2 cups boiling milk
20 g/¾ oz butter or margarine
20 g/¾ oz plain (all-purpose) flour

Put the tripe and onions in a casserole dish (Dutch oven) and season to taste with salt. Tie the peppercorns and four of the parsley sprigs in muslin (cheesecloth) and add to the casserole. Pour in the milk, cover and bake in a preheated oven at 160°C/325°F/gas mark 3 for the time recommended by the butcher, as butchers parboil tripe for a variable time before sale. Transfer the tripe to a warm serving dish and keep warm. Melt the butter or margarine in a pan, stir in the flour and cook for 1 minute. Whisk in the cooking liquor and cook, stirring, until the sauce thickens. Pour over the tripe and garnish with the remaining parsley sprigs.

Kidneys turbigo

SERVES 4

12 small onions or shallots
50 g/2 oz/¼ cup butter or margarine
5 lambs' kidneys, halved and cored
100 g/4 oz chipolata sausages
100 g/4 oz button mushrooms, quartered
10 ml/2 tsp plain (all-purpose) flour
5 ml/1 tsp tomato purée (paste)
15 ml/1 tbsp dry sherry
150 ml/¼ pt/⅔ cup Beef Stock (page 28)
1 bay leaf
Salt and freshly ground black pepper
45 ml/3 tbsp oil
4 slices of bread, cubed
15 ml/1 tbsp chopped parsley

Blanch the onions in boiling salted water for 1 minute, then drain. Heat the butter or margarine and fry (sauté) the kidneys until lightly browned. Remove them from the pan. Add the sausages to the pan and fry until browned on all sides, then add them to the kidneys. Add the onions and mushrooms to the pan and fry for 3 minutes. Remove the pan from the heat, stir in the flour, tomato purée, sherry and stock and bring to the boil. Add the bay leaf and season to taste. Slice the kidneys and sausages and add them to the pan. Cover and simmer gently for 20 minutes until tender.

Meanwhile, heat the oil and fry (sauté) the bread until crisp and golden brown. Transfer the kidneys and sausages to a warm serving plate, discard the bay leaf, surround with the croûtons and serve sprinkled with the parsley.

Sweet and sour kidneys

SERVES 4

30 ml/2 tbsp clear honey
45 ml/3 tbsp dry sherry
60 ml/4 tbsp soy sauce
300 ml/½ pt/1¼ cups beef consommé
1 garlic clove, crushed
A pinch of Chinese five spice powder
450 g/1 lb lambs' kidneys, halved and cored
25 g/1 oz/¼ cup plain (all-purpose) flour
Salt and freshly ground black pepper
50 g/2 oz/¼ cup butter or margarine
15 ml/1 tbsp cornflour (cornstarch)
15 ml/1 tbsp water
2 spring onions (scallions), sliced

Mix together the honey, sherry, soy sauce, consommé, garlic and five spice powder. Add the kidneys and leave to marinate for 1 hour. Remove the kidneys and pat dry on kitchen paper (paper towels). Season the flour with salt and pepper and coat the kidneys in the flour. Melt the butter or margarine and fry (sauté) the kidneys until just browned, then remove from the pan. Add the marinade to the pan and bring to the boil. Blend the cornflour and water, stir into the pan and cook until the sauce thickens. Return the kidneys to the pan and season to taste. Cook for 2 minutes until heated through and serve garnished with the spring onions.

Kidney and onion dumplings

SERVES 4

225 g/8 oz/2 cups self-raising (self-rising) flour
100 g/4 oz/1 cup shredded (chopped) suet
A pinch of salt
30 ml/2 tbsp water
4 large onions
Salt and freshly ground black pepper
4 lambs' kidneys
Gravy, to serve

Mix together the flour, suet and salt, then add the water and mix to a firm dough. Roll out on a lightly floured surface and cut into four squares. Scoop out the centres of the onions, season inside and put a kidney in each. Place an onion in each pastry square and seal round to enclose the onions completely. Place upside-down on a baking (cookie) sheet so that the joins are underneath. Bake in a preheated oven at 180°C/350°F/gas mark 4 for 1¼ hours until tender and lightly browned. Remove from the sheet carefully and serve with gravy.

Turkish-style kidneys

SERVES 4

15 g/½ oz/1 tbsp butter or margarine
1 onion, chopped
8 lambs' kidneys, skinned, cored and
    halved
15 ml/1 tbsp plain (all-purpose) flour
600 ml/1 pt/2½ cups Beef Stock
    (page 28)
15 ml/1 tbsp dry sherry
Salt and freshly ground black pepper
120 ml/4 fl oz/½ cup plain yoghurt
15 ml/1 tbsp chopped parsley
Boiled rice, to serve

Melt the butter or margarine and fry
(sauté) the onion until soft but not
brown. Add the kidneys and cook on
both sides for 2 minutes. Place the
mixture in a casserole dish (Dutch
oven). Stir the flour into the pan and
cook for 1 minute, then stir in the
stock and sherry and bring to the
boil, stirring continuously. Season to
taste, then simmer until thick and
smooth. Pour the gravy into the
casserole, cover and cook in a
preheated oven at 140°C/275°F/gas
mark 1 for 2½ hours. Stir in the
yoghurt, sprinkle with the parsley and
serve with boiled rice.

Kidney and bacon pasties

SERVES 6

450 g/1 lb Shortcrust Pastry (page 164)
175 g/6 oz lambs' kidneys, chopped
100 g/4 oz streaky bacon rashers
    (slices), rinded and chopped
225 g/8 oz minced (ground) beef
2 onions, chopped
5 ml/1 tsp Worcestershire sauce
Salt and freshly ground black pepper
1 egg, beaten

Roll out the pastry (paste) on a lightly
floured surface and cut into six
rounds. Mix together all the remaining
ingredients except the egg, seasoning
to taste with salt and pepper. Put
spoonfuls of the mixture on to the
pastry rounds and seal into pasties
with the beaten egg. Place on a
greased baking (cookie) sheet, brush
with the egg and bake in a preheated
oven at 220°C/425°F/gas mark 5 for
15 minutes, then reduce the heat to
180°C/350°F/gas mark 4 for a further
45 minutes.

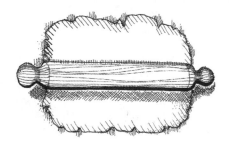

Kidney and mushroom lasagne

SERVES 4

1 onion, chopped
15 ml/1 tbsp oil
100 g/4 oz mushrooms, sliced
30 ml/2 tbsp dry sherry
15 ml/1 tbsp tomato purée (paste)
50 g/2 oz/½ cup plain (all-purpose) flour
450 ml/¾ pt/2 cups Vegetable Stock (page 28)
Salt and freshly ground black pepper
450 g/1 lb calves' or pigs' kidneys, sliced
40 g/1½ oz butter or margarine
600 ml/1 pt/2½ cups milk
2.5 ml/½ tsp grated nutmeg
6 no-need-to-precook lasagne sheets
25 g/1 oz/¼ cup Parmesan cheese, freshly grated

Fry (sauté) the onion in half the oil until soft but not brown, then add half the mushrooms and fry gently. Add the sherry, tomato purée, 15 ml/ 1 tbsp of the flour and the stock and season to taste. Bring to the boil and simmer for 10 minutes. Purée in a food processor or blender. Fry (sauté) the kidneys in the remaining oil, add the reserved mushrooms, then pour the sauce round them and simmer for 5 minutes. Melt the butter or margarine in a separate saucepan, then stir in the remaining flour and cook for 1 minute. Whisk in the milk and continue whisking until the sauce thickens. Add the nutmeg and season to taste. Layer the kidney mixture and the lasagne sheets in a shallow ovenproof dish, pour over the white sauce and sprinkle with the Parmesan. Bake in a preheated oven at 200°C/ 400°F/gas mark 6 for 30 minutes until golden brown on top.

Kidney flan

SERVES 4

350 g/12 oz Shortcrust Pastry (page 164)
25 g/1 oz/2 tbsp butter or margarine
1 onion, chopped
1 green (bell) pepper, chopped
6 lambs' kidneys, chopped
3 eggs, beaten
45 ml/3 tbsp milk
Salt and freshly ground black pepper

Roll out the pastry (paste) on a lightly floured surface and use to line a greased 20 cm/8 in flan tin (pie pan). Cover with greaseproof (waxed) paper and fill with baking beans and bake in a preheated oven at 200°C/400°F/ gas mark 6 for 10 minutes. Remove from the oven and remove the paper and beans. Reduce the oven temperature to 180°C/350°F/gas mark 4. While the pastry is cooking, melt the butter or margarine and fry (sauté) the onion until soft but not brown. Add the green pepper and kidneys and fry for 4 minutes, stirring continuously. Spread the mixture over the base of the flan. Beat the eggs with the milk and season to taste, then pour over the flan. Bake in the oven for 40 minutes until set. Serve hot.

Kidneys in cream

SERVES 4

25 g/1 oz/2 tbsp butter or margarine
8 lambs' kidneys, skinned, cored and
    halved
1 onion, chopped
1 garlic clove, crushed
15 ml/1 tbsp plain (all-purpose) flour
150 ml/¼ pt/⅔ cup Beef Stock (page 28)
150 ml/¼ pt/⅔ cup double (heavy) cream
Salt and freshly ground black pepper
Boiled rice, to serve

Melt the butter or margarine and fry
(sauté) the kidneys, onion and garlic
for 4 minutes until browned. Stir in
the flour and cook for 2 minutes, then
stir in the stock and cream and heat
gently without allowing the mixture to
boil. Season to taste and serve with
boiled rice.

Kidney pudding

SERVES 4

4 lambs' kidneys, chopped
5 ml/1 tsp shredded (chopped) suet
75 g/3 oz/1½ cups fresh breadcrumbs
10 ml/2 tsp chopped parsley
5 ml/1 tsp dried mixed herbs
A pinch of grated nutmeg
Salt and freshly ground black pepper
1 egg, beaten
75 ml/5 tbsp milk
Onion Gravy (see Beef Sausages with
    Onion Gravy, page 83), to serve

Mix together the kidneys, suet,
breadcrumbs, parsley, herbs and
nutmeg and season to taste. Mix
together the egg and milk and stir
into the breadcrumb mixture. Spoon
into a greased pudding basin, cover
with greaseproof (waxed) paper and
place in a large saucepan. Add boiling
water to the pan to come half-way up

the side of the basin. Cover the pan
and steam for 1½ hours, topping up
with boiling water as necessary. Serve
with Onion Gravy.

Veal kidney in mustard sauce

SERVES 4

50 g/2 oz/¼ cup butter or margarine
1 veal kidney, sliced
100 g/4 oz mushrooms, sliced
2 spring onions (scallions), cut into
    slivers
A few drops of lemon juice
1 garlic clove, crushed
Salt and freshly ground black pepper
4 slices of bread, halved
5 ml/1 tsp Dijon mustard
150 ml/¼ pt/⅔ cup single (light) cream

Melt half the butter or margarine and
fry (sauté) the kidney until browned.
Add the mushrooms, onions, lemon
juice and garlic and season to taste.
Cook for 5 minutes. Melt the
remaining butter or margarine and fry
the bread until crisp. Stir the mustard
into the cream in a separate
saucepan, bring the mixture to the
boil, then pour it over the kidneys.
Stir the juices together in the pan and
serve immediately with the fried
(sautéed) bread.

Poultry and game

Chicken has never been more popular. Economical, readily available, low in fat and quick to cook, there is no end of tasty recipes you can choose. Free-range and corn-fed chickens cost a little more but offer the best flavour, and obviously you will pay more for select cuts, although you cannot beat them for convenience. Remember that chicken breast is a delicate meat and can dry out during cooking so make sure it is cooked gently or has sufficient cooking liquid or sauce. For a change, use whole poussins (Cornish hens) instead of chicken pieces so that everyone can enjoy an individual bird.

Various cuts of turkey meat are also widely available – from breast roasts to legs and mince – so it is no longer just at Christmas that you can enjoy turkey meat. You can substitute an appropriate cut of turkey in most chicken recipes, perhaps allowing a little more cooking time.

Duck, pheasant, quail, partridge and other game birds used to be for special occasions only but they can now be bought ready prepared, or you can buy duck breasts, which make a delicious meal.

Chicken

Catalan chicken

SERVES 4

60 ml/4 tbsp oil
4 chicken breasts, skinned and boned
2 onions, sliced
1 garlic clove, crushed
350 g/12 oz/1½ cups long-grain rice
15 ml/1 tbsp tomato purée (paste)
2.5 ml/½ tsp turmeric
600 ml/1 pt/2½ cups Chicken Stock
   (page 28)
2.5 ml/½ tsp paprika
Salt and freshly ground black pepper
100 g/4 oz garlic sausage, cubed
1 green (bell) pepper, sliced
1 red pepper, sliced
50 g/2 oz stuffed green olives
15 ml/1 tbsp chopped parsley

Heat half the oil in a flameproof
casserole dish (Dutch oven) and fry
(sauté) the chicken until browned on
both sides. Remove from the pan and
keep warm. Add the onions and garlic
and fry until soft. Add the remaining
oil and the rice and cook to a golden
colour, then stir in the tomato purée,
turmeric, stock and paprika and
season to taste. Bring to the boil,
then add the chicken, garlic sausage
and peppers. Simmer over a low heat
for 30 minutes or until the rice is just
tender, stirring occasionally and
adding a little more hot stock if
necessary. Add the olives and heat
through, then serve sprinkled with the
parsley.

Chicken Rossini

SERVES 4

4 chicken breasts, skinned
Salt and freshly ground black pepper
100 g/4 oz firm pâté, cut into 4 slices
75 g/3 oz/⅓ cup butter or margarine
175 g/6 oz button mushrooms, sliced
45 ml/3 tbsp brandy
90 ml/6 tbsp chicken stock
30 ml/2 tbsp oil
4 slices of bread, diced
60 ml/4 tbsp double (heavy) cream

Flatten the chicken and season with
salt and pepper. Wrap each slice of
pâté in a chicken breast and secure
with cocktail sticks (toothpicks). Melt
50 g/2 oz/¼ cup of the butter or
margarine and fry (sauté) the chicken
until lightly browned, then transfer it
to a flameproof casserole dish (Dutch
oven). Fry the mushrooms for
1 minute, then add the brandy and
stock and bring to the boil. Season to
taste and pour over the chicken.
Cover and cook in a preheated oven
at 180°C/350°F/gas mark 4 for
40 minutes until cooked through.
Heat the oil and fry (sauté) the bread
on both sides until crispy and golden,
then drain and place on a warm
serving dish. Lift out the chicken from
the casserole, remove the cocktail
sticks (toothpicks) and place on top of
the croûtons. Stir the cream into the
sauce and season to taste. Bring back
to the boil, then spoon over the
chicken.

Orange chicken supreme

SERVES 4

4 chicken breasts, skinned
200 ml/7 fl oz/scant 1 cup water
2 dill (dill weed) sprigs
Salt and freshly ground black pepper
Finely pared rind and juice of 1 orange
50 g/2 oz/¼ cup butter or margarine
60 ml/4 tbsp double (heavy) cream
4 watercress sprigs

Place the chicken, water and dill in a saucepan and season with salt and pepper. Bring to the boil, then simmer gently for 15 minutes. Remove from the heat and leave to stand for 10 minutes, then transfer the chicken to a serving plate and keep warm. Place the orange rind and juice in a saucepan with the butter or margarine and simmer gently for 5 minutes until the mixture thickens slightly, then stir in the cream and simmer for a further 5 minutes. Season to taste and pour over the chicken. Serve garnished with the watercress sprigs.

Stir-fried chicken

SERVES 4

45 ml/3 tbsp oil
350 g/12 oz chicken breast, cut into strips
1 green (bell) pepper, cut into strips
100 g/4 oz carrots, finely sliced
175 g/6 oz white cabbage, finely shredded
225 g/8 oz/1 medium can of pineapple chunks in natural juice
10 ml/2 tsp soy sauce
15 ml/1 tbsp white wine vinegar
Boiled noodles, to serve

Heat 30 ml/2 tbsp of the oil in a frying pan (skillet) and fry (sauté) the chicken until white all over. Remove the chicken from the pan. Add the remaining oil to the pan with the green pepper and carrots and stir-fry for 2 minutes. Add the cabbage and stir-fry for 1 minute. Replace the chicken and stir in the pineapple and juice, soy sauce and wine vinegar. Simmer gently for 3 minutes and serve hot with noodles.

Chicken escalopes with cream

SERVES 4

100 g/4 oz/2 cups fresh breadcrumbs
30 ml/2 tbsp chopped parsley
4 chicken breasts
1 egg, beaten
15 ml/1 tbsp milk
Salt and freshly ground black pepper
45 ml/3 tbsp oil
50 g/2 oz/¼ cup butter or margarine
60 ml/4 tbsp dry white wine
10 ml/2 tsp lemon juice
60 ml/4 tbsp single (light) cream

Mix together the breadcrumbs and parsley. Flatten the chicken breasts with a rolling pin. Mix together the egg and milk and season to taste. Dip the chicken in the egg mixture, then press it into the breadcrumbs. Heat the oil and fry (sauté) the chicken for 8 minutes each side until cooked through. Lift out on to a warm serving dish and keep warm. Melt the butter or margarine in the pan, add the wine and lemon juice and stir well. Add the cream, stir and heat through and pour over the chicken breasts. Serve immediately.

Sweet and sour chicken

SERVES 4

15 g/¼ oz fresh yeast
150 ml/¼ pt/⅔ cup warm water
10 ml/2 tsp oil
100 g/4 oz/1 cup plain (all-purpose)
   flour
1 egg, separated
2 carrots, grated
150 g/5 oz/1 small can of pineapple
   pieces in natural juice
10 ml/2 tsp light brown sugar
15 ml/1 tbsp white wine vinegar
15 ml/1 tbsp soy sauce
300 ml/½ pt/1¼ cups cold water
15 ml/1 tbsp cornflour (cornstarch)
2 boneless chicken breasts, cubed
Oil, for deep-frying
Rice, noodles or beansprouts, to serve

Blend together the yeast, warm water, oil, flour and egg yolk. Leave to stand for 20 minutes. Whisk the egg white until stiff. Place the carrots, pineapple and juice, sugar, wine vinegar, soy sauce and cold water in a food processor or blender and process until smooth. Pour into a saucepan, bring to the boil and simmer for 10 minutes. Mix the cornflour with a little water, then stir it into the sauce and simmer, stirring, until it thickens. Fold the egg whites into the yeast mixture, dip the chicken into the batter and fry (sauté) in hot oil for 5 minutes until light, fluffy and golden brown. You may need to do this in batches. Serve with the sweet and sour sauce and rice, noodles or beansprouts.

Pink pineapple chicken

SERVES 4

100 g/4 oz/½ cup butter or margarine,
   softened
15 ml/1 tbsp plain (all-purpose) flour
30 ml/2 tbsp tomato purée (paste)
10 ml/2 tsp mustard powder
2.5 ml/½ tsp salt
Freshly ground black pepper
5 ml/1 tsp Worcestershire sauce
15 ml/1 tbsp vinegar
400 g/14 oz/1 large can of pineapple
   chunks in natural juice, chopped
4 chicken breasts
15 ml/1 tbsp cornflour (cornstarch)
15 ml/1 tbsp water
Boiled rice or potatoes, to serve

Mix together the butter or margarine, flour, tomato purée, mustard, salt, pepper, Worcestershire sauce and vinegar. Stir in a little chopped pineapple. Place the chicken breasts in a flameproof casserole dish (Dutch oven) and spread the mixture over the top. Pour the remaining pineapple and juice over and bake in a preheated oven at 180°C/350°F/gas mark 4 for 1 hour. Transfer the chicken to a serving dish and keep warm. Mix the cornflour with the water, stir into the sauce, bring to the boil and boil, stirring, until the sauce thickens. Pour the sauce over the chicken and serve with rice or potatoes.

Chicken with lemon and thyme

SERVES 4

15 ml/1 tbsp olive oil
1 garlic clove, crushed
Salt and freshly ground black pepper
4 boneless chicken breasts, cut into
    strips
5 ml/1 tsp thyme leaves
½ lemon, thinly sliced

Mix together the oil, garlic, salt and pepper in a shallow ovenproof dish. Add the chicken and turn until coated in the oil. Sprinkle with the thyme and arrange the lemon slices on top. Bake in a preheated oven at 200°C/400°F/ gas mark 6 for 15–20 minutes just until the chicken is cooked through. The cooking time will vary depending on the size of the chicken strips.

Chicken with roasted peppers

SERVES 4

1 red (bell) pepper, seeded and cut into
    strips
1 yellow pepper, seeded and cut into
    strips
3 garlic cloves, chopped
30 ml/2 tbsp olive oil
4 boneless chicken breasts, cut into
    strips
Salt and freshly ground black pepper
15 ml/1 tbsp chopped thyme

Toss the peppers and garlic with the oil in a roasting tin (pan) and cook in a preheated oven at 200°C/400°F/ gas mark 6 for 20 minutes until beginning to brown, stirring once during cooking. Season the chicken strips with salt and pepper, then stir them into the peppers with half the thyme. Return to the oven for a further 25 minutes until tender, stirring occasionally. Serve sprinkled with the remaining thyme.

Saffron chicken

SERVES 4

4 chicken portions
15 ml/1 tbsp oil
1 onion, sliced
1 sprig of thyme
1 bay leaf
300 ml/½ pt/1¼ cups plain yoghurt
A pinch of saffron powder
5 ml/1 tsp lemon juice
Freshly ground black pepper
Lemon wedges, to garnish

Fry (sauté) the chicken in the oil until just browned, then half-fill the pan with water, add the onion, thyme and bay leaf and simmer for about 20 minutes until the chicken is cooked. Transfer the chicken to a serving dish and keep warm. Mix the yoghurt, saffron and lemon juice with 250 ml/8 fl oz/1 cup of the strained cooking liquor and season to taste with pepper. Heat the sauce gently but do not allow it to boil or the yoghurt will separate. Pour the sauce over the chicken and garnish with lemon wedges.

Quick barbecued chicken

SERVES 4

120 ml/4 fl oz/½ cup tomato ketchup (catsup)
100 g/4 oz chutney, chopped
45 ml/3 tbsp dark brown sugar
4 chicken portions

Mix together the tomato ketchup, chutney and sugar, brush it over the chicken and leave it to stand for 1 hour. Brush again with any remaining mixture and place the chicken in a roasting tin (pan). Bake in a preheated oven at 190°C/375°F/gas mark 5 for 40 minutes until cooked through, turning occasionally and basting with more sauce if necessary.

Braised lemon chicken

SERVES 4

1 celery stick, chopped
1 onion, chopped
1 cooking (tart) apple, peeled, cored and sliced
50 g/2 oz/¼ cup butter or margarine, softened
5 ml/1 tsp French mustard
5 ml/1 tsp dried mixed herbs
Grated rind and juice of ½ lemon
Salt and freshly ground black pepper
4 chicken portions
300 ml/½ pt/1¼ cups Chicken Stock (page 28)

Place the celery, onion and apple in the bottom of an ovenproof dish. Mix the butter or margarine with the mustard, herbs, lemon rind and juice and season to taste. Make two slits across the top of each chicken portion and spread liberally with the lemon butter. Place the portions on top of the vegetables, add the stock and cover. Bake in a preheated oven at 200°C/400°F/gas mark 6 for 35 minutes, then remove the lid and return the dish to the oven for a further 10 minutes to brown.

Paprika chicken

SERVES 4

30 ml/2 tbsp oil
4 chicken portions
2 onions, sliced
50 g/2 oz mushrooms, sliced
4 tomatoes, skinned and sliced
1 garlic clove, crushed
15 ml/1 tbsp paprika
450 ml/¾ pt/2 cups Chicken Stock (page 28)
Salt and freshly ground black pepper
15 ml/1 tbsp cornflour (cornstarch)
15 ml/1 tbsp water
30 ml/2 tbsp chopped parsley
Mashed potatoes and a green vegetable, to serve

Heat the oil and fry (sauté) the chicken portions until lightly browned on all sides, then remove them from the pan. Add the onions and fry until browned, then add the mushrooms and tomatoes and cook for 2 minutes. Stir in the garlic and paprika, return the chicken portions, pour over the stock and season to taste. Bring to the boil, cover and simmer for 45 minutes until the chicken is cooked through. Transfer the chicken to a warm serving dish and keep warm. Mix the cornflour with the water, stir into the sauce, bring to the boil and boil, stirring, until the sauce thickens. Pour the sauce over the chicken, sprinkle with the parsley and serve with mashed potatoes and a green vegetable.

147

Chicken with prosciutto and polenta

SERVES 4

30 ml/2 tbsp chopped tarragon
150 g/5 oz/⅔ cup butter or margarine
Salt and freshly ground black pepper
4 boneless chicken breasts
8 slices of prosciutto
300 ml/½ pt/1¼ cups Chicken Stock
  (page 28)
1 quantity of Soft Polenta (page 201)

Mix the tarragon into the butter or margarine and season to taste with salt and pepper. Make a slit down the side of each chicken breast and fill with the flavoured butter. Fold the edges together and wrap in the slices of prosciutto, then chill until the butter is firm.

Arrange the chicken in a roasting tin (pan) and pour the stock over. Cook in a preheated oven at 200°C/400°F/gas mark 6 for about 30 minutes, basting occasionally, until tender. Remove the chicken from the tin and boil the stock until reduced by half. Serve the chicken with the sauce spooned over and the polenta served separately.

Sesame drumsticks

SERVES 4

8 chicken drumsticks
1 egg, beaten
100 g/4 oz/1 cup sesame seeds
2.5 ml/½ tsp chilli powder
Salt and freshly ground black pepper

Brush the chicken with egg. Mix together the sesame seeds and chilli powder and season to taste. Roll the chicken in the seeds. Place the chicken in a roasting tin (pan) and bake in a preheated oven at 180°C/350°F/gas mark 4 for 35 minutes until golden brown and cooked through.

Crunchy-coated chicken drumsticks

SERVES 4

75 g/3 oz/1½ cups fresh breadcrumbs
100 g/4 oz/1 cup cashew nuts or
  peanuts, chopped
Freshly ground black pepper
5 ml/1 tsp ground coriander (cilantro)
8 chicken drumsticks
1 egg, beaten

Mix together the breadcrumbs, nuts, pepper and coriander. Dip the chicken drumsticks in the egg, then in the breadcrumb mixture and bake in a preheated oven at 190°C/375°F/gas mark 5 for 30 minutes.

Coconut drumsticks

SERVES 4

100 g/4 oz/⅓ cup apricot jam (jelly)
60 ml/4 tbsp orange juice
8 chicken drumsticks
100 g/4 oz/1 cup desiccated (shredded)
  coconut

Warm the apricot jam and mix in the orange juice. Brush liberally over the drumsticks and coat them in the coconut. Place in a roasting tin (pan) and bake in a preheated oven at 190°C/375°F/gas mark 5 for 30 minutes, turning once or twice, until golden brown and cooked through.

Chicken satay with peanut sauce

SERVES 4

120 ml/4 fl oz/½ cup coconut cream
Salt and freshly ground black pepper
1 kg/2¼ lb chicken meat, cut into
 4 cm/1½ in cubes
60 ml/4 tbsp smooth peanut butter
2.5 ml/½ tsp chilli powder
5 ml/1 tsp grated lemon rind
10 ml/2 tsp light brown sugar
250 ml/8 fl oz/1 cup water
Juice of ½ lime

Mix the coconut cream with salt and pepper to taste and marinate the chicken pieces for 2 hours. Drain, reserving the marinade. Thread the meat on to skewers and grill (broil) under a medium grill (broiler) for 20 minutes, turning frequently and basting with the marinade until cooked through.

Meanwhile, mix together the peanut butter, chilli powder, lemon rind, sugar and water in a saucepan, bring to the boil and simmer for 20 minutes. Stir in the lime juice and serve with the satay sticks.

Gardener's chicken

SERVES 4

100 g/4 oz/½ cup butter or margarine
50 g/2 oz streaky bacon, rinded and
 chopped
2 onions, sliced
3 celery sticks, sliced
100 g/4 oz mushrooms, sliced
1 chicken, jointed
450 g/1 lb small new potatoes
225 g/½ lb turnips, sliced
400 g/14 oz/1 large can of tomatoes
1 bouquet garni sachet
Salt and freshly ground black pepper
15 ml/1 tbsp chopped parsley

Melt half the butter or margarine and fry (sauté) the bacon, onions, celery and mushrooms until soft but not brown. Transfer to a casserole dish (Dutch oven). Add the remaining butter or margarine to the pan and fry the chicken portions until lightly browned, then transfer to the casserole and add the potatoes, turnips, tomatoes and bouquet garni. Season to taste. Cover tightly and cook in a preheated oven at 150°C/300°F/gas mark 3 for 2 hours until tender. Discard the bouquet garni and serve sprinkled with the parsley.

Chicken Maryland

SERVES 4

175 g/6 oz/1½ cups plain (all-purpose)
  flour
Salt and freshly ground black pepper
1.5 kg/3 lb chicken, jointed
2 eggs, beaten
100 g/4 oz/2 cups fresh breadcrumbs
50 g/2 oz/¼ cup butter or margarine
30 ml/2 tbsp oil
4 bacon rashers (slices)
4 bananas
150 ml/¼ pt/⅔ cup milk
300 g/11 oz canned creamed sweetcorn
  (corn)
Salt and freshly ground black pepper

Season 50 g/2 oz/½ cup of the flour
with salt and pepper and use to coat
the chicken joints. Dip the joints in
the egg, then the breadcrumbs. Heat
the butter or margarine and oil and
fry (sauté) the chicken pieces until
lightly browned all over. Reduce the
heat and continue frying gently for
20 minutes or until cooked through.
Drain on kitchen paper (paper
towels), place on a warm serving dish
and keep warm.

Stretch the bacon rashers and cut
in half. Roll the pieces round a skewer
and grill (broil) until crisp, then place
on the serving dish. Halve the
bananas lengthways and fry in the hot
butter or margarine for 3 minutes,
turning once. Place on the serving
dish.

Whisk the remaining flour with the
milk and sweetcorn and season to
taste. Fry spoonfuls of the batter in
the hot butter or margarine until
browned, turning once. Place on the
serving dish, and serve the chicken
with the fritters, bacon rolls and
bananas.

Chicken with parsley dumplings

SERVES 4

30 ml/2 tbsp oil
1 chicken, jointed
2 onions, sliced
1 garlic clove, crushed
25 g/1 oz/¼ cup plain (all-purpose) flour
600 ml/1 pt/2½ cups Chicken Stock
  (page 28)
1 bay leaf
10 ml/2 tsp dried mixed herbs
Salt and freshly ground black pepper
100 g/4 oz/1 cup self-raising (self-rising)
  flour
50 g/2 oz/½ cup shredded (chopped)
  suet
30 ml/2 tbsp chopped parsley
1 egg, beaten

Heat the oil and fry (sauté) the
chicken pieces until browned on all
sides, then transfer them to a
casserole dish (Dutch oven). Fry the
onions and garlic until soft but not
brown, then transfer to the casserole.
Stir the flour into the pan and cook
for 1 minute, stirring. Stir in the
stock, bring to the boil and cook,
stirring, until the sauce thickens. Add
the bay leaf and herbs and season to
taste. Pour over the chicken, cover
and cook in a preheated oven at
180°C/350°F/gas mark 4 for 1 hour.
Mix the flour, suet and parsley and
bind together with the egg. Roll into
small dumplings and add to the
casserole. Cook, uncovered, for a
further 30 minutes. Discard the bay
leaf before serving.

Sweet curried chicken

SERVES 4

60 ml/4 tbsp clear honey
10 ml/2 tsp curry powder
1 chicken, jointed
Salt and freshly ground black pepper
50 g/2 oz/¼ cup butter or margarine
15 ml/1 tbsp plain (all-purpose) flour
300 ml/½ pt/1¼ cups Chicken Stock
    (page 28)
50 g/2 oz/⅓ cup sultanas (golden raisins)
15 ml/1 tbsp lemon juice
15 ml/1 tbsp chopped parsley
Boiled rice, to serve

Mix half the honey with the curry powder. Season the chicken portions with salt and pepper and marinate in the honey mixture overnight.

Melt the butter or margarine and remaining honey and fry (sauté) the chicken pieces until browned on all sides. Stir the flour into the pan and cook for 1 minute, then stir in the stock, sultanas and lemon juice and season to taste. Bring to the boil, cover and simmer for 20 minutes until the chicken is cooked through and tender, stirring occasionally and adding a little extra stock if necessary. Sprinkle with the parsley and serve with rice.

Quick chicken crunchies

SERVES 4

400 g/14 oz filo pastry (paste)
60 ml/4 tbsp olive oil
450 g/1 lb/4 cups cooked chicken, cut into 5 cm/2 in pieces
Corn oil, for deep-frying

Cover the pastry sheets you are not using with a damp cloth to avoid them drying out while you are working. Brush the pastry with the oil, then fold in half lengthways. Place a piece of chicken on one end and fold over and over into a small parcel. Fry (sauté) the chicken parcels in the hot oil for 3 minutes until golden brown and crispy. Drain well on kitchen paper (paper towels) and keep warm while you fry the remaining parcels.

Crunchy chicken bake

SERVES 4

450 g/1 lb/4 cups cooked chicken, diced
15 ml/1 tbsp lemon juice
120 ml/4 fl oz/½ cup Mayonnaise
    (page 277)
A pinch of salt
2 celery sticks, chopped
150 g/5 oz/1 small can of condensed cream of chicken soup
2 hard-boiled (hard-cooked) eggs, chopped
½ onion, finely chopped
25 g/1 oz/¼ cup flaked (slivered) almonds
50 g/2 oz/½ cup Cheddar cheese, grated
50 g/2 oz potato crisps (chips), crushed

Combine all the ingredients except the almonds, cheese and crisps and spoon into a baking dish. Top with the almonds, cheese and crisps and leave to chill in the fridge overnight. Return to room temperature, then bake in a preheated oven at 200°C/400°F/gas mark 6 for 25 minutes until hot and bubbly.

151

Chicken and broccoli stir-fry

SERVES 4

60 ml/4 tbsp oil
5 ml/1 tsp sesame oil
50 g/2 oz baby sweetcorn (corn) cobs, sliced
225 g/8 oz broccoli florets
225 g/8 oz/2 cups cooked chicken, cut into strips
30 ml/2 tbsp soy sauce
50 g/2 oz mangetout (snow peas)
50 g/2 oz/1 cup beansprouts
50 g/2 oz bamboo shoots, cut into strips

Heat the oils and fry (sauté) the sweetcorn and broccoli for 5 minutes over a high heat. Add the chicken and soy sauce and stir-fry for 3 minutes. Add the mangetout, beansprouts and bamboo shoots and stir-fry for 3 minutes. Serve immediately.

Orange and tarragon chicken

SERVES 4

450 g/1 lb/4 cups cooked chicken, cut into strips
90 ml/6 tbsp dry white wine
5 ml/1 tsp lemon juice
½ onion, grated
5 ml/1 tsp chopped tarragon
4 oranges, peeled and segmented
1 lettuce, shredded
1 bunch of watercress
50 g/2 oz/½ cup walnuts, toasted
75g/3 oz/⅓ cup full-fat soft cheese
150 ml/¼ pt/⅔ cup soured (dairy sour) cream
5 ml/1 tsp Tabasco sauce
Salt and freshly ground black pepper

Place the chicken, wine, lemon juice, onion, tarragon and oranges in a bowl and mix well. Cover and leave to marinate for 30 minutes. Arrange the lettuce and watercress on a serving plate. Remove the chicken and orange segments from the marinade, mix with the walnuts and spoon on to the lettuce. Mix together the cheese, soured cream and Tabasco sauce and season to taste. Stir in just enough marinade to give a pouring consistency. Pour over the chicken mixture and serve chilled.

Baked chicken with broccoli

SERVES 4

75 g/10 oz broccoli florets
50 g/2 oz/¼ cup butter or margarine
25 g/1 oz/¼ cup plain (all-purpose) flour
250 ml/8 fl oz/1 cup Chicken Stock (page 28)
60 ml/4 tbsp double (heavy) cream
30 ml/2 tbsp dry sherry
Salt and freshly ground black pepper
4 cooked chicken breasts, halved lengthways
50 g/2 oz/½ cup Parmesan cheese, freshly grated

Blanch the broccoli in boiling water for 5 minutes, then drain and arrange on the base of a casserole dish (Dutch oven). Melt the butter or margarine in a frying pan (skillet), stir in the flour and cook for 1 minute, stirring continuously. Remove from the heat and stir in the stock, bring to the boil, then stir in the cream and sherry and season to taste. Spoon half the sauce over the broccoli, then lay the chicken on top and pour over the remaining sauce. Sprinkle with the Parmesan and bake in a preheated oven at 180°C/ 350°F/gas mark 4 for 20 minutes until golden brown.

Chicken and sweetcorn samosas

SERVES 4

15 g/½ oz/1 tbsp butter or margarine
15 ml/½ oz/2 tbsp plain (all-purpose)
   flour
150 ml/¼ pt/⅔ cup milk
Salt and freshly ground black pepper
1 egg, beaten
100 g/4 oz/1 cup cooked chicken,
   chopped
50 g/2 oz sweetcorn (corn) kernels
450 g/1 lb Puff Pastry (page 165)
Oil, for deep-frying

Melt the butter or margarine in a saucepan, stir in the flour and cook for 1 minute. Whisk in the milk and bring to the boil, stirring continuously, until the sauce thickens. Season to taste, remove from the heat and beat in half the egg. Stir in the chicken and sweetcorn. Roll out the pastry (paste) as thinly as possible and divide into eight small rectangles. Divide the chicken mixture between the rectangles, glaze the edges with egg and fold over to make square parcels. Press the edges together to seal and glaze on both sides with egg. Chill for 30 minutes. Fry (sauté) in deep hot oil for 6 minutes until golden brown and well puffed, drain on kitchen paper (paper towels) and serve immediately.

Chicken stuffed pancakes

SERVES 4

150 g/5 oz/1¼ cups plain (all-purpose)
   flour
1 egg, beaten
300 ml/½ pt/1¼ cups milk
Salt and freshly ground black pepper
30 ml/2 tbsp oil
75 g/3 oz/⅓ cup butter or margarine
100 g/4 oz mushrooms, chopped
300 ml/½ pt/1¼ cups Chicken Stock
   (page 28)
2.5 ml/½ tsp dried mixed herbs
225 g/8 oz/2 cups cooked chicken,
   chopped

Beat 100 g/4 oz/1 cup of the flour with the egg, milk and a pinch of salt to make a batter. Heat the oil in a frying pan (skillet) and fry (sauté) eight pancakes. Melt half the butter or margarine in a frying pan and fry the mushrooms until soft, then stir in the remaining flour and gradually add the stock. Bring to the boil, stirring continuously, add the herbs and season to taste. Stir in the chicken, then remove from the heat and allow to cool. Divide the sauce between the pancakes and fold over the edges to make square parcels. Place them, folded-sides down, on a flat ovenproof dish, and place knobs of the remaining butter or margarine on top. Cover with foil and bake in a preheated oven at 200°C/400°F/gas mark 6 for 20 minutes until hot and golden.

Quick lemon chicken

SERVES 4

25 g/1 oz/2 tbsp butter or margarine
25 g/1 oz/¼ cup plain (all-purpose) flour
300 ml/½ pt/1¼ cups Chicken Stock
  (page 28)
300 ml/½ pt/1¼ cups milk
350 g/12 oz/3 cups cooked chicken, cut
  into strips
100 g/4 oz cooked French (green) beans
30 ml/2 tbsp lemon juice
A pinch of dried thyme
Salt and freshly ground black pepper
175 g/6 oz/¾ cup long-grain rice
15 ml/1 tbsp chopped parsley
100 g/4 oz carrots, cut into strips
25 g/1 oz/¼ cup flaked (slivered)
  almonds

Melt the butter or margarine, stir in
the flour and cook gently for
1 minute, stirring. Whisk in the stock
and milk, bring to the boil and
simmer, stirring continuously, until the
sauce thickens. Stir in the chicken,
beans, lemon juice and thyme and
season to taste. Cook for 10 minutes
until heated through.

Meanwhile, cook the rice in plenty
of boiling salted water until just
tender. Drain and toss with the
parsley, then arrange in a ring on a
warm serving plate. Blanch the carrots
in boiling salted water for 3 minutes.
Pour the chicken mixture into the
centre of the rice and garnish with the
carrots and almonds.

Chicken with pork and walnuts

SERVES 4

2 onions
25 g/1 oz/2 tbsp butter or margarine
100 g/4 oz mushrooms, sliced
5 ml/1 tsp soy sauce
225 g/8 oz/2 cups cooked chicken,
  chopped
225 g/8 oz/2 cups cooked pork,
  chopped
100 g/4 oz bamboo shoots
150 ml/¼ pt/⅔ cup Chicken Stock
  (page 28)
Salt and freshly ground black pepper
30 ml/2 tbsp oil
12 walnuts
Boiled rice, to serve

Chop one onion and slice the other
into rings. Melt the butter or
margarine and fry (sauté) the
chopped onion until soft but not
brown, then add the mushrooms and
fry for 1 minute. Stir in the soy sauce,
then add the chicken, pork, bamboo
shoots and stock and season to taste.
Bring to the boil, then simmer for
20 minutes, stirring occasionally.

Meanwhile, heat the oil and fry the
walnuts until golden. Remove from
the pan and keep warm. Fry the onion
rings in the same pan until soft and
golden. Arrange the chicken and pork
mixture on a warm serving plate and
garnish with the walnuts and onions.
Serve with boiled rice.

Poussins with rosemary

SERVES 4

4 small poussins (Cornish hens)
Salt and freshly ground black pepper
Juice of 1 lemon
1 sprig of rosemary
4 garlic cloves, chopped
45 ml/3 tbsp olive oil

Cut down each side of the backbones of the poussins and remove the backbones. Flatten the birds by pressing down on the breast bone and season on both sides with salt and pepper. Arrange skin-side down in a foil-lined baking tin (pan) and sprinkle with the rosemary leaves from the sprig, the garlic and oil. Leave to stand for at least 30 minutes. Bake in a preheated oven at 200°C/400°F/ gas mark 6 for 20 minutes. Turn the birds over and baste with the juices. Return to the oven for a further 25 minutes until cooked through and golden.

French mustard poussin

SERVES 4

75 g/3 oz/⅓ cup butter or margarine
4 poussins (Cornish hens)
20 ml/1½ tbsp Dijon mustard
150 ml/¼ pt/⅔ cup Chicken Stock (page 28)
30 ml/2 tbsp orange juice
30 ml/2 tbsp double (heavy) cream
15 ml/1 tbsp chopped parsley

Melt the butter or margarine and fry (sauté) the poussins until browned on all sides. Transfer them to a casserole dish (Dutch oven) just large enough to fit them. Mix the mustard into the pan, stirring to scrape up all the meat juices. Stir in the stock and orange juice, bring to the boil and pour over the poussins. Bake in a preheated oven at 180°C/350°F/gas mark 4 for 45 minutes until tender. Transfer the poussins to a warm serving dish. Pour the sauce into a saucepan, bring almost to the boil and stir in the cream, then pour around the poussins and serve sprinkled with the parsley.

Poussins with ham and cream

SERVES 4

75 g/3 oz/⅓ cup butter or margarine
2 poussins (Cornish hens), jointed into four
100 g/4 oz chicken liver, chopped
2 onions, chopped
100 g/4 oz gammon, chopped
150 ml/¼ pt/⅔ cup dry white wine
150 ml/¼ pt/⅔ cup single (light) cream
Freshly ground black pepper
Boiled rice, to serve

Melt the butter or margarine and fry (sauté) the leg portions gently for 2 minutes each side, then add the wing pieces. Add the liver to the pan with the onions and gammon and cook for 4 minutes, turning once. Stir in the wine and cook for 5 minutes, then slowly pour the cream over the poussins and simmer for 1 minute. Lift the poussins out on to a warm serving plate. Season the sauce with black pepper, stir well and pour over the poussins. Serve with boiled rice.

Turkey

Devilled turkey drummers

SERVES 4

4 turkey drumsticks
1 garlic clove, sliced lengthways
15 ml/1 tbsp oil
8 streaky bacon rashers (slices), rinded
100 g/4 oz/⅓ cup apricot jam (jelly)
250 ml/8 fl oz/1 cup tomato ketchup (catsup)
60 ml/4 tbsp soy sauce
45 ml/3 tbsp French mustard
60 ml/4 tbsp Worcestershire sauce
60 ml/4 tbsp lemon juice
Salt and freshly ground black pepper

Stick a garlic sliver in the thick end of each drumstick and brush with the oil. Roll up the bacon rashers. Melt the jam with the ketchup in a heavy saucepan. Stir in the soy sauce, mustard, Worcestershire sauce and lemon juice and season to taste. Bring to the boil and cook for 1 minute. Place the drumsticks in an ovenproof dish and cover with the sauce. Cover and bake in a preheated oven at 180°C/350°F/gas mark 4 for 2 hours until the drumsticks are well cooked through, basting occasionally with the sauce. Remove the lid and add the bacon rolls for the last 20 minutes cooking.

Spiced eastern turkey

SERVES 4

1.2 kg/2½ lb turkey legs
5 ml/1 tsp ground cumin
5 ml/1 tsp ground coriander (cilantro)
5 ml/1 tsp turmeric
2.5 ml/½ tsp ground ginger
300 ml/½ pt/1¼ cups plain yoghurt
30 ml/1 tbsp lemon juice
Salt and freshly ground black pepper
45 ml/3 tbsp oil
225 g/8 oz onions, sliced
45 ml/3 tbsp desiccated (shredded) coconut
30 ml/2 tbsp plain (all-purpose) flour
150 m/¼ pt/⅔ cup Chicken Stock (page 28)
15 ml/1 tbsp chopped parsley

Cut the meat off the bones and cut it into bite-sized pieces. Stir the spices into the yoghurt and lemon juice and season to taste. Stir in the meat, cover and chill for 3 hours.

Heat the oil and fry (sauté) the onion until lightly browned. Add the coconut and flour and fry, stirring, for 1 minute. Stir in the turkey, marinade and stock, bring to the boil and pour into a casserole dish (Dutch oven). Cover and bake in a preheated oven at 170°C/325°F/gas mark 3 for 1¼ hours until the turkey is tender. Adjust the seasoning if necessary and sprinkle with the parsley to serve.

Turkey and bean ragout

SERVES 4

50 g/2 oz/¼ cup butter or margarine
2 onions, chopped
15 ml/1 tbsp plain (all-purpose) flour
10 ml/2 tsp chilli powder
400 g/14 oz/1 large can of tomatoes,
    chopped
15 ml/1 tbsp Worcestershire sauce
30 ml/2 tbsp tomato purée (paste)
300 ml/½ pt/1¼ cups Chicken Stock
    (page 28) or turkey stock
10 ml/2 tsp caster (superfine) sugar
1 bay leaf
Salt and freshly ground black pepper
450 g/1 lb/4 cups cooked turkey, diced
200 g/7 oz/1 small can of pimientos,
    drained and chopped
200 g/7 oz/1 small can of red kidney
    beans, drained

Melt half the butter or margarine and
fry (sauté) the onions until soft but
not brown. Stir in the flour and chilli
powder and cook for 1 minute, then
stir in the tomatoes, Worcestershire
sauce, tomato purée, stock, sugar
and bay leaf and season to taste.
Bring to the boil, cover and simmer
for 30 minutes. Fry the turkey in the
remaining butter or margarine. Stir
into the sauce with the pimientos and
beans and simmer for a further
10 minutes.

Turkey roulade

SERVES 4

50 g/2 oz/¼ cup butter or margarine
50 g/2 oz/½ cup plain (all-purpose) flour
300 ml/½ pt/1¼ cups milk
100 g/4 oz/1 cup strong cheese, grated
3 eggs, separated
5 ml/1 tsp dried mixed herbs
225 g/8 oz/2 cups cooked mixed
    vegetables, chopped
225 g/8 oz/2 cups cooked turkey,
    chopped
50 g/2 oz/½ cup cooked ham, chopped
Grated rind and juice of ½ lemon
100 g/4 oz mushrooms, sliced
15 ml/1 tbsp snipped chives
Salt and freshly ground black pepper
2 tomatoes, sliced

Melt the butter or margarine, stir in
the flour and cook for 1 minute.
Whisk in the milk, bring to the boil
and boil, stirring, until the sauce
thickens. Remove from the heat and
stir in the cheese. Divide the mixture
in half and put half to one side. Stir
the egg yolks, herbs and vegetables
into the other half. Whisk the egg
whites until stiff, then fold them into
the mixture and pile into a greased
and lined 33 × 23 cm/13 × 9 in
Swiss roll tin (jelly roll pan). Bake in a
preheated oven at 190°C/375°F/gas
mark 5 for 30 minutes. Place the
remaining sauce in a saucepan, stir in
the turkey, ham, lemon rind and juice,
mushrooms and chives. Cover and
simmer gently for 15 minutes, then
season to taste. Turn out the cooked
soufflé on to a clean sheet of
greaseproof (waxed) paper and
remove the lining paper. Spread the
filling over and quickly roll up, using
the paper to help. Roll on to a serving
plate and garnish with the tomato
slices.

Thai-style turkey burgers

SERVES 4

450 g/1 lb minced (ground) turkey
15 ml/1 tbsp soy sauce
5 ml/1 tsp grated fresh root ginger
2 garlic cloves, crushed
Salt and freshly ground black pepper
30 ml/2 tbsp oil
Flat white rolls and salad, to serve

Mix together the turkey, soy sauce, ginger, garlic, salt and pepper until well blended. Using wetted hands, shape into eight burgers about 1 cm/ ½ in thick. Heat the oil in a frying pan (skillet) and fry (sauté) the burgers for about 5 minutes on each side until cooked through and golden brown. Serve in flat white rolls with salad.

Turkey slices with cider cream

SERVES 4

500 g/18 oz turkey breast, sliced into four
1 egg, beaten
100 g/4 oz/2 cups fresh breadcrumbs
100 g/4 oz/½ cup butter or margarine
300 ml/½ pt/1¼ cups dry cider
150 ml/¼ pt/⅔ cup double (heavy) cream
Salt and freshly ground black pepper
2 parsley sprigs

Dip the turkey breast slices in the egg, then in the breadcrumbs. Melt the butter or margarine and fry (sauté) the turkey until golden brown and cooked through. Transfer to a warm serving plate and keep warm. Stir the cider into the pan and bring to the boil, stirring to scrape up all the meat juices. Boil for 1 minute, then stir in the cream, season to taste and heat through. Pour over the turkey and serve garnished with the parsley sprigs.

Duck

Duck with plum sauce

SERVES 4

400 g/14 oz/1 large can of plums,
    drained and juice reserved
30 ml/2 tbsp tomato purée (paste)
25 g/1 oz/2 tbsp dark brown sugar
15 ml/1 tbsp red wine vinegar
5 ml/1 tsp Dijon mustard
1 garlic clove, crushed
Salt and freshly ground black pepper
1 duck, quartered, or 4 duck breasts

Place the plums, tomato purée, sugar,
wine vinegar, mustard and garlic in a
saucepan and warm gently to dissolve
the sugar. Season to taste, then purée
in a food processor or blender. Thin, if
necessary, with a little of the plum
juice. Pour the sauce over the duck in
a roasting tin (pan) and roast in a
preheated oven at 190°C/375°F/gas
mark 5 for 1½ hours until crisp and
golden, basting occasionally with the
sauce.

Honey duck

SERVES 4

450 g/1 lb pork sausagemeat
50 g/2 oz/1 cup fresh breadcrumbs
Grated rind and juice of 1 orange
2.5 ml/½ tsp dried mixed herbs
Salt and freshly ground black pepper
2.25 kg/5 lb duck
300 ml/½ pt/1¼ cups water
15 ml/1 tbsp clear honey
15 ml/1 tbsp plain (all-purpose) flour
450 ml/¾ pt/2 cups Vegetable Stock
    (page 28)
1 orange, sliced
1 bunch of watercress

Mix together the sausagemeat,
breadcrumbs, orange rind and herbs
and season to taste. Stuff the duck
with the mixture and skewer down the
loose skin. Place the duck on a rack in
a roasting tin (pan) and prick the skin
all over with a needle. Rub the skin
with salt and roast in a preheated
oven at 200°C/400°F/gas mark 6 for
30 minutes, then reduce the heat to
180°C/350°F/gas mark 4 and cook
for a further 1½ hours until just
cooked.

Mix together the orange juice and
honey and brush over the duck, then
return it to the oven for 15 minutes.
When ready, transfer the duck to a
warm serving plate and keep warm.
Pour most of the fat out of the tin,
leaving about 30 ml/2 tbsp. Stir in
the flour and cook for 1 minute, then
stir in the stock and boil, stirring, until
smooth and thick. Season to taste and
pour into a sauce boat. Serve the
duck garnished with the orange slices
and watercress.

Duck in orange liqueur sauce

SERVES 6

2 ducks
4 oranges
150 ml/¼ pt/⅔ cup red wine
15 ml/1 tbsp caster (superfine) sugar
300 ml/½ pt/1¼ cups Vegetable Stock (page 28)
Juice of ½ lemon
15 ml/1 tbsp cornflour (cornstarch)
15 ml/1 tbsp water
45 ml/3 tbsp orange liqueur

Place the ducks on their sides in a greased roasting tin (pan) and roast in a preheated oven at 200°C/400°F/ gas mark 6 for 40 minutes. Turn them on to the other side and roast for a further 30 minutes, then turn them on their backs and roast for a final 30 minutes until cooked, basting frequently.

Peel the oranges, remove the pith and divide into segments, reserving the juice that drips out as you work. Cut the rind into strips and boil in water for 5 minutes, then drain. Boil the wine and sugar until thickened, then add the reserved orange juice, the stock and lemon juice. Bring to the boil and boil for 5 minutes. Mix the cornflour (cornstarch) with the water and stir it into the sauce with the orange liqueur. Boil, stirring, until thickened, then pour the sauce over the ducks and garnish with the orange segments and rind.

Game

Pigeon with mushrooms

SERVES 4

100 g/4 oz/½ cup butter or margarine
3 onions, chopped
4 celery sticks, chopped
4 pigeons
Salt and freshly ground black pepper
225 g/8 oz mushrooms, sliced
120 ml/4 fl oz/½ cup brandy
100 g/4 oz canned chestnut purée

Melt the butter or margarine in a large saucepan and fry (sauté) the onions and celery until browned. Season the pigeons with salt and pepper and brown them in the pan, then cover and simmer gently for 30 minutes. Add the mushrooms and cook for 5 minutes, then add the brandy and simmer for 10 minutes. Season the chestnut purée with salt and pepper and place it in the bottom of a heated casserole dish (Dutch oven). Sit the pigeons on top of the purée. Lift out the vegetables with a slotted spoon and place them round the pigeons. Bring the pan juices back to the boil, then pour them over the pigeons. Cook in a preheated oven at 180°C/350°F/gas mark 5 for 20 minutes before serving.

Chicken and pork layer pie (page 171)

Pigeon casserole

SERVES 4

4 pigeons
Salt and freshly ground black pepper
450 ml/¾ pt/2 cups dry white wine
2 onions, chopped
2 carrots, chopped
1 bouquet garni sachet
50 g/2 oz/¼ cup butter or margarine
100 g/4 oz belly pork, rinded and diced
25 g/1 oz/¼ cup plain (all-purpose) flour
120 ml/4 fl oz/½ cup brandy
2 garlic cloves, crushed
Boiled red cabbage and chestnuts, to
　serve

Season the pigeons with salt and
pepper. Mix together the wine,
onions, carrots and bouquet garni and
marinate the pigeons in the mixture
overnight, turning two or three times.
Melt three-quarters of the butter or
margarine in a flameproof casserole
(Dutch oven) and fry (sauté) the pork
until crisp. Lift the pigeons out of the
marinade, pat dry on kitchen paper
(paper towels) and sprinkle with the
flour. Melt the remaining butter and
brown the pigeons all over. Pour the
brandy over them and set them alight
to burn off the excess fat. Strain the
marinade and add to the casserole
with the garlic and seasoning to taste.
Cover tightly and cook in a preheated
oven at 150°C/300°F/gas mark 2 for
2½ hours until very tender. Serve with
red cabbage and chestnuts.

Partridge with red cabbage

SERVES 4

60 ml/4 tbsp olive oil
4 partridges
2 onions, chopped
2 eating (dessert) apples, peeled, cored
　and chopped
2 celery sticks, chopped
90 ml/6 tbsp white wine vinegar
25 g/1 oz/2 tbsp demerara sugar
15 ml/1 tbsp orange juice
Salt and freshly ground black pepper
1 bouquet garni sachet

Heat the oil and fry (sauté) the
partridges until browned on all sides.
Remove from the pan. Fry the onions,
apples and celery until just beginning
to brown, then stir in the wine
vinegar, sugar and orange juice and
season to taste. Transfer the mixture
to a casserole dish (Dutch oven) and
top with the partridges. Add the
bouquet garni, cover tightly and bake
in a preheated oven at 150°C/300°F/
gas mark 2 for 3 hours until tender.
Discard the bouquet garni before
serving.

*Baked eggs in green peppers
(page 185) and Camembert puffs
with conserve (page 192)*

Grouse in milk

SERVES 2

25 g/1 oz/2 tbsp lard (shortening) or
    vegetable fat
1 grouse
2 bacon rashers (slices), rinded and
    chopped
50 g/2 oz belly pork, diced
100 g/4 oz mushrooms sliced
150 ml/¼ pt/⅔ cup milk
75 ml/5 tbsp water
2.5 ml/½ tsp ground mace
1 bouquet garni sachet
Salt and freshly ground black pepper

Heat the lard or vegetable fat in a
frying pan (skillet). Stuff the grouse
with the bacon and brown it in the fat,
then transfer it to a casserole dish
(Dutch oven). Fry (sauté) the pork until
browned. Add the mushrooms and fry
for 1 minute, then spoon over the
grouse. Bring the milk and water to the
boil, stir in the mace and pour into the
casserole. Add the bouquet garni and
season to taste. Cook in a preheated
oven at 150°C/300°F/gas mark 2 for
4 hours until tender. Discard the
bouquet garni before serving.

Roast pheasant

SERVES 4

2 pheasants
1 garlic clove, crushed
Salt and freshly ground black pepper
100 g/4 oz streaky bacon rashers
    (slices), rinded
300 ml/½ pt/1¼ cups dry red wine
100 g/4 oz/½ cup butter or margarine
5 ml/1 tsp chopped marjoram
5 ml/1 tsp chopped parsley

Clean the pheasants and dry on
kitchen paper (paper towels). Rub
with the garlic and season with salt
and pepper. Place in a roasting tin

(pan) and cover with the bacon. Mix
together the wine, butter or
margarine and herbs and pour over
the pheasants. Roast in a preheated
oven at 180°C/350°F/gas mark 4 for
1 hour until the birds are tender,
basting occasionally with the sauce.
Transfer the pheasants to a warm
serving plate and serve the sauce in a
sauce boat.

Rabbit and bacon casserole

SERVES 4

1 rabbit, jointed and soaked overnight in
    salted water
25 g/1 oz/¼ cup plain (all-purpose) flour
50 g/2 oz/1 cup fresh breadcrumbs
A pinch of dried marjoram
A pinch of dried sage
Salt and freshly ground black pepper
30 ml/2 tbsp milk
2 large onions, sliced
300 ml/½ pt/1¼ cups Chicken or
    Vegetable Stock (page 28)
225 g/8 oz bacon rashers (slices), rinded

Roll the rabbit pieces in the flour and
lay them in a casserole dish (Dutch
oven). Season the breadcrumbs with
the marjoram, sage and salt and
pepper, moisten with the milk and
sprinkle over the rabbit pieces. Lay
the onion slices over the top and add
enough of the boiling stock to just
cover. Lay the bacon on top, cover
and bake in a preheated oven at
180°C/350°F/gas mark 4 for
1½ hours, then remove the lid and
cook for a further 30 minutes to
allow the top to brown.

Pastry, pies and pizza

A hot pie makes a delicious and warming meal on a cold winter
day, and can often be partly prepared in advance. Cold pies for
slicing at a buffet or salad meal are guaranteed to be popular.
Shortcrust pastry (basic pie crust) doesn't take long to make, but
if you're busy and don't have much time to spare, make up a
batch to freeze, or keep a packet of ready-made pastry (paste) in
the freezer. Puff pastry, filo pastry or other pastries that take time
and care to prepare can also be made in advance, or bought in
from the local supermarket. The quality is excellent so, unless you
enjoy making your own pastry, just put it on the shopping list!
Pizza is now almost a way of life and makes a great snack, supper
or complete meal if teamed with garlic bread and a crisp, freshly
tossed salad. If you are pressed for time, use a ready-made pizza
base or a slice of French bread and experiment with your favourite
toppings – they may not be authentic Italian but who cares if they
taste good?

Pastry (Paste)

Shortcrust pastry

MAKES 350 G/12 OZ

225 g/8 oz/2 cups plain (all-purpose)
   flour
A pinch of salt
50 g/2 oz/¼ cup butter or margarine
50 g/2 oz/¼ cup lard (shortening) or
   vegetable fat
30–45 ml/2–3 tbsp cold water

Mix together the flour and salt, then
rub in the fats until the mixture
resembles fine breadcrumbs. Mix with
enough of the water to form a dough
that comes cleanly away from the side
of the bowl. Roll out on a lightly
floured surface and use as required.
The pastry can be wrapped tightly in
clingfilm (plastic wrap) and kept in the
freezer if it is made before it is
required.

Wholemeal shortcrust pastry

MAKES 350 G/12 OZ

Prepare as for Shortcrust Pastry, but
substitute wholemeal for plain (all-
purpose) flour. You will need to use a
little more water to bind the dough.

Enriched shortcrust pastry

MAKES 350 G/12 OZ

Prepare as for Shortcrust Pastry, but
blend in an egg yolk and reduce the
amount of water to bind the dough.

Suet crust pastry

MAKES 350 G/12 OZ

225 g/8 oz/2 cups plain (all-purpose)
   flour
5 ml/1 tsp baking powder
A pinch of salt
75 g/3 oz/¾ cup shredded (chopped)
   suet
30 ml/2 tbsp cold water

Mix together the flour, baking powder
and salt, then stir in the suet. Mix
with enough of the water to make a
soft dough.

Hot water crust pastry

MAKES 450 G/1 LB

350 g/12 oz/4 cups plain (all-purpose)
   flour
A pinch of salt
100 g/4 oz/½ cup lard (shortening) or
   vegetable fat
100 ml/4 fl oz/½ cup water

Mix together the flour and salt in a
warm bowl. Melt the lard or vegetable
fat gently in a saucepan, add the
water when just melted and bring to
the boil. Stir the liquid into the flour
with a wooden spoon and mix quickly
until blended. Turn out on to a floured
surface and knead until smooth. Use
at once and do not allow to cool.

Rough puff pastry

MAKES 400 G/14 OZ

225 g/8 oz/2 cups plain (all-purpose) flour
2.5 ml/½ tsp salt
75 g/3 oz lard (shortening) or vegetable fat, diced
75 g/3 oz/⅓ cup butter or margarine, diced
90–120 ml/6–8 tbsp cold water

Mix together the flour and salt, then add the fats and enough of the water to mix to a soft dough. Roll out on a lightly floured surface to a 30 × 15 cm/ 12 × 6 in rectangle. Fold the bottom third upwards and the top third downwards over it, turn the dough so that the fold is on the left and seal the edges. Roll, fold and seal twice more, keeping the folded edge on the left. If the pastry becomes too soft, chill between rollings.

Choux pastry

MAKES 150 G/5 OZ

50 g/2 oz/¼ cup unsalted (sweet) butter
60 ml/4 tbsp water
60 ml/4 tbsp milk
60 g/2½ oz plain (all-purpose) flour
A pinch of salt
2 eggs, beaten

Melt the butter with the water and milk in a small saucepan over a gentle heat, then bring to the boil. Remove from the heat, add all the flour and the salt in one go and beat until the pastry is smooth and comes away from the side of the pan. Leave to cool for a few minutes, then gradually beat in the eggs a little at a time until the pastry is shiny and firm enough to hold its shape.

Puff pastry

MAKES 900 G/2 LB

450 g/1 lb/4 cups plain (all-purpose) flour
5 ml/1 tsp salt
450 g/1 lb butter or margarine
10 ml/2 tsp lemon juice
250 ml/8 fl oz/1 cup ice-cold water

Mix together the flour and salt. Rub a quarter of the butter or margarine into the mixture until it resembles breadcrumbs, then mix to a dough with the lemon juice and just enough of the water. Turn out on to a floured surface and knead gently until smooth. Wrap in clingfilm (plastic wrap) and leave to rest in a cool place for 15 minutes. Roll out the dough on a lightly floured surface to a 28 × 15 cm/11 × 6 in rectangle. Roll out the butter into a 13 cm/5 in square and place on the top half of the dough, leaving a gap around the edges. Fold the pastry over, seal the edges and turn so that the folded edge is on the left. Roll the pastry into a 30 × 15 cm/12 × 6 in rectangle, keeping the edges straight. Fold the top third down and the bottom third up, then turn so that the folded edge is on the left. Seal the edges and roll out and turn once more, then wrap in clingfilm and chill for 20 minutes. Roll out four more times, leaving to rest and chill for 20 minutes between each rolling.

Pies

Steak and ale pie

SERVES 4

30 ml/2 tbsp oil
750 g/1¾ lb stewing or braising steak,
    cubed
1 onion, chopped
4 celery sticks, chopped
450 ml/¾ pt/2 cups Beef Stock (page 28)
Salt and freshly ground black pepper
25 g/1 oz/¼ cup plain (all-purpose) flour
15 ml/1 tbsp water
225 g/8 oz Puff Pastry (page 165)
1 egg, beaten
300 ml/½ pt/1¼ cups brown ale

Heat the oil and fry (sauté) the steak,
onion and celery until just browned.
Stir in the stock and season to taste.
Bring to the boil, cover and simmer
for 1 hour until the meat is tender.
Mix together the flour and water and
stir into the meat, then bring back to
the boil, stirring continuously, until the
gravy thickens. Turn the meat and
vegetables and half the gravy into a
900 ml/1½ pt pie dish and leave to
cool.

Roll out the pastry (paste) and use
to cover the pie. Brush with the egg
and bake in a preheated oven at
220°C/425°F/gas mark 7 for
10 minutes, then reduce the heat to
190°C/375°F/gas mark 5 for a further
20 minutes. Place the ale in a
saucepan and boil rapidly until
reduced by half. Before serving the
pie, lift off the crust and stir the hot
ale into the meat and vegetables.
Replace the pie crust. Heat the
remaining gravy to serve separately.

Old-fashioned steak and kidney pie

SERVES 4

25 g/1 oz/¼ cup plain (all-purpose) flour
A pinch of mustard powder
A pinch of ground mace
Salt and freshly ground black pepper
450 g/1 lb braising steak, cubed
100 g/4 oz ox kidney, cubed
100 g/4 oz mushrooms, chopped
1 onion, chopped
1 garlic clove, crushed
300 ml/½ pt/1¼ cups Beef Stock
    (page 28)
150 ml/¼ pt/⅔ cup port
2.5 ml/½ tsp Worcestershire sauce
1 hard-boiled (hard-cooked) egg, sliced
225 g/8 oz Shortcrust Pastry (page 164)
1 egg, beaten

Mix together the flour, mustard and
mace and season to taste. Toss the
steak and kidney in the seasoned
flour, then place in a casserole dish
(Dutch oven) with the mushrooms,
onion and garlic. Mix together the
stock, port and Worcestershire sauce
and pour over the meat. Cover and
cook in a preheated oven at 150°C/
300°F/gas mark 3 for 3 hours until
the meat is tender. Remove from the
oven, chill and skim any fat from the
top. Transfer the meat and gravy to
a pie dish and lay the egg slices over
the top. Roll out the pastry (paste) on
a lightly floured surface and use to
cover the pie. Brush with beaten egg,
then bake in a preheated oven at
200°C/400°F/gas mark 6 for
30 minutes until the pie is golden
brown.

Steak and mushroom pie with horseradish pastry

SERVES 6

15 ml/1 tbsp oil
2 onions, sliced
750 g/1¾ lb stewing or braising steak, cubed
175 g/6 oz/1½ cups plain (all-purpose) flour
45 ml/3 tbsp made mustard
1 garlic clove, crushed
A pinch of thyme
A pinch of sage
Salt and freshly ground black pepper
300 ml/½ pt/1¼ cups Beef Stock (page 28)
40 g/1½ oz/3 tbsp lard (shortening) or vegetable fat
40 g/1½ oz butter or margarine
5 ml/1 tsp horseradish sauce
30 ml/2 tbsp water
30 ml/2 tbsp milk

Heat the oil and fry (sauté) the onions until browned. Add the meat and brown well all over. Stir in 15 ml/ 1 tbsp of the flour, the mustard, garlic and herbs and season to taste. Add the stock, cover and simmer until the meat is tender. Pour into a 1.2 litre/ 2 pt/5 cup pie dish with an egg cup in the centre, cool quickly and chill overnight.

Rub the fats into the remaining flour until the mixture resembles fine breadcrumbs, then stir in the horseradish. Mix in just enough of the water to make a smooth pastry (paste). Roll out on a lightly floured surface and use to cover the pie dish. Trim and crimp the edges and use the trimmings for decoration. Brush with the milk and bake in a preheated oven at 200°C/400°F/gas mark 6 for 30 minutes until golden brown.

Beef batter pie

SERVES 4

450 g/1 lb minced (ground) beef
1 onion, chopped
300 ml/½ pt/1¼ cups Beef Stock (page 28)
10 ml/2 tsp Worcestershire sauce
Salt and freshly ground black pepper
225 g/8 oz/2 cups plain (all-purpose) flour
5 ml/1 tsp baking powder
25 g/1 oz cornflour (cornstarch)
75 g/3 oz/¾ cup shredded (chopped) suet
300 ml/½ pt/1¼ cups milk

Put the beef in a saucepan and fry (sauté) gently until browned. Add the onion and fry until soft. Stir in the stock and Worcestershire sauce and season to taste. Bring to the boil, simmer for 15 minutes, then transfer to a greased 1.2 litre/2 pt/5 cup pie dish. Beat the flour, baking powder, cornflour, suet and milk to a thick batter and season to taste. Pour over the meat and bake in a preheated oven at 180°C/350°F/gas mark 4 for 35 minutes until risen and golden brown.

Savoury beef roll

SERVES 4

450 g/1 lb minced (ground) beef
100 g/4 oz sausagemeat
50 g/2 oz/1 cup fresh breadcrumbs
1 onion, chopped
A pinch of ground ginger
2.5 ml/½ tsp dried mixed herbs
Salt and freshly ground black pepper
350 g/12 oz Shortcrust Pastry
   (page 164)
1 egg, beaten

Mix together the beef, sausagemeat, breadcrumbs, onion, ginger and herbs and season to taste. Shape into a roll, place in a greased baking tin (pan), cover and bake in a preheated oven at 190ºC/375ºF/gas mark 5 for 20 minutes. Roll out the pastry (paste) on a lightly floured surface to a rectangle large enough to enclose the meat. Remove the meat from the oven, lay it on the pastry and quickly seal the pastry round the meat in a roll. Place it seam-downwards on a greased baking (cookie) sheet, decorate with pastry trimmings and brush with the egg. Return to the oven and cook for 30 minutes until golden brown.

Corned beef pie

SERVES 4

15 ml/1 tbsp oil
2 onions, chopped
450 g/1 lb/1 large can of corned beef,
   flaked
100 g/4 oz cooked carrots, sliced
100 g/4 oz cooked fresh peas or frozen
   peas
1 egg, beaten
5 ml/1 tsp Tabasco sauce
Salt and freshly ground black pepper
350 g/12 oz Shortcrust Pastry
   (page 164)
15 ml/1 tbsp milk

Heat the oil and fry (sauté) the onions until soft but not brown. Remove from the heat, stir in the corned beef, carrots, peas, egg and Tabasco sauce and season to taste. Roll out the pastry (paste) and use half to line a greased 20 cm/8 in pie dish. Fill with the meat mixture, then top with the remaining pastry and decorate with the trimmings. Brush with the milk. Bake in a preheated oven at 200ºC/400ºF/gas mark 6 for 30 minutes.

Veal and ham pie

SERVES 6

900 g/2 lb lean veal, cubed
1 veal shin bone, sawn into pieces
900 ml/1½ pts/3¾ cups Chicken Stock
  (page 28)
Salt and freshly ground black pepper
15 ml/1 tbsp chopped parsley
225 g/8 oz/2 cups cooked ham, diced
3 hard-boiled (hard-cooked) eggs
Grated rind of 1 lemon
450 g/1 lb Puff Pastry (page 165)
1 egg, beaten

Put the veal and bones in a large saucepan with the stock. Season to taste and add the parsley. Cover and simmer for 2 hours, then leave to cool for 15 minutes. Scoop out the meat and cut into bite-sized pieces. Mix with the ham and put a layer of half the meats in a greased 1.2 litre/2 pt/ 5 cup oval pie dish. Put the eggs on top and pack the remaining meat around and over them. Sprinkle with the lemon rind and add just enough of the stock to cover the meat.

Roll out the pastry (paste) on a lightly floured surface and cut an oval to fit the dish and a 2.5 cm/1 in strip to go round the edge. Moisten the edges and press the strip round the dish, then moisten the strip and seal the lid on top. Make a hole in the centre, roll out the pastry trimmings and use to decorate the pie. Brush with the egg. Bake in a preheated oven at 230°C/450°F/gas mark 8 for 10 minutes, then reduce the heat to 200°C/400°F/gas mark 6 and bake for a further 20 minutes until the pastry is well risen and golden brown. Use a funnel to fill the pie with more hot stock, if needed. Serve hot or cold.

Tourte Bourguignonne

SERVES 4

225 g/8 oz minced (ground) veal
100 g/4 oz gammon, minced
100 g/4 oz pork fat, minced
45 ml/3 tbsp brandy
1 onion, chopped
1 garlic clove, chopped
2.5 ml/½ tsp grated nutmeg
2.5 ml/½ tsp ground cinnamon
2.5 ml/½ tsp ground mace
Salt and freshly ground black pepper
350 g/12 oz Shortcrust Pastry
  (page 164)
1 egg, separated
15 ml/1 tbsp water

Mix together all the ingredients except the pastry (paste), egg and water and leave in a cool place for at least 1 hour. Roll out the pastry on a lightly floured surface and use half to line a greased 20 cm/8 in flan ring on a baking (cookie) sheet. Brush the inside with egg white and fill with the meat mixture. Roll out the remaining pastry and use it to cover the pie, sealing the edges well, then roll out the trimmings and use them to decorate the top. Mix together the egg yolk and water and brush it over the pie, then make four holes to allow steam to escape. Bake in a preheated oven at 190°C/375°F/gas mark 5 for 50 minutes. Serve hot or cold.

Terrine en croûte

SERVES 8

450 g/1 lb streaky bacon rashers
(slices), rinded
750 g/1¾ lb belly pork, rinded
450 g/1 lb lean veal
225 g/8 oz pigs' liver
1 onion, chopped
15 ml/1 tbsp chopped parsley
A pinch of mace
1 garlic clove, crushed
3 green peppercorns
3 juniper berries, crushed
60 ml/4 tbsp Madeira
150 ml/¼ pt/⅔ cup dry white wine
450 g/1 lb Puff Pastry (page 165)
1 egg, beaten

Stretch out the bacon rashers thinly
with a knife and use to line a 1.2 litre/
2 pt/5 cup terrine dish, arranging
them across the bottom and down the
sides and leaving the ends hanging
over the sides. Mince together all the
remaining ingredients except the
Madeira, wine, egg and pastry (paste)
and marinate in the Madeira and wine
for 1 hour. Press the mixture firmly
into the terrine, then lap the ends of
the bacon rashers over the top to
cover completely. Cover and stand the
terrine in a roasting tin (pan) of hot
water. Bake in a preheated oven at
180°C/350°F/gas mark 4 for
1½ hours.

Remove the terrine from the tin,
uncover and leave to cool completely.
Roll out the pastry on a lightly floured
surface into a square, set the terrine
in the centre and wrap the pastry
neatly around to form a parcel,
sealing the edges with beaten egg.
Set on a greased baking (cookie)
sheet with the seam underneath and
brush with egg. Roll out any pastry
trimmings and use them to decorate
the top, then brush with egg again.
Bake in a preheated oven at
220°C/425°F/gas mark 7 for
30 minutes until golden brown.
Cool thoroughly before serving cut
into slices.

Sausage plait

SERVES 4

350 g/12 oz Shortcrust Pastry
(page 164)
15 ml/1 tbsp French mustard
450 g/1 lb pork sausagemeat
1 onion, chopped
5 ml/1 tsp dried mixed herbs
Salt and freshly ground black pepper
2 hard-boiled (hard-cooked) eggs, sliced
1 egg, beaten

Roll out the pastry (paste) on a lightly
floured surface to a 30 cm/12 in
square and spread with the mustard.
Mix together the sausagemeat, onion
and herbs and season to taste.
Spread half the mixture down the
centre third of the pastry, arrange the
hard-boiled eggs on top and cover
with the remaining mixture. Cut
diagonal slits in the sides of the
pastry to within 2.5 cm/1 in of the
filling. Brush the edges of the pastry
with beaten egg, and fold alternate
strips of pastry over the filling to
make a plait. Seal the ends, place on
a greased baking (cookie) sheet and
brush with egg. Bake in a preheated
oven at 200°C/400°F/gas mark 6 for
20 minutes, then reduce the heat to
180°C/350°F/gas mark 4 and cook
for a further 20 minutes until cooked
through and golden.

Chicken and pork layer pie

SERVES 4-6

275 g/10 oz/2½ cups plain (all-purpose) flour
A pinch of salt
40 g/1½ oz lard (shortening) or vegetable fat
75 g/3 oz/⅓ cup butter or margarine
2 eggs, beaten
350 g/12 oz lean pork, finely chopped
1 onion, finely chopped
100 g/4 oz belly pork, rinded and finely chopped
5 ml/1 tsp marjoram
Salt and freshly ground black pepper
100 g/4 oz/1 cup cooked chicken, cut into strips

Mix together the flour and salt, then rub in the fats until the mixture resembles fine breadcrumbs. Reserve half an egg for glazing, and mix to a firm pastry (paste) with the remainder. Cover and chill until required.

Mix together the pork, onion, belly pork and marjoram and season to taste. Cut a 2.5 cm/1 in double strip of greaseproof (waxed) paper and lay it along the length of a greased 450 g/1 lb loaf tin (pan), sticking out at each end. Divide the pastry into six pieces, and roll it out into rectangles to fit the sides, base and top of the tin. Seal the base and sides together and fill the tin with half the pork mixture. Layer the chicken on top, then add the remaining pork and put on the pastry lid, pinching round the edge to seal and make a pattern. Roll out any trimmings and decorate the top of the pie with pastry `leaves'. Glaze well with the reserved egg and cut three steam vents in the top. Bake in a preheated oven at 200°C/400°F/ gas mark 6 for 45 minutes, then reduce the heat to 170°C/325°F/gas mark 3 for a further 45 minutes. Leave to cool in the tin.

Fidget pie

SERVES 4

350 g/12 oz lean back bacon rashers (slices), rinded
450 g/1 lb potatoes, sliced
450 g/1 lb cooking (tart) apples, peeled, cored and sliced
Salt and freshly ground black pepper
150 ml/¼ pt/⅔ cup Chicken Stock (page 28)
225 g/8 oz Shortcrust Pastry (page 164)
1 egg, beaten

Cut each bacon rasher into three pieces, and arrange layers of bacon, potatoes and apples in a large greased pie dish. Season to taste and pour in the stock. Roll out the pastry (paste) and cut a lid to fit the dish and a 2.5 cm/1 in strip round the edge. Lay the strip round the edge, then moisten the strip and place the lid on top, sealing the edges together well. Roll out the trimmings and use to decorate the top. Brush with the egg and bake in a preheated oven at 190°C/375°F/gas mark 5 for 20 minutes, then reduce the heat to 180°C/350°F/gas mark 4 and continue to cook for a further 45 minutes until cooked through and golden brown.

Pork pie

SERVES 4

750 g/12 oz lean pork, cubed
A pinch of sage
A pinch of grated nutmeg
Salt
350 g/12 oz pork bones
450 g/1 lb Hot Water Crust Pastry
   (page 164)
300 ml/½ pt/1¼ cups Chicken Stock
   (page 28)
1 egg, beaten
10 ml/2 tsp powdered gelatine

Mix together the pork, sage, nutmeg
and salt, cover and chill. Put the
bones in a saucepan, just cover with
water, add a pinch of salt, bring to the
boil and simmer gently for 2 hours.
Drop a little stock on a chilled plate to
see if it jells firmly. If not, leave to
simmer for a little longer.

Make up the pastry (paste) and set
a quarter of it aside in a warm place.
Mould the remaining pastry over an
inverted 18 cm/7 in deep cake tin
(pan) or pie dish. Leave to cool, then
ease off the tin and turn upright. Fill
with the prepared meat and 30 ml/
2 tbsp of the stock. Top with the
remaining pastry and seal the edges.
Make a hole in the centre and
decorate with pastry trimmings. Place
on a greased baking (cookie) sheet
and bake in a preheated oven at
180°C/350°F/gas mark 4 for
2¼ hours. Brush with the egg to glaze
15 minutes before the end of the
cooking time. Allow to cool.

While the pie cools, soften the
gelatine in the stock, dissolve over a
gentle heat, then bring to the boil.
Use a funnel to pour the boiling stock
into the pie through the centre hole.

Chicken, apricot and cumin pie

SERVES 4–6

350 g/12 oz/3 cups plain (all-purpose)
   flour
A pinch of salt
75 g/3 oz/⅔ cup butter or margarine
150 ml/¼ pt/⅔ cup water
450 g/1 lb chicken breast, diced
150 g/5 oz no-need-to-soak dried
   apricots, chopped
1 onion, chopped
30 ml/2 tbsp chopped parsley
30 ml/2 tbsp chopped coriander (cilantro)
1 garlic clove, crushed
5 ml/1 tsp ground cumin
30 ml/2 tbsp white wine
Salt and freshly ground black pepper
1 egg, beaten

Sift the flour and salt into a bowl and
make a well in the centre. Melt the
butter or margarine with the water,
then pour into the flour and mix to a
soft dough. Knead until smooth, then
roll out three-quarters of the pastry
(paste) and use to line a greased
23 cm/9 in flan tin (pie pan).

Mix together all the remaining
ingredients except the egg, seasoning
generously with salt and pepper.
Spoon into the pastry case (pie shell).
Roll out the reserved pastry to make a
lid, moisten the edges and seal on to
the pie, fluting the edges if you wish.
Brush with the egg. Bake in a
preheated oven at 200°C/400°F/gas
mark 6 for 30 minutes, then reduce
the oven temperature to 180°C/
350°F/gas mark 4 and continue to
cook for a further 1 hour until golden
brown, covering with foil if the pastry
browns too quickly. Leave to cool,
then chill and serve cold, cut into
wedges.

Chicken and mushroom pie

SERVES 4

25 g/1 oz/2 tbsp butter or margarine
1 onion, chopped
100 g/4 oz mushrooms, sliced
25 g/1 oz/¼ cup plain (all-purpose) flour
150 ml/¼ pt/⅔ cup milk
150 ml/¼ pt/⅔ cup Chicken Stock
   (page 28)
100 g/4 oz cooked, peeled prawns
   (shrimp)
100 g/4 oz/1 cup cooked chicken, cubed
1 hard-boiled (hard-cooked) egg,
   chopped
2.5 ml/½ tsp paprika
Salt and freshly ground black pepper
350 g/12 oz Puff Pastry (page 165)
1 egg, beaten

Melt the butter or margarine and fry (sauté) the onion until soft but not brown. Stir in the mushrooms and cook for 1 minute, then stir in the flour and cook for a further 1 minute. Stir in the milk and stock, bring to the boil, stirring, and simmer until the sauce thickens. Stir in the prawns, chicken, chopped egg and paprika and season to taste. Leave to cool.

Roll out the pastry (paste) and use half to line a greased 18 cm/7 in pie dish. Fill with the chicken mixture and top with the remaining pastry. Seal the edges, roll out the trimmings and use to decorate the top. Brush with the egg to glaze and bake in a preheated oven at 230°C/450°F/gas mark 8 for 10 minutes, then reduce the heat to 190°C/375°F/gas mark 5 for a further 20 minutes until cooked through and golden.

Hot lamb and mushroom pie

SERVES 4

15 ml/1 tbsp plain (all-purpose) flour
Salt and freshly ground black pepper
450 g/1 lb shoulder of lamb, cubed
2 lambs' kidneys, chopped
15 ml/1 tbsp oil
1 onion, chopped
300 ml/½ pt/1¼ cups Beef Stock
   (page 28)
100 g/4 oz mushrooms, halved
225 g/8 oz Shortcrust Pastry (page 164)
1 egg, beaten

Season the flour with salt and pepper and roll the lamb cubes and kidney in the flour. Heat the oil and fry (sauté) the onion until soft but not brown. Add the meat and cook until lightly browned. Stir in the stock and mushrooms, bring to the boil, then simmer for about 30 minutes until the meat is tender. Season to taste and turn into an ovenproof dish. Roll out the pastry (paste) on a lightly floured surface and use it to cover the pie. Brush with the egg and bake in a preheated oven at 200°C/400°F/gas mark 6 for 30 minutes until golden brown.

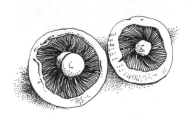

Game pie

SERVES 4

750 g/1¾ lb Hot Water Crust Pastry
(page 164)
350 g/12 oz pork sausagemeat
100 g/4 oz lean bacon, rinded and
cubed
175 g/6 oz stewing or braising steak,
cubed
1 pheasant, boned and the flesh
chopped
Salt and freshly ground black pepper
150–300 ml/¼–½ pt/⅔–1¼ cups hot
jellied stock, home-made or from the
chill cabinet
1 egg, beaten

Make up the pastry (paste) and use
three-quarters of it to line a greased
oval pie mould or round cake tin
(pan), pressing the pastry well into
the sides of the tin. Line the pastry
with a thin layer of sausagemeat. Mix
together the bacon, steak and
pheasant meat and season with salt
and pepper. Add about 60 ml/4 tbsp
of the stock and pack the meat into
the case. Cover with the remaining
pastry and seal the edges. Decorate
with pastry trimmings, make a hole in
the centre and brush with the egg.
Bake in a preheated oven at 220°C/
425°F/gas mark 7 for 30 minutes,
then reduce the heat to 190°C/
375°F/gas mark 5 for 30 minutes,
then reduce it again to 180°C/
350°F/gas mark 4 for a further
30 minutes. Cover the pie with
greaseproof (waxed) paper if it is
becoming too brown. Remove the pie
from the oven and fill with hot stock
through a funnel, then leave to cool
completely before removing from the
tin.

Country winter pie

SERVES 4

50 g/2 oz/¼ cup butter or margarine
175 g/6 oz leeks, sliced
175 g/6 oz carrots, sliced
175 g/6 oz celery sticks, sliced
175 g/6 oz parsnips, diced
225 g/8 oz/2 cups cooked ham, chopped
25 g/1 oz/¼ cup plain (all-purpose) flour
150 ml/¼ pt/⅔ cup milk
150 ml/¼ pt/⅔ cup Vegetable Stock
(page 28)
Salt and freshly ground black pepper
350 g/12 oz Shortcrust Pastry
(page 164)
1 egg, beaten

Melt the butter or margarine and fry
(sauté) the vegetables until soft but
not browned. Stir in the ham and flour
and cook for 1 minute, then stir in the
milk and stock, bring to the boil and
simmer, stirring, for a few minutes
until the sauce thickens. Season and
leave to cool.

Roll out the pastry (paste) on a
lightly floured surface and use half to
line a greased 20 cm/8 in pie dish. Fill
with the vegetable mixture and top
with the remaining pastry. Roll out the
trimmings and use to decorate the
top. Brush with the egg and cut a slit
in the centre. Bake in a preheated
oven at 200°C/400°F/gas mark 6 for
30 minutes until cooked through and
golden brown.

Rabbit pie

SERVES 6–8

2 rabbits, jointed
30 ml/2 tbsp vinegar
600 ml/1 pt/2½ cups Chicken Stock
  (page 28)
1 onion, chopped
1 leek, sliced
1 carrot, sliced
5 ml/1 tsp chopped thyme
15 ml/1 tbsp chopped parsley
Salt and freshly ground black pepper
100 g/4 oz gammon, diced
100 g/4 oz mushrooms, sliced
1 hard-boiled (hard-cooked) egg,
  chopped
50 g/2 oz/½ cup chestnuts, chopped
225 g/8 oz Shortcrust Pastry (page 164)
15 ml/1 tbsp milk

Soak the rabbits overnight in water
with the vinegar added. Drain and
transfer the meat to a saucepan. Add
just enough stock to cover the meat,
add the onion, leek, carrot and herbs
and season to taste. Bring to the boil,
then simmer gently for 30 minutes.
Leave to cool slightly. Lift out the
rabbits and remove the meat from the
bones. Mix the meat with the
gammon, mushrooms, egg and
chestnuts and place in a pie dish.
Season to taste with a little extra
parsley and thyme, if liked, and with
salt and pepper. Pour in a little
strained cooking liquor to about half-
way up the mixture. Roll out the
pastry (paste) on a lightly floured
surface and use to cover the pie.
Decorate with the pastry trimmings
and brush with the milk. Bake in a
preheated oven at 200°C/400°F/gas
mark 6 for 45 minutes until golden
brown.

Pigeon and steak pie

SERVES 6

600 ml/1 pt/2½ cups hot Chicken Stock
  (page 28)
100 g/4 oz/½ cup butter or margarine
100 g/4 oz/1 cup cooked ham, chopped
15 ml/1 tbsp chopped parsley
5 ml/1 tsp cayenne
Salt and freshly ground black pepper
1 egg yolk
3 pigeons, halved lengthways
450 g/1 lb rump steak, cut into 6 pieces
3 hard-boiled (hard-cooked) eggs,
  halved
225 g/8 oz Puff Pastry (page 165)
15 ml/1 tbsp milk

Boil the stock until reduced by half.
Mix together the butter or margarine,
ham, parsley and cayenne and season
to taste. Bind the mixture with the
egg yolk. Stuff the mixture into the
breast cavity of each bird. Place the
steak slices on the bottom of a 23
cm/9 in pie dish and lay the pigeon
halves, breast-side down, on top.
Arrange the eggs in between and
season with salt and pepper. Pour
over the stock. Roll out the pastry
(paste) and use to cover the pie.
Decorate the top with the pastry
trimmings. Brush with the milk and
make a hole in the centre for steam
to escape. Bake in a preheated oven
at 220°C/425°F/gas mark 7 for
15 minutes, then reduce the heat to
180°C/350°F/gas mark 4 and bake
for a further 1 hour.

175

Vegetable and parsley pie

SERVES 4

40 g/1½ oz/3 tbsp butter or margarine
4 carrots, sliced
25 g/1 oz/¼ cup plain (all-purpose) flour
300 ml/½ pt/1¼ cups milk, plus extra to glaze
Salt and freshly ground black pepper
100 g/4 oz cauliflower, separated into florets
100 g/4 oz broccoli, separated into florets
50 g/2 oz/½ cup cooked pearl barley
30 ml/2 tbsp chopped parsley
225 g/8 oz Wholemeal Shortcrust Pastry (page 164)

Melt the butter or margarine and fry (sauté) the carrots for 5 minutes. Stir in the flour and cook for 1 minute, then stir in the milk, bring to the boil and simmer, stirring continuously, until the sauce thickens. Season to taste with salt and pepper and remove from the heat. Bring a large pan of salted water to the boil, add the cauliflower and broccoli and blanch for 5 minutes, then drain. Add the vegetables to the sauce with the pearl barley and parsley and transfer the mixture into a 1.2 litre/2 pt/5 cup pie dish.

Roll out the pastry (paste) on a lightly floured surface and cut into a round large enough to cover the dish. Roll out the trimmings and cut a 2.5 cm/1 in strip long enough to go round the rim of the dish. Dampen the edge of the dish and press the strip round the edge, then dampen the strip of pastry and gently press on the pastry lid. Decorate with pastry trimmings and brush with milk. Bake in a preheated oven at 200°C/400°F/gas mark 6 for about 30 minutes until golden brown.

Filo mushroom tarts

SERVES 4

450 g/1 lb filo pastry (paste)
100 g/4 oz/½ cup butter or margarine, melted
15 ml/1 tbsp olive oil
35 g/1 oz pine nuts
100 g/4 oz chestnut mushrooms, sliced
100 g/4 oz shiitake mushrooms, sliced
100 g/4 oz button mushrooms, sliced
15 ml/1 tbsp chopped parsley
Salt and freshly ground black pepper
225 g/8 oz goats' cheese, sliced
Fresh mixed salad, to serve

Cut the filo sheets into 7.5 cm/3 in squares, brush with melted butter and use several overlapping layers to line four 10 cm/4 in tartlet tins, allowing the pastry to fold over the edges. Line with greaseproof (waxed) paper, then baking beans and bake in a preheated oven at 200°C/400°F/gas mark 6 for 8 minutes until golden brown. Remove from the oven, remove the paper and beans and leave to one side.

Melt the remaining butter or margarine with the oil and fry (sauté) the pine nuts gently until golden brown. Remove from the pan with a slotted spoon and drain on kitchen paper (paper towels). Add all the mushrooms to the pan and fry for about 5 minutes until soft, then stir in the parsley and season to taste. Divide the cheese between the pastry cases (pie shells), top with the mushrooms and sprinkle with pine nuts. Return the tarts to the oven at 180°C/350°F/gas mark 4 for 5 minutes until heated through, then serve at once with a mixed salad.

Steak and kidney pudding

SERVES 4

350 g/12 oz Suet Crust Pastry
(page 164)
25 g/1 oz/¼ cup plain (all-purpose) flour
Salt and freshly ground black pepper
450 g/1 lb beef steak, cut into
6 × 3 cm/2½ × 1¼ in strips
100 g/4 oz lambs' kidneys, cored and
diced
1 onion, finely chopped
150 ml/¼ pt/⅔ cup Beef Stock (page 28)

Roll out two-thirds of the pastry (paste) on a lightly floured surface and use to line a greased 1.2 litre/ 2 pt/5 cup pudding basin. Trim the edges. Season the flour with salt and pepper, then toss the meat in the flour until lightly coated. Wrap the pieces of steak around pieces of kidney and place the meat in the pudding basin. Add the onion, then pour in the stock. Roll out the remaining pastry to form a lid, dampen the edges and seal to the base. Cover with a floured cloth, tie with string and place in a saucepan. Add enough boiling water to come half way up the basin. Cover and boil for 2–3 hours, topping up with boiling water as necessary, until the pastry is cooked through and the meat is tender.

Savoury pudding

SERVES 4

100 g/4 oz/1 cup plain (all-purpose)
flour
100 g/4 oz/1 cup fine oatmeal
50 g/2 oz/1 cup fresh breadcrumbs
175 g/6 oz/1½ cups shredded (chopped)
suet
3 onions, chopped
A pinch of dried thyme
A pinch of dried marjoram
Salt and freshly ground black pepper
1 egg, beaten
20 ml/2 tbsp milk
Mashed potatoes and gravy, to serve

Mix together all the ingredients except the egg and milk, seasoning to taste with salt and pepper. Lightly beat the egg and milk, then stir in just enough of the mixture to give a soft dough. Spoon into a greased 20 cm/8 in roasting tin (pan) and bake in a preheated oven at 180°C/ 350°F/gas mark 4 for 1 hour. Serve with mashed potatoes and gravy.

Pizza

Pizza dough

MAKES 350 G/¾ LB

350 g/12 oz/3 cups strong plain (bread) flour
A pinch of salt
15 g/½ oz/1 sachet easy-blend dried yeast
15 ml/1 tsp caster (superfine) sugar
15 ml/1 tbsp olive oil
250 ml/8 fl oz/1 cup warm water

Mix together the flour, salt, yeast and sugar in a bowl or a food processor. Add the oil and gradually add enough of the warm water to mix to a smooth dough. Continue to knead until the dough is elastic and no longer sticky. Place in an oiled bowl, cover with oiled clingfilm (plastic wrap) and leave in a warm place for 1 hour, then use as required.

Pizza dough with caraway seeds

MAKES 450 G/1 LB

450 g/1 lb/4 cups strong plain (bread) flour
15 g/½ oz/1 sachet easy-blend dried yeast
5 ml/1 tsp caster (superfine) sugar
5 ml/1 tsp salt
5 ml/1 tsp ground caraway seeds
15 g/½ oz/1 tbsp lard (shortening) or vegetable fat, grated
300 ml/½ pt/1¼ cups warm water

Mix together the flour, yeast, sugar, salt and caraway seeds in a bowl or food processor. Stir in the lard or vegetable fat, then add enough of the warm water to mix to a smooth dough. Continue to knead until the dough is elastic and no longer sticky. Place in an oiled bowl, cover with oiled clingfilm (plastic wrap) and leave in a warm place for 1 hour, then use as required.

Crumbly yeast dough

MAKES 450 G/1 LB

400 g/14 oz/3½ cups plain (all-purpose) flour
15 g/½ oz/1 sachet easy-blend dried yeast
5 ml/1 tsp caster (superfine) sugar
5 ml/1 tsp salt
100 g/4 oz/½ cup butter or margarine, diced
30 ml/2 tbsp olive oil
300 ml/½ pt/1¼ cups warm milk

Mix the together flour, yeast, sugar and salt into a bowl or food processor, then rub in the butter or margarine until the mixture resembles breadcrumbs. Stir in the oil and enough of the warm milk to make a smooth dough. Continue to knead until the dough is elastic and no longer sticky. Place in an oiled bowl, cover with oiled clingfilm (plastic wrap) and leave in a warm place for 1 hour, then use as required.

Rich pizza pastry

MAKES 450 G/1 LB

400 g/1 lb/4 cups plain (all-purpose)
   flour
5 ml/1 tsp salt
5 ml/1 tsp caster (superfine) sugar
5 ml/1 tsp baking powder
150 g/5 oz/⅔ cup butter or margarine,
   diced
2 eggs, lightly beaten

Mix together the flour, salt, sugar and
baking powder. Rub in the butter or
margarine until the mixture resembles
breadcrumbs. Gradually work in
enough of the eggs to make a firm
and not sticky dough. Wrap in
clingfilm (plastic wrap) and chill for
1 hour before use.

Stuffed crust pizza dough

MAKES 450 G/1 LB

450 g/1 lb Pizza Dough (page 178)
225 g/8 oz/2 cups Mozzarella cheese,
   shredded

Roll out the dough into a circle or
rectangle on a lightly floured surface.
Sprinkle a line of cheese about
2.5 cm/1 in from the edge. Moisten
the edge of the dough and press over
the cheese to form a stuffed rim. Fill
and bake as required.

Four-cheese pizza

SERVES 4

450 g/1 lb Rich Pizza Pastry (left)
60 ml/4 tbsp tomato purée (paste)
8 tomatoes, skinned and sliced
100 g/4 oz Parma ham, cut into strips
100 g/4 oz button mushrooms, sliced
10 green olives, stoned (pitted)
5 ml/1 tsp dried oregano
Salt and freshly ground black pepper
50 g/2 oz/½ cup Gorgonzola cheese,
   grated
50 g/2 oz/½ cup Bel Paese cheese,
   shredded
50 g/2 oz/½ cup Mozzarella cheese,
   shredded
50 g/2 oz/½ cup Pecorino cheese, grated

Quarter the pastry (paste), then roll it
out into rounds on a lightly floured
surface and use to line four greased
pizza or flan tins (pie pans). Spread
the pastry with the tomato purée,
then cover with the tomatoes, ham,
mushrooms and olives. Sprinkle with
the oregano and season to taste.
Either sprinkle each of the cheeses
over a quarter of each pizza, or mix
them together and sprinkle them over
the top. Bake in a preheated oven at
200°C/400°F/gas mark 6 for about
20 minutes until hot and bubbling.
Serve immediately.

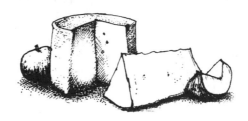

Pizza Bolognese

SERVES 4

60 ml/4 tbsp olive oil
1 onion, chopped
3 garlic cloves, chopped
450 g/1 lb minced (ground) beef or lamb
5 ml/1 tsp cayenne
5 ml/1 tsp curry powder
15 ml/1 tbsp dried oregano
200 g/7 oz/1 small can of tomatoes, chopped
30 ml/2 tbsp tomato purée (paste)
1 red (bell) pepper, chopped
2.5 ml/½ tsp mixed (apple-pie) spice
Salt and freshly ground black pepper
450 g/1 lb Rich Pizza Pastry (page 179)
50 g/2 oz/1 cup fresh breadcrumbs
8 tomatoes, skinned and sliced
225 g/8 oz/2 cups Emmental (Swiss) cheese, grated
15 ml/1 tbsp chopped parsley

Heat the oil and fry (sauté) the onion and garlic until soft, then add the mince and fry until brown and all the grains are separate. Stir in the cayenne, curry powder, oregano, tomatoes, tomato purée and red pepper. Season with the mixed spice and salt and pepper to taste. Cook over a medium heat for about 20 minutes until all the liquid has evaporated and the ingredients are thoroughly cooked.

Quarter the dough, roll it out on a lightly floured surface and use to line four greased pizza or flan tins (pie pans). Sprinkle with the breadcrumbs, then arrange the tomato slices over the top. Spoon the mince mixture over the tomatoes, sprinkle with the cheese and bake in a preheated oven at 200°C/400°F/gas mark 6 for 20 minutes. Serve sprinkled with the parsley.

Four seasons pizza

SERVES 4

450 g/1 lb Pizza Dough (page 178)
60 ml/4 tbsp tomato purée (paste)
15 ml/1 tbsp dried oregano
100 g/4 oz/1 cup Parmesan cheese, freshly grated
8 tomatoes, skinned and sliced
100 g/4 oz cooked, peeled prawns (shrimp)
100 g/4 oz Parma ham, cut into strips
100 g/4 oz salami
100 g/4 oz shelled mussels
100 g/4 oz button mushrooms, sliced
½ red (bell) pepper, cut into strips
½ green pepper, cut into strips
Salt and freshly ground black pepper
225 g/8 oz/2 cups Mozzarella cheese, shredded

Quarter the dough and roll it out into squares on a lightly floured surface. Place the dough on greased baking (cookie) sheets. Spread with the tomato purée, sprinkle with the oregano and Parmesan and arrange the tomato slices over the top. Arrange the prawns in one quarter of each dough piece, the ham in another, the salami in the third and the mussels and mushrooms in the fourth. Make a cross across the centre of the dough using a line of red pepper and a line of green pepper. Season to taste with salt and pepper and sprinkle with the Mozzarella. Bake in a preheated oven at 200°C/400°F/gas mark 6 for 20 minutes until browned and bubbling and serve immediately.

Neapolitan pizza

SERVES 4

25 g/1 oz/2 tbsp butter or margarine
2 onions, chopped
100 g/4 oz Parma ham, diced
15 ml/1 tbsp dried oregano
Salt and freshly ground black pepper
450 g/1 lb Crumbly Yeast Dough
  (page 178)
60 ml/4 tbsp tomato purée (paste)
8 tomatoes, skinned and sliced
50 g/2 oz/1 small can of anchovy fillets,
  drained
20 black olives, stoned (pitted)
225 g/8 oz Mozzarella cheese, sliced
15 ml/1 tbsp chopped parsley

Melt the butter or margarine and fry
(sauté) the onions until soft but not
brown. Add the ham and cook for
2 minutes, then season with the
oregano and salt and pepper to taste.
Remove from the heat and allow to
cool. Roll out the dough on a lightly
floured surface and place on a
greased baking (cookie) sheet or pizza
tin (pan). Spread with the tomato
purée and cover with the onions and
ham, the tomato slices, anchovies and
olives. Top with the Mozzarella and
bake in a preheated oven at 200°C/
400°F/gas mark 6 for 20 minutes.
Serve sprinkled with the parsley.

Spinach pizza

SERVES 4

450 g/1 lb young spinach, stalks
  removed
1 bunch of spring onions (scallions),
  chopped
30 ml/2 tbsp chopped parsley
2 garlic cloves, crushed
15 ml/1 tbsp olive oil
15 ml/1 tbsp tomato purée (paste)
5 ml/1 tsp cayenne
Salt and freshly ground black pepper
450 g/1 lb Pizza Dough (page 178)
1 tomato, skinned, seeded and chopped
4 eggs

Rinse the spinach and shake off any
excess water. Place in a large pan with
just the water clinging to the leaves,
cover and place over a medium heat
for a few minutes, shaking the pan
occasionally, until the leaves have
wilted. Drain and squeeze out any
excess water. Stir in the spring onions,
parsley, garlic, oil, tomato purée and
cayenne and season generously. Roll
out the dough on a lightly floured
surface and place on a greased baking
(cookie) sheet or pizza tin (pan). Fold
up the edges to make a rim. Spread
the spinach mixture over the top and
sprinkle with the tomatoes. Make four
small wells in the spinach mixture and
break in the eggs. Bake in a
preheated oven at 200°C/400°F/gas
mark 6 for 25–30 minutes until the
dough is risen and the eggs have set.

Focaccia

SERVES 4

45 ml/3 tbsp olive oil
4 large onions, sliced
3 garlic cloves, crushed
450 g/1 lb Pizza Dough (page 178)
Salt and freshly ground black pepper
50 g/2 oz black olives, stoned (pitted)

Heat the oil and fry (sauté) the onions and garlic over a low heat for about 20 minutes until soft but not browned. Roll out the dough on a lightly floured surface and place on a greased baking (cookie) sheet or large pizza tin (pan). Spread with the onion mixture and season generously with salt and pepper. Dot with the olives. Bake in a preheated oven at 200°C/ 400°F/ gas mark 6 for about 15 minutes until the dough is risen and the onions are lightly browned. Serve hot.

Summer calzone

SERVES 4

25 g/1 oz/2 tbsp butter or margarine
100 g/4 oz streaky bacon, rinded and diced
1 onion, chopped
200 g/7 oz young spinach leaves, torn into pieces
A pinch of cayenne
A pinch of grated nutmeg
Salt and freshly ground black pepper
400 g/14 oz/1 large can of tomatoes, chopped
450 g/1 lb Crumbly Yeast Dough (page 178)
225 g/8 oz/2 cups Mozzarella cheese, shredded
30 ml/2 tbsp snipped chives

Melt the butter or margarine and fry (sauté) the bacon and onion until soft but not brown. Add the spinach leaves, cayenne and nutmeg and season to taste. Cook for about 1 minute until the spinach wilts. Add the tomatoes, remove from the heat and leave to cool.

Quarter the dough, then roll it out into rounds on a lightly floured surface and use to line four greased pizza tins (pans) or flan tins (pie pans). Spread the tomato and spinach mixture on to half of each circle, then sprinkle the cheese and chives over. Moisten the edges, then fold over the empty half of the dough to seal into semi-circular pasties. Place on a greased baking (cookie) sheet and bake in a preheated oven at 200°C/ 400°F/gas mark 6 for about 20 minutes until hot and bubbling. Serve immediately.

Eggs and cheese

Speed is a great advantage of cooking with eggs and cheese, as a delicious meal can be put together in very little time. The variety of cheeses available expands every week, it seems, so you can experiment with different types to suit your own tastes.

To separate eggs, crack them over a bowl and carefully separate the shell halves. Tip the yolk from one half-shell to the other, allowing the white to slip into the bowl. The process of whisking eggs is designed to incorporate as much air as possible into the mixture, so use a large enough bowl and a balloon or electric whisk and whisk in a circular motion for best results. Egg whites must be whisked in a perfectly clean bowl. Add a pinch of salt to help the whites stiffen, and incorporate as much air as possible. Once the whites stiffen, keep the whisk in contact with the bowl until the mixture is very smooth and holds a peak when the whisk is lifted out of the bowl.

To boil eggs perfectly, use them at room temperature. Lower them gently into a saucepan of gently simmering water containing 15 ml/1 tbsp of vinegar and simmer for about 3 minutes for soft or 10 minutes for hard. For hard-boiled (hard-cooked) eggs, rinse under cold running water to prevent a dark ring forming around the yolk. To fry (sauté) eggs, heat a little oil in a frying pan (skillet), then slide in the eggs and fry for a few minutes until the base is lightly golden and crisp and the white is set, basting with the oil as you cook.

Spanish omelette

SERVES 4

45 ml/3 tbsp olive oil
2 potatoes, peeled and diced
1 large onion, sliced
Salt and freshly ground black pepper
4 eggs, beaten

Heat the oil in a frying pan (skillet) and fry (sauté) the potatoes for a few minutes until coated in oil. Add the onions and fry for about 15 minutes until the vegetables are soft but not brown. Drain off any excess oil. Add the eggs to the pan and stir quickly to mix with the vegetables, then shake the pan gently until the underside is golden and set. Using oven gloves, carefully cover the pan with a plate, invert the omelette on to the plate, then slide it back into the pan to cook the other side. Serve hot or cold, cut into wedges.

Garlic croûton omelette

SERVES 2

50 g/2 oz/¼ cup butter or margarine
2 slices of bread, cubed
1 garlic clove, crushed
5 eggs, beaten
Salt and freshly ground black pepper
15 ml/1 tbsp chopped parsley

Heat most of the butter or margarine in a frying pan (skillet) and fry (sauté) the bread cubes and garlic until crispy, stirring well. Remove from the pan and keep warm. Melt the remaining butter or margarine. Season the eggs with salt and pepper and pour into the pan. Cook until the base begins to set, lifting the sides to allow the uncooked mixture to run on to the base of the pan. When the omelette is almost set, sprinkle in the croûtons, cover and continue to cook until the omelette is just set on top and golden brown underneath. Serve immediately, sprinkled with the parsley.

Omelette

SERVES 2

Prepare as for Garlic croûton omelette, but omit the croûtons. When the egg is just set, flip over in half and serve immediately.

Piperade

SERVES 4

50 g/2 oz/¼ cup butter or margarine
2 green (bell) peppers, sliced
2 onions, sliced
1 garlic clove, crushed
450 g/1 lb tomatoes, skinned and
    chopped
Salt and freshly ground black pepper
6 eggs, beaten
45 ml/3 tbsp milk
4 bacon rashers (slices)

Melt the butter or margarine and fry (sauté) the peppers for 4 minutes. Add the onions and garlic and fry until soft but not brown. Add the tomatoes, season well and cook until the tomatoes are mushy. Beat the eggs with the milk and pour over the vegetables. Cook gently, stirring, until just set. Meanwhile, grill (broil) the bacon until crisp and browned. Transfer the eggs to a warm serving dish and serve topped with the bacon.

Frittata with goats' cheese and artichokes

SERVES 4

8 eggs
Salt and freshly ground black pepper
30 ml/2 tbsp olive oil
50 g/2 oz/½ cup lean ham, chopped
200 g/17 oz/1 small can of artichoke
  hearts, drained and sliced
15 ml/1 tbsp chopped parsley
5 ml/1 tsp chopped thyme
150 g/5 oz/1¼ cups goats' cheese, diced
Mixed salad leaves, to garnish

Beat the eggs lightly and season with salt and pepper. Heat the oil in a large flameproof frying pan (skillet), pour in the egg mixture and as the underside sets, gradually pull the edges towards the centre so that the uncooked egg runs underneath. When the top is still runny, sprinkle with the ham, artichokes, herbs and cheese and continue to cook for another 1–2 minutes, then transfer to a hot grill (broiler) for a few minutes until the top is set and golden. Serve cut into wedges, garnished with the salad leaves.

Eggs with black butter

SERVES 4

4 eggs
100 g/4 oz/½ cup butter or margarine
4 slices of bread
15 ml/1 tbsp chopped parsley
2 gherkins (cornichons), chopped
10 ml/2 tsp capers, chopped
Salt and freshly ground black pepper
30 ml/2 tbsp white wine vinegar
Boiled potatoes and green salad, to
  serve

Poach the eggs and keep them warm but do not let them overcook. Melt half the butter or margarine and fry (sauté) the bread until crisp, then drain it well on kitchen paper (paper towels). Arrange the bread on a serving plate and top with the eggs. Heat the remaining butter or margarine until a deep nut brown. Quickly stir in the parsley, gherkins and capers and season to taste, then pour over the eggs. Add the wine vinegar to the pan, boil to reduce by half, then pour it over the eggs. Serve with boiled potatoes and a green salad.

Baked eggs in green peppers

SERVES 4

2 large green (bell) peppers
15 ml/1 tbsp olive oil
75 g/3 oz/1½ cups fresh breadcrumbs
25 g/1 oz/2 tbsp butter or margarine
3 tomatoes, skinned and chopped
1 garlic clove, crushed
Salt and freshly ground black pepper
8 eggs
Boiled or fried rice, to serve

Halve the peppers and remove the core and seeds. Blanch in boiling water for 5 minutes, then drain. Brush the peppers inside and out with the oil, then stand them in a shallow baking tin (pan). Divide the breadcrumbs between the peppers, dot with half the butter or margarine, the tomatoes and garlic and season to taste. Break the eggs into the pepper halves, dot with the remaining butter or margarine and bake in a preheated oven at 180°C/350°F/gas mark 4 for 15 minutes until the eggs have set. Serve with boiled or fried rice.

Curried egg mousse

SERVES 4

4 hard-boiled (hard-cooked) eggs
150 ml/¼ pt/⅔ cup Mayonnaise
    (page 277)
10 ml/2 tsp oil
1 small onion, chopped
10 ml/2 tsp curry powder
150 ml/¼ pt/⅔ cup Chicken Stock
    (page 28)
5 ml/1 tsp apricot jam (jelly)
2.5 ml/½ tsp tomato purée (paste)
Juice of ½ lemon
30 ml/2 tbsp cold water
15 ml/1 tbsp powdered gelatine
60 ml/4 tbsp double (heavy) cream,
    whipped
Salt and freshly ground black pepper
2 watercress sprigs

Sieve the egg yolks and chop the
whites, then fold them into the
mayonnaise. Heat the oil and fry
(sauté) the onion until soft but not
brown. Add the curry powder and
cook for 1 minute. Add the stock,
jam, tomato purée and lemon juice,
bring to the boil and simmer for
5 minutes, stirring occasionally. Place
the water in a small bowl and sprinkle
the gelatine over. Stand the bowl in a
pan of hot water until the gelatine
dissolves. Leave to cool slightly, then
stir into the egg mayonnaise. Fold in
the cream and season to taste with
salt and pepper. Pour into a wetted
900 ml/1½ pt/3¾ cup ring mould and
leave to set. Unmould and serve
garnished with the watercress sprigs.

Eggs with cucumber sauce

SERVES 4

50 g/2 oz/¼ cup butter or margarine
1 cucumber, peeled and chopped
5 ml/1 tsp plain (all-purpose) flour
150 ml/¼ pt/⅔ cup hot Vegetable Stock
    (page 28)
30 ml/2 tbsp chopped dill (dill weed)
Salt and freshly ground black pepper
60 ml/4 tbsp double (heavy) cream
4 hard-boiled (hard-cooked) eggs, sliced

Melt the butter or margarine and fry
(sauté) the cucumber for 5 minutes.
Stir in the flour and cook for
1 minute, then stir in the stock and
half the dill. Season to taste. Bring to
the boil and simmer for 10 minutes,
then stir in the cream. Arrange the
eggs on a warm serving dish, pour
over the sauce and serve sprinkled
with the remaining dill.

Yorkshire pudding

SERVES 4

2 eggs, beaten
250 ml/8 fl oz/1 cup milk
A pinch of salt
100 g/4 oz/1 cup plain (all-purpose)
    flour
Oil, for greasing

Beat together the eggs and milk, then
gradually whisk in the salt and flour to
make a thickish batter. Leave to stand
for 30 minutes, if possible, then whisk
again. Grease a Yorkshire pudding tin
(pan) and preheat it in the oven to
200°C/400°F/gas mark 6. Pour in the
batter, then cook in the oven for
about 20 minutes until well risen and
golden brown.

Pancakes

SERVES 4

100 g/4 oz/1 cup plain (all-purpose)
    flour
A pinch of salt
300 ml/½ pt/1¼ cups milk
1 egg, beaten
15 ml/1 tbsp butter or margarine,
    melted
Oil, for frying
Lemon juice and caster (superfine) sugar,
    to serve (optional)

Whisk together the flour, salt, milk
and egg to a smooth batter. Whisk in
the melted butter or margarine. Leave
to stand for 30 minutes, if possible,
then whisk again before using. Heat a
little oil in the base of a small frying
pan (skillet) and pour in just enough
of the batter to cover the base of the
pan, tipping the pan to spread it over
the base. Cook for a few minutes until
the bottom begins to brown, then flip
over and cook the other side. Remove
from the pan and keep warm while
you fry (sauté) the remaining
pancakes. Serve rolled and sprinkled
with lemon juice and sugar, if liked, or
use a savoury filling.

Mushroom and egg pancakes

SERVES 4

100 g/4 oz/1 cup plain (all-purpose)
    flour
A pinch of salt
1 egg
300 ml/½ pt/1¼ cups milk
30 ml/2 tbsp oil
50 g/2 oz/¼ cup butter or margarine
100 g/4 oz mushrooms, sliced
1 garlic clove, crushed
15 ml/1 tbsp chopped parsley
5 ml/1 tsp thyme
30 ml/2 tbsp soured (dairy sour) cream
1 hard-boiled (hard-cooked) egg,
    chopped
Salt and freshly ground black pepper
25 g/1 oz/¼ cup Parmesan cheese,
    freshly grated

Mix together the flour and salt, make
a well in the centre and beat in the
egg, then whisk in the milk to make a
smooth batter. Heat half the oil and
fry (sauté) the pancakes until golden
brown on both sides, then layer them
in greaseproof (waxed) paper and
keep warm. Melt the butter or
margarine and fry the mushrooms and
garlic until soft, then stir in the herbs
and continue to cook until the
mushrooms are tender. Stir in the
soured cream and egg. Divide the
mixture between the pancakes, roll
them up, brush with the remaining
butter or margarine and sprinkle with
the Parmesan. Brown for a few
seconds under a hot grill (broiler)
before serving.

Buttered eggs with smoked salmon

SERVES 4

5 eggs, beaten
Salt and freshly ground black pepper
300 ml/½ pt/1¼ cups double (heavy)
    cream
100 g/4 oz smoked salmon, diced
25 g/1 oz/2 tbsp butter or margarine
15 ml/1 tbsp chopped parsley
A pinch of cayenne

Season the eggs to taste and beat in
15 ml/1 tbsp of the cream and the
smoked salmon. Melt the butter or
margarine and scramble the egg
mixture until just set. Transfer to a
warm serving dish and keep warm.
Bring the remaining cream to the boil
and pour it over the eggs. Serve at
once, garnished with the parsley and
dusted with the cayenne.

Mexican eggs

SERVES 4

5 eggs
100 g/4 oz/½ cup butter or margarine
2 onions, chopped
1 green (bell) pepper, chopped
300 g/11 oz canned sweetcorn (corn)
    kernels, drained
15 ml/1 tbsp tomato pickle
Salt and freshly ground black pepper
15 ml/1 tbsp plain (all-purpose) flour
250 ml/8 fl oz/1 cup milk
60 ml/4 tbsp double (heavy) cream
75 g/3 oz/¾ cup Cheddar cheese, grated

Soft boil the eggs, shell them and
keep them in warm water. Melt
50 g/2 oz/¼ cup of the butter or
margarine and fry (sauté) the onions
until soft and just beginning to brown,
then add the green pepper and
sweetcorn and heat through. Stir in

half the remaining butter or margarine
and the pickle and season to taste.
Shake over the heat until very hot,
then set aside and keep warm. Melt
the remaining butter or margarine,
stir in the flour and pour on the milk.
Whisk until the sauce boils and
thickens. Remove from the heat. Stir
the cream and nearly all the cheese
into the sauce. Turn the corn mixture
into an ovenproof dish, drain the eggs
and arrange on top and cover with
the sauce. Sprinkle with the remaining
cheese and brown under a hot grill
(broiler).

Spanish baked eggs

SERVES 4

25 g/4 oz/½ cup butter or margarine
2 onions, chopped
4 tomatoes, skinned and sliced
1 garlic clove, crushed
8 eggs
100 g/4 oz/1 cup Parmesan cheese,
    freshly grated
150 ml/¼ pt/⅔ cup double (heavy) cream
Salt and freshly ground black pepper

Melt the butter or margarine and fry
(sauté) the onions until soft but not
brown. Stir in the tomatoes and garlic
and fry for 2 minutes. Transfer to a
greased shallow ovenproof dish, break
in the eggs, sprinkle with the cheese
and pour the cream over. Season to
taste and bake in a preheated oven
at 180°C/350°F/gas mark 4 for
about 15 minutes until the egg whites
have set.

Onion and pepper tart

SERVES 4

175 g/6 oz/1½ cups plain (all-purpose)
flour
A pinch of salt
75 g/3 oz/⅓ cup butter or margarine
30 ml/2 tbsp cold water
15 ml/1 tbsp oil
1 onion, sliced
1 red (bell) pepper, sliced
2 eggs, beaten
150 ml/¼ pt/⅔ cup single (light) cream
50 g/2 oz/½ cup strong cheese, grated
Salt and freshly ground black pepper

Mix together the flour and salt, then
rub in the butter or margarine until
the mixture resembles fine
breadcrumbs. Add the water gradually
until the mixture forms a pastry
(paste) that comes away cleanly from
the side of the bowl. Roll out and use
to line a 20 cm/8 in flan ring. Heat
the oil in a frying pan (skillet) and fry
(sauté) the onion until soft but not
brown. Add the pepper and cook for
5 minutes, then spread the mixture in
the flan ring. Mix together the eggs,
cream and cheese and season to
taste. Pour over the flan and bake in a
preheated oven at 200°C/400°F/gas
mark 6 for 30 minutes until set and
risen.

Quiche Lorraine

SERVES 4

175 g/6 oz/1½ cups plain (all-purpose)
flour
Salt and freshly ground black pepper
75 g/3 oz/⅓ cup butter or margarine
30 ml/2 tbsp cold water
175 g/6 oz streaky bacon, rinded and
chopped
2 eggs, beaten
150 ml/¼ pt/⅔ cup single (light) cream
175 g/6 oz/1½ cups strong cheese,
grated

Season the flour with salt and pepper,
then rub in the butter or margarine
until the mixture resembles fine
breadcrumbs. Mix in enough of the
water to make a firm dough. Roll out
on a lightly floured surface and use to
line a 20 cm/8 in flan ring. Scatter the
bacon over the pastry (paste). Mix
together the eggs, cream and cheese
and pour the mixture into the flan
case (pie shell). Bake in a preheated
oven at 220°C/425°F/gas mark 7 for
8 minutes, then reduce the heat to
190°C/375°F/gas mark 5 for a further
30 minutes until firm and golden
brown. Serve hot or cold.

Leek and Stilton flan

SERVES 4

75 g/3 oz/¾ cup plain (all-purpose) flour
75g /3 oz/¾ cup wholemeal flour
100 g/4 oz/½ cup butter or margarine
50 g/2 oz/½ cup Stilton cheese, grated
30 ml/2 tbsp water
450 g/1 lb leeks, sliced
100 g/4 oz streaky bacon, rinded and
    chopped
150 ml/¼ pt/⅔ cup single (light) cream
2 eggs, beaten
2.5 ml/½ tsp made English mustard
Salt and freshly ground black pepper
Salad, to serve

Sift the flours into a bowl and rub in
75 g/3 oz/⅓ cup of the butter or
margarine and half the cheese until
the mixture resembles fine
breadcrumbs. Add the water gradually
until the mixture forms a pastry
(paste) that comes away cleanly from
the side of the bowl. Roll out and use
to line a 23 cm/9 in flan ring. Melt
the remaining butter or margarine in a
frying pan (skillet) and fry (sauté) the
leeks gently for 15 minutes until soft.
Allow to cool, then place the leeks in
the pastry case (pie shell) and
sprinkle with the bacon. Mix together
the cream, eggs, mustard, salt and
pepper and pour over the flan.
Sprinkle with the remaining cheese
and bake in a preheated oven at
200°C/400°F/gas mark 6 for
30 minutes. Serve hot with a salad.

Broad bean and cheese flan

SERVES 4

25 g/1 oz/2 tbsp lard (shortening) or
    vegetable fat
25 g/1 oz/2 tbsp butter or margarine
100 g/4 oz/1 cup wholemeal plain flour
30 ml/2 tbsp water
5 ml/1 tsp light brown sugar
5 ml/1 tsp oil
100 g/4 oz/½ cup curd (smooth cottage)
    cheese
2 eggs, beaten
200 ml/7 fl oz/scant 1 cup milk
Salt and freshly ground black pepper
10 ml/2 tsp chopped parsley
100 g/4 oz canned broad (fava) beans,
    drained
2 tomatoes, sliced

Rub the fats into the flour until the
mixture resembles fine breadcrumbs.
Mix together the water, sugar and oil
and use to bind the pastry (paste).
Leave to rest in the fridge for
30 minutes, then use to line a 20 cm/
8 in flan ring. Beat the cheese in a
bowl until soft. Mix together the eggs
and milk, season to taste with salt,
pepper and the parsley, then beat into
the cheese. Arrange the beans in the
base of the flan ring and pour the
cheese mixture on top. Arrange the
tomato slices over the top. Bake in a
preheated oven at 200°C/400°F/gas
mark 6 for 30 minutes until brown
and set.

Quiche Provençale

SERVES 4

225 g/8 oz/2 cups plain (all-purpose)
   flour
Salt and freshly ground black pepper
100 g/4 oz/½ cup butter or margarine
25 g/1 oz lard (shortening) or vegetable
   fat
1 egg yolk
30 ml/2 tbsp iced water
1 onion, sliced
1 garlic clove, crushed
100 g/4 oz mushrooms, sliced
1 courgette (zucchini), chopped
2 tomatoes, skinned and chopped
15 ml/1 tbsp chopped basil
5 ml/1 tsp dried mixed herbs
2 eggs, beaten
150 ml/¼ pt/⅔ cup single (light) cream
50g/2 oz/½ cup Cheddar cheese, grated
25 g/1 oz/¼ cup Gruyère (Swiss) cheese,
   grated

Mix together the flour and a pinch of
salt and rub in 75 g/3 oz/⅓ cup of the
butter or margarine and the lard or
vegetable fat until the mixture
resembles fine breadcrumbs. Stir in the
egg yolk and enough of the water to
make a firm dough. Roll out and use
to line a 23 cm/9 in flan ring and chill
for 30 minutes. Bake blind in a
preheated oven at 190°C/375°F/gas
mark 5 for 15 minutes. Melt the
remaining butter or margarine and
fry (sauté) the onion and garlic for
5 minutes. Add the vegetables and
herbs, season to taste and cook for
10 minutes. Beat together the eggs
and cream and stir in the cheeses.
Spoon the cooked mixture over the
flan case (pie shell) and pour in the
egg mixture. Bake for 30 minutes until
set and golden brown on top. Serve
hot or cold.

Parsnip, cheese and almond quiche

SERVES 6

225 g/8 oz Wholemeal Shortcrust Pastry
   (page 164)
450 g/1 lb parsnips, sliced
175 g/6 oz carrots, sliced
300 ml/½ pt/1¼ cups single (light) cream
Salt and freshly ground black pepper
3 eggs, beaten
45 ml/3 tbsp plain yoghurt
50 g/2 oz/½ cup Cheddar cheese, grated
50 g/2 oz/½ cup flaked (slivered)
   almonds

Roll out the pastry (paste) and use to
line a 25 cm/10 in flan ring. Bake
blind in a preheated oven at 200°C/
400°F/gas mark 6 for 20 minutes.
Put the parsnips, carrots and cream in
a saucepan, season to taste, bring to
the boil and simmer for 20 minutes
until the vegetables are tender. Purée
in a food processor or blender until
not quite smooth, then blend in the
eggs and yoghurt. Pour the mixture
into the flan case (pie shell), sprinkle
on the cheese and almonds and
return to the oven for 20 minutes
until risen and firm. Serve hot or cold.

Gruyère cheese roll

SERVES 4

6 eggs
Salt and freshly ground black pepper
175 g/6 oz/1½ cups Gruyère (Swiss)
    cheese, grated
40 ml/2½ tbsp plain (all-purpose) flour
25 g/1 oz/2 tbsp butter or margarine
150 ml/¼ pt/⅔ cup milk
30 ml/2 tbsp double (heavy) cream
30 ml/2 tbsp chopped parsley

Separate 5 of the eggs. Season the yolks lightly with salt and pepper and beat until pale. Beat in two-thirds of the cheese and 25 g/1 oz/¼ cup of the flour. Whisk the 5 egg whites with a pinch of salt until semi-stiff. Stir 45 ml/3 tbsp into the yolk mixture, then fold in the rest. Spread the mixture in a greased and lined Swiss roll tin (jelly roll pan) and bake in a preheated oven at 180°C/350°F/gas mark 4 for 15 minutes until firm.

Meanwhile, melt the butter or margarine in a saucepan, stir in the remaining flour and cook for 1 minute. Whisk in the milk and cream and cook, stirring, until the sauce thickens. Remove from the heat. Beat the remaining whole egg and add it to the sauce with the remaining cheese and half the parsley. Remove the roll from the oven, turn out of the tin on to a sheet of greaseproof (waxed) paper and peel off the lining paper. Spread the filling over the inverted roll, leaving a 2.5 cm/1 in gap at the end. Roll up so that the cut end is underneath and place on the tin. Return the roll to the oven for 10 minutes and serve at once, sprinkled with the remaining parsley.

Cheese pudding

SERVES 4

300 ml/½ pt/1¼ cups milk
50 g/2 oz/1 cup fresh breadcrumbs
2 eggs, separated
40 g/1½ oz/⅓ cup Cheshire cheese,
    grated
50 g/2 oz/½ cup Parmesan cheese,
    freshly grated
15 ml/1 tbsp butter or margarine,
    softened
A pinch of ground mace
Salt and freshly ground black pepper

Bring the milk to the boil and pour it over the breadcrumbs in a bowl. Leave to stand for 10 minutes. Beat in the egg yolks, then the cheeses and butter or margarine. Add the mace and season to taste. Whisk the egg whites until just stiff, stir a spoonful into the cheese mixture, then fold in the rest. Turn the mixture into a greased deep pie dish and bake in a preheated oven at 180°C/350°F/gas mark 4 for 30 minutes.

Camembert puffs with conserve

SERVES 4

350 g/12 oz Camembert, cut into 8
    wedges and chilled
15 ml/1 tbsp plain (all-purpose) flour
2 eggs, beaten
100 g/4 oz/1 cup fresh breadcrumbs
Corn oil, for deep-frying
60 ml/4 tbsp gooseberry or cherry jam
    (jelly)

Dust the chilled cheese wedges with the flour, then dip in the egg and coat with the breadcrumbs. Fry (sauté) in deep hot oil for 4 minutes, then drain well on kitchen paper (paper towels) and serve immediately with the jam.

Blue cheese tarts with red onions

SERVES 4

900 g/2 lb red onions, very thinly sliced
150 ml/¼ pt/⅔ cup olive oil
15 ml/1 tbsp caster (superfine) sugar
Salt and freshly ground black pepper
225 g/8 oz Puff Pastry (page 165)
1 egg
150 g/5 oz/1¼ cup blue cheese, crumbled
50 g/2 oz/¼ cup Mascarpone cheese

Place the onions and oil in a heavy-based pan over a very low heat, cover and cook gently for about 45 minutes, stirring regularly, until very soft. Add the sugar and season with salt and pepper. Cover and continue to cook gently for about 1 hour until the onions have caramelised. It is important to cook them slowly otherwise they will burn before they go soft and dark.

Roll out the pastry (paste) on a lightly floured surface and use to line four greased 10 cm/4 in tart tins (pans). Chill while you complete the filling. Beat the egg with the Mascarpone and blue cheeses. Spoon into the pastry shells and bake in a preheated oven at 200°C/400°F/gas mark 6 for about 20 minutes until golden brown. Serve hot with a spoonful of the onion preserve.

Light cheese soufflé

SERVES 4

25 g/1 oz/2 tbsp butter or margarine
25 g/1 oz/¼ cup plain (all-purpose) flour
150 ml/¼ pt/⅔ cup milk
75 g/3 oz/¾ cup Cheddar cheese, grated
3 eggs, separated
A pinch of cayenne
Salt and freshly ground black pepper

Melt the butter or margarine, stir in the flour and cook for 1 minute. Whisk in the milk and cook, stirring, until the sauce thickens. Remove from the heat, allow to cool slightly, then stir in the cheese. Gradually beat in the egg yolks, cayenne and seasoning. Whisk the egg whites until stiff, stir a spoonful into the cheese mixture, then fold in the rest. Turn the mixture into a greased soufflé dish and score a circular slit round the top of the mixture about 2 cm/¾ in from the edge. Bake in a preheated oven at 200°C/400°F/gas mark 6 for 30 minutes until risen and golden. Serve immediately.

Cheese and spinach cutlets

SERVES 4

450 g/1 lb frozen chopped spinach
25 g/1 oz/2 tbsp butter or margarine
3 egg yolks, beaten
225 g/8 oz/2 cups Cheddar cheese, grated
A pinch of grated nutmeg
Salt and freshly ground black pepper
100 g/4 oz/2 cups fresh breadcrumbs

Heat the spinach in a saucepan until thawed, then bring to the boil and simmer for 3 minutes until tender and dry. Drain well and stir in half the butter or margarine. Spread the mixture on a plate and leave to cool for 10 minutes, then mix in 2 egg yolks, the cheese and nutmeg and season to taste with salt and pepper. Chill for 15 minutes. Shape into eight oval patties and pinch one end to make a cutlet shape. Coat with beaten egg yolk, then breadcrumbs, then repeat. Grill (broil) gently until golden brown, turning once. Melt the remaining butter or margarine and sprinkle on the cutlets.

Délices au Gruyère

SERVES 4

50 g/2 oz/¼ cup butter or margarine
50 g/2 oz/½ cup plain (all-purpose) flour
450 ml/¾ pt/2 cups boiling milk
100 g/4 oz/1 cup Gruyère (Swiss)
   cheese, grated
A pinch of grated nutmeg
2 egg yolks
Salt and freshly ground black pepper
1 egg, beaten
30 ml/2 tbsp cold milk
15 ml/1 tbsp olive oil
100 g/4 oz/2 cups fresh breadcrumbs
Corn oil, for deep-frying
1 lemon, cut into wedges
4 parsley sprigs

Melt the butter or margarine in the
top of a double saucepan, stir in half
the flour and cook until smooth.
Whisk in the boiling milk and simmer
until thickened. Stir in the cheese and
nutmeg and cook until the cheese has
melted. Remove from the heat, stir in
the egg yolks and season to taste.
Continue to cook over the hot water
for 2 minutes without letting the
mixture boil. Spread in a greased
rectangular baking tin (pan) and leave
to cool.

Just before serving, cut into
rectangles and dip in the remaining
flour. Beat the whole egg with the
cold milk and oil, then dip the
rectangles in the mixture and roll in
the breadcrumbs. Fry (sauté) in deep
hot oil until golden brown and serve
immediately garnished with the lemon
wedges and parsley sprigs.

Feta with roast tomatoes and herbs

SERVES 4

300 g/12 oz/3 cups Feta cheese, cut into
   chunks
2 garlic cloves, sliced
2 rosemary sprigs
2 thyme sprigs
2 bay leaves
120 ml/4 fl oz/½ cup olive oil
450 g/1 lb ripe plum tomatoes, halved
   lengthways
25 g/1 oz basil leaves, torn
25 g/1 oz parsley, chopped
25 g/1 oz thyme leaves
Salt and freshly ground black pepper
Crusty bread, to serve

Put the cheese, garlic, rosemary,
thyme and bay leaves in a screw-
topped jar and pour over the olive oil
to cover. Chill for 2–3 days.

Arrange the tomatoes in a roasting
tin (pan) and sprinkle with the basil,
parsley and thyme. Sprinkle with a
little of the oil from the Feta jar and
season generously with salt and
pepper. Roast in a preheated oven at
250°C/475°F/gas mark 9 for
15 minutes, then reduce the oven
temperature to 150°C/300°F/gas
mark 2 and cook for a further 1 hour.
Remove from the oven and leave to
cool. Serve the tomatoes with the
drained Feta cheese and with chunks
of crusty bread.

Pulses, grains and pasta

There is almost no limit to the versatility of these ingredients: they can be a base for vegetarian meals, served as a side dish or accompaniment or used to extend casseroles or bakes.

If you use pulses regularly, you may want to buy them dried, which is very economical. Most need soaking overnight in cold water, then boiling for between 20 minutes and 2 hours until tender – there will be full instructions on the packets. Dried red kidney beans must be boiled rapidly for 5 minutes before simmering to kill the natural toxins they contain. Canned pulses are much easier and generally very good quality.

There's now a wide range of rices to choose from. If you buy a rice labelled 'quick-cook' or 'easy', it means exactly that, and you will have to reduce the cooking time and keep an eye on the rice to make sure it does not go soggy. The easiest way to test if rice is cooked is to lift out a few grains on a slotted spoon and press them between your finger and thumb, or bite them. As soon as they are just tender, stop cooking.

Pasta has long been popular and is now available in a vast range of shapes and sizes, both fresh and dried. Fresh pasta can always be substituted for dried in any recipe, but needs cooking for only 2–3 minutes, instead of about 10. There are no hard and fast rules on which shape of pasta to serve with which sauce, but generally speaking you should match a robust sauce with a chunky pasta and a delicate sauce with a slender pasta. Again, the best test for when it is done is the taste test: pasta is cooked when it is *al dente* – just tender but with a hint of bite. Check the Vegetarian dishes (pages 230–248) for more recipes.

Pulses

Home-made baked beans

SERVES 4

450 g/1 lb/2⅔ cups haricot (navy)
    beans, soaked overnight and drained
2 bay leaves
4 cloves
30 ml/2 tbsp black treacle (molasses)
300 ml/½ pt/1¼ cups water
15 ml/1 tbsp plain (all-purpose) flour
15 ml/1 tbsp milk
A pinch of basil
Salt and freshly ground black pepper
225 g/8 oz tomatoes, skinned and
    chopped

Place the beans in a saucepan, just
cover with fresh water and add the
bay leaves and cloves. Bring to the
boil and simmer for 1½ hours, then
drain and discard the cloves and bay
leaves. Dilute the treacle with the
water and mix the flour to a thin
paste with the milk. Add this to the
molasses with the basil and season
with salt and pepper. Put the beans in
a greased casserole dish (Dutch
oven), cover with the tomatoes and
sauce and bake in a preheated oven
at 180°C/350°F/gas mark 4 for
1 hour until the beans are tender.

Cassoulet

SERVES 4

450 g/1 lb/2⅔ cups haricot (navy)
    beans, soaked overnight and drained
175 g/6 oz belly pork, rinded and
    chopped
4 garlic cloves, chopped
1.2 litres/2 pts/5 cups water
30 ml/2 tbsp oil
900 g/2 lb shoulder of lamb, boned and
    cubed
2 bay leaves
5 parsley stalks
2 blades of mace
6 whole black peppercorns
400 g/14 oz/1 large can of tomatoes
30 ml/2 tsp tomato purée (paste)
100 g/4 oz/2 cups fresh wholemeal
    breadcrumbs

Place the beans, pork and garlic in a
flameproof casserole dish (Dutch
oven), pour on the water, bring to the
boil, cover and simmer for 1 hour.
Heat the oil and fry (sauté) the lamb
until just browned, then add it to the
casserole. Tie the herbs and spices
together in a square of muslin
(cheesecloth) or cotton and hang
them from the edge of the casserole.
Simmer gently for 2 hours, stirring
occasionally and adding extra water if
necessary. Stir in the tomatoes and
tomato purée and cook for a further
1 hour until the sauce is thick and
creamy. Sprinkle the breadcrumbs
over the top of the casserole, then
bake in a preheated oven at 190°C/
360°F/gas mark 5 until brown and
crispy on top.

Chick pea curry

SERVES 4

50 g/2oz/¼ cup butter or margarine
1 large onion, sliced
10 ml/2 tsp curry powder
5 ml/1 tsp turmeric
A pinch of ground ginger
15 ml/1 tbsp desiccated (shredded)
   coconut
60 ml/4 tbsp boiling water
225 g/8 oz/1 small can of chick peas
   (garbanzos), drained
300 ml/½ pt/1¼ cups Vegetable Stock
   (page 28)
15 g/½ oz/1 tbsp sultanas (golden
   raisins)
1 bay leaf
1 red (bell) pepper, sliced
1 leek, sliced
Salt and freshly ground black pepper
Boiled rice, to serve

Melt the butter or margarine and fry
(sauté) the onion until soft but not
brown. Stir in the spices and cook for
1 minute. Infuse the coconut in the
boiling water for 10 minutes, then
strain the liquid into the pan and
discard the coconut. Add the chick
peas, stock, sultanas and bay leaf,
bring to the boil, cover and simmer
for 25 minutes. Add the red pepper
and leek, season to taste and cook for
a further 20 minutes until the
vegetables are tender and the sauce
is thick. Serve hot with boiled rice.

Haricot beans Provençale

SERVES 4

15 ml/1 tbsp olive oil
2 onions, sliced
1 garlic clove, chopped
400 g/14 oz/1 large can of tomatoes,
   drained
225 g/8 oz/1 medium can of haricot
   (navy) beans
Salt and freshly ground black pepper
15 ml/1 tbsp chopped parsley

Heat the oil in a saucepan and fry
(sauté) the onions and garlic until soft
but not brown. Add the tomatoes and
beans and season to taste. Continue
to cook until heated through, then
serve sprinkled with the parsley.

Pease pudding

SERVES 4

225 g/8 oz/1⅛ cups split peas, soaked
   for 30 minutes and drained
50 g/2 oz/¼ cup butter or margarine
1 large onion, chopped
1 egg, beaten
Salt and freshly ground black pepper

Place the peas in a saucepan and just
cover with cold water. Bring to the
boil and simmer until tender, then
drain. Melt in the butter or margarine
and fry (sauté) the onion until soft but
not browned. Stir in the peas and egg
and season to taste. Turn into a lightly
greased casserole dish (Dutch oven)
and bake at 180°C/350°F/gas mark 4
for 30 minutes. Serve hot, cut into
slices, with roast meats.

Aduki burgers

SERVES 4

175 g/6 oz/1 cup aduki beans, soaked
  overnight
2 carrots, grated
25 g/1 oz/¼ cup cashew nuts, chopped
50 g/2 oz/1 cup wholemeal breadcrumbs
A few drops of soy sauce
2.5 ml/½ tsp yeast extract
Salt and freshly ground black pepper
1 egg, beaten
30 ml/2 tsp oil
Wholemeal baps and salad, to serve

Drain and rinse the beans and cook in
boiling salted water for 30 minutes.
Drain well and mash. Add the carrots,
nuts, breadcrumbs, soy sauce, yeast
extract and seasoning to taste and
mash together. Add enough of the
egg to bind the mixture and shape it
into four burgers. Chill for 30 minutes
before shallow frying in the oil. Serve
hot in wholemeal baps with salad.

Boston beans

SERVES 4

30 ml/2 tbsp oil
225 g/8 oz belly pork, rinded and cubed
1 onion, chopped
1 garlic clove, chopped
400 g/14 oz/1 large can of tomatoes
10 ml/2 tsp tomato purée (paste)
450 g/1 lb/2⅔ cups haricot (navy)
  beans, soaked overnight and drained
600 ml/1 pt/2½ cups Vegetable Stock
  (page 28)

Heat the oil and fry (sauté) the pork
lightly in a large saucepan until
browned. Lift out the meat with a
draining spoon. Fry the onion and
garlic, then add the tomatoes, tomato
purée, beans and meat. Stir well to
break up the tomatoes. Add the

stock, bring to the boil, part-cover
and simmer for 40 minutes until the
beans are tender and the sauce is
thick and creamy.

Chick pea goulash

SERVES 4

45 ml/3 tbsp olive oil
2 shallots, chopped
1 garlic clove, crushed
1 carrot, chopped
15 ml/1 tbsp paprika
400 g/14 oz/1 large can of chick peas
  (garbanzos)
60 ml/4 tbsp passata (sieved tomatoes)
15 ml/1 tbsp tomato purée (paste)
15 ml/1 tbsp chopped parsley
Salt and freshly ground black pepper
225 g/8 oz ribbon noodles
150 ml/¼ pt/⅔ cup crème fraîche

Heat the oil and fry (sauté) the
shallots, garlic and carrot until soft
but not brown. Stir in the paprika,
then the chick peas and their liquid
and fry for 1 minute. Stir in the
passata, tomato purée and parsley,
bring to the boil, then simmer for
about 10 minutes until thickened.
Season to taste. Meanwhile, bring a
large pan of salted water to the boil,
add the noodles and cook until
tender. Drain well, then arrange on a
serving plate. Spoon the goulash over
the noodles and garnish with the
crème fraîche.

Lentil stew with dumplings

SERVES 4

225 g/8 oz/1⅓ cups lentils, soaked
600 ml/1 pt/2½ cups Vegetable Stock
  (page 28)
225 g/8 oz baby carrots
100 g/4 oz mushrooms, sliced
2 large onions, finely chopped
30 ml/2 tbsp vinegar
5 ml/1 tsp thyme
Salt and freshly ground black pepper
100 g/4 oz/1 cup self-raising (self-rising)
  flour
50 g/2 oz/½ cup shredded (chopped)
  suet
½ small onion, finely chopped
15 ml/1 tbsp chopped parsley
30 ml/2 tbsp water
Water or stock, for cooking the
  dumplings

Drain the lentils and place in a large saucepan with the stock, carrots, mushrooms, onions, vinegar and thyme. Season to taste, bring to the boil and simmer for 30 minutes until the lentils are tender. Continue cooking, stirring frequently, until the lentils go mushy, adding more stock if necessary.

To make the dumplings, mix together all the remaining ingredients, adding enough of the water to make a firm dough. Roll the mixture into small dumplings and cook separately in boiling water or stock for about 30 minutes, then add them to the stew to heat through before serving.

Lentil rissoles

SERVES 4

100 g/4 oz/½ cup brown rice
200 g/7 oz/1 small can of lentils
45 ml/3 tbsp oil
2 shallots, finely chopped
50 g/2 oz mushrooms, finely chopped
2.5 ml/½ tsp paprika
2.5 ml/½ tsp dried mixed herbs
100 g/4 oz/2 cups fresh white
  breadcrumbs
Salt and freshly ground black pepper
1 egg, beaten
Plain (all-purpose) flour, for dusting
Oil, for shallow-frying
Tomato ketchup (catsup), to serve

Place the rice in a saucepan and cover with cold water. Bring to the boil and simmer for about 10 minutes until soft. Add the lentils and continue to simmer gently for about 10 minutes until the mixture is very soft, adding a little more water if necessary and stirring occasionally, but finishing with a fairly dry mixture.

Meanwhile, heat the measured oil and fry (sauté) the shallots and mushrooms until soft. Remove everything from the heat and stir the mushroom mixture into the lentils with the paprika, herbs, breadcrumbs, salt and pepper. Stir in the egg to bind the mixture. Shape into 16 rissoles and dust with flour. Heat the oil and fry for about 5 minutes on each side until heated through and golden. Serve with tomato ketchup.

Lentil dhal

SERVES 4

225 g/8 oz/1⅓ cups lentils
600 ml/1 pt/2½ cups Vegetable Stock
    (page 28)
2.5 ml/½ tsp turmeric
25 g/1 oz/2 tbsp butter or margarine
1 onion, chopped
1 green (bell) pepper, chopped
2 garlic cloves
2.5 ml/½ tsp chilli powder
2.5 ml/½ tsp cumin seeds

Put the lentils, stock and turmeric in a
saucepan, bring to the boil and
simmer for 20 minutes until almost
tender and much of the liquid has
been absorbed. Meanwhile, melt the
butter or margarine in a saucepan and
fry (sauté) the onion, green pepper,
whole garlic cloves, chilli powder and
cumin seeds until the onion is golden
brown. Remove the garlic, add the
lentils and simmer gently, stirring,
for 5 minutes.

Vegetable dhal

SERVES 4

225 g/8 oz/1⅓ cups lentils
1.2 litres/2 pts/5 cups Vegetable Stock
    (page 28)
1 bay leaf
30 ml/2 tbsp oil
1 garlic clove, chopped
1 large onion chopped
½ red (bell) pepper, thinly sliced
½ yellow pepper, thinly sliced
2.5 ml/½ tsp turmeric
10 ml/2 tsp curry powder
2.5 ml/½ tsp ground coriander (cilantro)
1 small cauliflower, separated into florets
100 g/4 oz French (green) beans,
    roughly chopped

Cook the lentils in the stock with the
bay leaf for 20 minutes until soft,
then drain and remove the bay leaf.
Heat the oil and fry (sauté) the garlic
and onion until soft but not brown,
then stir in the peppers and spices
and cook for 2 minutes. Stir in the
cauliflower and cook for 3 minutes.
Stir in the beans and lentils and cook
for 5 minutes until the sauce is well
combined but the vegetables remain
crisp.

Grains

Soft polenta

SERVES 4

350 ml/12 fl oz/1⅓ cups water
150 ml/¼ pt/⅔ cup milk
150 ml/¼ pt/⅔ cup single (light) cream
1 garlic clove, crushed
50 g/2 oz/½ cup polenta
Salt and freshly ground black pepper

Put the water, milk and half the cream in a heavy-based saucepan and bring to the boil. Add the garlic and gradually whisk in the polenta over a low heat, whisking continuously, until the grain is absorbed. Lower the heat and continue to cook for a further 30 minutes, stirring continuously to ensure that the polenta does not stick. Season generously with salt and pepper. Beat in the remaining cream and serve hot.

Yellow rice

SERVES 4

750 ml/1¼ pts/3 cups water
200 g/7 oz/scant 1 cup long-grain rice
1 cinnamon stick
2.5 ml/½ tsp turmeric
A pinch of salt
15 g/½ oz/1 tbsp butter or margarine
75 g/3 oz/½ cup raisins (optional)

Bring the water to the boil in a large saucepan, sprinkle in the rice and add the remaining ingredients. Return the water to the boil, stir once, then cover and simmer for about 10 minutes until the rice is just tender. Drain off any excess water and discard the cinnamon. Serve hot as a side dish or cold with salads.

Baked polenta

SERVES 4

450 ml/¾ pt/2 cups milk
100 g/4 oz/1 cup polenta
50 g/2 oz/¼ cup butter or margarine
3 eggs, separated
5 ml/1 tsp salt
2.5 ml/½ tsp baking powder

Bring the milk almost to the boil in a saucepan, then sprinkle in the polenta and stir until thickened. Melt half the butter or margarine and stir it into the pan, then remove from the heat and leave to cool for 5 minutes. Beat the egg yolks with the salt until pale, then stir into the polenta. Whisk the egg whites with the baking powder until stiff, then fold into the polenta using a metal spoon. Turn the mixture into a greased 1.5 litre/2½ pt/6 cup ovenproof dish and bake in a preheated oven at 180°C/350°F/gas mark 4 for 40 minutes until golden brown. Serve dotted with the remaining butter or margarine.

Vegetable rice with herbs

SERVES 4

50 g/2 oz/¼ cup butter or margarine
1 onion, chopped
225 g/8 oz broccoli florets
225 g/8 oz cauliflower florets
2 carrots, sliced
1 leek, sliced
250 ml/8 fl oz/1 cup dry white wine
225 g/8 oz/1 cup brown rice
900 ml/1½ pts/3¾ cups hot Vegetable
   Stock (page 28)
Salt and freshly ground black pepper
15 ml/1 tbsp grated lemon rind
1 garlic clove, crushed
25 g/1 oz/¼ cup flaked (slivered)
   almonds
3 eggs, beaten
30 ml/2 tbsp chopped parsley
30 ml/2 tbsp chopped tarragon
30 ml/2 tbsp chopped chervil
30 ml/2 tbsp chopped sorrel

Melt the butter or margarine and fry (sauté) the onion, broccoli and cauliflower until the onion is soft. Add the carrots, leek, wine and rice and stir well to coat in the butter. Add the stock, season to taste and bring to the boil. Transfer to a casserole dish (Dutch oven), cover and bake in a preheated oven at 200°C/400°F/gas mark 6 for 25 minutes. Mix together the lemon rind, garlic and almonds and sprinkle over the top. Pour the eggs over and sprinkle with the herbs. Return to the oven for a further 10 minutes, then serve immediately.

Smoked haddock kedgeree

SERVES 4

350 g/12 oz smoked haddock
350 g/12 oz/1½ cups long-grain rice
5 ml/1 tsp lemon juice
2 hard-boiled (hard-cooked) eggs,
   coarsely chopped
50 g/2 oz/¼ cup butter or margarine
Salt and freshly ground black pepper
150 ml/¼ pt/⅔ cup single (light) cream
15 ml/1 tbsp chopped parsley

Place the haddock in a saucepan and almost cover with water. Bring just to the boil, cover and simmer very gently for about 10 minutes until the fish flakes when tested with a fork. Drain the fish, reserving the cooking liquor. Remove any bones and skin from the fish and flake the flesh with a fork. Make the cooking liquor up to 450 ml/¾ pt/2 cups with water and place in a pan with the rice and lemon juice. Bring to the boil, cover and simmer for about 15 minutes until the rice is just tender. Drain off any excess water and transfer the rice to an ovenproof dish. Gently stir in the fish, eggs and butter or margarine and season with salt and pepper. Warm the cream and stir into the rice. Bake in a preheated oven at 150°C/300°F/ gas mark 3 for about 10 minutes until heated through. Serve sprinkled with the parsley.

Rice with yoghurt and herbs

SERVES 4

225 g/8 oz/1 cup long-grain rice
30 ml/2 tbsp oil
6 spring onions (scallions), sliced
225 g/8 oz tomatoes, skinned and sliced
150 ml/¼ pt/⅔ cup plain yoghurt
15 ml/1 tbsp chopped dill (dill weed)
15 ml/1 tbsp snipped chives
15 ml/1 tbsp chopped tarragon
Salt and freshly ground black pepper

Cook the rice in boiling salted water until just tender. Drain and rinse in hot water. Heat the oil and fry (sauté) the spring onions until just beginning to brown, then carefully stir in the tomatoes and rice. Mix together the yoghurt and herbs, stir into the rice mixture and season to taste. Heat through gently before serving.

Brown rice with leeks

SERVES 4

25 g/1 oz/2 tbsp butter or margarine
15 ml/1 tbsp corn oil
4 leeks, sliced
225 g/8 oz/1 cup brown rice
450 ml/¾ pt/2 cups hot Chicken Stock (page 28)
Salt and freshly ground black pepper
15 ml/1 tbsp snipped chives
150 ml/¼ pt/⅔ cup plain yoghurt

Melt the butter or margarine with the oil in a saucepan and fry (sauté) the leeks until soft. Add the rice and stir until coated, then pour in the stock and season with salt and pepper. Return to the boil, cover and simmer for about 40 minutes until the rice is tender and stock has been absorbed. Sprinkle with the chives and pour the yoghurt over the top.

Tomato rice

SERVES 4

225 g/8 oz/1 cup long-grain rice, soaked in cold water for 30 minutes
45 ml/3 tbsp oil
1 onion, sliced
1 garlic clove, crushed
25 g/1 oz fresh root ginger, grated
400 g/14 oz/1 large can of tomatoes, chopped
Salt and freshly ground black pepper
15 ml/1 tbsp coriander (cilantro)

Drain the rice thoroughly. Heat the oil and fry (sauté) the onion until just beginning to brown, then add the garlic and ginger and fry for 2 minutes. Stir in the rice and fry for 2 minutes. Add the tomatoes and season to taste. Cover and simmer for 10 minutes until the rice is just tender. Transfer to a warm serving dish and sprinkle with the coriander.

Pilau rice

SERVES 4

50 g/2 oz/¼ cup butter or margarine
225 g/8 oz/1 cup long-grain rice
600 ml/1 pt/2½ cups Chicken Stock (page 28)
Salt and freshly ground black pepper
15 ml/1 tbsp chopped coriander (cilantro)
15 ml/1 tbsp chopped flatleaf parsley
300 ml/½ pt/1¼ cups plain yoghurt

Melt the butter in a casserole (Dutch oven). Add the rice and cook for 1 minute, stirring. Stir in the stock, salt and pepper, bring to the boil, cover and simmer gently for 15 minutes until the rice is tender and has absorbed all the liquid. Stir in half the herbs and season to taste. Serve hot, with the yoghurt spooned over and sprinkle with the remaining herbs.

Chinese-style fried rice

SERVES 4

30 ml/2 tbsp oil
½ bunch of spring onions (scallions)
100 g/4 oz mushrooms, sliced
1 small red (bell) pepper, chopped
450 g/1 lb/4 cups cooked long-grain rice
100 g/4 oz/1 cup peeled prawns
   (shrimp)
45 ml/3 tbsp frozen peas
1.5 ml/¼ tsp cayenne
2.5 ml/½ tsp ground ginger
Salt and freshly ground black pepper

Heat the oil and fry the onions,
mushrooms and peppers for about
5 minutes until soft but not browned.
Add the rice and fry for about
4 minutes until well blended, stirring
continuously. Add the remaining
ingredients and stir together until
piping hot.

Egg fried rice

SERVES 4

15 ml/1 tbsp oil
1 egg, lightly beaten
350 g/12 oz/3 cups cooked long-grain
   rice
15 ml/1 tbsp soy sauce
10 ml/2 tsp Chinese five spice powder
45 ml/3 tbsp frozen peas
Salt and freshly ground black pepper

Heat the oil in a large frying pan
(skillet) and add the egg, whisking
lightly with a fork. Stir in the rice and
mix together for a few minutes so that
the egg is distributed through the
rice. Add the soy sauce, five spice
powder and peas and season to taste
with salt and pepper. Continue to
cook for about 5 minutes until heated
through.

Milanese risotto

SERVES 4

2.5 ml/½ tsp saffron threads
15 ml/1 tbsp olive oil
50 g/2 oz/¼ cup unsalted (sweet) butter
1 onion, finely chopped
2 garlic cloves, crushed
350 g/12 oz/1½ cups risotto rice
150 ml/¼ pt/⅔ cup dry white wine
1.2 litres/2 pts/5 cups hot Chicken or
   Vegetable Stock (page 28)
100 g/4 oz/1 cup Parmesan cheese,
   freshly grated
Salt and freshly ground black pepper

Place the saffron in a small bowl with
about 15 ml/1 tbsp boiling water and
leave to soak. Heat the oil and half
the butter in a large pan and fry
(sauté) the onion and garlic until soft
but not brown. Add the rice and stir
until it is coated with oil, hot and
shiny. Add the wine and boil for a
minute until it has evaporated. Add
the hot stock a little at a time, stirring
continuously and allowing the stock to
be absorbed by the rice before adding
any more. It should take about
15–20 minutes to add all the stock,
by which time the rice will be tender.
Stir in the saffron and soaking liquid,
the remaining butter and half the
Parmesan and heat through. Season
to taste. Remove from the heat, cover
and leave to stand for 5 minutes.
Serve sprinkled with the remaining
Parmesan.

Seafood risotto

SERVES 4

15 ml/2 tbsp oil
350 g/12 oz/1½ cups risotto rice
2 onions, sliced
Salt and freshly ground black pepper
900 ml/1½ pts/3¾ cups hot Chicken
    Stock (page 28)
50 g/2 oz/¼ cup butter or margarine
100 g/4 oz cooked, peeled prawns
    (shrimp)
100 g/4 oz shelled, cooked mussels
5 ml/1 tsp turmeric
A pinch of grated nutmeg
5 ml/1 tsp light brown sugar
5 ml/1 tsp lemon juice
30 ml/2 tbsp double (heavy) cream
50 g/2 oz/½ cup Parmesan cheese,
    freshly grated

Heat the oil and turn the rice and onions in it until well coated. Season to taste. Stir in a third of the stock, bring to the boil and simmer until the liquid has been absorbed. Add more stock and simmer, continuing until the rice is tender and moist and all the stock has been used; this should take 15–20 minutes. Stir in half the butter or margarine. Melt the remaining butter or margarine in a saucepan and stir in the prawns, mussels, turmeric, nutmeg, sugar, lemon juice and cream. Heat through gently. Turn the rice into a warm serving dish, pile the seafood mixture on top, cover and leave to stand for 5 minutes. Serve sprinkled with the Parmesan.

Red pepper risotto

SERVES 4

50 g/2 oz/¼ cup unsalted (sweet) butter
1 onion, finely chopped
1 garlic clove, crushed
400 g/14 oz/1 large jar of pimientos, cut
    into strips
1 sun-dried tomato, chopped
450 g/1 lb/2 cups risotto rice
1.5 litres/2½ pts/6 cups hot Chicken or
    Vegetable Stock (page 28)
Salt and freshly ground black pepper
50 g/2 oz/½ cup Parmesan cheese,
    freshly grated

Melt the butter in a large heavy-based frying pan (skillet) and fry (sauté) the onion and garlic for a few minutes until soft but not brown. Add the pimientos and sun-dried tomato and stir until heated through. Add the rice and stir until it is coated in hot oil. Add the stock a few spoonfuls at a time, allowing the stock to be absorbed before adding any more. This should take about 20 minutes. Season to taste, cover and leave to stand for 3 minutes before serving sprinkled with the Parmesan.

Pasta

Tuscan-style macaroni

SERVES 4

60 ml/4 tbsp olive oil
450 g/1 lb/4 cups cooked veal or
  chicken, diced
1 onion, chopped
225 g/8 oz button mushrooms, sliced
15 ml/1 tbsp plain (all-purpose) flour
250 ml/8 fl oz/1 cup Chicken Stock
  (page 28)
150 ml/¼ pt/⅔ cup dry white wine
150 ml/¼ pt/⅔ cup crème fraîche
5 ml/1 tsp Worcestershire sauce
Salt and freshly ground black pepper
100 g/4 oz/1 cup blue cheese, crumbled
350 g/12 oz macaroni
100 g/4 oz/1 cup Pecorino cheese, grated
15 ml/1 tbsp snipped chives

Heat the oil and fry (sauté) the meat
for 3 minutes, then remove and keep
warm. Fry the onion until soft but not
brown, then add the mushrooms and
fry for 1 minute. Sprinkle in the flour
and cook for 1 minute, then stir in the
stock and wine, bring to the boil and
simmer, stirring, until the sauce has
thickened. Fold in the crème fraîche
and do not allow the mixture to boil
again. Add the Worcestershire sauce
and season to taste. Stir in the blue
cheese and meat and keep the sauce
warm without allowing it to boil.
  Meanwhile, cook the macaroni in
boiling salted water for 15 minutes
until just tender. Drain and rinse in
hot water. Turn the macaroni on to a
serving dish, pour the sauce over and
sprinkle with the Pecorino cheese and
chives.

Fettuccine with tomatoes

SERVES 4

2 red (bell) peppers, seeded and cut
  into strips
15 ml/1 tbsp olive oil
1 shallot, sliced
1 garlic clove, crushed
120 ml/4 fl oz/½ cup water
400 g/14 oz/1 large can of chopped
  tomatoes
A few basil leaves, torn into shreds
Salt and freshly ground black pepper
350 g/12 oz spinach fettuccine
225 g/8 oz young spinach leaves,
  shredded and rinsed
120 ml/4 fl oz/½ cup crème fraîche

Toss the pepper strips in the oil in a
flameproof and ovenproof pan, then
roast in a preheated oven at 200°C/
200°F/gas mark 6 for 15 minutes
until beginning to brown. Stir in the
shallot, garlic and water and return to
the oven for a further 20 minutes
until all the vegetables are very soft.
Transfer to direct heat and stir in the
tomatoes and basil and season to
taste. Leave to simmer, stirring
occasionally.
  Meanwhile, bring a large pan of
salted water to the boil, add the
fettuccine and boil for about
10 minutes until al dente. Meanwhile,
put the spinach in a large pan with
just the water clinging to the leaves.
Cook over a medium heat just until
wilted. Remove from the heat and
drain. Arrange the spinach on a warm
serving plate. Drain the fettucine. Stir
the crème fraîche into the sauce, toss
with the fettuccine, spoon over the
spinach and serve at once.

Penne with carrots and pepper

SERVES 4

350 g/12 oz penne
60 ml/4 tbsp olive oil
1 onion, chopped
450 g/1 lb carrots, coarsely grated
1 red (bell) pepper, cut into strips
1 garlic clove, chopped
Salt and freshly ground black pepper
45 ml/3 tbsp chopped flatleaf parsley
50 g/2 oz/½ cup Parmesan cheese, freshly grated

Bring a large pan of salted water to the boil, add the penne and boil for about 10 minutes just until al dente. Meanwhile, heat the oil and fry (sauté) the onion until soft but not brown. Add the carrots, red pepper and garlic and stir-fry for about 5 minutes until just tender. Drain the penne, reserving about 120 ml/ 4 fl oz/½ cup of the cooking liquid. Return the pasta to the hot pan and stir in the sauce and the reserved cooking liquid. Season well, stir in the parsley and Parmesan and serve at once.

Pasta with mushrooms and soured cream

SERVES 4

25 g/1 oz/2 tbsp butter or margarine
30 ml/2 tbsp olive oil
450 g/1 lb mushrooms, chopped
2 garlic cloves, crushed
5 ml/1 tsp anchovy essence (extract)
Salt and freshly ground black pepper
300 ml/½ pt/1¼ cups soured (dairy sour) cream
90 ml/6 tbsp chopped parsley
350 g/12 oz pasta shapes

Melt the butter or margarine with the oil and fry (sauté) the mushrooms and garlic for 5 minutes, stirring continuously. Season to taste with the anchovy essence, salt and pepper and cook for 3 minutes. Stir in the soured cream and 60 ml/4 tbsp of the parsley and heat through gently without boiling.

Meanwhile cook the pasta in boiling salted water until just tender, then drain and rinse in hot water and turn into a serving dish. Pour the sauce over and sprinkle with the remaining parsley.

Rigatoni with salmon and dill

SERVES 4

350 g/12 oz rigatoni
30 ml/2 tbsp olive oil
30 ml/2 tbsp butter or margarine
2 shallots, sliced
1 bunch of asparagus, cut into chunks
100 g/4 oz smoked salmon trimmings
45 ml/3 tbsp chopped dill (dill weed)
Salt and freshly ground black pepper
30 ml/2 tbsp soured (dairy sour) cream

Bring a large pan of salted water to the boil, add the rigatoni and boil for about 10 minutes until al dente. Meanwhile, heat the oil and butter or margarine and fry (sauté) the shallots for a few minutes until translucent. Add the asparagus and fry for about 5 minutes until just tender. Stir in the salmon pieces and most of the dill and season to taste. Drain the pasta, then mix it with the salmon mixture until well blended. Serve topped with the soured cream and sprinkled with the remaining dill.

Creamy pasta

SERVES 4

225 g/8 oz pasta shells
5 ml/1 tbsp oil
25 g/1 oz/2 tbsp butter or margarine
100 g/4 oz mushrooms, sliced
100 g/4 oz/1 cup cooked ham, cut into
    strips
150 ml/¼ pt/⅔ cup double (heavy) cream
175 g/6 oz/1½ cups Cheddar cheese,
    grated
15 ml/1 tbsp chopped parsley
Salt and freshly ground black pepper
25 g/1 oz/¼ cup Parmesan cheese,
    freshly grated

Cook the pasta in boiling salted water
with the oil until just tender, then
drain and rinse in hot water. Melt the
butter or margarine, add the
mushrooms and ham and fry (sauté)
until soft. Add the pasta and cook
over a gentle heat for 2 minutes. Mix
together the cream, Cheddar cheese
and parsley, stir into the pasta and
season to taste. Turn into a warm
serving dish and sprinkle with the
Parmesan.

Pepper vermicelli

SERVES 4

30 ml/2 tbsp olive oil
1 onion, sliced
1 red (bell) pepper, sliced
1 green pepper, sliced
1 yellow pepper, sliced
30 ml/2 tbsp red wine
400 g/14 oz/1 large can of tomatoes,
    chopped
5 ml/1 tsp sugar
Salt and freshly ground black pepper
350 g/12 oz vermicelli
15 ml/1 tbsp chopped parsley

Heat the oil and fry (sauté) the onion
and peppers until soft. Stir in the wine

and heat until it has evaporated, then
add the tomatoes and sugar and
simmer for 20 minutes. Season to
taste. Mean while, cook the vermicelli
in boiling salted water until just
tender, then drain and rinse in hot
water and turn into a warm serving
dish. Mix in the hot sauce and serve
sprinkled with the parsley.

Pasta with sun-dried tomatoes and mushrooms

SERVES 4

350 g/12 oz pasta shells
60 ml/4 tbsp olive oil
3 shallots, chopped
225 g/8 oz chestnut mushrooms,
    quartered
1 garlic clove, crushed
4 sun-dried tomato halves, thinly sliced
Salt and freshly ground black pepper
50 g/2 oz/½ cup Parmesan cheese,
    freshly grated

Bring a large pan of salted water to
the boil, add the pasta and boil for
about 10 minutes just until al dente.
Meanwhile, heat the oil and fry
(sauté) the shallots until just soft. Add
the mushrooms and garlic and fry
gently for about 10 minutes until soft.
Add the sun-dried tomatoes. Drain
the pasta well, reserving 120 ml/
4 fl oz/½ cup of the cooking liquid,
then return the pasta to the hot pan
and stir in the mushroom sauce and
the reserved cooking liquid. Season
well and serve sprinkled with the
Parmesan.

Japanese tofu pasta

SERVES 4

25 g/1 oz/2 tbsp butter or margarine
175 g/6 oz/⅔ cup tofu, diced
1 onion, chopped
1 red (bell) pepper, diced
1 green pepper, diced
15 g/1 oz/¼ cup wholewheat flour
2 tomatoes, skinned, seeded and
    chopped
2 gherkins (cornichons), diced
250 ml/8 fl oz/1 cup red wine
250 ml/8 fl oz/1 cup Vegetable Stock
    (page 28)
350 g/12 oz tagliatelle
5 ml/1 tsp paprika
2.5 ml/½ tsp curry powder
Salt and freshly ground black pepper
150 ml/¼ pt/⅔ cup crème fraîche
15 ml/1 tbsp snipped chives

Melt the butter or margarine and fry
(sauté) the tofu for 2 minutes, then
add the onion and peppers and fry
until beginning to soften. Stir in the
flour and cook for 1 minute, then add
the tomatoes and gherkins and stir in
the wine and stock. Bring to the boil,
cover and simmer for 10 minutes.
Meanwhile, cook the tagliatelle in
boiling salted water until just tender,
drain and rinse in hot water. Turn into
a warm serving dish. Add the paprika
and curry powder to the sauce and
season to taste. Stir in the crème
fraîche, pour the sauce over the pasta
and serve sprinkled with the chives.

Pepper spaghetti

SERVES 4

60 ml/4 tbsp olive oil
350 g/12 oz rump or sirloin steak, diced
100 g/4 oz streaky bacon, rinded and
    diced
1 onion, chopped
1 red (bell) pepper, chopped
1 green pepper, chopped
400 g/14 oz/1 large can of tomatoes,
    chopped
50 g/2 oz green olives, stoned (pitted)
150 ml/¼ pt/⅔ cup Beef Stock (page 28)
15 ml/1 tbsp cornflour (cornstarch)
2.5 ml/½ tsp cayenne
2.5 ml/½ tsp curry powder
Salt and freshly ground black pepper
30 ml/2 tbsp snipped chives
350 g/12 oz spaghetti

Heat the oil and fry (sauté) the steak
until browned. Add the bacon and
onion and fry until soft, then add the
peppers and cook until soft. Stir in the
tomatoes, olives and nearly all the
stock. Mix the cornflour with the
remaining stock, then stir into the
sauce, bring to the boil and simmer,
stirring, until the sauce thickens. Add
the cayenne and curry powder and
season to taste. Stir in the chives and
meat and heat gently.

Meanwhile cook the spaghetti in
boiling salted water for 15 minutes
until just tender. Drain and rinse in
hot water. Turn the spaghetti into a
warm serving dish, pour over the
sauce and serve immediately.

Spaghetti pancakes with vegetable filling

SERVES 4

150 g/5 oz wholewheat spaghetti
5 eggs, beaten
A pinch of grated nutmeg
50 g/2 oz/½ cup Parmesan cheese, freshly grated
Salt and freshly ground black pepper
60 ml/4 tbsp oil
25 g/1 oz/2 tbsp butter or margarine
1 onion, chopped
1 red (bell) pepper, sliced
1 courgette (zucchini), sliced
150 g/5 oz mangetout (snow peas)
3 tomatoes, skinned, seeded and chopped
250 ml/8 fl oz/1 cup Vegetable Stock (page 28)
15 ml/1 tbsp cornflour (cornstarch)
30 ml/2 tbsp water
30 ml/2 tbsp soy sauce
30 ml/2 tbsp cider vinegar
15 ml/1 tbsp clear honey
30 ml/2 tbsp snipped chives

Break the spaghetti into roughly 7.5 cm/3 in lengths, then cook it in boiling salted water until just tender, drain and rinse in hot water. Beat the eggs with the nutmeg and cheese and season to taste. Stir in the spaghetti. Heat 15 ml/1 tbsp of the oil and fry (sauté) a quarter of the spaghetti batter on both sides, then remove from the pan and keep warm while cooking three more pancakes.

Heat the butter or margarine and fry the onion until soft. Add the red pepper, courgette and mangetout and fry for 2 minutes, stirring. Add the tomatoes and stock, cover and simmer for 5 minutes. Mix the cornflour with the water and stir into the vegetable mixture until the mixture thickens. Add the soy sauce, vinegar and honey and season to taste. Divide the mixture between the pancakes and fold them in half. Serve sprinkled with the chives.

Spaghetti carbonara

SERVES 4

30 ml/2 tbsp oil
1 onion, chopped
1 garlic clove, crushed
25 g/1 oz/2 tbsp butter or margarine
175 g/6 oz lean bacon, rinded and chopped
90 ml/6 tbsp dry white wine
350 g/12 oz spaghetti
3 egg yolks
75 g/3 oz/¾ cup Parmesan cheese, freshly grated
15 ml/1 tbsp chopped parsley
Salt and freshly ground black pepper

Heat the oil and fry (sauté) the onion and garlic until soft but not brown. Add the butter or margarine and bacon and fry until crisp. Add the wine, bring to the boil and simmer until the wine has evaporated. Meanwhile, cook the spaghetti in boiling salted water until just tender, then drain and rinse in hot water. Beat the egg yolks with the cheese and parsley and season to taste. Toss the spaghetti with the egg mixture, then mix in the bacon mixture. The heat from the spaghetti will be sufficient to cook the eggs. Serve immediately.

Spaghetti with garlic butter

SERVES 4

600 ml/1 pt/2½ cups water
6 garlic cloves, peeled
100 g/4 oz/½ cup butter or margarine
90 ml/6 tbsp chopped parsley
350 g/12 oz spaghetti
Salt and freshly ground black pepper
100 g/4 oz/1 cup Parmesan cheese,
   freshly grated

Bring the water to the boil, add the garlic and boil for 5 minutes, then drain and crush the garlic. Melt the butter or margarine and stir in the garlic and parsley and cook over a low heat for 2 minutes. Meanwhile, cook the spaghetti in boiling salted water until just tender, then drain and rinse in hot water. Toss the spaghetti in the garlic butter, season to taste and turn into a warm serving dish. Serve sprinkled with the Parmesan.

Pasta puttanesca

SERVES 4

30 ml/2 tbsp olive oil
2 garlic cloves, crushed
4 ripe tomatoes, skinned and chopped
1 sun-dried tomato, chopped
12 black olives, stoned (pitted) and halved
3 anchovy fillets, chopped
15 ml/1 tbsp capers, chopped
15 ml/1 tbsp chilli flakes
30 ml/2 tbsp chopped flatleaf parsley
Salt and freshly ground black pepper
350 g/12 oz penne
15 ml/1 tbsp freshly grated Parmesan
   cheese

Heat the oil in a large pan and add the garlic, tomatoes, sun-dried tomato, olives, anchovies, capers and chilli. Add half the parsley and season

to taste. Bring to the boil, then simmer for about 10 minutes until thick and well blended, stirring regularly. Meanwhile, bring a large pan of salted water to the boil, add the penne and boil for about 10 minutes until al dente. Drain well. Toss the pasta with the sauce and serve sprinkled with the Parmesan.

Pasta and chicken

SERVES 4

225 g/8 oz broccoli florets
75 g/3 oz/⅓ cup butter or margarine
25 g/1 oz/¼ cup plain (all-purpose) flour
450 ml/¾ pt/2 cups Chicken Stock
   (page 28)
150 ml/¼ pt/⅔ cup double (heavy) cream
5 ml/1 tsp dried oregano
Salt and freshly ground black pepper
350 g/12 oz rigatoni
450 g/1 lb/4 cups cooked chicken, cut
   into strips
75 g/3 oz/¾ cup Parmesan cheese,
   freshly grated

Cook the broccoli in boiling salted water until just tender, then drain and chop. Heat 50 g/2 oz/¼ cup of the butter or margarine, stir in the flour and cook for 1 minute. Whisk in the stock and cook, stirring, until the sauce thickens. Simmer for 5 minutes, then stir in the broccoli, cream and oregano and season to taste.

Meanwhile, cook the rigatoni in boiling salted water until just tender, drain and rinse in hot water, then toss in the remaining butter or margarine. Put a layer of pasta in an ovenproof dish, followed by layers of chicken, sauce and a sprinkling of the Parmesan. Bake in a preheated oven at 220°C/425°F/gas mark 7 for 20 minutes.

211

Macaroni with four cheeses

SERVES 4

350 g/12 oz macaroni
A pinch of grated nutmeg
75 g/3 oz/¾ cup Parmesan cheese,
  freshly grated
300 ml/½ pt/1¼ cups Béchamel Sauce
  (page 251)
Salt and freshly ground black pepper
75 g/3 oz/¾ cup Gouda or Edam (Dutch)
  cheese, diced
75 g/3 oz/¾ cup Gruyère (Swiss) cheese,
  diced
75 g/3 oz/¾ cup Mozzarella cheese, diced
50 g/2 oz/¼ cup butter or margarine

Cook the pasta in boiling salted water
for about 15 minutes until just tender,
then drain and rinse in hot water and
turn into a well greased ovenproof
dish. Mix the nutmeg and half the
Parmesan into the Béchamel Sauce
and season to taste. Stir in the
Gouda, Gruyère and Mozzarella
cheeses, then stir into the macaroni.
Dot with the butter or margarine and
sprinkle with the remaining Parmesan.
Bake in a preheated oven at 220°C/
425°F/gas mark 7 for 15 minutes
until brown and crispy on top.

Spaghetti with Mozzarella

SERVES 4

4 tomatoes, skinned, seeded and
  chopped
60 ml/4 tbsp capers, chopped
225 g/8 oz/2 cups Mozzarella cheese,
  chopped
2 egg yolks
150 ml/¼ pt/⅔ cup double (heavy) cream
350 g/12 oz spaghetti
Salt and freshly ground black pepper

Mix together the tomatoes, capers,
cheese, egg yolks and cream. Cook
the spaghetti in boiling salted water
until just tender, then drain and rinse
in hot water. Stir the tomato mixture
gently into the spaghetti over a low
heat until the cheese melts, season to
taste and serve immediately.

Spinach-stuffed cannelloni

SERVES 4

225 g/8 oz frozen spinach, thawed
100 g/4 oz/½ cup full-fat soft cheese
Salt and freshly ground black pepper
12 cannelloni tubes
40 g/1½ oz butter or margarine
40 g/1½ oz plain (all-purpose) flour
600 ml/1 pt/2½ cups milk
2.5 ml/½ tsp grated nutmeg
25 g/1 oz/½ cup fresh wholemeal
  breadcrumbs

Purée the spinach and full-fat soft
cheese in a food processor or blender.
Season to taste. Fill the cannelloni
tubes with this mixture and place in a
shallow ovenproof dish. Melt the
butter or margarine in a saucepan,
stir in the flour and cook for
1 minute. Whisk in the milk and cook,
stirring, until thickened. Add the
nutmeg and season to taste. Pour the
sauce over the cannelloni, sprinkle
with the breadcrumbs and bake in a
preheated oven at 200°C/400°F/gas
mark 6 for 40 minutes until golden
brown.

Pasta with Napolitana sauce

SERVES 4

400 g/14 oz/1 large can of tomatoes, chopped
15 ml/1 tbsp oil
1 onion, chopped
15 ml/1 tbsp tomato purée (paste)
10 ml/2 tsp dried oregano
A pinch of sugar
450 g/1 lb pasta shapes
400 g/14 oz/1 large can of baked beans
100 g/4 oz/1 cup Parma ham, chopped
Salt and freshly ground black pepper
50 g/2 oz/1 cup fresh breadcrumbs
50 g/2 oz/½ cup Mozzarella cheese, grated

Put the tomatoes, oil, onion, tomato purée, oregano and sugar in a saucepan, bring to the boil and simmer for 25 minutes. Purée in a food processor or blender if you like a smooth sauce. Cook the pasta in boiling water for 15 minutes until just tender, then drain and rinse in hot water. Mix the pasta with the beans, ham and sauce, season to taste and spoon into a large ovenproof dish. Mix together the breadcrumbs and cheese and sprinkle on the top. Bake in a preheated oven at 180°C/350°F/ gas mark 4 for 30 minutes until golden brown and crispy on top.

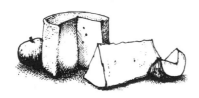

Beef lasagne

SERVES 4

15 ml/1 tbsp olive oil
1 onion, chopped
1 garlic clove, chopped
1 carrot, chopped
1 celery stick, chopped
450 g/1 lb minced (ground) beef
150 ml/¼ pt/⅔ cup red wine
400 g/14 oz/1 large can of tomatoes, chopped
60 ml/4 tbsp tomato purée (paste)
10 ml/2 tsp dried oregano
Salt and freshly ground black pepper
25 g/1 oz/2 tbsp butter or margarine
15 ml/1 tbsp plain (all-purpose) flour
300 ml/½ pt/1¼ cups milk
175 g/6 oz no-need-to-precook lasagne sheets
225 g/8 oz Mozzarella cheese, sliced
50 g/2 oz/½ cup Parmesan cheese, freshly grated

Heat the oil and fry (sauté) the onion, garlic, carrot and celery until soft but not brown, then stir in the mince and fry until browned and all the grains are separate. Add the wine and cook for 2 minutes, then add the tomatoes, tomato purée and oregano and season to taste. Simmer gently for at least 30 minutes until thick.

Meanwhile, melt the butter or margarine in a saucepan, stir in the flour and cook for 1 minute. Whisk in the milk and cook, stirring, until the sauce thickens. Season to taste. Arrange alternate layers of meat, lasagne and sauce into a shallow ovenproof dish, finishing with a layer of sauce. Cover with the Mozzarella and sprinkle with the Parmesan. Bake in a preheated oven at 190°C/375°F/ gas mark 5 for 20 minutes until browned and bubbling on top.

Kidney bean and vegetable lasagne

SERVES 4

50 g/2 oz/¼ cup butter or margarine
60 g/2½ oz wholemeal flour
600 ml/1 pt/2½ cups milk
Salt and freshly ground black pepper
100 g/4 oz/1 cup strong cheese, grated
30 ml/2 tbsp oil
1 leek, sliced
1 garlic clove, chopped
1 celery stick, sliced
50 g/2 oz mushrooms, sliced
15 ml/1 tbsp dry sherry
A few drops of soy sauce
450 ml/¾ pt/2 cups Vegetable Stock
    (page 28)
225 g/8 oz/1 small can of kidney beans,
    rinsed and drained
225 g/8 oz courgettes (zucchini), sliced
6 no-need-to-precook lasagne sheets

Melt the butter or margarine in a large pan and fry (sauté) the flour for 1 minute. Gradually stir in the milk and bring to the boil, stirring. Remove from the heat and season well. Stir in half the cheese. Heat the oil and fry the leek, garlic, celery and mushrooms until soft and just brown. Stir in the sherry, then the remaining flour. Add the soy sauce to the stock and stir into the pan. Bring to the boil, add the kidney beans and simmer for 15 minutes.

Place half the courgette slices on the base of an ovenproof dish. Pour half the vegetable sauce over the top. Lay half the lasagne on top, then pour on the remaining vegetable sauce. Cover with lasagne, then the cheese sauce, and finally the remaining cheese. Bake in a preheated oven at 190°C/375°F/gas mark 5 for 30 minutes.

Prawn cannelloni

SERVES 4

25 g/1 oz/2 tbsp butter or margarine
1 bunch of spring onions (scallions),
    sliced
450 g/1 lb cooked, peeled prawns
    (shrimp)
225 g/8 oz/1 small can of tomatoes,
    drained, juice reserved and chopped
100 g/4 oz button mushrooms, sliced
150 ml/¼ pt/⅔ cup dry white wine
15 ml/1 tbsp plain (all-purpose) flour
A pinch of mixed (apple-pie) spice
Salt and freshly ground black pepper
450 g/1 lb cannelloni
75 ml/5 tbsp tomato purée (paste)
225 g/8 oz Mozzarella cheese, sliced

Melt the butter or margarine and fry (sauté) the onions until soft but not brown. Add the prawns, tomatoes and mushrooms. Blend the wine with the flour and stir into the pan. Bring to the boil, stirring, and simmer until the sauce thickens. Add the spice and season to taste. Leave to cool. Cook the cannelloni in boiling salted water for 5 minutes until just tender, then drain and rinse in hot water. Stuff with the prawn mixture and lay in a greased ovenproof dish. Mix the tomato purée with the juice from the tomatoes, pour over the cannelloni, then place the Mozzarella on top. Bake in a preheated oven at 200°C/400°F/gas mark 6 for 15 minutes.

Vegetables

Though some vegetables, such as the youngest carrots or the first new potatoes of the season, are at their best simply boiled and served with a knob of butter or a sprinkling of fresh herbs, it would be very dull just to serve all vegetables plain boiled! Try out some of the interesting options offered here for all your favourite vegetables, and some you may not have tried before.

Scalloped artichokes

SERVES 4

6 Jerusalem artichokes, peeled and
  sliced
50 g/2 oz/¼ cup butter or margarine
50 g/2 oz/1 cup fresh breadcrumbs
300 ml/½ pt/1¼ cups Béchamel Sauce
  (page 251)
A pinch of cayenne

Boil the artichokes in lightly salted
water for 15 minutes, then drain.
Grease four scallop shells or soufflé
dishes, melt the remaining butter or
margarine and stir in the
breadcrumbs. Line the dishes with
about two-thirds of the breadcrumb
mixture. Mix the artichokes with
enough of the sauce to coat them
well, season to taste with the cayenne
and divide them between the dishes.
Cover with the reserved breadcrumbs
and bake in a preheated oven at
180°C/350°F/gas mark 4 until golden
brown on top.

Malaysian-style asparagus

SERVES 4

15 ml/1 tbsp oil
450 g/1 lb asparagus, cut into chunks
10 ml/2 tsp soy sauce
5 ml/1 tsp fresh root ginger, finely
  chopped
1 garlic clove, crushed
150 ml/¼ pt/⅔ cup crème fraîche
Salt and freshly ground black pepper
15 ml/1 tbsp chopped coriander
  (cilantro)

Heat the oil and fry (sauté) the
asparagus, soy sauce, ginger and
garlic for a few minutes until well
mixed. Reduce the heat, cover and

cook for about 5 minutes until the
asparagus is tender. Stir in the crème
fraîche and season with salt and
pepper. Cook over a gentle heat until
warmed through, without allowing the
mixture to boil. Serve sprinkled with
the coriander.

Baked aubergine rolls

SERVES 4

2 aubergines (eggplants), thinly sliced
  lengthways
Salt and freshly ground black pepper
75 ml/5 tbsp olive oil
2 garlic cloves, crushed
75 ml/5 tbsp Pesto Sauce (page 254)
225 g/8 oz/2 cups Mozzarella cheese,
  shredded
A few basil leaves, torn into pieces

Arrange the aubergine slices in a
colander and sprinkle with salt. Leave
to stand for 30 minutes to extract the
bitter juices. Rinse well, then pat dry
on kitchen paper (paper towels). Heat
the oil and garlic in a large frying pan
(skillet) and fry (sauté) the aubergine
slices a few at a time until just
beginning to brown on both sides.
Drain on kitchen paper while you fry
the remaining slices. Spread the slices
with the pesto, then sprinkle on the
Mozzarella and basil and season well.
Roll up and secure with cocktail sticks
(toothpicks). Arrange in a greased
baking tin (pan) and brush with the oil
from the frying pan. Bake in a
preheated oven at 180°C/350°F/gas
mark 4 for 10 minutes until the
cheese has melted and the aubergines
are golden. Serve immediately.

French beans with bacon

SERVES 4

25 g/1 oz/2 tbsp butter or margarine
½ leek, sliced
3 streaky bacon rashers (slices), rinded
  and cut into strips
225 g/8 oz French (green) beans, cut
  into 2.5 cm/1 in pieces
¼ iceberg lettuce, shredded

Melt the butter or margarine in a large pan and fry (sauté) the leek until soft but not brown. Add the bacon and fry until browned. Blanch the beans in boiling water for 1 minute, then drain and add to the pan. Stir-fry for 2 minutes, then stir in the lettuce and cook for 30 seconds. Turn out on to a warm serving dish and serve immediately.

Green beans with pears

SERVES 4

450 ml/¾ pt/2 cups Vegetable Stock
  (page 28)
4 hard pears, peeled, cored and sliced
A twist of lemon peel
225 g/8 oz French (green) beans, sliced
15 ml/1 tbsp tarragon vinegar
30 ml/2 tbsp demerara sugar
Salt and freshly ground black pepper

Bring the stock to the boil, then add the pears and lemon peel and simmer for 10 minutes. Add the beans and simmer for 20 minutes. Add the vinegar and sugar and season to taste with salt and pepper. Continue simmering until the liquid is almost all absorbed. Serve immediately.

French beans with almonds

SERVES 4

350 g/12 oz French (green) beans
25 g/1 oz/2 tbsp butter or margarine
50 g/2 oz/½ cup flaked (slivered)
  almonds
Freshly ground black pepper

Cook the beans in boiling salted water for 7 minutes, then drain. Melt the butter or margarine and fry (sauté) the almonds until just browned. Mix them with the beans, season with pepper and serve immediately.

Beetroot with soured cream

SERVES 4

6 cooked beetroot (red beet), sliced
150 ml/¼ pt/⅔ cup soured (dairy sour)
  cream
Grated rind of ½ lemon
15 ml/1 tbsp chopped parsley
25 g/1 oz/½ cup fresh breadcrumbs
25 g/1 oz/¼ cup Parmesan cheese,
  freshly grated
50 g/2 oz/¼ cup butter or margarine
Salt and freshly ground black pepper

Arrange the beetroot in an ovenproof dish and pour the soured cream over. Mix together the lemon rind, parsley, breadcrumbs and cheese and sprinkle over the beetroot. Dot with the butter or margarine and season to taste. Place under a hot grill (broiler) until brown and bubbling.

Broccoli with lemon

SERVES 4

450 g/1 lb broccoli florets
Grated rind and juice of 1 lemon
5 ml/1 tsp sugar
Salt
30 ml/2 tbsp cornflour (cornstarch)
30 ml/2 tbsp water

Cook the broccoli in boiling salted water for 10 minutes, then drain and reserve 300 ml/½ pt/1¼ cups of the cooking liquid. Keep the broccoli warm while making the sauce. Add the lemon rind, juice and sugar to the cooking liquid and season to taste with salt. Mix the cornflour and water to a paste, then stir it into the liquid. Bring to the boil, stirring continuously, and simmer until the sauce becomes thick and clear. Pour the sauce over the broccoli and serve.

Broccoli with black bean sauce

SERVES 4

225 g/8 oz broccoli florets
45 ml/3 tbsp oil
2 chilli peppers, chopped
½ leek, chopped
½ red (bell) pepper, chopped
50 g/2 oz canned black beans, chopped
200 ml/7 fl oz/scant 1 cup Vegetable Stock (page 28)
15 ml/1 tbsp soy sauce
15 ml/1 tbsp cornflour (cornstarch)

Steam the broccoli for 7–8 minutes, then transfer to a warm serving dish and keep warm. Heat the oil in a large pan and fry (sauté) the chilli peppers, leek and red pepper until soft, then add the beans, stock and soy sauce and cook for 2 minutes. Blend the

cornflour with a little cold water, then add to the sauce and cook for 1 minute. Pour the sauce over the broccoli and serve.

Red cabbage with apple

SERVES 4

1 red cabbage, shredded
2 cooking (tart) apples, peeled, cored and cubed
50 g/2 oz/¼ cup butter or margarine
2 or 3 cloves
Salt and freshly ground black pepper
15 ml/1 tbsp redcurrant jelly (clear conserve)
15 ml/1 tbsp vinegar
30 ml/2 tbsp plain (all-purpose) flour

Put the cabbage in a large saucepan with just enough water to cover, add the apples, butter or margarine and cloves and season with salt and pepper. Bring to the boil and simmer gently for 2 hours until the cabbage is tender and the apples have virtually disappeared. Warm the redcurrant jelly, add the vinegar and mix with the flour. Add a little juice from the pan, then stir into the cabbage mixture and heat until the sauce thickens.

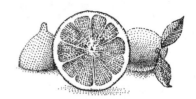

Glazed carrots

SERVES 4

700 g/1½ lb carrots
50 g/2 oz/¼ cup butter or margarine
15 ml/1 tbsp sugar
2.5 ml/½ tsp salt
450 ml/¾ pt/2 cups Vegetable Stock
   (page 28)

If the carrots are young, leave them
whole; old carrots should be scraped
and quartered. Melt the butter or
margarine in a saucepan and add the
carrots, sugar and salt. Pour in
enough of the stock to come half-way
up the carrots, bring to the boil and
simmer for 15 minutes, shaking the
pan occasionally, until the carrots are
cooked through and the liquid has
disappeared, leaving only the glaze.
Stir the carrots well in the glaze before
serving.

Herbed carrots

SERVES 4

50 g/2 oz/¼ cup butter or margarine
8 large carrots, thinly sliced
1 onion, chopped
15 ml/1 tbsp cornflour (cornstarch)
300 ml/½ pt/1¼ cups Vegetable Stock
   (page 28)
15 ml/1 tbsp chopped mixed herbs
Salt and freshly ground black pepper

Melt the butter or margarine in a
saucepan and fry (sauté) the carrots
and onion for 5 minutes. Stir in the
cornflour and cook for 1 minute. Stir
in the stock and simmer, stirring, until
the sauce thickens. Add the herbs,
season to taste and simmer for about
20 minutes until the carrots are
tender, adding a little more stock if
necessary.

Sweet and sour carrots

SERVES 4

450 g/1 lb young carrots, cut into
   chunks
45 ml/3 tbsp vinegar
10 ml/2 tsp light brown sugar
25 g/1 oz/2 tbsp butter or margarine

Place the carrots in a saucepan and
just cover with water, bring to the boil
and cook for about 15 minutes until
tender. Add the vinegar, sugar and
butter or margarine and continue
cooking until the liquid has
evaporated.

Carrots Bourguignonne

SERVES 4

450 g/1 lb carrots, sliced
75 g/3 oz/⅓ cup butter or margarine
2 large onions, sliced
30 ml/2 tbsp plain (all-purpose) flour
300 ml/½ pt/1¼ cups Vegetable Stock
   (page 28)
Salt and freshly ground black pepper

Place the carrots in a saucepan and
just cover with water, bring to the boil
and cook for about 15 minutes until
tender, then drain. Meanwhile, melt
the butter or margarine and fry
(sauté) the onions until soft. Add the
carrots, mix in the flour and stir until
it browns. Add the stock and season
to taste, then simmer for 15 minutes
and serve.

Cauliflower fritters

SERVES 4

100 g/4 oz/1 cup plain (all-purpose)
    flour
A pinch of salt
1 egg, beaten
150 ml/¼ pt/⅔ cup milk
350 g/12 oz cauliflower florets
Corn oil, for deep-frying

Beat together the flour, salt, egg and
milk to make a batter and leave in a
cool place. Cook the cauliflower in
boiling salted water for about
10 minutes until just tender, then
drain. Dip the cauliflower in the batter
and fry (sauté) in batches in hot oil
for a few minutes until crisp and
golden. Drain well before serving.

Cauliflower with chillies and peppers

SERVES 4

45 ml/3 tbsp oil
1 onion, sliced
2.5 ml/½ tsp turmeric
1 cauliflower, separated into florets
Salt
2 green chillies, seeded and sliced
1 red (bell) pepper, sliced
1 green pepper, sliced
1 yellow pepper, sliced

Heat the oil and fry (sauté) the onion
until soft. Add the turmeric and cook
for 1 minute. Add the cauliflower and
season to taste with salt. Cover and
cook gently for 10 minutes until the
cauliflower is almost cooked. Stir in
the chillies and peppers and cook for
a further 5 minutes until tender. Serve
with curries.

Cauliflower Polonaise

SERVES 4

1 cauliflower, separated into florets
50 g/2 oz/¼ cup butter or margarine
1 garlic clove, crushed
50 g/2 oz/1 cup fresh breadcrumbs
15 ml/1 tbsp chopped parsley
1 hard-boiled (hard-cooked) egg, finely
    chopped

Cook the cauliflower in plenty of
boiling salted water for 10 minutes
until just tender. Drain and place in a
warm serving dish. Meanwhile, melt
the butter or margarine and fry
(sauté) the garlic for 1 minute. Add
the breadcrumbs and fry until lightly
browned. Stir in the parsley and egg,
heat through and pour over the
cauliflower.

Braised celery hearts with orange

SERVES 4

25 g/1 oz/2 tbsp butter or margarine
1 onion, chopped
1 carrot, sliced
2 celery hearts
300 ml/½ pt/1¼ cups Chicken Stock
    (page 28)
Grated rind and juice of 1 orange
Salt and freshly ground black pepper

Melt the butter or margarine in a
saucepan and fry (sauté) the onion
until soft but not brown. Stir in the
carrot, celery and stock. Add the
orange rind and juice and season to
taste. Pour into an ovenproof dish,
cover and bake in a preheated oven
at 170°C/325°F/gas mark 3 for
1½ hours. Serve hot with lamb or
pork.

Italian-style celery

SERVES 4

1 head of celery, diced
25 g/1 oz/2 tbsp butter or margarine
1 onion, finely chopped
1 garlic clove, chopped
½ green (bell) pepper, finely chopped
4 tomatoes, skinned and cut into wedges
15 ml/1 tbsp chopped parsley
A pinch of basil
A pinch of cayenne
Salt and freshly ground black pepper

Cook the celery in boiling water until tender, then drain. Melt the butter or margarine and fry (sauté) the onion, garlic and green pepper until soft. Stir in the celery, tomatoes, parsley, basil and cayenne and season to taste. Cook for 10 minutes until tender.

Baked celeriac with Parmesan

SERVES 4

1 celeriac (celery root), sliced
1 garlic clove, crushed
450 ml/¾ pt/2 cups single (light) cream
Salt and freshly ground black pepper
50 g/2 oz/½ cup Parmesan cheese, freshly grated
25 g/1 oz/½ cup fresh breadcrumbs

Cook the celeriac in boiling salted water for 4 minutes, then drain. Stir the garlic into the cream. Layer the celeriac with the cream in a greased ovenproof dish, seasoning generously with salt and pepper as you go. Sprinkle with the Parmesan and breadcrumbs and bake in a preheated oven at 190°C/375°F gas mark 5 for about 45 minutes until the celeriac is tender and the top is golden brown.

Stuffed courgettes

SERVES 4

6 courgettes (zucchini)
50 g/2 oz/¼ cup butter or margarine
1 onion, chopped
2.5 ml/½ tsp paprika
30 ml/2 tbsp tomato purée (paste)
4 tomatoes, chopped
2.5 ml/½ tsp dried oregano
2.5 ml/½ tsp chopped basil
175 g/6 oz/1½ cups cooked long-grain rice
100 g/4 oz/1 cup strong Cheddar cheese, grated

Trim the stalks and boil the courgettes, whole and unpeeled, for 5 minutes. Drain, rinse in cold water and halve lengthways. Scoop out and discard the seeds. Scoop out and reserve most of the flesh, leaving a wall inside the skin. Melt the butter or margarine in a saucepan and fry (sauté) the onion until soft but not brown. Add the courgette flesh and all the other ingredients except the cheese and simmer gently for 5 minutes. Fill the courgettes with the mixture, place them in a greased ovenproof dish, sprinkle with the cheese and bake in a preheated oven at 190°C/375°F/gas mark 5 for 20 minutes until browned and crispy on top.

Fennel with cheese

SERVES 4

3 fennel bulbs, sliced
50 g/2 oz/¼ cup butter or margarine
100 g/4 oz/1 cup Gruyère (Swiss)
  cheese, grated

Cook the fennel in boiling water for
12 minutes until tender, then drain.
Rub half the butter or margarine over
an ovenproof dish and lay the fennel
in the dish. Dot with the remaining
butter or margarine and sprinkle with
the cheese. Bake in a preheated oven
at 180°C/350°F/gas mark 4 for
20 minutes until browned.

Mangetout and cashew stir-fry

SERVES 4

15 ml/1 tbsp oil
½ red (bell) pepper, thinly sliced
½ yellow pepper, thinly sliced
2.5 cm/1 in piece of root ginger,
  chopped
50 g/2 oz/½ cup cashew nuts
225 g/8 oz mangetout (snow peas)
100 g/4 oz/2 cups beansprouts
30 ml/2 tbsp dry sherry
A few drops soy sauce
5 ml/1 tsp tomato purée (paste)

Heat the oil in a frying pan (skillet)
and fry (sauté) the peppers and
ginger for 2 minutes. Add the nuts
and stir-fry for 1 minute. Add the
remaining ingredients and stir-fry for
about 3 minutes until everything is
well blended and the vegetables are
coated in the sauce. Serve at once.

Orange baked marrow

SERVES 4

1 marrow (squash), peeled and thickly
  sliced
25 g/1 oz/2 tbsp butter or margarine
30 ml/2 tbsp clear honey
30 ml/2 tbsp orange juice
15 ml/1 tbsp lemon juice
5 ml/1 tsp ground cinnamon
2.5 ml/½ tsp ground ginger
5 ml/1 tsp grated orange peel

Lay the marrow slices in a greased
ovenproof dish. Melt the butter or
margarine and stir in the honey and
orange and lemon juices. Pour over
the marrow. Sprinkle with the spices
and orange peel and bake in a
preheated oven at 180°C/350°F/gas
mark 4 for 40 minutes, basting
occasionally. Serve with rich meat or
poultry.

Creamed parsnips in breadcrumbs

SERVES 4

25 g/1 oz/2 tbsp butter or margarine
450 g/1 lb parsnips, boiled and mashed
15 ml/1 tsp single (light) cream or milk
Salt and freshly ground black pepper
2 eggs, beaten
100 g/4 oz/2 cups fresh breadcrumbs
Oil, for deep-frying

Melt the butter or margarine, add the
parsnips and milk and season to
taste. Stir over a low heat until it
begins to bubble, then remove from
the heat and beat in 1 egg. Allow to
cool, then shape into small balls. Roll
in the beaten egg, then in the
breadcrumbs and fry (sauté) in deep
hot oil until golden brown.

Stuffed mushrooms

SERVES 4

225 g/8 oz/1 cup split peas, soaked for
   30 minutes, then drained
100 g/4 oz/2 cups wholemeal
   breadcrumbs
1 carrot, chopped
1 onion, chopped
1 potato, chopped
15 ml/1 tbsp oil
2.5 ml/½ tsp French mustard
2.5 ml/½ tsp yeast extract
10 ml/2 tsp chopped parsley
1 sage leaf, chopped
15 ml/1 tbsp dry sherry
15 ml/1 tbsp water
8 large open mushrooms

Boil the peas in water until soft, then
drain and mash. Reserve half the
breadcrumbs, then mix together all
the remaining ingredients except the
mushrooms with the peas. Chop the
mushroom stalks and stir them into
the mixture. Lay the mushrooms,
black-side up, in a shallow ovenproof
dish. Divide the stuffing between the
mushrooms and sprinkle with the
reserved breadcrumbs. Bake in a
preheated oven at 190°C/375°F/gas
mark 5 for 20 minutes until cooked
through and crispy on top.

Fried mushrooms Kiev

SERVES 4

24 open cap mushrooms
100 g/4 oz/½ cup unsalted (sweet)
   butter, softened
2 garlic cloves, crushed
30 ml/2 tbsp chopped parsley
Salt and freshly ground black pepper
2 eggs, beaten
75 g/3 oz/1½ cups fresh breadcrumbs
Corn oil, for deep-frying
A few parsley sprigs

Remove the stalks from the
mushrooms and chop them finely.
Keep the caps whole. Mix the stalks
with the butter, garlic and parsley and
season to taste. Spoon the mixture
into the mushroom caps, press them
together in pairs and secure with
cocktail sticks (toothpicks). Dip the
mushrooms in the egg, then the
breadcrumbs, then the egg and
breadcrumbs again. Chill for 1 hour.
Fry (sauté) the mushrooms in deep
hot oil until golden brown. Drain well,
remove the cocktail sticks and serve
garnished with parsley.

Mushrooms in tomato and oregano

SERVES 4

45 ml/3 tbsp olive oil
1 onion, chopped
1 garlic clove, chopped
350 g/12 oz button mushrooms, sliced
400 g/14 oz/1 large can of tomatoes,
   drained and chopped
60 ml/4 tbsp dry white wine
2.5 ml/½ tsp dried oregano
1 bouquet garni sachet
Salt and freshly ground black pepper
15 ml/1 tbsp chopped parsley

Heat the oil and fry (sauté) the onion
and garlic until browned. Add the
mushrooms and toss well in the oil,
then stir in the tomatoes, wine,
oregano and bouquet garni and
season to taste. Simmer gently for
15 minutes, then remove the bouquet
garni, sprinkle with the parsley and
serve hot.

Fried potatoes and onions

SERVES 4

45 ml/3 tbsp oil
450 g/1 lb potatoes, thinly sliced
4 onions, sliced
Salt and freshly ground black pepper

Heat the oil in a frying pan (skillet), then layer the potatoes and onions in the pan, seasoning each layer well with salt and pepper. Fry (sauté) gently, turning so that the potatoes and onions are cooked through and crispy and browned on the top and bottom. Serve with grilled (broiled) meats and gherkins (cornichons).

Roasted onions with sage

SERVES 4

4 large onions
60 ml/4 tbsp olive oil
10 ml/2 tsp chopped sage
Salt and freshly ground black pepper
50 g/2 oz/1 cup breadcrumbs
1 garlic clove, crushed

Halve the onions crossways and arrange in a 23 cm/9 in roasting tin (pan), pointed-ends down, so that they fit fairly tightly. Drizzle with 45 ml/3 tbsp of the oil, sprinkle with half the sage and season with salt and pepper. Cover with foil and bake in a preheated oven at 180°C/ 350°F/gas mark 4 for about 45 minutes until tender and golden. Meanwhile, mix together the remaining oil and sage, the breadcrumbs and garlic and season lightly. Remove the foil and sprinkle the breadcrumb mixture over the cooked onions, then return to the

oven for a further 10–15 minutes until browned.

Baked potatoes in soured cream

SERVES 4

450 g/1 lb potatoes, sliced
300 ml/½ pt/1¼ cups Vegetable Stock (page 28)
5 ml/1 tsp ground caraway
Salt and freshly ground black pepper
2 onions, chopped
1 bunch of spring onions (scallions), sliced
450 ml/¾ pt/2 cups soured (dairy sour) cream
2 eggs, beaten
100 g/4 oz/1 cup Emmental (Swiss) cheese, grated
4 tomatoes, skinned, seeded and sliced
30 ml/2 tbsp snipped chives
25 g/1 oz/2 tbsp butter or margarine, diced

Place the potatoes in a shallow ovenproof dish. Pour the stock over, then add the caraway and season to taste with salt and pepper. Sprinkle with the onions and spring onions and bake in a preheated oven at 200°C/ 400°F/gas mark 6 for 25 minutes. Meanwhile, mix together the soured cream, eggs and cheese. Spread the tomatoes over the potatoes and pour the cream mixture over. Sprinkle with the chives and dot with the butter or margarine. Return to the oven for a further 20 minutes.

Cassoulet (page 196)

New potatoes with lemon and herbs

SERVES 4

750 g/12 oz new potatoes
120 ml/4 fl oz/½ cup olive oil
25 g/1 oz/2 tbsp butter or margarine
2 garlic cloves, crushed
15 ml/1 tbsp thyme leaves
5 ml/1 tsp grated lemon rind
Salt and freshly ground black pepper
15 ml/1 tbsp chopped parsley

Cook the potatoes in their skins in boiling salted water for about 15 minutes or until tender. Drain and cool. Heat the oil and butter or margarine with the garlic, thyme and lemon rind, then fry (sauté) the potatoes until hot and browned. Season and serve sprinkled with the parsley.

Baked potatoes with chick peas

SERVES 4

4 large potatoes, scrubbed
100 g/4 oz canned chick peas
  (garbanzos), drained
50 g/2 oz/¼ cup butter or margarine
Salt and freshly ground black pepper
50 g/2 oz/½ cup Cheddar cheese, grated

Prick the potatoes all over with a fork and bake in a preheated oven at 200°C/400°F/gas mark 6 for about 1 hour until soft. Purée the chick peas. Halve the potatoes and scoop out the flesh. Mash well, then mix in the butter or margarine, chick peas and seasoning. Pile back into the potato shells, sprinkle with the cheese and brown in the oven for 10 minutes.

*Cauliflower with chillies
and peppers (page 220)*

Baked potatoes with anchovies

SERVES 4

50 g/2 oz/¼ cup butter or margarine
1 Spanish onion, chopped
4 potatoes, cut into julienne strips
150 ml/¼ pt/⅔ cup single (light) cream
150 ml/¼ pt/⅔ cup milk
Salt and freshly ground black pepper
50 g/2 oz/1 small can of anchovy fillets,
  drained
50 g/2 oz/1 cup fresh breadcrumbs

Heat the butter or margarine and fry (sauté) the onion until soft. Add the potatoes and fry for 3 minutes, stirring well. Stir in the cream and milk and season lightly to taste. Simmer gently for 5 minutes until the potatoes begin to soften. Transfer half the mixture to a shallow ovenproof dish, arrange the anchovy fillets over the top, cover with the remaining potato mixture and sprinkle with the breadcrumbs. Bake in a preheated oven at 200°C/400°F/gas mark 6 for 20 minutes until cooked through and crispy on top.

Potato scones

SERVES 4

450 g/1 lb cooked potato, mashed
25 g/1 oz/2 tbsp butter or margarine
50 g/2 oz/½ cup Cheddar cheese, grated
75 g/3 oz/¾ cup plain (all-purpose) flour
Salt and freshly ground black pepper
30 ml/2 tbsp oil

Mix together the potato, butter or margarine, cheese and flour and season to taste with salt and pepper. Divide into pieces, shape into flat rounds and fry (sauté) in the oil for about 3 minutes each side until golden. Serve immediately.

Baked potato and onion layer

SERVES 4

900 g/2 lb potatoes, thinly sliced
2 onions, sliced
50 g/2 oz/¼ cup butter or margarine, grated
225 g/8 oz/2 cups Cheddar cheese, grated
300 ml/½ pt/1¼ cups milk
Salt and freshly ground black pepper

Layer the potatoes, onions, butter or margarine and cheese in an ovenproof dish, ending with a layer of cheese. Season the milk with salt and pepper and pour it over the potatoes. Bake in a preheated oven at 190°C/375°F/gas mark 5 for 1½ hours until the potatoes are cooked through and crispy on top.

Roast potatoes

SERVES 4

900 g/2 lb potatoes, cut into chunks
Salt
60 ml/4 tbsp melted lard (shortening) or oil

Cook the potatoes in boiling salted water for 5 minutes, then drain. Shake in the sieve (strainer) to roughen the surfaces. Toss the potatoes with the lard or oil in a roasting tin (pan) until coated, then roast in a preheated oven at 200°C/400°F/gas mark 6 for about 1 hour until crisp and golden on the outside and soft in the centre, turning once or twice during cooking.

Note:
For the best flavour, roast in the same tin as the meat if you are cooking a joint, as long as you have not added water to the tin.

Pumpkin bake

SERVES 4

450 g/1 lb pumpkin, rinded and chopped
100 g/4 oz/½ cup butter or margarine
1 onion, chopped
175 g/6 oz carrots, chopped
100 g/4 oz celery, chopped
175 g/6 oz/3 cups fresh breadcrumbs
5 ml/1 tsp chopped basil
5 ml/1 tsp thyme leaves
Salt and freshly ground black pepper
450 ml/¾ pt/2 cups plain yoghurt
45 ml/3 tbsp sesame oil
100 g/4 oz/½ cup Cheddar cheese, grated
1 egg, beaten
30 ml/2 tbsp snipped chives
50 g/2 oz sesame seeds, toasted

Steam the pumpkin until tender, then drain. Melt the butter or margarine and fry (sauté) the onions, carrots and celery until soft but not brown. Add the breadcrumbs and herbs and season to taste. Put half the pumpkin in a greased ovenproof dish, spread with the stuffing mixture and top with the remaining pumpkin. Stir the yoghurt, oil and cheese over a low heat until the cheese melts. Season with a little salt. Stir a spoonful of the sauce into the egg, then stir the egg into the sauce and add the chives. Pour the sauce over the pumpkin and sprinkle with the sesame seeds. Bake in a preheated oven at 180°C/350°F/gas mark 4 for 30 minutes.

Sweet roast pumpkin

SERVES 4

900 g/2 lb pumpkin
75 ml/5 tbsp olive oil
15 ml/1 tbsp caster (superfine) sugar
Salt and freshly ground black pepper

Skin and seed the pumpkin and cut into chunks. Melt the oil in a roasting tin (pan) and season with the sugar and plenty of salt and pepper. When the oil is hot, add the pumpkin and cook until browned on all sides. Transfer the tin to a preheated oven and roast at 200°C/400°F/gas mark 6 for about 30 minutes until the pumpkin is tender.

Sauerkraut and potatoes

SERVES 4

450 g/1 lb potatoes, sliced
30 ml/2 tbsp oil
2 onions, sliced
100 g/4 oz bacon, chopped
450 g/1 lb bottled sauerkraut
Salt and freshly ground black pepper
15 ml/1 tbsp cornflour (cornstarch)

Cook the potatoes in boiling salted water until just tender. Do not drain. Meanwhile, heat the oil and fry (sauté) the onions and bacon until soft and brown. When the potatoes are ready, stir in the sauerkraut, onions and bacon and season to taste with a little salt and plenty of black pepper. Mix the cornflour with a little cold water and stir into the pan. Bring to the boil, stirring, then simmer for 20 minutes until thick. Serve with frankfurters and gherkins (cornichons).

Spinach Florentine

SERVES 4

25 g/1 oz/2 tbsp butter or margarine
40 g/1½ oz plain (all-purpose) flour
450 ml/¾ pt/2 cups milk
Salt and freshly ground black pepper
225 g/8 oz frozen spinach, thawed and finely chopped
4 eggs

Melt the butter or margarine, stir in the flour and cook for 1 minute. Whisk in the milk and cook, stirring, until the sauce thickens. Season to taste. Mix a third of the sauce with the spinach and adjust the seasoning if necessary. Pour the mixture into a shallow ovenproof dish and make four wells in the mixture. Break an egg into each one, cover with the remaining sauce and bake in a preheated oven at 190°C/375°F/gas mark 5 for 25 minutes.

Tomatoes duxelle

SERVES 4

4 large tomatoes
25 g/1 oz/2 tbsp butter or margarine
1 onion, finely chopped
50 g/2 oz mushrooms, finely chopped
25 g/1 oz/½ cup fresh breadcrumbs
15 ml/1 tbsp chopped parsley
1 egg yolk, beaten
Salt and freshly ground black pepper

Cut the stalk ends off the tomatoes and reserve. Scoop out the seeds. Melt the butter or margarine and fry (sauté) the onion until soft. Add the mushrooms and cook for 2 minutes. Stir in the breadcrumbs, parsley and egg yolk and season to taste with salt and pepper. Fill the tomato shells with the mixture, replace the lids and place in an ovenproof dish. Bake at 190°C/375°F/gas mark 5 for 25 minutes.

Creamed swede

SERVES 4

450 g/1 lb swede (rutabaga), chopped
50 g/2 oz/¼ cup butter or margarine
60 ml/4 tbsp single (light) cream
A pinch of ground nutmeg
Salt and freshly ground black pepper

Cook the swede in boiling salted water for about 15 minutes until tender, then drain well. Return to the saucepan and add the butter or margarine and cream and mash well. Season to taste with nutmeg, salt and pepper and serve hot.

Ratatouille

SERVES 4

25 g/1 oz/2 tbsp butter or margarine
45 ml/3 tbsp olive oil
2 onions, thinly sliced
2 garlic cloves, crushed
3 aubergines (eggplants), thinly sliced
1 green (bell) pepper, chopped
1 red pepper, chopped
5 courgettes (zucchini)
400 g/14 oz/1 large can of tomatoes
5 ml/1 tsp chopped basil
5 ml/1 tsp rosemary leaves
2 bay leaves
Salt and freshly ground black pepper
30 ml/2 tbsp chopped parsley

Melt the butter or margarine with the oil in a flameproof casserole dish (Dutch oven), and fry (sauté) the onions and garlic until soft but not brown. Add the aubergines, peppers and courgettes and fry for 5 minutes, stirring frequently. Add the tomatoes and their juice and the herbs and season to taste. Sprinkle with the parsley and bring to the boil. Cover and simmer for 45 minutes until the vegetables are cooked.

Sweetcorn fritters

SERVES 4

2 eggs, separated
Salt and freshly ground black pepper
225 g/8 oz frozen or canned sweetcorn (corn)
5 ml/1 tsp baking powder
50 g/2 oz/1 cup fresh breadcrumbs
Oil, for shallow-frying

Whisk the egg yolks with salt and pepper and stir in the sweetcorn and baking powder. Whisk the egg whites until stiff, then fold them into the mixture with the breadcrumbs. Fry (sauté) spoonfuls of the mixture in hot shallow oil for a few minutes, turning once during cooking. Serve hot with chicken dishes.

Stuffed tomatoes

SERVES 4

4 large tomatoes
100 g/4 oz/½ cup full-fat soft cheese
60 ml/4 tbsp plain yoghurt
5 cm/2 in piece of cucumber, finely chopped
15 ml/1 tbsp chopped mint
Salt and freshly ground black pepper

Cut a slice off the top of each tomato and hollow out the inside. Discard the seeds and juice and chop the flesh. Beat together the cheese and yoghurt, then stir in the tomato, cucumber and mint and season to taste with salt and pepper. Fill the tomatoes with the mixture and serve.

Vegetable fritters

SERVES 4

225 g/8 oz broccoli florets
225 g/8 oz cauliflower florets
225 g/8 oz carrots, cubed
225 g/8 oz celeriac (celery root), cubed
100 g/4 oz/1 cup wholemeal flour
200 ml/7 fl oz/scant 1 cup lager
15 ml/1 tbsp olive oil
5 ml/1 tsp caster (superfine) sugar
A pinch of salt
1 egg, separated
45 ml/3 tbsp corn oil
For the sauce:
25 g/1 oz/2 tbsp butter or margarine
1 onion, chopped
100 g/4 oz/½ small can of tomatoes
15 ml/1 tbsp plain (all-purpose) flour
30 ml/2 tbsp tomato purée (paste)
150 ml/¼ pt/⅔ cup dry white wine
150 ml/¼ pt/⅔ cup Vegetable Stock
  (page 28)
150 ml/¼ pt/⅔ cup single (light) cream
15 ml/1 tbsp dried oregano
Salt and freshly ground black pepper

Blanch the vegetables in boiling salted water for 5 minutes, then drain well. Mix together the wholemeal flour, lager, olive oil, sugar, salt and egg yolk and leave to stand for 15 minutes. Whisk the egg white until stiff, then fold into the batter. Turn the vegetables in the batter, then fry (sauté) in the hot corn oil until golden brown. Drain well and keep warm.

To make the sauce, heat the butter or margarine and fry the onion until soft but not brown. Add the tomatoes, flour and tomato purée, then stir in the wine and stock. Bring to the boil, cover and simmer for 5 minutes, stirring frequently. Add the cream and oregano and season to taste. Pour on to individual plates, top with the vegetables and serve immediately.

Roasted Mediterranean vegetables

SERVES 4

4 onions
1 red (bell) pepper
1 green (bell) pepper
8 new potatoes
120 ml/4 fl oz/½ cup olive oil
30 ml/2 tbsp coarse salt
4 courgettes (zucchini)
8 baby aubergines (eggplants)

Leave all the vegetables whole, scrub and dry well. Remove the outer skin from the onions and slice off the top and tail. Remove the stem and seeds from the peppers. Place the onions, peppers and potatoes in a roasting tin (pan) and pour over the olive oil, then toss so that the vegetables are well coated in oil. Sprinkle with coarse salt. Roast in a preheated oven at 200°C/400°F/gas mark 6 for 30 minutes. Add the courgettes and aubergines to the pan and toss in the oil. Return all the vegetables to the oven for a further 45 minutes until the vegetables are tender and lightly charred on the edges. Serve hot or cold.

229

Vegetarian dishes

An increasing number of people are becoming vegetarian, and
even more people are cutting down on their intake of red meats,
in particular, and perhaps choosing to have a 'vegetarian' day
each week. But even those who never intend to give up eating
meat will find recipes here to enjoy. Of course, you'll find plenty of
other recipes in the book that are suitable for vegetarians,
especially in the Vegetables (page 215–229) and Pulses, Grains
and Pasta (page 195–214) chapters. Please note that these
recipes do contain dairy products so you may wish to substitute
appropriate vegan or vegetarian products.

Aubergine with Parmesan and Mozzarella

SERVES 4

1–2 garlic cloves, crushed
30 ml/2 tbsp olive oil
Salt and freshly ground black pepper
2 medium aubergines (eggplants), peeled and thickly sliced
30 ml/2 tbsp torn basil leaves
25 g/1 oz/¼ cup Parmesan cheese, freshly grated
2 tomatoes, skinned and thinly sliced
100 g/4 oz Mozzarella cheese, thinly sliced

Blend the garlic into the oil and season with salt and pepper. Brush over the aubergine slices on both sides, then arrange them in a single layer on baking (cookie) sheets and cook in a preheated oven at 220°C/425°F/gas mark 7 for about 10 minutes until the bases are lightly browned. Turn them over and cook for a further 10 minutes until golden. Arrange half the aubergine slices in a 23 cm/9 in baking dish, sprinkle with half the basil and a third of the Parmesan. Top with the tomatoes, the remaining basil, half the Mozzarella and half the remaining Parmesan. Cover with the remaining aubergine slices and top with the remaining Mozzarella and Parmesan. Reduce the oven temperature to 180°C/350°F/gas mark 4, cover with foil and bake for 30 minutes, then remove the foil and bake for a further 10 minutes until golden.

Aubergine and vegetable medley

SERVES 4

1 aubergine (eggplant), sliced
Salt and freshly ground black pepper
15 ml/1 tbsp oil
2 leeks, sliced
1 large potato, sliced
50 g/2 oz mushrooms, sliced
½ small cabbage, sliced
400 g/14 oz/1 large can of tomatoes
5 ml/1 tsp paprika
75 g/3 oz/¾ cup smoked cheese, sliced
50 g/2 oz/1 cup fresh breadcrumbs
50 g/2 oz/½ cup cashew nuts, ground
25 g/1 oz/2 tbsp butter or margarine, melted

Lay the aubergine slices on a plate, sprinkle with salt, cover and leave for 30 minutes. Heat the oil and fry (sauté) the leeks until soft. Place the potatoes in a layer in a base of an ovenproof dish. Add the leeks, then the mushrooms and cabbage. Drain the aubergine and place on top. Purée the tomatoes and their juice with the paprika in a food processor or blender and pour over the vegetables. Layer the cheese on top. Mix the breadcrumbs and nuts with the melted butter or margarine and season to taste. Sprinkle over the vegetables and bake in a preheated oven at 180°C/350°F/gas mark 4 for 1¼ hours.

Stuffed aubergines

SERVES 4

2 large aubergines (eggplants), halved
45 ml/3 tbsp olive oil
2 garlic cloves, crushed
1 onion, chopped
4 tomatoes, skinned, seeded and
    chopped
250 ml/8 fl oz/1 cup Vegetable Stock
    (page 28)
225 g/8 oz soya granules
175 g/6 oz/¾ cup low-fat quark
30 ml/2 tbsp tomato purée (paste)
5 ml/1 tsp chopped basil
5 ml/1 tsp dried oregano
15 ml/1 tbsp snipped chives
15 ml/1 tbsp chopped parsley
2 eggs, beaten
100 g/4 oz/1 cup Emmental (Swiss)
    cheese, grated
Salt and freshly ground black pepper

Cook the aubergines in boiling salted
water for 5 minutes, then drain.
Scoop out a little of the flesh to make
a boat shape, and chop the flesh.
Heat the oil and fry (sauté) the garlic
and onion until soft but not brown.
Add the chopped aubergine, tomatoes
and stock, bring to the boil, cover and
simmer for 5 minutes. Prepare the
soya granules according to the
instructions on the packet. Mix with
the quark, tomato purée, herbs, eggs
and cheese and season to taste. Place
the aubergines cut-side up in an
ovenproof dish. Spoon the mixture
into the hollows, piling the rest on
top. Pour over the tomato sauce and
bake in a preheated oven at 200°C/
400°F/gas mark 6 for 20 minutes.
Serve immediately.

Aubergine bake

SERVES 4

90 ml/6 tbsp olive oil
1 onion, sliced
2 garlic cloves, crushed
400 g/14 oz/1 large can of tomatoes,
    chopped
15 ml/1 tbsp chopped parsley
Salt and freshly ground black pepper
4 aubergines (eggplants), thinly sliced
350 g/11 oz Mozzarella cheese,
    shredded
15 ml/1 tbsp chopped marjoram
15 ml/1 tbsp chopped basil
150 ml/¼ pt/⅔ cup White Sauce
    (page 250)
25 g/1 oz/¼ cup Parmesan cheese,
    freshly grated

Heat 45 ml/3 tbsp of the oil and fry
(sauté) the onion and garlic until soft
but not brown. Add the tomatoes and
parsley, season with salt and pepper
and leave to simmer for about
15 minutes until thickened slightly.
Meanwhile, bring a large pan of salted
water to the boil, add the aubergines
and boil for 2 minutes, then drain well
and pat dry on kitchen paper (paper
towels). Spoon half the tomato sauce
into the bottom of a shallow
ovenproof dish. Cover with half the
aubergines and top with half the
Mozzarella. Sprinkle with the
marjoram and basil and season with
salt and pepper. Repeat the layers,
then pour the White Sauce over and
sprinkle with the Parmesan. Cook in a
preheated oven at 200°C/400°F/gas
mark 6 for about 30 minutes until
heated through and golden on top.

Mixed curried beans

SERVES 4

100 g/4 oz/½ cup butter or margarine
2 onions, chopped
2 garlic cloves, crushed
15 ml/1 tbsp ground coriander (cilantro)
5 ml/1 tsp garam masala
5 ml/1 tsp chilli powder
400 g/14 oz/1 large can of tomatoes, chopped
5 ml/1 tsp sugar
300 g/11 oz/1 medium can of red kidney beans, drained
300 g/11 oz/1 medium can of borlotti beans, drained
300 g/11 oz/1 medium can of haricot (navy) beans, drained
Salt and freshly ground black pepper

Melt the butter or margarine and fry (sauté) the onions until just browned. Add the garlic and fry for 1 minute, then add the coriander, garam masala and chilli powder and fry for a few seconds. Stir in the tomatoes and sugar and simmer for 10 minutes. Stir in the beans, season to taste and heat through thoroughly before serving.

Tyropitakia

SERVES 4

225 g/8 oz/2 cups Feta cheese, crumbled
225 g/8 oz/1 cup ricotta or cottage cheese
30 ml/2 tbsp chopped parsley
10 ml/2 tsp chopped mint
Freshly ground black pepper
2 eggs, beaten
400 g/14 oz filo pastry (paste)
60 ml/4 tbsp oil

Mix the cheeses with the herbs and season to taste with pepper. Stir in the eggs. Cut the filo pastry into 13 cm/5 in wide strips, and cover the strips you are not working with with a damp cloth to avoid them drying out while you are working. Take one strip at a time, brush it lightly with oil and fold it in half lengthways. Place 5 ml/ 1 tsp of the cheese mixture on the end of the strip and fold it over into triangles. Place the finished triangles on a greased baking (cookie) sheet, brush the tops with a little oil and bake in a preheated oven at 180°C/ 350°F/gas mark 4 for 35 minutes until golden brown.

Chick pea and tomato casserole

SERVES 4

30 ml/2 tbsp olive oil
1 celery stick, chopped
1 carrot, chopped
1 onion, chopped
2 garlic cloves, chopped
100 g/4 oz shallots, cut into wedges
45 ml/3 tbsp dry white wine
400 g/14 oz/1 large can tomatoes, chopped
10 ml/2 tsp dried oregano
400 g/14 oz/1 large can of chick peas (garbanzos), drained
400 g/14 oz/1 large can of cannellini beans
Salt and freshly ground black pepper
15 ml/1 tbsp chopped parsley

Heat the oil and fry (sauté) the celery, carrot, onion and garlic until soft but not brown. Add the shallots and fry until just golden. Add the wine and cook for 2 minutes until it has evaporated. Stir in the tomatoes and oregano and bring to a simmer, then stir in the chick peas and beans and simmer gently for about 15 minutes until the sauce is thick. Season to taste and serve sprinkled with the parsley.

Chick pea and mushroom curry

SERVES 4

50 g/2 oz/⅓ cup split peas, soaked
   overnight
30 ml/2 tbsp oil
25 g/1 oz/2 tbsp butter or margarine
2 garlic cloves, crushed
2 onions, chopped
15 ml/1 tbsp curry powder
45 ml/3 tbsp tomato purée (paste)
50 g/2 oz creamed coconut, grated
225 g/8 oz button mushrooms,
   quartered
400 g/14 oz/1 large can of chick peas
   (garbanzos)
Salt and freshly ground black pepper
Boiled rice, to serve

Cook the split peas in boiling water
until tender, then drain. Heat the oil
and butter or margarine and fry
(sauté) the garlic and onions until soft
but not brown. Stir in the curry
powder to taste and cook for
1 minute, then stir in the tomato
purée, coconut and mushrooms and
cook for 5 minutes. Add the chick
peas and season to taste. Cover and
simmer for 10 minutes until all the
ingredients are tender and well
combined. Serve with boiled rice.

Corn pudding

SERVES 4

15 ml/1 tbsp plain (all-purpose) flour
300 ml/½ pt/1¼ cups milk
350 g/12 oz/1 large can of sweetcorn
   (corn), drained
1 egg white, whisked
Salt and freshly ground black pepper

Mix the flour to a paste with a little
milk, then mix in all the ingredients,
seasoning to taste with salt and

pepper. Turn into a greased soufflé
dish, cover with foil and bake in a
preheated oven at 180°C/350°F/ gas
mark 4 for 30 minutes until the
centre is set.

Cheese round

SERVES 4

2 onions, chopped
175 g/6 oz/1½ cups strong cheese,
   grated
15 ml/1 tbsp chopped parsley
30 ml/2 tbsp mustard pickle
Salt and freshly ground black pepper
400 g/14 oz Shortcrust Pastry
   (page 164)
1 egg, beaten
15 ml/1 tbsp sesame seeds

Mix together the onions, cheese,
parsley and pickle and season to
taste. Roll out the pastry (paste) on a
lightly floured surface to a large
rectangle. Spread the filling over the
pastry to within 1 cm/½ in of the
edge, then roll up like a Swiss (jelly)
roll and make cuts along the roll to
three-quarters of the width. Shape
into a ring and seal the ends with
egg. Place on a greased baking
(cookie) sheet, brush with the egg
and sprinkle with the sesame seeds.
Bake in a preheated oven at 200°C/
400°F/ gas mark 6 for 30 minutes.

Savoury choux fritters

SERVES 4

300 ml/½ pt/1¼ cups Vegetable Stock
   (page 28)
50 g/2 oz/¼ cup butter or margarine
A pinch of grated nutmeg
Salt and freshly ground black pepper
150 g/5 oz/1¼ cups wholemeal flour
45 ml/3 tbsp cornflour (cornstarch)
100 g/4 oz/½ cup wheatgerm
4 eggs, beaten
100 g/4 oz/1 cup Parmesan cheese,
   freshly grated
30 ml/2 tbsp snipped chives
Corn oil, for deep-frying
Mixed green salad, to serve

Place the stock, butter or margarine
and nutmeg in a saucepan and season
to taste. Bring just to the boil, then
stir in the flour, cornflour and
wheatgerm and beat until the mixture
comes cleanly away from the side of
the pan. Beat in the eggs a little at a
time, then beat in the cheese and
chives. Heat the oil and drop
spoonfuls of the mixture into the hot
oil and fry (sauté) until golden. Drain
well and serve hot or cold with a
mixed green salad.

Courgette fritters

SERVES 4

100 g/4 oz/1 cup self-raising (self-rising)
   flour
2 eggs, beaten
50 ml/4 tbsp milk
Salt and freshly ground black pepper
225 g/8 oz courgettes (zucchini), grated
15 ml/1 tbsp dried oregano
30 ml/2 tbsp olive oil

Whisk the flour, eggs and milk to a
thick batter and season with salt and
pepper. Mix in the courgettes and

oregano. Heat the oil in a large frying
pan (skillet) and fry (sauté) spoonfuls
of the mixture for a few minutes each
side until golden brown. Remove
from the pan and keep warm while
you fry the remaining fritters. Serve
immediately.

Cucumber and cheese mousse

SERVES 4

1 cucumber, diced
Salt
175 g/6 oz/¾ cup full-fat soft cheese
5 ml/1 tsp chopped onion
Salt and freshly ground black pepper
15 ml/1 tbsp powdered gelatine
150 ml/¼ pt/⅔ cup water
30 ml/2 tbsp white wine vinegar
15 ml/1 tbsp caster (superfine) sugar
A pinch of ground mace
150 ml/¼ pt/⅔ cup double (heavy)
   cream, whipped

Sprinkle the cucumber with salt and
leave pressed between two plates for
30 minutes. Mix together the cheese
and onion and season to taste.
Dissolve the gelatine in the water over
a pan of hot water and stir into the
cheese. Drain the cucumber and mix
with the wine vinegar, sugar and
mace. Fold the cucumber and cream
into the cheese mixture, spoon into a
greased 900 ml/1½ pt/3¾ cup ring
mould and leave to set.

Leek and Swiss cheese roly poly

SERVES 4

200 g/7 oz/1¾ cups wholemeal flour
3 eggs
15 ml/1 tbsp oil
250 ml/8 fl oz/1 cup lukewarm water
Salt and freshly ground black pepper
5 ml/1 tsp ground caraway seeds
2.5 ml/½ tsp ground coriander (cilantro)
2.5 ml/½ tsp clear honey
30 ml/2 tbsp cider vinegar
50 g/2 oz/¼ cup butter or margarine
2 onions, chopped
2 leeks, sliced
2 garlic cloves, crushed
250 ml/8 fl oz/1 cup quark or full-fat
    soft cheese
100 g/4 oz/1 cup Emmental (Swiss)
    cheese, grated
45 ml/3 tbsp fresh breadcrumbs
A pinch of grated nutmeg
30 ml/2 tbsp snipped chives
1 egg yolk
15 ml/1 tbsp water

Sift the flour into a bowl and add
1 egg, the oil, water and 5 ml/1 tsp
salt. Add the caraway seeds,
coriander, honey and cider vinegar
and knead to a smooth dough. Cover
and leave for 30 minutes.

Meanwhile, heat the butter or
margarine and fry (sauté) the onions
and leeks until translucent. Add the
garlic and 5 ml/1 tsp salt and fry
briefly, then remove from the heat and
leave to cool. Beat the quark or soft
cheese with the remaining eggs, then
fold in the vegetables. Add the grated
cheese, breadcrumbs, nutmeg and
chives and season to taste with salt
and pepper. Roll out the dough on a
sheet of greaseproof (waxed) paper to
5 mm/¼ in thick. Spread the quark

mixture over the dough, then use the
paper to help you roll the dough into
a tube. Carefully transfer it to a
greased baking (cookie) sheet and
bake in a preheated oven at 200°C/
400°F/gas mark 6 for 30 minutes.
Beat the egg yolk with the water.
Remove the roly poly from the oven
and brush the egg mixture over the
surface. Return it to the oven for a
further 10 minutes to brown, then
serve hot.

Pasta with peas and fennel

SERVES 4

150 ml/¼ pt/⅔ cup olive oil
400 g/14 oz fennel bulbs, diced
4 leeks, white parts only, finely chopped
150 ml/¼ pt/⅔ cup water
100 g/4 oz shelled peas
Salt and freshly ground black pepper
400 g/14 oz pasta shapes
50 g/2 oz/½ cup Parmesan cheese,
    freshly grated

Heat the oil in a pan and fry (sauté)
the fennel and leeks for about
2 minutes. Add the water, bring to
the boil, cover and simmer gently for
20 minutes. Add the peas and season
with salt and pepper. Uncover and
simmer for 10 minutes until the peas
are tender. Meanwhile, bring a large
pan of salted water to the boil, add
the pasta and simmer for about
10 minutes until the pasta is just
cooked. Drain well, then toss in the
sauce and serve sprinkled with the
Parmesan.

Mushroom and almond croustade

SERVES 4

100 g/4 oz/2 cups fresh breadcrumbs
100 g/4 oz/1 cup ground almonds
50 g/2 oz/¼ cup butter or margarine
100 g/4 oz/1 cup flaked (slivered)
    almonds
1 garlic clove, crushed
2.5 ml/½ tsp dried mixed herbs
450 g/1 lb button mushrooms
450 ml/¾ pt/2 cups soya milk
1 bay leaf
25 g/1 oz/¼ cup plain (all-purpose) flour
150 ml/¼ pt/⅔ cup dry white wine
A pinch of grated nutmeg
Salt and freshly ground black pepper
15 ml/1 tbsp chopped parsley

Mix together the breadcrumbs and ground almonds and rub in the butter or margarine until the mixture resembles breadcrumbs. Add the flaked almonds, garlic and herbs. Press the mixture into a greased pie dish and bake in a preheated oven at 230°C/450°F/gas mark 8 for 15 minutes until crisp. Keep warm. Meanwhile, put the mushrooms, milk and bay leaf in a saucepan, bring to the boil and simmer for 5 minutes until the mushrooms are tender. Remove the bay leaf. Blend the flour with the wine and stir in a little of the hot milk, then mix it into the sauce, stirring well. Simmer for 5 minutes, then add the nutmeg and season to taste with salt and pepper. Spoon on to the warm base and serve sprinkled with the parsley.

Red onion and cheese tarts

SERVES 4

250 g/9 oz Puff Pastry (page 165)
30 ml/2 tbsp olive oil
2 red onions, sliced
1 orange (bell) pepper, seeded and
    sliced
1 garlic clove, crushed
4 tomatoes, skinned, seeded and sliced
150 ml/¼ pt/⅔ cup passata (sieved
    tomatoes)
Salt and freshly ground black pepper
175 g/6 oz/1½ cups Mozzarella cheese,
    shredded
A few rosemary sprigs

Roll out the pastry (paste) and cut it into 15 cm/6 in squares. Place on a dampened baking (cookie) sheet and fold up the sides to contain the filling. Heat the oil and fry (sauté) the onions, orange pepper, garlic and tomatoes until just beginning to soften. Remove from the heat, stir in the passata and season to taste with salt and pepper. Divide the mixture between the pastry squares, then sprinkle with the Mozzarella and add a few rosemary leaves to each square. Bake in a preheated oven at 200°C/400°F/gas mark 6 for about 15 minutes until cooked through and golden.

Crunchy croquettes

SERVES 4

25 g/1 oz/2 tbsp butter or margarine
1 onion, chopped
450 g/1 lb cooked peas
175 g/6 oz/3 cups fresh breadcrumbs
30 ml/2 tbsp chopped parsley
5 ml/1 tsp green peppercorns, crushed
30 ml/2 tbsp rolled oats
A pinch of grated nutmeg
15 ml/1 tbsp soy sauce
15 ml/1 tbsp Dijon mustard
Salt and freshly ground black pepper
4 eggs, beaten
150 g/5 oz/1¼ cups wholemeal flour
Oil, for shallow-frying

Melt the butter or margarine and fry (sauté) the onion until golden brown. Purée the peas in a food processor or blender. Mix together the peas, onion, half the breadcrumbs, the parsley, peppercorns, oats, nutmeg, soy sauce and mustard and season to taste with salt and pepper. Bind with 2 of the eggs. Shape into rissoles, then roll in the flour, dip in the remaining eggs and then the remaining breadcrumbs. Fry (sauté) in hot oil until golden brown, drain and serve immediately.

Mushroom kebabs

SERVES 4

16 large button mushrooms
2 red (bell) peppers, cut into 6
1 courgette (zucchini), sliced
1 banana, sliced
Salt and freshly ground black pepper
50 g/2 oz/¼ cup butter or margarine, melted

Thread the mushrooms, peppers, courgette and banana on to four skewers, beginning and ending with a mushroom. Season to taste with salt and pepper and brush with the butter or margarine. Cook under a low grill (broiler) for 15 minutes, turning and basting frequently, until the pepper and courgette are tender.

Savoury onion dumplings

SERVES 4

4 large onions
25 g/1 oz/2 tbsp butter or margarine
30 ml/2 tbsp chopped parsley
50 g/2 oz/1 cup fresh breadcrumbs
2 eggs, beaten
2.5 ml/½ tsp paprika
Salt and freshly ground black pepper
450 g/1 lb Shortcrust Pastry (page 164)

Hollow out the onions, leaving the shells about 1 cm/½ in thick and cook the shells in boiling water for 6 minutes, then drain. Chop the onion centres. Melt the butter or margarine and fry (sauté) the chopped onion until soft but not brown, then remove from the heat and mix in the parsley, breadcrumbs, 1 egg and the paprika and season to taste with salt and pepper. Press the stuffing into the onion shells. Roll out the pastry (paste) and cut into four rounds. Place the onions in the centre of each round and pull up the pastry to cover, brushing the edges with beaten egg to seal. Place on a greased baking (cookie) sheet, brush with egg and bake in a preheated oven at 190°C/375°F/gas mark 5 for 40 minutes.

Stuffed peppers with herbes de Provence

SERVES 4

4 green (bell) peppers
2 onions, chopped
225 g/8 oz mushrooms, chopped
2 eggs, beaten
100 g/4 oz/1 cup Emmental (Swiss) cheese, grated
50 g/2 oz/1 cup fresh breadcrumbs
30 ml/2 tbsp chopped parsley
A pinch of grated nutmeg
Salt and freshly ground black pepper
4 tomatoes, skinned, seeded and chopped
250 ml/8 fl oz/1 cup crème fraîche
250 ml/8 fl oz/1 cup dry white wine
15 ml/1 tbsp Herbes de Provence (basil, rosemary, garlic)

Cut a lid off each pepper and remove the seeds. Mix together the onions, mushrooms, eggs, cheese, breadcrumbs, parsley and nutmeg and season to taste with salt and pepper. Fill the peppers with the mixture and stand them in an ovenproof dish just large enough to hold them. Mix together the tomatoes, crème fraîche and wine, season with the herbs, then pour over the peppers and bake in a preheated oven at 200°C/400°F/gas mark 6 for 20 minutes.

Potato fritters Aix-la-Chapel

SERVES 4

450 g/1 lb potatoes
225 g/8 oz/2 cups wholemeal flour
1 egg, beaten
A pinch of grated nutmeg
Salt and freshly ground black pepper
60 ml/4 tbsp oil
50 g/2 oz/¼ cup butter or margarine
1 onion, chopped
1 small white cabbage, shredded
250 ml/8 fl oz/1 cup dry white wine
250 ml/8 fl oz/1 cup Vegetable Stock (page 28)
15 ml/1 tbsp cider vinegar
5 ml/1 tsp caraway seeds
A pinch of sugar
Snipped chives, to garnish

Cook the potatoes in boiling salted water until tender, then drain and mash. Stir in the flour, egg and nutmeg and season to taste with salt and pepper, then roll into thick fritters. Heat the oil and fry (sauté) the fritters until golden brown on both sides. Meanwhile, melt the butter or margarine and fry the onion until soft but not brown. Add the cabbage and fry for 2 minutes, then pour in the wine, stock, cider vinegar, caraway seeds and sugar. Bring to the boil, then simmer for 30 minutes. Sprinkle the cabbage with the chives and serve with the hot fritters.

Country hot-pot

SERVES 4

175 g/6 oz soya cubes
300 ml/½ pt/1¼ cups Vegetable Stock
   (page 28)
50 g/2 oz/¼ cup butter or margarine
1 onion, chopped
1 leek, sliced
2 carrots, cubed
4 potatoes, cubed
30 ml/2 tbsp tomato purée (paste)
25 g/1 oz/¼ cup wholemeal flour
250 ml/8 fl oz/1 cup red wine
5 ml/1 tsp marjoram
5 ml/1 tsp thyme
225 g/8 oz button mushrooms
150 ml/¼ pt/⅔ cup single (light) cream
100 g/4 oz/1 cup blue cheese, crumbled
Salt and freshly ground black pepper
15 ml/1 tbsp chopped parsley

Soak the soya cubes in the stock for
30 minutes, then drain, reserving the
stock. Heat the butter or margarine
and fry (sauté) the soya until just
browned, then add the vegetables
and fry for 2 minutes. Stir in the
tomato purée and flour, then the
wine, reserved stock, herbs and
mushrooms. Bring to the boil and
simmer for 30 minutes. Stir in the
cream and cheese, season to taste
and serve sprinkled with the parsley.

Hungarian soya goulash

SERVES 4

175 g/6 oz soya cubes
600 ml/1 pt/2½ cups Vegetable Stock
   (page 28)
250 ml/8 fl oz/1 cup red wine
45 ml/3 tbsp olive oil
225 g/8 oz mushrooms, sliced
2 onions, sliced
1 red (bell) pepper, sliced
1 green pepper, sliced
30 ml/2 tbsp tomato purée (paste)
2 tomatoes, skinned, seeded and
   chopped
Grated rind of 1 lemon
2 garlic cloves, crushed
5 ml/1 tsp marjoram
5 ml/1 tsp paprika
Salt and freshly ground black pepper
250 ml/8 fl oz/1 cup soured (dairy sour)
   cream
30 ml/2 tbsp snipped chives

Cover the soya cubes with the stock
and wine and leave to marinate for
30 minutes. Drain well, reserving the
marinade. Heat the oil and fry (sauté)
the soya cubes for 2 minutes, then
add the mushrooms, onions and
peppers and fry until soft. Stir in the
tomato purée and flour, then the
tomatoes and marinade and bring to
the boil. Add the lemon rind, garlic,
marjoram and paprika and season to
taste. Simmer for 30 minutes, then
serve garnished with the soured
cream and chives.

Pitta crunch

SERVES 4

4 vegetarian sausages, sliced
4 red eating (dessert) apples, cored and
  sliced
450 g/1 lb/2 cups cottage cheese
2 celery sticks, chopped
Freshly ground black pepper
4 wholemeal pitta breads

Grill (broil) the sausages until crispy,
then drain on kitchen paper (paper
towels) and cut into small pieces. Mix
together the sausages, apples, cheese
and celery and season well with
pepper. Warm the pitta breads under
the grill (broiler), cut in half and
gently open up. Stuff with the filling
and heat through in a preheated oven
at 180°C/350°F/gas mark 4 for
10 minutes before serving.

Soya risotto

SERVES 4

50 g/2 oz/¼ cup butter or margarine
1 onion, chopped
2 carrots, diced
½ celeriac (celery root), diced
1 leek, sliced
1 courgette (zucchini), diced
250 ml/8 fl oz/1 cup dry white wine
Juice of 1 lemon
8 soya sausages
225 g/8 oz/1 cup brown rice
1 litre/1¾ pts/4¼ cups Vegetable Stock
  (page 28)
4 tomatoes, skinned, seeded and
  chopped
250 ml/8 fl oz/1 cup crème fraîche
Salt and freshly ground black pepper
15 ml/1 tbsp snipped chives

Melt the butter or margarine and fry
(sauté) the vegetables until soft. Stir
in the wine and lemon juice, bring to
the boil, cover and simmer for
5 minutes. Add the sausages and rice
and fry until the rice is coated. Pour
in 150 ml/¼ pt/⅔ cup of the stock,
bring to the boil and simmer,
uncovered, until the liquid is
absorbed. Continue gradually adding
the stock until the rice is tender; this
will take about 20 minutes. Add the
tomatoes and crème fraîche, season
to taste and reheat, but do not allow
the risotto to boil. Cover and leave to
stand for 5 minutes, then serve
sprinkled with the chives.

Spinach and cheese quenelles

SERVES 4

225 g/8 oz spinach, stalks removed and
  chopped
225 g/8 oz/1 cup full-fat soft cheese
75 g/3 oz/1½ cups fresh breadcrumbs
15 g/½ oz wheatgerm
1 egg, beaten
1 small onion, chopped
1 garlic clove, crushed
25 g/1 oz/¼ cup Parmesan cheese,
  freshly grated
2.5 ml/½ tsp chopped basil
A pinch of grated nutmeg
Salt and freshly ground black pepper
50 g/2 oz/½ cup wholemeal flour
Tomato Sauce (page 253)

Mix together all the ingredients
except the flour and Tomato Sauce,
seasoning to taste. Roll into 2.5 cm/
1 in balls, roll lightly in the flour and
chill. Bring a saucepan of salted water
to the boil, then drop in the spinach
balls and simmer until they rise to the
surface. Remove with a slotted spoon
and serve with Tomato Sauce.

Spinach and herb loaf

SERVES 4

25 g/1 oz/2 tbsp butter or margarine
1 onion, chopped
450 g/1 lb spinach, stalks removed and
    roughly chopped
300ml/½ pt/1¼ cups Vegetable Stock
    (page 28)
225 g/8 oz/4 cups fresh breadcrumbs
15 ml/1 tbsp chopped parsley
15 ml/1 tbsp snipped chives
5 ml/1 tsp chopped tarragon
2 garlic cloves, crushed
Salt and freshly ground black pepper
250 ml/8 fl oz/1 cup crème fraîche
4 eggs, beaten
25 g/1 oz/¼ cup wholemeal flour

Melt the butter or margarine and fry
(sauté) the onion until soft but not
brown. Stir in the spinach and fry for
2 minutes. Place the stock in a large
bowl, add the breadcrumbs, the
spinach mixture, herbs and garlic and
season to taste. Fold in the crème
fraîche, eggs and flour and knead to a
firm mixture. Transfer to a greased
900 g/2 lb loaf tin (pan) and bake in
a preheated oven at 220°C/425°F/
gas mark 7 for 40 minutes.

Tofu ragout

SERVES 4

225 g/8 oz tofu, cut into strips
750 ml/1¼ pts/3 cups hot Vegetable
    Stock (page 28)
Plain (all-purpose) flour, for dusting
30 ml/2 tbsp oil
25 g/1 oz/¼ cup butter or margarine
1 onion, chopped
1 green (bell) pepper, chopped
100 g/4 oz mushrooms, sliced
250 ml/8 fl oz/1 cup dry white wine
150 ml/¼ pt/⅔ cup crème fraîche
15 ml/1 tbsp cornflour (cornstarch)
30 ml/2 tbsp water
A pinch of grated nutmeg
5 ml/1 tsp soy sauce
Salt and freshly ground black pepper
50 g/2 oz/½ cup Parmesan cheese,
    freshly grated
30 ml/2 tbsp chopped parsley

Soak the tofu in 500 ml/17 fl oz/
2¼ cups of the hot stock for
15 minutes. Remove, drain well and
toss in a little flour. Heat the oil and
fry (sauté) the tofu until golden.
Meanwhile, melt the butter or
margarine and fry the onion and
green pepper until soft but not brown.
Add the mushrooms, wine, remaining
stock, crème fraîche and tofu. Simmer
over a low heat for 10 minutes but do
not allow to boil. Combine the
cornflour and water and stir into the
ragout to thicken slightly. Add the
nutmeg and soy sauce and season to
taste. Stir in the Parmesan and serve
sprinkled with the parsley.

Sweet potato and parsnip cakes

SERVES 4

450 g/1 lb sweet potatoes, diced
225 g/8 oz parsnips, diced
15 ml/1 tbsp plain (all-purpose) flour
2.5 ml/½ tsp grated nutmeg
Salt and freshly ground black pepper
30 ml/2 tbsp milk
50 g/2 oz/½ cup rolled oats
50 g/2 oz/½ cup coarse oatmeal
30 ml/2 tbsp oil
Green salad, to serve

Cook the sweet potatoes and parsnips in boiling salted water for 15 minutes until just tender, then drain and purée in a food processor or blender with the flour and nutmeg (or mash with a potato masher). Season to taste and shape into eight rounds. Brush with the milk and roll in the oats and oatmeal. Heat the oil and fry (sauté) the cakes for 10 minutes until golden on both sides. Serve warm with a green salad.

Vegetable burgers

SERVES 4

4 wholemeal rolls, halved
60 ml/4 tbsp tartare sauce
4 lettuce leaves
4 radicchio leaves
1 tomato, sliced
100 g/4 oz tofu, sliced
25 g/1 oz/¼ cup plain (all-purpose) flour
1 egg, beaten
50 g/2 oz/1 cup fresh breadcrumbs
30 ml/2 tbsp oil
1 onion, sliced
½ box of cress
60 ml/4 tbsp crème fraîche
30 ml/2 tbsp French mustard
15 ml/1 tbsp soy sauce
Salt and freshly ground black pepper

Toast the rolls and spread the bottom halves with the tartare sauce. Place a lettuce leaf, radicchio leaf and tomato slice in each. Coat the tofu slices in flour, then dip in the egg, then the breadcrumbs. Heat the oil and fry (sauté) the slices until golden brown. Drain well and place on top of the tomato. Garnish with the onion and cress. Mix together the crème fraîche, mustard and soy sauce and season to taste. Spread over the burgers and top with the second half of the roll.

Vegetable soufflé

SERVES 4

225 g/8 oz potatoes, diced
2 carrots, chopped
100 g/4 oz parsnips, chopped
100 g/4 oz cauliflower florets
100 g/4 oz broccoli florets
75 ml/5 tbsp single (light) cream
3 eggs, separated
100 g/4 oz/1 cup Cheddar cheese, grated
Salt and freshly ground black pepper

Cook the vegetables in boiling salted water until tender, then drain and mash. Beat in the cream, egg yolks and cheese and season to taste with salt and pepper. Whisk the egg whites until stiff, then fold into the vegetables. Spoon into a greased 18 cm/7 in soufflé dish and bake in a preheated oven at 200°C/400°F/gas mark 6 for 20 minutes until well risen and lightly brown. Serve immediately.

Barley cake garni

SERVES 4

50 g/2 oz/¼ cup butter or margarine
1 onion, chopped
1 red (bell) pepper, chopped
225 g/8 oz/generous 1 cup pearl barley
900 ml/1½ pts/3¾ cups Vegetable Stock
  (page 28)
150 ml/¼ pt/⅔ cup dry white wine
2 garlic cloves, crushed
Salt and freshly ground black pepper
450 ml/¾ pt/2 cups Béchamel Sauce
  (page 251)
225 g/8 oz/2 cups Emmental (Swiss)
  cheese, grated
25 g/1 oz/½ cup fresh breadcrumbs
30 ml/2 tbsp snipped chives
30 ml/2 tbsp chopped parsley
A pinch of grated nutmeg
3 eggs, separated
1 boiled potato, sliced
2 tomatoes, skinned, seeded and sliced
½ cucumber, sliced
4 radishes, sliced
15 ml/1 tbsp powdered gelatine

Melt the butter or margarine and fry
(sauté) the onion and pepper until
soft but not brown. Add the barley
and fry for 1 minute, then stir in
600 ml/1 pt/2½ cups of the stock, the
wine and garlic and season to taste
with salt and pepper. Bring to the
boil, cover and simmer for
40 minutes, then take off the lid and
boil until all the liquid has evaporated.
Leave to cool.

Fold in the Béchamel Sauce,
cheese, breadcrumbs, chives, parsley
and nutmeg and season to taste with
salt and pepper. Stir in the egg yolks.
Whisk the egg whites until stiff, then
fold them into the mixture. Spoon the
mixture into a greased 20 cm/8 in
cake tin (pan) and bake in a
preheated oven at 200°C/400°F/gas

mark 6 for 40 minutes. Leave to cool.
Decorate the cake with the potato,
tomatoes, cucumber and radish slices.
Dissolve the gelatine in the remaining
stock and pour over the top. Leave to
cool before serving.

Nut roast

SERVES 4

50 g/2 oz/¼ cup butter or margarine
3 onions
350 g/12 oz/3 cups chopped mixed nuts
225 g/8 oz/4 cups fresh breadcrumbs
600 ml/1 pt/2½ cups Vegetable Stock
  (page 28)
10 ml/2 tsp yeast extract
10 ml/2 tsp dried mixed herbs
Salt and freshly ground black pepper
1 tomato, sliced

Melt the butter or margarine. Chop
two of the onions and fry (sauté) until
soft but not brown. Remove from the
heat and stir in the nuts, most of the
breadcrumbs, the stock, yeast extract
and herbs and season to taste with
salt and pepper. Press the mixture
into a greased shallow baking dish,
sprinkle with the reserved
breadcrumbs and bake in a preheated
oven at 180°C/350°F/gas mark 4 for
50 minutes until golden brown. Slice
the remaining onion into rings and
serve the loaf garnished with onion
rings and tomato slices.

Milanese oat cutlets

SERVES 4

50 g/2 oz/¼ cup butter or margarine
3 onions, chopped
750 ml/1¼ pts/3 cups Vegetable Stock
  (page 28)
175 g/6 oz/1½ cups rolled oats
15 ml/1 tbsp dried mixed herbs
Salt and freshly ground black pepper
3 eggs, beaten
30 ml/1 tbsp Dijon mustard
30 ml/2 tbsp snipped chives
25 g/1 oz/½ cup fresh breadcrumbs
45 ml/3 tbsp oil
1 red (bell) pepper, chopped
100 g/4 oz sweetcorn (corn) kernels
90 ml/6 tbsp tomato ketchup (catsup)
100 ml/4 fl oz/½ cup crème fraîche
5 ml/1 tsp curry powder
5 ml/1 tsp paprika
A few drops of Tabasco sauce
A pinch of sugar

Melt half the butter or margarine and
fry (sauté) 2 of the onions until soft
but not brown. Add 600 ml/1 pt/
2½ cups of the stock, the oats and
herbs and season to taste with salt
and pepper. Bring to the boil, cover
and simmer for 30 minutes. Remove
from the heat and allow to cool, then
stir in the eggs, mustard, chives and
breadcrumbs and shape into cutlets.
Heat the oil and fry the cutlets until
golden brown on both sides, then
transfer to a warm serving plate and
keep warm.

Meanwhile, melt the remaining
butter or margarine and fry (sauté)
the remaining onion and the red
pepper until soft but not brown. Add
the sweetcorn, ketchup and remaining
stock, then stir in the crème fraîche,
curry powder, paprika, Tabasco and
sugar and season to taste with salt

and pepper. Heat through gently, but
do not allow the sauce to boil. Pour
over the cutlets and serve.

Peanut roast

SERVES 4

225 g/8 oz/2 cups peanuts, finely
  chopped
100 g/4 oz/2 cups wholemeal
  breadcrumbs
50 g/2 oz/½ cup rolled oats
1 onion, finely chopped
1 carrot, grated
5 ml/1 tsp chopped sage
Salt and freshly ground black pepper
10 ml/2 tsp yeast extract
10 ml/2 tsp hot water
250 ml/8 fl oz/1 cup milk
25 g/1 oz/¼ cup Cheddar cheese, grated
400 g/14 oz/1 large can of tomatoes,
  chopped
1 garlic clove, crushed
2.5 ml/½ tsp dried mixed herbs
2.5 ml/½ tsp sugar

Mix together the peanuts, breadcrumbs, oats, onion, carrot and sage
and season to taste. Dissolve the
yeast extract in the hot water, then
stir into the nut mixture and add
enough of the milk to give a soft
consistency. Turn into a greased
900 g/2 lb loaf tin (pan), sprinkle
with the cheese and bake in a
preheated oven at 190°C/375°F/gas
mark 5 for 45 minutes. Put the
tomatoes, garlic, herbs and sugar in a
saucepan, bring to the boil and
simmer for 10 minutes. Serve hot
with the peanut roast.

Turlu guvec

SERVES 4

1 aubergine (eggplant), peeled and
  cubed
Salt and freshly ground black pepper
1 green (bell) pepper, sliced
100 g/4 oz okra, stalks removed
4 courgettes (zucchini), sliced
225 g/8 oz French (green) beans,
  chopped
225 g/8 oz peas
400 g/14 oz/1 large can of tomatoes,
  chopped
1 bunch of parsley, chopped
10 ml/2 tsp paprika
60 ml/4 tbsp oil
4 tomatoes, sliced

Sprinkle the aubergine with salt in a
colander and leave for 1 hour, then
rinse and drain. Mix together all the
vegetables with the parsley, paprika
and oil in a large casserole dish
(Dutch oven) and season to taste with
salt and pepper. Arrange the tomato
slices on top and bake in a preheated
oven at 190°C/375°F/gas mark 5 for
1¼ hours until most of the liquid has
been absorbed and the tomatoes are
browned on top.

Millet pilaf

SERVES 4

350 g/12 oz millet
30 ml/2 tbsp olive oil
1 onion, chopped
2 garlic cloves, crushed
900 ml/1½ pts/3¾ cups Vegetable Stock
  (page 28)
1 red (bell) pepper, sliced
50 g/2 oz/⅓ cup sultanas (golden raisins)
50 g/2 oz/½ cup shelled pistachio nuts

Place the millet in a heavy-based pan
and shake over a high heat until the

millet begins to pop. Remove the
millet from the pan. Heat the oil and
fry (sauté) the onion and garlic until
soft but not brown. Add the millet
and stock, bring to the boil, cover and
simmer for 10 minutes. Add the red
pepper and sultanas and cook for a
further 10 minutes until the millet is
softened and the stock is absorbed.
Serve sprinkled with the pistachios.

Filo vegetable pie

SERVES 4

900 g/2 lb courgettes (zucchini),
  chopped
250 ml/8 fl oz/1 cup oil
225 g/8 oz/2 cups Feta cheese,
  crumbled
3 eggs, beaten
25 g/1 oz/½ cup fresh breadcrumbs
15 ml/1 tbsp chopped dill (dill weed)
Salt and freshly ground black pepper
400 g/14 oz filo pastry (paste)

Place the courgettes in a pan with half
the oil, cover and simmer gently until
very soft, then leave to cool. Add the
cheese, eggs, breadcrumbs and dill
and season to taste. Cover the pastry
sheets you are not working with with
a damp cloth to prevent them drying
out. Brush the pastry sheets with oil
and layer two-thirds of the pastry over
a greased baking (cookie) sheet.
Cover with the filling, then top with
the remaining oiled pastry sheets and
seal the edges together well. Brush
the top with oil, then bake in a
preheated oven at 180°C/350°F/gas
mark 4 for 35 minutes until golden
brown.

Stir-fry pancake stack

SERVES 4

50 g/2 oz/½ cup cashew nuts, ground
300 ml/½ pt/1¼ cups milk
50 g/2 oz/½ cup plain (all-purpose) flour
1 egg, beaten
60 ml/4 tbsp oil
½ red (bell) pepper, sliced
½ green pepper, sliced
1 garlic clove, chopped
1 leek, sliced, OR 6 spring onions
   (scallions), chopped
1 courgette (zucchini), sliced
1 tomato, sliced
225 g/8 oz/4 cups beansprouts
30 ml/2 tbsp soy sauce
45 ml/3 tbsp sherry

Beat the nuts, milk, flour and egg to a batter. Heat a little of the oil in a frying pan (skillet) and use the batter to make six pancakes. Set aside. Blanch the peppers in boiling water for 2 minutes, then drain and rinse with cold water. Heat the remaining oil and fry (sauté) the garlic until browned. Stir in the leek or spring onions, then add the courgette and peppers and cook for 1 minute. Add the tomato, beansprouts, soy sauce and sherry, stir well and heat through. Place one pancake in a flat ovenproof dish, spread a fifth of the cooked mixture on top and then place another pancake on top. Continue layering pancakes and filling, finishing with a pancake. Cover with foil and bake in a preheated oven at 190°C/375°F/gas mark 5 for 10 minutes. Cut into wedges and serve immediately.

Quick tofu quiche

SERVES 4

175 g/6 oz/1½ cups wholemeal flour
25 g/1 oz/2 tbsp light brown sugar
25 g/1 oz/2 tbsp butter or margarine
10 ml/2 tsp fresh yeast
30 ml/2 tbsp cold water
1 egg, beaten
A pinch of salt
15 ml/1 tbsp oil
1 onion, chopped
1 garlic clove, chopped
50 g/2 oz mushrooms, chopped
A few drops of soy sauce
225 g/8 oz tofu, mashed
75 g/3 oz/¾ cup Cheddar cheese, grated
2 eggs, beaten
120 ml/4 fl oz/½ cup milk
1 carrot, grated
25 g/1 oz/¼ cup sesame seeds

Mix together the flour and sugar and rub in the butter or margarine. Dissolve the yeast in the water and add the egg and salt. Mix into the dry ingredients and knead until the dough is firm. Use to line a 20 cm/8 in flan ring. Heat the oil and fry (sauté) the onion, garlic, mushrooms and soy sauce until soft. Stir in the tofu, cheese, eggs and milk and pour them over the vegetables. Sprinkle with the carrot and sesame seeds. Leave to rest for 10 minutes, then bake in a preheated oven at 200°C/400°F/gas mark 6 for 25 minutes.

Tofu and vegetable kebabs

SERVES 4

350 g/12 oz smoked tofu, cubed
1 green (bell) pepper, seeded and cut into squares
1 orange pepper, seeded and cut into squares
1 courgette (zucchini), sliced
Grated rind and juice of 1 lemon
60 ml/4 tbsp olive oil
15 ml/1 tbsp chopped parsley
Salt and freshly ground black pepper
100 g/4 oz/1 cup cashew nuts
15 g/½ oz/1 tbsp butter or margarine
2 garlic cloves, crushed
1 shallot, finely chopped
5 ml/1 tsp ground coriander (cilantro)
5 ml/1 tsp ground cumin
15 ml/1 tbsp soft brown sugar
15 ml/1 tbsp desiccated (shredded) coconut
150 ml/¼ pt/⅔ cup crème fraîche

Thread the tofu and vegetables on to soaked wooden skewers and arrange in a shallow dish. Mix together the lemon rind and juice, the oil and parsley and season with salt and pepper. Brush over the kebabs and leave to marinate for 30 minutes. Toss the nuts in a dry frying pan (skillet) for a minute or two until golden brown, then remove from the pan and chop. Melt the butter or margarine in a saucepan and fry the garlic and shallot for a few minutes until soft but not brown. Remove from the heat and leave to cool slightly. Stir in the nuts and the remaining ingredients. Grill (broil) the kebabs for about 20 minutes, turning and basting with the marinade, until cooked through and golden. Serve with the cold sauce.

Sauces, butters and stuffings

Here is a range of sauces – savoury and sweet – that can be used in conjunction with so many other recipes, as accompaniments or to liven up a simple meal. Sauces you use regularly can sometimes be frozen so they are ready at a moment's notice. A small sauce whisk is usually the best utensil to use when making sauces as it will keep them free from lumps.

Sauces

All-in-one white sauce

MAKES 300 ML/½ PT/1¼ CUPS

25 g/1 oz/2 tbsp butter or margarine
25 g/1 oz/¼ cup plain (all-purpose) flour
300 ml/½ pt/1¼ cups milk
Salt and freshly ground black pepper

Place the butter or margarine, flour and milk in a saucepan and whisk over a medium heat until the mixture begins to thicken. Reduce the heat and continue to cook for 3 minutes, stirring continuously to make sure the sauce is smooth. If any lumps do form, remove from the heat and whisk vigorously. Season to taste with salt and pepper.

Note:
This makes a fairly thick sauce. For a thinner sauce, reduce the quantities to 15 g/½ oz/2 tbsp of flour and 15 g/½ oz/1 tbsp of butter or margarine.

Cheese sauce

MAKES 300 ML/½ PT/1¼ CUPS

300 ml/½ pt/1¼ cups All-in-one White
    Sauce
50 g/2 oz/¼ cup Cheddar cheese, grated
5 ml/1 tsp made mustard

Make the white sauce. Remove from the heat and stir in the grated cheese and mustard.

Mushroom sauce

MAKES 300 ML/½ PT/1¼ CUPS

100 g/4 oz mushrooms
300 ml/½ pt/1¼ cups milk
25 g/1 oz/2 tbsp butter or margarine
25 g/1 oz/¼ cup plain (all-purpose) flour
Salt and freshly ground black pepper

Simmer the mushrooms in the milk for 2 minutes. Strain and chop the mushrooms and reserve the milk. Melt the butter or margarine in a saucepan, add the flour and cook for 2–4 minutes, stirring constantly and without letting the flour brown. Stir in the flavoured milk, bring to the boil, stirring continuously, and simmer gently for 5 minutes. Add the mushrooms and season to taste with salt and pepper.

Mustard sauce

MAKES 300 ML/½ PT/1¼ CUPS

300 ml/½ pt/1¼ cups All-in-one White
    Sauce
15 ml/1 tbsp French mustard
5 ml/1 tsp white vinegar
5 ml/1 tsp caster (superfine) sugar
15 g/½ oz/1 tbsp butter or margarine,
    diced

Make the white sauce. Mix together the mustard, vinegar, sugar and butter or margarine and whisk it into the hot sauce but do not allow the sauce to boil.

Parsley sauce

MAKES 300 ML/½ PT/1¼ CUPS

300 ml/½ pt/1¼ cups All-in-one White
   Sauce
15 ml/1 tbsp finely chopped parsley
25 g/1 oz/2 tbsp butter or margarine,
   diced

Make the white sauce. Remove from
the heat when the sauce is boiling
and stir in the parsley, then whisk in
the butter or margarine.

Prawn sauce

MAKES 300 ML/½ PT/1¼ CUPS

15 g/½ oz/1 tbsp butter or margarine
15 ml/1 tbsp plain (all-purpose) flour
150 ml/¼ pt/⅔ cup hot milk
150 ml/¼ pt/⅔ cup Fish Stock (page 29)
50 g/2 oz cooked, peeled prawns
   (shrimp)
5 ml/1 tsp lemon juice
A pinch of cayenne
Freshly ground black pepper

Melt the butter or margarine in a
saucepan, add the flour and cook for
2–3 minutes, stirring constantly and
without letting the flour brown.
Continue stirring as you add the milk
and stock, bring to the boil and
simmer gently for 5 minutes, stirring
regularly. Add the prawns and lemon
juice and season to taste with
cayenne and pepper.

Béchamel sauce

MAKES 300 ML/½ PT/1¼ CUPS

300 ml/½ pt/1¼ cups milk
1 bay leaf
1 small onion
1 sprig of parsley
6 white peppercorns
25 g/1 oz/2 tbsp butter or margarine
25 g/1 oz/2 tbsp plain (all-purpose) flour
Salt and freshly ground black pepper
15 ml/1 tbsp single (light) cream
   (optional)

Place the milk in a small saucepan
with the bay leaf, onion, parsley and
peppercorns. Bring to the boil, then
remove from the heat, cover and
leave to infuse for 30 minutes. Melt
the butter or margarine in a clean
pan, stir in the flour and cook for
1 minute until foaming. Remove from
the heat and strain in the milk, then
return to the heat, bring to the boil
and simmer gently for 3 minutes,
stirring continuously. Season to taste
with salt and pepper. Stir in the
cream, if liked, but do not allow the
sauce to boil.

Hollandaise sauce

MAKES 300 ML/½ PT/1¼ CUPS

10 ml/2 tsp lemon juice
10 ml/2 tsp white wine vinegar
15 ml/1 tbsp water
5 black peppercorns
1 bay leaf
3 egg yolks
175 g/6 oz/¾ cup butter or margarine,
   diced
Salt and freshly ground black pepper

Put the lemon juice, vinegar, water, peppercorns and bay leaf into a saucepan. Bring to the boil and simmer gently until the liquid has reduced by half. Leave to cool, then strain. Put the egg yolks and vinegar mixture into a double saucepan or basin standing over a pan of simmering water and whisk until thick and foamy. Do not allow the mixture to become too hot or the eggs will curdle. Whisk in the butter or margarine a piece at a time until the sauce is thick and shiny and the consistency of mayonnaise. Season with salt and pepper and serve at once with vegetable and egg dishes.

Curry sauce

MAKES 450 ML/¾ PT/2 CUPS

50 g/2 oz/¼ cup butter or margarine
1 onion, finely chopped
15 ml/1 tbsp curry powder
15 ml/1 tbsp plain (all-purpose) flour
300 ml/½ pt/1¼ cups milk
150 ml/¼ pt/⅔ cup Chicken Stock
   (page 28)
30 ml/2 tbsp sweet chutney, chopped
Salt and freshly ground black pepper

Melt the butter or margarine and fry (sauté) the onion until soft but not brown. Stir in the curry powder and flour and cook for 2 minutes. Stir in the milk and stock, bring to the boil and simmer until thickened, stirring continuously. Add the chutney and season to taste with salt and pepper. Serve with plain vegetables or chicken.

Italian sauce

MAKES 450 ML/¾ PT/2 CUPS

25 g/1 oz/2 tbsp butter or margarine
2 shallots, chopped
50 g/2 oz mushrooms, sliced
1 bay leaf
2.5 ml/½ tsp chopped parsley
15 ml/1 tbsp plain (all-purpose) flour
300 ml/½ pt/1¼ cups dry white wine
150 ml/¼ pt/⅔ cup Chicken or Vegetable
   Stock (page 28)

Melt the butter or margarine and fry (sauté) the shallots, mushrooms, bay leaf and parsley for about 3 minutes. Stir in the flour, wine and stock, bring to the boil and simmer for 5 minutes until the sauce has reduced and thickened. Remove the bay leaf. Serve with meat or fish dishes.

Madeira sauce

MAKES 450 ML/¾ PT/2 CUPS

25 g/1 oz/2 tbsp butter or margarine
25 g/1 oz/¼ cup plain (all-purpose) flour
150 ml/¼ pt/⅔ cup hot milk
150 ml/¼ pt/⅔ cup Vegetable Stock
  (page 28)
150 ml/¼ pt/⅔ cup Madeira
Salt and freshly ground black pepper

Melt the butter or margarine in a saucepan, add the flour and cook for 2–3 minutes, stirring continuously. Continue stirring as you add the milk and stock, bring to the boil and stir until quite smooth. Add the Madeira and cook for a further 4 minutes. Season to taste with salt and pepper and serve with hot ham or bacon dishes.

Tomato sauce

MAKES 300 ML/½ PT/1¼ CUPS

30 ml/2 tbsp olive oil
1 onion, finely chopped
1 garlic clove, crushed
1 carrot, finely chopped
1 celery stick, finely chopped
450 g/1 lb ripe tomatoes, skinned,
  seeded and chopped
1 bay leaf
30 ml/2 tbsp tomato purée (paste)
  (optional)
Salt and freshly ground black pepper

Heat the oil and fry (sauté) the onion, garlic, carrot and celery until soft but not brown. Add the tomatoes and bay leaf and bring to the boil. Add the tomato purée if the tomatoes are not particularly ripe. Simmer gently for about 30 minutes, stirring occasionally, until the tomatoes are tender and the sauce is thick. Discard the bay leaf and season to taste.

Purée in a food processor or blender if you like a smooth sauce and thin down to the consistency you prefer with water or tomato juice, if necessary.

Spanish sauce

MAKES 450 ML/¾ PT/2 CUPS

25 g/1 oz/2 tbsp butter or margarine
50 g/2 oz lean bacon rashers (slices),
  rinded and finely chopped
1 onion, sliced
1 carrot, sliced
50 g/2 oz mushrooms, sliced
25 g/1 oz/¼ cup plain (all-purpose) flour
300 ml/½ pt/1¼ cups Vegetable Stock
  (page 28)
2 tomatoes, skinned and quartered
30 ml/2 tbsp dry sherry
Salt and freshly ground black pepper

Melt the butter or margarine in a saucepan and fry (sauté) the bacon, onion, carrot and mushrooms until just brown. Stir in the flour and cook slowly until the mixture is smooth and browned. Add the stock, stir well, and simmer for 30 minutes. Add the tomatoes and sherry and cook for a further 10 minutes. Strain, season to taste with salt and pepper and reheat before serving.

Pesto sauce

SERVES 4

50 g/2 oz basil leaves
2 garlic cloves, crushed
15 ml/1 tbsp pine nuts
90 ml/6 tbsp olive oil
25 g/1 oz/2 tbsp Parmesan cheese,
    freshly grated
Salt and freshly ground black pepper

Purée the basil leaves, garlic, pine
nuts and oil in a blender or food
processor until smooth. Stir in the
Parmesan and season to taste. Serve
with hot pasta.

Tomato and lentil sauce

MAKES 300 ML/½ PT/1¼ CUPS

100 g/4 oz/⅔ cup lentils
15 ml/1 tbsp oil
1 onion, sliced
½ green (bell) pepper, seeded and sliced
400 g/14 oz/1 large can of tomatoes
5 ml/1 tsp dried mixed herbs
5 ml/1 tsp chopped basil
Salt and freshly ground black pepper

Place the lentils in a saucepan and
just cover with water. Bring to the boil
and simmer for 30 minutes until
tender, then drain well. Heat the oil in
a saucepan and fry (sauté) the onion
and green pepper until soft but not
brown. Add the tomatoes and simmer
for 10 minutes. Add the lentils and
herbs and season to taste. Purée in a
food processor or blender and serve
with pasta.

Apple sauce

MAKES 450 ML/¾ PT/2 CUPS

450 g/1 lb cooking (tart) apples, peeled,
    cored and sliced
50 g/2 oz/¼ cup caster (superfine) sugar
Grated rind and juice of ½ lemon
45 ml/3 tbsp water
25 g/1 oz/2 tbsp butter or margarine

Place the apples, sugar lemon rind
and water in a saucepan and simmer
for about 15 minutes until very soft.
Purée in a food processor or blender
or rub through a sieve (strainer).
Reheat with the lemon juice and
butter or margarine until hot. Serve
with pork, duck or goose.

Barbecue sauce

MAKES 450 ML/¾ PT/2 CUPS

50 g/2 oz/¼ cup butter or margarine
1 onion, chopped
5 ml/1 tsp tomato purée (paste)
30 ml/2 tbsp red wine vinegar
30 ml/2 tbsp light brown sugar
10 ml/2 tsp mustard powder
30 ml/2 tbsp Worcestershire sauce
150 ml/¼ pt/⅔ cup water

Melt the butter or margarine and fry
(sauté) the onion until soft but not
brown. Stir in the remaining
ingredients, bring to the boil and
simmer for 10 minutes. Serve with
grilled (broiled) meats, sausages or
beefburgers.

Bread sauce

MAKES 300 ML/½ PT/1¼ CUPS

300 ml/½ pt/1¼ cups milk
1 small onion
2 cloves
75 g/3 oz/1½ cups fresh breadcrumbs
15 g/½ oz/1 tbsp butter or margarine
Salt and freshly ground black pepper

Bring the milk to the boil with the onion and cloves, cover and simmer gently for 15 minutes. Place the breadcrumbs in a clean pan and strain in the milk. Stir in the butter or margarine and season to taste. Reheat gently but do not allow the sauce to boil. Serve hot with poultry.

Black butter sauce

MAKES 100 ML/4 FL OZ/½ CUP

100 g/4 oz/½ cup unsalted (semi-sweet) butter
30 ml/2 tbsp white wine vinegar
Salt and freshly ground black pepper

Heat the butter until nut brown, then immediately remove from the heat. Add the vinegar and season to taste with salt and pepper. Reheat without boiling and serve hot with fish.

Cranberry sauce

MAKES 450 ML/¾ PT/2 CUPS

175 g/6 oz/¾ cup caster (superfine) sugar
150 ml/¼ pt/⅔ cup water
225 g/8 oz fresh or frozen cranberries
Grated rind of 1 orange

Bring the sugar and water to the boil and simmer for 4 minutes. Add the cranberries and orange rind, cover and simmer gently for about 5 minutes until all the cranberries have popped. Serve hot or cold with poultry.

Brown sauce

MAKES 300 ML/½ PT/1¼ CUPS

50 g/2 oz/¼ cup butter or margarine
2 onions, finely chopped
15 g/½ oz/1 tbsp wholemeal flour
300 ml/½ pt/1¼ cups Beef Stock (page 28)
5 ml/1 tsp Worcestershire sauce
Salt and freshly ground black pepper

Melt the butter or margarine in a large saucepan and fry (sauté) the onions until well browned. Add the flour and cook, stirring continuously, until browned. Gradually stir in the stock and cook for 5 minutes. Season to taste with the Worcestershire sauce and salt and pepper. Serve with grilled (broiled) meats.

Chestnut sauce

MAKES 450 ML/¾ PT/2 CUPS

100 g/4 oz/½ small can of chestnuts, drained
Salt and freshly ground black pepper
15 ml/1 tbsp cornflour (cornstarch)
300 ml/½ pt/1¼ cups milk

Purée the chestnuts in a food processor or blender, then season to taste with salt and pepper. Blend the cornflour to a paste with a little milk. Pour the remainder of the milk into a saucepan and bring to the boil, then stir in the cornflour paste and chestnuts, bring to the boil and simmer for 5 minutes. Serve with poultry or game.

Dill sauce

MAKES 300 ML/½ PT/1¼ CUPS

6 dill (dill weed) sprigs
150 ml/¼ pt/⅔ cup single (light) cream
1 egg yolk
5 ml/1 tsp Dijon mustard
A pinch of salt
150 ml/¼ pt/⅔ cup olive oil
10 ml/2 tsp white wine vinegar

Chop 15 ml/1 tbsp of the dill leaves. Put the remaining sprigs and the cream in a saucepan, bring to the boil, then remove from the heat and leave to infuse for 15 minutes. Strain and leave to cool. Whisk together the egg yolk, mustard and salt, then gradually whisk in the oil a little at a time. Stir in the wine vinegar. Stir in the cream and chopped dill and serve with vegetable dishes.

Cucumber raita

SERVES 4

½ cucumber, peeled and grated
150 ml/¼ pt/⅔ cup plain yoghurt
30 ml/2 tbsp snipped chives

Mix together the cucumber and yoghurt and sprinkle with the chives. Serve with curry or spiced foods as a side dish.

Mint sauce

MAKES 150 ML/¼ PT/⅔ CUP

60 ml/4 tbsp chopped fresh mint
10 ml/2 tsp sugar
15 ml/1 tbsp boiling water
30 ml/2 tbsp wine vinegar

Mix together the mint, sugar and water and stir until the sugar dissolves. Add the wine vinegar and leave to stand for at least 2 hours before serving with lamb.

Horseradish sauce

MAKES 150 ML/¼ PT/⅔ CUP

30 ml/2 tbsp grated fresh horseradish
5 ml/1 tsp caster (superfine) sugar
10 ml/2 tsp white wine vinegar
A pinch of salt
A pinch of mustard powder
150 ml/¼ pt/⅔ cup double (heavy)
    cream, lightly whipped

Mix together the horseradish, sugar, vinegar, salt and mustard. Fold the mixture into the whipped cream and chill before serving with beef or smoked fish dishes.

Tartare sauce

MAKES 150 ML/¼ PT/⅔ CUP

150 ml/¼ pt/⅔ cup Mayonnaise
    (page 277)
5 ml/1 tsp chopped gherkin (cornichon)
5 ml/1 tsp chopped parsley
5 ml/1 tsp chopped drained capers
5 ml/1 tsp snipped chives
10 ml/2 tsp lemon juice

Mix together all the ingredients and leave to stand for at least 1 hour before serving with fried (sautéed) fish.

Orange mint sauce

MAKES 150 ML/¼ PT/⅔ CUP

1 bunch of mint
15 ml/1 tbsp boiling water
10 ml/2 tsp caster (superfine) sugar
30 ml/2 tbsp white wine vinegar
60 ml/4 tbsp orange juice

Chop the mint in a food processor or blender, then add the remaining ingredients and blend again. Serve with lamb or other meats.

Red onion and cheese tarts (page 237)

Yoghurt sauce with herbs

MAKES 150 ML/¼ PT/⅔ CUP

1 garlic clove, crushed
150 ml/¼ pt/⅔ cup plain yoghurt
15 ml/1 tbsp chopped dill (dill weed)
15 ml/1 tbsp chopped tarragon
Salt and freshly ground black pepper

Beat the garlic clove well into the yoghurt until thoroughly combined. Mix in the herbs and season to taste. Chill before serving with grilled (broiled) or roast meats.

Minted yoghurt

MAKES 150 ML/¼ PT/⅔ CUP

½ cucumber, peeled and grated
150 ml/¼ pt/⅔ cup plain yoghurt or crème fraîche
1 garlic clove, crushed
30 ml/2 tbsp chopped mint
Salt and freshly ground black pepper

Squeeze any excess water out of the cucumber, then purée all the ingredients together in a food processor or blender. Chill before serving with roast lamb, curry or other spicy dishes.

Sweet white sauce

MAKES 300 ML/½ PT/1¼ CUPS

50 g/2 oz/¼ cup butter or margarine
10 g/2 tsp cornflour (cornstarch)
5 ml/1 tsp caster (superfine) sugar
300 ml/½ pt/1¼ cups milk

Melt the butter or margarine in a saucepan and stir in the cornflour. Cook for 1 minute, then stir in the sugar and milk, bring to the boil, stirring continuously, and cook for a further 3 minutes.

Nut sauce

MAKES 300 ML/½ PT/1¼ CUPS

300 ml/½ pt/1¼ cups Sweet White Sauce
15 g/1 tbsp chopped mixed nuts

Make the white sauce, stir in the nuts and heat through for 3–4 minutes.

Custard sauce

MAKES 300 ML/½ PT/1¼ CUPS

300 ml/½ pt/1¼ cups milk
1 egg, beaten
15 g/½ oz/1 tbsp caster (superfine) sugar

Bring the milk to just below boiling point. Whisk together the egg and sugar in a heatproof bowl. Pour the hot milk into the egg mixture, stirring continuously. Rinse the pan, then strain the custard back into the pan and heat gently, stirring, for about 5 minutes until the custard thickens.

Carob sauce

MAKES 200 ML/8 FL OZ/1 CUP

100 g/4 oz/1 cup carob powder
250 ml/8 fl oz/1 cup water
15 g/1 oz/2 tbsp butter or margarine
60 ml/4 tbsp clear honey
1 egg, beaten
5 ml/1 tsp vanilla essence (extract)

Mix the carob and water in a small saucepan, bring to the boil and simmer, stirring, for 8 minutes to make a smooth syrup. Stir in the remaining ingredients and simmer over a low heat until thick and smooth. Leave to cool, then store in the fridge.

Olive and feta salad (page 266)

Brandy sauce

MAKES 300 ML/½ PT/1¼ CUPS

10 ml/2 tsp cornflour (cornstarch)
300 ml/½ pt/1¼ cups milk
15 ml/1 tbsp soft brown sugar
2 egg yolks, lightly beaten
90 ml/6 tbsp brandy

Mix the cornflour to a paste with a little of the milk. Bring the rest of the milk to the boil, then remove from the heat and whisk in the cornflour mixture. Return to the heat and bring to the boil, stirring continuously, then simmer, stirring, for 2 minutes until thick and smooth. Remove from the heat and whisk in the egg yolks and brandy. Return to a very gentle heat and stir for a few minutes until the sauce thickens, but do not allow the sauce to boil.

Chocolate sauce

MAKES 300 ML/½ PT/1¼ CUPS

300 ml/½ pt/1¼ cups milk
10 ml/2 tsp cocoa (unsweetened chocolate) powder
1 egg yolk
15 ml/1 tbsp caster (superfine) sugar
A few drops of vanilla essence (extract)

Bring the milk and cocoa to the boil. Beat the egg yolk well with the sugar. Pour the boiling milk on to the egg and sugar mixture, whisking well. Return the mixture to the pan and stir over a low heat until the sauce boils. Add a few drops of vanilla essence and serve.

Sweet jam sauce

MAKES 300 ML/½ PT/1¼ CUPS

300 ml/½ pt/1¼ cups water
5 ml/1 tsp cornflour (cornstarch)
45 ml/3 tbsp raspberry or strawberry jam (jelly)
5 ml/1 tsp lemon juice

Mix the water and cornflour and bring to the boil, stirring. Add the jam and lemon juice and boil for 1 minute, then rub the sauce through a fine sieve (strainer). Serve hot or cold.

Lemon sauce

MAKES 600 ML/1 PT/2½ CUPS

5 ml/1 tsp cornflour (cornstarch)
600 ml/1 pt/2½ cups milk
1 egg yolk
Grated rind and juice of 1 lemon
50 g/2 oz caster (superfine) sugar

Mix the cornflour with all but 30 ml/ 2 tbsp of the milk. Beat the remaining milk with the egg yolk. Bring the cornflour, milk, lemon rind and juice and sugar to the boil. Remove from the heat and stir in the egg yolk and milk. Reheat but do not allow to boil.

Sauce cassis

MAKES 450 ML/¾ PT/2 CUPS

225 g/8 oz/1 small can of blackcurrants
10 ml/2 tsp cornflour (cornstarch)

Purée the fruit and its juice in a food processor or blender, then make up to 450 ml/¾ pt/2 cups with water, if necessary. Mix the cornflour with 15 ml/1 tbsp of the purée, then mix this into the purée. Bring to the boil, stirring, then serve warm or pour on fruit and leave to set.

Orange sauce

MAKES 600 ML/1 PT/2½ CUPS

5 ml/1 tsp cornflour (cornstarch)
600 ml/1 pt/2½ cups milk
1 egg yolk
Grated rind and juice of 1 orange
25 g/1 oz/2 tbsp caster (superfine) sugar

Mix the cornflour with all but 30 ml/
2 tbsp of the milk. Beat the remaining
milk with the egg yolk. Bring the
cornflour, milk, orange rind and juice
and sugar to the boil. Remove from
the heat and stir in the egg yolk and
milk. Reheat but do not allow to boil.

Fluffy almond sauce

MAKES 600 ML/1 PT/2½ CUPS

25 g/1 oz/¼ cup ground almonds
600 ml/1 pt/2½ cups milk
15 ml/1 tbsp plain (all-purpose) flour
15 ml/1 tbsp caster (superfine) sugar
1 egg, separated

Beat together the almonds, milk, flour,
sugar and egg yolk in a saucepan,
bring to the boil and cook, stirring
until the sauce thickens. Allow to cool
slightly, then whisk well. Whisk the
egg white until stiff, then fold it into
the sauce and serve warm.

Butters

Herb butter

MAKES 100 G/4 OZ/½ CUP

100 g/4 oz/½ cup unsalted (sweet)
   butter
10 ml/1 tsp chopped mint
10 ml/1 tsp chopped dill (dill weed)
10 ml/2 tsp chopped tarragon
10 ml/2 tbsp snipped chives
15 ml/1 tbsp lemon juice
Salt and freshly ground black pepper

Purée all the ingredients together in
food processor or blender. Shape into
a cylinder and wrap in greaseproof
(waxed) paper. Chill before serving
slices with grilled (broiled) meats.

Variations:
You can use a selection of any of your
favourite herbs in this recipe.

Chive butter

MAKES 50 G/2 OZ/¼ CUP

50 g/2 oz/¼ cup unsalted (sweet) butter
30 ml/2 tbsp snipped chives
Juice of ½ lemon
Salt and freshly ground black pepper

Purée all the ingredients together in
food processor or blender. Shape into
a cylinder and wrap in greaseproof
(waxed) paper. Chill before serving
slices with grilled (broiled) meats.

Garlic butter

MAKES 50 G/2 OZ/¼ CUP

50 g/2 oz/¼ cup unsalted (sweet) butter
2 garlic cloves, crushed
30 ml/2 tbsp chopped parsley
Juice of ½ lemon

Purée all the ingredients together in a food processor or blender. Chill before serving with grilled (broiled) pork or on garlic bread.

Peanut butter

MAKES 225 G/8 OZ/1 CUP

225 g/8 oz/2 cups peanuts
10 ml/2 tsp oil

Purée the peanuts in a food processor or blender for 20 seconds until they form a paste. Scrape down, add the oil and process for a further 20 seconds. Store in a screw-topped jar in the fridge.

Sage and shallot butter

MAKES 50 G/2 OZ/¼ CUP

50 g/2 oz/¼ cup unsalted (sweet) butter
15 ml/1 tbsp chopped sage
5 ml/1 tsp lemon juice
1 shallot, finely chopped
Salt and freshly ground black pepper

Purée all the ingredients together in a food processor or blender. Chill before serving with grilled (broiled) meats.

Stuffings

Apple and walnut stuffing

MAKES 225 G/8 OZ

25 g/1 oz/½ cup fresh breadcrumbs
50 g/2 oz/½ cup walnuts, chopped
1 onion, chopped
2 eating (dessert) apples, peeled and chopped
30 ml/2 tbsp chopped parsley
25 g/1 oz/2 tbsp butter or margarine, melted
1 egg, beaten
Salt and freshly ground black pepper

Thoroughly mix together all the ingredients, seasoning to taste with salt and pepper. Use to stuff poultry or pork or make into small balls and bake or fry (sauté) in a little oil for about 5 minutes until browned all over.

Celery and apple stuffing

MAKES 100 G/4 OZ

25 g/1 oz/½ cup fresh breadcrumbs
1 cooking (tart) apple, peeled and chopped
2 celery sticks, finely chopped
25 g/1 oz mushrooms, chopped
1 egg, beaten
A pinch of paprika
Salt and freshly ground black pepper

Mix together the breadcrumbs, apple, celery and mushrooms. Season the egg with the paprika and salt and pepper and use it to bind the stuffing ingredients. Use to stuff pork or other meats.

Herb stuffing

MAKES 175 G/6 OZ

100 g/4 oz/2 cups fresh breadcrumbs
50 g/2 oz/½ cup shredded (chopped)
    suet
30 ml/2 tbsp chopped parsley
2.5 ml/½ tsp dried mixed herbs
A pinch of grated lemon rind
A pinch of cayenne
Salt and freshly ground black pepper
1 egg, beaten

Thoroughly mix together all the ingredients. Use to stuff chicken, meat or vegetables or to make stuffing balls for frying (sautéing).

Herby sausagemeat

MAKES 225 G/8 OZ

25 g/1 oz/½ cup fresh breadcrumbs
5 ml/1 tsp dried mixed herbs
1 onion, finely chopped
1 garlic clove, finely chopped
225 g/8 oz belly pork, finely chopped
2.5 ml/1 tsp French mustard
15 ml/1 tbsp lemon juice
1 egg, beaten

Thoroughly mix all the ingredients, binding with the beaten egg. The finished sausagemeat holds its shape well and can be used for stuffings and sausage rolls.

Tomato and pepper stuffing

MAKES 100 G/4 OZ

25 g/1 oz/2 tbsp butter or margarine
1 small leek, sliced
1 garlic clove, crushed
½ red (bell) pepper, chopped
15 ml/1 tbsp chopped parsley
25 g/1 oz/½ cup fresh breadcrumbs
2 tomatoes, skinned and chopped
Salt and freshly ground black pepper

Melt the butter or margarine and fry (sauté) the leek until soft. Add the garlic and fry until browned, then remove from the heat. Blanch the pepper in boiling water for 2 minutes, then drain and mix into the garlic mixture. Stir in the parsley, breadcrumbs and tomatoes and season to taste with salt and pepper. Use to stuff meat or poultry.

Salads and salad dressings

Gone are the days when a salad meant a limp lettuce leaf and half a tomato! Now there's such a variety of produce in the supermarket and greengrocer that we're spoilt for choice. Take advantage of the range of produce and try variations on all the recipes using different salad leaves – from lollo rosso to oak leaf and frissée – and try new ingredients so that your salads are exciting and adventurous.

A simple mixed green salad is just that – a combination of the freshest and tastiest leaves available, introducing those with stronger flavours – like rocket or watercress – in smaller quantities. Don't be afraid to experiment, and use these recipes as a guide to some excellent taste combinations. You will find both simple salads that are ideal for side dishes and also some more substantial salads that can be served with crusty bread as a meal in themselves.

If you have the time, you can make your own salad dressings, the advantage being that you can make them in small quantities if you wish, although there are also plenty of high-quality, ready-made dressings you can buy.

Salads

Artichoke and prosciutto salad

SERVES 4

225 g/8 oz/1 can of artichokes, drained
and quartered
4 tomatoes, cut into wedges
25 g/1 oz sun-dried tomatoes, chopped
25 g/1 oz stoned (pitted) black olives
50 g/2 oz Parma ham, cut into strips
A few basil leaves, torn into pieces
For the dressing:
45 ml/3 tbsp extra virgin olive oil
15 ml/1 tbsp white wine vinegar
1 garlic clove, crushed
2.5 ml/½ tsp Dijon mustard
A pinch of sugar
Salt and freshly ground black pepper

Gently toss together all the salad
ingredients. To make the dressing,
whisk together the ingredients,
seasoning to taste with salt and
pepper. Pour over the salad and toss
together before serving.

Aubergine and pepper salad

SERVES 4

450 g/1 lb small aubergines (eggplants)
1 red (bell) pepper
1 yellow pepper
2 large onions
2 large potatoes
2 large tomatoes
60 ml/4 tbsp olive oil
Salt and freshly ground black pepper
45 ml/3 tbsp chopped parsley

Rub all the vegetables with a little of
the oil and place the aubergines,

peppers, onions and potatoes in a
baking tin (pan). Bake in a preheated
oven at 180°C/350°F/gas mark 4 for
45 minutes, then add the tomatoes
and bake for a further 15 minutes
until all the vegetables are cooked.
Leave to cool slightly, then peel the
peppers and tomatoes. Cut all the
vegetables into strips and arrange in a
serving dish. Drizzle with the
remaining oil, season to taste with salt
and pepper and sprinkle with the
parsley. Serve at room temperature.

Avocado and Dolcelatte salad

SERVES 4

1 little gem lettuce, shredded
A handful of rocket leaves
A handful of baby spinach leaves
1 large grapefruit
2 avocados
175 g/6 oz Dolcelatte cheese, thinly
sliced
75 ml/5 tbsp olive oil
25 ml/1½ tbsp white wine vinegar
Salt and freshly ground black pepper

Arrange the lettuce, rocket and
spinach on a serving plate. Holding
the fruit over a bowl to catch the
juice, peel the grapefruit and cut the
flesh from the membranes with a
sharp knife. Peel, stone (pit) and slice
the avocados and toss in the reserved
grapefruit juice. Arrange the avocado
slices, grapefruit and Dolcelatte slices
on top of the lettuce. Whisk together
the olive oil and wine vinegar and
season to taste. Drizzle over the salad
just before serving.

Avocado and bacon salad

SERVES 4

6 streaky bacon rashers (slices), rinded and chopped
2 avocados, peeled and stoned (pitted)
15 ml/1 tbsp lemon juice
30 ml/2 tbsp olive oil
Salt and freshly ground black pepper

Fry (sauté) the bacon pieces until crisp. Slice 1½ of the avocados and place the remainder in a food processor or blender. Purée with the lemon juice, oil and salt and pepper to taste until thick. Arrange the avocado slices around a serving dish and pile the purée in the centre. Sprinkle the bacon pieces on top and chill before serving.

Red bean and broccoli salad

SERVES 4

225 g/8 oz broccoli florets
400 g/14 oz/1 large can of red kidney beans, rinsed and drained
1 red onion, sliced into rings
2 celery sticks, chopped
150 ml/¼ pt/⅔ cup French Dressing (page 276)
Salt and freshly ground black pepper

Blanch the broccoli in boiling salted water for 2 minutes, then drain and refresh in cold water. Mix with the beans, onion and celery. Season the French Dressing to taste with salt and pepper, then pour over the salad and toss together well before serving.

Broccoli niçoise

SERVES 4

350 g/12 oz broccoli florets
200 g/7 oz/1 small can of tuna, drained and flaked
2 hard-boiled (hard-cooked) eggs, cut into wedges
50 g/2 oz/1 small can of anchovy fillets, drained
8 black olives, stoned (pitted)
150 ml/¼ pt/⅔ cup French Dressing (page 276)

Cook the broccoli in boiling salted water until just tender, then drain and rinse in cold water. Arrange the broccoli over the base of a serving dish and place the tuna on top. Arrange the eggs, anchovy fillets and olives on the tuna and pour the French Dressing over. Toss gently before serving.

Quick bean salad

SERVES 4

400 g/14 oz/1 large can of red kidney beans, drained and rinsed
400 g/14 oz/1 large can of cannellini beans, drained and rinsed
400 g/14 oz/1 large can of haricot (navy) beans, drained and rinsed
45 ml/3 tbsp oil
30 ml/2 tbsp white wine vinegar
2.5 ml/½ tsp French mustard
Salt and freshly ground black pepper
2 tomatoes, cut into wedges
15 ml/1 tbsp chopped parsley

Empty the beans into a salad bowl. Whisk together the oil, wine vinegar and mustard and season to taste. Toss the beans in the dressing. Arrange the tomatoes round the edge of the bowl and sprinkle the parsley on top.

Coleslaw

SERVES 4

1 small white cabbage, shredded
2 shallots, grated
1–2 carrots, grated
1 eating (dessert) apple, grated
50 g/2 oz/⅓ cup raisins
30 ml/2 tbsp milk
150 ml/¼ pt/⅔ cup Mayonnaise
(page 277)
Salt and freshly ground black pepper

Mix together the vegetables and fruit (you can vary the quantity of ingredients to suit your own taste). Mix enough of the milk into the mayonnaise to make it a slightly looser consistency, then season to taste with salt and pepper. Pour over the vegetables and toss until well blended.

Pineapple slaw

SERVES 4

450 g/1 lb white cabbage, shredded
1 pineapple, cored and cubed
1 eating (dessert) apple, cored and
quartered
75 g/3 oz/¾ cup walnut halves
60 ml/4 tbsp Mayonnaise (page 277)
120 ml/4 fl oz/½ cup plain yoghurt
10 ml/2 tsp clear honey
15 ml/1 tbsp lemon juice
Salt and freshly ground black pepper

Mix together the cabbage, pineapple and apple. Reserve a few walnuts for garnish and mix in the remainder. Mix together the mayonnaise and yoghurt, then stir in the honey and lemon juice and season to taste with salt and pepper. Toss the slaw with the dressing, cover and chill. Toss and season again just before serving.

Beansprout and fruit salad

SERVES 4

175 g/6 oz pasta shapes
Salt
200 g/7 oz/1 small can of pineapple
chunks
120 ml/4 fl oz/½ cup olive oil
30 ml/2 tbsp orange juice
15 ml/1 tbsp soy sauce
A pinch of ground ginger
2 carrots, grated
½ cucumber, sliced
175 g/6 oz/3 cups beansprouts

Cook the pasta in boiling salted water until just tender, then drain. Drain the pineapple, reserving the juice. Mix 30 ml/2 tbsp of the pineapple juice with the oil, orange juice, soy sauce and ginger and mix with the pasta while it is still warm. Leave to cool. Add the carrots, cucumber and pineapple chunks and toss, then add the beansprouts and mix in lightly before serving.

Red cabbage slaw

SERVES 4

1 small red cabbage, shredded
2 carrots, grated
1 red (bell) pepper, chopped
2.5 ml/½ tsp celery seed
120 ml/4 fl oz cider vinegar
30 ml/2 tbsp clear honey
45 ml/3 tbsp Mayonnaise (page 277)

Mix together the cabbage, carrots, red pepper and celery seed. Blend the cider vinegar with the honey and mayonnaise and toss the salad in the dressing.

Grated carrot salad

SERVES 4

450 g/1 lb carrots, grated
30 ml/2 tbsp chopped coriander
    (cilantro)
5 ml/1 tsp ground cumin
30 ml/2 tbsp lime juice
5 ml/1 tsp chopped jalapeño peppers
30 ml/2 tbsp olive oil
Salt and freshly ground black pepper

Toss the carrots and coriander
together. Mix the cumin, lime juice
and peppers into the oil and season
with salt and pepper. Whisk until
blended. Pour over the carrots and
toss together well before serving.

Olive and feta salad

SERVES 4

For the salad:
8 hard-boiled (hard-cooked) eggs, cut
    into wedges
1 radicchio, shredded
1 small iceberg lettuce, shredded
2 large tomatoes, diced
100 g/4 oz black olives, stoned (pitted)
30 ml/2 tbsp capers
225 g/8 oz/2 cups goats' cheese, flaked
175 g/6 oz/1½ cups Feta cheese, flaked
1 large onion, sliced
For the dressing:
90 ml/6 tbsp olive oil
90 ml/6 tbsp red wine vinegar
5 ml/1 tsp dried oregano
15 ml/1 tbsp chopped lemon balm
15 ml/1 tbsp snipped chives
15 ml/1 tbsp chopped mint
Salt and freshly ground black pepper

Gently toss together all the salad
ingredients. To make the dressing, mix
the oil with the remaining ingredients,
seasoning to taste. Toss the salad in
the dressing and serve.

Carrot and orange salad

SERVES 4

175 g/6 oz carrots, grated
2 oranges, peeled and diced
100 g/8 oz/2 cups walnuts, chopped
30 ml/2 tbsp chopped chervil
15 ml/1 tbsp lemon juice
15 ml/1 tbsp groundnut (peanut) oil
Salt and freshly ground black pepper

Mix together the carrots, oranges,
walnuts and chervil. Whisk together
the lemon juice and oil and season to
taste with salt and pepper. Pour over
the salad and toss together well
before serving.

Israeli carrot salad

SERVES 4

300 ml/½ pt/1¼ cups orange juice
6 carrots, grated
½ white cabbage, shredded
100 g/4 oz/⅔ cup raisins
50 g/2 oz/½ cup sesame seeds
1 orange, peeled and sliced

Purée the orange juice and carrots in
a food processor or blender. Mix in
the cabbage, raisins and sesame
seeds, turn into a serving bowl and
garnish with the orange slices.

Cauliflower salad

SERVES 4

1 small cauliflower, separated into florets
60 ml/4 tbsp French Dressing
  (page 276)
3 celery sticks, chopped
2 red pimientos, chopped
2 gherkins (cornichons), chopped
1 shallot, finely chopped
10 ml/2 tsp orange juice
Salt and freshly ground black pepper

Marinate the cauliflower in the French
Dressing for 2 hours, then drain and
mix with the remaining ingredients,
seasoning to taste with salt and
pepper.

Danish chef's salad

SERVES 4

½ cos (romaine) lettuce, sliced
1 bunch of radishes, sliced
¼ cucumber, sliced
1 onion, sliced
225 g/8 oz/2 cups cooked ham,
  shredded
100 g/4 oz/½ cup Danish blue cheese,
  cubed
60 ml/4 tbsp oil
30 ml/2 tbsp white wine vinegar
A pinch of mustard powder
A pinch of caster (superfine) sugar
Salt and freshly ground black pepper

Layer the lettuce, radishes, cucumber,
onion, ham and cheese in a glass
serving bowl and toss lightly. Put the
oil and wine vinegar in a screw-topped
jar, add the mustard, sugar, salt and
pepper and shake well to mix. Pour
over the salad and toss gently just
before serving.

Cucumber salad with fennel

SERVES 4

1 small cucumber, cut into chunks
2 tangerines, peeled and segmented
1 small fennel bulb, thinly sliced
1 hard-boiled (hard-cooked) egg, sliced
15 ml/1 tbsp chopped mint
30 ml/2 tbsp French Dressing (page 276)

Gently mix together the cucumber,
tangerine segments, fennel, egg and
mint. Spoon the French Dressing over
and toss together lightly before
serving.

Minted courgette salad

SERVES 4

450 g/1 lb courgettes (zucchini), finely
  chopped
10 ml/2 tsp salt
50 g/2 oz/½ cup flaked (slivered)
  almonds
100 g/4 oz/⅔ cup sultanas (golden
  raisins)
90 ml/6 tbsp olive oil
30 ml/2 tbsp lemon juice
15 ml/1 tbsp chopped mint
Freshly ground black pepper

Put the courgettes in a colander,
sprinkle with the salt and leave to
stand for 1 hour, then rinse, drain and
pat dry on kitchen paper (paper
towels). Mix with the almonds and
sultanas. Mix together the oil, lemon
juice and mint and toss the salad in
the dressing. Season well with pepper
before serving.

Smoked haddock salad

SERVES 4

225 g/8 oz smoked haddock, flaked
Salt and freshly ground black pepper
15 ml/1 tbsp chopped dill (dill weed)
150 ml/¼ pt/⅔ cup Mayonnaise
  (page 277)
½ iceberg lettuce, shredded
1 bunch of watercress
2 hard-boiled (hard-cooked) eggs,
  quartered
1 cooked beetroot (red beet), diced

Season the fish with salt and pepper
to taste. Mix the dill with the
mayonnaise and stir in the fish.
Arrange the lettuce and watercress
round a serving dish and pile the fish
in the centre. Garnish with the hard-
boiled eggs and beetroot just before
serving.

Lemon fennel salad

SERVES 4

1 lemon
30 ml/2 tbsp olive oil
30 ml/2 tbsp plain yoghurt
10 ml/2 tsp sugar
Salt and freshly ground black pepper
1 head of fennel, thinly sliced
6 black olives, stoned (pitted)

Halve the lemon. Slice one half thickly
and trim away the peel. Purée the
flesh with 15 ml/1 tsp of juice from
the other lemon half, the oil, yoghurt,
sugar, salt and pepper. Process until
thick. Toss the fennel slices in the
dressing and garnish with the olives.

Smoked cod mayonnaise

SERVES 4

450 g/1 lb smoked cod or other white
  fish fillets, flaked
300 ml/½ pt/1¼ cups Mayonnaise
  (page 277)
225 g/8 oz cooked small new potatoes
1 hard-boiled (hard-cooked) egg, sliced
30 ml/2 tbsp chopped dill (dill weed)

Mix the fish with half the mayonnaise
and pile on to a serving plate. Toss
the potatoes with the remaining
mayonnaise and spoon round the fish.
Arrange the egg slices decoratively on
top and sprinkle with the dill.

Lobster mayonnaise salad

SERVES 4

1 cooked lobster
1 cos (romaine) lettuce, heart reserved
  and outer leaves shredded
300 ml/½ pt/1¼ cups Mayonnaise
  (page 277)
2 hard-boiled (hard-cooked) eggs, cut
  into wedges

Remove the flesh from the shell and
cut it into chunks. Keep the flesh from
the claws whole and put it to one side
with the coral for garnishing. Mix the
shredded lettuce with the lobster
meat and enough of the mayonnaise
to moisten. Pile this into a deep dish
or salad bowl. Arrange the hard-
boiled eggs around the bowl. Separate
the heart of the lettuce and use the
leaves with the claw meat and coral to
decorate the top of the salad. Pour
over the remaining mayonnaise.

Scandinavian herring salad

SERVES 4

4 cooked beetroot (red beets), diced
4 cooked potatoes, diced
3 gherkins (cornichons), diced
4 rollmop herrings with onions in the centre, chopped
30 ml/2 tbsp Mayonnaise (page 277)
Salt and freshly ground black pepper

Thoroughly mix together all the ingredients, seasoning to taste with salt and pepper.

Mediterranean pepper salad

SERVES 4

45 ml/3 tbsp olive oil
1 red onion, cut into wedges
2 red (bell) peppers, seeded and cut into strips
2 orange or yellow peppers, seeded and cut into strips
2 courgettes (zucchini), sliced
2 garlic cloves, sliced
50 g/2 oz/1 small can of anchovy fillets, drained
15 ml/1 tbsp balsamic vinegar
25 g/1 oz stoned (pitted) black olives
Freshly ground black pepper
A few fresh basil leaves

Heat the oil and fry (sauté) the onion, peppers, courgettes and garlic for about 15 minutes until soft and just beginning to brown. Crush the anchovy fillets into the vinegar, stir into the pan with the olives and stir until all the ingredients are well coated. Season with pepper. Remove from the heat and leave to cool, then serve garnished with basil leaves.

Californian fruit salad

SERVES 4

1 iceberg lettuce, shredded
200 g/7 oz/1 small can of pineapple chunks in juice, drained
200 g/7 oz/1 small can of peaches in juice, drained
4 celery sticks, chopped
25 g/1 oz/¼ cup flaked (slivered) almonds
30 ml/2 tbsp Mayonnaise (page 277)
A sprig of mint

Arrange the lettuce in the base of a salad bowl. Thoroughly mix together the remaining ingredients and spoon into the bowl. Serve garnished with the mint sprig.

Green salad with blue cheese

SERVES 4

100 g/4 oz white cabbage, finely shredded
100 g/4 oz broccoli florets
100 g/4 oz courgettes (zucchini), thinly sliced
1 green (bell) pepper, sliced
1 celery stick, sliced
150 ml/¼ pt/⅔ cup Blue Cheese Dressing (page 277)
50 g/2 oz/½ cup Stilton cheese, crumbled

Thoroughly mix together all the salad ingredients, then pour the dressing over. Top with the cheese and chill well. Toss gently before serving.

Mushroom and watercress salad

SERVES 4

60 ml/4 tbsp oil
15 ml/1 tbsp white wine vinegar
Salt and freshly ground black pepper
350 g/12 oz mushrooms, sliced
100 g/4 oz watercress leaves
15 ml/1 tbsp chopped parsley
15 ml/1 tbsp snipped chives

Beat together the oil and wine vinegar and season to taste. Mix together the mushrooms, watercress and parsley. Pour the dressing over just before serving, toss well and sprinkle with the chives.

Potato and frankfurter salad

SERVES 4

900 g/2 lb small new potatoes
6 cooked frankfurters, cut into bite-sized pieces
5 spring onions (scallions), sliced
50 g/2 oz/½ cup flaked (slivered) almonds, toasted
15 ml/1 tbsp snipped chives
½ red (bell) pepper, chopped
90 ml/6 tbsp Mayonnaise (page 277)
45 ml/3 tbsp plain yoghurt
A few drops of Tabasco sauce
Salt and freshly ground black pepper
Cook the potatoes in boiling salted water until tender, then drain. Mix together the potatoes, frankfurters, onions, almonds, chives and red pepper. Mix together the mayonnaise, yoghurt and Tabasco sauce and season to taste with salt and pepper. Toss the salad in the dressing and turn into a serving dish.

Pear salad with walnuts

SERVES 4

1 small iceberg lettuce, shredded
2 pears, peeled, cored and sliced
15 ml/1 tbsp lemon juice
2 celery sticks, chopped
50 g/2 oz/½ cup walnuts, chopped
50 g/2 oz/⅓ cup raisins
225 g/8 oz/1 cup cottage cheese
150 ml/¼ pt/⅔ cup Mayonnaise (page 277)

Arrange the lettuce on a serving plate. Brush the pears with the lemon juice to prevent them browning and arrange them on the plate. Thoroughly mix together the remaining ingredients and pile on to the pears.

Bacon and potato salad

SERVES 4

4 bacon rashers (slices), rinded
75 g/3 oz/¾ cup Cheddar cheese, diced
2 cocktail gherkins (cornichons), chopped
1 onion, finely chopped
350 g/12 oz boiled potatoes, diced
5 ml/1 tsp chopped parsley
30 ml/2 tbsp olive oil
15 ml/1 tbsp white wine vinegar

Grill (broil) the bacon until crisp, then dice it and leave to cool. Mix together the cheese, gherkins, onion, potatoes and parsley, then mix in the cooled bacon. Mix together the oil and wine vinegar and sprinkle over the salad.

Spinach salad with hot bacon and almonds

SERVES 4

225 g/8 oz young spinach leaves
50 g/2 oz rocket or other salad leaves
60 ml/4 tbsp olive oil
50 g/2 oz flaked (slivered) almonds
4 streaky bacon rashers (slices), rinded
    and chopped
45 ml/3 tbsp lemon juice
Salt and freshly ground black pepper

Arrange the spinach and rocket in a salad bowl. Heat the oil and fry (sauté) the almonds and bacon until golden brown. Add the lemon juice and season to taste with salt and pepper. Pour over the salad leaves, toss well and serve immediately.

Creole potato salad

SERVES 4

450 g/1 lb potatoes
100 g/4 oz cooked, peeled prawns
    (shrimp)
2 hard-boiled (hard-cooked) eggs,
    chopped
1 green (bell) pepper, chopped
45 ml/3 tbsp French Dressing
    (page 276)
A pinch of paprika
Salt and freshly ground black pepper

Cook the potatoes in boiling salted water until tender, then drain and dice. Mix with the prawns while still warm. Mix in the eggs, green pepper and French Dressing and season to taste with the paprika and salt and pepper.

Lemon rice with fresh herbs

SERVES 4

100 g/4 oz/½ cup long-grain rice
30 ml/2 tbsp olive oil
10 ml/2 tsp white wine vinegar
5 ml/1 tsp lemon juice
45 ml/3 tbsp chopped parsley
45 ml/3 tbsp snipped chives
Salt and freshly ground black pepper

Cook the rice in boiling salted water until just tender, then drain and rinse in cold water. Mix in the oil, wine vinegar and lemon juice and leave to cool, then stir in the herbs and season to taste with salt and pepper.

Spring potato salad with tofu dressing

SERVES 4

100 g/4 oz canned green lentils
1 garlic clove, roughly chopped
225 g/8 oz boiled new potatoes, diced
½ cucumber, diced
6 cherry tomatoes
3 hard-boiled (hard-cooked) eggs, cut
    into wedges
100 g/4 oz/½ cup firm tofu
10 ml/2 tsp white wine vinegar
5 ml/1 tsp French mustard
2.5 ml/½ tsp light brown sugar
5 ml/1 tsp olive oil
15 ml/1 tbsp chopped tarragon
Salt and freshly ground black pepper

Combine the lentils, garlic, potatoes, cucumber and tomatoes in a salad bowl and arrange the eggs round the edge. Purée the tofu, wine vinegar, mustard, sugar, oil and tarragon in a food processor or blender, then pour over the salad. Season to taste with salt and pepper.

Tomato, Mozzarella and basil salad

SERVES 4

4 ripe tomatoes, sliced
200 g/7 oz Mozzarella cheese, sliced
12 fresh basil leaves, torn into pieces
120 ml/4 fl oz/½ cup olive oil
Salt and freshly ground black pepper

Arrange the tomato and Mozzarella slices alternately on a serving place and sprinkle with the basil. Drizzle the olive oil over and season with salt and pepper.

Provençale baked potato salad

SERVES 4

50 g/2 oz/1 small can of anchovy fillets, drained
2.5 ml/½ tsp dried mixed herbs
5 ml/1 tsp chopped parsley
15 ml/1 tbsp olive oil
450 g/1 lb potatoes, sliced
1 onion, sliced
225 g/8 oz tomatoes, sliced
A little butter or margarine

Mash the anchovies with the dried herbs, parsley and oil. Arrange a third of the potatoes over the base of a greased 1.2 litre/2 pt/5 cup ovenproof dish, cover with half the onion slices and half the tomatoes, spread with half the anchovy paste, then repeat the layers. Top with the remaining potatoes. Dot with butter or margarine, then bake in a preheated oven at 190°C/375°F/gas mark 5 for 1 hour until cooked through and golden brown. Leave to cool before serving.

Rice and vegetable salad

SERVES 4

100 g/4 oz/½ cup long-grain rice
90 ml/6 tbsp French Dressing (page 276)
1 carrot, grated
50 g/2 oz cooked peas
2 celery sticks, chopped
1 red-skinned eating (dessert) apple, cored and chopped
15 ml/1 tbsp snipped chives
10 ml/2 tsp chopped parsley
Salt and freshly ground black pepper

Cook the rice in boiling salted water until just tender, then drain and rinse in hot water. Mix with enough of the French Dressing to moisten it well, then stir in the vegetables, apple, chives and parsley and season lightly with salt and pepper. Turn into a serving bowl and chill before serving.

Sweetcorn salad

SERVES 4

400 g/14 oz/1 large can of sweetcorn (corn), drained
1 shallot, chopped
50 g/2 oz/⅓ cup sultanas (golden raisins)
1 orange (bell) pepper, chopped
60 ml/4 tbsp oil
15 ml/1 tbsp white wine vinegar
15 ml/1 tbsp Worcestershire sauce
15 ml/1 tbsp tomato ketchup (catsup)
15 ml/1 tbsp light brown sugar
15 ml/1 tbsp snipped chives, to garnish

Mix together the sweetcorn, shallot, sultanas and pepper. Whisk together the remaining ingredients, pour over the salad and toss gently. Serve sprinkled with the chives.

Sunshine salad

SERVES 4

2 hard-boiled (hard-cooked) eggs
200 g/7 oz/1 small can of sweetcorn
   (corn), drained
50 g/2 oz mushrooms, chopped
100 g/4 oz carrots, grated
5 ml/1 tsp lemon juice
2.5 ml/½ tsp French mustard
15 ml/1 tbsp soured (dairy sour) cream
Freshly ground black pepper
15 ml/1 tbsp chopped parsley

Separate the yolks from the whites of
the eggs. Chop the whites, mix with
the sweetcorn and mushrooms and
turn into a serving dish. Mix the
carrots with the lemon juice, then
arrange them round the bowl.
Crumble the egg yolks and whisk
together with the mustard and soured
cream. Pour the dressing over the
salad, season to taste with pepper
and serve garnished with the parsley.

Rainbow salad

SERVES 4

120 ml/4 fl oz/½ cup olive oil
60 ml/4 tbsp lemon juice
2.5 ml/½ tsp caster (superfine) sugar
Salt and freshly ground black pepper
2 carrots, grated
100 g/4 oz button mushrooms, sliced
½ cucumber, seeded and cut into
   matchsticks
5 tomatoes, quartered
4 celery sticks, sliced
2 spring onions (scallions), chopped
15 ml/1 tbsp snipped chives, to garnish
15 ml/1 tbsp chopped parsley, to garnish
½ onion, cut into rings, to garnish

Mix together the oil, lemon juice,
sugar, salt and pepper. Toss the
carrots with 30 ml/2 tbsp of this

dressing and arrange in a strip on a
flat platter. Lay the mushrooms,
cucumber, tomatoes, celery and
spring onions in strips alongside.
Sprinkle each strip with one of the
garnishes. Serve the remaining
dressing in a jug.

Chicken salad with apple and mustard dressing

SERVES 4

60 ml/4 tbsp sunflower oil
15 ml/1 tbsp olive oil
45 ml/3 tbsp apple juice
1 garlic clove, crushed
5 ml/1 tsp wholegrain mustard
Salt and freshly ground black pepper
200 g/7 oz/1 small can of lentils, drained
225 g/8 oz mixed salad leaves
4 cooked chicken breasts, skinned and
   sliced
100 g/4 oz/1 cup walnuts, toasted

Whisk together the oils, apple juice,
garlic and mustard and season to
taste. Toss the lentils in 15 ml/1 tbsp
of the dressing. Arrange the salad
leaves on a serving plate, lay the
chicken on top and spoon the lentils
into the centre. Sprinkle with the
walnuts and pour the remaining
dressing over.

Waldorf salad

SERVES 4

2 red-skinned eating (dessert) apples,
    sliced
30 ml/2 tbsp lemon juice
50 g/2 oz/½ cup walnuts, chopped
½ head of Chinese leaves (stem lettuce),
    sliced
90 ml/6 tbsp olive oil
45 ml/3 tbsp white wine vinegar
5 ml/1 tsp caster (superfine) sugar
Salt and freshly ground black pepper

Sprinkle the apple slices with the
lemon juice to prevent browning, then
mix them with the walnuts and
Chinese leaves. Whisk together the
oil, wine vinegar, sugar, salt and
pepper until thick and well blended.
Toss the salad in the dressing just
before serving.

Smoked chicken salad

SERVES 4

2 red-skinned eating (dessert) apples,
    cubed
15 ml/1 tbsp lemon juice
225 g/8 oz smoked chicken, cut into
    strips
2 celery sticks, chopped
1 red (bell) pepper, sliced
½ green pepper, sliced
50 g/2 oz/½ cup walnut halves
60 ml/4 tbsp olive oil
30 ml/2 tbsp white wine vinegar
10 ml/2 tsp French mustard
Salt and freshly ground black pepper

Toss the apple slices in the lemon
juice to prevent browning. Mix
together the apples, chicken, celery,
peppers and walnuts. Whisk together
the oil, wine vinegar and mustard and
season to taste. Toss the salad in the
dressing just before serving.

Chicken and almond salad

SERVES 4

350 g/12 oz/3 cups cooked chicken,
    diced
50 g/2 oz/½ cup almonds, toasted
300 g/11 oz/1 medium can of pineapple
    chunks in juice, drained
½ green (bell) pepper, chopped
½ red pepper, chopped
2 small chicory hearts, chopped
30 ml/2 tbsp Mayonnaise (page 277)
Freshly ground black pepper

Mix together all the ingredients, toss
in the mayonnaise and season to taste
with pepper.

Curried chicken salad

SERVES 4

350 g/12 oz/3 cups cooked chicken,
    sliced
2 bananas, sliced
15 ml/1 tsp lemon juice
50 g/2 oz/⅓ cup sultanas (golden raisins)
50 g/2 oz/⅓ cup no-need-to-soak dried
    apricots, chopped
50 g/2 oz/½ cup cashew nuts
45 ml/3 tbsp Mayonnaise (page 277)
1 shallot, finely chopped
5 ml/1 tsp curry powder
1 eating (dessert) apple, peeled, cored
    and grated
10 ml/2 tsp sweet chutney
Salt and freshly ground black pepper

Place the chicken in a serving bowl
and mix with the bananas, lemon
juice, sultanas, apricots and nuts. Mix
together the mayonnaise, shallot,
curry powder, apple and chutney and
season to taste. Toss the salad in the
dressing just before serving.

Curried ham and yoghurt salad

SERVES 4

100 g/4 oz button mushroom, sliced
225 g/8 oz/2 cups cooked ham, diced
25 g/1 oz/3 tbsp raisins
1 eating (dessert) apple, peeled, cored
  and chopped
15 ml/1 tbsp lemon juice
150 ml/¼ pt/⅔ cup plain yoghurt
5 ml/1 tsp curry powder
15 ml/1 tbsp chopped parsley
50 g/2 oz sweet chutney

Mix together the mushrooms, ham and raisins. Toss the apple in the lemon juice, then add it to the mixture. Mix together the yoghurt and curry powder and pour it over the salad, tossing gently. Sprinkle with the parsley and serve the salad with the chutney.

Tuna and tomato salad

SERVES 4

200 g/7 oz/1 small can of tuna, drained
4 tomatoes, cut into wedges
½ cucumber, cut into chunks
2 shallots, sliced
2 little gem lettuces, cut into chunks
1 red (bell) pepper, seeded and cut into
  strips
50 g/2 oz/1 small can of anchovies,
  drained
25 g/1 oz stoned (pitted) black olives
30 ml/2 tbsp chopped parsley
75 ml/5 tbsp French Dressing (page 276)
Ciabatta bread, to serve

Mix together all the salad ingredients, pour the dressing over and toss together gently. Serve with ciabatta bread.

Prawn and mushroom pasta salad

SERVES 4

175 g/6 oz pasta shapes
1 avocado, peeled, stoned (pitted) and
  sliced
15 ml/1 tbsp lemon juice
225 g/8 oz cooked, peeled prawns
  (shrimp)
100 g/4 oz button mushrooms, sliced
30 ml/2 tbsp Mayonnaise (page 277)
30 ml/2 tbsp soured (dairy sour) cream
1 garlic clove, crushed
10 ml/2 tsp snipped chives
Salt and freshly ground black pepper

Cook the pasta in boiling salted water until just tender, then drain and rinse in cold water. Toss the avocado in the lemon juice, then add it to the pasta. Reserve a few prawns for garnish, then add the remainder to the pasta with the mushrooms. Mix together the mayonnaise, cream, garlic and chives and season to taste. Fold the dressing into the pasta and turn out into a serving dish. Chill before serving garnished with the reserved prawns.

Dressings

Oil and vinegar dressing

MAKES 150 ML/¼ PT/⅓ CUP

120 ml/4 fl oz/½ cup olive oil
60 ml/4 tbsp white wine vinegar
Salt and freshly ground black pepper

Thoroughly whisk the ingredients together, or place in a small screw-topped jar and shake until well blended.

French dressing

MAKES 200 ML/7 FL OZ/SCANT 1 CUP

30 ml/2 tbsp red wine vinegar
120 ml/4 fl oz/½ cup olive oil
5 ml/1 tsp salt
5 ml/1 tsp Dijon mustard
Salt and freshly ground black pepper

Thoroughly whisk the ingredients together, or place in a small screw-topped jar and shake until well blended.

Vinaigrette dressing

MAKES 150 ML/¼ PT/⅓ CUP

120 ml/4 fl oz/½ cup olive oil
60 ml/4 tbsp olive oil
15 ml/1 tbsp Dijon mustard
10 ml/2 tsp caster (superfine) sugar
15 ml/1 tbsp finely chopped shallot
15 ml/1 tbsp chopped parsley

Thoroughly whisk the ingredients together, or place in a small screw-topped jar and shake until well blended.

Tomato vinaigrette

SERVES 4

150 ml/¼ pt/⅔ cup olive oil
2 shallots, finely chopped
2 garlic cloves, crushed
30 ml/2 tbsp white wine vinegar
400 g/14 oz/1 large can of tomatoes, chopped
300 ml/½ pt/1¼ cups passata (sieved tomatoes)
15 ml/1 tbsp torn basil leaves
15 ml/1 tbsp chopped tarragon
5 ml/1 tsp balsamic vinegar
Salt and freshly ground black pepper

Heat 30 ml/2 tbsp of the oil and fry (sauté) the shallots and garlic for a few minutes until soft but not brown. Add the wine vinegar and cook for a few minutes until syrupy. Add all the remaining ingredients except the balsamic vinegar and seasoning and simmer gently for 1 hour. Remove from the heat, stir in the balsamic vinegar and season to taste with salt and pepper. Leave to cool, then rub through a sieve (strainer) and store in an airtight jar in the fridge until required.

Mayonnaise

MAKES 450 ML/¾ PT/2 CUPS

1 egg
1 egg yolk
2.5 ml/½ tsp salt
2.5 ml/½ tsp mustard powder
30 ml/2 tbsp lemon juice
15 ml/1 tbsp white wine vinegar
375 ml/13 fl oz/1½ cups oil

Purée the egg, egg yolk, salt, mustard, lemon juice, wine vinegar and a third of the oil in a food processor or blender or whisk them thoroughly in a large bowl. While the blender is running, slowly pour in the remaining oil through the feed tube until the mayonnaise emulsifies. If you are not using a processor or blender, continue to whisk by hand while you gradually pour in the oil.

Note:
All fresh mayonnaise recipes contain raw eggs.

Blue cheese mayonnaise

MAKES 150 ML/¼ PT/⅔ CUP

½ onion, chopped
5 ml/1 tsp Worcestershire sauce
50 g/2 oz/½ cup blue cheese, crumbled
150 ml/¼ pt/⅔ cup Mayonnaise
Salt and freshly ground black pepper

Mix the onion, Worcestershire sauce and cheese into the mayonnaise and season to taste with salt and pepper.

Garlic mayonnaise

MAKES 150 ML/¼ PT/⅓ CUP

150 ml/¼ pt/⅔ cup Mayonnaise
1 garlic clove, crushed

If you are using ready-made mayonnaise, crush the garlic thoroughly and mix it into the mayonnaise. If you are making the mayonnaise from the recipe, add the crushed garlic with the egg before you start adding the oil.

Green mayonnaise

MAKES 450 ML/¾ PT/2 CUPS

1 egg
1 egg yolk
2.5 ml/½ tsp salt
2.5 ml/½ tsp Dijon mustard
30 ml/2 tbsp lemon juice
15 ml/1 tbsp white wine vinegar
375 ml/13 fl oz/1½ cups oil
15 ml/1 tbsp chopped parsley
1 bunch of watercress, stalks removed
1 spring onion (scallion), chopped

Purée the egg, egg yolk, salt, mustard, lemon juice, wine vinegar and a third of the oil in a food processor or blender or whisk them thoroughly in a large bowl. While the blender is running, slowly pour in most of the remaining oil through the feed tube until the mayonnaise begins to thicken. Stop the processor, add the parsley, watercress leaves and spring onion and process until mixed, then gradually add the remaining oil. If you are not using a processor or blender, continue to whisk by hand while you gradually pour in the oil.

Dill mayonnaise with soured cream

MAKES 300 ML/½ PT/1¼ CUPS

150 ml/¼ pt/⅔ cup Mayonnaise
  (page 277)
90 ml/6 tbsp soured (dairy sour) cream
15 ml/1 tbsp lemon juice
30 ml/2 tbsp chopped dill (dill weed)
A pinch of mustard powder
A few drops of chilli sauce

Thoroughly whisk the ingredients together.

Toasted sesame seed mayonnaise

MAKES 300 ML/½ PT/1¼ CUPS

5 ml/1 tsp sesame seeds
1 garlic clove, crushed
2 egg yolks
7.5 ml/1½ tsp French mustard
5 ml/1 tsp white wine vinegar
Salt and freshly ground black pepper
250 ml/8 fl oz/1 cup sunflower oil
75 ml/5 tbsp sesame oil

Toast the sesame seeds in a dry frying pan (skillet) for a few minutes until golden, shaking the pan continuously. Set aside. Whisk together the garlic, egg yolks, mustard, wine vinegar and a pinch of salt, then gradually whisk in the sunflower oil until the mixture begins to thicken. Whisk in the sesame oil, stir in the sesame seeds and season to taste with salt and pepper.

Green onion dressing

MAKES 150 ML/¼ PT/⅔ CUP

120 ml/4 fl oz/½ cup Mayonnaise
  (page 277)
60 ml/4 tbsp plain yoghurt
1 spring onion (scallion), cut into
  2.5 cm/1 in lengths
10 ml/2 tsp white wine vinegar
5 ml/1 tsp lemon juice
5 ml/1 tsp chopped parsley leaves
A pinch of sugar
A pinch of salt
A pinch of cayenne
½ garlic clove

Place all the ingredients except the garlic into a food processor or blender. Squeeze the garlic over the mixture through a garlic press. Process until the onion and parsley leaves are finely chopped. Cover and chill for 1 hour before use.

Thousand island dressing

MAKES 200 ML/7 FL OZ/SCANT 1 CUP

150 ml/¼ pt/⅔ cup Mayonnaise
  (page 277)
30 ml/2 tbsp milk
15 ml/1 tbsp tomato purée (paste)
15 ml/1 tbsp finely chopped red (bell)
  pepper
15 ml/1 tbsp finely chopped green
  pepper
15 ml/1 tbsp finely chopped gherkin
  (cornichon)
1 hard-boiled (hard-cooked) egg, finely
  chopped

Thoroughly mix all the ingredients together and chill until required.

Soft cheese dressing

MAKES 150 ML/¼ PT/⅔ CUP

100 g/4 oz/½ cup full-fat soft cheese
5 ml/1 tsp Dijon mustard
30 ml/2 tbsp oil
30 ml/2 tbsp milk
30 ml/2 tbsp vinegar
Salt and freshly ground black pepper

Beat the cheese until smooth, then
work in the mustard. Gradually beat in
the oil, followed by the milk and
vinegar and season to taste with salt
and pepper.

Curry dressing

MAKES 450 ML/¾ PT/2 CUPS

15 ml/1 tbsp oil
1 small onion, chopped
15 ml/1 tbsp curry powder
150 ml/¼ pt/⅔ cup Vegetable Stock
　(page 28)
15 ml/1 tbsp apricot jam (jelly)
5 ml/1 tsp lemon juice
150 ml/¼ pt/⅔ cup Mayonnaise
　(page 277)
150 ml/¼ pt/⅔ cup soured (dairy sour)
　cream
Salt and freshly ground black pepper

Heat the oil and fry (sauté) the onion
until soft but not brown. Add the
curry powder and cook for 2 minutes,
then stir in the stock and bring to the
boil. Add the jam and lemon juice and
simmer for 5 minutes, then leave to
cool. Stir the mayonnaise and soured
cream into the dressing and season to
taste with salt and pepper.

Creamy mustard dressing

MAKES 150 ML/¼ PT/⅔ CUP

75 ml/5 tbsp plain yoghurt
60 ml/4 tbsp single (light) cream
15 ml/1 tbsp Dijon mustard
Salt and freshly ground black pepper

Thoroughly mix all the ingredients
together, seasoning to taste with salt
and pepper. Chill until required.

Soured cream dressing

MAKES 150 ML/¼ PT/⅔ CUP

2 hard-boiled (hard-cooked) egg yolks,
　sieved (strained)
150 ml/¼ pt/⅔ cup soured (dairy sour)
　cream
5 ml/1 tsp tarragon vinegar
Salt and freshly ground black pepper

Mix the egg yolks to a smooth paste
with the soured cream, add the
vinegar and season to taste with salt
and pepper.

Sharp yoghurt dressing

MAKES 150 ML/¼ PT/⅔ CUP

120 ml/4 fl oz/½ cup plain yoghurt
30 ml/2 tbsp soured (dairy sour) cream
2.5 ml/½ tsp made English mustard
15 ml/1 tbsp lemon juice
Salt and freshly ground black pepper

Thoroughly mix all the ingredients
together, seasoning to taste with salt
and pepper. Chill until required.

Hot desserts

In this chapter, you'll find some delicious versions of old favourites as well as unusual and exotic desserts suitable for special occasions. You can introduce plenty of your own variations to the principles of these recipes. For example, the great steamed pudding can be varied in any number of ways by adding spices to the main mixture, or by using different jams (jellies) in the base of the dish. Don't be afraid to try out different ideas – recipes are not carved in stone but are designed to give you ideas so that you can experiment.

Nursery slices

SERVES 4

600 ml/1 pt/2½ cups milk
175 g/6 oz/1 cup semolina (cream of
    wheat)
50 g/2 oz/⅓ cup sultanas (golden raisins)
100 g/4 oz/½ cup caster (superfine)
    sugar
A pinch of salt
2 eggs, beaten
50 g/2 oz/¼ cup butter or margarine,
    plus extra for frying (sautéing)

Bring the milk almost to the boil in a
saucepan, then stir in 100 g/4 oz/
⅔ cup of the semolina and cook over
a low heat, stirring, for 2 minutes.
Add the sultanas and continue to
cook for a few minutes until the
mixture is thick and creamy. Remove
from the heat and stir in half the
sugar, the salt and eggs. Pour into a
greased 900 g/2 lb loaf tin (pan) and
leave to set. When cold, turn out of
the tin and slice thickly. Roll each slice
in the remaining semolina and fry
(sauté) on both sides in the hot butter
or margarine until golden brown.
Drain and serve hot, sprinkled with
the remaining sugar.

Cointreau banana melts

SERVES 4

100 g/4 oz/1 cup desiccated (shredded)
    coconut
2 bananas, mashed
75 g/3 oz/⅓ cup soft brown sugar
A few drops of vanilla essence (extract)
30 ml/2 tbsp Cointreau
A pinch of baking powder
Corn oil, for deep-frying

Reserve a quarter of the coconut,
then mix the remaining coconut with
all the remaining ingredients. Roll
5 ml/1 tsp quantities of the mixture
into balls, roll in the reserved coconut,
then fry (sauté) in deep hot oil for
3 minutes until golden brown on all
sides. Drain well on kitchen paper
(paper towels) and serve immediately.

Fruit in rum batter

SERVES 4

300 ml/½ pt/1¼ cups milk
60 ml/4 tbsp rum
A pinch of salt
30 ml/2 tbsp caster (superfine) sugar,
    plus extra for sprinkling
225 g/8 oz/2 cups plain (all-purpose)
    flour
5 ml/1 tsp baking powder
30 ml/2 tbsp oil
200 g/7 oz/1 small can of pineapple
    pieces, drained
200 g/7 oz/1 small can of peach slices,
    drained
Corn oil, for deep-frying
A pinch of ground cinnamon

Beat the milk with the rum, salt,
sugar, flour, baking powder and oil to
make a batter. Pat the fruit dry on
kitchen paper (paper towels), then dip
it into the batter and fry (sauté) in
deep hot oil for 3 minutes until
golden brown on all sides. Mix a
spoonful of sugar with the cinnamon
and sprinkle over the fruit, then serve
immediately.

Spotted dick

SERVES 4

225 g/8 oz/2 cups shredded (chopped)
  suet
450 g/1 lb/4 cups plain (all-purpose)
  flour
5 ml/1 tsp baking powder
100 g/4 oz/½ cup caster (superfine) sugar
350 g/12 oz/2 cups dates, stoned
  (pitted) and chopped
45 ml/3 tbsp milk
Custard Sauce (page 257), to serve

Thoroughly mix together all the dry
ingredients, then work to a light
dough with the milk. Spoon into a
greased 600 ml/1 pt/2½ cup pudding
basin and cover with pleated
greaseproof (waxed) paper. Place in a
saucepan and add enough water to
come half-way up the side of the
basin. Bring to the boil, cover and boil
for 3 hours, topping up with boiling
water as necessary. Serve with
Custard Sauce.

Italian cream fritters

SERVES 4

3 eggs
25 g/1 oz/2 tbsp caster (superfine)
  sugar, plus extra for sprinkling
75 g/3 oz/¾ cup cornflour (cornstarch)
Grated rind of 1 lemon
450 ml/¾ pt/2 cups milk
25 g/1 oz/2 tbsp butter or margarine
A pinch of salt
75 g/3 oz/1½ cups fresh breadcrumbs
Oil, for shallow-frying
90 ml/6 tbsp apricot jam (jelly)

Beat 1 of the eggs and reserve. Mix
the remaining 2 eggs with the sugar
in a saucepan, then beat in the
cornflour and lemon rind. Stir in the
milk, butter or margarine and salt and

bring to the boil, stirring. Cook over a
low heat for 3 minutes, stirring
continuously, until thick. Pour into a
wetted 18 cm/7 in square tin (pan)
and leave in a cool place to set. Cut
into squares and dip each in the
beaten egg, then in the breadcrumbs.
Fry (sauté) in the hot oil until golden
on all sides, then drain on kitchen
paper (paper towels) and serve
sprinkled with caster sugar with a
spoonful of apricot jam on top.

Brandy apple doughnuts

SERVES 4

3 eating (dessert) apples, peeled, cored
  and thickly sliced
15 ml/1 tbsp brandy or rum
250 ml/8 fl oz/1 cup warm water
45 ml/3 tbsp condensed milk
A pinch of salt
1 egg, separated
225 g/8 oz/2 cups plain (all-purpose)
  flour
2.5 ml/½ tsp baking powder
Corn oil, for deep-frying
Caster sugar and ground cinnamon, for
  sprinkling

Lay the apples on a plate, sprinkle
with the brandy or rum and leave to
soak for 15 minutes. Mix together the
water, condensed milk, salt and egg
yolk, then whisk in the flour and
baking powder. Whisk the egg white
until stiff, then fold it into the mixture
to make a very thick batter. Dip the
apple slices in the batter, then fry
(sauté) in deep hot oil for about
4 minutes until golden brown. Drain
well on kitchen paper (paper towels)
and serve sprinkled with sugar and
cinnamon.

Banoffee pie

SERVES 4

175 g/6 oz/1 small can of condensed
  milk
50 g/2 oz/¼ cup butter or margarine
25 g/1 oz/2 tbsp caster (superfine) sugar
225 g/8 oz digestive biscuits (graham
  crackers), crushed
1 large banana, sliced
150 ml/¼ pt/⅔ cup double (heavy)
  cream, whipped

Stand the unopened tin of condensed
milk in a saucepan of simmering water
and simmer for 1½ hours, topping up
with boiling water as necessary.
Carefully remove from the heat, leave
to cool for 10 minutes, then open the
can. Melt the butter or margarine and
mix in the sugar and biscuit (cookie)
crumbs. Press into the base of a
greased 20 cm/8 in cake tin (pan).
Spread the sliced banana over the
base and pour on the condensed milk,
which will have turned to a toffee
consistency. Spread the whipped
cream over the top. Serve warm or at
room temperature.

Note:
Caramelised cans of condensed milk
will last indefinitely, so you can boil
several cans at the same time and
store them in the cupboard. Make
sure you mark the cans with indelible
pen as the labels will come off during
boiling.

Treacle sponge

SERVES 4

45 ml/3 tbsp golden (light corn) syrup
15 ml/1 tbsp fresh breadcrumbs
100 g/4 oz/½ cup butter or margarine
100 g/4 oz/½ cup caster (superfine)
  sugar
Grated rind of 1 lemon
2 eggs, beaten
100 g/4 oz/1 cup self-raising (self-rising)
  flour
A pinch of salt
75 ml/5 tbsp milk

Mix together the syrup and
breadcrumbs and spoon into a
greased 450 g/1 lb pudding basin.
Cream the butter or margarine until
soft, then blend in the sugar and
lemon rind and beat until light and
fluffy. Beat in the eggs, a little at a
time, then fold in the flour and salt
with enough of the milk to make a
soft dropping consistency. Spoon into
the basin and cover with pleated
greaseproof (waxed) paper. Place in a
large saucepan and add enough
boiling water to come half-way up the
side of the basin. Cover and steam for
1½ hours, topping up with boiling
water as necessary, until spongy to
the touch.

283

Christmas pudding

MAKES TWO 900 G/2 LB PUDDINGS

50 g/2 oz/½ cup plain (all-purpose) flour
5 ml/1 tsp salt
5 ml/1 tsp mixed (apple-pie) spice
2.5 ml/½ tsp grated nutmeg
2.5 ml/½ tsp ground cinnamon
450 g/1 lb/2⅔ cups raisins, chopped
225 g/8 oz/1⅓ cups currants
225 g/8 oz/1⅓ cups sultanas (golden raisins)
50 g/2 oz/⅓ cup mixed peel
50 g/2 oz/½ cup flaked (slivered) almonds, chopped
50 g/2 oz/½ cup ground almonds
450 g/1 lb/2 cups shredded (chopped) suet
225 g/8 oz/4 cups fresh breadcrumbs
100 g/4 oz/½ cup soft brown sugar
6 eggs, lightly beaten
75 ml/5 tbsp brandy
250 ml/8 fl oz/1 cup milk

Mix the flour, salt and spices in a large bowl. Stir in the dried fruit, mixed peel and almonds and stir until the fruit is well coated in the flour. Stir in the ground almonds, suet, breadcrumbs and sugar. Stir in the eggs, brandy and milk, mixing well to a soft dropping consistency. Spoon into two well-greased 900 g/2 lb pudding basins and cover with pleated greaseproof (waxed) paper. Place in one or two large saucepans and add enough boiling water to come half-way up the side of the basins. Cover and steam for 4 hours, topping up with boiling water as necessary. Cover with clean paper and cloth and store in a cool, dry place. When ready to serve, steam in the same way for 2 hours, topping up with boiling water as necessary.

Fat-free Christmas pudding

SERVES 6

225 g/8 oz/4 cups wholemeal breadcrumbs
100 g/4 oz/½ cup Muscovado sugar
100 g/4 oz/⅔ cup sultanas (golden raisins)
100 g/4 oz/⅔ cup raisins
25 g/1 oz/¼ cup almonds, finely chopped
25 g/1 oz/¼ cup brazil nuts, finely chopped
1 eating (dessert) apple, peeled, cored and grated
1 banana, chopped
10 ml/2 tsp ground cinnamon
Grated rind and juice of 1 lemon
A pinch of salt
2 eggs, beaten
150 ml/¼ pt/⅔ cup milk

Mix together all the dry ingredients, then stir in the eggs. Add enough of the milk to make a firm but not stiff mixture. Spoon into a greased 1.2 litre/2 pt/5 cup pudding basin and cover with pleated greaseproof (waxed) paper. Place in a large saucepan and add enough boiling water to come half-way up the side of the basin. Cover and steam for 4½ hours, topping up with boiling water as necessary.

Date and lemon pudding

SERVES 4

2 lemons
75 ml/5 tbsp water
75 g/3 oz/⅓ cup caster (superfine) sugar
100 g/4 oz/½ cup soft margarine
100 g/4 oz/1 cup self-raising (self-rising) flour
50 g/2 oz/¼ cup soft brown sugar
2 eggs, beaten
25 g/1 oz/½ cup fresh breadcrumbs
100 g/4 oz/⅔ cup dates, stoned (pitted) and chopped

Grate the rind from the lemons, quarter the fruits and place the flesh in a food processor or blender and purée. Make up to 300 ml/½ pt/ 1¼ cups with water. Place in a saucepan, add the caster sugar and heat on a low temperature until the sugar dissolves, then boil rapidly for 3 minutes. Mix together the margarine, flour, brown sugar, eggs, breadcrumbs and dates until smooth. Turn into a well greased1.2 litre/2 pt/ 5 cup pudding basin, pour the sauce over and cover with pleated kitchen foil. Place in a large saucepan and add enough boiling water to come half-way up the side of the basin. Cover and steam for 1½ hours until the top is dry and spongy, topping up with boiling water as necessary. Turn out with care as the sauce will pour round the pudding.

Golden surprise pudding

SERVES 4–6

225 g/8 oz/⅔ cup golden (light corn) syrup
1 lemon
175 g/6 oz/1½ cups self-raising (self-rising) flour
A pinch of salt
5 ml/1 tsp baking powder
100 g/4 oz/1 cup shredded (chopped) suet
30–45 ml/2–3 tbsp water
100 g/4 oz/2 cups fresh breadcrumbs
Custard Sauce (page 257), to serve

Put 45 ml/3 tbsp of the syrup in the bottom of a greased 900 ml/1½ pt/ 3¾ cup pudding basin. Grate the rind from the lemon, remove the pith and slice the flesh thinly. Lay the lemon slices over the syrup. Mix together the flour, salt, baking powder, suet, lemon rind and half the suet. Mix to a light dough with a little of the water. Roll out the dough and cut into four pieces, increasing in size. Roll out the smallest piece and lay it in the bottom of the basin. Spoon some syrup over the dough and sprinkle with breadcrumbs. Repeat with the remaining layers, finishing with the final layer of dough. Cover with pleated greaseproof (waxed) paper and foil. Place in a large saucepan and add enough boiling water to come half-way up the side of the basin. Cover and and steam the pudding for 2 hours, topping up with boiling water as necessary. Turn out and serve hot with Custard Sauce.

285

Ginger pudding

SERVES 4

225 g/8 oz/2 cups plain (all-purpose)
    flour
A pinch of salt
5 ml/1 tsp ground ginger
75 g/3 oz/¾ cup shredded (chopped)
    suet
50 g/2 oz/¼ cup caster (superfine) sugar
100 g/4 oz/⅓ cup golden (light corn)
    syrup, warmed
1 egg, beaten
A pinch of bicarbonate of soda (baking
    soda)
45 ml/3 tbsp warm milk
45 ml/3 tbsp golden (light corn) syrup
Custard Sauce (page 257), to serve

Mix together the flour, salt, ginger,
suet and sugar. Mix together the
syrup and egg and use to bind the
dry ingredients. Dissolve the
bicarbonate of soda in the milk and
mix in to give a dropping consistency.
Spoon the extra syrup into a greased
1.2 litre/2 pt/5 cup pudding basin,
then spoon in the mixture and cover
with pleated greaseproof (waxed)
paper. Place in a large saucepan and
add enough boiling water to come
half-way up the side of the basin.
Cover and steam for 2 hours, topping
up with boiling water as necessary,
until springy to the touch. Turn out on
to a serving plate and serve with
Custard Sauce.

Steamed orange pudding

SERVES 4

120 g/5 oz/⅔ cup caster (superfine)
    sugar
100 g/4 oz/½ cup butter or margarine
2 eggs
100 g/4 oz/1 cup plain (all-purpose)
    flour
2.5 ml/½ tsp baking powder
30 ml/2 tbsp orange juice
Grated rind of 1 orange
10 ml/2 tsp arrowroot

Cream 100 g/4 oz/½ cup of the sugar
with the butter or margarine and
eggs, then beat in the flour and
baking powder, followed by the
orange juice and half the orange rind.
Pour the mixture into a greased
1.2 litre/2 pt/5 cup pudding basin
and cover with pleated greaseproof
(waxed) paper. Place in a large
saucepan and add enough boiling
water to come half-way up the side of
the basin. Cover and steam for
1½ hours, topping up with boiling
water as necessary, until springy to
the touch.

Mix the remaining sugar and
orange rind in a saucepan and heat
gently until the sugar has dissolved.
Mix the arrowroot with a little cold
water, then stir it into the pan, bring
to the boil and boil until the mixture
thickens. Add a little more sugar and
orange juice to taste, if necessary, and
serve the sauce with the orange
pudding.

French apple flan

SERVES 4

175 g/6 oz/1½ cups plain (all-purpose)
  flour
A pinch of salt
100 g/4 oz/½ cup butter or margarine
175 g/6 oz/¾ cup caster (superfine)
  sugar
1 egg yolk
15 ml/1 tbsp water
900 g/2 lb cooking (tart) apples, peeled,
  cored and chopped
2 red eating (dessert) apples, sliced
Juice of 1 lemon
15 ml/1 tbsp apricot jam (jelly), sieved
Single (light) or whipped double (heavy)
  cream, to serve

Mix together the flour and salt, then
rub in 75 g/3 oz/⅓ cup of the butter
or margarine until the mixture
resembles fine breadcrumbs. Stir in
30 ml/1 tbsp of the sugar, then bind
together to a pastry (paste) with the
egg yolk and a little of the cold water.
Cover and chill.

Melt the remaining butter or
margarine in a saucepan, add the
cooking apples and half the remaining
sugar. Cover and simmer for
10 minutes. Strain the apples,
reserving the juice, then purée the
apples in a food processor or blender.
Sprinkle the apple slices with lemon
juice to prevent browning. Roll out the
pastry and use to line a greased
10 cm/7 in flan tin (pie pan). Prick
the base with a fork and spoon in the
apple purée, then arrange the apple
slices in overlapping circles on the
top. Dissolve the remaining sugar in
the reserved apple juice, 30 ml/2 tbsp
of the lemon juice and the jam. Bring
to the boil and boil for 5 minutes,
then brush generously over the apple
slices. Bake in a preheated oven at
200°C/400°F/gas mark 6 for
40 minutes until golden brown. Serve
hot or cold with cream.

Rhubarb pudding with brown sugar sauce

SERVES 4

225 g/8 oz/2 cups self-raising (self-
  rising) flour
A pinch of salt
2.5 ml/½ tsp ground ginger
100 g/4 oz/½ cup butter or margarine
175 g/6 oz/¾ cup soft brown sugar
225 g/8 oz rhubarb, chopped
2 eggs, beaten
30 ml/2 tbsp single (light) cream

Mix together the flour, salt and ginger,
then rub in half the butter or
margarine until the mixture resembles
fine breadcrumbs. Stir in 100 g/4 oz/
½ cup of the sugar, the rhubarb and
eggs. Spoon the mixture into a
greased 1.2 litre/2 pt/5 cup pudding
basin and cover with pleated
greaseproof (waxed) paper. Place in a
large saucepan and add enough
boiling water to come half-way up the
side of the basin. Cover and steam for
1½ hours, topping up with boiling
water as necessary, until springy to
the touch.

To make the sauce, melt the
remaining butter or margarine and stir
in the remaining sugar and the cream
until the sugar has dissolved. Serve
the sauce warm with the hot pudding.

Fig pudding

SERVES 4

50 g/2 oz/½ cup plain (all-purpose) flour
50 g/2 oz/½ cup shredded (chopped)
    suet
50 g/2 oz/1 cup fresh breadcrumbs
25 g/1 oz/2 tbsp caster (superfine) sugar
A pinch of salt
100 g/4 oz/⅔ cup dried figs, chopped
A pinch of bicarbonate of soda (baking
    soda)
30 ml/2 tbsp milk
Single (light) cream, to serve

Mix together all the ingredients, using
enough of the milk to make a soft
dropping consistency. Spoon into a
greased 600 ml/1 pt/2½ cup pudding
basin and cover with pleated
greaseproof (waxed) paper. Place in a
large saucepan and add enough
boiling water to come half-way up the
side of the basin. Cover and steam for
2 hours, topping up with boiling water
as necessary, until springy to the
touch. Turn out and serve with cream.

Crunchy apricot
pudding

SERVES 4

900 g/2 lb/2 large cans of apricot halves
    in syrup, drained and halved
100 g/4 oz/½ cup butter or margarine
A pinch of salt
5 ml/1 tsp ground cinnamon
2.5 ml/½ tsp grated nutmeg
90 ml/6 tbsp clear honey
6 large slices of bread, crusts removed
50 g/2 oz cornflakes
Cream or ice cream, to serve

Mix 150 ml/¼ pt/⅔ cup of the apricot
syrup with the butter or margarine,
salt, cinnamon, nutmeg and honey in
a large saucepan and heat gently until

well mixed. Toast the bread and cut
into 1 cm/½ in cubes. Add the bread,
apricots and cornflakes to the syrup
and toss all the ingredients together
lightly. Spoon the mixture into a large
greased ovenproof dish and bake in a
preheated oven at 180°C/350°F/gas
mark 4 for 30 minutes. Serve hot or
cold with cream or ice cream.

Baked stuffed apples
with lemon butter
sauce

SERVES 4

4 cooking (tart) apples
100 g/4 oz/⅔ cup dates, stoned (pitted)
    and chopped
15 ml/1 tbsp golden (light corn) syrup
15 g/½ oz/1 tbsp butter or margarine
25 g/1 oz/2 tbsp demerara sugar
15 ml/1 tbsp cornflour (cornstarch)
Juice of 1 lemon

Core the apples and make a horizontal
score in the skins all round. Stuff the
centre with the dates and bake in a
preheated oven at 180°C/350°F/gas
mark 4 for 45 minutes until soft and
golden round the edges. Place the
syrup, butter or margarine, sugar and
cornflour in a saucepan. Make the
lemon juice up to 150 ml/¼ pt/⅔ cup
with water and add to the pan. Bring
to the boil, stirring continuously, then
simmer for 10 minutes and serve with
the baked apples.

Baked fruit dumplings

SERVES 4

275 g/10 oz/2½ cups plain (all-purpose)
    flour
A pinch of salt
75 g/3 oz/⅓ cup butter or margarine
50 g/2 oz/¼ cup lard (shortening) or
    vegetable fat
15 ml/1 tbsp caster (superfine) sugar
60 ml/4 tbsp water
4 cooking (tart) apples, peeled and
    cored
50 g/2 oz/¼ cup soft brown sugar
5 ml/1 tsp ground cinnamon
30 ml/2 tbsp milk

Mix together the flour and salt, then rub in the fats until the mixture resembles fine breadcrumbs. Stir in 5 ml/1 tsp of the caster sugar and add just enough of the water to bind to a pastry (paste). Roll out on a lightly floured surface and cut into four rounds, each large enough to cover an apple, and place an apple in the centre of each round. Mix together the brown sugar and cinnamon and use the mixture to fill the holes in the centre of the apples. Dampen the edges of the pastry and draw it up to cover each apple, sealing the edges together well. Place on a greased baking (cookie) sheet with the joins underneath. Brush with the milk and sprinkle with the remaining caster sugar. Bake in a preheated oven at 200°C/400°F/gas mark 6 for 40 minutes until golden.

Apple Betty

SERVES 4

750 g/1¾ lb cooking (tart) apples,
    peeled, cored and sliced
30 ml/2 tbsp water
1 lemon
1 orange
100 g/4 oz/⅔ cup sultanas (golden
    raisins)
25 g/1 oz/2 tbsp soft brown sugar
100 g/4 oz/1 cup wholemeal
    breadcrumbs
50 g/2 oz/½ cup walnuts, finely chopped
25 g/1 oz/2 tbsp butter or margarine,
    chopped
2.5 ml/½ tsp ground cinnamon
Cream or Custard Sauce (page 257),
    to serve

Cook the apples in the water for 10 minutes until just soft. Grate the rind from the lemon. Cut the lemon and orange into quarters and purée the flesh in a food processor or blender. Add the sultanas, half the sugar and the lemon rind and blend to mix. Add the apples. Place half the mixture in the base of a deep ovenproof dish. Mix together the breadcrumbs and nuts and spread half the mixture over the top, followed by half the remaining sugar. Then add the rest of the apple mixture, the remaining breadcrumb mixture and the remaining sugar. Dot the butter or margarine on top and sprinkle with the cinnamon. Bake in a preheated oven at 190°C/375°F/gas mark 5 for 35 minutes until crisp on top. Serve hot with cream or Custard Sauce.

Apple crunch

SERVES 4

900 g/2 lb cooking (tart) apples, peeled,
cored and sliced
50 g/2 oz/¼ cup granulated sugar
2.5 ml/½ tsp ground cinnamon
175 g/6 oz/1½ cups plain (all-purpose)
flour
5 ml/1 tsp baking powder
100 g/4 oz/½ cup butter or margarine
100 g/4 oz/½ cup soft brown sugar
50 g/2 oz/½ cup chopped mixed nuts
Ice cream, to serve

Place the apple slices in a greased
ovenproof dish and sprinkle with
granulated sugar and cinnamon to
taste. Mix together the flour and
baking powder and rub in the butter
or margarine until the mixture
resembles fine breadcrumbs. Stir in
the brown sugar and nuts and spread
the mixture over the apples. Bake in a
preheated oven at 220°C/425°F/gas
mark 7 for 30 minutes until brown
and crisp. Serve hot or cold with ice
cream.

Crunchy-topped apple layer pie

SERVES 4–6

450 g/1 lb cooking (tart) apples, peeled,
cored and sliced
30 ml/2 tbsp orange juice
15 ml/1 tbsp caster (superfine) sugar
100 g/4 oz/½ cup butter or margarine
175 g/6 oz/1½ cups plain (all-purpose)
flour
A pinch of salt
45 ml/3 tbsp cold water
25 g/1 oz/¼ cup ground almonds
15 ml/1 tbsp clear honey
15 ml/1 tbsp hot water
Custard Sauce (page 257), to serve

Arrange the apples on the base of a
greased 20 cm/8 in ovenproof dish
and sprinkle with the orange juice and
sugar. Rub the butter or margarine
into the flour and salt until the
mixture resembles fine breadcrumbs,
then mix in enough of the water to
make a smooth pastry (paste). Roll
out on a lightly floured surface to fit
the dish and place on top of the
apples. Mix together the almonds,
honey and hot water and spread
evenly over the pastry. Bake in a
preheated oven at 190°C/375°F/gas
mark 5 for 30 minutes until the top is
crisp. Serve hot with Custard Sauce.

Coffee custard pudding

SERVES 4

100 g/4 oz/½ cup butter or margarine
175 g/6 oz/¾ cup soft brown sugar
1 egg, beaten
75 ml/5 tbsp strong black coffee
100 g/4 oz/1 cup plain (all-purpose)
flour
5 ml/1 tsp baking powder
25 g/1 oz/¼ cup walnuts, chopped
300 ml/½ pt/1¼ cups milk
Cream or Custard Sauce (page 257),
to serve

Cream the butter or margarine and
100 g/4 oz/½ cup of the sugar, then
beat in the egg and coffee. Stir in the
flour, baking powder and walnuts.
Spoon the mixture into a greased
1.2 litre/2 pt/5 cup pudding basin.
Mix the remaining sugar with the milk
and pour over the pudding. Bake in a
preheated oven at 170°C/325°F/gas
mark 3 for 1½ hours until set and
springy with a sauce underneath.
Serve with cream or Custard Sauce.

Carrot pudding

SERVES 4

50 g/2 oz/¼ cup butter or margarine
25 g/1 oz/2 tbsp lard (shortening) or
  vegetable fat
175 g/6 oz/1½ cups plain (all-purpose)
  flour
45 ml/3 tbsp water
50 g/2 oz carrots, grated
50 g/2 oz/1 cup fresh breadcrumbs
300 ml/½ pt/1¼ cups hot milk
50 g/2 oz/½ cup caster (superfine) sugar
Grated rind and juice of 1 lemon
25 g/1 oz/3 tbsp raisins, chopped
10 ml/2 tbsp mixed (apple-pie) spice
2 eggs, beaten

Rub the fats into the flour until the
mixture resembles fine breadcrumbs,
then mix to a pastry (paste) with the
water. Roll out on a lightly floured
surface and use to line a 20 cm/8 in
pie dish. Mix together the remaining
ingredients, pour into the pie dish and
bake in a preheated oven at 190°C/
375°F/gas mark 5 for 40 minutes
until set.

Fluffy pear and apricot pudding

SERVES 4

600 ml/1 pt/2½ cups milk
100 g/4 oz/2 cups fresh white
  breadcrumbs
15 g/½ oz/1 tbsp butter or margarine
Grated rind of 1 lemon
25 g/1 oz/2 tbsp caster (superfine) sugar
2 eggs, separated
1 firm pear, peeled, cored and sliced
50 g/2 oz/⅓ cup no-need-to-soak dried
  apricots, chopped
15 ml/1 tbsp soft brown sugar

Heat the milk in a saucepan, then
remove from the heat and stir in the
breadcrumbs, butter or margarine,
lemon rind and caster sugar. Leave to
stand for 20 minutes until most of the
milk has been absorbed. Add the egg
yolks and beat well. Whisk the egg
whites until stiff, then fold them into
the mixture. Place the pear slices in
the base of a greased shallow
ovenproof dish. Sprinkle with the
apricots and brown sugar and pour
the milk mixture on top. Bake in a
preheated oven at 180°C/350°F/gas
mark 4 for 30 minutes until well risen
and golden brown.

Luxury bread and butter pudding

SERVES 4

300 ml/½ pt/1¼ cups milk
150 ml/¼ pt/⅔ cup double (heavy) cream
2.5 ml/½ tsp vanilla essence (extract)
2 eggs, beaten
50 g/2 oz/¼ cup caster (superfine) sugar
8 slices of bread, crusts removed,
  quartered
25 g/1 oz/2 tbsp butter or margarine,
  softened
50 g/2 oz/⅓ cup raisins
Grated rind of 1 lemon

Mix together the milk, cream and
vanilla essence in a saucepan, bring to
the boil, then remove from the heat
and leave to cool. Beat the eggs with
the sugar until pale and thick, then
whisk in the milk. Spread the bread
with the butter or margarine and layer
in a greased 1.2 litre/2 pt/5 cup pie
dish with the raisins and lemon rind.
Pour in the custard and bake in a
preheated oven at 180°C/350°F/gas
mark 4 for 40 minutes until set and
golden brown on top.

Apple and rhubarb crumble

SERVES 4

450 g/1 lb cooking (tart) apples, peeled, cored and thinly sliced
300 g/12 oz rhubarb, cut into chunks
15 g/1 oz/2 tbsp light brown sugar
75 g/3 oz/⅓ cup butter or margarine
100 g/4 oz/1 cup plain (all-purpose) flour
50 g/2 oz/½ cup wholemeal flour
50 g/2 oz/¼ cup caster (superfine) sugar
1.5 ml/¼ tsp ground cinnamon
Single (light) cream or Custard Sauce (page 257), to serve

Put the fruit in a 1.2 litre/2 pt/5 cup ovenproof dish and sprinkle with the brown sugar. Rub the butter or margarine into the flours until the mixture resembles breadcrumbs, then stir in the caster sugar and cinnamon. Sprinkle over the fruit. Bake in a preheated oven at 200°C/400°F/gas mark 6 for 30 minutes until crisp and golden brown. Serve with cream or Custard Sauce.

Apple charlotte

SERVES 4–6

450 g/1 lb cooking (tart) apples, peeled, cored and sliced
Grated rind and juice of 1 lemon
100 g/4 oz/½ cup caster (superfine) sugar, plus extra for sprinkling
10 slices of white bread, crusts removed
75 g/3 oz/⅓ cup butter or margarine, melted
Cream, to serve

Place the apples, lemon rind and juice and sugar in a saucepan and simmer for about 10–15 minutes to a thick purée, then leave to cool. Cut one bread slice into a round to fit the bottom of a greased 1.2 litre/2 pt/5 cup soufflé dish. Dip the bread in the melted butter or margarine and lay it in the dish. Cut another round to fit the top of the dish and keep it aside. Dip the remaining slices in the butter or margarine and use to line the sides of the dish, filling any gaps with small pieces of bread. Spoon in the purée and cover with the reserved bread, dipped in butter or margarine. Cover with foil and bake in a preheated oven at 180°C/350°F/gas mark 4 for 40 minutes until golden. Sprinkle with sugar and serve with cream.

Hot chocolate soufflé

SERVES 4

75 g/3 oz/⅓ cup butter or margarine
50 g/2 oz/½ cup plain (all-purpose) flour
15 ml/1 tbsp cocoa (unsweetened chocolate) powder
2.5 ml/½ tsp ground cinnamon
450 ml/¾ pt/2 cups milk
4 eggs, separated
50 g/2 oz caster (superfine) sugar
15 ml/1 tbsp icing (confectioners') sugar

Melt the butter or margarine, stir in the flour, cocoa and cinnamon and blend well over a low heat. Stir in the milk, stirring continuously, until the sauce thickens. Remove from the heat and leave to cool slightly. Beat the egg yolks into the sauce. Whisk the egg whites lightly, then add the sugar and whisk again until they hold soft peaks. Fold into the sauce, then turn the mixture into a greased 1.2 litre/ 2 pt/5 cup soufflé dish with a collar of paper round the side. Stand the dish in a roasting tin (pan) and add enough water to come half-way up the side of the dish. Bake in a preheated oven at 190°C/375°F/gas mark 5 for 45 minutes until well risen. Sprinkle with the icing sugar and serve immediately.

Rich chocolate pudding

SERVES 4

100 g/4 oz/⅔ cup soft brown sugar
100 g/4 oz/1 cup self-raising (self-rising)
    flour
5 ml/1 tsp baking powder
50 g/2 oz/¼ cup cocoa (unsweetened
    chocolate) powder
100 g/4 oz/½ cup butter or margarine
2 eggs
10 ml/2 tsp caster (superfine) sugar
5 ml/1 tsp cornflour (cornstarch)
150 ml/¼ pt/⅔ cup water
Cream or Custard Sauce (page 257),
    to serve

Mix together the brown sugar, flour, baking powder and 25 g/1 oz/2 tbsp of the cocoa, then rub in the butter or margarine and mix in the eggs. Turn the mixture into a greased 1.2 litre/ 2 pt/5 cup casserole dish (Dutch oven). Mix together the caster sugar, cornflour and water with the remaining cocoa, pour on top of the pudding mixture and leave to stand for 5 minutes. Bake in a preheated oven at 190°C/375°F/gas mark 5 for 45 minutes. Turn out on to a serving dish. The pudding will be moist and soggy on the top with a crisper base. Serve with cream or Custard Sauce.

Rimside tarts

SERVES 4

100 g/4 oz/½ cup butter or margarine
225 g/8 oz/2 cups plain (all-purpose)
    flour
45 ml/3 tbsp water
50 g/2 oz/1 cup fresh breadcrumbs
90 ml/6 tbsp orange marmalade
225 g/8 oz/1⅓ cups currants

Rub the butter or margarine into the flour until the mixture resembles fine breadcrumbs. Mix in the water to make a smooth pastry (paste). Roll out the pastry and use it to line two greased 18 cm/7 in sandwich tins (pans). Roll out the trimmings and cut into strips. Mix together the breadcrumbs, marmalade and currants and add a little water, if necessary, to keep the mixture fairly moist. Divide the filling between the tins and arrange the strips of pastry in a lattice pattern on top. Bake in a preheated oven at 200°C/400°F/gas mark 6 for 25 minutes until golden.

Jack tart

SERVES 4

90 g/3½ oz/scant ½ cup butter or
    margarine
40 g/1½ oz/3 tbsp lard (shortening) or
    vegetable fat
175 g/6 oz/1½ cups plain (all-purpose)
    flour
30 ml/2 tbsp water
60 ml/4 tbsp raspberry jam (jelly)
50 g/2 oz/¼ cup caster (superfine) sugar
100 g/4 oz/1 cup rolled oats
A few drops of almond essence (extract)

Rub 40 g/1½ oz/3 tbsp of the butter or margarine and the lard or vegetable fat into the flour and mix to a pastry (paste) with the water. Roll out on a lightly floured surface and use to line a greased 20 cm/8 in pie dish. Spread the jam over the pastry. Melt the remaining butter and stir in the sugar, oats and almond essence. Spoon over the jam, spread with a fork and bake in a preheated oven at 200°C/400°F/gas mark 6 for 25 minutes until lightly browned.

Orange delight

SERVES 4

100 g/4 oz/½ cup butter or margarine
50 g/2 oz/¼ cup lard (shortening) or
   vegetable fat
275 g/10 oz/2½ cups plain (all-purpose)
   flour
45 ml/3 tbsp water
60 ml/4 tbsp lemon curd
2 oranges, peeled and sliced
25 g/1 oz/¼ cup cornflour (cornstarch)
2.5 ml/½ tsp salt
2.5 ml/½ tsp baking powder
50 g/2 oz/¼ cup caster (superfine) sugar
1 egg

Rub half the butter or margarine and
the lard or vegetable fat into 225 g/
8 oz/2 cups of the flour until the
mixture resembles fine breadcrumbs.
Mix to a pastry (paste) with the water.
Roll out on a lightly floured surface
and use to line a greased 23 cm/9 in
sandwich tin (pan). Spread the pastry
with the lemon curd, then layer the
orange slices over the top. Mix the
remaining flour with the cornflour, salt
and baking powder. Cream the
remaining butter or margarine with
the sugar and egg. Stir in the flour
mixture and beat until smooth. Spread
the mixture over the oranges. Bake in
a preheated oven at 190°C/375°F/
gas mark 5 for 30 minutes until
golden and springy to the touch.

Apricot and orange pancakes

SERVES 4

25 g/1 oz/¼ cup ground almonds
100 g/4 oz/1 cup plain (all-purpose)
   flour
A pinch of salt
1 egg
300 ml/½ pt/1¼ cups milk
Grated rind of 1 orange
25 g/1 oz/2 tbsp butter or margarine,
   melted
Oil, for shallow-frying
2 oranges
50 g/2 oz/⅓ cup no-need-to-soak dried
   apricots, chopped
Single (light) cream, to serve

Beat together the almonds, flour, salt,
egg, milk, orange rind and melted
butter or margarine to make a batter.
Heat some oil in a frying pan (skillet)
and use the batter to make eight
pancakes. As they are cooked, place
them in a stack separated by sheets
of greaseproof (waxed) paper and
keep them warm. Peel the oranges
and remove all the pith and pips.
Purée with the apricots in a food
processor or blender. Spread the
mixture over each pancake, then roll
them up and place them in a shallow
ovenproof dish. Cover with foil and
reheat in a preheated oven at
200°C/400°F/gas mark 6 for
20 minutes. Serve hot with cream.

Buckwheat pancakes with cherries and butterscotch sauce

SERVES 4

100 g/4 oz/1 cup buckwheat flour
3 eggs, beaten
Salt
250 ml/8 fl oz/1 cup milk
75 g/3 oz/⅓ cup caster (superfine) sugar
30 ml/2 tbsp oil
25 g/1 oz/2 tbsp butter or margarine
450 ml/¾ pt/2 cups red wine
225 g/8 oz cherries, stoned (pitted)
A pinch of ground cloves
2.5 ml/½ tsp ground cinnamon
15 ml/1 tbsp green peppercorns, crushed
5 ml/1 tsp cornflour (cornstarch)
30 ml/2 tbsp water

Beat the flour into the eggs and add the salt, milk and 10 ml/2 tsp of the sugar. Heat the oil and pour in enough batter just to cover the base of the pan. Cook for a few minutes until set and lightly browned, then toss or flip over and cook the other side. Remove from the pan and keep the pancake warm while you cook seven more in the same way.

Heat the butter or margarine with half the remaining sugar for about 4 minutes until the sauce is smooth and bubbly. Boil the wine with the remaining sugar and the cherries for 2 minutes. Stir in the cloves, cinnamon and peppercorns. Mix the cornflour (cornstarch) and water to a paste and stir into the sauce. Simmer, stirring, for a few minutes until thick and glossy. Fill the pancakes with the cherry mixture and pour the sauce over.

Pear, oat and walnut pudding

SERVES 4

150 g/5 oz/⅔ cup butter or margarine
150 g/5 oz/⅔ cup soft brown sugar
3 pears, peeled, halved and cored
6 whole walnuts
25 g/1 oz/¼ cup walnuts, ground
2 eggs
100 g/4 oz/1 cup self-raising (self-rising) flour
5 ml/1 tsp mixed (apple-pie) spice
15 ml/1 tbsp milk
25 g/1 oz/¼ cup rolled oats
Cream or Custard Sauce (page 257), to serve

Grease the base of an ovenproof dish with some of the butter or margarine and sprinkle with 15 ml/1 tbsp of the sugar. Place a walnut in the dip in each pear half and arrange the pears, flat-side down, on the base of the dish. Cream the remaining butter or margarine and sugar until smooth, then mix in the ground walnuts, eggs, flour, spice, milk and oats. Spoon the mixture over the pears and bake in a preheated oven at 190°C/375°F/gas mark 5 for 35 minutes until well risen and golden brown. Turn out of the dish and serve with cream or Custard Sauce.

Two-layer lemon bake

SERVES 4

50 g/2 oz/¼ cup butter or margarine
100 g/4 oz/½ cup caster (superfine)
    sugar
45 ml/3 tbsp lemon juice
5 ml/1 tsp grated lemon rind
2 eggs, separated
50 g/2 oz/⅓ cup semolina (cream of
    wheat)
450 ml/¾ pt/2 cups milk

Melt the butter or margarine, then stir in the sugar, lemon juice and rind. Remove from the heat and beat in the egg yolks and semolina. Stir in the milk and mix to a smooth batter. Whisk the egg whites until stiff, then fold them into the mixture. Pour into a greased ovenproof dish and stand the dish in a roasting tin (pan). Add enough water to come half-way up the sides of the dish. Bake in a preheated oven at 180°C/350°F/gas mark 4 for 45 minutes until risen and golden. Serve hot or cold.

Queen of puddings

SERVES 4

4 eggs, separated
600 ml/1 pt/2½ cups milk
100 g/4 oz/2 cups fresh breadcrumbs
90 ml/6 tbsp raspberry jam (jelly)
75 g/3 oz/⅓ cup caster (superfine) sugar,
    plus extra for sprinkling

Beat 1 whole egg and 3 egg yolks, then stir in the milk and breadcrumbs. Spread the jam over the bottom of a greased 20 cm/8 in pie dish, spoon the egg mixture on top and leave to stand for 30 minutes. Bake in a preheated oven at 150°C/300°F/gas mark 2 for 1 hour until set. Whisk the egg whites until stiff, then fold in half the sugar. Whisk again, then fold in the remaining sugar. Pile the meringue mixture on top of the custard, sprinkle with sugar and return to the oven for 20 minutes until the meringue is set and lightly browned.

Austrian lattice pie

SERVES 4

350 g/12 oz raspberries
75 g/3 oz/⅓ cup caster (superfine) sugar
15 g/½ oz/1 tbsp butter or margarine
5 ml/1 tsp ground cinnamon
225 g/8 oz Shortcrust Pastry (page 164)
50 g/2 oz/½ cup ground almonds
1 egg white, lightly beaten
Single (light) cream, to serve

Place the raspberries, 50 g/2 oz/ ¼ cup of the sugar, the butter or margarine and cinnamon in a saucepan and heat gently for about 5 minutes until the fruit is soft. Roll out the pastry (paste) on a lightly floured surface and use to line a greased 18 cm/7 in flan ring. Sprinkle the base with the ground almonds and spread the raspberry mixture on top. Roll out the pastry trimmings, cut into 1 cm/½ in strips and arrange on top of the pie in a lattice pattern. Brush over the whole pie with egg white and sprinkle with the remaining sugar. Bake in a preheated oven at 190°C/375°F/gas mark 5 for 30 minutes until golden. Serve warm with cream.

Baked rice pudding

SERVES 4

50 g/2 oz/¼ cup short-grain rice
600 ml/1 pt/2½ cups milk
25 g/1 oz/2 tbsp caster (superfine) sugar
Grated rind of ½ lemon
Grated nutmeg, for sprinkling
15 g/½ oz/1 tbsp butter or margarine

Put the rice in a greased 900 ml/
1½ pt ovenproof dish and stir in the
milk. Leave to soak for 30 minutes.
Stir in the sugar and lemon rind,
sprinkle with nutmeg and dot with the
butter or margarine. Bake in a
preheated oven at 150°C/300°F/gas
mark 2 for 30 minutes, stir, then bake
for a further 2 hours until creamy.

Rhubarb batter

SERVES 4

450 g/1 lb rhubarb, chopped
45 ml/3 tbsp orange juice
225 g/8 oz/⅔ cup clear honey
25 g/1 oz/2 tbsp butter or margarine
1 egg, beaten
2.5 ml/½ tsp vanilla essence (extract)
30 ml/2 tbsp soured (dairy sour) cream
100 g/4 oz/1 cup wholemeal flour
A pinch of salt
2.5 ml/½ tsp bicarbonate of soda
(baking soda)

Spread the rhubarb over the base of a
greased 20 cm/8 in pie dish. Mix
together the orange juice and half the
honey and trickle it over the rhubarb.
Dot with the butter or margarine. Mix
together the egg, the remaining
honey, the vanilla essence and soured
cream. Stir in the flour, salt and
bicarbonate of soda and spread the
batter over the rhubarb. Bake in a
preheated oven at 180°C/350°F/gas
mark 4 for 30 minutes until golden.

Toffee fruit cobbler

SERVES 4

100 g/4 oz/½ cup butter or margarine
175 g/6 oz/1½ cups self-raising (self-
rising) flour
150 ml/¼ pt/⅔ cup milk
2 cooking (tart) apples, peeled, cored
and sliced
15 ml/1 tbsp water
400 g/14 oz/1 large can of raspberries,
drained
150 ml/¼ pt/⅔ cup double (heavy) cream
25 g/1 oz/2 tbsp demerara sugar

Rub 50 g/2 oz/¼ cup of the butter or
margarine into the flour until the
mixture resembles fine breadcrumbs.
Mix to a soft dough with the milk,
then roll out on a lightly floured
surface and cut into 5 cm/2 in
rounds. Place them on a greased
baking (cookie) sheet and bake in a
preheated oven at 220°C/425°F/gas
mark 7 for 10 minutes until golden.
Meanwhile, cook the apples in the
water for 10 minutes until soft, then
drain away any excess juice, stir in the
raspberries and spoon the fruit into a
flameproof bowl. Split the scones,
spread with the remaining butter or
margarine and arrange round the
edge of the dish. Pour the cream in
the centre and sprinkle with the sugar.
Place under a hot grill (broiler) for a
few minutes until the sugar has
caramelised, then serve immediately.

Trigona

SERVES 4

225 g/8 oz/2 cups walnuts, chopped
100 g/4 oz/2 cups fresh breadcrumbs
5 ml/1 tsp ground cinnamon
350 g/12 oz/1½ cups caster (superfine)
   sugar
300 ml/½ pt/1¼ cups water
150 ml/¼ pt/⅔ cup clear honey
1 egg yolk
225 g/8 oz filo pastry (paste)
175 g/6 oz/¾ cup butter or margarine,
   melted

Mix together the walnuts, breadcrumbs and cinnamon. Boil 50 g/2 oz
of the sugar with 50 ml/2 fl oz of the
water and 15 ml/1 tbsp of the honey
for 5 minutes. Remove from the heat
and stir in the walnut mixture and the
egg yolk. Cut the pastry sheets into
13 cm/5 in strips and cover the
sheets you are not using with a damp
cloth to avoid them drying out while
you are working. Brush the pastry
strips with butter or margarine, fold in
half lengthways and brush again.
Place a 5 ml/1 tsp quantity of the
filling on one end and fold into a
triangle, then fold over and over to
the end of the strip. Place the finished
triangles on a greased baking (cookie)
sheet and brush with the remaining
butter. Bake in a preheated oven at
180°C/350°F/ gas mark 4 for
30 minutes until crisp and golden.

To make the sauce, boil the
remaining water with the remaining
honey and sugar until it thickens to a
syrup. Pour the warmed syrup over
the triangles.

Hot walnut pudding with butterscotch sauce

SERVES 4

4 eggs, separated
175 g/6 oz/¾ cup caster (superfine)
   sugar
100 g/4 oz/1 cup walnuts, chopped
Grated rind and juice of 1 orange
100 g/4 oz/1 cup self-raising (self-rising)
   flour
For the sauce:
100 g/4 oz/½ cup butter or margarine,
   softened
100 g/4 oz/½ cup soft brown sugar
25 g/1 oz/¼ cup plain (all-purpose) flour
90 ml/6 tbsp milk

Beat the egg yolks with the caster
sugar until thick, then add the walnuts
and orange rind and juice and stir in
the self-raising flour. Whisk the egg
whites until stiff, then fold them into
the mixture and turn into a greased
and lined 18 cm/7 in square cake tin
(pan). Bake in a preheated oven at
180°C/350°F/gas mark 4 for
45 minutes until springy to the touch.

To make the sauce, beat together
the butter or margarine, brown sugar
and plain flour in a saucepan, then
heat gently until the butter melts
and the mixture bubbles. Cook for
4 minutes, stirring continuously. Stir in
the milk and bring to the boil, stirring
continuously, until the sauce is thick
and smooth. Serve the pudding warm
with the hot sauce.

Lemon meringue pie

SERVES 6

175 g/6 oz/1½ cups plain (all-purpose) flour
A pinch of salt
90 g/3½ oz/scant ½ cup butter or margarine, diced
25 g/1 oz/3 tbsp icing (confectioners') sugar
3 eggs
Finely grated rind and juice of 2 lemons
30 ml/2 tbsp cornflour (cornstarch)
150 g/5 oz/⅔ cup caster (superfine) sugar

Sift the flour and salt into a bowl. Add 75 g/3 oz/⅓ cup of the butter or margarine and rub in with the fingertips until the mixture resembles breadcrumbs. Stir in the icing sugar. Beat one of the eggs and mix in to form a soft but not sticky dough. Knead gently on a lightly floured surface. Wrap in clingfilm (plastic wrap) and chill for 30 minutes.

Roll out and use to line a 20 cm/ 8 in flan tin (pie pan). Fill with crumpled foil and bake in a preheated oven at 200°C/400°F/gas mark 6 for 10 minutes. Remove the foil and bake for a further 5 minutes to dry out.

Make the lemon rind and juice up to 300 ml/½ pt/1¼ cups with water. Blend a little with the cornflour in a saucepan. Stir in the remaining liquid and 25 g/1 oz/2 tbsp of the caster sugar. Separate the remaining eggs and whisk the egg yolks into the saucepan. Add the remaining butter or margarine. Bring to the boil and cook for 2 minutes, stirring all the time, until thickened. Turn into the cooked flan case (pie shell).

Whisk the egg whites until stiff. Whisk in half the remaining sugar and whisk again until stiff and glossy. Fold in the remaining caster sugar and pile the meringue on top of the lemon mixture, spreading right to the edges. Reduce the oven temperature to 190°C/375°F/gas mark 5 and cook the pie for about 20 minutes until crisp on top and pale golden brown. Serve warm or cold.

Treacle tart

SERVES 4

175 g/6 oz/1½ cups plain (all-purpose) flour
10 ml/2 tsp caster (superfine) sugar
75 g/3 oz/⅓ cup butter or margarine
1 egg yolk
225 g/8 oz/⅔ cup golden (light corn) syrup
50 g/2 oz/1 cup fresh breadcrumbs
15 ml/1 tbsp lemon juice
Cream, Custard Sauce (page 257) or ice cream, to serve

Mix together the flour and sugar and rub in the butter or margarine until the mixture resembles coarse breadcrumbs. Mix to a firm pastry (paste) with the egg yolk, wrap in clingfilm (plastic wrap) and chill for 30 minutes. Roll out on a lightly floured surface and use to line a greased 20 cm/8 in pie dish. Warm the syrup, then stir in the breadcrumbs and lemon juice and leave to cool. Pour into the pastry base and bake in a preheated oven at 180°C/350°F/gas mark 4 for 35 minutes until set and golden. Serve hot or cold with cream, Custard Sauce or ice cream.

Cold desserts

This collection of cold desserts gives you a great choice when looking for something for a warm summer day, to follow a rich main course, or a sweet you can prepare in advance so that you can enjoy your time with guests. There are plenty of light mousses as well as richer desserts to try out for special occasions.

If you always keep a tub of good-quality ice cream in the freezer, you need never be short of an interesting dessert at the last minute. Team it with grated chocolate, a melted Mars bar, sliced or canned fruit or even just a drizzle of honey and a wafer biscuit (cookie) and serve with a flourish.

Brandied berry compôte

SERVES 4–6

100 g/4 oz gooseberries
225 g/8 oz blackcurrants
225 g/8 oz redcurrants
225 g/8 oz blackberries
225 g/8 oz raspberries
60 ml/4 tbsp blackcurrant juice
30 ml/2 tbsp lemon juice
45 ml/3 tbsp brandy
25 g/1 oz/3 tbsp icing (confectioners')
  sugar, sifted
50 g/2 oz/¼ cup almonds, toasted
2 mint sprigs
150 ml/¼ pt/⅔ cup double (heavy) cream

Place the prepared fruit in a serving bowl. Mix together the blackcurrant juice, lemon juice and brandy and pour it over the fruit. Sprinkle with the icing sugar and chill for at least 3 hours. Sprinkle with the toasted almonds, garnish with the mint sprigs and serve with the cream.

Brandied peaches

SERVES 4

4 ripe peaches
30 ml/2 tbsp lemon juice
25 g/1 oz/2 tbsp caster (superfine) sugar
60 ml/4 tbsp brandy
300 ml/½ pt/1¼ cups whipping cream,
  whipped

Blanch the peaches in boiling water, then remove the skins. Toss the peaches in the lemon juice, place in a serving dish and prick with a fork. Sprinkle with the sugar and brandy. Cover and chill for several hours until the flavours have developed. Serve with the whipped cream.

Fruit and nut oranges

SERVES 4

4 large oranges
300 ml/½ pt/1¼ cups double (heavy)
  cream
30 ml/2 tbsp orange juice
75 g/3 oz/¾ cup walnuts, chopped
50 g/2 oz/¼ cup glacé (candied) cherries,
  finely chopped
50 g/2 oz plain (semi-sweet) chocolate,
  grated
5 ml/1 tsp orange liqueur

Cut a slice from the top of each orange and cut out the flesh with a sharp knife. Chop the flesh and spoon it back into the orange shells. Whip the cream with the orange juice, then stir in the nuts, cherries, chocolate and liqueur. Spoon the mixture into the oranges and chill before serving.

Strawberry and Cointreau crush

SERVES 4

225 g/8 oz strawberries
25 g/1 oz/2 tbsp caster (superfine) sugar
30 ml/2 tbsp Cointreau
300 ml/½ pt/1¼ cups double (heavy)
  cream, whipped

Reserve four strawberries for decoration, then crush the remainder with the sugar. Whisk the Cointreau into the cream, then fold in the strawberry mixture. Spoon into individual glass dishes and top with a strawberry. Chill before serving.

Chartreuse fruit salad

SERVES 4

1 eating (dessert) apple, cored and
  sliced
225 g/8 oz seedless grapes
225 g/8 oz kiwi fruit, sliced
1 melon, cut into balls
100 g/4 oz/½ cup granulated sugar
150 ml/¼ pt/⅔ cup water
15 ml/1 tbsp lemon juice
15 ml/1 tbsp green Chartreuse

Mix the prepared fruits in a serving
bowl. Bring the sugar and water to
the boil and boil for 3 minutes. Leave
to cool, then stir in the lemon juice
and Chartreuse and pour over the
fruit. Chill until required, stirring
occasionally.

Caramel oranges in Grand Marnier

SERVES 4

6 oranges
175 g/6 oz/¾ cup caster (superfine)
  sugar
150 ml/¼ pt/⅔ cup cold water
Juice of ½ lemon
30 ml/2 tbsp Grand Marnier

Cut away all the peel and pith from
the oranges, slice the flesh crossways
and arrange in a serving dish. Cut
away the pith from 6 pieces of rind
and slice finely. Put in a saucepan and
cover with water. Bring to the boil,
then simmer for 15 minutes and drain
well. Put the sugar in a heavy-based
saucepan and stir over a low heat
until it has dissolved and caramelised.
Remove from the heat and carefully
stir in the cold water, which will make
the mixture bubble. When the
bubbling has stopped, return to the
heat and stir until the caramel has
dissolved and a syrup has formed.
Add the prepared peel, bring to the
boil and simmer for 3 minutes. Allow
to cool slightly, then stir in the lemon
juice and Grand Marnier. Spoon the
sauce over the oranges, cover and
chill before serving.

Pears in red wine

SERVES 4

150 ml/¼ pt/⅔ cup red wine
150 ml/¼ pt/⅔ cup water
100 g/4 oz/½ cup caster (superfine)
  sugar
4 firm pears, peeled but stalks left on
5 ml/1 tsp arrowroot (optional)

Mix together the wine, water and
sugar in a heavy-based saucepan and
dissolve over a gentle heat, then boil
until syrupy, without stirring. Stand
the pears, stalks upwards, in the pan.
Cut a circle of greaseproof (waxed)
paper with holes in for the stalks to
poke through and place it over the
pears. Boil for 5–8 minutes, basting
occasionally, until the pears are just
tender. Carefully remove the pears to
a serving dish. If the syrup is thin,
bring it back to the boil, then mix the
arrowroot with a little cold water and
stir it into the syrup. Boil for about
5 minutes until thick and clear, then
allow to cool. Spoon over and around
the pears and serve.

Peach cream

SERVES 4

25 g/1 oz/2 tbsp short-grain rice
300 ml/½ pt/1¼ cups milk
100 g/14 oz/1 large can of peach slices,
     drained and juice reserved
15 ml/1 tbsp powdered gelatine
300 ml/½ pt/1¼ cups double (heavy)
     cream, whipped

Put the rice and milk in a saucepan, bring to the boil and simmer for about 20 minutes until the rice is soft and thick. Mix 45 ml/3 tbsp of the peach juice with the gelatine in a small bowl, then stand the bowl in a pan of hot water until dissolved. Reserve a few peach slices for decoration and purée the remaining peaches and the juice in a food processor or blender. Pour in the gelatine and blend again, then lightly blend in half the cream, pour the mixture into a serving dish and allow to set. Decorate with the remaining cream and the peach slices.

Raspberry crowdie

SERVES 4

50 g/2 oz/½ cup coarse oatmeal
600 ml/1 pt/2½ cups double (heavy)
     cream, whipped
25 g/1 oz/2 tbsp caster (superfine) sugar
15 ml/1 tbsp whisky
100 g/4 oz raspberries

Toss the oatmeal in a heavy-based pan over a moderate heat for 3 minutes, then leave to cool slightly. Stir the oatmeal into the cream with the sugar, whisky and raspberries. Spoon into individual bowls and serve.

Fruit brûlée

SERVES 4

225 g/8 oz soft summer fruits
     (raspberries, strawberries,
     blackcurrants, redcurrants)
30 ml/2 tbsp maraschino
600 ml/1 pt/2½ cups crème fraîche
100 g/4 oz/½ cup demerara sugar

Divide the fruit between four flameproof ramekins (custard cups) and sprinkle with the maraschino. Spoon the crème fraîche over the top and chill for at least 2 hours. Sprinkle with the sugar and brown under a hot grill (broiler) for a few minutes until the sugar has just melted. Cool and chill before serving.

Chocolate dessert

SERVES 4

50 g/2 oz/½ cup plain (semi-sweet)
     chocolate
30 ml/2 tbsp water
25 g/1 oz/2 tbsp caster (superfine) sugar
2.5 ml/½ tsp vanilla essence (extract)
600 ml/1 pt/2½ cups double (heavy)
     cream, whipped
25 g/1 oz/¼ cup flaked (slivered)
     almonds, toasted

Melt the chocolate and water over a low heat. Stir in the sugar and vanilla essence and leave to cool slightly. Fold in the whipped cream, turn into a serving dish and chill for at least 4 hours. Sprinkle with the almonds before serving.

Orange crème caramel

SERVES 4

1 orange
175 g/6 oz/¾ cup caster (superfine)
    sugar
45 ml/3 tbsp water
500 ml/17 fl oz/2¼ cups milk
2.5 cm/1 in piece of cinnamon stick
3 cloves
2 eggs
1 egg yolk
5 ml/1 tsp vanilla essence (extract)

Use a vegetable peeler to pare off a strip of orange rind from round the centre of the orange, then cut it into fine julienne strips. Finely grate the remaining orange rind. Place in a bowl and pour over some boiling water, then leave to soak. Place 100 g/4 oz/½ cup of the sugar in a saucepan with the water and stir over a gentle heat until the sugar has dissolved. Raise the heat and boil without stirring for about 5 minutes until the syrup turns golden. While it is boiling, drain the orange rind, pat dry on kitchen paper (paper towels) and divide between four ramekin dishes (custard cups). Once the caramel is ready, pour it into the dishes and set aside.

To make the custard, put the milk, grated orange rind, cinnamon and cloves in a saucepan and bring almost to the boil. Remove from the heat, cover and leave to stand for 20 minutes. Strain and discard the spices and orange rind. Beat the eggs, egg yolk, vanilla and remaining sugar until blended but not too frothy, then whisk in the warm milk. Divide between the ramekin dishes. Stand them in a large baking tin (pan) and add enough boiling water to come half-way up the side of the dishes. Bake in a preheated oven at 160°C/325°F/gas mark 3 for about 50 minutes until the custards are just set around the edges. Leave to cool in the water for 1 hour, then loosen round the edges with a knife and turn out on to serving plates.

Crème caramel

SERVES 4

Prepare as for Orange Crème Caramel but omit the orange rind.

Chocolate mousse

SERVES 4

450 g/1 lb/4 cups plain (semi-sweet)
    chocolate
Grated rind and juice of 1 orange
50 g/2 oz/¼ cup butter or margarine
30 ml/2 tbsp brandy
2 eggs, separated
2 egg yolks
150 ml/¼ pt/⅔ cup whipping cream,
    whipped
25 g/1 oz/¼ cup milk (sweet) chocolate,
    grated

Melt the chocolate in a bowl over a pan of hot water, then stir in the orange rind and juice and the butter or margarine. Remove from the heat and stir in the brandy. Beat the egg yolks thoroughly together, then strain the chocolate mixture into the eggs, beating well all the time. Leave to cool. Beat the egg whites until stiff, then gently fold them into the chocolate mixture. Pour into individual glass dishes and chill for at least 2 hours before serving. Decorate with the cream and grated chocolate.

Apricot and orange mousse

SERVES 4

225 g/8 oz/1⅓ cups no-need-to-soak dried apricots
30 ml/2 tbsp apricot brandy
150 ml/¼ pt/⅔ cup frozen concentrated orange juice
150 ml/¼ pt/⅔ cup whipping cream
3 egg whites
25 g/1 oz/¼ cup flaked (slivered) almonds
8 ratafia biscuits (cookies)

Place the apricots in a pan and just cover with cold water. Bring to the boil, then simmer gently for about 15 minutes until soft and plump. Drain, reserving the liquid. Purée the apricots with the apricot brandy and orange juice, then transfer to a dish. Whisk the cream until it holds soft peaks, then fold it into the fruit. Whisk the egg whites until stiff, then fold them in. Spoon into a serving bowl and sprinkle with the almonds. Cover with clingfilm (plastic wrap) and chill before serving with ratafia biscuits.

Cider syllabub

SERVES 4

90 ml/6 tbsp dry cider
Grated rind and juice of 1 lemon
75 g/3 oz/¾ cup caster (superfine) sugar
300 ml/½ pt/1¼ cups double (heavy) cream, whipped
8 shortbread fingers

Mix together the cider, lemon rind and juice and sugar and leave to stand for at least 2 hours. Stir in the whipped cream and whisk until the mixture stands in soft peaks. Spoon into individual glasses and chill well before serving with the shortbread fingers.

Rhubarb fool

SERVES 4

1.5 kg/3 lb rhubarb, sliced
225 g/8 oz/1 cup soft brown sugar
90 ml/6 tbsp water
45 ml/3 tbsp lemon juice
225 g/8 oz marshmallows
300 ml/½ pt/1¼ cups whipping cream, whipped
8 brandy snaps, to serve

Cook the rhubarb, sugar and water gently for about 20 minutes until the rhubarb is soft. Add the lemon juice and marshmallows and heat gently until the marshmallows dissolve, then beat well, pour into a serving dish and leave to cool. Fold in the whipped cream and chill until required. Serve with the brandy snaps.

Mocha delight

SERVES 4

100 g/4 oz/1 cup fresh brown breadcrumbs
175 g/6 oz/¾ cup demerara sugar
5 ml/1 tsp instant coffee powder
50 g/2 oz/¼ cup drinking (sweetened) chocolate powder
150 ml/¼ pt/⅔ cup double (heavy) cream
150 ml/¼ pt/⅔ cup single (light) cream
25 g/1 oz/¼ cup plain (semi-sweet) chocolate

Mix together the breadcrumbs, sugar, coffee and drinking chocolate. Whip the creams together lightly. Layer the breadcrumb mixture and cream alternately in a glass bowl, finishing with a layer of cream. Sprinkle with the grated chocolate and chill for several hours, preferably overnight, before serving.

Coffee cream charlotte

SERVES 4

30 ml/2 tbsp apricot jam (jelly), sieved (strained)
20 sponge fingers
4 eggs, separated
100 g/4 oz/⅔ cup icing (confectioners') sugar
60 ml/4 tbsp coffee essence (extract)
45 ml/3 tbsp rum
300 ml/½ pt/1¼ cups double (heavy) cream, lightly whipped
150 ml/¼ pt/⅔ cup whipping cream, whipped
50 g/2 oz/½ cup plain (semi-sweet) chocolate, grated

Warm the jam slightly and brush it over the sides of a 15 cm/6 in springform cake tin (pan). Trim the ends of the sponge fingers and stand them round the edge. Whisk the egg whites until very stiff. Whisk together the egg yolks, icing sugar, coffee essence and rum, then fold in the egg whites and double cream. Spoon the mixture into the cake tin and freeze for 5 hours. When ready to serve, carefully loosen round the side of the tin with a palette knife and turn out. Decorate with whirls of whipped cream and sprinkle the grated chocolate over.

Hazelnut and gooseberry fool

SERVES 4

450 g/1 lb gooseberries
75 g/3 oz/⅓ cup caster (superfine) sugar
15 ml/1 tbsp custard powder
300 ml/½ pt/1¼ cups milk
150 ml/¼ pt/⅔ cup hazelnut (filbert) yoghurt
25 g/1 oz/¼ cup hazelnuts, chopped
Shortbread biscuits (cookies), to serve

Cook the gooseberries with 50 g/ 2 oz/¼ cup of the sugar and a little water for about 15 minutes until soft, then purée in a food processor or blender. Mix the custard powder with the remaining sugar and a little of the milk. Bring the remaining milk to the boil, pour on to the custard mixture then return to the heat and stir until the custard boils and thickens. Leave to cool. Mix together the custard, gooseberry purée and hazelnut yoghurt, pour into individual glasses and decorate with the chopped hazelnuts. Serve with shortbread biscuits.

Butterscotch puddings

SERVES 4

50 g/2 oz/¼ cup butter or margarine
75 g/3 oz/⅓ cup demerara sugar
75 g/3 oz/½ cup fine semolina (cream of wheat)
300 ml/½ pt/1¼ cups milk
150 ml/¼ pt/⅔ cup whipping cream, whipped
6 strawberries, sliced

Melt the butter or margarine, stir in the sugar and semolina and cook gently for 3 minutes. Gradually stir in the milk and continue stirring until the mixture boils and thickens. Simmer for 3 minutes, then pour into individual glasses and chill. When cold, decorate with the cream and strawberries.

Burgundy wine trifle

SERVES 4

225 g/8 oz plums, stoned (pitted)
150 ml/¼ pt/⅔ cup water
1 blackcurrant jelly (jello) tablet
60 ml/4 tbsp Burgundy or other red wine
4 macaroons
150 ml/¼ pt/⅔ cup double (heavy) cream, whipped
25 g/1 oz/¼ cup hazelnuts (filberts), toasted and chopped

Place the plums and water in a saucepan and simmer until soft. Pour the fruit into a measuring jug and add enough of the juice, and water if necessary, to make up to 450 ml/¾ pt/2 cups. Return the fruit and juice to the saucepan, bring to the boil, add the jelly and stir until dissolved. Add the burgundy and leave to cool. Crumble the macaroons into a serving dish, pour the jelly over and leave to set. When set, top with the cream and sprinkle with the hazelnuts.

Simple lemon soufflés

SERVES 4–6

1 lemon jelly (jello) tablet
Grated rind and juice of 1 lemon
150 ml/¼ pt/⅔ cup double (heavy) cream
15 ml/1 tbsp milk
2 eggs, separated
150 ml/¼ pt/⅔ cup whipping cream, whipped
50 g/2 oz/½ cup plain (semi-sweet) chocolate, grated

Dissolve the jelly in 150 ml/¼ pt/ ⅔ cup of water over a low heat, then make up to 450 ml/¾ pt/2 cups with cold water. Add the lemon rind and juice and put in a cool place until the jelly is beginning to set. Whip the cream and milk until thick. Whisk the egg whites until very stiff. When the jelly is just beginning to set, whisk in the egg yolks until fluffy, then fold in the cream and egg whites. Spoon into individual bowls and leave to set. When cold, decorate with the whipped cream and grated chocolate.

Hazelnut pavlova

SERVES 4

3 egg whites
175 g/6 oz/¾ cup caster (superfine) sugar
75 g/3 oz/¾ cup hazelnuts (filberts), ground
A few drops of white wine vinegar
300 ml/½ pt/1¼ cups whipping cream, whipped
225 g/8 oz soft fruit (strawberries, raspberries, kiwi fruits, canned mandarins etc.)

Whisk the egg whites until they form soft peaks. Add half the sugar and whisk again until stiff. Using a metal spoon, fold in the remaining sugar, the nuts and wine vinegar. Pipe or spoon the meringue into a round about 20 cm/8 in diameter on a greased and lined baking (cookie) sheet. Bake in a preheated oven at 190°C/375°F/gas mark 5 for 20 minutes until brown and crisp on top. Turn off the oven and leave the door ajar, but leave the meringue in the oven until cool. When ready to serve, spread half the cream in the base of the pavlova, cover with the fruit and pipe stars of cream around the edge.

307

Blackberry soufflé

SERVES 4

450 g/1 lb blackberries
120 ml/4 fl oz/½ cup water
4 eggs, separated
100 g/4 oz/½ cup caster (superfine) sugar
15 ml/1 tbsp powdered gelatine
300 ml/½ pt/1¼ cups whipping cream, whipped

Reserve a few of the blackberries for decoration and cook the remainder in 75 ml/5 tbsp of the water for 10 minutes. Purée in a food processor or blender. Whisk the egg yolks and sugar in a large bowl over a pan of hot water until thick and creamy, then remove from the heat and continue whisking until cool. Dissolve the gelatine in a bowl in the remaining water and stand it over hot water to melt. Whisk the egg whites until stiff. Stir the gelatine into the fruit purée, then fold this into the egg yolk mixture. Fold in half the whipped cream, then the egg whites. Make a collar of greaseproof (waxed) paper round an 18 cm/7 in soufflé dish, pour the mixture into the dish and leave to set in the fridge for 5–6 hours or overnight. Remove the greaseproof collar, use the remaining cream to pipe rosettes round the top and decorate with the reserved blackberries.

Note:
You can use other soft fruits such as raspberries or strawberries for this recipe.

Summer pudding with chantilly cream

SERVES 4–6

6–8 slices of stale white bread, crusts removed
100 g/4 oz/½ cup caster (superfine) sugar
75 ml/5 tbsp water
750 g/1¾ lb soft summer fruits (raspberries, strawberries, blackcurrants, redcurrants)
150 ml/¼ pt/⅔ cup double (heavy) cream, whipped
½ egg white, whisked
15 g/½ oz icing (confectioners') sugar
A few drops of vanilla essence (extract)

Slice the bread into strips and use most of them to line a greased 1.2 litre/2 pt/5 cup pudding basin, lining the basin tightly. Dissolve the sugar in the water over a low heat, then add the fruit and simmer for 10 minutes. Spoon the hot fruit into the basin, reserving a little of the juice, and cover with the reserved bread. Put a saucer on top of the basin, weigh down with weights or food cans, then chill overnight.

Mix together the whipped cream and whisked egg white and fold in the icing sugar and vanilla essence. Chill. When ready to serve, turn out the pudding on to a serving plate and spoon the reserved juice over any parts of the bread that have not absorbed the fruit juice. Serve with the chantilly cream.

Frosted chocolate pudding

SERVES 4

100 g/4 oz/1 cup plain (semi-sweet)
    chocolate
225 g/8 oz/1 cup cottage cheese, sieved
    (strained)
2 eggs, separated
50 g/2 oz/¼ cup caster (superfine) sugar
5 ml/1 tsp vanilla essence (extract)
2.5 ml/½ tsp almond essence
225 g/8 oz plain cake, cubed
150 ml/¼ pt/⅔ cup whipping cream,
    whipped

Melt the chocolate in a bowl over a
pan of hot water. Remove from the
heat and beat in the cottage cheese
and egg yolks. Whisk the egg whites
until stiff, then beat in the sugar. Fold
into the chocolate mixture with the
essences, then fold in the cake cubes.
Stand the bowl over the pan of
simmering water and cook for
15 minutes. Spoon into glasses and
chill. Serve with the whipped cream.

Coffee and banana krispie pie

SERVES 4

25 g/1 oz/2 tbsp butter or margarine
30 ml/2 tbsp golden (light corn) syrup
50 g/2 oz crisp rice cereal
175 g/6 oz marshmallows
45 ml/3 tbsp hot water
15 ml/1 tbsp instant coffee powder
300 ml/½ pt/1¼ cups double (heavy)
    cream, whipped
3 bananas, sliced

Melt the butter or margarine and
syrup in a saucepan, then remove
from the heat and stir in the cereal.
Press the mixture into a 20 cm/8 in
pie dish and chill. Put the marshmallows, hot water and coffee powder
into a bowl over a pan of hot water.
Simmer until the marshmallows have
melted, stirring occasionally, then
leave to cool. Fold the cream into the
coffee mixture with two sliced
bananas. Cool until thick, then pour
on to the crisp base and chill until
firm. Decorate with the remaining
banana.

Peaches in bittersweet cream

SERVES 4

150 ml/¼ pt/⅔ cup water
100 g/4 oz/½ cup granulated sugar
4 peaches, peeled and sliced
75 ml/5 tbsp double (heavy) cream,
    lightly whipped
150 ml/¼ pt/⅔ cup plain yoghurt
25 g/1 oz/2 tbsp demerara sugar
25 g/1 oz/2 tbsp soft brown sugar

Put the water and granulated sugar in
a saucepan and heat gently, stirring,
until the sugar has dissolved. Bring to
the boil and simmer for 5 minutes.
Add the peaches, cover and simmer
for 5 minutes until tender. Remove
the peaches from the syrup and
transfer them to a large serving dish.
Mix together the cream and yoghurt
and spread over the peaches. Mix
together the demerara and soft brown
sugars and sprinkle them thickly over
the cream. Cover and chill for several
hours until the sugar melts on the
top.

Chocolate fruit and nut dessert

SERVES 4–6

100 g/4 oz/1 cup hazelnuts (filberts),
toasted and chopped
100 g/4 oz/1 cup blanched almonds,
chopped
25 g/1 oz/¼ cup pine nuts
50 g/2 oz/⅓ cup chopped mixed
(candied) peel, chopped
50 g/2 oz/½ cup plain (all-purpose) flour
25 g/1 oz/¼ cup cocoa (unsweetened
chocolate) powder
A pinch of ground cloves
A pinch of ground cinnamon
A pinch of white pepper
100 g/4 oz/½ cup caster (superfine)
sugar
100 g/4 oz/⅓ cup clear honey
25 g/1 oz/2 tbsp unsalted (sweet) butter
15 ml/1 tbsp icing (confectioners') sugar

Mix together the nuts and mixed peel
and stir in the flour, cocoa and spices.
Dissolve the sugar, honey and butter
or margarine in a heavy-based
saucepan, then boil, without stirring,
until a drop in cold water will form a
soft ball between the fingers.
Immediately stir the syrup into the
fruit and nut mixture and press it into
a greased and lined 20 cm/8 in cake
tin (pan). Bake in a preheated oven at
150°C/300°F/gas mark 2 for
35 minutes. Leave to cool in the tin
for 30 minutes, then turn out and
leave until cold. Dust with the icing
sugar and serve cut into thin wedges.

Apple strudel

SERVES 4

5 crisp eating (dessert) apples, peeled,
cored and chopped
100 g/4 oz/1 cup blanched almonds,
toasted and chopped
100 g/4 oz/⅔ cup raisins
15 ml/1 tbsp ground cinnamon
A pinch of salt
A pinch of grated nutmeg
225 g/8 oz/1 cup caster (superfine)
sugar
5 ml/1 tsp vanilla essence (extract)
6 filo pastry (paste) sheets
100 g/4 oz/½ cup butter or margarine,
melted
15 ml/1 tbsp icing (confectioners') sugar

Stir together the apples, almonds,
raisins, cinnamon, salt, nutmeg, sugar
and vanilla essence. Lay a sheet of filo
pastry on a clean tea towel (dish
cloth) and brush with melted butter or
margarine. Lay a second sheet beside
it, overlapping the edges and brush
with butter. Lay two more sheets on
top in the opposite direction and
brush with butter. Lay the final two
sheets on top, in the opposite
direction, and brush with butter. Fold
the edges in 1 cm/½ in. Spread the
fruit mixture evenly over the pastry,
right up to the folded edges. Roll up
carefully from the narrow end, using
the towel to help. Roll on to a greased
and lined baking (cookie) sheet with
the join underneath and tuck in the
ends. Brush with the remaining butter
or margarine and bake in a preheated
oven at 180°C/350°F/gas mark 4 for
30 minutes until crisp and golden. Lift
carefully from the paper on to a wire
rack to cool and serve sprinkled with
the icing sugar.

Caribbean bananas

SERVES 4

4 bananas
50 g/2 oz/¼ cup soft brown sugar
30 ml/2 tbsp orange juice
A pinch of grated nutmeg
A pinch of ground cinnamon
30 ml/2 tbsp rum
25 g/1 oz/2 tbsp butter or margarine
Cream or ice cream, to serve

Halve the bananas lengthways and place in a baking dish. Mix together the sugar, orange juice, spices and rum and pour over the fruit. Dot with the butter or margarine and bake in a preheated oven at 230°C/450°F/gas mark 8 for 15 minutes, basting from time to time. Serve hot with cream or ice cream.

Banana and ginger cheesecake flan

SERVES 4

75 g/3 oz/⅓ cup butter or margarine
225 g/8 oz gingernut biscuits (cookies), crushed
225 g/8 oz/1 cup cottage cheese, sieved (strained)
150 ml/¼ pt/⅔ cup plain yoghurt
30 ml/2 tbsp clear honey
3 bananas, mashed
Juice of ½ lemon
15 ml/1 tbsp powdered gelatine
30 ml/2 tbsp water
6 slices of preserved ginger
150 ml/¼ pt/⅔ cup whipping cream, whipped

Melt the butter or margarine, remove from the heat and stir in the biscuit crumbs. Press into the base and sides of a 20 cm/8 in flan tin (pie pan). Leave to cool. Mix together the cottage cheese, yoghurt, honey, bananas and lemon juice. Dissolve the gelatine in the water, then stir it into the mixture, pour it into the flan case and leave to set. Arrange the slices of ginger on top and decorate with piped stars of whipped cream. Chill before serving.

Apricot cream meringue

SERVES 4

3 eggs, separated
225 g/8 oz/1 cup caster (superfine) sugar
400 g/14 oz/1 large can of apricots
150 ml/¼ pt/⅔ cup milk
5 ml/1 tsp cornflour (cornstarch)
2.5 ml/½ tsp vanilla essence (extract)

Whisk the egg whites until stiff, then whisk in 175 g/6 oz/¾ cup of the sugar. Spoon or pipe into a circle on wetted greaseproof (waxed) paper on a baking (cookie) sheet and build up the edges to form a case. Bake in a preheated oven at 140°C/275°F/gas mark 1 for 1 hour until the meringue is crisp, then turn off the oven and leave the meringue in the oven until it cools. Mix the milk with 150 ml/ ¼ pt/⅔ cup juice from the can of apricots, stir in the cornflour and heat gently. Whisk the egg yolks and remaining sugar and pour on a little of the hot liquid. Return to the pan and stir over a low heat until creamy. Leave to cool, then stir in the vanilla essence. Just before serving, arrange half the drained fruit in the meringue case, cover with the custard and top with the remaining apricots.

Honey meringues

SERVES 4

6 egg whites
350 g/12 oz/1¼ cups caster (superfine)
    sugar
30 ml/2 tbsp clear honey
100 g/4 oz/1 cup hazelnuts (filberts),
    chopped
10 ml/2 tsp brandy
300 ml/½ pt/1¼ cups double (heavy)
    cream, whipped

Whisk the egg whites until stiff, then
whisk in half the sugar and fold in the
remainder. Pipe or drop 5 ml/1 tsp
quantities of the mixture on to a
lightly greased baking (cookie) sheet.
Bake in a preheated oven at 140°C/
275°F/gas mark 1 for 50 minutes,
then leave to cool. Fold the honey,
hazelnuts and brandy into the cream
and sandwich the meringues together
with the cream filling.

Chocolate cream tart

SERVES 4

50 g/2 oz/¼ cup butter or margarine
50 g/2 oz/¼ cup caster (superfine) sugar
15 ml/1 tbsp golden (light corn) syrup
175 g/6 oz digestive biscuits (graham
    crackers), crushed
175 g/6 oz/1½ cups plain (semi-sweet)
    chocolate
3 eggs, separated
10 ml/2 tsp brandy
150 ml/¼ pt/⅔ cup double (heavy)
    cream, whipped
25 g/1 oz/¼ cup walnuts, chopped

Melt the butter or margarine, sugar
and syrup and stir in the biscuit
crumbs. Press into a 20 cm/8 in flan
tin (pie pan) and bake in a preheated
oven at 180°C/350°F/gas mark 4 for
15 minutes. Chill until firm and crisp.
Melt the chocolate in a heatproof

bowl over a pan of simmering water.
Remove from the heat and stir in the
egg yolks and brandy. Leave to cool,
then fold in the cream. Whisk the egg
whites until stiff, then fold them into
the mixture. Pour into the crumb case
and chill until firm. Sprinkle with the
walnuts before serving.

Cheesecake torte

SERVES 4

150 ml/¼ pt/⅔ cup double (heavy)
    cream, whipped
25 g/1 oz/¼ cup cornflour (cornstarch)
450 g/1 lb/2 cups cottage cheese, sieved
    (strained)
4 egg whites
175 g/6 oz/¾ cup caster (superfine) sugar
5 ml/1 tsp vanilla essence (extract)
25 g/1 oz/2 tbsp butter or margarine
100 g/4 oz digestive biscuits (graham
    crackers), crushed
2 kiwi fruit, sliced
50 g/2 oz/½ cup flaked (slivered)
    almonds, toasted
150 ml/¼ pt/⅔ cup whipping cream,
    whipped

Mix the double cream with the
cornflour and cheese. Whisk the egg
whites until stiff, then whisk in the
sugar and continue to whisk until it
holds soft peaks. Fold into the cheese
mixture with the vanilla essence. Rub
the butter or margarine over the base
and sides of a 23 cm/9 in loose-
bottomed flan tin (pie pan) and
sprinkle with the biscuit crumbs. Pour
in the cheese mixture and bake in a
preheated oven at 180°C/350°F/gas
mark 4 for 1 hour. Allow to cool
slightly, then remove from the tin and
leave to cool completely. Arrange the
kiwi fruit over the top, sprinkle with
the almonds and serve with the
whipped cream.

Lemon fridge cake

SERVES 4

6 eggs
150 g/5 oz/⅔ cup caster (superfine)
   sugar
15 ml/1 tbsp water
100 g/4 oz/1 cup self-raising (self-rising)
   flour
1 egg yolk
175 g/6 oz/1 cup icing (confectioners')
   sugar
15 g/½ oz/1 tbsp powdered gelatine
Grated rind and juice of 1 lemon
150 ml/¼ pt/⅔ cup double (heavy) cream

Cream three of the eggs with the caster sugar until pale and thick, then add the water and fold in the flour. Spoon into two greased 20 cm/8 in round cake tins (pans) and bake in a preheated oven at 180°C/350°F/gas mark 4 for 12 minutes until springy to the touch. Turn out on to a wire rack and leave to cool.

Whisk the remaining eggs and the egg yolk with the icing sugar until frothy. Soften the gelatine in the lemon juice in a small bowl. Stand the bowl in a pan of hot water and leave until dissolved. Whisk the cream until stiff. Stir the gelatine and lemon rind into the egg mixture, then fold in the whipped cream. Return one of the sponge cakes to its tin, then spoon the cream mixture over the top. Cover with the other cake and chill before serving.

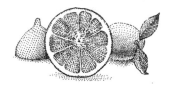

Linzertorte

SERVES 4

175 g/6 oz/¾ cup soft margarine
50 g/2 oz/¼ cup caster (superfine) sugar
50 g/2 oz/½ cup ground almonds
Grated rind of 1 lemon
1 egg
225 g/8 oz/2 cups plain (all-purpose)
   flour
2.5 ml/½ tsp ground cinnamon
450 g/1 lb raspberries
100 g/4 oz/½ cup granulated sugar
30 ml/2 tbsp redcurrant jelly (clear
   conserve)
30 ml/2 tbsp icing (confectioners') sugar

Cream together the margarine, caster sugar, almonds, lemon rind, egg and 15 ml/1 tbsp of the flour until well blended, then mix in the remaining flour and the cinnamon to form a soft dough. Turn out on to a lightly floured surface and knead lightly until smooth. Roll out two-thirds of the dough and use to line a greased 20 cm/8 in flan tin (pie pan) placed on a baking (cookie) sheet. Chill for 30 minutes. Roll out the remaining dough and cut into 1 cm/½ in strips.

Place the raspberries in a saucepan with the granulated sugar and simmer gently for about 10 minutes until soft. Spoon into the pastry (paste) case and arrange the pastry strips across the top in a lattice pattern, damping the edges of the pastry so they stick to the sides. Bake in a preheated oven at 190°C/ 375°F/gas mark 5 for 30 minutes. Warm the redcurrant jelly, brush it over the top to glaze, then leave to cool. Serve dusted with the icing sugar.

Pear and hazelnut shortcake

SERVES 8

100 g/4 oz/½ cup butter or margarine
50 g/2 oz/¼ cup caster (superfine) sugar
75 g/3 oz/¾ cup ground hazelnuts
(filberts)
140 g/5 oz/1¼ cups plain (all-purpose)
flour
15 ml/1 tbsp water
150 ml/¼ pt/⅔ cup double (heavy) or
whipping cream, whipped
2 pears, peeled, cored and sliced
15 ml/1 tbsp icing (confectioners') sugar,
sifted

Beat the butter or margarine until soft, then beat in the sugar, nuts and flour. Add the water and mix to a soft dough. Divide the dough in half and form each into a ball. Pat each ball into a round about 18 cm/7 in in diameter, place the rounds on a greased baking (cookie) sheet and bake in a preheated oven at 190°C/375°F/gas mark 5 for 10 minutes until lightly golden round the edges. Cut one round into eight segments. Allow to cool on the baking sheet.

An hour before the shortcake is needed, place the whole round on a serving plate. Spread half the cream on top, then cover with the pear slices. Put the remaining cream in a piping bag with a large star nozzle and pipe eight large rosettes on top of the pears. Lay each triangle of pastry (paste) on top of the rosettes of cream so that it rests at an angle. Sprinkle with the icing sugar and serve within an hour.

Orange savarin

SERVES 4–6

15 ml/1 tbsp easy-blend dried yeast
100 g/4 oz/½ cup granulated sugar
100 g/4 oz/1 cup strong plain (bread)
flour
75 g/3 oz/⅓ cup butter or margarine
85 ml/3 fl oz warm milk
2 eggs, beaten
150 ml/¼ pt/⅔ cup water
1 orange
10 ml/2 tsp rum or brandy
150 ml/¼ pt/⅔ cup double or whipping
cream, whipped

Stir the yeast and 5 ml/1 tsp of the granulated sugar into the flour, then rub in the butter or margarine. Blend to a light dough with the milk and eggs. Pour into a 20 cm/8 in savarin or ring mould, cover with a damp cloth and leave to rise in a warm place for 45 minutes. Bake in a preheated oven at 230°C/450°F/gas mark 8 for 30 minutes.

Meanwhile, make the sauce by dissolving the remaining sugar in the water over a gentle heat. Use a potato peeler to remove 4 strips of orange rind and put these in the sugar syrup. Bring to the boil, boil for 1 minute, then add the rum or brandy and remove from the heat. Turn the savarin out of the mould, pour the sauce over and leave to soak in. Slice half the orange and cut the rest into small pieces. Arrange the slices round the edge and the pieces in the centre of the savarin. Serve with the whipped cream.

Vanilla ice cream

MAKES 900 ML/1½ PTS/3¾ CUPS

2 eggs
100 g/4 oz/½ cup caster (superfine)
   sugar
600 ml/1 pt/2½ cups warm milk
300 ml/½ pt/1¼ cups double (heavy)
   cream
7.5 ml/1½ tsp vanilla essence (extract)

Beat the eggs and sugar until liquid
then stir in the milk and strain into a
bowl over a pan of simmering water.
Stir over a gentle heat for 20 minutes
until the custard is as thick as single
(light) cream. Pour into a clean bowl,
cover and leave to cool. Whip the
cream until very thick but not too stiff,
then mix it lightly with the egg
custard and vanilla essence. Turn into
a freezer container and freeze for
1 hour. Turn out into a chilled bowl
and beat until smooth. Return it to
the container and freeze until firm.

Fruity ice cream

MAKES 600 ML/1 PT/2½ CUPS

300 ml/½ pt/1¼ cups puréed soft or
   stewed fruit
300 ml/½ pt/1¼ cups double (heavy)
   cream
5 ml/1 tsp lemon juice

Sieve (strain) the fruit purée if it
contains any lumps or pips. Whip the
cream until very thick but not too stiff,
then blend in the purée and lemon
juice. Pour into a freezer container
and freeze for 1 hour. Turn out into a
chilled bowl and beat until smooth.
Return it to the container and freeze
until firm.

Christmas pudding ice cream

SERVES 8

50 g/2 oz/¼ cup butter or margarine
175 g/6 oz/1 cup raisins
100 g/4 oz/⅔ cup sultanas (golden
   raisins)
50 g/2 oz/⅓ cup currants
50 g/2 oz/⅓ cup chopped mixed
   (candied) peel
2.5 ml/½ tsp almond essence (extract)
Grated rind and juice of 1 orange
Grated rind of 1 lemon
1 cooking (tart) apple, peeled, cored
   and finely chopped
100 g/4 oz canned pineapple, drained
   and crushed
5 ml/1 tsp mixed (apple-pie) spice
50 g/2 oz/¼ cup caster (superfine) sugar
50 g/2 oz/½ cup walnuts, chopped
30 ml/2 tbsp brandy or rum
1 litre/1¾ pts/4¼ cups soft-scoop ice
   cream

Mix together all the ingredients
except the ice cream in a large
saucepan. Bring to the boil, cover and
simmer gently for 30 minutes. Leave
to cool. Spoon the ice cream into a
bowl and whisk. Fold in the fruit
mixture, then pour into a freezer
container. Freeze for about 1 hour
until beginning to freeze, then stir
well. Continue to freeze until firm.

315

Orange almond ice cream

SERVES 4

4 eggs
75 ml/5 tbsp clear honey
A few drops of vanilla essence
150 ml/¼ pt/⅔ cup whipping cream, whipped
45 ml/3 tbsp orange liqueur
25 g/1 oz/2 tbsp butter or margarine
25 g/1 oz/¼ cup flaked (slivered) almonds

Whisk the eggs with the honey and vanilla essence until creamy, then fold in the cream and liqueur. Turn into a freezer container and freeze for 1 hour. Turn out into a chilled bowl and beat until smooth, then return it to the container and freeze until firm. Just before serving, melt the butter or margarine and fry (sauté) the flaked almonds until just beginning to brown. Sprinkle on top of the ice cream.

Chocolate ice cream

SERVES 6–8

4 egg yolks
100 g/4 oz/½ cup caster (superfine) sugar
600 ml/1 pt/2½ cups warm milk
75 g/3 oz/¾ cup plain (semi-sweet) chocolate, grated
5 ml/1 tsp vanilla essence (extract)
150 ml/¼ pt/⅔ cup double (heavy) cream, whipped

Beat the egg yolks and sugar until liquid, then stir in the milk and strain into a bowl over a pan of simmering water. Stir over a gentle heat for 20 minutes until the custard is as thick as single (light) cream. Pour into a clean bowl and whisk in the chocolate and vanilla essence until smooth. Leave to cool. Fold the whipped cream into the custard. Turn it into a freezer container and freeze for 1 hour. Turn out into a chilled bowl and beat until smooth, then return it to the container and freeze for a further 1 hour. Beat again, then return to the container and freeze until firm.

Chocolate mint ice cream

SERVES 4

4 egg yolks
300 ml/½ pt/1¼ cups milk
175 g/6 oz/¾ cup caster (superfine) sugar
100 g/4 oz/1 cup plain (semi-sweet) chocolate, grated
30 ml/2 tbsp crème de menthe
50 g/2 oz chocolate mint crisps, chopped
250 ml/8 fl oz/1 cup double (heavy) cream
30 ml/2 tbsp iced water

Beat the egg yolks and sugar until pale and fluffy, then whisk in the milk. Cook the mixture over a low heat, stirring continuously, until the custard is thick enough to coat the back of a wooden spoon. Remove from the heat and leave to cool for 5 minutes. Mix the chocolate into the custard and stir until melted, then leave to cool and chill. Stir in the crème de menthe and mint crisps. Whisk the cream with the iced water until it forms soft peaks. Fold into the chocolate custard, then pour into a freezer container and freeze for about 1 hour until beginning to set. Turn out into a chilled bowl, whisk well, then return to the container and freeze until firm.

Kirsch and kiwi fruit ice cream

SERVES 4

6 eggs, separated
225 g/8 oz/1 cup caster (superfine) sugar
30 ml/2 tbsp boiling water
600 ml/1 pt/2½ cups double (heavy) cream, whipped
8 kiwi fruit
60 ml/4 tbsp kirsch
5 ml/1 tsp vanilla essence (extract)

Whisk the egg whites with 30 ml/ 2 tbsp of the sugar. Whisk the egg yolks with the remaining sugar and the boiling water. Fold the two mixtures together, then fold in the cream. Thinly slice one kiwi fruit and reserve for decoration. Purée the remaining kiwi fruit in a food processor or blender and sieve (strain) to remove the pips. Stir the fruit into the mixture with the kirsch and vanilla essence. Pour into a freezer container and freeze until firm. Serve garnished with slices of kiwi fruit.

Raspberry bombe

SERVES 4

225 g/8 oz raspberries
25 g/1 oz/2 tbsp icing (confectioners') sugar
300 ml/½ pt/1¼ cups double (heavy) cream
150 ml/¼ pt/⅔ cup single (light) cream
100 g/4 oz meringues, broken into pieces

Reserve a few raspberries for decoration and purée the remainder with the icing sugar in a food processor or blender. Rub through a sieve (strainer) to remove the pips.

Whip the creams together until they form soft peaks, then fold in the meringues. Lightly fold in half the raspberry purée to give a marbled effect, then turn into a 1.2 litre/2 pt/ 5 cup pudding basin, cover and freeze until firm. Transfer to the fridge 30 minutes before serving. Turn out, pour over the remaining purée and decorate with the reserved raspberries.

Pineapple ice

SERVES 4

1 pineapple, halved lengthways
175 g/6 oz/¾ cup granulated sugar
450 ml/¾ pt/2 cups water
1 egg white

Remove the core from the pineapple and scoop out the flesh, keeping the shells intact. Chill the shells in the fridge. Purée the pineapple flesh in a food processor or blender. Dissolve the sugar in the water in a saucepan, then bring to the boil and boil for 5 minutes to make a syrup. Leave to cool. Mix the pineapple pulp into the syrup, pour into a freezer container and freeze for 3 hours. Whisk the egg white until stiff, then whisk in the ice cream. Return to the freezer container and freeze until firm. Transfer to the fridge 10 minutes before serving to soften the ice cream, then scoop into the pineapple shells to serve.

Apple sorbet with mint

SERVES 4

4 eating (dessert) apples, peeled, cored
  and finely chopped
250 ml/8 fl oz/1 cup white wine
100 ml/4 fl oz/½ cup water
75 ml/5 tbsp clear honey
Juice of 1 lemon
6 mint leaves, finely chopped

Purée the apples, wine and water in a
food processor or blender, then stir in
the honey and lemon juice. Freeze for
1 hour. Stir well, then freeze again
and continue to stir the sorbet
occasionally while it is freezing. Just
before it sets, stir in the mint. Whisk
the sorbet and serve in individual
glasses.

Orange and ginger sorbet

SERVES 4

450 ml/¾ pt/2 cups orange juice
4 chunks of stem ginger
6 egg whites
1 orange, peeled and sliced

Purée the orange juice and ginger in a
food processor or blender. Pour into a
shallow container and freeze until the
mixture begins to harden. Remove
from the freezer and mix well. Whisk
the egg whites until stiff, then fold
into the orange mixture. Return to the
freezer until firm. Transfer to the
fridge 30 minutes before serving and
serve decorated with the orange
slices.

Lemon water ice

SERVES 4

450 g/1 lb/2 cups granulated sugar
600 ml/1 pt/2½ cups water
Peeled rind and juice of 2 lemons
2 egg whites
A few mint leaves, to garnish

Place the sugar, water, peeled lemon
rind and lemon juice in a saucepan
and stir over a low heat until the
sugar has dissolved. Bring to the boil
and boil for 6 minutes to make a
syrup. Allow to cool, then strain.
Whisk the egg whites until stiff, then
fold in the lemon syrup, pour into a
freezer container and freeze for
1 hour. Turn out into a chilled bowl
and whisk, then freeze and whisk
again. Serve decorated with mint
leaves.

Breads and teabreads

Since there is such a wide selection of interesting breads in the supermarkets, it is no longer necessary to make your own. But it can be great fun – and very therapeutic if you abandon the food processor and knead the dough by hand. In any event, you can't beat the smell of freshly baked bread drifting out of the kitchen. For convenience, the recipes use easy-blend dried yeast, which you simply mix with the dry ingredients before making the dough. If you use ordinary dried yeast, use the same quantity but mix it with 5 ml/1 tsp of sugar and half the warm liquid and leave for 10 minutes in a warm place until frothy before mixing into the dry ingredients to make the dough. If using fresh yeast, substitute twice the amount of fresh yeast for the dried yeast listed in the recipes, blend with a little sugar and warm liquid and leave to stand before mixing your dough.

Rising times vary depending on the temperature. Dough will take about 1 hour to rise in a warm place, 2 hours at ordinary room temperature, 12 hours in a cool place or up to 24 hours in a fridge. You can use this to your advantage if you make up the dough and leave it to rise in a suitable place ready to be baked when you need it, but remember to allow the dough to return to room temperature before kneading it again.

Most bread recipes can be used to make whatever shape of bread you prefer. Use a loaf tin (pan) for a standard-shaped loaf or shape the dough and bake it on a greased baking (cookie) sheet. You can tell when a loaf is cooked as it will sound hollow when tapped on the base.

Wholemeal bread

MAKES TWO 900 G/2 LB LOAVES

1.5 kg/3 lb/12 cups strong wholemeal (bread) flour
30 ml/2 tbsp salt
30 ml/2 tbsp easy-blend dried yeast
5 ml/1 tsp sugar
25 g/1 oz/2 tbsp lard (shortening) or vegetable fat
900 ml/1½ pts/3¾ cups warm water
30 ml/2 tbsp sesame or caraway seeds

Mix together the flour, salt, yeast and sugar and rub in the lard or vegetable fat. Blend in enough of the warm water to make a firm dough that leaves the side of the bowl cleanly. Knead on a lightly floured surface or in a processor until elastic and no longer sticky. Place the dough in an oiled bowl, cover with oiled clingfilm (plastic wrap) and leave to rise in a warm place for about 1 hour until doubled in size and springy to the touch. Knead the dough again until firm, divide in half and place in two greased 450 g/1 lb loaf tins (pans). Cover and leave to prove for about 1 hour until the dough rises just above the tops of the tins. Brush the tops with water and sprinkle with the sesame or caraway seeds. Bake in a preheated oven at 230°C/450°F/gas mark 8 for about 40 minutes until golden brown.

Variations:
You can shape this loaf how you like. Omit the seeds if you wish, or substitute chopped nuts, cracked wheat or poppy seeds. If you make smaller loaves or rolls, reduce the cooking time.

White bread

MAKES TWO 900 G/2 LB LOAVES

1.5 kg/3 lb/12 cups strong plain (bread) flour
30 ml/2 tbsp salt
15 ml/1 tbsp/1 sachet easy-blend dried yeast
5 ml/1 tsp sugar
25 g/1 oz/2 tbsp lard (shortening) or vegetable fat
900 ml/1½ pts/3¾ cups warm water

Mix together the flour, salt, yeast and sugar and rub in the lard or vegetable fat. Blend in enough of the warm water to make a firm dough that leaves the side of the bowl cleanly. Knead on a lightly floured surface or in a processor until elastic and no longer sticky. Place the dough in an oiled bowl, cover with oiled clingfilm (plastic wrap) and leave to rise in a warm place for about 1 hour until doubled in size and springy to the touch. Knead the dough again until firm, divide in half and place in two greased 450 g/1 lb loaf tins (pans). Cover and leave to prove for about 1 hour until the dough rises just above the tops of the tins. Bake in a preheated oven at 230°C/450°F/gas mark 8 for about 40 minutes until golden brown.

Variations:
You can shape this loaf how you like – into rolls, four small loaves or other loaf shapes. If you make smaller loaves or rolls, reduce the cooking time.

Toffee fruit cobbler (page 297)

Brown milk bread

MAKES ONE 700 G/1½ LB LOAF

450 g/1 lb/4 cups wholemeal flour
100 g/4 oz/1 cup strong plain (bread) flour
A pinch of salt
10 ml/2 tsp baking powder
100 g/4 oz/½ cup butter or margarine
300 ml/½ pt/1¼ cups milk

Mix together the flours, salt and baking powder and rub in the butter or margarine. Mix to a dough with the milk. Place in a loaf tin (pan) and bake in a preheated oven at 220ºC/425ºF/gas mark 7 for about 20 minutes until well risen and golden.

Milk rolls

MAKES 12 ROLLS

450 g/1 lb/4 cups strong plain (bread) flour
5 ml/1 tsp salt
15 ml/1 tbsp/1 sachet easy-blend dried yeast
10 ml/2 tsp sugar
50 g/2 oz/¼ cup butter or margarine
1 egg, beaten
300 ml/½ pt/1¼ cups warm milk, plus extra for brushing

Mix together the flour, salt, yeast and sugar, then rub in the butter or margarine. Add the egg and warm milk and mix to a firm dough. Knead until the dough is pliable and no longer sticky. Place in an oiled bowl, cover with oiled clingfilm (plastic wrap) and leave to rise in a warm place for about 1 hour until doubled in size and springy. Knead again, shape into rolls and place them on a greased baking (cookie) sheet. Cover and leave to prove for 1 hour. Brush the tops with milk and bake in a preheated oven at 230ºC/450ºF/gas mark 8 for about 15 minutes.

Buttered rolls

MAKES 12 ROLLS

1 quantity of White Bread dough
100 g/4 oz/½ cup butter or margarine, diced

Make the bread dough and leave it to rise until doubled in size and springy to the touch. Knead the dough again and work in the butter or margarine. Shape into rolls and place them, well apart, on a greased baking (cookied) sheet. Cover and leave to prove, then bake in a preheated oven at 230ºC/450ºF/gas mark 8 for 20 minutes.

French rolls

MAKES 12 ROLLS

450 g/1 lb/4 cups strong plain (all-purpose) flour
10 ml/2 tsp easy-blend dried yeast
25 g/1 oz/2 tbsp butter or margarine
1 egg, well beaten
150 ml/¼ pt/⅔ cup warm milk

Mix together the flour and yeast, then rub in the butter or margarine. Beat in the egg and milk to make a smooth dough but do not knead. Place in an oiled bowl, cover with oiled clingfilm (plastic wrap) and leave to rise in a warm place for about 1 hour until doubled in size. Shape into rolls and place them on a greased baking (cookie) tray. Bake in a preheated oven at 230ºC/450ºF/gas mark 8 for about 20 minutes.

Chocolate, fruit and nut dessert (page 310)

Brioche

MAKES FOUR 400 G/14 OZ LOAVES

750 g/1¾ lb/7 cups wholemeal flour
225 g/8 oz/2 cups strong plain (bread) flour
2.5 ml/½ tsp salt
30 ml/2 tbsp easy-blend dried yeast
400 g/14 oz/1¾ cups butter or margarine, melted
40 g/1½ oz clear honey
8 eggs, beaten
75 ml/5 tbsp warm milk
75 ml/5 tbsp warm water

Mix together the flours, salt and yeast, then rub in the butter or margarine and honey. Reserve a little of the egg for brushing and add the remaining eggs and enough of the warm milk and water to mix to a soft dough. Place in an oiled bowl, cover with oiled clingfilm (plastic wrap) and leave to rise in a warm place for about 1 hour until doubled in size and springy to the touch. Knead lightly, then divide the dough into four. Place in greased brioche tins (pans), cover and leave to prove in a warm place for 40 minutes. Brush with egg, then bake in a preheated oven at 220°C/425°F/gas mark 7 for 30 minutes.

Raisin loaf

MAKES TWO 450 G/1 LB LOAVES

900 g/2 lb/8 cups strong plain (bread) flour
15 ml/1 tbsp/1 sachet easy-blend dried yeast
10 ml/2 tsp mixed (apple-pie) spice
5 ml/1 tsp sugar
50 g/2 oz/¼ cup butter or margarine
450 g/1 lb/2⅔ cups raisins
450 ml/¾ pt/2 cups warm water

Mix together the flour, yeast, spice and sugar, then rub in the butter or margarine and stir in the raisins. Add the warm water and mix to a smooth dough. Knead until the dough is pliable and no longer sticky. Place in an oiled bowl, cover with oiled clingfilm (plastic wrap) and leave to rise in a warm place for about 1 hour until doubled in size and springy to the touch. Knead again, and place in two greased 450 g/1 lb loaf tins (pans). Cover and leave to prove for 1 hour. Bake in a preheated oven at 230°C/450°F/gas mark 8 for about 20 minutes.

Spiced buns

MAKES 12 BUNS

450 g/1 lb/4 cups strong plain (bread) flour
25 g/1 oz/2 tbsp caster (superfine) sugar
15 ml/1 tbsp/1 sachet easy-blend dried yeast
175 g/6 oz/¾ cup butter or margarine
350 g/12 oz/2 cups currants
15 ml/1 tbsp caraway seeds
150 ml/¼ pt/⅔ cup warm milk
15 ml/1 tbsp clear honey

Mix together the flour, sugar and yeast, then rub in the butter or margarine and stir in the currants and caraway seeds. Add the enough of the warm milk to mix to a soft dough. Knead until the dough is pliable and no longer sticky. Place in an oiled bowl, cover with oiled clingfilm (plastic wrap) and leave to rise in a warm place for 1 hour until the dough has doubled in size. Knead gently, then shape into rolls and place them on a greased baking (cookie) sheet. Cover and leave to rise for 1 hour. Bake in a preheated oven at 230°C/450°F/gas mark 8 for about 15 minutes. Remove from the oven and brush the warm buns with the honey. Leave to cool.

Coffee time rolls

MAKES 12

600 ml/1 pt/2½ cups milk
225 g/8 oz/1 cup butter or margarine
175 g/6 oz/¾ cup caster (superfine) sugar, plus extra for sprinkling
225 g/8 oz/2 cups strong plain (bread) flour
20 ml/1½ tbsp rosewater
9 eggs, separated

Boil the milk, butter and sugar and mix the flour and rosewater into the boiling liquid. Stir in the well-beaten egg yolks and 7 of the whites. Place the dough in little heaps on a greased baking tin, brush with egg white and sprinkle with a little sugar. Bake in a preheated oven at 180°C/350°F/gas mark 4 for about 20 minutes.

Currant loaf

MAKES ONE 900 G/2 LB LOAF

150 g/5 oz/⅔ cup butter or margarine
450 g/1 lb/4 cups wholemeal flour
15 ml/1 tbsp baking powder
A pinch of salt
175 g/6 oz/¾ cup soft brown sugar
175 g/6 oz/1 cup currants
50 g/2 oz/⅓ cup chopped mixed (candied) peel
2 eggs
15 ml/1 tbsp milk

Rub the butter or margarine into the flour, baking powder and salt. Add the sugar, currants and mixed peel. Beat the eggs and milk together and thoroughly mix them into the other ingredients. Add a little more milk if the mixture is too dry. Place in a greased loaf tin (pan) and bake in a preheated oven at 180°C/350°F/gas mark 4 for 30–40 minutes.

Sally Lunn

MAKES TWO 15 CM/6 IN CAKES

225 g/8 oz/2 cups strong plain (bread) flour
A pinch of salt
15 ml/1 tbsp/1 sachet easy-blend dried yeast
5 ml/1 tsp caster (superfine) sugar
50 g/2 oz/¼ cup butter or margarine, melted
150 ml/¼ pt/⅔ cup warm milk
1 egg, beaten
15 ml/1 tbsp granulated sugar
15 ml/1 tbsp water
50 g/2 oz/¼ cup clotted cream, to serve

Mix together the flour, salt, yeast and caster sugar, then add the melted butter or margarine and the egg and mix to a soft dough. Knead until the dough is pliable and no longer sticky. Place in an oiled bowl, cover with oiled clingfilm (plastic wrap) and leave to rise in a warm place for 1 hour until doubled in size. Knead the dough lightly, then place in two greased 15 cm/6 in cake tins (pans) and bake in a preheated oven at 220°C/450°F/gas mark 7 for 20 minutes until golden brown. While the loaves are baking, boil the granulated sugar and water in a small pan for 2 minutes. Remove the loaves from the oven and brush with the syrup. Leave to cool. To serve, cut the cakes into layers and toast lightly. Spread with clotted cream, reshape the cake and serve cut into wedges.

Chelsea buns

MAKES 9 BUNS

225 g/8 oz/2 cups strong plain (all-
purpose) flour
2.5 ml/½ tsp salt
10 ml/2 tsp easy-blend dried yeast
5 ml/1 tsp caster (superfine) sugar
15 g/½ oz/1 tbsp butter or margarine
1 egg, beaten
100 ml/4 fl oz/½ cup warm milk
15 ml/1 tbsp melted butter
75 g/3 oz/½ cup dried mixed fruit (fruit
cake mix)
15 g/½ oz/1 tbsp chopped mixed
(candied) peel
50 g/2 oz/¼ cup soft brown sugar
15 ml/1 tbsp clear honey

Mix together the flour, salt, yeast and
caster sugar, then rub in the butter or
margarine. Add the egg and enough
of the warm milk to make a smooth
dough. Knead until the dough is
pliable and no longer sticky. Place in
an oiled bowl, cover with oiled
clingfilm (plastic wrap) and leave in a
warm place for about 1 hour until
doubled in size. Knead the dough
again, then roll out on a lightly floured
surface into a 33 × 23 cm/13 × 9 in
rectangle. Brush with the melted
butter. Mix together the fruit, mixed
peel and brown sugar and spread it
over the dough. Roll up from one long
side like a Swiss (jelly) roll and
moisten the edges to seal. Cut into
about nine slices. Place them well
apart on a greased baking (cookie)
sheet, cover with oiled clingfilm
(plastic wrap) and leave in a warm
place for 1 hour. Bake in a preheated
oven at 190°C/350°F/gas mark 5 for
about 20 minutes. Remove from the
oven and brush the warm buns with
the honey. Leave to cool.

Hot cross buns

MAKES 18 BUNS

15 ml/1 tbsp/1 sachet easy-blend dried
yeast
100 g/4 oz/½ cup caster (superfine)
sugar
300 ml/½ pt/⅔ cup warm milk
75 g/3 oz/⅓ cup butter or margarine
450 g/1 lb/4 cups strong plain (bread)
flour
50 g/2 oz/⅓ cup chopped mixed
(candied) peel
175 g/6 oz/1 cup currants
5 ml/1 tsp mixed (apple-pie) spice
15 ml/1 tbsp honey

Mix together the yeast, 5 ml/1 tsp of
the sugar and a little of the warm milk
and leave in a warm place for about
10 minutes until frothy. Rub the
butter or margarine into the flour,
then stir in the remaining sugar, the
mixed peel, currants and spice. Stir in
the yeast mixture and the remaining
warm milk and mix to a soft dough.
Knead lightly until the dough is pliable
and no longer sticky. Place in an oiled
bowl, cover with oiled clingfilm (plastic
wrap) and leave to rise in a warm
place for about 1 hour until doubled
in size and springy to the touch.
Knead the dough again, then shape
into buns and place on a greased
baking (cookie) sheet. Cover with
clingfilm and leave to rise for 1 hour.
Cut a cross on the top of each bun
with a sharp knife. Bake in a
preheated oven at 200°C/400°F/gas
mark 6 for about 20 minutes.
Remove from the oven and brush the
warm buns with the honey. Leave to
cool.

Almond stollen

MAKES THREE 400 G/14 OZ LOAVES

250 g/9 oz/1¼ cups strong plain (bread) flour
250 g/9 oz/1¼ cups wholemeal flour
25 g/1 oz/¼ cup rye flour
50 g/2 oz/¼ cup soft brown sugar
15 g/½ oz/1 sachet easy-blend dried yeast
75 g/3 oz/⅓ cup butter or margarine
2 eggs, beaten
300 ml/½ pt/1¼ cups warm water
150 g/5 oz/scant 1 cup currants
175 g/6 oz/1 cup sultanas (golden raisins)
2.5 ml/½ tsp ground cinnamon
50 g/2 oz/¼ cup grated lemon rind
Grated rind and juice of 1 orange
100 g/4 oz Almond Paste (page 356)
15 ml/1 tbsp clear honey
15 ml/1 tbsp melted butter or margarine
30 ml/2 tbsp flaked (slivered) almonds, toasted

Mix together the flours, sugar and yeast, then rub in the butter or margarine. Reserve a little of the beaten egg for brushing. Stir the remaining eggs and the warm water into the flours and sugar and mix to a dough. Knead until the dough is pliable and elastic. Mix the fruit, cinnamon, lemon rind and orange juice and rind into the dough. Place in an oiled bowl, cover with oiled clingfilm (plastic wrap) and leave to rise in a warm place for 1 hour until doubled in size.

Knead again, divide into three and roll out into ovals about 10 in/25 cm long. Brush the edges with the reserved egg. Roll out the almond paste into three ovals a little smaller than the pieces of dough and place one piece in the centre of each piece of dough. Fold the dough over like a turnover, allowing a 2.5 cm/1 in overlap, and seal the edges. Place on a greased baking (cookie) sheet, cover with oiled clingfilm and leave in a warm place to rise for 40 minutes. Bake in a preheated oven at 220°C/425°F/gas mark 7 for 30 minutes. Mix together the honey and melted butter or margarine and use to glaze the warm loaves. Sprinkle with the almonds, then leave to cool.

Tea cakes

MAKES 12 CAKES

450 g/1 lb/4 cups strong plain (bread) flour
15 g/½ oz/1 sachet easy-blend dried yeast
50 g/2 oz/¼ cup caster (superfine) sugar
5 ml/1 tsp salt
25 g/1 oz/2 tbsp butter or margarine
50 g/2 oz/⅓ cup sultanas (golden raisins)
300 ml/½ pt/1¼ cups warm milk, plus extra for brushing

Mix together the flour, yeast, sugar and salt. Rub in the butter or margarine until the mixture resembles breadcrumbs, then stir in the sultanas. Stir in warm milk and mix to a soft dough. Knead until the dough is pliable and no longer sticky. Place in an oiled bowl, cover with oiled clingfilm (plastic wrap) and leave to rise in a warm place until doubled in size and springy to the touch. Knead again, then shape into rounds and place on a greased baking (cookie) sheet. Brush the tops with milk, cover with clingfilm and leave to rise for 1 hour. Bake in a preheated oven at 200°C/400°F/gas mark 6 for 20 minutes. Leave to cool, then serve toasted and buttered.

Autumn mist crown

MAKES TWO 750 G/1½ LB LOAVES

500 g/18 oz/4½ cups wholemeal flour
20 ml/4 tsp baking powder
150 g/5 oz/⅔ cup soft brown sugar
5 ml/1 tsp salt
2.5 ml/½ tsp ground mace
75 g/3 oz/⅓ cup vegetable fat
3 egg whites
300 ml/½ pt/1¼ cups milk
175 g/6 oz/1½ cups wholemeal cake crumbs
50 g/2 oz/½ cup hazelnuts (filberts), ground
100 g/4 oz marrons glacés, chopped
5 ml/1 tsp ground ginger
30 ml/2 tbsp rum or brandy
1 egg, beaten
30 ml/2 tbsp clear honey

Mix together the flour, baking powder, 75 g/3 oz/⅓ cup of the sugar, the salt and mace. Rub in the fat. Mix in the egg whites and milk and knead to a soft and pliable dough. Roll out on a lightly floured surface into two 30 × 20 cm/12 × 8 in rectangles.

Mix together the cake crumbs, hazelnuts, marrons glacés, ginger, rum or brandy and the remaining sugar. Mix with enough of the egg to give a spreading consistency. Brush the dough with the remaining egg and spread with the filling, leaving 2.5 cm/1 in free at the edges. Make into a roll and join the ends together into a circle. Place the rounds on greased baking sheets, snip the tops with scissors for decoration and brush with the remaining egg. Cover and leave to rest for 10 minutes, then bake in a preheated oven at 230°C/450°F/gas mark 8 for 30 minutes. Brush with the honey to glaze, leave to cool and serve sliced.

Malt bread

MAKES TWO 450 G/1 LB LOAVES

450 g/1 lb/4 cups wholemeal flour
15 g/½ oz/1 sachet easy-blend dried yeast
5 ml/1 tsp salt
15 g/½ oz/1 tbsp butter or margarine
300 ml/½ pt/1¼ cups warm water
30 ml/2 tbsp clear honey
15 ml/1 tbsp black treacle (molasses)
30 ml/2 tbsp liquid malt extract
175 g/6 oz/1 cups sultanas (golden raisins)
50 g/2 oz/⅓ cup dates, stoned (pitted) and chopped
15 ml/1 tbsp golden (light corn) syrup

Mix together the flour, yeast and salt, then rub in the butter or margarine. Mix the water, honey, treacle and malt extract. Pour this into the dry ingredients and knead until the dough is smooth. Mix in the dried fruits. Place in an oiled bowl, cover with oiled clingfilm (plastic wrap) and leave to rise in a warm place for 1 hour until doubled in size and springy to the touch. Knead again, then shape into loaves and place in four greased 450 g/1 lb loaf tins (pans). Cover with clingfilm and leave to rise for 1 hour. Bake in a preheated oven at 180°C/350°F/gas mark 4 for 35 minutes, making sure the loaves do not get too dark. Remove from the oven and brush with the syrup. Leave to cool.

Cottage tea bread

MAKES TWO 450 G/1 LB LOAVES

450 g/1 lb/4 cups wholemeal flour
15 g/½ oz/1 sachet easy-blend dried
　yeast
2.5 ml/½ tsp salt
15 g/½ oz/1 tbsp butter or margarine
15 ml/1 tbsp soft brown sugar
1 small egg, beaten
300 ml/½ pt/1¼ cups warm water
175 g/6 oz/1 cup currants
100 g/4 oz/⅔ cups sultanas (golden
　raisins)
75 g/3 oz/½ cup raisins
50 g/2 oz/⅓ cup chopped mixed
　(candied) peel
2.5 ml/½ tsp mixed (apple-pie) spice
To glaze:
15 ml/1 tbsp water
15 ml/1 tbsp lemon juice
A pinch of mixed (apple-pie) spice

Mix together the flour, yeast and salt,
then rub in the butter or margarine.
Stir in the sugar, then beat in the egg
and enough of the warm water to mix
to a soft dough. Knead until the
dough is smooth and elastic. Mix in
the fruit, mixed peel and spice. Place
in an oiled bowl, cover with oiled
clingfilm (plastic wrap) and leave to
rise in a warm place for 1 hour until
doubled in size and springy. Knead
again, cover and leave to rest for
15 minutes. Place the dough in two
greased 450 g/1 lb loaf tins (pans),
cover and leave in a warm place for
45 minutes. Bake in a preheated oven
at 220°C/425°F/gas mark 7 for
25 minutes until golden.
　To make the glaze, mix together
the water, lemon juice and spice and
brush over the top of the warm
loaves.

Malted banana loaf

MAKES TWO 450 G/1 LB LOAVES

150 g/5 oz/⅔ cups Muscovado sugar
175 g/6 oz/¾ cup butter or margarine
30 ml/2 tbsp liquid malt extract
3 eggs, beaten
225 g/8 oz/2 cups wholemeal flour
15 ml/1 tbsp baking powder
2.5 ml/½ tsp ground cinnamon
50 g/2 oz/½ cup hazelnuts (filberts),
　chopped
2 bananas, mashed
50 g/2 oz/⅓ cup no-need-to-soak dried
　apricots, chopped
5 ml/1 tsp rum

Cream together the sugar and butter
or margarine until light. Dissolve the
malt extract in the eggs and add to
the creamed mixture a little at a time,
beating well between each addition.
Mix in the flour, baking powder and
cinnamon. Reserve a few hazelnuts,
then mix in the remainder with the
bananas, apricots and rum. Divide in
half and shape into two greased
450 g/1 lb loaf tins (pans). Sprinkle
with the reserved hazelnuts and bake
in a preheated oven at 180°C/350°F/
gas mark 4 for 35 minutes until firm
and golden.

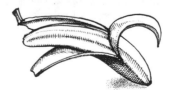

Nut bread

MAKES THREE 450 G/1 LB LOAVES

450 g/1 lb/4 cups wholemeal flour
100 g/4 oz/½ cup rolled oats
5 ml/1 tsp salt
10 ml/2 tsp soy flour (optional)
25 g/1 oz/2 sachets of easy-blend dried
  yeast
40 g/1½ oz/2½ tbsp soft brown sugar
15 ml/1 tbsp malt extract
600 ml/1 pt/2½ cups warm water
225 g/8 oz/2 cups chopped mixed nuts
175 g/6 oz/1 cup currants
100 g/4 oz/⅔ cup dates, chopped
100 g/4 oz/⅔ cup raisins
5 ml/1 tsp ground cinnamon
20 g/¾ oz/1 tbsp vegetable fat
1 egg, beaten
15 ml/1 tbsp clear honey
15 ml/1 tbsp golden (light corn) syrup

Mix together the flour, oats, salt, soy flour if using, yeast and sugar. Dissolve the malt extract in the warm water, then mix enough into the dry ingredients to make a smooth dough. Knead until no longer sticky. Reserve a few nuts for decoration, then mix the remaining nuts, the fruit, cinnamon and fat into the dough. Place in an oiled bowl, cover with oiled clingfilm (plastic wrap) and leave to rise for about 1 hour until doubled in size.

Knead again, shape the dough into three flat rounds and mark each into eight. Place on greased baking (cookie) sheets, brush the tops with beaten egg and sprinkle with the reserved nuts. Cover and leave to prove in a warm place for 40 minutes. Bake in a preheated oven at 230°C/ 450°F/gas mark 8 for 30 minutes. Mix the honey and syrup and brush over the baked loaves to glaze.

Herb bread

MAKES TWO 450 G/1 LB LOAVES

900 g/2 lb/8 cups wholemeal flour
25 g/1 oz/2 sachets easy-blend dried
  yeast
5 ml/1 tsp salt
50 g/2 oz/¼ cup vegetable fat
40 g/1½ oz/2½ tbsp soft brown sugar
600 ml/1 pt/2½ cups warm water
5 ml/1 tsp chopped thyme
5 ml/2 tsp chopped parsley
2.5 ml/½ tsp chopped marjoram
2. 5 ml/½ tsp dried oregano
5 ml/1 tsp poppy seeds

Mix together the flour, yeast and salt, then and rub in the fat and stir in the sugar. Mix in the warm water, then work in the herbs and knead until the dough is pliable and no longer sticky. Place in an oiled bowl, cover with oiled clingfilm (plastic wrap) and leave to rise for about 1 hour until doubled in size and springy to the touch. Knead again and shape into two greased 450 g/1 lb loaf tins (pans) or shape and place on baking (cookie) sheets. Cover and leave to prove in a warm place for 45 minutes. Sprinkle with the poppy seeds and bake in a preheated oven at 230°C/450°F/gas mark 8 for 30 minutes until firm and golden.

Kentucky sweet corn bread

MAKES THREE 450 G/1 LB LOAVES

450 g/1 lb/4 cups fine cornmeal
225 g/8 oz/2 cups wholemeal flour
15 ml/1 tbsp baking powder
2.5 ml/½ tsp salt
10 ml/2 tsp clear honey
2 eggs
60 ml/4 tbsp oil
450 ml/¾ pt/2 cups milk
225 g/8 oz sweetcorn (corn) kernels
50 g/2 oz millet flakes (optional)

Mix the together cornmeal, flour, baking powder and salt. Mix together the honey, 1 egg, the oil and milk and mix it into the dry ingredients. Knead until the dough is soft and pliable, then mix in the sweetcorn. Divide into three, shape into long batons and place on a greased baking (cookie) sheet. Brush with beaten egg and sprinkle with the millet flakes, if using. Cover with oiled clingfilm (plastic wrap) and leave to rest for 15 minutes, then bake in a preheated oven at 220°C/ 425°F/gas mark 7 for 30 minutes until golden and firm.

Pitta bread

MAKES 4 BREADS

450 g/1 lb/4 cups strong plain (bread) flour
15 g/½ oz/1 sachet easy-blend dried yeast
10 ml/2 tsp salt
2.5 ml/½ tsp clear honey
30 ml/2 tbsp olive oil
300 ml/½ pt/1¼ cups warm water

Mix together the flour, yeast and salt. Stir in the honey and oil and enough of the warm water to make a smooth dough. Knead until elastic and no

longer sticky. Place in an oiled bowl, cover with oiled clingfilm (plastic wrap) and leave to rise in a warm place for 1 hour until doubled in size and springy to the touch.
Knead the dough again, divide into four and roll into balls. Cover and leave to rise again for 30 minutes. Roll out into ovals about 3 mm/⅛ in thick, lay them on greased baking (cookie) sheets, cover and leave for a further 30 minutes. Bake in a preheated oven at 240°C/475°F/gas mark 9 for 10 minutes. Remove from the oven and wrap in a cloth immediately to soften the bread, then leave to cool on a wire rack.

Soda bread

MAKES ONE 450 G/1 LB LOAF

250 g/9 oz/2¼ cups wholemeal flour
2.5 ml/½ tsp salt
2.5 ml/½ tsp bicarbonate of soda (baking soda)
40 g/1½ oz/3 tbsp butter or margarine
300 ml/½ pt/1¼ cups buttermilk
1 egg, beaten

Mix together the flour, salt and bicarbonate of soda, then rub in the butter or margarine. Mix in enough of the buttermilk to make a soft dough. Shape into a round and place on a greased baking (cookie) sheet. Mark into quarters, brush with egg, cover and leave to rest for 30 minutes before baking. Bake in a preheated oven at 230°C/450°F/gas mark 8 for 25 minutes or until the base sounds hollow when tapped.

Cakes

Whatever type of cake you prefer – rich fruit or light sponge – there are plenty of choices here for you to try, ideal for family teas, offering to special guests or just enjoying with a cup of tea. For the best results, use a cake tin (pan) of a similar size to the one specified in the recipe. Grease and line the tin where appropriate so that the cake slides out easily and is not damaged. Loose-bottomed cake tins make this even easier.

There are several ways to test whether a cake is done, depending on the type of cake. A sponge-type cake will be well risen and golden brown; the top should spring back if pressed gently with a fingertip. A thin skewer inserted into the centre of a fruit cake should come out clean. Most cakes will begin to shrink from the sides of the tin.

Sponges and light cakes are best eaten as soon after baking as possible. Heavier cakes or fruit cakes can be stored in a airtight container. Most cakes can be frozen if well wrapped as soon as they are completely cold. They will keep for about three months.

Classic fat-free sponge cake

MAKES ONE 18 CM/7 IN CAKE

3 eggs, separated
75 g/3 oz/⅓ cup caster sugar, plus extra
    for sprinkling
75 g/3 oz/¾ cup plain (all-purpose) flour
A pinch of salt
2.5 ml/½ tsp baking powder
Raspberry jam (jelly) and icing
    (confectioners') sugar, to finish

Whisk together the egg yolks and sugar for about 5 minutes until very pale and fluffy. Whisk the egg whites until stiff. Mix together the flour, salt and baking powder. Fold the egg whites and flour alternately into the egg yolk mixture using a metal spoon. Divide the mixture between two greased and lined 18 cm/7 in cake tins (pans) and bake in a preheated oven at 180°C/350°F/gas mark 4 for about 20 minutes until well risen and springy to the touch. Leave to cool in the tins for a few minutes, then turn out on to a sheet of greaseproof (waxed) paper sprinkled with caster sugar. When cool, sandwich together with jam and sprinkle with icing sugar.

Swiss roll

MAKES ONE 18 CM/7 IN CAKE

Prepare as for Classic Fat-free Sponge Cake, but bake the cake in a Swiss roll tin (jelly roll pan). Turn out on to the greaseproof (waxed) paper sprinkled with caster sugar and use the paper to help you roll up the warm cake from the long side. Leave to cool. Gently unroll the cake, spread with jam and re-roll. Serve sprinkled with icing (confectioners') sugar.

Coffee-iced walnut cake

MAKES ONE 20 CM/8 IN CAKE

4 eggs
100 g/4 oz/½ cup caster (superfine)
    sugar
100 g/4 oz/1 cup self-raising (self-rising)
    flour
100 g/4 oz/1 cup walnuts, ground
For the icing (frosting):
50 g/2 oz/⅓ cup icing (confectioners')
    sugar
1 egg white
100 g/4 oz/½ cup unsalted (sweet)
    butter, diced
5 ml/1 tsp instant coffee powder
5 ml/1 tsp boiling water

Place the eggs and caster sugar in a large bowl over a pan of hot water, making sure the bowl does not touch the water. Whisk until light and frothy and thick enough to leave a trail from the whisk. Remove from the heat and lightly fold in the flour and nuts using a metal spoon. Pour into a greased loose-bottomed 20 cm/8 in cake tin (pan) and bake in a preheated oven at 190°C/375°F/gas mark 5 for 20 minutes until golden brown. Leave to cool.

To make the icing, place the icing sugar and egg white in a bowl over a pan of hot water and whisk for about 10 minutes until thick and glossy. Remove from the heat and beat in the butter. Mix together the coffee and water and stir this into the icing. Chill for 30 minutes, then spread over the top and sides of the cake.

Victoria sandwich

MAKES ONE 18 CM/7 IN CAKE

100 g/4 oz/½ cup butter or margarine
100 g/4 oz/½ cup caster (superfine)
  sugar
2 eggs, beaten
100 g/4 oz/1 cup plain (all-purpose)
  flour
A pinch of salt
2.5 ml/½ tsp baking powder
60 ml/4 tbsp jam (jelly)
300 ml/½ pt/1¼ cups double (heavy)
  cream, whipped
30 ml/2 tbsp icing (confectioners') sugar,
  sifted

Cream together the butter or
margarine and sugar until light. Beat
in the eggs, then lightly stir in the
flour, salt and baking powder. Spoon
into two greased and lined 18 cm/7 in
sandwich tins (pans) and bake in a
preheated oven at 180°C/350°F/gas
mark 4 for 25 minutes until lightly
browned and springy to the touch.
Turn out on to a wire rack to cool.
When cold, sandwich together with
the jam and cream and sprinkle with
the icing sugar.

Orange sandwich cake

MAKES ONE 18 CM/7 IN CAKE

100 g/4 oz/½ cup butter or margarine
100 g/4 oz/½ cup caster (superfine)
  sugar
2 eggs, beaten
100 g/4 oz/1 cup plain (all-purpose)
  flour
Grated rind of 1 orange
A pinch of salt
2.5 ml/½ tsp baking powder
175 g/6 oz/1¾ cup Orange Butter Icing
  (page 352)

Cream together the butter or
margarine and sugar until light and
fluffy. Beat in the eggs, adding a
spoonful of the flour if the mixture
begins to curdle. Mix in the orange
rind. Sift together the flour, salt and
baking powder and mix lightly into the
mixture. Divide the mixture between
two greased and lined 18 cm/7 in
sandwich tins (pans) and bake at
180°C/350°F/gas mark 4 for
25 minutes until lightly browned.
Leave to cool. Sandwich together with
the Orange Butter Icing.

Madeira cake

MAKES ONE 20 CM/8 IN CAKE

175 g/6 oz/¾ cup butter or margarine
175 g/6 oz/¾ cup caster (superfine)
  sugar
3 eggs, beaten
225 g/8 oz/2 cups plain (all-purpose)
  flour
7.5 ml/1½ tsp baking powder
30 ml/2 tbsp milk
Grated rind of 1 lemon
10 ml/2 tsp vanilla essence (extract)

Cream the butter or margarine until
soft, then beat in the sugar. Mix in
the eggs, one at a time, adding a
little flour between each addition if
the mixture shows signs of curdling.
Mix in the remaining ingredients and
stir until well blended. Spoon into a
greased and lined 20 cm/8 in cake tin
(pan) and bake in a preheated oven
at 160°C/325°F/gas mark 3 for
1½ hours until a skewer inserted in
the centre comes out clean. Leave to
cool in the tin for 5 minutes before
turning out.

Hazelnut torte

MAKES ONE 15 CM/6 IN CAKE

2 eggs
125 g/5 oz/⅔ cup caster (superfine)
   sugar
100 g/4 oz/1 cup hazelnuts (filberts),
   ground
300 ml/½ pt/1¼ cups double (heavy)
   cream, whipped
50 g/2 oz/¼ cup butter or margarine
60 ml/4 tbsp milk
50 g/2 oz/½ cup cocoa (unsweetened
   chocolate) powder
5 ml/1 tsp vanilla essence (extract)
225 g/8 oz/1⅓ cups icing (confectioners')
   sugar
12 whole hazelnuts (filberts)

Whisk together the eggs and caster
sugar until light and fluffy. Fold in the
ground hazelnuts. Spoon the mixture
into two greased 15 cm/6 in tins
(pans) and bake in a preheated oven
at 200°C/400°F/gas mark 6 for
15 minutes until golden brown and
springy to the touch. Leave to cool in
the tins. Sandwich the layers together
with most of the whipped cream.
Place the butter or margarine and
milk in a saucepan and heat until
boiling. Stir in the cocoa and simmer
for 30 seconds. Remove from the
heat and stir in the vanilla essence,
then beat in the icing sugar. Spread
the icing on top of the cake. Decorate
with the remaining whipped cream
and the hazelnuts.

Chocolate fudge cake

MAKES ONE 20 CM/8 IN CAKE

For the cake:
60 ml/4 tbsp cocoa (unsweetened
   chocolate) powder
100 g/4 oz/½ cup butter or margarine
120 ml/4 fl oz/½ cup sunflower oil
250 ml/8 fl oz/1 cup water
350 g/12 oz/1½ cups caster (superfine)
   sugar
225 g/8 oz/2 cups self-raising (self-
   rising) flour
2 eggs, beaten
120 ml/4 fl oz/½ cup milk
2.5 ml/½ tsp bicarbonate of soda
   (baking soda)
5 ml/1 tsp vanilla essence (extract)
For the icing (frosting):
60 ml/4 tbsp cocoa powder
100 g/4 oz/½ cup butter or margarine
60 ml/4 tbsp evaporated milk
450 g/1 lb/2⅔ cups icing (confectioners')
   sugar
5 ml/1 tsp vanilla essence (extract)
100 g/4 oz/1 cup plain (semi-sweet)
   chocolate

To make the cake, put the cocoa,
butter or margarine, oil and water in a
pan and bring to the boil. Remove
from the heat and stir in the sugar
and flour. Beat together the eggs,
milk, bicarbonate of soda and vanilla
essence, then add to the mixture in
the pan. Pour into a greased and
lined 20 cm/8 in cake tin (pan) and
bake in a preheated oven at 180°C/
350°F/gas mark 4 for 1 hour until
well risen and springy to the touch.

   To make the icing, bring all the
ingredients to the boil and beat until
smooth, then pour over the cake while
still warm and leave to set.

Chocolate layer cake

MAKES ONE 20 CM/8 IN CAKE

For the cake:
100 g/4 oz/½ cup butter or margarine
100 g/4 oz/½ cup caster (superfine)
   sugar
2 eggs, lightly beaten
30 ml/2 tbsp cocoa (unsweetened
   chocolate) powder
100 g/4 oz/1 cup self-raising (self-rising)
   flour
A pinch of salt
For the filling:
30 g/1½ oz/3 tbsp butter or margarine
75 g/3 oz/½ cup icing (confectioners')
   sugar
10 ml/2 tsp coffee essence (extract)
15 ml/1 tbsp milk

To make the cake, cream together the
butter and sugar until light and fluffy.
Beat in the eggs a little at a time.
Blend the cocoa with just enough
water to make a paste, then mix this
into the bowl with the flour and salt.
Spoon the mixture into a greased and
lined 20 cm/8 in cake tin (pan) and
bake in a preheated oven at 180°C/
350°F/gas mark 4 for 30 minutes
until well risen and springy to the
touch.
   To make the filling, beat the butter
or margarine until creamy, then
gradually work in the icing sugar,
coffee essence and milk until you have
a smooth and creamy texture. Halve
the cake horizontally, then sandwich
the two halves together with the
filling.

Chocolate roulade

MAKES ONE 30 CM/12 IN ROULADE

5 eggs, separated
150 g/5 oz/⅔ cup caster (superfine)
   sugar
225 g/8 oz/2 cups plain (semi-sweet)
   chocolate, grated
75 ml/5 tbsp water
5 ml/1 tsp instant coffee powder
300 ml/½ pt/1¼ cups double (heavy)
   cream
Icing (confectioners') sugar, for dusting

Line a Swiss roll tin (jelly roll pan) with
greaseproof (waxed) paper, brush with
oil and sprinkle with flour, then
30 ml/2 tbsp of the caster sugar. Beat
the egg yolks and remaining sugar
until pale and fluffy. Melt the
chocolate, water and coffee in a
heavy-based pan, then stir into the
egg yolks. Whisk the egg whites until
stiff, then gently fold them into the
chocolate mixture. Spread evenly in
the prepared tin and bake in a
preheated oven at 200°C/400°F/gas
mark 6 for 12–15 minutes until
springy to the touch. Lift the cake out
of the tin, still on the paper, place on
a wire rack and cover with a damp tea
towel (dish cloth) until cool. Whip the
cream and spread over the roulade.
Roll up from the long side, peeling off
the paper as you roll. Dust with the
icing sugar to finish.

Moist chocolate cake

MAKES ONE 20 CM/8 IN CAKE

200 g/7 oz/1¾ cups plain (all-purpose) flour
30 ml/2 tbsp cocoa (unsweetened chocolate) powder
5 ml/1 tsp bicarbonate of soda (baking soda)
5 ml/1 tsp baking powder
125 g/5 oz/⅔ cup caster (superfine) sugar
30 ml/2 tbsp golden (light corn) syrup
2 eggs, beaten
150 ml/¼ pt/⅔ cup oil
150 ml/¼ pt/⅔ cup milk
150 ml/¼ pt/⅔ cup double (heavy) or whipping cream, whipped

Beat together all the ingredients except the cream to make a batter. Pour into two greased and lined 20 cm/8 in cake tins (pans) and bake in a preheated oven at 160°C/325°F/ gas mark 3 for 35 minutes until springy to the touch. Remove from the tins and leave to cool. Sandwich together with the whipped cream.

Mud pie

MAKES ONE 20 CM/8 IN CAKE

225 g/8 oz/2 cups plain (semi-sweet) chocolate
225 g/8 oz/1 cup butter or margarine
225 g/8 oz/1 cup caster (superfine) sugar
4 eggs, lightly beaten
15 ml/1 tbsp cornflour (cornstarch)

Melt the chocolate and butter or margarine in a heatproof bowl set over a pan of gently simmering water. Remove from the heat and stir in the sugar until dissolved, then beat in the eggs and cornflour. Spoon into a greased and lined 20 cm/8 in cake tin

(pan) and stand the tin in a roasting tray. Add enough hot water to come half-way up the side of the tin. Bake in a preheated oven at 180°C/350°F/ gas mark 4 for 1 hour. Remove from the tray of water and leave to cool in the tin, then chill until ready to turn out and serve.

Chocolate biscuit cake

MAKES ONE 450 G/1 LB CAKE

2 eggs, beaten
25 g/1 oz/2 tbsp caster (superfine) sugar
225 g/8 oz/1 cup butter or margarine, melted
15 ml/1 tbsp rum or brandy
225 g/8 oz/2 cups plain (semi-sweet) chocolate, melted
225 g/8 oz rich tea biscuits (cookies), broken into small pieces

Beat together the eggs and caster sugar, then stir in the butter or margarine, brandy and chocolate. Stir in the biscuit pieces and fold together so they are all covered with the chocolate mixture. Pour into a 450 g/ 1 lb loaf tin (pan) lined with overlapping foil and shake gently to help the mixture settle. Leave in the fridge overnight, then turn out and serve in thin slices.

Note:
This cake contains raw eggs.

Gingerbread

MAKES ONE 23 CM/9 IN CAKE

450 g/1 lb/4 cups plain (all-purpose)
   flour
15 ml/1 tbsp ground ginger
15 ml/1 tbsp baking powder
5 ml/1 tsp bicarbonate of soda (baking
   soda)
5 ml/1 tsp salt
225 g/8 oz/1 cup demerara sugar
175 g/6 oz/¾ cup butter or margarine
175 g/6 oz/½ cup black treacle
   (molasses)
175 g/6 oz/½ cup golden (light corn)
   syrup
300 ml/½ pt/1¼ cups milk
1 egg, beaten

Mix together the flour, ginger, baking
powder, bicarbonate of soda and salt.
Gently heat the sugar, butter or
margarine, treacle and syrup in a
saucepan until the butter or
margarine has just melted, then stir
into the dry ingredients with the milk
and egg. Beat well, then pour the
mixture into a greased and lined
23 cm/9 in square cake tin (pan) and
bake in a preheated oven at 180°C/
350°F/gas mark 4 for 1½ hours until
well risen and springy to the touch.
Leave to cool. Store for a few days in
an airtight container before cutting
into chunks to serve.

St Clement's cheesecake

MAKES ONE 20 CM/8 IN CAKE

50 g/2 oz/¼ cup butter or margarine
100 g/4 oz digestive biscuits (graham
   crackers), crushed
2 eggs, separated
A pinch of salt
100 g/4 oz/½ cup caster (superfine)
   sugar
45 ml/3 tbsp orange juice
45 ml/3 tbsp lemon juice
15 ml/1 tbsp powdered gelatine
30 ml/2 tbsp cold water
350 g/12 oz/1½ cups cottage cheese,
   sieved (strained)
150 ml/¼ pt/⅔ cup double (heavy)
   cream, whipped
1 orange, peeled and sliced

Rub a 20 cm/8 in loose-bottomed
cake tin (pan) with the butter or
margarine and sprinkle with the
biscuit (cookie) crumbs. Beat the egg
yolks with the salt and half the sugar
until thick and creamy. Put into a bowl
with the orange and lemon juices and
stir over a pan of hot water until the
mixture begins to thicken and will
coat the back of a spoon. Dissolve the
gelatine in the cold water and heat
gently until syrupy. Stir into the fruit
juice mixture, then leave to cool. Stir
in the cottage cheese and cream.
Whisk the egg whites until stiff and
fold in the remaining sugar. Fold into
the cheesecake mixture and pour into
the tin. Chill until firm. Turn out to
serve and sprinkle with any loose
crumbs. Serve garnished with the
orange slices.

Raspberry cheesecake

MAKES ONE 15 CM/6 IN CAKE

75 g/3 oz/⅓ cup butter or margarine, melted
175 g/6 oz digestive biscuits (graham crackers), crushed
3 eggs, separated
300 ml/½ pt/1¼ cups milk
25 g/1 oz/2 tbsp caster (superfine) sugar
15 ml/1 tbsp powdered gelatine
30 ml/2 tbsp cold water
225 g/8 oz/1 cup full-fat soft cheese
Grated rind and juice of ½ lemon
450 g/1 lb raspberries, hulled

Mix together the butter or margarine and biscuit (cookie) crumbs and press the mixture into the base of a loose-bottomed 15 cm/6 in cake tin (pan). Chill while making the filling.

Whisk the egg yolks, then pour into a saucepan with the milk and heat gently, stirring continuously, until the custard thickens. Remove from the heat and stir in the sugar. Whisk the egg whites until stiff. Soften the gelatine in the water, then dissolve over a pan of hot water. Beat the cheese until soft, then whisk in the gelatine, custard and lemon rind and juice and continue whisking until the mixture thickens. Fold in the egg whites and spoon the mixture over the base. Leave in a cool place to set. Just before serving, remove the cheesecake from the tin and cover with the raspberries.

Baked lemon and kiwi cheesecake

SERVES 4–6

For the base:
50 g/2 oz/¼ cup butter or margarine
225 g/8 oz digestive biscuits (graham cracker), crushed
25 g/1 oz/2 tbsp caster (superfine) sugar
5 ml/1 tsp ground cinnamon
For the filling:
2 eggs, separated
100 g/4 oz/½ cup caster (superfine) sugar
350 g/12 oz/1½ cups full-fat soft cheese
Grated rind and juice of 1 lemon
150 ml/¼ pt/⅔ cup double (heavy) cream

To make the base, melt the butter or margarine, then mix in the biscuit (cookie) crumbs, sugar and cinnamon. Press the mixture into the base of a greased 20 cm/8 in loose-based flan tin (pie pan). Chill.

To make the filling, beat the egg yolks with the sugar until thick. Mix in the cheese and lemon rind and juice. Whisk the egg whites until they form soft peaks, then fold into the mixture. Whip the cream until stiff, then fold into the mixture. Spoon the filling into the prepared base. Bake in a preheated oven at 160°C/325°F/gas mark 3 for 1 hour until firm and lightly golden. Turn off the oven and leave the cheesecake in the oven to cool. When cold, remove from the tin and chill before serving.

Ginger and lemon cheesecake

MAKES ONE 20 CM/8 IN CAKE

50 g/2 oz/¼ cup butter or margarine
175 g/6 oz gingernut biscuits (cookies),
  crushed
15 ml/1 tbsp powdered gelatine
30 ml/2 tbsp water
2 lemons
100 g/4 oz/½ cup cottage cheese
100 g/4 oz/½ cup full-fat soft cheese
50 g/2 oz /¼ cup caster (superfine) sugar
150 ml/¼ pt/⅔ cup plain yoghurt
150 ml/¼ pt/⅔ cup double (heavy) cream

Melt the butter or margarine and stir
in the biscuit (cookie) crumbs. Press
into the base of a 20 cm/8 in flan tin
(pie pan). Mix the gelatine and water
in a small bowl and stand the bowl in
a pan of hot water until dissolved.
Pare three strips of lemon rind from
one lemon. Grate the remaining rind
of both lemons. Quarter the lemons,
remove the pips and skin and purée
the flesh in a food processor or
blender. Add the cheeses and process
to mix. Add the sugar, yoghurt and
cream and process again. Pour in the
gelatine mixture and process. Pour
into the prepared base and leave in
the fridge to set for 1 hour. Decorate
with the strips of lemon rind.

Pineapple cheesecake

MAKES ONE 20 CM/8 IN CAKE

175 g/6 oz digestive biscuits (graham
  crackers), crushed
75 g/3 oz/⅓ cup butter or margarine,
  melted
3 eggs, separated
75 g/3 oz/⅓ cup caster (superfine) sugar
425 g/15 oz/1 large can of pineapple,
  drained and chopped
150 ml/¼ pt/⅔ cup pineapple juice
225 g/8 oz/2 cups Cheddar cheese,
  finely grated
150 ml/¼ pt/⅔ cup milk
150 ml/¼ pt/⅔ cup single (light) cream
150 ml/¼ pt/⅔ cup double (heavy) cream
15 ml/1 tbsp powdered gelatine
150 ml/¼ pt/⅔ cup whipping cream,
  whipped

Stir the biscuit (cookie) crumbs into
the melted butter or margarine and
press the mixture into a greased and
lined 20 cm/8 in loose-bottomed cake
tin (pan). Chill until firm.

Reserve some of the pineapple for
decoration and spread the rest over
the biscuit base. Whisk the egg yolks,
sugar and half the pineapple juice in a
bowl over a pan of hot water until
thick. Mix together the cheese and
milk. Whisk the single and double
creams until thick. Add to the cheese,
then stir into the egg mixture.
Dissolve the gelatine in the remaining
juice in a small bowl set over a pan of
hot water, leave to cool slightly, then
stir into the mixture and chill until
almost setting. Whisk the egg whites
until stiff, then fold them into the
mixture. Pour into the tin and chill
until set. Turn out and decorate with
the whipped cream and reserved
pineapple.

Apricot cheesecake

MAKES ONE 18 CM/7 IN CAKE

75 g/3 oz/⅓ cup butter or margarine
100 g/4 oz/1 cup plain (all-purpose)
flour
100 g/4 oz/½ cup caster (superfine)
sugar
25 g/1 oz/¼ cup hazelnuts (filberts),
ground
45 ml/3 tbsp cold water
100 g/4 oz/⅔ cup no-need-to-soak dried
apricots, chopped
Grated rind and juice of 1 lemon
100 g/4 oz/½ cup curd (smooth cottage)
cheese
100 g/4 oz/½ cup full-fat soft cheese
25 g/1 oz/¼ cup cornflour (cornstarch)
2 eggs, separated
15 ml/1 tbsp icing (confectioners') sugar

Rub the butter or margarine into the
flour until the mixture resembles
breadcrumbs. Stir in half the sugar
and the hazelnuts, then add enough
of the water to make a firm pastry
(paste). Roll out and use to line an
18 cm/7 in loose-bottomed flan tin
(pie pan) and spread the apricots over
the base. Purée the lemon rind and
juice and cheeses in a food processor
or blender. Blend in the remaining
sugar, the cornflour and egg yolks
until smooth and creamy. Whisk the
egg whites until stiff, then fold them
into the mixture and spread it over
the flan. Bake in a preheated oven at
180°C/350°F/gas mark 5 for
30 minutes until well risen and golden
brown. Allow to cool slightly, then
sieve the icing sugar over the top and
serve warm or cold.

Honey and almond cake

MAKES ONE 20 CM/8 IN SQUARE CAKE

225 g/8 oz carrots, grated
75 g/3 oz/¾ cup almonds, chopped
2 eggs, beaten
100 ml/4 fl oz/½ cup clear honey
60 ml/4 tbsp oil
150 ml/¼ pt/⅔ cup milk
150 g/5 oz/1¼ cups wholemeal flour
10 ml/2 tsp salt
10 ml/2 tsp bicarbonate of soda (baking
soda)
15 ml/1 tbsp ground cinnamon
Lemon Glacé Icing (page 353) (optional)

Mix together the carrots and nuts.
Beat the eggs with the honey, oil and
milk, then mix into the carrot mixture.
Mix together the flour, salt,
bicarbonate of soda and cinnamon
and stir into the carrot mixture.
Spread the batter evenly in a greased
20 cm/8 in square cake tin (pan) and
bake in a preheated oven at 150°C/
300°F/gas mark 2 for 1¼ hours until
springy to the touch. Allow to cool in
the tin for 10 minutes, then turn out
on to a wire rack to finish cooling. Ice
when cool, if liked.

Dutch fried apple cake

MAKES ONE 20 CM/8 IN CAKE

100 g/4 oz/½ cup unsalted (sweet) butter
175 g/6 oz digestive biscuits (graham crackers), crushed
2 eating (dessert) apples, peeled, cored and sliced
100 g/4 oz/⅔ cup sultanas (golden raisins)
225 g/8 oz/2 cups Gouda or Edam (Dutch) cheese, finely grated
25 g/1 oz/¼ cup plain (all-purpose) flour
75 ml/5 tbsp single (light) cream
2.5 ml/½ tsp mixed (apple-pie) spice
Grated rind and juice of 1 lemon
3 eggs, separated
100 g/4 oz/½ cup caster (superfine) sugar
2 red-skinned eating (dessert) apples, sliced
30 ml/2 tbsp apricot jam (jelly), sieved (strained)

Melt half the butter in a saucepan and stir in the biscuit (cookie) crumbs. Press the mixture into the base of a loose-bottomed 20 cm/8 in cake tin (pan). Fry (sauté) the apples in the remaining butter until soft and golden. Drain off any excess fat, allow to cool slightly, then spread over the biscuit base and sprinkle with the sultanas. Mix together the cheese, flour, cream, spice and lemon rind and juice. Mix together the egg yolks and sugar, then stir into the cheese mixture until well blended. Whisk the egg whites until stiff, then fold them into the mixture. Turn the cheese mixture gently into the tin and bake in a preheated oven at 180°C/350°F/gas mark 4 for 40 minutes until firm. Cool in the tin on a wire rack. When cold, arrange the red-skinned apple slices in rings around the top of the cake. Warm the apricot jam until liquid, then brush it over the top.

Yorkshire parkin

MAKES ONE 15 CM/6 IN CAKE

100 g/4 oz/⅓ cup golden (light corn) syrup
30 ml/2 tbsp black treacle (molasses)
75 g/3 oz/⅓ cup butter or margarine
75 g/3 oz/⅓ cup soft brown sugar
175 g/6 oz/1¼ cups medium oatmeal
75 g/3 oz/¾ cup self-raising (self-rising) flour
5 ml/1 tsp ground ginger
A pinch of salt
1 egg, beaten
15 ml/1 tbsp milk

Gently heat the syrup, treacle, butter or margarine and sugar in a saucepan until the butter or margarine has melted. Remove from the heat and blend in the oatmeal, flour, ginger and salt. Add the egg and milk. Spoon into a greased and lined 15 cm/6 in square cake tin (pan) and bake in a preheated oven at 140°C/275°F/gas mark 1 for 1½ hours until springy to the touch. Leave on a wire rack to cool.

Carrot and almond cake

MAKES ONE 18 CM/7 IN CAKE

For the cake:
5 eggs, separated
200 g/7 oz/scant 1 cup soft brown sugar
15 ml/1 tbsp lemon juice
275 g/10 oz young carrots, grated
225 g/8 oz/2 cups ground almonds
25 g/1 oz/¼ cup wholemeal flour
5 ml/1 tsp ground cinnamon
For the topping:
25 g/1 oz/2 tbsp butter or margarine, melted
65 g/2½ oz/generous ¼ cup soft brown sugar
20 ml/1½ tbsp single (light) cream
75 g/3 oz/¾ cup chopped mixed nuts

To make the cake, beat the egg yolks until frothy. Beat in the sugar until smooth and creamy, then beat in the lemon juice. Beat in a third of the carrots, then a third of the almonds, and continue in this way until they are all included. Stir in the flour and cinnamon. Whisk the egg whites until stiff, then fold into the mixture. Turn the mixture into a greased and lined deep 18 cm/7 in cake tin (pan) and bake in a preheated oven at 180°C/ 350°F/gas mark 4 for 1 hour. Cover the cake loosely with greaseproof (waxed) paper and reduce the heat to 160°C/325°F/gas mark 3 for a further 15 minutes or until the cake shrinks slightly from the sides of the tin and the centre is still moist. Cool the cake in the tin until just warm, then turn out on to a wire rack to finish cooling.

To make the topping, combine the melted butter or margarine, sugar, cream and nuts. Cover the cake with this mixture and heat under the grill (broiler) until golden brown

Toffee-top cherry cake

MAKES ONE 20 CM/8 IN SQUARE CAKE

100 g/4 oz/1 cup almonds
225 g/8 oz/1 cup glacé (candied) cherries, halved
225 g/8 oz/1 cup butter or margarine
225 g/8 oz/1 cup caster (superfine) sugar
3 eggs, beaten
100 g/4 oz/1 cup self-raising (self-rising) flour
50 g/2 oz/½ cup ground almonds
5 ml/1 tsp baking powder
5 ml/1 tsp almond essence (extract)

Grease and line a 20 cm/8 in square cake tin (pan) and sprinkle the almonds and cherries over the base. Melt 50 g/2 oz/¼ cup of the butter or margarine with 50 g/2 oz/¼ cup of the sugar, then pour the mixture over the cherries and almonds. Beat the remaining butter or margarine and sugar until light and fluffy, then beat in the eggs and mix in the flour, ground almonds, baking powder and almond essence. Spoon the mixture into the tin and level the top. Bake in a preheated oven at 160°C/325°F/ gas mark 3 for 1 hour until springy to the touch. Allow to cool in the tin for a few minutes, then turn out carefully on to a wire rack to finish cooling, using the lining paper to help.

Apple cake

MAKES ONE 20 CM/8 IN CAKE

175 g/6 oz/1½ cups self-raising (self-rising) flour
5 ml/1 tsp baking powder
A pinch of salt
150 g/5 oz/⅔ cup caster (superfine) sugar
150 g/5 oz/⅔ cup butter or margarine
1 egg, beaten
175 ml/6 fl oz/¾ cup milk
3 eating (dessert) apples, peeled, cored and sliced
2.5 ml/½ tsp ground cinnamon
15 ml/1 tbsp clear honey

Mix together the flour, baking powder and salt, then stir in the sugar. Rub in the butter or margarine until the mixture resembles fine breadcrumbs. Mix in the egg and milk and pour the mixture into a greased 20 cm/8 in cake tin (pan). Press the apple slices into the top, sprinkle with the cinnamon and brush with the honey. Bake in a preheated oven at 200°C/400°F/gas mark 6 for 45 minutes until firm and golden.

Coconut and carrot cake

MAKES ONE 20 CM/8 IN CAKE

350 g/12 oz/3 cups wholemeal flour
5 ml/1 tsp baking powder
225 g/8 oz/1 cup soft brown sugar
5 ml/1 tsp ground cinnamon
2.5 ml/½ tsp grated nutmeg
350 g/12 oz carrots, grated
50 g/2 oz/½ cup desiccated (shredded) coconut
3 eggs, beaten
75 ml/5 tbsp milk
200 ml/7 fl oz/scant 1 cup oil
15 ml/1 tbsp icing (confectioners') sugar

Mix together the flour, baking powder, brown sugar, cinnamon and nutmeg. Stir in the carrots and coconut, then the eggs, milk and oil. Spoon into a greased and lined 20 cm/8 in loose-bottomed cake tin (pan) and bake in a preheated oven at 180°C/350°F/gas mark 4 for 1½ hours until firm. Leave to cool in the tin, then turn out and sprinkle with the icing sugar.

Banana cake

MAKES ONE 18 × 7.5 CM/8 × 3 IN CAKE

450 g/1 lb ripe bananas, mashed
50 g/2 oz/½ cup chopped mixed nuts
100 ml/4 fl oz/½ cup sunflower oil
100 g/4 oz/⅔ cup raisins
75 g/3 oz/¾ cup rolled oats
125 g/5 oz/1¼ cups wholemeal flour
2.5 ml/½ tsp almond essence (extract)
A pinch of salt

Mix together all the ingredients to a soft, moist mixture. Spoon into a greased 450 g/1 lb loaf tin (pan) and bake in a preheated oven at 190°C/375°F/gas mark 5 for 1 hour until firm and golden. Cool in the tin for 10 minutes before turning out.

Sticky treacle and cinnamon square

MAKES ONE 25 CM/10 IN SQUARE CAKE

100 g/4 oz/½ cup butter or margarine
175 g/6 oz/½ cup golden (light corn) syrup
175 g/6 oz/½ cup black treacle (molasses)
100 g/4 oz/½ cup soft brown sugar
275 g/10 oz/2½ cups plain (all-purpose) flour
10 ml/2 tsp ground cinnamon
5 ml/1 tsp bicarbonate of soda (baking soda)
2 eggs, beaten
150 ml/¼ pt/⅔ cup hot water

Melt the butter or margarine, syrup, treacle and sugar, then mix them into the flour, cinnamon and bicarbonate of soda. Beat in the eggs and hot water. Pour the mixture into a greased and lined 25 cm/10 in square cake tin (pan) and bake in a preheated oven at 180°C/350°F/gas mark 4 for 45 minutes until well risen and firm.

Honeyed rhubarb cake

MAKES TWO 450 G/1 LB CAKES

100 ml/4 fl oz/½ cup oil
225 g/8 oz/¾ cup clear honey
1 egg
15 ml/1 tbsp bicarbonate of soda (baking soda)
150 ml/¼ pt/⅔ cup plain yoghurt
350 g/12 oz/3 cups wholemeal flour
10 ml/2 tsp salt
350 g/12 oz rhubarb, finely chopped
5 ml/1 tsp vanilla essence (extract)
50 g/2 oz/½ cup chopped mixed nuts
75 g/3 oz/⅓ cup Muscovado sugar
5 ml/1 tsp ground cinnamon
25 g/1 oz/2 tbsp butter or margarine

Mix together the oil and honey, add the egg and beat well. Dissolve the bicarbonate of soda in the yoghurt, then add it to the honey mixture alternately with the flour and salt. Stir in the rhubarb, vanilla essence and nuts. Spoon into two greased 450 g/ 1 lb loaf tins (pans). Mix together the sugar, cinnamon and butter or margarine and spread over the cake mixture. Bake in a preheated oven at 170°C/325°F/gas mark 3 for 1 hour until firm and golden.

Cumberland cake

MAKES ONE 20 CM/8 IN CAKE

225 g/8 oz/1 cup lard (shortening) or vegetable fat
225 g/8 oz/1 cup caster (superfine) sugar
225 g/8 oz/⅔ cup golden (light corn) syrup
5 ml/1 tsp bicarbonate of soda (baking soda)
15 ml/1 tbsp milk
450 g/1 lb/4 cups plain (all-purpose) flour
2.5 ml/½ tsp ground cinnamon
5 ml/1 tsp ground ginger
225 g/8 oz/1⅓ cups currants
50 g/2 oz grated lemon rind
1 egg, beaten

Melt the lard or vegetable fat, sugar and syrup in a saucepan. Dissolve the bicarbonate of soda in the milk and stir into the syrup. Beat in the dry ingredients, then the egg and a little more milk if necessary to give a soft consistency. Turn the mixture into a greased 20 cm/8 in cake tin (pan) and bake in a preheated oven at 180°C/350°F/gas mark 4 for 2 hours until firm.

Traditional Christmas cake

MAKES ONE 23 CM/9 IN CAKE

350 g/12 oz/1½ cups butter or
   margarine, softened
350 g/12 oz/1½ cups soft brown sugar
6 eggs
450 g/1 lb/4 cups plain (all-purpose)
   flour
A pinch of salt
5 ml/1 tsp mixed (apple-pie) spice
225 g/8 oz/1⅓ cups raisins
450 g/1 lb/2⅔ cups sultanas (golden
   raisins)
225 g/8 oz/1⅓ cups currants
175 g/6 oz/1 cup chopped mixed
   (candied) peel
50 g/2 oz /¼ cup glacé (candied)
   cherries, chopped
100 g/4 oz/1 cup almonds, chopped
30 ml/2 tbsp black treacle (molasses)
45 ml/3 tbsp brandy
Almond paste (see Marzipan Petit Fours,
   page 396) and Royal Icing (page
   354), to decorate (optional)

Cream the butter or margarine and
sugar until soft, then beat in the
eggs, one at a time. Fold in the flour,
salt and spice, then mix in the
remaining ingredients. Spoon into a
greased and lined 23 cm/9 in cake tin
(pan) and bake at 140°C/275°F/gas
mark 1 for 6½ hours. Leave to cool
completely, then wrap in foil and store
in an airtight container for at least
3 weeks before covering with almond
paste and decorating with Royal Icing,
if liked.

Cherry cobblestone cake

MAKES ONE 900 G/2 LB LOAF CAKE

175 g/6 oz/¾ cup soft margarine
175 g/6 oz/¾ cup caster (superfine)
   sugar
3 eggs, beaten
225 g/8 oz/2 cups plain (all-purpose)
   flour
2.5 ml/½ tsp baking powder
100 g/4 oz/⅔ cup sultanas (golden
   raisins)
125 g/5 oz/⅔ cup glacé (candied)
   cherries, quartered
225 g/8 oz fresh cherries, halved
30 ml/2 tbsp apricot jam (jelly)

Beat the margarine until soft, then
beat in the sugar. Mix in the eggs,
then the flour, baking powder,
sultanas and glacé cherries. Spoon
into a greased 900 g/2 lb loaf tin
(pan) and bake in a preheated oven
at 170°C/325°F/gas mark 3 for
2½ hours until a skewer inserted in
the centre comes out clean. Leave in
the tin for 5 minutes, then turn out
on to a wire rack to cool. Arrange the
fresh cherries in a row on top of the
cake. Boil the apricot jam, then sieve
(strain) it and brush it over the top of
the cake to glaze.

Dundee cake

MAKES ONE 20 CM/8 IN CAKE

225 g/8 oz/1 cup butter or margarine
225 g/8 oz/1 cup caster (superfine)
sugar
4 eggs, beaten
225 g/8 oz/2 cups plain (all-purpose)
flour
A pinch of salt
350 g/12 oz/2 cups sultanas (golden
raisins)
350 g/12 oz/2 cups currants
175 g/6 oz/1 cup chopped mixed
(candied) peel
100 g/4 oz/½ cup glacé (candied)
cherries, chopped
Grated rind of ½ lemon
75 g/3 oz/¾ cup whole almonds

Cream the butter or margarine and
sugar until light and fluffy. Beat in the
eggs, one at a time, then fold in the
flour and salt. Mix in the sultanas,
currants, peel, glacé cherries and
lemon rind. Chop 25 g/1 oz/¼ cup of
the almonds and mix them into the
cake. Split the remaining almonds.
Spoon the mixture into a greased and
lined 20 cm/8 in cake tin (pan) and
arrange the almonds, rounded-side
up, over the cake. Tie a band of
brown paper round the tin extending
5 cm/2 in above the top and bake in
a preheated oven at 150°C/300°F/
gas mark 3 for 2½ hours until a
skewer inserted in the centre comes
out clean. Reduce the heat to 140°C/
275°F/gas mark 1 and cook for a
further 1 hour, covering the cake with
a sheet of greaseproof (waxed) paper
if it begins to brown too quickly. Allow
to cool in the tin for 30 minutes, then
turn out on to a wire rack to finish
cooling. The cake is best kept in an
airtight container for two weeks before
eating.

Sugar-free fruit cake

MAKES ONE 18 CM/7 IN CAKE

175 g/6 oz/1½ cups plain (all-purpose)
flour
175 g/6 oz/1½ cups wholemeal flour
10 ml/2 tsp baking powder
5 ml/1 tsp mixed (apple-pie) spice
100 g/4 oz/½ cup butter or margarine
75 g/3 oz/½ cup currants
75 g/3 oz/½ cup raisins
75 g/3 oz/½ cup dates, stoned (pitted)
and chopped
1 ripe banana, mashed
2 eggs, beaten
60 ml/4 tbsp orange juice

Mix together the flours, baking
powder and spice and rub in the
butter or margarine. Stir in the fruit
and eggs and add enough of the
orange juice to make a soft dropping
consistency. Spoon into a greased
18 cm/7 in cake tin (pan) and bake in
a preheated oven at 180°C/350°F/
gas mark 4 for 1¼ hours until springy
to the touch.

Quick chocolate krispies

MAKES 20

3 Mars bars, cut into pieces
75 g/3 oz/⅓ cup butter or margarine
75 g/3 oz crisp rice cereal

Melt the Mars bars and butter or
margarine and stir in the cereal. Place
spoonfuls into cake cases, or press
the mixture into a
20 cm/8 in square tin (pan). Allow to
cool, then cut into squares.

Variation:
If you make the square cake, cover it
with melted chocolate and allow to set
before cutting into squares.

Sweetheart cake

MAKES TWO 20 CM/8 IN SQUARE CAKES

450 g/1 lb Puff Pastry (page 165)
450 g/1 lb/2⅔ cups currants
Juice of 1 lemon
50 g/2 oz/¼ cup soft brown sugar
50 g/2 oz/¼ cup butter or hard block
   margarine, grated
Water
30 ml/2 tbsp caster (superfine) sugar

Divide the pastry (paste) into four equal pieces, roll out on a lightly floured surface and use two pieces to line two greased 20 cm/8 in square cake tins (pans). Sprinkle with the currants. Mix the lemon juice with the brown sugar and sprinkle over the currants. Cover with the butter, then top with the remaining pastry, sealing the edges together. Brush the pastry lids with cold water, sprinkle generously with caster sugar and bake in a preheated oven at 200°C/420°F/ gas mark 7 for 30 minutes until the tops are lightly browned.

Almond macaroons

MAKES 20

100 g/4 oz/1 cup ground almonds
175 g/6 oz/¾ cup caster (superfine)
   sugar
2 egg whites
A few drops of vanilla essence (extract)
10 whole almonds, split

Mix together the ground almonds and sugar. Whisk the egg whites until stiff, then fold in the sugar and almonds and the vanilla essence. Shape into small balls and place on a greased baking tray lined with rice paper. Flatten each ball slightly and place a split almond on top. Bake in a preheated oven at 180°C/350°F/gas

mark 4 for 20 minutes until golden brown round the edges and slightly moist in the centre.

Apple and blackcurrant crumble bars

MAKES 20

175 g/6 oz/1½ cups plain (all-purpose)
   flour
5 ml/1 tsp baking powder
2.5 ml/½ tsp salt
175 g/6 oz/¾ cup butter or margarine
225 g/8 oz/1 cup soft brown sugar
100 g/4 oz/1 cup rolled oats
225 g/8 oz blackcurrants
450 g/1 lb cooking (tart) apples, peeled,
   cored and chopped
30 ml/2 tbsp cornflour (cornstarch)
10 ml/2 tsp ground cinnamon
2.5 ml/½ tsp grated nutmeg
2.5 ml/½ tsp allspice

Mix together the flour, baking powder and salt and rub in the butter or margarine. Mix in the sugar and oats and press half the mixture into a greased 33 × 23 cm/13 × 9 in baking tin (pan). Top with the blackcurrants. Mix together the apples, cornflour and spices and spread over the blackcurrants. Top with the remaining mixture and bake in a preheated oven at 180°C/350°F/ gas mark 4 for 35 minutes. Leave in the tin to cool before cutting into bars.

Bakewell fingers

MAKES 16

175 g/6 oz/¾ cup butter or margarine
25 g/1 oz/2 tbsp lard (shortening) or
   vegetable fat
175 g/6 oz/1½ cups plain (all-purpose)
   flour
45 ml/ tbsp water
30 ml/2 tbsp raspberry jam (jelly)
100 g/4 oz/½ cup caster (superfine)
   sugar
2 eggs, beaten
50 g/2 oz/½ cup ground almonds
100 g/4 oz/1 cup self-raising (self-rising)
   flour
25 g/1 oz/3 tbsp icing (confectioners')
   sugar

Rub 50 g/2 oz/¼ cup of the butter or margarine and the all lard or vegetable fat into the plain flour until the mixture resembles breadcrumbs. Mix in just enough of the water to make a firm pastry (paste), roll it out on a lightly floured surface and use to line a greased Swiss roll tin (jelly roll pan). Spread the jam over the pastry. Beat the remaining butter or margarine until soft, then beat in the sugar, followed by the eggs, ground almonds and self-raising flour. Spoon the mixture into the tin, covering the jam and pastry completely. Roll out the pastry trimmings and cut into long strips. Twist these and lay them over the top of the sponge mixture. Bake in a preheated oven at 190°C/375°F/gas mark 5 for 25 minutes until golden. Allow to cool slightly, then cut into fingers and leave in the tin to cool completely. Mix the icing sugar with enough water to make a smooth paste and pipe icing lines over the fingers.

Date slices

MAKES 16

225 g/8 oz/1⅓ cups dates, stoned
   (pitted) and chopped
30 ml/2 tbsp clear honey
30 ml/2 tbsp lemon juice
225 g/8 oz/2 cups wholemeal flour
225 g/8 oz/2 cups rolled oats
225 g/8 oz/1 cup butter or margarine
75 g/3 oz/⅓ cup soft brown sugar

Put the dates, honey and lemon juice in a saucepan and simmer gently until the dates are soft. Allow to cool slightly. Mix together the flour and oats, rub in the butter or margarine and mix in the sugar. Press half the flour mixture into a greased and lined shallow 20 cm/8 in square tin (pan), spread the date mixture on top, then cover with the remaining flour mixture and press down firmly. Bake in a preheated oven at 190°C/ 370°F/gas mark 5 for 35 minutes. Cut into slices while still warm, then leave to cool in the tin.

Flapjacks

MAKES 16

75 g/3 oz/⅓ cup butter or margarine
50 g/2 oz/3 tbsp golden (light corn)
   syrup
100 g/4 oz/½ cup soft brown sugar
175 g/6 oz/¾ cup rolled oats

Melt the butter or margarine with the syrup, then mix into the sugar and oats. Press into a greased 20 cm/8 in shallow square tin (pan) and bake in a preheated oven at 180°C/350°F/gas mark 4 for 20 minutes. Cut into fingers while still warm.

Chocolate éclairs

MAKES 12

50 g/2 oz/¼ cup butter or margarine
75 ml/5 tbsp milk
75 ml/5 tbsp water
50 g/2 oz/½ cup plain (all-purpose) flour
A pinch of salt
2 eggs, beaten
300 ml/½ pt/1¼ cups double (heavy)
 cream, whipped
225 g/8 oz Chocolate Glacé Icing
 (page 353)

Melt the butter or margarine with the milk and water over a low heat, then turn up the heat and bring to the boil. Remove from the heat and stir in the flour and salt, then beat just until the pastry (paste) comes away from the side of the pan. Cool slightly, then beat in the eggs a little at a time. Spoon the mixture into a piping bag with a 1 cm/ ½ in plain nozzle (icing tip) and pipe lengths on to a greased baking (cookie) sheet. Bake in a preheated oven at 220°C/425°F/gas mark 7 for 20 minutes. Remove from the oven and slit the éclairs lengthways to allow the steam to escape, then leave to cool. When cool, fill with the whipped cream and top with Chocolate Glacé Icing.

Cider squares

MAKES 16

225 g/8 oz1⅓ cups sultanas (golden
 raisins)
150 ml/¼ pt/⅔ cup dry cider
100 g/4 oz/½ cup butter or margarine
100 g/4 oz/½ cup soft brown sugar
2 eggs, beaten
225 g/8 oz/2 cups plain (all-purpose)
 flour
5 ml/1 tsp bicarbonate of soda (baking
 soda)

Soak the sultanas in the cider overnight. Cream the butter or margarine and sugar until pale and fluffy, then beat in the eggs, half the flour and the bicarbonate of soda. Mix in the sultanas and cider, then fold in the remaining flour. Pour into a greased 18 cm/7 in square cake tin (pan) and bake in a preheated oven at 180°C/350°F/gas mark 4 for 1 hour until well risen and firm. Allow to cool in the tin for 30 minutes, then turn out on to a wire rack to finish cooling. Cut into squares when cool.

American muffins

MAKES 12

225 g/8 oz/2 cups plain (all-purpose)
 flour
100 g/4 oz/½ cup caster (superfine)
 sugar
10 ml/2 tsp baking powder
2.5 ml/½ tsp salt
1 egg
250 ml/8 fl oz/1 cup milk
120 ml/4 fl oz/½ cup oil

Mix together the flour, sugar, baking powder and salt. Beat together the egg, milk and oil. Make a well in the centre of the dry ingredients, pour in the egg mixture and stir together just until the dry ingredients are mixed in. The mixture should still be lumpy. Spoon into greased muffin tins (pans) and bake in a preheated oven at 200°C/400°F/ gas mark 6 for 20 minutes until well risen and springy to the touch.

Chocolate chip muffins

MAKES 12

175 g/6 oz/1½ cups plain (all-purpose) flour
40 g/1½ oz cocoa (unsweetened chocolate) powder
100 g/4 oz/½ cup caster (superfine) sugar
10 ml/2 tsp baking powder
2.5 ml/½ tsp salt
100 g/4 oz/1 cup chocolate chips
1 egg
250 ml/8 fl oz/1 cup milk
120 ml/4 fl oz/½ cup oil
2.5 ml/½ tsp vanilla essence (extract)

Mix together the flour, cocoa, sugar, baking powder, salt and chocolate chips. Beat together the egg, milk, oil and vanilla essence. Make a well in the centre of the dry ingredients, pour in the egg mixture and stir together until well mixed but still lumpy. Spoon into greased muffin tins (pans) and bake in a preheated oven at 200°C/ 400°F/gas mark 6 for 20 minutes until well risen and springy to the touch.

Blueberry muffins

MAKES 12

225 g/8 oz/2 cups plain (all-purpose) flour
100 g/4 oz/½ cup caster (superfine) sugar
10 ml/2 tsp baking powder
2.5 ml/½ tsp salt
2.5 ml/½ tsp ground cinnamon
200 g/7 oz fresh or thawed frozen blueberries
1 egg
250 ml/8 fl oz/1 cup milk
120 ml/4 fl oz/½ cup sunflower oil

Mix together the flour, sugar, baking powder, salt and cinnamon. Stir in the blueberries and make a well in the centre of the mixture. Mix together the egg, milk and oil and pour into the dry ingredients. Stir the ingredients just until the dry ingredients are mixed in. The mixture should still be lumpy. Spoon into greased muffin tins (pans) and bake in a preheated oven at 200°C/400°F/ gas mark 6 for 20 minutes until well risen and golden.

Chocolate fingers

MAKES 20

100 g/4 oz/½ cup soft margarine
100 g/4 oz/½ cup caster (superfine) sugar
100 g/4 oz/1 cup self-raising (self-rising) flour
2 eggs, beaten
50 g/2 oz/½ cup plain (semi-sweet) chocolate
15 ml/1 tbsp golden (light corn) syrup
50 g/2 oz/⅓ cup icing (confectioners') sugar
30 ml/2 tbsp hot water

Beat the margarine until soft, then beat in the caster sugar, then the flour and finally the eggs. Turn the mixture into a greased and floured Swiss roll tin (jelly roll pan) and bake in a preheated oven at 180°C/350°F/gas mark 4 for 20 minutes. Melt the chocolate in a small bowl over a saucepan of hot water. Stir in the syrup and icing sugar and mix well. Add enough of the hot water to make the mixture smooth and thick. Spread the warm icing (frosting) on the cake and mark with a fork to make a pattern. Cut the cake into fingers with a bread knife dipped in hot water.

Fudge-topped chocolate brownies

MAKES 16

For the brownies:
225 g/8 oz/1 cup granulated sugar
3 eggs
75 ml/5 tbsp oil
5 ml/1 tsp vanilla essence (extract)
100 g/4 oz/1 cup plain (all-purpose)
    flour
A pinch of baking powder
A pinch of salt
50 g/2 oz/¼ cup cocoa (unsweetened
    chocolate) powder
100 g/4 oz/1 cup walnuts, chopped
For the fudge topping:
225 g/8 oz/1 cup soft brown sugar
75 ml/5 tbsp double (heavy) cream
25 g/1 oz/2 tbsp butter or margarine
A pinch of salt
A few drops of vanilla essence (extract)

To make the brownies, beat together
the sugar, eggs, oil and vanilla
essence. Sieve the flour, baking
powder, salt and the cocoa into the
mixture, add the walnuts and beat all
together for 1 minute. Pour the
mixture into a greased and lined
20 cm/8 in square cake tin (pan) and
bake in a preheated oven at 180°C/
350°F/gas mark 4 for 30 minutes
until just firm. Leave to cool in the tin.

To make the fudge topping, put the
sugar, cream, butter or margarine and
salt in a saucepan and dissolve over a
low heat, stirring, then bring to the
boil. Remove from the heat, stir in the
vanilla essence and beat well until
thick. Spread over the brownies, leave
to set, then cut into squares.

Special frangipan tartlets

MAKES 24

150 g/5 oz/⅔ cup butter or margarine
200 g/7 oz/1¾ cups plain (all-purpose)
    flour
10 ml/2 tsp grated orange rind
30 ml/2 tbsp orange juice
50 g/2 oz/¼ cup caster (superfine) sugar
1 egg
25 g/1 oz/¼ cup ground almonds
100 g/4 oz/⅔ cup icing (confectioners')
    sugar, sifted
15 ml/1 tbsp water
12 glacé (candied) cherries, halved

Rub 75 g/3 oz/⅓ cup of the butter or
margarine into 175 g/6 oz/1½ cups of
the flour until the mixture resembles
breadcrumbs. Mix in the orange rind,
then bind with the juice until the
mixture forms a pastry (paste). Roll
out on a lightly floured surface, cut
into rounds and line 24 greased bun
tins (patty pans). Cream the
remaining butter or margarine with
the caster sugar, mix in the egg, then
the remaining flour and the ground
almonds. Divide the mixture between
the pastry cases and bake in a
preheated oven at 200°C/400°F/gas
mark 6 for 15 minutes. Leave to cool.
Put the icing sugar in a bowl and
gradually mix in the water a drop at a
time to make a smooth icing. Spread
over the cakes and top each one with
half a cherry.

Icings, frostings and fillings

Here are all the basic recipes you need for a range of cake icings (frostings) and fillings as well as some more unusual options that are ideal for jazzing up a plain cake or making a special cake that bit more special.

Butter icing

MAKES 350 G/12 OZ/1½ CUPS

100 g/4 oz/½ cup butter or margarine
225 g/8 oz/1⅓ cup icing (confectioners')
 sugar, sifted
10 ml/2 tsp hot water

Beat the butter or margarine until soft, then beat in the icing sugar. Add 5 ml/1 tsp of the hot water and mix again, adding the remainder if necessary to make the icing (frosting) soft enough to spread or pipe. Depending on the fat you use, you may need to add a little more icing sugar.

Orange butter icing

MAKES 350 G/12 OZ/1½ CUPS

Prepare as for Butter Icing, but substitute orange juice for the water and add 15 ml/1 tbsp finely grated orange rind.

Lemon butter icing

MAKES 350 G/12 OZ/1½ CUPS

Prepare as for Butter Icing, but substitute lemon juice for the water and add 15 ml/1 tbsp finely grated lemon rind.

Chocolate butter icing

MAKES 350 G/12 OZ/1½ CUPS

Prepare as for Butter Icing, but dissolve 30 ml/2 tbsp cocoa (unsweetened chocolate) powder in the hot water.

Coffee butter icing

MAKES 350 G/12 OZ/1½ CUPS

Prepare as for Butter Icing, but substitute strong coffee for the water.

Rich butter icing

FILLS AND ICES ONE 20 CM/8 IN CAKE

50 g/2 oz/¼ cup butter or margarine,
 softened
A pinch of salt
75 ml/5 tbsp double (heavy) cream
450 g/1 lb/2⅔ cups icing (confectioners')
 sugar
5 ml/1 tsp vanilla essence (extract)

Cream the butter or margarine with the salt. Warm the cream, but do not allow it to boil. Beat the warm cream into the butter alternately with the sugar, blending well. Beat in the vanilla essence and continue beating until the icing (frosting) is cold, creamy and thick enough to spread.

Caramel icing

COVERS ONE 20 CM/8 IN CAKE

75 g/3 oz/⅓ cup butter or margarine
75 ml/5 tbsp single (light) cream
25 g/1 oz/2 tbsp caster (superfine) sugar
175 g/6 oz/1 cup icing (confectioners')
 sugar

Melt the butter or margarine with the cream in a saucepan. Heat the caster sugar gently in another saucepan until it turns golden brown. Pour the cream mixture into the caster sugar and heat, stirring, until the caramel has dissolved. Beat in the icing sugar until smooth, then use the icing (frosting) immediately.

Almond stollen (page 325)

Chocolate icing

COVERS THE TOPS OF 2 × 20 CM/8 IN CAKES

50 g/2 oz/½ cup plain (semi-sweet)
  chocolate, grated
15 ml/1 tbsp milk
275 g/10 oz/1⅔ cups icing
  (confectioners') sugar
100 g/4 oz/½ cup butter or margarine,
  softened
A few drops of vanilla essence (extract)

Place the chocolate in a bowl over a
pan of hot water, add the milk and stir
until the chocolate has melted, then
leave to cool. Gradually beat in the
icing sugar, then beat in the butter or
margarine and vanilla essence and use
the icing (frosting) at once.

Glacé icing

MAKES 100 G/4 OZ/½ CUP

100 g/4 oz/½ cup icing (confectioners')
  sugar
15 ml/1 tbsp hot water
A few drops of flavouring (optional)
A few drops of food colouring (optional)

Sift the icing sugar into a bowl and
add the water, a few drops at a time,
until the icing is smooth. Add
flavouring and colouring to taste, if
using, mixing in a little more icing
sugar if necessary. Pour over the cake
and spread with a knife dipped in hot
water. Do not move the cake until the
icing (frosting) has set.

Almond glacé icing

MAKES 100 G/4 OZ/½ CUP

Prepare as for Glacé Icing, but add a
few drops of almond essence (extract)
and a few drops of lemon juice.

Lemon glacé icing

MAKES 100 G/4 OZ/½ CUP

Prepare as for Glacé Icing, but add
5 ml/1 tsp grated lemon rind, a few
drops of lemon juice and a few drops
of yellow food colouring (optional).

Orange glacé icing

MAKES 100 G/4 OZ/½ CUP

Prepare as for Glacé Icing, but add
5 ml/1 tsp grated orange rind, a few
drops of orange juice and a few drops
of orange food colouring (optional).

Pineapple glacé icing

MAKES 100 G/4 OZ/½ CUP

Prepare as for Glacé Icing, but add a
few drops of pineapple essence
(extract) and a few drops of yellow
food colouring (optional).

Chocolate glacé icing

MAKES 100 G/4 OZ/½ CUP

Prepare as for Glacé Icing, but blend
10 ml/2 tsp cocoa (unsweetened
chocolate) powder with 15 ml/1 tbsp
water and mix into the icing (frosting).

*Carrot and almond cake (page 341)
and Muesli biscuits (page 365)*

Fondant icing

COVERS ONE 18 CM/7 IN CAKE

350 g/12 oz/2 cups icing (confectioners')
  sugar, plus extra for dusting
15 ml/1 tbsp liquid glucose
1 egg white
Cornflour (cornstarch), for dusting

Sift the icing sugar into a bowl, make a well in the centre and mix in the glucose with a palette knife, then with the hands. Turn out on to a work surface sprinkled with icing sugar and work into a ball.

It is best to use the icing (frosting), on a cake already covered with Almond Paste (page 356). Roll out the icing on a work surface sprinkled with icing sugar until it is 7 cm/3 in larger than the cake. Brush the almond paste with egg white. Lift the icing and mould it over the cake with fingers dipped in a mixture of cornflour and icing sugar. Trim the edges to neaten.

Royal icing

COVERS THE TOP AND SIDES OF ONE
20 CM/8 IN CAKE

5 ml/1 tsp lemon juice
2 egg whites
450 g/1 lb/2⅔ cups icing (confectioners')
  sugar
A few drops of glycerine (optional)
2 drops of blue food colouring (optional)

Mix together the lemon juice and egg whites and gradually beat in the icing sugar until the icing (frosting) is smooth and white and will coat the back of a spoon. Add the glycerine, if wished, to prevent the icing becoming too brittle. A very little blue food colouring will prevent the icing developing a yellowish tinge when stored. Cover with a damp cloth and leave to stand for 20 minutes to allow any air bubbles to rise to the surface.

Note:
This consistency can be poured on to the cake and smoothed with a knife dipped in hot water. For piping, mix in extra icing sugar until the icing is stiff enough to stand in peaks.

American frosting

COVERS ONE 15 CM/6 IN CAKE

175 g/6 oz/¾ cup granulated sugar
30 ml/2 tbsp water
A pinch of cream of tartar
1 egg white
A few drops of flavouring (optional)
A few drops of food colouring (optional)

Put the sugar and water in a large bowl over a pan of hot water and stir until the sugar dissolves. Remove the bowl from the pan and add the cream of tartar and egg white. Return the bowl to the pan over the heat and bring to the boil. Whisk for 5 minutes or until the mixture forms peaks. Take the bowl off the pan and add flavouring and colouring, if liked. Continue whisking until the frosting has a thick consistency, then spread on the cake with a round-bladed knife.

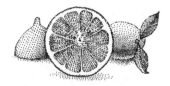

Cherry and nut frosting

FILLS AND COVERS ONE
20 CM/8 IN CAKE

25 g/1 oz/3 tbsp raisins, chopped
25 g/1 oz/2 tbsp glacé (candied)
 cherries, chopped
25 g/1 oz/¼ cup chopped mixed nuts
2 dried figs, chopped
1 egg white
175 g/6 oz/¾ cup caster (superfine)
 sugar
A pinch of cream of tartar
30 ml/2 tbsp cold water
A pinch of salt
2.5 ml/½ tsp vanilla essence (extract)

Mix together the raisins, cherries, nuts and figs. Place the egg white, sugar, cream of tartar, water and salt in a bowl over a pan of boiling water and beat for about 7 minutes until the mixture forms soft peaks. Remove from the heat and beat in the vanilla essence. Combine 150 ml/¼ pt/ ⅔ cup of the frosting with the fruit and nuts and use to fill a plain cake. Use the remaining frosting to cover the top and sides of the cake.

Chocolate frosting

COVERS ONE 20 CM/8 IN CAKE

25 g/1 oz/¼ cup plain (semi-sweet)
 chocolate, grated
30 ml/2 tbsp single (light) cream
75 g/3 oz/½ cup icing (confectioners')
 sugar

Stand the chocolate in a bowl over a pan of hot water, add the cream and stir until all the chocolate has melted. Add the sugar and whisk until smooth. Spread over the cake while warm, then allow to set.

Honey butter frosting

COVERS ONE 20 CM/8 IN CAKE

75 g/3 oz/⅓ cup butter or margarine
175 g/6 oz/1 cup icing (confectioners')
 sugar
15 ml/1 tbsp clear honey
15 ml/1 tbsp lemon juice

Beat the butter or margarine until soft, then beat in half the icing sugar. Beat in the honey and lemon juice, followed by the remaining icing sugar until you have a soft icing that will form peaks when spread over the cake.

Apricot topping

COVERS ONE 20 CM/8 IN CAKE

450 g/1 lb/2½ cups no-need-to-soak
 dried apricots, chopped
1 thin slice of lemon rind, chopped
60 ml/4 tbsp clear honey

Mix together all the ingredients in a saucepan and heat gently for about 5 minutes until the honey has dissolved and the fruit is juicy. Purée the mixture in a food processor or blender. Return to the saucepan and cook gently for 8 minutes, stirring to prevent the topping burning. Leave to cool and store in an airtight jar in the fridge. Use to sandwich together or spread over the top of plain cakes.

Butterscotch topping

COVERS ONE 20 CM/8 IN CAKE

150 g/5 oz/scant ½ cup clear honey
60 ml/4 tbsp water
25 g/1 oz/2 tbsp butter or margarine
50 g/2 oz/½ cup chopped mixed nuts,
    finely chopped or ground

Boil the honey and water together over a low heat to 112°C/234°F or until a drop in cold water forms a soft ball. Remove from the heat and stir in the butter or margarine and nuts. Leave to cool slightly before spreading over plain or chocolate cakes.

Melba topping

MAKES 450 ML/¾ PT/2 CUPS

900 g/2 lb raspberries
100 g/4 oz/⅓ cup clear honey
120 ml/4 fl oz/½ cup water

Rub the raspberries through a sieve (strainer), then put to one side. Boil the honey and water together gently for 12 minutes, then add the raspberries and cook for 1 minute. Leave to cool, then chill before using spread over plain cakes or drizzled over ice cream.

Blender cream

MAKES 300 ML/½ PT/1¼ CUPS

150 ml/¼ pt/⅔ cup milk
150 g/5 oz/⅔ cup unsalted (sweet)
    butter, diced

Place the milk in a saucepan, add the butter and heat gently until the butter melts, but do not allow the mixture to boil. Pour into a food processor or blender and blend well. Pour into a jug, cover and chill in the fridge for several hours or overnight before use.

Almond paste

COVERS TOP AND SIDES OF ONE
23 CM/9 IN CAKE

175 g/6 oz/¾ cup caster (superfine)
    sugar
175 g/6 oz/1 cup icing (confectioners')
    sugar
350 g/12 oz/3 cups ground almonds
2 eggs, beaten
A few drops of almond essence (extract)
5 ml/½ tsp lemon juice

Mix the sugars together and stir in the almonds. Make a well in the centre and beat in the eggs, one at a time. Add the almond essence and lemon juice and knead the paste until smooth. Wrap in clingfilm (plastic wrap) if not being used at once.

Confectioners' custard

MAKES 350 ML/12 FL OZ/1⅓ CUPS

25 g/1 oz/2 tbsp butter or margarine
25 g/1 oz/¼ cup plain (all-purpose) flour
300 ml/½ pt/1¼ cups milk
50 g/2 oz/¼ cup caster (superfine) sugar
1 egg
1 egg yolk
A pinch of salt
A few drops of vanilla essence (extract)

Melt the butter or margarine in a saucepan, stir in the flour and cook for 1 minute. Whisk in the milk and cook, stirring, for 5 minutes until the sauce is smooth and glossy. Remove from the heat, add the sugar and beat for a few minutes, then add the remaining ingredients. Beat the custard well and cook without boiling until very thick. Leave to cool.

Rum butter

MAKES 225 G/8 OZ/1 CUP

100 g/4 oz/½ cup butter or margarine,
  diced
100 g/4 oz/½ cup light brown sugar
10 ml/2 tsp rum or brandy

Beat the butter or margarine and
sugar with a wooden spoon or process
in a food processor or blender until
smooth. Beat in the rum until the
mixture is soft and light. Store in
small jars or tubs.

Brandy butter

MAKES 225 G/8 OZ/1 CUP

Prepare as for Rum Butter, but
substitute brandy for the rum.

Rich brandy and orange butter

MAKES 450 G/1 LB

100 g/4 oz/½ cup butter or margarine
350 g/12 oz/1½ cups light brown sugar
1 egg yolk
Grated rind of 1 orange
120 ml/4 fl oz/½ cup brandy

Beat the butter or margarine and
sugar with a wooden spoon or process
in a food processor or blender until
smooth, then beat in the remaining
ingredients until creamy. Store in the
fridge for up to three weeks.

Biscuits, cookies and scones

Quick and easy to make, home-made biscuits (cookies) make a great impression on guests and are good fun to try. They rarely last long, so the fact that they are best eaten fresh is not really a problem. You can freeze them in a hard container, separated by sheets of greaseproof (waxed) paper, or you can make up a quantity of mixture and freeze it ready for baking.

Scones (biscuits) are always best eaten fresh, so there's no substitute for home-made.

Iced chocolate biscuits

MAKES 24

225 g/8 oz/1 cup caster (superfine) sugar
175 g/6 oz/1½ cups ground almonds
75 g/3 oz/¾ cup plain (semi-sweet) chocolate, grated
2 egg whites
100 g/4 oz/1 cup icing (confectioners') sugar
15 ml/1 tbsp cocoa (unsweetened chocolate) powder
15 ml/1 tbsp hot water

Mix together the caster sugar, almonds and chocolate. Whisk the egg whites until stiff, then fold them into the mixture. Place spoonfuls of the mixture on a greased baking (cookie) sheet and bake in a preheated oven at 180°C/350°F/gas mark 4 for 10 minutes. Transfer to a wire rack to cool. When the biscuits (cookies) are cool, sift together the icing sugar and cocoa and mix to a glacé icing with the hot water. Spread over the biscuits and leave to set.

Chocolate mint squares

MAKES 16

50 g/2 oz/¼ cup butter or margarine
50 g/2 oz/3 tbsp golden (light corn) syrup
50 g/2 oz/¼ cup soft soft brown sugar
100 g/4 oz/1 cup plain (semi-sweet) chocolate
100 g/4 oz crisp rice cereal
175 g/6 oz marshmallows
A few drops of peppermint essence (extract)

Melt the butter or margarine, syrup, sugar and chocolate over a low heat. Stir in the cereal. Melt the marsh-mallows in a separate pan and add peppermint essence to taste. Press half the cereal mixture into the base of a 20 cm/8 in square baking tin (pan). Spread the mint marshmallow over the top, then cover with the remaining cereal mixture. Chill until firm, then cut into squares.

Chocolate biscuits

MAKES 24

30 ml/2 tbsp cocoa (unsweetened chocolate) powder
60 ml/4 tbsp boiling water
200 g/7 oz/scant 1 cup butter or margarine
175 g/3 oz/⅓ cup caster (superfine) sugar
225 g/8 oz/2 cups self-raising (self-rising) flour
75 g/3 oz/¾ cup desiccated (shredded) coconut
225 g/8 oz cornflakes, crushed
75 g/3 oz/¾ cup milk (sweet) chocolate

Dissolve the cocoa in the boiling water, then allow to cool slightly while you cream together the butter or margarine and sugar until soft. Work in the flour, coconut and cornflake crumbs. Roll into 7.5 cm/3 in balls, place on a greased baking (cookie) sheet and press flat with a fork. Bake in a preheated oven at 180°C/350°F/gas mark 4 for 15 minutes until firming around the edges, then remove from the oven and place on a wire rack. Melt the chocolate in a heatproof bowl set over a pan of simmering water. Sandwich the biscuits (cookies) together with the melted chocolate.

No-bake chocolate biscuits

MAKES 24

120 ml/4 fl oz/½ cup milk
50 g/2 oz/½ cup cocoa (unsweetened chocolate) powder
225 g/8 oz/1 cup butter or margarine
450 g/1 lb/2 cups caster (superfine) sugar
225 g/8 oz/2 cups rolled oats
50 g/2 oz/½ cup desiccated (shredded) coconut
A pinch of salt
5 ml/1 tsp vanilla essence (extract)

Place the milk, cocoa, butter or margarine and sugar in a saucepan and bring to the boil, then simmer for 5 minutes. Remove from the heat and stir in the remaining ingredients until well blended. Drop 5 ml/1 tsp quantities of the mixture on to a greased baking sheet and allow to cool. Store the biscuits (cookies) in the fridge.

Orange and chocolate chip cookies

MAKES 30

50 g/2 oz/¼ cup butter or margarine
75 g/3 oz/⅓ cup lard (shortening) or vegetable fat
175 g/6 oz/¾ cup soft brown sugar
200 g/7 oz/1¾ cups wholemeal flour
75 g/3 oz/¾ cup ground almonds or hazelnuts (filberts)
10 ml/2 tsp baking powder
75 g/3 oz/¾ cup chocolate chips
Grated rind of 2 oranges
15 ml/1 tbsp orange juice
1 egg, beaten
30 ml/2 tbsp demerara sugar

Beat the fats with the sugar until soft, then add all the remaining ingredients

except the demerara sugar and mix well. Roll out on a lightly floured surface, cut into 5 cm/2 in rounds and sprinkle with the demerara sugar. Bake in a preheated oven at 180°C/350°F/gas mark 4 for 20 minutes until lightly golden. Transfer to a wire rack to cool.

Hazelnut coffee macaroons

MAKES 20

2 egg whites
100 g/4 oz/½ cup caster (superfine) sugar
50 g/2 oz/½ cup plain (all-purpose) flour
2.5 ml/½ tsp instant coffee powder
100 g/4 oz/1 cup hazelnuts (filberts) finely chopped
20 hazelnuts, to decorate

Whisk egg whites until stiff, then whisk in half the sugar and fold in the remainder. Sift the flour and coffee over the surface and fold in with the nuts. Drop spoonfuls on to greased and floured baking (cookie) sheets and top each one with a whole nut. Bake in a preheated oven at 150°C/300°F/gas mark 2 for 30 minutes until just firm. Transfer to a wire rack to cool.

Coffee sandwich biscuits

MAKES ABOUT 36

For the biscuits (cookies):
450 g/1 lb/4 cups plain (all-purpose) flour
A pinch of salt
100 g/4 oz/½ cup soft brown sugar
175 g/6 oz/¾ cup butter or margarine
25 g/1 oz/¼ cup lard (shortening) or vegetable fat
100 g/4 oz/⅓ cup golden (light corn) syrup
5 ml/1 tsp bicarbonate of soda (baking soda)
60 ml/4 tbsp strong black coffee
2.5 ml/½ tsp vanilla essence (extract)
For the filling:
10 ml/2 tsp instant coffee powder
10 ml/2 tsp boiling water
50 g/2 oz/¼ cup caster (superfine) sugar
50 g/2 oz/¼ cup butter or margarine
15 ml/1 tbsp milk

To make the biscuits, mix together the flour, salt and sugar, then rub in the fats until the mixture resembles coarse breadcrumbs. Mix in the syrup. Dissolve the bicarbonate of soda in a little of the coffee and add it to the flour with the remaining coffee and the vanilla essence. Mix to a soft dough, then wrap in clingfilm (plastic wrap) and chill overnight.

Roll out the dough on a lightly floured surface and cut into about 72 rectangular biscuits. Place on greased baking (cookie) sheets and bake in a preheated oven at 200°C/400°F/gas mark 6 for 10 minutes until golden. Transfer to a wire rack to cool.

To make the filling, dissolve the coffee powder in the boiling water in a small saucepan, then add the remaining ingredients and bring to the boil. Boil for 5 minutes. Remove from the heat and beat well until smooth and thick. Sandwich the biscuits together in pairs with the filling.

Digestive biscuits

MAKES 24

175 g/6 oz/1½ cups wholemeal plain flour
50 g/2 oz/½ cup plain (all-purpose) flour
50 g/2 oz/½ cup medium oatmeal
2.5 ml/½ tsp salt
5 ml/1 tsp baking powder
100 g/4 oz/½ cup butter or margarine
30 ml/2 tbsp soft brown sugar
60 ml/4 tbsp milk

Mix together the flours, oatmeal, salt and baking powder. Rub in the butter or margarine, then mix in the sugar. Mix to a dough with the milk and knead well. Roll out on a lightly floured surface and cut into rounds. Place on a greased baking (cookie) sheet and bake in a preheated oven at 180°C/350°F/gas mark 4 for 15 minutes. Transfer the biscuits (cookies) to a wire rack to cool.

Shortbread

MAKES 8

100 g/4 oz/½ cup butter or margarine
50 g/2 oz/¼ cup caster (superfine) sugar
100 g/4 oz/1 cup plain (all-purpose) flour

Cream the butter or margarine and sugar until pale and fluffy, then gradually add the flour and mix to a smooth paste. Roll or press out into a 15 cm/6 in round on a greased baking (cookie) sheet, crimp the edges and prick lightly with a fork. Mark into eight wedges without cutting right through. Bake in a preheated oven at 160°C/325°F/gas mark 3 for 35 minutes until pale golden. Transfer to a wire rack to cool.

Wholemeal honey shortbread

SERVES 4–6

100 g/4 oz/½ cup soft brown sugar
100 g/4 oz/⅓ cup clear honey
225 g/8 oz/1 cup butter or margarine
225 g/8 oz/1 cup lard (shortening) or vegetable fat
750 g/1¾ lb/7 cups wholemeal flour
30 ml/2 tbsp demerara sugar

Beat the sugar, honey and fats to a paste, then blend in the flour until smooth. Roll out on a lightly floured surface to a rectangle about 5 mm/¼ in thick, place on a greased baking (cookie) sheet and prick all over with a fork. Mark into fingers without cutting right through. Bake in a preheated oven at 200°C/400°F/gas mark 6 for 15 minutes until golden brown. Sprinkle with the demerara sugar. Transfer to a wire rack to cool.

Viennese whirls

MAKES 12

25 g/1 oz/2 tbsp butter or margarine
100 g/4 oz/½ cup soft brown sugar
225 g/8 oz/2 cups wholemeal flour
50 g/2 oz/½ cup ground almonds
100 g/4 oz/⅓ cup raspberry jam (jelly)

Cream together the butter or margarine and sugar until light and fluffy. Mix in the flour and almonds until soft and well blended. Pipe the mixture into biscuits (cookies), well apart, through a star nozzle (icing tip) on to a greased baking (cookie) sheet. Bake in a preheated oven at 200°C/400°F/gas mark 6 for 15 minutes until golden brown. Transfer to a wire rack to cool, then sandwich together with the jam.

Florentines

MAKES 40

100 g/4 oz/½ cup butter or margarine
100 g/4 oz/½ cup caster (superfine) sugar
15 ml/1 tbsp double (heavy cream)
100 g/4 oz/1 cup chopped mixed nuts
75 g/3 oz/½ cup sultanas (golden raisins)
50 g/2 oz/¼ cup glacé (candied) cherries

Melt the butter or margarine, sugar and cream in a pan over a low heat. Remove from the heat and stir in the nuts, sultanas and glacé cherries. Drop 5 ml/1 tsp quantities, well apart, on to greased baking (cookie) sheets lined with rice paper. Bake in a preheated oven at 180°C/350°F/gas mark 4 for 10 minutes. Leave to cool on the sheets for 5 minutes, then transfer to a wire rack to finishing cooling, trimming off the excess rice paper.

Langues de chat

MAKES 30

50 g/2 oz/¼ cup unsalted (sweet) butter
50 g/2 oz/¼ cup caster (superfine) sugar
A few drops of vanilla essence (extract)
2 egg whites
50 g/2 oz/½ cup plain (all-purpose) flour

Cream together the butter and sugar with the vanilla essence until light and fluffy. Beat the egg whites until fluffy but not stiff, then fold them into the butter mixture a little at a time. Lightly fold in the flour. Spoon the batter into an icing bag with a plain 1 cm/½ in nozzle (icing tip) and pipe 7.5 cm/3 in lengths on to a greased and flour-dusted baking (cookie) sheet. Bake in a preheated oven at 200°C/425°F/gas mark 7 for about 6 minutes until just beginning to brown at the edges. Leave to cool on the sheets for a few minutes, then transfer to a wire rack to finish cooling.

Crack nuts

MAKES 24

225 g/8 oz/2 cups plain (all-purpose) flour
225 g/8 oz/1 cup caster (superfine) sugar, plus extra for sprinkling
100 g/4 oz/½ cup butter or margarine
3 eggs, beaten
30 ml/2 tbsp caraway seeds
1 egg white

Blend together the flour, sugar and butter or margarine, then add the eggs and caraway seeds and mix to a dough. Roll out on a lightly floured surface as thinly as possible, then cut into 5 cm/2 in rounds and place on a greased baking (cookie) sheet. Brush with egg white and sprinkle with caster sugar. Bake in a preheated oven at 160°C/325°F/gas mark 3 for 10 minutes until just golden. Transfer to a wire rack to cool.

Ginger nuts

MAKES 24

175 g/6 oz/1½ cups plain (all-purpose) flour
100 g/4 oz/1 cup fine oatmeal
75 g/3 oz/⅓ cup caster (superfine) sugar
5 ml/1 tsp ground ginger
5 ml/1 tsp mixed (apple-pie) spice
5 ml/1 tsp bicarbonate of soda (baking soda)
50 g/2 oz/¼ cup lard (shortening) or vegetable fat
175 g/6 oz/½ cup black treacle (molasses)
A little milk

Mix together all the dry ingredients. Rub in the lard or vegetable fat, then mix to a pliable dough with the treacle. Roll out to 1 cm/½ in thick, cut into 5 cm/2 in rounds and place on a greased baking (cookie) sheet. Brush with milk and bake in a preheated oven at 180°C/350°F/gas mark 4 for 15 minutes until just browning at the edges. Transfer to a wire rack to cool.

Ginger biscuits

MAKES 16

3 eggs, separated
175 g/6 oz/¾ cup caster (superfine)
  sugar
75 g/3 oz/¾ cup plain (all-purpose) flour
5 ml/1 tsp ground ginger

Beat the egg yolks with the sugar
until thick. Whisk the egg whites until
stiff, then fold them into the mixture.
Stir in the flour and ginger. Place
spoonfuls on a greased baking
(cookie) sheet and bake in a
preheated oven at 150°C/300°F/gas
mark 2 for 15 minutes until the
biscuits (cookies) are just beginning to
brown at the edges. Transfer to a wire
rack to cool.

Coconut cookies

MAKES ABOUT 20

150 g/5 oz/⅔ cup caster (superfine)
  sugar
150 g/5 oz/⅔ cup soft margarine
1 egg
50 g/2 oz creamed coconut, warmed
275 g/10 oz/2½ cups plain (all-purpose)
  flour
5 ml/1 tsp baking powder
15 ml/1 tbsp desiccated (shredded)
  coconut

Work together all the ingredients
except the desiccated coconut to
make a dough. Shape into a roll, wrap
in greaseproof (waxed) paper and chill
until firm. Cut into 1 cm/½ in slices
and arrange on a greased baking
(cookie) sheet, then dust with the
coconut. Bake in a preheated oven at
190°C/375°F/gas mark 5 for
10–12 minutes until golden. Transfer
to a wire rack to cool.

Almond crunch biscuits

MAKES 18

200 g/7 oz/1¾ cup flaked (slivered)
  almonds
225 g/8 oz/1 cup caster (superfine)
  sugar
120 ml/4 fl oz/½ cup water
100 g/4 oz/½ cup butter or margarine
150 g/5 oz/1¼ cups plain (semi-sweet)
  chocolate

Toast the almonds in a dry frying pan
(skillet) for a few minutes, tossing
continuously, until golden. Place the
sugar, water and butter or margarine
in a saucepan and melt over a low
heat. Bring to the boil, then boil for
8 minutes until you have dark syrup.
Remove from the heat immediately
and quickly mix in the almonds.
Quickly spoon 15 ml/1 tbsp quantities
of the mixture on to a baking (cookie)
sheet covered with greased kitchen
foil and flatten into rounds. If the
mixture begins to thicken before you
have finished, warm it very gently to
loosen it. Leave to cool and set
slightly while you melt the chocolate
in a heatproof bowl set over a pan of
simmering water. Turn the biscuits
(cookies) over and spread the
chocolate on the smooth sides of the
biscuits, then mark into patterns with
a fork and leave to set.

Muesli biscuits

MAKES 30

100 g/4 oz/½ cup butter or margarine
100 g/4 oz/⅓ cup clear honey
75 g/3 oz/⅓ cup Muscovado sugar
100 g/4 oz/1 cup wholemeal flour
100 g/4 oz/1 cup rolled oats
50 g/2 oz/⅓ cup raisins
50 g/2 oz/⅓ cup sultanas (golden raisins)
50 g/2 oz/⅓ cup dates, chopped
50 g/2 oz/⅓ cup no-need-to-soak dried
  apricots, chopped
25 g/1 oz/¼ cup walnuts, chopped
25 g/1 oz/¼ cup hazelnuts (filberts),
  chopped

Melt the butter or margarine, honey
and sugar, then stir in the remaining
ingredients. Roll out on a lightly
floured surface, cut into 5 cm/2 in
rounds and arrange on a greased
baking (cookie) sheet. Bake in a
preheated oven at 180°C/350°F/gas
mark 4 for 20 minutes until the
biscuits (cookies) are lightly browned.
Transfer to a wire rack to cool.

Note:
You can vary the ingredients to match
what you have in your storecupboard.

Oatmeal biscuits

MAKES 16

125 g/5 oz/1¼ cups wholemeal flour
2.5 ml/½ tsp bicarbonate of soda (baking
  soda)
A pinch of salt
100 g/4 oz/½ cup butter or margarine
50 g/2 oz/½ cup oatmeal
50 g/2 oz/¼ cup soft brown sugar
1 egg, beaten
15 ml/1 tbsp water

Mix together the flour, bicarbonate of
soda and salt, then rub in the butter
or margarine. Mix in the oatmeal and

sugar. Beat the egg with the water
and add it to the mixture to make a
stiff paste, adding a little more water
if necessary. Roll out, cut into rounds
and place on a greased and floured
baking (cookie) sheet. Bake in a
preheated oven at 180°C/350°F/gas
mark 4 for 20 minutes. Transfer the
biscuits (cookies) to a wire rack to
cool.

Oatcakes

MAKES 8

175 g/6 oz/1½ cups fine oatmeal, plus
  extra for dusting
50 g/2 oz/¼ cup wholemeal flour
Salt
A pinch of bicarbonate of soda (baking
  soda)
25 g/1 oz/2 tbsp butter or margarine
120 ml/4 fl oz/½ cup hot water

Mix together the oatmeal, flour, salt
and bicarbonate of soda. Melt the
butter or margarine and add to the
dry ingredients with enough of the hot
water to make a stiff dough. Turn out
on to a surface dusted with oatmeal
and knead until smooth. Divide in half
and roll out into large rounds as thinly
as possible. Cut each round into
quarters and place on an ungreased
baking (cookie) sheet dusted with
oatmeal. Bake in a preheated oven at
180°C/350°F/gas mark 4 for
20 minutes until the edges begin to
brown. Cool on the sheets and store
in an airtight container.

Orange and walnut biscuits

MAKES 16

100 g/4 oz/½ cup butter or margarine
75 g/3 oz/⅜ cup caster (superfine) sugar
Grated rind of ½ orange
150 g/5 oz/1¼ cups self-raising (self-rising) flour
50 g/2 oz/½ cup walnuts, ground

Beat together the butter or margarine, 50 g/2 oz/¼ cup of the sugar and the orange rind until smooth and creamy. Add the flour and nuts and beat again until the mixture begins to hold together. Form into balls and flatten on to a greased baking (cookie) sheet. Bake in a preheated oven at 190°C/375°F/gas mark 5 for 10 minutes until brown at the edges. Sprinkle the biscuits (cookies) with the remaining sugar and leave to cool slightly before removing from the sheet. Transfer to a wire rack to finish cooling.

Peanut jacks

MAKES ABOUT 15

100 g/4 oz/½ cup butter or margarine
1 egg
30 ml/2 tbsp golden (light corn) syrup
100 g/4 oz/1 cup rolled oats
50 g/2 oz/¼ cup demerara sugar
50 g/2 oz/½ cup peanuts, chopped

Cream together the butter or margarine, egg and syrup. Work in the oats, sugar and nuts. Drop spoonfuls on to a greased baking (cookie) sheet and bake in a preheated oven at 180°C/350°F/gas mark 4 for 12–15 minutes until golden. Transfer to a wire rack to cool.

Nut biscuits

MAKES 24

50 g/2 oz/¼ cup butter or margarine
225 g/8 oz/2 cups plain (all-purpose) flour
5 ml/1 tsp baking powder
A pinch of salt
50 g/2 oz/½ cup chopped mixed nuts
150 ml/¼ pt/⅔ cup warm milk

Rub the butter or margarine into the flour, baking powder and salt. Add the nuts and mix in just enough of the milk to make a firm paste. Roll out on a lightly floured surface and cut into 5 cm/2 in rounds. Place on a greased baking sheet and bake in a preheated oven at 180°C/350°F/gas mark 4 for 15 minutes until golden. Transfer the biscuits (cookies) to a wire rack to cool.

Rice biscuits

MAKES 24

75 g/3 oz/⅓ cup caster (superfine) sugar
2 eggs
50 g/2 oz/¼ cup butter or margarine
225 g/8 oz/2 cups rice flour
25 g/1 oz/2 tbsp currants

Beat together the sugar, eggs and butter or margarine. Mix the flour and currants and add to the mixture, beating well. Roll out and cut into rounds. Place them on a greased and floured baking (cookie) sheet and bake in a preheated oven at 150°C/300°F/gas mark 2 for 20 minutes. Transfer the biscuits (cookies) to a wire rack to cool.

Mincemeat bites

MAKES ABOUT 12

175 g/6 oz/¾ cup butter or margarine,
  softened
225 g/8 oz/2 cups plain (all-purpose)
  flour
100 g/4 oz/½ cup caster (superfine)
  sugar
60 ml/4 tbsp mincemeat

Mash together the butter or
margarine, flour and sugar with a
fork. Work in the mincemeat to form
a soft dough. Roll out on a lightly
floured surface. Cut into rounds. Prick
with a fork and bake at 180°C/350°F/
gas mark 4 for about 20 minutes.
Transfer to a wire rack to cool.

Spiced biscuits

MAKES 24

225 g/8 oz/2 cups plain (all-purpose)
  flour
100 g/4 oz/1 cup flaked (slivered)
  almonds
5 ml/1 tsp mixed (apple-pie) spice
175 g/6 oz/¾ cup caster (superfine)
  sugar
225 g/8 oz/1 cup granulated sugar
30 ml/2 tbsp water

Mix together the flour, almonds, spice
and caster sugar. Bring the granulated
sugar and water to the boil, then add
the flour mixture and mix to a paste.
Mould the paste into a shape like a
large rolling pin and place it on
greased baking parchment on a
baking (cookie) sheet. Bake in a
preheated oven at 220°C/425°F/gas
mark 7 for 10 minutes. When baked,
cut into slices while still hot and lay
each biscuit (cookie) separately to
cool.

Peppermint fingers

MAKES 18

50 g/2 oz/¼ cup butter or margarine
50 g/2 oz/¼ cup caster (superfine) sugar
100 g/4 oz/1 cup plain (all-purpose)
  flour
175 g/6 oz/1 cup icing (confectioners')
  sugar
30 ml/2 tbsp hot water
2.5 ml/½ tsp peppermint essence
  (extract)
175 g/6 oz/1½ cups plain (semi-sweet)
  chocolate

Whisk together the butter or
margarine and sugar until pale and
fluffy, then stir in the flour and knead
to a smooth dough. Press into a small
Swiss roll tin (jelly roll pan), prick with
a fork and bake in a preheated oven
at 180°C/350°F/gas mark 4 for
10 minutes until golden brown. Leave
to cool. Mix the icing (confectioners')
sugar with enough of the water and
the peppermint essence to make a
spreading consistency. Spread on top
of the biscuit (cookie) base. Leave to
cool. Melt the chocolate in a bowl
over a pan of hot water and spread
over the icing. Cut into fingers when
cold.

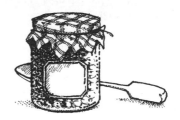

True lovers' knots

MAKES 12

225 g/8 oz Puff Pastry (page 165)
75 g/3 oz/¼ cup jam (jelly)

Roll out the pastry (paste) to a thin sheet and cut into 9 cm/3½ in squares. Fold each corner into the centre and press in the sides to form a knot shape. Place on a baking (cookie) sheet and bake in a preheated oven at 200°C/400°F/gas mark 6 for 10 minutes. When cool, place a spoonful of jam in the centre of each knot.

Brandy snaps

MAKES 12

50 g/2 oz/¼ cup butter or margarine
50 g/2 oz/¼ cup caster (superfine) sugar
50 g/2 oz/3 tbsp golden (light corn) syrup
50 g/2 oz/½ cup plain (all-purpose) flour
2.5 ml/½ tsp ground ginger

Put the butter or margarine, sugar and syrup in saucepan and beat slowly over a low heat until melted. Remove from the heat and mix in the flour and ginger. Place spoonfuls of the mixture on greased baking (cookie) sheets, allowing plenty of space for the mixture to spread. Bake in a preheated oven at 180°C/350°F/gas mark 4 for 10 minutes until golden brown. Leave to firm for a minute, then remove with a palette knife and roll round the greased handle of a wooden spoon. Slip off the spoon and leave to cool on a wire rack. If the mixture becomes too hard to shape, return to the oven for 1–2 minutes to soften.

Caraway nibbles

MAKES 24

50 g/2 oz/¼ cup butter or margarine
225 g/8 oz/2 cups plain (all-purpose) flour
50 g/2 oz/¼ cup caster (superfine) sugar
1 egg
15 ml/1 tbsp single (light) cream
5 ml/1 tsp caraway seeds

Rub the butter or margarine into the flour. Add the sugar and mix to a paste with the egg and cream. Stir in the caraway seeds. Place spoonfuls on a greased baking (cookie) sheet and bake in a preheated oven at 220°C/425°F/gas mark 7 for 10 minutes. Transfer to a wire rack to cool.

Butterscotch crisps

MAKES 48

100 g/4 oz/½ cup butter or margarine
100 g/4 oz/½ cup Muscovado sugar
1 egg, beaten
A few drops of vanilla essence (extract)
225 g/8 oz/2 cups plain (all-purpose) flour
8 ml/1½ tsp baking powder
A pinch of salt

Cream the butter or margarine and sugar until light. Beat in the egg and vanilla essence. Sift together the flour, baking powder and salt and mix into the creamed mixture. Shape the dough into three rolls about 5 cm/2 in in diameter, wrap in greaseproof (waxed) paper and chill overnight. Cut into slices 3 mm/⅛ in thick, place on ungreased baking (cookie) sheets and bake in a preheated oven at 190°C/375°F/gas mark 5 for 10 minutes until lightly browned.

Yarmouth biscuits

MAKES 24

100 g/4 oz/1 cup plain (all-purpose)
  flour
225 g/8 oz/1 cup caster (superfine)
  sugar
100 g/4 oz/½ cup butter or margarine
175 g/6 oz/1 cup currants
2 eggs, beaten

Mix together the flour and sugar and
rub in the butter or margarine. Mix in
the currants and beat to a pastry
(paste) with the eggs. Roll out and
cut into rounds. Place on greased
baking parchment on a baking
(cookie) sheet and bake in a
preheated oven at 220°C/425°F/gas
mark 7 for 10 minutes. Transfer the
biscuits (cookies) to a wire rack to
cool.

Cherry biscuits

MAKES 16

175 g/6 oz/1½ cups plain (all-purpose)
  flour
25 g/1 oz/¼ cup cornflour (cornstarch)
100 g/4 oz/½ cup caster (superfine)
  sugar
100 g/4 oz/½ cup soft margarine
50 g/2 oz/¼ cup glacé (candied) cherries,
  chopped

Mix together the flours and 75 g/
3 oz/⅓ cup of the sugar, then rub in
the margarine until the mixture
resembles fine breadcrumbs. Stir in
the glacé cherries and mix well. Press
the mixture into a greased Swiss roll
tin (jelly roll pan) and bake in a
preheated oven at 160°C/325°F/gas
mark 3 for 20 minutes. Sprinkle the
biscuits (cookies) with the reserved
sugar while hot and mark into fingers.
Leave to cool in the tin.

Simple scones

MAKES 10–12

225 g/8 oz/2 cups plain (all-purpose)
  flour
A pinch of salt
2.5 ml/½ tsp bicarbonate of soda (baking
  soda)
5 ml/1 tsp cream of tartar
50 g/2 oz/¼ cup butter or margarine,
  diced
30 ml/2 tbsp milk
30 ml/2 tbsp water

Mix together the flour, salt,
bicarbonate of soda and cream of
tartar, then rub in the butter or
margarine. Slowly add enough of the
milk and water to make a soft dough.
Knead quickly until smooth, then roll
out on a lightly floured surface to
1 cm/½ in thick and cut into 5 cm/
2 in rounds with a biscuit (cookie)
cutter. Place on a greased baking
(cookie) sheet and bake in a
preheated oven at 220°C/425°F/gas
mark 7 for about 10 minutes until the
scones (biscuits) are well risen and
golden brown.

Wholemeal scones

MAKES 16

450 g/1 lb/4 cups wholemeal flour
15 ml/1 tbsp baking powder
75 g/3 oz/⅓ cup soft brown sugar
5 ml/1 tsp salt
90 ml/6 tbsp sunflower oil
300 ml/½ pt/1¼ cups milk
1 egg, beaten

Mix together the flour, baking powder, sugar and salt, then stir in the oil. Gradually add enough of the milk to make a soft dough. Roll out on a lightly floured surface to about 2.5 cm/1 in thick, then cut into rounds with a 5 cm/2 in biscuit (cookie) cutter. Place the rounds on a greased baking (cookie) sheet and brush with the egg. Leave to rest for 10 minutes, then bake the scones (biscuits) in a preheated oven at 200°C/400°F/gas mark 6 for 15 minutes.

Apple and coconut scones

MAKES 12

50 g/2 oz/¼ cup butter or margarine
225 g/8 oz/2 cups self-raising (self-rising) flour
25 g/1 oz/2 tbsp caster (superfine) sugar
30 ml/2 tbsp desiccated (shredded) coconut
1 eating (dessert) apple, peeled, cored and chopped
150 ml/¼ pt/⅔ cup plain yoghurt
30 ml/2 tbsp milk

Rub the butter or margarine into the flour. Stir in the sugar, coconut and apple, then blend in the yoghurt to make a soft dough, adding a little of the milk if necessary. Roll out on a lightly floured surface to about 2.5 cm/1 in thick and cut into rounds with a biscuit (cookie) cutter. Place on a greased baking (cookie) sheet and bake in a preheated oven at 220°C/425°F/gas mark 7 for 10–15 minutes until the scones (biscuits) are well risen and golden.

Muesli scones

MAKES 8–10

100 g/4 oz/1 cup muesli
150 ml/¼ pt/⅔ cup water
50 g/2 oz/¼ cup butter or margarine
100 g/4 oz/1 cup plain (all-purpose) flour
10 ml/2 tsp baking powder
50 g/2 oz/⅓ cup raisins
1 egg, beaten

Soak the muesli in the water for 30 minutes. Rub the butter or margarine into the flour and baking powder until the mixture resembles breadcrumbs, then stir in the raisins and soaked muesli and mix to a soft dough. Shape into a 20 cm/8 in round and flatten on to a greased baking (cookie) sheet. Cut partially through into eight or ten sections and brush with the beaten egg. Bake in a preheated oven at 200°C/400°F/gas mark 6 for about 20 minutes until the scones (biscuits) are golden brown.

West Country scones

MAKES 12

100 g/4 oz/½ cup butter or margarine
450 g/1 lb/4 cups self-raising (self-rising) flour
A pinch of salt
10 ml/2 tsp baking powder
300 ml/½ pt/1¼ cups milk
Jam (jelly) and clotted cream, to serve

Rub the butter or margarine into the flour, salt and baking powder. Mix with the milk to a soft dough. Roll out on a lightly floured surface to about 2.5 cm/1 in thick and cut into rounds with a 5 cm/2 in biscuit (cookie) cutter. Place on a greased baking (cookie) sheet and bake in a preheated oven at 200°C/400°F/gas mark 6 for 10 minutes. Serve the scones (biscuits) with jam and clotted cream.

Maple, date and cherry fingers

MAKES 12

50 g/2 oz/¼ cup butter or margarine
50 g/2 oz/3 tbsp maple syrup
50 g/2 oz/¼ cup caster (superfine) sugar
100 g/4 oz sponge finger biscuits (cookies), crushed
50 g/2 oz/¼ cup glacé cherries, chopped
100 g/4 oz/⅔ cup dates, stoned (pitted) and chopped

Melt the butter or margarine, syrup and sugar, then stir in the biscuit crumbs. Spoon into a shallow 20 cm/8 in square baking tin (pan), sprinkle with the cherries and dates, then press them down into the mixture. Chill until firm, then cut into fingers.

Honey no-bakes

MAKES ABOUT 12

50 g/2 oz/¼ cup butter or margarine
50 g/2 oz/3 tbsp clear honey
50 g/2 oz/¼ cup caster (superfine) sugar
100 g/4 oz broken biscuit (cookies), crushed
100 g/4 oz/1 cup chopped mixed nuts

Melt the butter or margarine, honey and sugar, then stir in the biscuit crumbs and 75 g/3 oz/¾ cup of the nuts. Leave the mixture to chill. Meanwhile, toast the remaining nuts in a dry saucepan for a few minutes until golden, then leave to cool. Roll the biscuit mixture into about 12 balls, then roll in the toasted nuts.

Jams, jellies and marmalades

You can make jams (jellies) and marmalades with almost any fruit, although some are more successful than others, largely due to the amount of pectin, the setting agent, they contain. You can make preserves in small quantities just as easily as large ones. So try making a jar or two of jam or marmalade to indulge yourself or as gifts.

Jam sugar contains added pectin and is the best one to use. Preserving sugar also contains pectin but is slightly coarser so can take longer to dissolve. Granulated sugar also works well. Brown sugar, honey and syrup all give distinctive flavours, but do not set as well, so if you want to try these, substitute them for one-quarter of the sugar in the recipe, then use ordinary sugar for the remainder.

To keep soft-skinned fruits whole, mix them with the sugar and leave to stand overnight before continuing the recipe. Always cook the fruit first, if necessary, dissolve the sugar gently, then boil rapidly, without stirring, to setting point at 104°C/220°F. This will take 10–25 minutes. If you do not have a thermometer, place a saucer in the fridge to chill while the jam is boiling. After the minimum cooking time, place a spoonful of the jam on the chilled saucer and leave it to cool for a few seconds, then press it with your finger. If it wrinkles, the jam has reached setting point. If not, boil for another 5 minutes and test again.

Clean jars thoroughly in hot, soapy water, then rinse in hot water. Place the bottles on a wire rack in the bottom of a large saucepan and cover with hot water. Bring to the boil, then boil for 10 minutes. Carefully remove from the pan and turn upside-down on a clean tea towel (dish cloth) to drain. Dry and warm the jars in a preheated oven at 110°C/225°F/gas mark ¼ until ready to use.

Orchard jam

MAKES 1 KG/2¼ LB

600 ml/1 pt/2½ cups water
400 g/14 oz/1¾ cups jam sugar
Grated rind and juice of 1 small orange
225 g/8 oz/1½ cups raisins
700 g/1½ lb cooking (tart) apples,
  peeled, cored and diced
1.5 ml/¼ tsp ground cloves
1.5 ml/¼ tsp ground cinnamon

Bring the water gently to the boil with the sugar, stirring, until the sugar dissolves. Add the orange rind and juice and the raisins and simmer for 15 minutes. Add the apples and spices and boil for a further 15 minutes until setting point is reached, then pour the jam (jelly) into warmed jars, leave to cool, then seal and label.

Apple and ginger jam

MAKES 1.5 KG/3 LB

900 g/2 lb cooking (tart) apples, peeled,
  cored and sliced
700 g/1½ lb/3 cups jam sugar
40 g/1½ oz crystallised ginger, finely
  chopped
450 ml/¾ pt/2 cups water
Grated rind and juice of 1 lemon

Place layers of apple, sugar and ginger in a bowl, pour over the water and leave to stand overnight. Place in a pan and bring to the boil, stirring, until the sugar dissolves, then simmer for 30 minutes. Add the lemon rind and juice, bring back to the boil and simmer for a further 30 minutes until the fruit and syrup are transparent. Stir the jam (jelly) well, pour into warmed jars and leave to cool, then seal and label.

Apple and blackberry jam

MAKES 1.5 KG/3 LB

450 g/1 lb cooking (tart) apples, peeled,
  cored and sliced
300 ml/½ pt/1¼ cups water
450 g/1 lb blackberries
900 g/2 lb/4 cups jam sugar, warmed

Place the apples and water in a pan and simmer gently for about 15 minutes until soft. Add the blackberries, bring to the boil and simmer for about 5 minutes until the blackberries are soft. Stir in the warm sugar until dissolved, then boil for about 10 minutes to setting point. Stir the jam (jelly) well, pour into warmed jars and leave to cool, then seal and label.

Fresh apricot jam

MAKES 1.5 KG/3 LB

700 g/1½ lb apricots, halved and stoned
  (pitted)
300 ml/½ pt/1¼ cups water
15 g/½ oz/1 tbsp butter or margarine
900 g/2 lb/4 cups jam sugar, warmed

Put the apricots and water in a pan and simmer for 10 minutes. Stir in the butter or margarine and warmed sugar until dissolved, then boil for about 20 minutes to setting point. Stir well, pour into warmed jars and leave to cool, then seal and label. To use this jam (jelly) for brushing on cakes before adding almond paste or icing (frosting), purée the jam, then rub it through a sieve (strainer) so that it is completely smooth.

Dried apricot jam

MAKES 1.5 KG/3 LB

450 g/1 lb/2⅔ cups no-need-to-soak
  dried apricots
400 ml/14 fl oz/1¾ cups water
Juice of 1 small lemon
900 g/2 lb/4 cups jam sugar, warmed

Put the apricots, water and lemon
juice in a pan, bring to the boil and
simmer for about 20 minutes until the
fruit is soft. Stir in the warmed sugar
until dissolved, then boil for about
15 minutes to setting point. Stir the
jam (jelly) well, pour into warmed jars
and leave to cool, then seal and label.

Banana jam

MAKES 900 G/2 LB

450 g/1 lb bananas, sliced
900 ml/1½ pts/3¾ cups orange or apple
  juice
Juice of 1 lemon
350 g/12 oz/1½ cups light brown sugar

Stir all the ingredients over a low heat
until the sugar has dissolved. Bring to
the boil, then simmer gently, stirring
occasionally, for about 10 minutes
until the mixture thickens. Stir the jam
(jelly) well, pour into warmed jars and
leave to cool, then seal and label.

Blackberry jam

MAKES 1.5 KG/3 LB

900 g/2 lb blackberries
15 g/½ oz/1 tbsp butter or margarine
900 g/2 lb/4 cups jam sugar, warmed

Bring the blackberries slowly to the
boil over a low heat, adding a little
water if there is very little juice. Add
the butter or margarine and simmer
for about 10 minutes until the fruit is
soft. Stir in the warmed sugar until
dissolved, then boil for about 10
minutes to setting point. Stir the jam
(jelly) well, pour into warmed jars,
then seal and label.

Gooseberry jam

MAKES 1.5 KG/3 LB

700 g/1½ lb gooseberries, topped and
  tailed
300 ml/½ pt/1¼ cups water
900 g/2 lb/4 cups granulated or
  preserving sugar, warmed

Put the gooseberries and water in a
saucepan and simmer until the fruit is
soft and most of the water has been
absorbed. Stir in the warmed sugar
until dissolved, then boil for about
15 minutes to setting point. Skim the
jam (jelly), pour into warmed jars and
leave to cool, then seal and label.

Cherry jam

MAKES 1.75 KG/4 LB

1.5 kg/3 lb morello cherries
Juice of 2 lemons
900 g/2 lb/4 cups jam sugar, warmed

Put the cherries and lemon juice in a pan and simmer for about 15 minutes until the fruit is soft. Stir in the warmed sugar until dissolved, then boil for about 15 minutes to setting point. Stir the jam (jelly) well, pour into warmed jars and leave to cool, then seal and label.

Blackcurrant jam

MAKES 1.5 KG/3 LB

700 g/1½ lb blackcurrants
600 ml/1 pt/2½ cups water
1.5 kg/3 lb/6 cups granulated or
    preserving sugar, warmed

Put the blackcurrants and water in a pan and simmer for 10 minutes until soft. Stir in the warmed sugar until dissolved, then boil for about 5 minutes to setting point. Stir the jam (jelly) well, pour into warmed jars and leave to cool, then seal and label.

Plum jam

MAKES 1.75 KG/4 LB

900 g/2 lb plums, halved and stoned
    (pitted)
250 ml/8 fl oz/1 cup water
900 g/2 lb/4 cups granulated or
    preserving sugar, warmed

Put the plums and water in a pan and simmer for about 10 minutes until tender. Stir in the warmed sugar until dissolved, then boil for about 15 minutes to setting point. Skim the jam (jelly), pour into warmed jars and leave to cool, then seal and label.

Raspberry jam

MAKES 2.25 KG/5 LB

900 g/2 lb raspberries
900 g/2 lb/4 cups cups jam sugar,
    warmed

Place the raspberries in a saucepan and simmer gently for a few minutes until the juice begins to flow. Stir in the warmed sugar until dissolved, then boil for about 10 minutes to setting point. Stir the jam (jelly) well, pour into warmed jars and leave to cool, then seal and label.

Strawberry jam

MAKES 2.25 KG/5 LB

1.75 kg/4 lb strawberries
1.5 kg/3 lb/6 cups jam sugar, warmed
Juice of 1 lemon
25 g/1 oz/2 tbsp butter or margarine

Layer the strawberries and sugar in a bowl and leave to stand in a cool place for 24 hours. Pour into a pan with the lemon juice, bring to the boil, stirring carefully to avoid breaking up the fruit, then boil rapidly for about 10 minutes to setting point. Stir in the butter, then leave the jam (jelly) in the pan until fairly cool, when a thin skin begins to form on top. Stir gently, spoon into warmed jars and leave to cool, then seal and label.

Blackberry jelly

MAKES 1.5 KG/3 LB

1.75 kg/4 lb blackberries
Juice of 2 lemons
300 ml/½ pt/1¼ cups water
A pinch of ground cinnamon
About 900 g/2 lb/4 cups jam sugar,
   warmed

Put the blackberries in a pan with the lemon juice, water and cinnamon and simmer for 30 minutes until the fruit is very soft. Strain through a jelly bag, allowing the juice to drip naturally into a bowl as if you squeeze the pulp the jelly will be cloudy. Measure the juice and return it to the pan. Stir in 450 g/1 lb/2 cups of warmed sugar to each 600 ml/1 pt/2½ cups of juice until dissolved, then boil for 15 minutes to setting point. Pour into warmed jars and leave to cool, then seal and label.

Apple jelly

MAKES 1.5 KG/3 LB

1.75 kg/4 lb cooking (tart) apples,
   roughly chopped
2.25 litres/4 pts/10 cups water
About 900 g/2 lb/4 cups jam sugar,
   warmed

Put the apples and water in a pan and boil for about 15 minutes until the apples are soft. Strain through a jelly bag, allowing the juice to drip naturally into a bowl as if you squeeze the pulp the jelly will be cloudy.

Measure the juice and return it to the pan. Stir in 450 g/1 lb/2 cups of warmed sugar to each 600 ml/1 pt/2½ cups of juice until dissolved, then boil for about 10 minutes to setting point. Pour into warmed jars and leave to cool, then seal and label.

Note:
You can use any kind of apples for this recipe, including crab apples, or a mixture of cooking (tart) and eating (dessert) apples.

Apple mint jelly

MAKES 1.75 KG/4 LB

2.75 kg/6 lb cooking (tart) apples,
   roughly chopped
1.2 litres/2 pts/5 cups water
About 1.5 kg/3 lb/6 cups jam sugar,
   warmed
A bunch of mint
15 ml/1 tbsp lemon juice

Put the apples and water in a pan and boil until soft. Strain through a jelly bag, allowing the juice to drip naturally into a bowl as if you squeeze the pulp the jelly will be cloudy. Measure the juice and return it to the pan. Stir in 450 g/1 lb/2 cups of warmed sugar to each 600 ml/1 pt/2½ cups of juice until dissolved, then add half the mint and the lemon juice and boil for about 10 minutes to setting point. Remove the sprigs of mint, chop the remainder and stir it into the jelly. Pour into warmed jars and leave to cool, then seal and label.

Redcurrant jelly

MAKES 900 G/2 LB

1.5 kg/3 lb redcurrants
1.25 litres/2¼ pts/5½ cups water
About 900 g/2 lb/4 cups jam sugar,
   warmed

Put the redcurrants and water in a
pan, bring to the boil and simmer for
20 minutes until the fruit is pulpy.
Strain the juice through a jelly bag,
allowing the juice to drip naturally into
a bowl as if you squeeze the pulp the
jelly will be cloudy. Measure the juice,
return it to the pan and add 450 g/
1 lb/2 cups of sugar for each 600 ml/
1 pt/2½ cups juice. Stir over a low
heat until the sugar has dissolved,
then boil for 10 minutes to setting
point. Skim, pour into warmed jars
and leave to cool, then seal and label.

Grapefruit marmalade

MAKES 1.5 KG/3 LB

450 g/1 lb grapefruit
1–2 lemons
1.75 litres/3 pts/7½ cups cold water
1.5 kg/3 lb/6 cups jam sugar, warmed

Halve the grapefruit, then squeeze out
and reserve the juice. Tie the pips in a
muslin (cheesecloth) bag. Chop the
peel and soak it in 1.5 litres/2½ pts/
6 cups of the water overnight. Put the
water, peel, bag of pips and remaining
water in a preserving pan and simmer
for 1½ hours until the peel is soft.
Discard the bag of pips. Stir in the
warmed sugar until dissolved, then
boil for about 20 minutes to setting
point. Skim, then leave to cool
slightly, Stir well, pour into warmed
jars and leave to cool, then seal and
label.

Orange marmalade

MAKES 1.5 KG/3 LB

450 g/1 lb Seville oranges
1 small lemon
1.2 litres/2 pts/5 cups cold water
900 g/2 lb/4 cups jam sugar, warmed

It speeds up preparation considerably
if you use a food processor. Halve the
oranges and lemon, squeeze out the
juice, and strain through a large-mesh
sieve (strainer) into a preserving pan
or large saucepan. Tip the contents of
the sieve with all the pips into a
muslin (cheesecloth) bag or jelly (jello)
bag, tie it securely and add it to the
pan. Chop the peel and attached pith
and add it to the pan with the water.
Bring to the boil, then simmer for
about 1½ hours until the peel is soft.
Squeeze any thick juices (which
contain the setting agent, pectin)
from the bag of pips into the pan,
then discard the bag. Stir in the
warmed sugar until dissolved, then
bring to a rolling boil and boil for
20 minutes to setting point. Skim off
any scum, then leave to cool slightly.
Stir well, pour into warmed jars and
leave to cool, then seal and label.

Whisky marmalade

MAKES 1.5 KG/3 LB

Prepare as for Orange Marmalade,
but add 60 ml/4 tbsp whisky with the
sugar.

Orange jelly marmalade

MAKES 1.7 KG/4 LB

900 g/2 lb Seville oranges
2 lemons
3 litres/5 pts/12½ cups water
1.5 kg/3 lb/6 cups jam sugar, warmed

Wash and scald the oranges and lemons in boiling water. Squeeze the juice from the lemons and reserve. Peel the oranges. Shred the orange peel finely and place in a pan with 900 ml/1½ pts/3¾ cups of the water, cover and cook gently for 1½ hours. Coarsely chop the rest of the fruit and place in another pan with the pith, lemon juice and remaining water. Simmer gently for 2 hours. Drain the liquid from the peel and add to the other pan. Strain the pulp through a scalded jelly bag, then return the juice to the pan with the sugar and stir until dissolved. Add the peel shreds. Bring to the boil and boil for about 20 minutes to setting point. Skim, leave to cool slightly, then pour into warmed jars. Leave to cool, then seal and label.

Three fruit marmalade

MAKES 1.5 KG/4 LB

2 grapefruit
2 oranges
1.2 litres/2 pts/5 cups water
Juice of 2 lemons
900 g/2 lb/4 cups jam sugar, warmed

Quarter the grapefruit and remove the skin, pith and pips. Chop the flesh and place in a pan. Quarter the oranges and remove the pips. Remove the flesh from half the segments, chop finely and add to the pan. Slice the remaining segments and add to the pan. Tie all the pips in a muslin (cheesecloth) bag and place in the pan. Add the water and lemon juice, bring to the boil and simmer for about 2 hours until the rind is soft. Remove the bag of pips. Stir in the sugar until dissolved, then boil for about 10 minutes to setting point. Skim, leave to cool slightly, then stir well and pour into warmed jars. Leave to cool, then seal and label.

Lemon curd

MAKES 450 G/1 LB

75 g/3 oz/⅓ cup butter or margarine
225 g/8 oz/1 cup caster (superfine) sugar
Grated rind and juice of 2 lemons
2 eggs, beaten

Place the butter or margarine, sugar, lemon rind and juice in a bowl over a pan of boiling water and stir until the sugar has dissolved. Stir in the eggs and continue stirring for about 10 minutes until the mixture is thick enough to coat the back of a spoon. Pour into warmed jars and leave to cool, then seal and label. Store in the fridge and use within a month.

Orange curd

MAKES 450 G/1 LB

Prepare as for Lemon Curd, but substitute orange for the lemon rind and juice.

Pickles and chutneys

Pickling used to be a necessity, to make use of gluts of fruits and vegetables, but modern cooks don't do a lot of preserving as we tend not to grown our own and can buy everything we need all year round. However, it can be fun to make your own preserves, and these recipes give smaller quantities than are usually given for preserving to make them more suitable for the modern cook. If you do have quantities of home-grown produce or really enjoy preserving, you can easily increase the quantities in the recipes. To make the recipes even easier, you can always substitute ready-prepared pickling vinegar for the vinegar and pickling spices. Always sterilise, then warm jars before pouring in hot chutney and do not cover with a circle of paper, as you would with jam. Use plastic lids, never metal, as metal will react with the vinegar in the pickle and spoil the preserve. Leave chutneys to cool before putting on the lid, and always label the jars with the name of the preserve and the date.
Instructions for sterilising jars are on page 372.

Pickled onions

MAKES 900 G/2 LB

900 g/2 lb pickling onions or shallots
100 g/4 oz/½ cup salt
1.2 litres/4 pts/5 cups water
600 ml/1 pt/2½ cups malt vinegar
15 g/½ oz/2 tbsp pickling spice tied in
    muslin (cheesecloth)
10 ml/2 tsp caster (superfine) sugar

Pour boiling water over the onions or
shallots. One at a time, lift them out
carefully with a slotted spoon and peel
them. Bring the salt and water to the
boil, then remove from the heat and
leave to cool. Pour over the peeled
onions and leave to stand for 48 hours.
Drain the onions, then pack them into
screw-topped jars. Boil the vinegar and
spice for 5 minutes, then remove the
spice and stir in the sugar. Leave to
cool, then pour the vinegar over the
onions or shallots, seal, label and leave
for 1 month before eating.

Pickled red cabbage

MAKES 1.5 KG/3 LB

1 small red cabbage
Salt
600 ml/1 pt/2½ cups distilled malt vinegar
25 g/1 oz/¼ cup pickling spice tied in
    muslin (cheesecloth)
5 ml/1 tsp mustard powder

Quarter the cabbage and cut out the
centre stalk. Shred the cabbage finely,
put on a large flat dish and sprinkle
fairly generously with salt. Leave to
stand in a cool place for 24 hours.
Drain the cabbage thoroughly, then
pack it into jars. Boil the vinegar with
the spice and mustard for 5 minutes,
then leave until cold and remove the
spice. Pour over the cabbage, leave to
cool, then seal the jars and label.

Pear chutney

MAKES 900 G/2 LB

450 g/1 lb pears, peeled, cored and
    chopped
1 onion, chopped
5 ml/1 tsp salt
175 g/6 oz/¾ cup granulated sugar
5 ml/1 tsp ground ginger
100 g/4 oz/⅔ cup dates, stoned (pitted)
    and chopped
50 g/2 oz/⅓ cup sultanas (golden raisins)
5 ml/1 tsp mustard powder
300 ml/½ pt/1¼ cups malt vinegar

Put all the ingredients in a pan, bring
to the boil, then simmer for about
20 minutes until thick and brown.
Pour into warmed jars and leave to
cool, then seal and label.

Apple chutney

MAKES 1.5 KG/3 LB

900 g/2 lb cooking (tart) apples, peeled,
    cored and chopped
225 g/8 oz/1⅓ cups sultanas (golden
    raisins), chopped
1 onion, finely chopped
Grated rind and juice of 1 lemon
5 ml/1 tsp ground ginger
450 ml/¾ pt/2 cups malt vinegar
5 ml/1 tsp caraway seeds
450 g/1 lb light brown sugar

Put the apples, sultanas, onion, lemon
rind and juice, ginger and half the
vinegar in a pan, bring to the boil and
simmer for 20 minutes until the
mixture is soft. Add the caraway
seeds. Mix together the sugar and
remaining vinegar, add to the pan and
simmer for about 15 minutes until the
chutney thickens. Pour into warmed
jars and leave to cool, then seal and
label.

Banana chutney

MAKES 900 G/2 LB

6 bananas, sliced
400 g/14 oz onions, finely chopped
225 g/8 oz/1⅓ cups cups dates, stoned
 (pitted) and finely chopped
75 g/3 oz/¾ cup crystallised ginger,
 chopped
5 ml/1 tsp salt
15 ml/1 tbsp pickling spice tied in muslin
 (cheesecloth)
600 ml/1 pt/2½ cups vinegar
225 g/8 oz/1 cup granulated sugar

Put the bananas, onions, dates,
ginger, salt, spice and vinegar into a
pan, bring to the boil and boil for
5 minutes. Remove the spice, stir in
the sugar and simmer over a low heat
for about 25 minutes until rich and
brown. Spoon into warmed jars and
leave to cool, then seal and label.

Spiced orange chutney

MAKES 900 G/2 LB

450 g/1 lb cooking (tart) apples, peeled,
 cored and chopped
1 orange, chopped
175 g/6 oz/1 cup dates, stoned (pitted)
 and minced
175 g/6 oz ripe tomatoes, sliced
400 g/14 oz/1¾ cups cups granulated
 sugar
750 ml/1¼ pts/3 cups malt vinegar
15 ml/1 tbsp chopped chillies
5 ml/1 tsp salt

Put all the ingredients in a saucepan,
bring to the boil, then simmer for
about 30 minutes until thick and
brown. Spoon into warmed jars and
leave to cool, then seal and label.

Old-fashioned fruit chutney

MAKES 900 G/2 LB

450 g/1 lb pears, peeled, cored and
 chopped
450 g/1 lb cooking (tart) apples, peeled,
 cored and chopped
2 onions, chopped
600 ml/1 pt/2½ cups vinegar
225 g/8 oz/1½ cups dates, chopped
15 ml/1 tbsp salt
450 g/1 lb golden (light corn) syrup
A pinch of ground ginger
15 ml/1 tbsp mustard powder

Put the pears, apples, onions and
vinegar in a pan, bring to the boil and
simmer for about 15 minutes until
tender. Stir in the remaining
ingredients and boil for about
20 minutes until thick and golden.
Stir well, then pour into warmed jars
and leave to cool, then seal and label.

Plum chutney

MAKES 1.5 KG/3 LB

900 g/2 lb plums, stoned (pitted) and
 quartered
450 g/1 lb carrots, grated
600 ml/1 pt/2½ cups vinegar
350 g/12 oz/2 cups raisins
450 g/1 lb/2 cups light brown sugar
1 garlic clove, crushed
5 ml/1 tsp chilli powder
15 ml/1 tbsp ground ginger
30 ml/2 tbsp salt

Mix together the plums, carrots and
vinegar, bring to the boil, then simmer
for about 10 minutes until tender. Stir
in all the remaining ingredients and
simmer for about 20 minutes until
thick. Stir well, then spoon into
warmed jars and leave to cool. Seal
and label.

Autumn chutney

MAKES 900 G/2 LB

300 ml/½ pt/1¼ cups malt vinegar
15 ml/1 tbsp pickling spice tied in muslin
(cheesecloth)
5 ml/1 tsp mustard powder
5 ml/1 tsp salt
2.5 ml/½ tsp ground ginger
225 g/8 oz/⅔ cup golden (light corn)
syrup
2 firm pears, peeled, cored and chopped
1 large cooking (tart) apples, peeled,
cored and chopped
1 onion, chopped
100 g/4 oz/⅔ cup dates, stoned (pitted)
and chopped

Put the vinegar, spice, salt, mustard,
ginger and syrup in a pan, bring to
the boil and boil for 5 minutes. Add
the pears, apple, onion and dates and
simmer for about 25 minutes until
thick and brown. Remove the spice.
Spoon the chutney into warmed jars
and leave to cool, then seal and label.

Green tomato chutney

MAKES 1.5 KG/3 LB

1.5 kg/3 lb green tomatoes, finely
chopped
1 onion, finely chopped
225 g/8 oz cooking (tart) apples,
peeled, cored and finely chopped
15 ml/1 tbsp pickling spice tied in muslin
(cheesecloth)
600 ml/1 pt/2½ cups malt vinegar
100 g/4 oz/½ cup light brown sugar
10 ml/2 tsp salt

Put all the ingredients in a pan and
boil gently for about 45 minutes until
soft and thick. Remove the spice and
pour the chutney into warmed jars.
Leave to cool, then seal and label.

Spicy red tomato chutney

MAKES 900 G/2 LB

375 g/12 oz ripe tomatoes, skinned and
chopped
2 cooking (tart) apples, peeled, cored
and chopped
1 onion, chopped
100 g/4 oz/⅔ cup sultanas (golden
raisins)
100 g/4 oz/½ cup crystallised ginger,
chopped
5 ml/1 tsp salt
3 red chillies, chopped
100 g/4 oz/½ cup granulated sugar
300 ml/½ pt/1¼ cups malt vinegar

Put all the ingredients in a saucepan,
bring to the boil, then simmer for
about 35 minutes until thick and rich.
Spoon into warmed jars and leave to
cool, then seal and label.

Mango chutney

MAKES 1.5 KG/3 LB

1.5 kg/3 lb mangoes, peeled, stoned
(pitted) and chopped
15 ml/1 tbsp salt
15 ml/1 tbsp tamarind paste
50 g/2 oz fresh root ginger, peeled and
grated
15 ml/1 tbsp dried red chillies, seeded
and chopped
450 ml/¾ pt/2 cups wine vinegar
700 g/1½ lb/3 cups soft brown sugar
100 g/4 oz/⅔ cup sultanas (golden
raisins)
5 ml/1 tsp ground allspice

Place the mango flesh in a sieve
(strainer), sprinkle with salt and leave
to stand for 2 hours. Rinse well under
cold water, then pat dry on kitchen
paper (paper towels) and place in a
large saucepan. Add the remaining
ingredients, bring to the boil, then
simmer gently for about 30 minutes
until the chutney is thick and well
blended, stirring occasionally. Spoon
into warmed jars and leave to cool,
then cover and label.

Tomato ketchup

MAKES 1.5 KG/3 LB

1.5 kg/3 lb ripe tomatoes, quartered
100 g/4 oz/½ cup granulated or
preserving sugar
150 ml/¼ pt/⅔ cup malt vinegar
15 ml/1 tbsp pickling spice tied in muslin
(cheesecloth)
5 ml/1 tsp paprika
5 ml/1 tsp salt
A pinch of cayenne

Put the tomatoes in a pan and cook
over a gentle heat for about
10 minutes until the juices run, then
bring to the boil and simmer for about
15 minutes until reduced to a pulp.
Rub them through a sieve (strainer),
then return the purée to a clean pan.
Stir in the remaining ingredients, bring
to the boil and simmer for about
20 minutes until the mixture has a
sauce consistency. Remove the spice,
pour the ketchup (catsup) into
warmed jars and leave to cool, then
seal and label.

Drinks, syrups and sweets

Here are some new ideas for drinks for children, to quench your thirst on a hot summer day, and to serve at parties for those who are driving and those who are not.

The fruit syrups are easily made and can be used with ice creams and desserts or diluted as fruity cordials.

For those who like the taste of home-made treats, there are also some simple sweets (candies) to make for yourself, as gifts, or for the local fête.

Drinks

Lemon squash

MAKES 1.75 LITRES/3 PTS/7½ CUPS

Grated rind and juice of 8 lemons
1.75 kg/4 lb/8 cups caster (superfine) or
  granulated sugar
1.5 litres/2½ pts/6 cups boiling water
Ice cubes and lemon slices, to serve

Place the lemon rind, sugar and water
in a large saucepan and boil for
10 minutes. Leave to cool, add the
lemon juice, then strain and dilute to
taste. Serve with ice and garnished
with slices of lemon.

Orange squash

MAKES 1.75 LITRES/3 PTS/7½ CUPS

Prepare as for Lemon Squash, but
substitute the grated rind and juice of
6 oranges for the lemons and reduce
the amount of sugar to 1.2 kg/3 lb.

Honey and lemon squash

MAKES 600 ML/1 PT/2½ CUPS

600 ml/1 pt/2½ cups Honey Syrup (page
  389)
60 ml/4 tbsp Lemon Squash
600 ml/1 pt/2½ cups soda water
Ice cubes, to serve

Mix together all the ingredients and
serve with ice.

Apple and fig cordial

MAKES 900 ML/1½ PTS/3¾ CUPS

100 g/4 oz/⅔ cup dried figs, soaked in
  cold water overnight
450 g/1 lb cooking (tart) apples, peeled
  and chopped
1.2 litres/2 pts/5 cups boiling water
75 g/3 oz/⅓ cup caster (superfine) sugar
Grated rind and juice of ½ lemon
Ice cubes and a sprig of mint, to serve

Drain and chop the figs. Place the
fruit and water in a large saucepan,
bring to the boil, then simmer for
15 minutes. Strain the liquor back
into a saucepan, add the sugar and
lemon rind and juice, return to the
boil, then simmer for a further
10 minutes, carefully tasting and
adding more sugar if necessary. Allow
to cool and serve with ice and
garnished with a sprig of mint.

Brazilian banana milkshake

SERVES 2

600 ml/1 pt/2½ cups cold milk
150 ml/¼ pt/⅔ cup banana yoghurt
1 banana, mashed
25 g/1 oz/¼ cup walnuts, chopped

Blend together the milk, yoghurt and
banana in a food processor or blender
or whisk until smooth. Serve sprinkled
with the walnuts.

Strawberry milkshake

SERVES 2

600 ml/1 pt/2½ cups cold milk
200 g/7 oz/1 small can of strawberries in
  juice, drained
2 scoops of strawberry or vanilla ice
  cream

Blend together all the ingredients in a
food processor or blender until frothy.

Chocolate milkshake

SERVES 2

30 ml/2 tbsp drinking (sweetened)
  chocolate powder
10 ml/2 tsp boiling water
600 ml/1 pt/2½ cups cold milk
2 scoops of vanilla ice cream

Dissolve the drinking chocolate in the
boiling water, then blend with the milk
and ice cream in a food processor or
blender until frothy.

Hawaiian iced coffee

SERVES 2

300 g/11 oz/1 medium can of pineapple
  chunks in juice
300 ml/½ pt/1¼ cups milk
10 ml/2 tsp instant coffee granules
10 ml/2 tsp hot water
1 scoop of vanilla ice cream
5 ml/1 tsp caster (superfine) sugar
  (optional)

Place the pineapple and juice in a
food processor or blender and process
for 10 seconds. Add the milk and
process again. Mix the coffee with the
hot water, add to the processor with
the ice cream and process until frothy.
Taste and sprinkle in a little sugar if
necessary.

Banana whip

MAKES 600 ML/1 PT/2½ CUPS

450 ml/¾ pt/2 cups milk
1 ripe banana, chopped
1 scoop of vanilla ice cream
Ice cubes, to serve

Process the milk, banana and ice
cream in a food processor or blender
until frothy. Pour into tall glasses and
serve with ice cubes.

Orangeade

MAKES 1.75 LITRES/3 PTS/7½ CUPS

Grated rind and juice of 4 oranges
100 g/4 oz/½ cup caster (superfine)
  sugar
300 ml/½ pt/1¼ cups boiling water
1 bottle of soda water
Ice cubes and orange slices, to serve

Place the orange rind and juice, sugar
and boiling water in a jug and stir
until the sugar has dissolved, then
strain and mix in the soda water to
taste. Serve with ice and garnished
with slices of orange.

Peach and apricot tea

SERVES 4

900 ml/1½ pts/3¾ cups Indian tea
30 ml/2 tbsp caster (superfine) sugar
1 peach, stoned (pitted) and sliced
2 apricots, stoned (pitted) and sliced
Ice cubes, to serve

Make the tea and stir in the sugar.
Leave to cool, then chill. Strain the
tea into glasses and add the peach
and apricot slices and some ice cubes.
Drink the tea, then eat the fruit to
finish.

Pineapple crush

MAKES 4 GLASSES

Juice of 1 grapefruit
1 orange
1 lemon
1 celery stick, chopped
300 g/11 oz/1 medium can of pineapple
  in juice
120 ml/4 fl oz/½ cup water
Crushed ice and fruit slices, to serve

Place the grapefruit juice in a food
processor or blender. Peel the orange
and lemon, remove the pith and add
the flesh to the processor with the
celery, pineapple and juice and water.
Process until frothy, then pour into tall
glasses and add crushed ice. Garnish
with sliced fruits of your choice.

Spiced tomato juice

MAKES 1 LITRE/1¾ PTS/4¼ CUPS

4 cloves
3 celery tops with leaves
750 ml/1¼ pts/3 cups tomato juice
250 ml/8 fl oz/1 cup water
15 ml/1 tbsp granulated sugar
5 ml/1 tsp Worcestershire sauce
A pinch of cayenne
2.5 ml/½ tsp salt
10 ml/2 tsp lemon juice

Tie the cloves and celery tops in a
piece of muslin (cheesecloth). Put in a
saucepan with all the remaining
ingredients, bring to the boil and
simmer, uncovered, for 20 minutes.
Strain into a jug, cool and chill. The
juice can be stored in the fridge in a
screw-topped jar for 3–4 days.

Yoghurt smoothie

SERVES 4

600 ml/1 pt/2½ cups cold milk
300 ml/½ pt/1¼ cups fruit yoghurt

Blend the ingredients in a food
processor or blender or whisk until
smooth.

Hot snow foam

SERVES 2

600 ml/1 pt/2½ cups milk
6 marshmallows, chopped
5 ml/1 tsp ground cinnamon

Heat the milk, stir in the chopped
marshmallows and heat until they
begin to melt. Pour into cups and
serve dusted with the cinnamon.

Wine refresher

MAKES 1.75 LITRES/3 PTS/7½ CUPS

600 ml/1 pt/2½ cups dry red wine
225 g/8 oz/1 cup caster (superfine)
  sugar
1 lemon, finely sliced
¼ cucumber, sliced
600 ml/1 pt/2½ cups soda water
600 ml/1 pt/2½ cups lemonade
Ice cubes, to serve

Place the wine, sugar and lemon and
cucumber slices in a jug and stir until
the sugar has dissolved. Stand the jug
in a bowl of ice and leave for an hour
or so or until needed, then strain and
add the soda water and lemonade.
Serve with ice.

Red wine cup

MAKES 1.75 LITRES/3 PTS/7½ CUPS

2 oranges, thinly sliced
750 ml/1¼ pts/3 cups dry red wine
50 g/2 oz/¼ cup caster (superfine) sugar
1 lemon, thinly sliced
¼ cucumber, sliced
150 ml/¼ pt/⅔ cup brandy
1 bottle of soda water
Ice cubes, to serve

Reserve a few orange slices for garnish, then place the remainder in a jug with the wine, sugar and lemon and stir until the sugar has dissolved. Add the cucumber and brandy. Stand the jug in a bowl of ice for an hour or so or until needed, then strain and add the soda water to taste. Serve with ice in tall glasses garnished with the reserved orange slices.

Lemonade surprise

MAKES 4 GLASSES

Juice of 1 lemon
15 ml/1 tbsp Orange Syrup (page 390)
150 ml/¼ pt/⅔ cup dry sherry
Chopped ice
5 ml/1 tsp Strawberry Syrup (page 390)
15 ml/1 tbsp port
900 ml/1½ pts/3¾ cups soda water

Place the lemon juice, Orange Syrup and sherry in a cocktail shaker and fill with chopped ice. Mix together, then divide between tall glasses. Add the Strawberry Syrup and port, then dilute to taste with the soda water.

Port and wine punch

SERVES 6–8

1.2 litres/2 pts/5 cups dry red wine
100 ml/4 fl oz/½ cup port
60 ml/4 tbsp cherry brandy
Juice of 1½ lemons
Juice of 3 oranges
75 g/3 oz/⅓ cup caster (superfine) sugar
1.2 litres/2 pts/5 cups soda water
A large block of ice, to serve
Sliced fresh fruit, to garnish

Mix together all the ingredients except the sugar and soda water. Add the sugar to taste and stir until it dissolves. Pour the mixture over the ice in a punch bowl. Add the soda water just before serving and float some fruit slices on top.

Cider-brandy cup

MAKES 1.75 LITRES/3 PTS/7½ CUPS

1.2 litres/2 pts/5 cups dry cider
2 oranges, sliced
150 ml/¼ pt/⅔ cup brandy
Juice of 1 lemon
1 bottle of soda water
Ice cubes, to serve

Place the cider, the slices from 1 orange, the brandy and lemon juice in a jug and stand the jug in a bowl of ice for an hour or so or until needed, then strain into a serving jug and add soda water to taste. Serve with ice and garnish with the remaining orange slices.

Maraschino-splashed cider cup

MAKES 1.75 LITRES/3 PTS/7½ CUPS

½ cucumber, sliced
1.2 litres/2 pts/5 cups dry cider
100 g/4 oz/½ cup caster (superfine)
    sugar
Grated rind of 1 lemon
150 ml/¼ pt/⅔ cup Maraschino
1 bottle of soda water
Ice cubes, to serve

Reserve a few slices of cucumber for garnish, then put the remaining cucumber in a jug with the cider, sugar and lemon rind and stir until the sugar has dissolved. Stand the jug in a bowl of ice for an hour or so or until needed, then strain into a serving jug and add the Maraschino and soda water to taste. Serve with ice and garnished with a slice of cucumber.

Egg and coconut nogg

MAKES 2 GLASSES

2 eggs, thoroughly washed
150 ml/¼ pt/⅔ cup milk
10 ml/2 tsp caster (superfine) sugar
30 ml/2 tbsp dry sherry
25 g/1 oz creamed coconut, grated
A pinch of grated nutmeg

Place one whole egg, including the shell, in a food processor or blender. Add the other egg without its shell and the milk and sugar and process until frothy and smooth. Add the sherry and coconut and blend again. Dust with the nutmeg and serve.

Note:
This recipe uses raw eggs.

Mulled cider

SERVES 4

1.2 litres/2 pts/5 cups medium dry cider
50 g/2 oz/¼ cup Muscovado sugar
A pinch of salt
4 cloves
5 cm/2 in piece of cinnamon stick
4 whole allspice
A strip of orange peel

Put the cider, sugar and salt in a saucepan. Tie the spices and orange peel loosely in a piece of muslin (cheesecloth) and add to the pan. Bring gently to the boil, cover and simmer for 15 minutes. Serve hot in mugs.

Syrups

Sugar syrup

MAKES 600 ML/1 PT/2½ CUPS

450 g/1 lb/2 cups caster (superfine)
    sugar
600 ml/1 pt/2½ cups water

Bring the sugar and water to the boil, then simmer for 10 minutes. Skim the froth from the top and leave to cool, then bottle in screw-topped jars.

Honey syrup

MAKES 600 ML/1 PT/2½ CUPS

450 g/1 lb/1⅓ cups clear honey
Juice of 3 lemons
450 ml/¾ pt/2 cups water

Mix together the honey and lemon juice, then add enough of the water to make a syrupy consistency. Store in screw-topped jars.

Lemon syrup

MAKES 600 ML/1 PT/2½ CUPS

350 g/12 oz/1½ cups caster (superfine)
  sugar
600 ml/1 pt/2½ cups boiling water
Finely pared rind and juice of 2 lemons
25 g/1 oz citric acid

Warm the sugar and water until the
sugar has dissolved, then bring to the
boil and simmer for 15 minutes. Add
the lemon rind and juice and the citric
acid. Stir well, then strain into screw-
topped jars.

Orange syrup

MAKES 600 ML/1 PT/2½ CUPS

Finely pared rind and juice of 6 oranges
450 g/1 lb/2 cups caster (superfine)
  sugar

Place the orange rind and juice and
sugar in a heavy-based saucepan and
stir over a low heat until the sugar
has dissolved. Simmer gently for
15 minutes, skim and leave to cool.
Store in screw-topped jars.

Strawberry syrup

MAKES 600 ML/1 PT/2½ CUPS

450 g/1 lb strawberries
1.2 litres/2 pts/5 cups boiling water
450 g/1 lb/2 cups caster (superfine)
  sugar

Crush the strawberries in a bowl, then
pour in the boiling water. Stir well and
leave to stand for 24 hours, then
strain through a fine sieve (strainer)
or cloth into a saucepan. Stir in the
sugar, bring to the boil and simmer
until syrupy. Store in screw-topped
jars.

Elderberry syrup

MAKES 600 ML/1 PT/2½ CUPS

Prepare as for Strawberry Syrup, but
substitute elderberries for the
strawberries.

Raspberry syrup

MAKES 600 ML/1 PT/2½ CUPS

Prepare as for Strawberry Syrup, but
substitute raspberries for the
strawberries.

Redcurrant syrup

MAKES 600 ML/1 PT/2½ CUPS

Prepare as for Strawberry Syrup, but
substitute redcurrants for the
strawberries.

Sweets (Candies)

Butterscotch

MAKES 450 G/1 LB

450 g/1 lb/2 cups demerara sugar
150 ml/¼ pt/⅔ cup water
50 g/2 oz/¼ cup butter or margarine, diced

Dissolve the sugar and water in a heavy-based saucepan. Boil, without stirring, to 137°C/280°F or until a drop forms a ball when dropped into cold water. Stir in the butter or margarine a piece at a time, then pour into a greased 18 cm/7 in square tin (pan) and leave to cool before marking into squares.

Chocolate fudge

MAKES 450 G/1 LB

450 g/1 lb/2 cups caster (superfine) sugar
10 ml/2 tsp cocoa (unsweetened chocolate) powder
150 ml/¼ pt/⅔ cup milk
50 g/2 oz/¼ cup butter or margarine
45 ml/3 tbsp water
A few drops of vanilla essence (extract)

Place all the ingredients in a heavy-based saucepan and boil to 115°C/240°F or until a drop just sets when dropped into cold water. Remove from the heat and beat with a wooden spoon until creamy and almost cold. Pour into a greased 18 cm/7 in square tin (pan) and leave to set before cutting into squares.

Butterscotch fudge

MAKES 450 G/1 LB

450 g/1 lb/2 cups caster (superfine) sugar
150 ml/¼ pt/⅔ cup evaporated milk
150 ml/¼ pt/⅔ cup milk
50 g/2 oz/¼ cup butter or margarine
45 ml/3 tbsp water
A few drops of butterscotch essence (extract)

Place all the ingredients except the butterscotch essence in a heavy-based saucepan and boil to 115°C/240°F or until a drop just sets when dropped into cold water. Remove from the heat, add the essence and beat well until the mixture thickens. Pour into a greased 18 cm/7 in square tin (pan) and leave to set before cutting into squares.

Toffee

MAKES 450 G/1 LB

450 g/1 lb/2⅔ cups light brown sugar
50 g/2 oz/¼ cup butter or margarine

Dissolve the sugar and butter or margarine in a heavy-based saucepan. Boil to 143°C/290°F or until a drop cracks when dropped into cold water. Pour into a greased 18 cm/7 in square tin (pan) and leave to set. Cut into squares and store in an airtight container.

Everton toffee

MAKES 450 G/1 LB

100 g/4 oz/½ cup butter or margarine
225 g/8 oz/1 cup light brown sugar
225 g/8 oz/⅔ cup black treacle
(molasses)

Dissolve the butter or margarine and sugar with the treacle in a heavy-based saucepan. Boil to 143°C/290°F or until a drop cracks when dropped into cold water. Pour into a greased 18 cm/7 in square tin (pan), mark into squares and leave to set.

Toffee apples

MAKES 12

12 eating (dessert) apples, washed and dried
12 wooden sticks
175 g/6 oz/½ cup golden (light corn) syrup
350 g/12 oz/1½ cups light brown sugar
25 g/1 oz/2 tbsp butter or margarine
150 ml/¼ pt/⅔ cup water
5 ml/1 tsp vinegar

Press a wooden stick firmly into the core of each apple. Dissolve all the remaining ingredients in a heavy-based saucepan. Boil to 143°C/290°F or until a drop cracks when dropped into cold water. While it is boiling, prepare a bowl of iced water and a greased baking (cookie) sheet. When the toffee has reached the right temperature, remove it from the heat. Working quickly, twist the apples in the toffee until coated, then dip in the cold water, then stand them on the baking (cookie) sheet to set. When cold, wrap carefully in cellophane if the apples are not to be eaten straight away, otherwise the toffee will soften.

Toffee brazils

MAKES 900 G/2 LB

100 g/4 oz/½ cup butter or margarine
450 g/1 lb/2 cups light brown sugar
225 g/8 oz/⅔ cup black treacle
(molasses)
450 g/1 lb/4 cups brazil nuts, shelled and halved

Melt the butter or margarine in a saucepan, add the sugar and treacle and boil to 143°C/290°F or until a drop cracks when dropped into cold water. Turn into a greased 20 cm/8 in square tin (pan) and allow to cool a little. When the toffee is beginning to set, press the nuts into it and mark into squares with a knife. Snap the toffee into pieces when cold and store in an airtight container.

Almond crunch

MAKES 36

75 g/3 oz/⅓ cup butter or margarine
60 ml/4 tbsp clear honey
75 g/3 oz/¾ cup flaked (slivered) almonds

Melt the butter or margarine in a heavy-based saucepan, stir in the honey and almonds and cook over a medium heat, stirring continuously, for 7 minutes until the mixture is golden brown. Spread the mixture in a greased 20 cm/8 in square tin (pan) and cut into squares at once with a sharp greased knife. Leave to cool, chill in the fridge, then store in a covered container.

Coffee brazils

MAKES 450 G/1 LB

450 g/1 lb/4 cups ground almonds
100 g/4 oz/⅔ cup icing (confectioners')
  sugar
A few drops of coffee essence (extract)
  OR 5 ml/1 tsp very strong black
  coffee
25 g/1 oz/2 tbsp butter or margarine
100 g/4 oz/½ cup caster (superfine)
  sugar
15 ml/1 tbsp water
450 g/1 lb/4 cups brazil nuts, shelled

Mix the ground almonds and icing
sugar with the coffee essence or black
coffee. Mix in the butter or margarine
and work to a smooth paste. Dissolve
the caster sugar in the water, then
boil for 5 minutes to make a syrup.
Cover the nuts with the almond paste
and press them into compact shapes.
Spear them with a fine skewer (a hat
pin is ideal if you can find one!), then
dip them into the boiling syrup, twist
to remove drips and leave them on
greased baking parchment to harden.

Chocolate pineapple

MAKES 350 G/12 OZ

200 g/7 oz/1¾ cups plain (semi-sweet)
  chocolate
300 g/11 oz canned pineapple chunks,
  drained
Crystallised violets, to decorate

Melt the chocolate in a bowl over a
pan of hot water. Hold the pineapple
chunks with two forks, dip them into
the chocolate and turn to coat evenly.
Leave to dry on greaseproof (waxed)
paper and decorate with crystallised
violets.

Coconut fondants

MAKES 30

225 g/8 oz/1 cup caster (superfine)
  sugar
75 ml/5 tbsp water
15 ml/1 tbsp liquid glucose
100 g/4 oz/1 cup desiccated (shredded)
  coconut
A few drops of red food colouring

Dissolve the sugar and water over a
low heat, stirring, then add the
glucose. Boil to 110°C/230°F or until
a drop in cold water forms a soft ball
between the fingers. Pour into a large
greased tin (pan) and leave until cool
enough to handle. Work the fondant
with a wooden spoon until it becomes
white and creamy, then knead it until
smooth. Stir in the desiccated
coconut. Place small balls of half the
mixture on greased baking parchment
to dry. Colour the remainder with a
few drops of food colouring and make
them into balls in the same way.

Coffee fondants

MAKES 30

Prepare as for Coconut Fondants, but
substitute a few drops of coffee
essence (extract) or 5 ml/1 tsp very
strong black coffee for the coconut.
Omit the food colouring.

Rum truffles

MAKES 12

75 g/3 oz/¾ cup plain (semi-sweet)
chocolate
1 egg yolk
15 g/½ oz/1 tbsp butter or margarine
5 ml/1 tsp rum
5 ml/1 tsp single (light) cream
50 g/2 oz/½ cup chocolate vermicelli

Melt the chocolate in a bowl over a
pan of hot water. Beat in the egg
yolk, butter or margarine, rum and
cream and beat until thick, then chill
in the fridge until firm. Shape into
12 balls and toss in the vermicelli.
Place in paper petit four cases to
serve.

Marrons glacé

MAKES 350 G/12 OZ

450 g/1 lb chestnuts
450 g/1 lb/2 cups caster (superfine)
sugar
150 ml/¼ pt/⅔ cup water
A few drops of vanilla essence (extract)

Peel the chestnuts and boil them in
water for a few minutes until the skins
come off easily, then boil them gently
until they are soft but not broken.
Dissolve the sugar in the water with
the vanilla essence, then boil until the
mixture thickens to a syrup. Add the
chestnuts and bring back to the boil
for 4 minutes. Carefully remove the
chestnuts from the syrup with a
slotted spoon, bring the syrup back to
the boil and continue boiling until the
syrup thickens again. Replace the
chestnuts and boil again for
3 minutes. Drain and serve, or store
in the syrup in an airtight jar.

Coconut ice

MAKES 500 G/1¼ LB

450 g/1 lb/2 cups granulated sugar
150 ml/¼ pt/⅔ cup milk
175 g/6 oz/1½ cups desiccated
(shredded) coconut
A few drops of vanilla essence (extract)
A few drops of red food colouring

Dissolve the sugar and milk in a
heavy-based saucepan, then boil to
115°C/240°F or until the mixture
begins to thicken. Remove from the
heat and stir in the coconut and
vanilla essence. Pour half the mixture
into a greased loaf tin (pan). Stir the
food colouring into the other half and
pour it on top. When cold, turn out
and cut into bars.

Fruit and nut caramels

MAKES 36

75 g/3 oz/⅓ cup butter or margarine
150 g/5 oz/scant ½ cup golden (light
corn) syrup
175 g/6 oz/½ cup clear honey
100 g/4 oz/1 cup walnuts, chopped
100 g/4 oz/⅔ cup dates, stoned (pitted)
and chopped

Melt the butter or margarine in a
heavy-based saucepan. Add the syrup
and honey, bring to the boil and boil
to 137°C/270°F or until a drop in
cold water forms a soft ball between
the fingers. Remove from the heat,
stir in the walnuts and dates and beat
until opaque. Pour into a greased and
lined shallow 20 cm × 13 cm/
8 in × 5 in tin (pan) and leave to
cool. When almost set, cut through
into squares. Store in waxed paper.

Maple-glazed nuts

MAKES 300 G/11 OZ

120 ml/4 fl oz/½ cup maple syrup
2.5 ml/½ tsp ground cinnamon
10 ml/2 tsp butter or margarine
A pinch of salt
5 ml/1 tsp vanilla essence (extract)
225 g/8 oz/2 cups walnut halves

Stir the syrup, cinnamon, butter or margarine and salt over a medium heat until the mixture is lightly browned and syrupy. Stir in the vanilla essence, then add the nuts and turn them over until evenly covered with glaze. Spread on greaseproof (waxed) paper to cool.

Caramel grapes

MAKES 450 G/1 LB

450 g/1 lb/2 cups caster (superfine) sugar
A pinch of cream of tartar
300 ml/½ pt/1¼ cups water
225 g/8 oz seedless grapes, washed, dried and divided into pairs

Dissolve the sugar and cream of tartar in the water in a heavy-based saucepan, then boil to 150°C/300°F or until a drop hardens in cold water. Remove from the heat and quickly dip the pairs of grapes into the syrup, holding them with a fork. Place them on a greased baking (cookie) sheet to harden, then put them into paper petit four cases to serve. Serve within a few hours otherwise the caramel will go sticky.

Peppermint creams

MAKES 24

225 g/8 oz/1⅓ cups icing (confectioners') sugar
1 egg white, whisked until stiff
2.5 ml/½ tsp peppermint essence (extract)

Mix together the ingredients to make a stiff paste, adding a few drops of water if it is too dry. Roll out on a lightly floured surface to about 1 cm/½ in thick and cut into small rounds. Leave on baking parchment to dry.

Peanut brittle

MAKES 450 G/1 LB

350 g/12 oz/1½ cups granulated sugar
225 g/8 oz/⅔ cup golden (light corn) syrup
150 ml/¼ pt/⅔ cup water
10 ml/2 tsp liquid glucose
25 g/1 oz/2 tbsp butter or margarine
75 g/3 oz/¾ cup peanuts, toasted
2.5 ml/½ tsp lemon essence (extract)
10 ml/2 tsp bicarbonate of soda (baking soda)

Dissolve the sugar and syrup in the water in a heavy-based saucepan. Bring to the boil and simmer to 150°C/300°F or until a drop hardens in cold water. Add the butter or margarine, nuts and lemon essence, then stir in the bicarbonate of soda. The mixture will froth for a few minutes. Pour it on to a greased baking (cookie) sheet and leave to cool. Break into pieces when set.

Popcorn

MAKES TWO 1.2 LITRE/2 PT BOWLS

150 ml/¼ pt/⅔ cup oil
60 ml/4 tbsp popping corn
Flavouring of your choice, such as caster
    (superfine) sugar, brown sugar, honey,
    salt, maple syrup

Heat the oil in a large lidded
saucepan, add the corn and replace
the lid tightly. Shake the pan gently
over a medium heat for about
2 minutes until all the popping stops.
Do not open the lid while the corn is
still popping. Drain the popcorn on
kitchen paper (paper towels) and
sprinkle with the flavouring of your
choice.

Nut surprise

MAKES 24

100 g/4 oz/1 cup milk (sweet) chocolate
75 g/3 oz/⅓ cup butter or margarine
75 g/3 oz/⅓ cup demerara sugar
25 g/1 oz golden (light corn) syrup
175 g/6 oz/1½ cups chopped mixed nuts
1 egg yolk
A few drops of vanilla essence (extract)
25 g/1 oz/¼ cup plain (all-purpose) flour

Melt the chocolate in a bowl over a
pan of hot water, then spread it over
the base of a greased and lined
22 cm × 18 cm/9 in × 7 in baking
tin (pan). Cream together the butter
or margarine, sugar and syrup, then
stir in the nuts, egg yolk, vanilla
essence and flour. Press over the
chocolate and bake in a preheated
oven at 180°C/350°F/gas mark 4 for
about 15 minutes. Allow to cool in
the tin, then cut into squares.

Marzipan petit fours

MAKES 450 G/1 LB

225 g/8 oz/1 cup icing (confectioners')
    sugar
225 g/8 oz/1 cup caster (superfine)
    sugar
450 g/1 lb/4 cups ground almonds
2 eggs, beaten
5 ml/1 tsp vanilla essence (extract)
A few drops of lemon juice (optional)
A few drops of food colouring
Cloves and angelica to decorate

Mix together the icing and caster
sugars and the ground almonds. Stir
in the eggs and vanilla essence and
mix to a stiff dough. If the dough is
too stiff, add a few drops of lemon
juice. Knead lightly. Colour small
pieces of the marzipan and roll into
fruit shapes. Use cloves or pieces of
angelica as stems. Place the petit
fours in paper cases to serve.

Note:
You can use the uncoloured almond
paste to cover cakes.

Index